Collins

DICTIONARY
of SCOTTISH HISTORY

Collins

DICTIONARY
of SCOTTISH HISTORY

Ian Donnachie & George Hewitt

HarperCollins*Publishers*

HarperCollins Publishers
Westerhill Road, Bishopbriggs, Glasgow G64 2QT

www.**fire**and**water**.com

First published by HarperCollins in 2001 under license from
   Dunedin Multimedia Ltd
   69 Merchiston Crescent
   Edinburgh
   EH10 5AQ

Reprint 10 9 8 7 6 5 4 3 2 1 0

ISBN 0 00 712185 7

A catalogue record for this book is available from The British Library

Printed and bound in Great Britain by
Omnia Books Ltd, Glasgow

CONTENTS

To
Claire, Agnes
and everyone with
a love of Scotland's past

PREFACE

Interest in Scotland's past is greater than ever, thanks to the new agendas being explored by devolved government, the cultural industries, education and the media. For example, Scottish history touches and informs heritage and tourism, and television, film and theatre draw extensively on Scotland's story. The subject has an enormous readership which generates demand for a wide range of books and other publications on Scottish history. One of the fastest growing sectors, family and community history, sustains widespread interest in tracing Scottish kin both in the country itself and among its diaspora, notably in the United States, Canada, Australia and New Zealand.

Scottish history is being given a more adequate place in the school curriculum on increasingly equal footing with British, European and global themes. Web and CDRom-based materials are helping to strengthen the resource base for the subject in the school context and beyond. The teaching of Scottish history has also grown in the universities, including a widely acclaimed off-campus course developed by Dundee and the Open University, available for study globally.

Equally significant is the upsurge of research in Scottish history across all eras, including aspects of medieval and early modern, previously neglected, and with new agendas addressing such issues as gender, environment and culture. Scholars are not only extending the boundaries of the subject but actively promoting it internationally.

This book is therefore designed for a wide audience and we have tailored our coverage to include not only major personalities and events, but also key themes, topics and debates in which these are positioned. Extensive cross-referencing allows the reader to follow many paths and see the relationships between people, events and themes. All the major entries provide reference to further reading. Our selection was governed by relative historical importance and the findings of recent research. Cultural developments and figures are included when they can be considered of major historical significance.

We are indebted to James Carney at HarperCollins for embracing this project with such enthusiasm, to Rob Clyde and Dunedin Multimedia Ltd for skilled editorial and page-making inputs, and to Lillian Porch and Maggie Hyslop for assistance with the text. We are grateful to the libraries whose resources we have drawn on, notably the British Library, Edinburgh University Library,

Mitchell Library, Glasgow, National Library of Scotland and St Andrews University Library.

Ian Donnachie and George Hewitt
September 2001

A

Act anent Peace and War (1703)
The anger aroused in the Scottish
PARLIAMENT by the English Act of
Settlement (1701) resulted in two
provocative responses, the ACT OF
SECURITY and the Act anent Peace
and War. In the latter, Scotland
asserted its right, following the
death of Queen ANNE (1665—
1714), to an independent foreign
policy free of English control.
While this claim was indubitably an
angry gesture against the Act of
Settlement, indignation at Scotland
being unwillingly and disadvantageously dragged into her neighbour's continental wars stretched
back as far as the CROMWELLIAN
UNION. Faced with the more serious
constitutional implications of the
Act of Security, as well as a growing
need to obtain supply from the
Scottish Assembly, DOUGLAS (1662—
1711), the Royal Commissioner,
was reluctantly advised by his political mentors in London to accept
the measure. Undoubtedly the
passing of this Act was another
factor in convincing English politicians of the necessity of a Treaty of
UNION.
•*Dickinson, W.C. and Donaldson, G.
(eds.), A Source Book of Scottish
History III, Nelson, 1961.*
•*Ferguson, W., Scotland's Relations
with England, John Donald, 1977.*

Act of Classes (1649)   The defeat
at Preston in August 1648 of all
those who supported the
ENGAGEMENT presented the more
fanatical Presbyterians with the
opportunity of seizing power.
Thus, led by Archibald CAMPBELL,
eighth Earl and first Marquis of
Argyll (1607—61), and Cassillis,
(c.1599—1658) the anti-Engagers
took over the reins of government.
In January 1649, at the insistence
of the English, swingeing legislation was passed against Engagers
and other 'malignants' who were
divided into four categories or
'classes'. Accordingly, the leading
Engagers, as well as all followers of
GRAHAM (1612—50), were disbarred
from holding any public position
for life. Lesser figures were disqualified for either ten or five years.
Not surprisingly, with much of the
support for the new government
coming from the clergy, lay patronage was abolished shortly afterwards. The Act was a short-lived
measure, being rescinded in June
1651 in a vain attempt to restore
unity in the country in the face of
English invasions.
•*Dickinson, W.C. and Donaldson, G.
(eds.), A Source Book of Scottish
History III, Nelson, 1961.*
•*Donaldson, G., Scotland: James V to
James VII, Oliver & Boyd, 1965.*
•*Stevenson, D., Revolution and Counter Revolution in Scotland, 1644—51,
Royal Historical Society, 1977.*

Act of Revocation (1625) In July 1625, CHARLES I (1600–49), following a long-established Stewart tradition, issued a revocation in which all grants of royal and ecclesiastical property made since 1540 were to be restored to the Crown. Essentially the king's main objective was to obtain the necessary wherewithal to provide the clergy with adequate stipends. At the same time he also hoped to give a slight boost to his own finances. What he seems to have had no intention of doing was of permanently depriving landowners of their properties. Unfortunately the whole business was conducted in such a confused and haphazard manner than it created deep suspicion and resentment among the land-owning classes. This hostility deepened in 1627 when Charles, upset at the poor response to his initial demand, threatened actions of reduction against all those concerned. Certainly the Act of Revocation did provide the basis for a system of endowment which was to survive in the CHURCH OF SCOTLAND until this century. On the other hand it was introduced in such a way that it caused irreparable damage to the king's reputation among a highly influential section of Scottish society.

• *Dickinson, W.C. and Donaldson, G. (eds.), A Source Book of Scottish History III, Nelson, 1961.*

• *Donaldson, G., Scotland: James V to James VII, Oliver & Boyd, 1965.*

Act of Security (1704) Talks regarding a possible Treaty of UNION collapsed early in 1703 and DOUGLAS (1662–1711), the Royal Commissioner, found himself facing the combined opposition of the pro-JACOBITE Cavalier faction and the Country Party, the haven for all the dissident elements in Scottish politics. Resentment was largely directed against the extremely unpopular Act of Settlement (1701), whereby the Westminster Parliament had settled the succession on Sophia, Electress of Hanover (1630–1714), or her issue, and in so doing completely disregarded Scottish opinion over this vital issue. Thus, the parliamentary crisis of 1703, while certainly not eased by English governmental mishandling, was essentially a consequence of a piece of contentious legislation that had created an angry reaction in Scotland. The subsequent Act of Security stated that Parliament would nominate the successor of Queen ANNE (1665–1714), who should be Protestant and descended from the Scottish royal family. Moreover, unless there was legislation guaranteeing the independence of the Scottish Assembly and, in effect, drastically limiting the royal prerogative, Queen Anne's successor would not be the Hanoverian candidate adopted by the English. In September 1703, Queensberry, although instructed to give his assent to the controversial ACT ANENT PEACE AND WAR, refused to allow the Act of Security on to the statute book. HAY (1645–1715) now replaced Queensberry as commissioner, to the accompaniment of rumours of Jacobite plots and unrest. By this date, with the continental situation still uncertain, it had become imperative that the Scottish Parliament voted the necessary money for the upkeep of the small military force permanently based in Scotland.

Accordingly, in August 1704, Tweeddale accepted the Act of Security.

The English Parliament quickly retaliated with the ALIEN ACT (1705) and Anglo-Scottish relations were plunged into that critical phase that preceded the negotiations that ultimately produced the Treaty of Union.

• *Dickinson, W C. and Donaldson, G. (eds.), A Source Book of Scottish History III, Nelson, 1961.*

• *Ferguson, W., Scotland's Relations with England, John Donald, 1977.*

Adam, Robert, see ENLIGHTENMENT; NEW TOWN OF EDINBURGH; TELFORD

Agriculture In sixteenth-century Scotland agriculture, both Lowland and Highland, had inherited much from the past — notably in the form and structure of land-holdings, land use and modes of cultivation. Earlier growth in POPULATION and the consequent demand for land had almost certainly been checked, as in England, by the BLACK DEATH of the mid-fourteenth century, but had probably recovered its momentum by the sixteenth and seventeenth centuries. The overall trend before the AGRICULTURAL REVOLUTION of the eighteenth century was towards expansion and this was expressed in three key ways: (i) the creation of new settlements; (ii) the splitting of townships into two or more separate units; and (iii) the expansion of townships by overflow onto previously uncultivated land — invariably farming what had been the 'outfield' — beyond the original settlement itself. This expansion both extended and modified three of the most traditional institutions in the Scottish countryside — the 'INFIELD-OUTFIELD' system (with common grazings beyond), multiple tenancy and the RUNRIG mode of cultivation. The seventeenth century saw the beginnings of change in agriculture, though over the country as a whole the emphasis remained on pastoral farming, especially in the HIGHLANDS, where a combination of soil, climate and primitive technology made arable farming precarious. Over much of the Lowlands, notably in the west, pastoral agriculture was also the norm. The East Lowlands, from Berwick to Orkney, was becoming an increasingly important cereal-producing district. A significant trade in cattle from the Highlands to the Lowlands was well-established by the end of the seventeenth century — and this was given further impetus by the freer movement of trade resulting from the Treaty of UNION in 1707.

Agricultural Revolution, the Although in some regards evolutionary, a revolution occurred mainly in the eighteenth century — along broadly similar lines to those in England and parts of continental Europe. At first it affected the Lowlands where landowners undertook 'IMPROVEMENT' of their estates by continuing to consolidate holdings through ENCLOSURE into more economically efficient units or farms. They also made other innovations, such as better crop rotations, new strains of grasses, cereals and root crops, new breeds of livestock and the introduction in a limited way of machinery. Gradually agricultural modernization extended to the HIGHLANDS where traditional pastoral land use was readily adapted to sheep grazing — leading ultimately to the CLEARANCES. The BOARD OF AGRICULTURE and agricultural societies, such as the HIGHLAND AND AGRICULTURAL SOCIETY, helped spread new ideas. Market considerations — of modest importance until then — became increasingly significant during the late-eighteenth and early-nineteenth centuries when demand was stimulated by the FRENCH REVOLUTION and the NAPOLEONIC WARS (1793–1815, with minor interruptions). Both Lowland and to a lesser extent Highland agriculture (the latter having more in common with the cultural mores and land use of the west of Ireland) shared the English experience. During the nineteenth century lowland agriculture in particular became increasingly exposed to the same natural and fiscal restraints operating south of the border, as well as being much influenced by the rise of an international market in primary products as new lands were opened up for settlement and farming in North America, South America and Australasia.

Although the prosperity of cereal-growing districts from Berwick in the south to Orkney in the north was underpinned by the demand for barley from the DISTILLING and BREWING industries, and despite the supposed protection of the Corn Laws (designed to assist English wheat farmers), Scottish agriculture experienced mixed fortunes during the first half of the nineteenth century. The so-called 'Golden Age' of British agriculture between the repeal of the Corn Laws (1846) and the 'Great Depression' that set in with the rise of American cereal imports after 1870, seems to have been characterized by a move to more mixed farming. This probably saved Scottish agriculture from the worst effects of the depression that gripped much of British farming until the close of the century. Regional specialization — such as dairying and cheesemaking in Ayrshire, Dumfries and Galloway or fruit farming in the Clyde Valley and Strathmore — became important with the growth of nearby urban markets and improved transport brought by the RAILWAYS. The establishment of colleges of agriculture and greater scientific research helped improve farming practice.

The twentieth century was also typified by periodic booms and slumps and by an overall decline of arable land in favour of increased numbers of livestock. The two world wars were economic highpoints because of the need to feed the country, while the DEPRESSION of the late 1920s and early 1930s marked a prominent slump. Even then, some belated efforts were made to counter rural depopulation and invigorate agriculture through the extension of smallholdings under government-sponsored Land Settlement Schemes associated with the Special Areas initiatives. Indeed, while nineteenth-century parliamentary investigations into agricultural conditions and crofting in the Highlands had limited impact because of prevailing laisser faire ideas, of necessity government intervention greatly increased during the wars. Protective subsidies and the establishment of marketing boards both greatly assisted the farmer. A series of Agricultural Acts (notably that of 1947) introduced a major and sustained policy of support for farm prices and this was extended after Britain joined the European Economic Community in 1973.

After 1885 the Secretary (of State) for Scotland exercised increasing responsibility for agriculture, at first through a Board of Agriculture and ultimately the Department of Agriculture and Fisheries for Scotland, a major department of the Scottish Office.

Despite some limited mechanization, Scottish agriculture remained relatively labour-intensive well into the twentieth century. As late as 1939 there were still 100,000 persons in regular agricultural employment. The condition of rural workers was always tenuous, though ameliorated to some extent by the farm workers' trade unions. The landowners remained a powerful force — both in the Lowlands and the Highlands — though the break-up of some of the larger estates and the rise of owner-occupation was progressive after the 1920s. Finally, regional variations within Scotland remain notable, from the largely mechanized arable farms of Lothian to the traditional crofts of Lewis, both areas in their own way reflecting the change and continuity in Scottish farming over the centuries.

• Anthony, R., Herds and Hinds: Farm Labour in Lowland Scotland 1900–39, Tuckwell Press, 1997.

• Devine, T.M., The Transformation of Rural Scotland, Edinburgh University Press, 1994.

• Parry, M.L. and Slater, T.R., The Making of the Scottish Countryside, Croom Helm, 1980.

• Symon, J.A., Scottish Farming: Past and Present, Oliver & Boyd, 1959.

• Whyte, I., Agriculture and Society in Seventeenth-Century Scotland, John Donald, 1979.

Alexander I (c.1077—1124)

Alexander I, fifth son of MALCOLM III (Canmore) and MARGARET, succeeded his brother, EDGAR, in 1107. He was probably named after Alexander, pope at the time of his mother's marriage. He apparently gave homage to Henry I of England, whose illegitimate daughter, Sybil, he married. While Alexander is said to have followed a more independent line than his immediate predecessors, he also continued Edgar's policy of introducing NORMAN settlers, allocating them land from royal estates and erecting castles, for example, at Stirling. Alexander may well have been a pious individual as he is said to have been one of the few laymen present when the relics of St Cuthbert were examined and re-interred at Durham Cathedral in 1104. There is a suggestion on the part of modern scholars that this was merely propaganda designed to continue his family's association with the saint and the shrine, hence legitimizing Scottish interest in that part of northern England. However, Alexander evidently continued the reform of the church, appointing Thurgot, Prior of Durham, as Bishop of St Andrews (consecrated 1109) and establishing Augustinian MONASTIC HOUSES both there and at Scone, as well as possibly on Inchcolm. St Andrews was to become one of the leading religious centres in the country. It seems likely that Alexander's brother David played an important role in the kingdom. When Alexander died in 1124, DAVID I as king certainly continued many of the policies his brother had initiated.

• *Stringer, K.J. (ed.), Essays on the Nobility of Medieval Scotland, John Donald Publishers Ltd, 1985.*

Alexander II (1198—1249) Son of WILLIAM I, Alexander was born at Haddington and succeeded to the throne in 1214. The following year he joined English barons in their revolt against King John of England. Henry III's accession to the English throne allowed an uneasy rapprochement between the two countries, and the boundaries between England and Scotland were agreed by the Treaty of York in 1237. By this compromise treaty, Alexander agreed to give up his claims to overlordship in old Northumbria and to exchange lands he held in central England for territory in Cumberland. During his reign, he consolidated royal authority in Scotland, ruthlessly quelling rebellion and insurrections in Moray, Argyll, Caithness and Galloway. Having failed to recover the Western Isles by diplomacy, he set out to retrieve them by force, but died suddenly on the Isle of Kerrera, and was buried at Melrose.

Alexander was a generous patron of the Church, founding the abbeys at Balmerino and Pluscarden, and the Blackfriars monastery at Perth. He was also responsible for the castles of Eilean Donan and Kildrummy.

In 1221 he married Joanna, sister of Henry III, and in 1239, after her death, he married Marie de Courcy, with whom he had a son, ALEXANDER III, who succeeded him.

Alexander III (1241—1286) The only son of Alexander II (1214—49) and his second wife Marie de Courcy. While his minority witnessed some signs of noble unrest, for example, the seizure of the boy king by the pro-English Durward family in 1257, recent assessments of his reign play down the traditional view that such turbulence was either typical or very significant. Certainly Alexander, once he entered his majority, would appear to have ruled effectively in partnership with such powerful magnates as the Comyns and Stewarts. Whether this period of royal government was a 'Golden Age' is another matter, since this verdict is largely one taken by chroniclers later surveying the reign with somewhat rose-tinted spectacles.

There was some expansion of burghs and royal finances but unquestionably the greatest achievement of Alexander III was the acquisition of the Hebrides and the Isle of Man following the defeat of Hakon IV of Norway at LARGS in October 1263 and the subsequent Treaty of PERTH in July 1266.

Dynastically speaking, Alexander's reign ended disastrously. Both sons by his first wife Margaret, daughter of Henry III, predeceased him; his daughter Margaret, who also died before him, had married Eric II of Norway and it was their daughter, MARGARET, 'THE MAID OF NORWAY' (c.1283—1290) who was left as heir following her father's death, at Kinghorn, Fife, on 19 March 1286 as a result of a riding accident.

• *Duncan, A.A.M., Scotland: The Making of the Kingdom, Oliver & Boyd, 1975.*

• *Reid, N. (ed.), Scotland in the Reign of Alexander III, John Donald, 1990.*

Alien Act, see UNION, TREATY OF

American War of Independence
The American Revolutionary War (1775–83) impinged on Scotland in several ways, affecting politics, the economy and society in varying degrees. Historically there were long-established links between Scotland and the North American colonies, both in terms of EMIGRATION and trade, the latter becoming more significant with the rise of the TOBACCO trade, centred on Glasgow. Indeed, as Lenman indicates, the Glasgow merchant community was apparently in favour of compromise with the American colonists during the crisis sparked off by the Stamp Act passed by Parliament in 1765. Glasgow helped to secure the repeal of the Act in 1766, and in 1775 Glasgow and London merchants again sought conciliation in the interest of trade.

Such was the importance of America that most of the major figures of the Scottish Enlightenment had an opinion on it. David HUME (1711—76) declared himself 'American in my principles', but he preferred to get rid of the colonies before their aspirations caught on nearer home. Lord KAMES (1696—1782) was also initially sympathetic, corresponding with Benjamin Franklin (1706—90) about American representation in the British Parliament, but by 1774 he took the view that the colonies ought to be taxed whether or not they were politically represented. Others, including the painter Allan Ramsay (1713—84), William Robertson (1721—93), Principal of Edinburgh University, and the philosopher Adam FERGUSSON (1723—1816), indicated that the Scots were generally loyal supporters of the status quo and had little sympathy for the rebellious colonies. This was seen in PRESS reports of the time, which favoured recruitment for service in America, and in loyal addresses emanating from the burghs.

Many Scottish REGIMENTS served in the war, notably six new Highland regiments raised in 1777–8 expressly to fight the rebels. These were joined by many Scottish emigrants, though in the southern colonies Scots could be found on both sides — Loyalist and Patriot. As events had it, the American victory at Saratoga marked a turning point and the French entered the war in 1778. The British were ultimately overwhelmed by superior tactics and the problems of supplying a huge force at such a distance.

The American War of Independence acted as something of a catalyst to economic change, by encouraging a switch of resources from the commercial to the industrial sector that was already underway before the conflict. This can best be seen in the rise of the cotton industry, the raw material being obtained mainly from the plantations of the southern colonies, with which Scotland maintained strong trading and social links long after the Declaration of Independence. It might well be said that the American Revolution also influenced the spread of democratic ideas, which were briefly voiced by Thomas Muir (1765—99) and others in the aftermath of the French Revolution.

• *Brock, W.R., Scotus Americanus: A Survey of the Sources for Links between Scotland and America in the Eighteenth Century, Edinburgh University Press, 1982.*
• *Hook, A., Scotland and America: A Study of Cultural Relations, 1750– 1835, Blackie & Sons, 1975.*
• *Lenman, B., Integration, Enlightenment and Industrialisation. Scotland 1746–1832, Edward Arnold, 1981.*

Anderson, John (1726—96) John Anderson was an archetypal Scottish figure celebrated for his radical views on EDUCATION and for establishing a second university in Glasgow — predecessor of the Royal College of Science and Technology and the University of Strathclyde. A son of the manse at Roseneath, he was educated at the University of Glasgow, becoming professor of Oriental languages (1756) before switching to natural philosophy, or physics (1760). It was from Anderson that James WATT (1736–1819) received the model of Newcomen's steam-engine for repair.

Like many of his contemporaries, Anderson had a practical flair for teaching and for the applied sciences and he communicated his enthusiasm through twice-weekly classes to working men throughout his academic life. His main publication, *Institutes of Physics* (1786), went through five editions before his death. Anderson had an interesting, if short-lived, flirtation with RADICALISM and with the events of the FRENCH REVOLUTION, visiting Paris in 1791 to present the National Convention with a model

gun of his own design — what was called 'The Gift of Science to Liberty'. During his stay a six-pounder based on the model was demonstrated, one onlooker being John Paul Jones (1747—92), reputed founder of the American navy. Anderson was present in Paris when Louis XVI was brought back to the city from Varennes.

Under Anderson's will he left an endowment for the education of the 'unacademical classes' and this led to the establishment of Anderson's University or Institute. From a simple start teaching physics and chemistry, it soon embraced medicine and various other subjects. The second professor in charge of the university, George Birkbeck (1776–1841), started free classes for artisans in mechanics and chemistry, leading to the establishment of the Mechanics Institute — an early pioneer of adult and continuing education.

• *Butt, J., John Anderson's Legacy, Tuckwell Press, 1996.*

Anne (1665—1714) Second daughter of JAMES VII (1633–1701) and his first wife Anne Hyde (1637–61), Anne married Prince George of Denmark (1653–1708) in 1683 and was the last Stewart monarch to rule. The REVOLUTION SETTLEMENT had ensured her succession to the throne on the death of WILLIAM III (1650–1702) and Mary (1662—94). However, her failure to produce any surviving heirs was to cause a major breach in Anglo-Scottish relations at her accession in 1702, a situation largely the result of the English Parliament bestowing the succession on Sophia, Electress of Hanover (1630–1714), and her family without consulting its Scottish counterpart. There followed the retaliatory ACT OF SECURITY and ANENT PEACE AND WAR before the crisis was eventually resolved by the signing of the Treaty of UNION. Her reign ended inauspiciously in Scotland with growing demands for an end to the Union and clandestine support for the JACOBITE cause.

•*Ferguson, W., Scotland 1689 to the Present, Oliver & Boyd, 1968.*

Anti-Corn Law League The League was established with its headquarters in Manchester in 1839 to advocate free trade — and especially the abolition of tariffs on imported grain under the Corn Laws. These — it was widely believed — kept food prices artificially high. Like CHARTISM, the League was one of the first truly national reform movements and sought to consolidate the activities of numerous anti-Corn Law associations. Its leaders were Richard Cobden (1804–65) and John Bright (1811–89).

The Scottish movement had close associations with Chartism and many leading Chartists were directors of local anti-Corn Law associations before the League was formally established. In Glasgow, for example, William Weir, editor of the *Glasgow Argus*, played a prominent role as early as 1838. But the relationship between the two reform movements was far from easy and there was some fear in Scotland that the League was a tool of middle-class WHIGS and LIBERALS, and distracting attention from the wider objectives of political reform and universal suffrage. Although many Scottish Chartists wanted cheaper food, they suspected that industrialists were merely interested in lowering wages. Scottish suspicions were reflected in an apparent reluctance to contribute financially — though this changed later. At its peak the League proved very popular in BURGHS and industrial centres and even made some impact in rural districts in Fife and the Lothians most at risk from repeal.

Unlike Chartism, the Anti-Corn Law League was of single purpose, the *Scotch Reformers Gazette* declaring in 1839 that, 'The all-engrossing topic of the present day is the repeal of the Corn Laws. Of all the baneful bequests handed down to us by blood-stained Toryism, these laws are the most unjustifiable, the most iniquitous and the most oppressive.' The League was also well-organized and made good use of propaganda — the popular PRESS, monster meetings, pamphleteering — and succeeded in generating mass support.

In 1840 the League combined parliamentary reform and the extension of suffrage with its free trade programme, but an umbrella organization embracing Chartism, the Complete Suffrage League, had limited success.

J.B. Smith (1794–1879), for a time the League's president, stood for Dundee in the General Election of 1841 but the Liberal vote was split by the intervention of a local RADICAL candidate and he lost to the CONSERVATIVE candidate in a three-cornered fight. Another prominent figure was Sydney Smith, an Edinburgh solicitor, who was not only a leading missionary but also later secretary of the League.

In common with other popular movements, the League made most headway in times of harvest failure and social distress during 1839—41. Later it was the disastrous failure of the potato harvest and the resulting FAMINE in Ireland and the Scottish HIGHLANDS during 1845—6 that brought the League ultimate success in the repeal of the Corn Laws in June 1846.

•*Hutchison, I.G.C., A Political History of Scotland 1832—1924, John Donald, 1986.*

•*McCord, N., The Anti-Corn Law League 1836—1846, Unwin University Books, 1968.*

Arbroath, Declaration of (6 April 1320) The name commonly used to describe the letter sent to Pope John XXII by Scottish nobles, denouncing the tyrannies of Edward I's reign and re-asserting Scotland's ancient right to independence. Sealed by eight earls and 31 barons, it was written at Arbroath Abbey by its abbot, Bernard of Linton. The letter was a passionate attempt to dissuade the pope from supporting the English crown's claims of sovereignty over Scotland, pledging allegiance to ROBERT I and to the cause of Scottish independence: 'for so long as a hundred of us remain alive, we will yield in no least way to English dominion. For we fight, not for glory nor for riches nor for honour, but only and alone for freedom, which no good man surrenders but with his life.' On receipt of the letter, the pope rescinded punitive measures he had taken against the Scots and called on Edward II to make peace.

Argyll, Earl of, see CAMPBELL, ARCHIBALD, EIGHTH EARL OF ARGYLL

Argyll Rising, see CAMPBELL, ARCHIBALD, NINTH EARL OF ARGYLL

Arran, Earls of, see HAMILTON, SECOND EARL OF ARRAN

Arrol, Sir William (1839—1913) Arrol's name is linked to the heyday of Scottish heavy ENGINEERING, notably the reconstructed Tay Bridge, and more famous still, the Forth Bridge, a massive monument to its builders. His career was mapped out from the beginning for his father was a COTTON spinner and eventually mill manager, and his uncle a mechanical engineer in Paisley. Arrol himself started out in cotton but was then apprenticed to a local blacksmith, often the starting point for aspiring engineers. When he had completed his apprenticeship he went to work in England, prior to his return to Scotland to begin what proved to be a meteoric rise in the engineering industry.

By 1868 Arrol had his own business, working mainly in the IRON industry. He soon diversified into bridge building, mainly for RAILWAY companies, most notably the Clyde viaduct into the new Central Station (1878—9). This led ultimately to the contracts for the second Tay Bridge, and the much more prestigious Forth Bridge, designed by Sir Benjamin Baker to be a third of a mile long and costing the then massive sum of £3 million. Much of the work at the bridge sites was under his personal supervision. The Tay opened in 1887 and the Forth in 1890 (when Arrol was knighted), and these successes led to more major contracts for Arrol's firm. He was already heading a massive and diverse enterprise involved in construction, hydraulic and structural engineering, as well as having personal interests in BANKING, shipping and SHIPBUILDING.

Politically Arrol began as a LIBERAL but because he opposed HOME RULE he switched to the CONSERVATIVES and was MP for South Ayrshire (1895–1906). Arrol was one of the great makers of Victorian enterprise and his career might well be contrasted with that of his near contemporary, Andrew CARNEGIE, who rather than staying at home emigrated to make his fortune in the United States.

Asquith, Herbert Henry (1852–1928) H.H. Asquith, the LIBERAL politician and Prime Minister (1908–16), although born in Lancashire, had long-standing Scottish connections as MP for East Fife (1886–1918) and Paisley (1920–4). He was Home Secretary under Gladstone (1809–98) from 1892 to 1895. Following the Liberal victory in the General Election of 1906, Asquith served as Chancellor of the Exchequer under CAMPBELL-BANNERMAN (1836–1908). Asquith's time as Prime Minister was fraught with challenges and difficulties, including the 1909 budget, crises over the House of Lords in 1910–11, troubles in Ulster, charges of corruption in government, the suffrage question, and the outbreak of WORLD WAR I.

During the war he placed great trust in the military experts, but the failure of the Dardanelles expedition and the stalemate on the Western Front, characterized by the events at the Battle of the Somme, brought little credit either to the Coalition Government or his leadership. After a vigorous press campaign he resigned in December 1916 and was replaced by Lloyd George (1863–1945). Although he remained leader of the Liberal Party until 1926 and gave his support to the minority Labour Government led by Ramsay MACDONALD (1866–1937) in 1924, he never again held high office.

• *Cassar, G.H., Asquith as War Leader, Hambledon Press, 1994.*
• *Jenkins, R., Asquith, Collins, 1978.*
• *Koss, S., Asquith, Allen Lane, 1976.*

Auld Alliance The term used to describe Scotland's political links with France and a feature of Franco-Scottish relations, intermittently until the Reformation in the mid-sixteenth century.

The first such alliance was signed in October 1295 on the eve of the WARS OF INDEPENDENCE, lasting until the French defeat by the English at Courtrai in 1303 brought it to an end. The Treaty of Corbeil (1326) was similar to that of 1295, with both sides promising mutual assistance against England, and there were further renewals, all with little impact on Anglo-Scottish relations, in 1371 and 1391.

Although there were subsequent formal renewals in the fifteenth century, in 1428, 1448 and 1484, the Auld Alliance by this date was working less effectively as foreign relations took on a more international aspect epitomized by the alliance with Burgundy in 1449, whereby JAMES II married Mary of Gueldres, niece of Philip IV.

It was renewed on several occasions thereafter, notably by JAMES IV (1473–1513), whose adherence to it was to result in his melancholy fate at FLODDEN. Subsequently there was less enthusiasm for it, a fact borne out by the failure of Albany (c.1484–1536) to persuade the Scottish nobility to invade England in 1522 and 1523. However, it took a fresh lease of life following the French marriages of JAMES V (1512–42), although his war against Henry VIII (1491–1547) was not specifically in support of France.

The zenith of the alliance came during the minority of MARY, QUEEN OF SCOTS (1542–87), and in the aftermath of the ROUGH WOOING. It was resentment at the English invasions and fear of conquest by that country that prompted the signing of the TREATY OF HADDINGTON with France in 1548 and saw Scotland becoming a virtual French satellite. But, although French influence was to reach unprecedented heights during the regency of MARY OF GUISE (1515–60), the outbreak of the REFORMATION brought a dramatic political transformation. Thus the dependence of the reformers on English assistance, not to mention economic motives for such an alignment, produced by 1560 what effectively amounted to a diplomatic revolution. Thereafter, Scotland and England, despite various vicissitudes in their relationship, grew closer together and the Auld Alliance was forsaken.

• *Donaldson, G., Scotland: James V to James VII, Oliver & Boyd, 1965.*
• *Ferguson, W., Scotland's Relations with England, John Donald, 1977.*
• *Nicholson, R., The Later Middle Ages, Oliver & Boyd, 1974.*
• *Grant, A., Independence and Nationhood, Oliver & Boyd, 1984.*

Australia, see EMIGRATION, MACQUARIE, LACHLAN

B

Baird, John, see RADICAL WAR

Baird, John Logie (1888—1946)
Baird was born at Helensburgh, Dumbartonshire, the son of a local minister. He studied electrical engineering at the Royal Technical College and then went to the University of Glasgow, where the start of World War I interrupted his studies. He was never very fit and was turned down for military service on health grounds, spending most of the war as superintendent engineer of the Clyde Valley Electrical Power Company — a pioneer of electrical generation and power transmission in Scotland. After the war he tried a variety of business enterprises but was forced to abandon them due to his recurring ill-health. In 1922 he moved to Hastings.

Baird then began his scientific research on television, his laboratory an attic and his equipment odd pieces of junk, including a tea chest, biscuit tin, pieces of cardboard, darning needles, string and sealing wax. By 1924 he had transmitted the image of a Maltese cross over several feet. Moving to attic rooms in London's Soho he continued his experiments, despite ill-health and virtual poverty. In 1926 he made his breakthrough and was able to give a demonstration of his system to a group of fifty scientists. Thereafter events moved rapidly

and 1927 saw a television demonstration over telephone lines linking London and Glasgow, and the foundation of the Baird Television Development Company and the Television Society, of which Baird became a fellow. In 1928 the first transatlantic TV pictures were successfully transmitted and the same year Baird gave the first demonstration of colour TV.

An experimental TV service was inaugurated by the BBC in 1929 and Baird himself continued to be associated with many of the early developments in outside broadcasting during the early thirties. In 1935 the Selsdon Committee recommended that the BBC should produce the programmes for a full-scale, regular, public TV service — as was already provided by radio. The Baird system, using 240 lines, was to be used alongside the all-electronic Marconi-EMl system, which transmitted on 405 lines. The BBC used both systems until 1937 when Baird's was ultimately dropped.

Baird's company continued to manufacture TV sets on the electronic system, but he apparently took little interest. Becoming increasingly disillusioned he retreated into top secret war and other experimental work. He died in 1946.

•*Hallett, M., John Logie Baird and Television, Priory Press, 1978.*

• McArthur, R,T. and Waddell, P., The Secret Life of John Logie Baird, Hutchinson, 1986.

Balfour, Arthur James (1848—1930) Balfour came of a well-connected family, which, thanks to his grandfather, had made its fortune in India and bought into the landed gentry through the purchase of Whittinghame, East Lothian. The family had also maintained its position in society by a series of judicious marriages. His father, a director of the North British Railway and the MP for Haddington (1841—47), married a daughter of the second Marquis of Salisbury, and this relationship was to prove highly influential in shaping Balfour's political career.

Educated at Eton and Trinity College, Cambridge, Balfour at first devoted himself to philosophy then, under the influence of his uncle, the third Marquis of Salisbury (1830—1903), entered politics as CONSERVATIVE MP for Hertford in 1874. He held this seat until 1885, becoming member for Manchester East (1885—1906), and then for the City of London (1906—22). He was soon moving in high circles and was prominent in the 'Fourth Party', a Conservative ginger group, whose number included Lord Randolph Churchill (1849—94). When his uncle formed a government in 1885 he was appointed president of the Local Government Board. With the return of the Conservatives in the General Election of 1886 Balfour became Secretary for Scotland, Chief Secretary for Ireland (1887—91), then Leader of the Commons and First Lord of the Treasury (1891—2). He held these last two posts again under Salisbury (1895—1902).

Balfour became Prime Minister following Salisbury's retiral in 1902. Although highly intelligent and able in his previous offices, he was less successful as Prime Minister, giving an impression of indecision and proving unable to control the debate centring on tariff reform and free trade within his party. He resigned in 1905 and was defeated early the following year, when the reforming LIBERAL Government under CAMPBELL-BANNERMAN (1836—1908) was elected. He was Leader of the Opposition (1906—11), resigning the leadership of the Conservative Party following two narrow General Election defeats in 1910.

In 1914, following the outbreak of WORLD WAR I, Balfour became a member of the Committee of Imperial Defence and attended the War Cabinet (1914—15). Thereafter he was successively First Lord of the Admiralty (1915—16), Foreign Secretary (1916—19), and Lord President of the Council, (1919—22 and 1925—9). Balfour was Foreign Secretary at a vital time, leading a diplomatic mission to the United States and issuing the Balfour Declaration in favour of a Jewish homeland in Palestine in 1917 — as well as being a delegate to the Versailles peace conference in 1919. He was made an earl in 1922 and continued to be active in politics throughout the rest of his life. Balfour's career might be compared with that of his Liberal contemporary, Lord ROSEBERY (1847—1929).

• Mackay, R.F., Balfour: Intellectual Statesman, Oxford University Press, 1985.

• Zebel, S.H., Balfour: A Political Biography, Cambridge University Press, 1973.

Balliol, John, King of Scots (1250–1313) His family originated from Bailleul in Normandy, becoming prominent in Scotland during the reign of DAVID I (c.1084–1153). Following the death of MARGARET, 'MAID OF NORWAY' (c.1283–90), John, son of DEVORGILLA (c.1209–89) and John Baillol, was one of the leading COMPETITORS. Edward I in his adjudication in the 'Great Cause' favoured Baillol in preference to the other main candidate ROBERT BRUCE 'THE COMPETITOR' (1210–95), and he was crowned King of Scots on 30 November 1292.

Baillol's reign has suffered a bad press largely as a result of a propaganda campaign by the Bruce family and it is difficult to form a balanced assessment of his performance as a ruler. However, the existing evidence would suggest a monarch with a genuine concern for the dispensation of justice and for the strengthening of royal authority. At least this would appear to have been the case until his reign was undermined by the malign influence of Edward I and his assertions of overlordship.

Initially, Edward I's inteference took the form of insisting that Scottish legal appeals should be heard in England. However, it was his attempts in 1295 to recruit Scottish military assistance for his war against France which provoked a major crisis. The formation of the first AULD ALLIANCE resulted in the English invasion of 1296 in which Edward's army swept all before them. Baillol capitulated at Montrose on 26 July 1296 when, in a ceremony resembling a court martial, he was humiliatingly stripped of all his royal trappings of power to become the 'Toom Tabard' of subsequent accounts. At the same time the Stone of Destiny, the Scottish regalia and various records were seized by Edward I, and the Great Seal was destroyed.

Confined to the Tower of London, Baillol was released, after papal intercession, in July 1299 but on the understanding that he played no political role. By 1301 he had returned to his family estates in France where he was to remain until his death in 1313.

• Nicholson, R., Scotland: The Later Middle Ages, Oliver & Boyd, 1974.
• Watson, F., Under the Hammer: Edward I and Scotland, 1286–1307, Tuckwell Press, 1998.

banking The development of banking was critical to the modernization and economic growth of Scotland during and after the AGRICULTURAL REVOLUTION and INDUSTRIAL REVOLUTION of the eighteenth and nineteenth centuries. The first bank, the Bank of Scotland, though opposed by William PATERSON, was modelled on the Bank of England. It was created by an Act of the Scottish PARLIAMENT in 1695 – the same year the Act founding the ill-fated COMPANY OF SCOTLAND was passed. The 'Old Bank', as it became popularly known, was given a monopoly of banking in Scotland for twenty-one years – not actually broken until 1727 with the foundation of the 'New Bank', the Royal Bank of Scotland. The Royal Bank had originated in the Equivalent Company (itself incorporated in 1724), which had arisen from the complicated financial settlement necessitated by the Treaty of UNION. One of the first deposits was a payment by the government of £20,000 to provide income for the activities of the BOARD OF TRUSTEES. The third institution, the British Linen Company, was incorporated in 1746 – but by the 1760s its activities had begun to include a more specific banking function.

Alongside the three chartered companies there developed a second group of banking institutions, the private banks, often partnerships and located exclusively in Edinburgh. Many were merchants attracted by the potential profits of banking, notably through the granting of cash credits or overdrafts and the negotiation of bills of exchange. John Coutts & Co. was a typical merchant house that successfully entered banking and laid the origins of Forbes, Hunter & Co. (1773), one of the most important private banks. Towards the end of the eighteenth century some of this group even began to issue their own notes.

Finally, there were the provincial banks – again invariably partnerships – established to serve local communities outside Edinburgh. These provided banking services and finance for agriculture and industry. The first companies were formed in Aberdeen (1747) and Glasgow, where the Ship Bank (1749) and the Arms Bank (1750) both became important. They were followed by nearly a dozen others before 1790. At the peak of activity around 1820 there were over thirty, a third being in Glasgow and the west of Scotland.

Scotland pioneered many aspects of banking, including limited liability, widespread use of paper money to meet the demand for credit, the development of branch banking, granting a cash credit, encouraging deposits by paying interest, and joint-stock banking. The Savings Bank movement, initiated in 1810 at Ruthwell, Dumfriesshire, by the Rev. Henry Duncan (1774–1846) later spread to other parts of Scotland and beyond. These developments were not made without difficulties – including major financial crises and bank failures in 1772, 1793, 1825, 1857 and 1878.

During the nineteenth century a new group of joint-stock banks developed to join the three older institutions, ultimately supplanting the private and provincial banks by establishing branch systems. This led to another significant feature – the early consolidation by mergers of the Scottish banking system. Following the failure of the Western Bank of Scotland (1857) and the City of Glasgow Bank (1878) there were a total of ten banks, three public and seven joint stock. Subsequent amalgamations in the twentieth century reduced the number to three – the Bank of Scotland, the Royal Bank of Scotland and the Clydesdale Bank. All three became integrated in the national and international banking community – but Scottish banking retained many distinctive features derived from its long history. The most obvious, perhaps, is note issue, a long traditional feature north of the Border.

• Cameron, A., The Bank of Scotland, 1695–1995: A Very Singular Institution, Mainstream, 1995.

• Checkland, S.G., Scottish Banking: A History, 1695—1973, Collins, 1975.
• Gaskin, M., The Scottish Banks, Allen & Unwin, 1965.
• Munn, C.W., The Scottish Provincial Banking Companies 1747—1864, John Donald, 1981.

Bannockburn, Battle of (24 June 1314) In June 1313 the English governor of Stirling castle under siege from Edward BRUCE (c.1276—1318) offered to surrender the fortress if he had not been relieved by English forces by midsummer 1314.

This arrangement and the general situation in Scotland spurred Edward II into action and in March 1314 military and naval preparations were begun for an English offensive. By June 23 the two armies faced each other about two miles south of Stirling castle at the Bannockburn, a tributary of the River Forth, the English with a force of about 15,000 infantry and 2,500 calvary outnumbering the Scottish one of about 8,000 infantry and 500 calvary. BRUCE, recognizing that the English army was disadvantageously positioned in a marshy section of the Bannockburn, abandoned his customary guerrilla tactics and launched an all-out attack on the English. This paid dividends since the English cavalry made little headway against Edward Bruce, and the English archers, usually so effective, were soon in trouble against the small Scottish units commanded by Sir Robert KEITH (d.1346). As the afternoon progressed it became obvious to Edward II that he was suffering a major defeat and with the remnants of his forces he fled south pursued by the victorious Scottish forces.

Bannockburn was a crucial victory for Bruce in the WARS OF INDEPENDENCE. Within Scotland it made his opponents recognize his invincibility and greatly consolidated his position. Nonetheless it did not end the struggle with England which was to last for another fourteen years.

• Barrow, G.W.S., Robert Bruce and the Community of the Realm of Scotland, Edinburgh University Press, 1988.
• Nicholson, R., Scotland: The Later Middle Ages, Oliver & Boyd, 1974.
• Sadler, J., Scottish Battles, Canongate Books, 1996.

Barbour, John (d.1395) Author of various works, he is best remembered for his long narrative poem 'The Brus' written in 1375 during the reign of ROBERT II (1316—90). Although it took certain liberties with the material available it was nonetheless based on oral and written testimony and must be regarded as an invaluable historical source for the period 1286 to 1329.

An ecclesiastic, he was archdeacon of the diocese of Aberdeen, he was also an important royal official. With his contemporary John of Fordun (c.1320—84), Barbour began a tradition of scholarly patriotic writing which was to reach its apogee with the *Scotichronicon* of Walter Bower (d.1449). A more populist version of Scottish history was forthcoming later in the reign of JAMES III (1452—88) with Blind Harry's *The Wallace*.

• Duncan, A.A.M. (ed.), The Bruce, Canongate Classics, 1997.
• Nicholson, R., Scotland: The Later Middle Ages, Oliver & Boyd, 1974.

baron courts   Baron courts were survivors of the medieval system where the Crown devolved judicial and territorial powers to its great landowners or 'barons' in return for certain services. Thus the baron, or more likely his deputy, the baillie, presided over a jury of varying size either nominated by him or chosen by the court itself. By the sixteenth and seventeenth centuries much of the work of the laird and his 'birlay-men' concerned agricultural matters like repairs to dykes, disputes over land or compulsory labour on the baron's farm. The other main business was minor social misdemeanours such as assaults, drunkenness or sabbath breaking, with the normal punishment for most offences being a fine or possibly forfeiture of goods. The powers of the baron courts were greatly reduced during the CROMWELLIAN UNION and although they were not abolished under the terms of the HERITABLE JURISDICTIONS ACT (1747) they gradually fell into disuse.
• *Dickinson, W.C. (ed.), The Court Book of the Barony of Carnwath, 1523—2, Scottish History Society, 1937.*

Beardmore, William, Lord Invernairn (1856—1936)   Beardmore became one of the giants of the Scottish ENGINEERING industry during the heyday of its prosperity before 1914. Educated at Ayr Academy and the High School of Glasgow, he later attended the Royal College of Science and Technology, Glasgow and the Royal School of Mines, London. While serving his apprenticeship at Parkhead Forge in Glasgow he went to evening classes at ANDERSON'S COLLEGE to study mathematics and chemistry. When his father died in 1879 Beardmore became a partner with his uncle and later founded the firm of William Beardmore & Co.

Beardmore became one of the most famous engineering and shipbuilding enterprises in the world, constructing merchant ships, battleships, cruisers, destroyers and submarines — as well as diversifying into airships and planes before and during WORLD WAR I. After 1919 Beardmore's enterprise initially maintained its pre-war momentum, mainly constructing liners, but it soon ran into trouble with the onset of the DEPRESSION. He tried locomotive building and motor car manufacture, but neither were particularly successful given the economic slump. He left the firm in 1929 — a year before its shipbuilding activity was effectively moth-balled under a national shipbuilding agreement.

William Beardmore was knighted in 1914 and raised to the peerage as Lord Invernairn in 1921. The archetypal Scottish industrialist — autocratic in his dealings with his workforce — is appropriately commemorated in the Beardmore Glacier in Antarctica, named in his honour by Sir Ernest Shackleton (1874—1922).
• *Hume, J.R. and Moss, M., Beardmore: The History of a Scottish Industrial Giant, Heinemann Educational, 1979.*

Beaton, David   (c.1494—1546) Born in Markinch, Fife, the fifth of a family of fourteen children, he was the uncle of James Beaton (1517—1603), archbishop of Glasgow and the nephew of James Beaton (c.1480—1539), archbishop of St Andrews. He studied at St

Andrews, Glasgow, Paris and Orléans and, through the influence of his uncle James Beaton, became Commendator of Arbroath Abbey in 1523. He was appointed Bishop of Mirepoix in France in 1537 and made a cardinal a year later, the first a reward for his services to the AULD ALLIANCE and the second for his loyalty to Rome. He succeeded as Archbishop of St Andrews in 1539 and became Chancellor in the government of ARRAN (c.1516—75) early in 1543. His adherence to the papal cause and his Francophile sentiments, which had been influential in preventing the meeting of JAMES V (1512—42) and Henry VIII (1491—1547) at York in 1541, initially resulted in his imprisonment by his pro-English opponents. However, he soon retrieved his position and by the end of 1543 the pro-French faction led by MARY OF GUISE (1515—60) and himself dominated the Arran administration. The proposed Anglo-Scottish marriage treaty was repudiated, French arms and money arrived in the country and the cardinal was appointed papal legate. Although active against heresy and responsible for the execution of WISHART (1513—46), his affluence and worldly outlook, not to mention his several illegitimate children, did little to enhance the reputation of the Church as it faced the early challenge of the reformers. As has been aptly said, he was in some ways a Scottish equivalent of the English cardinal Wolsey (c.1473—1530). On 29 May 1546 he was murdered at ST ANDREWS CASTLE by a group of Fife lairds including KIRKCALDY OF GRANGE (c.1520—73). One of their motives was certainly vengeance

for Wishart's death, but personal grievances and Beaton's pro-French policies were also contributory factors in his assassination.
• *Sanderson, M.H.B., Cardinal of Scotland: David Beaton (1494—1546), John Donald, 1986.*

Bell, Henry (1767—1830) Bell was the son of a prominent West Lothian millwright, though he himself was apprenticed as a mason before taking up his father's trade. He served under various engineers before going south to London as an apprentice to the young civil engineer John RENNIE (1761—1821), who had earlier been associated with the work of James WATT (1736—1819). In 1790 Bell settled in Glasgow, which was already becoming an ENGINEERING and SHIPBUILDING centre, and was able to enter a partnership soon after.

Bell apparently began his experiments with steam navigation about 1798 and in 1800 fitted a steam-engine in a small vessel. His appeals for government assistance fell on deaf ears, and he had also to face the challenge of foreign competition from the United States, where Robert Fulton sailed a steamboat on the Hudson River in 1807. Nevertheless, in 1812 the COMET, a 30-ton vessel driven by a 3-hp steam-engine, built to Bell's design, began the first commercial service on the Clyde. This was maintained until 1820 when the COMET was wrecked. Although Bell had his precursors, notably another Scottish engineer, William SYMINGTON (1763—1831), he can nevertheless claim to be one of the leading pioneers of steam shipping who found practical solutions to many of the problems involved.

• *Osborne, B.D., The Ingenious Mr Bell, Argyll Publishing, 1995.*

Berwick, Treaty of (1560) Towards the end of 1559 the LORDS OF THE CONGREGATION despite their initial early successes were beginning to find themselves hard pressed by the forces of MARY OF GUISE (1515–60). By December her French army had taken Stirling, causing the reformers to withdraw their followers to Glasgow and St Andrews respectively. To their politically-minded supporters such as MAITLAND OF LETHINGTON (c.1525–73) and to KNOX (c.1512–72) as well, direct intervention by England, instead of intermittent clandestine financial aid, was becoming imperative. But while most of Elizabeth's (1533–1603) government favoured such a course, the Queen herself hesitated. Partly, this was through a fear that support for a rebellion in Scotland might cause awkward repercussions among Catholics in England. Moreover, armed involvement would be costly and, besides, why should she weaken her precarious finances any further by helping a religious movement whose doctrines she disagreed with and whose leader she personally disliked? Undoubtedly what convinced her she should risk intervening was the deteriorating political situation in Scotland and the realization that if the Lords of the Congregation were eliminated the country could be used as a base for providing further French support for the dynastic claims of MARY (1542–87). Thus in January 1560, before any agreement was actually signed, an English fleet was taking effective action against the French in the Firth of Forth.

Then on 27 February the treaty was completed between the two sides at Berwick, both nations agreeing to adopt a policy of mutual assistance against France. Certainly English military aid improved the fortunes of the reformers, who by April were besieging Leith with their English allies. At the same time the impact of the early stages of the French religious wars on that country's foreign policy should not be overlooked or underestimated.

The Treaty is often regarded as a 'diplomatic revolution' marking the beginning of that Anglo-Scottish co-operation that was to culminate in the UNION OF THE CROWNS. None the less, it is questionable whether, in 1560, either the Scots or English attached quite so much significance to it.

• *Dickinson, W.C., Scotland from Earliest Times to 1603, Oxford University Press, 1977.*
• *Donaldson, G., Scotland: James V to James VII, Oliver & Boyd, 1965.*
• *Ferguson, W., Scotland's Relations with England, John Donald, 1977.*

Birgham, Treaty of (1290) With Scotland plunged into a minority following the death of ALEXANDER III (1241–86), Edward I was understandably enthusiastic about the possibilities of arranging a marriage between his son Edward and MARGARET, MAID OF NORWAY (c.1283–90). Discussions on such a union commenced at Salisbury in November 1289 between English, Norwegian and Scottish commisioners, one of the latter being ROBERT BRUCE, lord of Annandale (1210–95). The decisions reached at Salisbury were ultimately ratified at Birgham, near Roxburgh on 18 July 1290 and, again at Northampton on 28 August. It was agreed that a dynastic union between the two kingdoms should take place but without, according to the terms, at least any diminution of 'the rights, liberties and customs' of Scotland. Whether or not Edward I would have adhered to these terms was never put to the test since the Maid of Norway died en route to Scotland shortly after the signing of this treaty.

•*Barrow, G.W.S., Robert Bruce and the Community of the Realm of Scotland, Edinburgh University Press, 1988.*

Bishops' War, the (1639) The controversial resolutions passed by the GLASGOW ASSEMBLY in November 1638 convinced Charles I (1600—49) that a show of force was the only way by which he could restore his position in Scotland. At the same time the Covenanting leadership, which included both ARGYLL (1607—61) and MONTROSE (1612—50), was preparing itself for this eventuality with extensive recruiting among Scottish veterans returning from the Thirty Years War in Europe. One of them, Alexander LESLIE (c.1580—1661), was placed in command of the Scottish army. Unquestionably Charles had an elaborate strategical plan in which the main feature was a large scale BORDER offensive but which also comprised a naval assault on the northeast by HAMILTON (1606—49) and diversionary Irish activity on the western seaboard. Unfortunately for the king, the Irish support never materialized, Hamilton's capture of Aberdeen was insignificant (it was soon recovered anyway by Montrose) and his main army was so weak and ineffectual that he quickly sought a

truce rather than face further humiliation. Hostilities ended with the Pacification of Berwick on 18 June, at which both sides agreed to disband their armies and the king promised to attend both PARLIAMENT and GENERAL ASSEMBLY, which were to be summoned later in the year.

•*Dickinson, W.C. and Donaldson, G. (eds.), A Source Book of Scottish History III, Nelson, 1961.*

•*Donaldson, G., Scotland: James V to James VII, Oliver & Boyd, 1965.*

•*Stevenson, D., The Scottish Revolution, 1637—44, David & Charles, 1973.*

Black, Dr Joseph (1728—99) Joseph Black was born in 1728 at Bordeaux, the son of a wine merchant from Belfast and a Scottish mother from Aberdeenshire. In 1740 Black was sent to school in Belfast, continuing his education after 1746 at the University of Glasgow. There he studied MEDICINE under another great scientist of the Scottish ENLIGHTENMENT, William CULLEN (1710—90). In 1750 he went to Edinburgh to pursue his studies and also began to take an interest in chemistry. After detailed experiments he produced an important thesis, *'Dehumore acido a cibis orto, et Magnesia alba'*, which laid the foundations of quantitative analysis in chemistry and of pneumatic chemistry itself. When Cullen moved to Edinburgh in 1756, Black became Professor of Anatomy and Chemistry at Glasgow. Although Black spent most of the next ten years either teaching or practising medicine, he also maintained an interest in chemistry and physics, and undertook pioneering research into

29

latent heat (1757—61). The results of these experiments contributed to the development of thermal science — as well as giving a useful impetus to James WATT's (1736—1819) improvements to the steam-engine. For many years the two men maintained an animated correspondence on matters of mutual interest.

In 1766 Black joined his former teacher, Cullen, at the University of Edinburgh, where he was appointed Professor of Medicine and Chemistry. Thereafter he established a considerable reputation as a teacher and savant — moving in a circle of powerful intellectuals that included Adam SMITH (1723—90), David HUME (1711—90) and Adam FERGUSSON (1723—1816), among others. Smith wrote that, 'no man had less nonsense in his head than Dr Black', and certainly his achievements were widely recognized by honours from France and Russia as well as his native land. Black was, therefore, one of an elite group who dominated the Scottish Enlightenment, displaying characteristic enthusiasm for applied science as much as knowledge for its own sake.

• *Crowther, J.G., Scientists of the Industrial Revolution, Cresset Press, 1962.*
• *Robinson, E. and McKie, D. (eds.), Partners in Science: The Letters of James Watt and Joseph Black, Constable, 1970.*

Black Death The bubonic plague reached Europe from China via the Middle East (Asia Minor) and began to spread over western Europe during the late 1340s. It is impossible to know with any degree of accuracy the population of Scotland during the medieval period and the scarcity of evidence has so far prevented modern scholars investigating the effects of the Black Death on Scotland in detail. In 1349 the Scots were evidently delighted to hear of the fate that overtaken the English as the plague took its relentless toll, sweeping from the Channel and Bristol Channel ports through the Midlands and on into the northern counties. This was regarded as just retribution and at the same time the Scots gathered their forces around Selkirk, 'laughing at their enemies' and preparing to invade. But as Zeigler notes, it was their last laugh, because just as they prepared to march 'a fearful mortality fell upon them and the Scots were scattered by sudden and savage death so that within a short period, some five thousand died'. The army dispersed, men dying on the roadside or taking the infection back to their homes in the more populated parts of the country. Actual evidence on the impact is hard to come by though it is known that 24 canons of the priory of St Andrews also died in 1349. The Scottish winter possibly helped retard the plague's progress but this was short-lived and during 1350 it spread rapidly over the whole country. Demographers think we can assume that because of the dispersed settlement pattern the effects of the plague were less severe than in England, where data for upland areas suggest mortality rates of 33-50 per cent, as compared to a possible 25-30 per cent in Scotland. The most striking feature of all the surviving accounts is the statement that a third of the population perished, though this may have been an exaggeration. Two chroniclers, John of Fordun and Andrew of Wyntoun, left descriptions of its impact, which can be read in the archive sources, while the later Book of Pluscarden says a third of the people died — with the poor suffering far more than the rich. On a political level it would be reasonable to assume that relatively small losses were sustained by the elite but the plague nevertheless affected Anglo-Scottish relations in that the English failed to capitalize on the lasting success that might have been possible following the Scots defeat at NEVILLE'S CROSS and the capture of DAVID II. A second major epidemic struck in 1361—62, but it may well have remained endemic thereafter. Another severe outbreak of bubonic plague occurred in the mid-1640s, after which it largely disappeared from Scotland. This could well be explained by changes in climate or other environmental factors.

•*Anderson, M. (ed.), British Population History from the Black Death to the Present Day, Cambridge University Press, 1996.*

•*Flinn, M. (ed.), Scottish Population History, Cambridge University Press, 1977.*

•*Zeigler, P., The Black Death, Alan Sutton Publishing Ltd, 1991.*

Blackwood's Magazine, see PRESS

Board of Agriculture (I) The Board of Agriculture, established under William Pitt (1759—1806), was the brainchild of the great Scottish improver, Sir John SINCLAIR (1754—1835). Arthur Young (1741—1820), the prominent agricultural essayist and traveller, became its first secretary.

Sinclair himself played a significant part in the Board's activities, serving as president on two occasions in 1798 and 1806—13. The Board's role was essentially propagandist and under its aegis an important series of volumes, *The General Views of Agriculture*, covering the counties and districts of Scotland, was published (1794—1813). Through its publications the Board greatly influenced the progress of agricultural IMPROVEMENT and the ENCLOSURE movement in Scotland.

Board of Agriculture (II) Another Board of Agriculture was established under the Agriculture (Scotland) Act in 1911 to advise the Secretary of State for Scotland on agricultural matters. Later, more wide-ranging responsibilities were exercised by the Department of Agriculture and Fisheries within the SCOTTISH OFFICE.

Board of Trustees. The Board of Trustees for Fisheries and Manufactures was established by PARLIAMENT in 1727 to administer revenues which were part of the Equivalent settlement under the Treaty of UNION. This favoured the FISHING and LINEN industries. Initially unsuccessful in the former, it concentrated after 1740 on the promotion of flax cultivation and the development of linen manufacture. Bounties or subsidies were offered for flax growing and the mechanization of the industry was also encouraged. The Board was also concerned with the promotion of the WOOLLEN industry and with CANAL building — notably the Forth and Clyde Canal. The Board of Trustees was finally wound up in 1844, its residual funds being devoted to the National Gallery of

Scotland. Historically the Board of Trustees was an early example of government intervention in the economy and played an important role in IMPROVEMENT and industrialization in the Scottish Lowlands.

Bonnymuir Scene of a skirmish on 5 April 1820 between armed RADICALS and troops, sometimes referred to as the 'Battle of Bonnymuir'. The party of Radicals were on their way to seize cannon at the CARRON COMPANY Ironworks, near Falkirk, and their interception proved to be the major incident in the short-lived RADICAL WAR.

Book of Discipline, First The blueprint for the reformed Kirk, detailing its financial arrangements, organization, educational policy and provisions for the poor, was drafted by KNOX (c.1512—72) and some of his colleagues between 29 April and 20 May 1560.

Accordingly, the wealth of the old CHURCH, with the exception of the MONASTERIES, was to be transferred to the new body. The rents and feu duties of the bishoprics were to provide for the upkeep of the universities and the newly-created office of the superintendent, while the existing teinds were to be used for clerical stipends, poor relief and educational purposes.

The central feature of the polity of the Kirk was to be a ministry whose members would be elected by individual congregations and who would be assisted by elders chosen annually. The latter's duties, apart from the important task of assisting the ministers in matters of discipline, included presenting an annual report on the clergy to the superintendents. Originally it planned to have ten such officials, with the administrative, but not the sacramental, authority of bishops, although, in fact, only five such appointments were ever made by the State. There was also a rather vague reference in the Book to a 'Council of the Church', which eventually emerged in the somewhat different form of the GENERAL ASSEMBLY of the 1560s.

In its educational programme the Kirk envisaged every parish having its own school with a schoolmaster or, in some instances, the local minister teaching the rudiments of grammar and Latin. Large towns, it was planned, would have colleges offering courses in higher education while the universities would also come under the Kirk's control.

The reformers were less specific in their remedies for tackling the problems of poverty but it was certainly made clear that the responsibility for poor relief lay with the Church. Thus, it should be the duty of its officials to make arrangements for supporting their less fortunate brethren.

Despite subsequent controversy over the structure of the post-Reformation church, the original proposals, including some supplementary instructions regarding the Confession of Faith, were all very gradually introduced in the years after 1560. The one notable exception was the plans for endowment. Here, with the laity so much in control of ecclesiastical finances, it was necessary to devise other arrangements. See also BOOK OF DISCIPLINE, SECOND.

•*Cowan, I.B., The Scottish Reformation, Weidenfeld & Nicolson, 1982.*

• *Donaldson, G., Scotland: James V to James VII, Oliver & Boyd, 1965.*
• *Donaldson, G., The Scottish Reformation, Cambridge University Press, 1960.*

Book of Discipline, Second The return of Andrew MELVILLE (1545–1622) from Switzerland in 1574 precipitated a crisis in the relations between the Kirk and the administration of the Regent MORTON (c.1516–81). By 1578 Melville and his radical colleagues had drafted their Second Book of Discipline, which reiterated many of the proposals in the FIRST BOOK OF DISCIPLINE but also contained several new demands. One of the main differences between the two Books was the Melvillians' desire to have bishops removed from the reformed Church, their duties to be undertaken by committees of ministers soon to become known as presbyteries. Another change affected the GENERAL ASSEMBLY, where attendance was to be restricted to ministers and elders. There was also an important and controversial alteration to the financial provisions made for the Kirk in that there was now a claim being made to all the revenues of the old church. Its collection was to be the responsibility of deacons, who would also see to its redistribution to the clergy, the poor and the schools. Finally, as well as a further call for lay PATRONAGE to be abolished, the doctrine of the 'Two Kingdoms' was firmly asserted. According to the latter, the Kirk should have sole control over all ecclesiastical affairs and, while the church should not interfere in civil matters, its members could none the less provide advice to the secular authorities.

The Second Book, like its predecessor, was rejected by PARLIAMENT. This was hardly surprising since its endowment proposals offended all members of the laity in possession of income belonging to the Kirk, while its anti-episcopal policy was completely at variance with the wishes of the Crown. In fact the religious controversy which now developed between the Kirk and the State was not resolved until the REVOLUTION SETTLEMENT, 1689–90.

• *Dickinson, W C. and Donaldson, G. (eds.), A Source Book of Scottish History III, Nelson, 1961.*
• *Kirk, J. (ed.), The Second Book of Discipline, St Andrew Press, 1980.*

Borders While the precise frontier with England remained uncertain along some stretches until after the UNION OF THE CROWNS (1603) — hence the term 'Debateable Land' for certain sections — both governments had set up fairly well defined administrative units or marches by a much earlier date. Administratively the Scottish borders consisted of the West March, comprising Dumfriesshire, the Stewartries of Annandale and Kirkcudbright as well as much of Wigtownshire, the Middle March, namely Peebleshire, Roxburghshire and Selkirkshire, and the East March covering mostly Berwickshire, known as the Merse. In addition there was Liddesdale, which was frequently treated as a separate entity.

The existing system of local government with its BURGH franchises operated, after a fashion, in the Borders. However, the intractable problems peculiar to a region notorious for its internecine feuding and general turbulence had resulted in additional administrative arrangements being necessary. Therefore, the key officials for much of the sixteenth century were the wardens or, in the case of Liddesdale, keepers, appointed and paid by the government to oversee each March. While not actually hereditary these positions tended to be a perquisite of certain powerful border families and their various branches. Thus the Homes and Kerrs were usually in charge of the East and Middle Marches respectively while the rivalry persisting between the Maxwells and the Johnstones was reflected in the alterations in wardenship in the West March.

The responsibilities of the wardens were very wide ranging but their two most important functions were undoubtedly administering justice and conducting negotiations with their English counterparts. This latter role was probably their most serious task, involving as it did holding 'days of truce' at which the English and Scottish officials co-operated in the enforcement of law and order along the frontier.

Although wardens received increasing military support from Scottish governments, especially in the latter part of the sixteenth century, their authority on certain occasions was superseded either by the appointment of a lieutenant responsible for the marches or by the nomination of a number of border commissioners. Lieutenancies were usually created in order to improve internal conditions within an area, whereas commissioners were more normally involved in handling Anglo-Scottish relations.

At the same time the Crown sometimes felt obliged to make its own presence felt more forcibly in these parts. In fact all Stewart governments in the sixteenth century indulged in such 'border raids'. The formula generally was that certain members of the PRIVY COUNCIL, possibly accompanied by the ruler or regent, and supported by a military levy, descended on a specific section of the countryside. After the armed force had detained as many known malefactors as it could find, justice was meted out at the specially convened courts or justice ayres. Peebles and Dumfries were frequently the centres selected for this purpose. The more affluent border families were compelled to subscribe to a General Bond whereby their lands or goods were offered as security for their good behaviour or that of their subordinates; lesser men gave pledges, often themselves, on the same basis as their superiors.

Despite the complex machinery that existed for controlling the borders it remained a problem area throughout the sixteenth century. Bonds were soon ignored once the conciliar visit was over while pledges were frequently worthless because of weaknesses and inefficiency in the custodial arrangements. The solution to all these difficulties came with the accession of JAMES VI (1566–1625) to the English throne in 1603. Thereafter, as a result of Anglo-Scottish co-operation that saw the formation of a joint border commission and the stationing of a small military force along the frontier, there was a vast improvement in conditions.

• *Fraser, G.M., The Steel Bonnets, Pan Books, 1974.*
• *Rae, T.I., The Administration of the Scottish Frontier, 1513—1603, Edinburgh University Press, 1966.*

Bothwell Bridge, Battle of (22 June 1679)   The policy of billeting the HIGHLAND HOST on the landowners in southwest Scotland who had refused to give sureties for their tenants had little effect on the support forthcoming for the COVENANTERS. Coventicles held in 1678 were better attended than ever and at one, for example, at Irongray, Dumfriesshire, there were 14,000 participants. In fact, by 1679 the Covenanting leaders were prepared to challenge the authorities outright. The murder of Archbishop SHARP (1618—79) in May, followed by the success at Drumclog the next month, produced a great upsurge in support for the dissidents. By 22 June a vast Covenanting army was camped beside Bothwell Bridge, near Hamilton, but it was a force that had serious divisions within its ranks. On the one hand, there were the moderates, including most of the ministers present, who were prepared to recognize royal authority and only sought a free PARLIAMENT and a GENERAL ASSEMBLY; and on the other hand, there were the extremists who deplored the indulgences and their acceptance by some of the clergy. The loyalty to the Crown of this latter faction was seriously in doubt. The battle itself resulted in a decisive victory for the royal army commanded by Monmouth (1649—85) who easily swept aside the rebel's defences on the bridge. Between 600 and 700 Covenanters were killed and another 1,200 were taken prisoner. The defeat, accompanied as it was by Monmouth's leniency, signalled the collapse of the main Covenanting resistance leaving only a hard core of irreconcilables, soon to be known as the CAMERONIANS, to continue the struggle.
• *Cowan, I.B., The Scottish Covenanters, Weidenfeld & Nicolson, 1976.*

Bothwell, Earls of, see HEPBURN, JAMES, 4TH EARL OF BOTHWELL; STEWART, FRANCIS, 5TH EARL OF BOTHWELL

Boyd Orr, John, Lord (1880—1971)   Boyd Orr, one of the most prominent scientists of his generation, was born at Kilmaurs, Ayrshire, in 1880. He began his schooling at West Kilbride, then went to Kilmarnock Academy, returning home later as a pupil teacher. In 1899 he won a scholarship to the University of Glasgow, graduating MA in 1902. He taught for three years and with his savings re-entered university to study science and medicine. He then worked as a Carnegie research fellow under E.P. Cathcart, head of physiological chemistry at the Institute of Physiology in Glasgow, obtaining his MD in 1914.

Meantime, in 1913, an Institute of Nutrition had been established at Aberdeen and Boyd Orr was appointed to direct it. Laboratories were built and work commenced on a modest scale before the intervention of WORLD WAR I. After war service, during which he was awarded the MC and DSO, Boyd Orr returned to the Rowett Institute at Aberdeen and began his influential work on nutritional science. He was soon advocating that health and nutrition in Britain should be linked to a national food and agricultural policy — his views being articulated in numerous publications, notably *Food, Health and Income* (1936). His work was recognized by his appointment as an FRS in 1932 and a knighthood in 1935. Boyd Orr later acted as advisor to the government on food policy during WORLD WAR II. It was during this time that he developed his ideas for a World Food Plan and greatly influenced the establishment of the Food and Agricultural Organization (FAO) — of which he ultimately became first director-general (1945–48). He resigned from the Rowett Institute and was briefly Professor of Agriculture at Aberdeen, then Rector and Chancellor of the University of Glasgow.

Bitterly disappointed when the UN rejected his world food proposals, he resigned from FAO and began his work for world peace. He continued to advise developing countries on agriculture and food. He was awarded the Nobel peace price in 1949, the same year he was created Lord Boyd Orr. Much honoured in his lifetime, Boyd Orr remained an unassuming man, whose commitment to his ideals much influenced both the development of the Welfare State in Britain and post-war co-operation internationally. He published an autobiography, *As I Recall*, in 1966.

Braxfield, Lord, see MACQUEEN

Breadalbane, earl of (John Campbell) see GLENCOE MASSACRE

brewing Brewing is as ancient as DISTILLING, and generated a major industry in the Lowlands, closely associated with AGRICULTURE — from which it derived its most important raw material — barley. Before the eighteenth century brewing was widespread. The city of Aberdeen alone had nearly 150 brewers in 1693, and at the same time there were over 500 in the county of Fife. Most publicans were brewers, and even the houses of the gentry brewed their own ale — seen in a fine survival at Traquair House, Peeblesshire, which maintains the tradition. Much of the beer offered for sale even to 'the better sort of citizens' was so bad that it would 'distemper a stranger's body'.

In the aftermath of the Treaty of UNION there was a major revolt against the MALT TAX — and the increasing efficiency of the customs and excise accelerated a trend towards larger, mass-production breweries at the expense of the small producer. Several important breweries were established during the eighteenth century — notably J. & R. Tennant of Wellpark Brewery, Glasgow (c.1745) and William Younger of Holyrood in Edinburgh (1749). These became large and important firms — dominating the Scottish industry virtually from the outset.

During the INDUSTRIAL REVOLUTION the Scottish brewing industry expanded to meet the needs of a growing POPULATION — both in country towns and the cities. Beer — a bulky commodity — was expensive to transport, hence the size of a brewery invariably reflected the size of its local market. Edinburgh became an important brewing centre — thanks to good water and grain supplies from nearby Lothian and Fife, which were in the vanguard of improvement. Elsewhere the industry was important in Alloa, Falkirk and Glasgow. By 1800 there were over 200 public breweries and output was 400,000 barrels, paying £75,000 in excise.

During the nineteenth century brewing underwent continuous expansion, thanks to rapid advances in science and technology. The trend after 1850 was towards larger breweries in the main centres of Edinburgh, Alloa and Glasgow. The capital of the industry rose from £600,000 in 1850 to over £6 million in 1900. Breweries got larger and that number fell from 220 in 1860 to 125 in 1900. The 'Brewery Boom' of the 1880s and 90s brought several important firms into being, notably William McEwan of Fountainbridge, Edinburgh. Despite the activities of the TEMPERANCE movement, a record 2.2 million barrels were brewed in 1899. By this time larger scale brewing had been pioneered by Tennant in Glasgow and Jeffrey in Edinburgh and a long-term shift towards bright beers had begun.

After WORLD WAR I the number of breweries continued its steady decline: by 1930 there were 45, producing 1.3 million barrels. Amalgamations and rationalization became a major feature of the industry, especially in the 1950s and 60s. By the 1970s a hugely expanded market was met by only a handful of large-production companies, although several of the traditional brewers survived — partly thanks to the resurgence in demand for traditional cask-conditioned ales of the kind produced in Victorian times.

•*Donnachie, I., A History of the Brewing Industry in Scotland, John Donald, 1979.*
•*McMaster, C., Alloa Ale: A History of the Brewing Industry in Alloa, Alloa Brewery Co. Ltd, 1985.*

Brewster, Rev. Patrick (1788–1859) Brewster, a prominent supporter of CHARTISM, the ANTI-CORN LAW LEAGUE, and other reform movements of his day, was born in Jedburgh, the son of the rector of the grammar school. Educated at the University of Edinburgh, he entered the ministry, being ordained to the Abbey Church of Paisley in 1818, and remaining there until his death over forty years later. Paisley — with its rapidly growing workforce — was a major centre of RADICALISM and this may well have influenced Brewster to support POOR LAW reform, the abolition of slavery and Catholic emancipation. His views certainly aroused hostility and brought him into conflict with the Church authorities, but his determination to voice his views suggests that he had considerable local support — as well friends in high places.

Brewster soon moved on to the national stage as a powerful proponent of 'moral-force' Chartism, which essentially rejected the violence advocated by Feargus O'Connor (1796–1855), Dr John TAYLOR (1805–42), and other more 'physical-force' Chartists. During the period 1838–42 he was a notable Chartist leader and orator, being associated with both the Complete Suffrage Movement and the National Charter Association. However, he became increasingly disillusioned with the rejection of moderation and turned from Chartism to the Anti-Corn Law

League and Scottish Poor Law reform. Although well connected with the establishment — and perhaps for this reason — he continued to speak out about political and social inequality, and was also a prolific author and pamphleteer on these issues.

In many ways the typical middle-class Chartist, Brewster was prepared to go along with the movement so long as its methods remained moderate and pacific. At the same time he remained remarkably radical in his espousal of wide-ranging reforms to improve the lot of the under-privileged living in his own parish and beyond.

• Wilson, A., The Chartist Movement in Scotland, Manchester University Press, 1970.

British Fisheries Society The British Fisheries Society was incorporated in 1786 as a jointstock company dedicated to the IMPROVEMENT of the HIGHLANDS — an aim it shared with its near contemporary, the HIGHLAND AND AGRICULTURAL SOCIETY and the much older-established Board of Trustees for Fisheries and Manufactures. The society was established at a relatively favourable time for the Highlands with the return of the FORFEITED ESTATES to their owners and a prevalent optimism about the potential for the development of the land and other natural resources. This was seen as the only way to halt further CLEARANCES and stem the flow of EMIGRATION, which some landlords feared would deprive them of rents and labour.

Development was to centre on the building of PLANNED VILLAGES where the Highlanders would live, and while FISHING was to be the main economic activity other trades and crafts would be encouraged. The original subscribers — apart from a clutch of landowners — included many prominent figures, English as well as Scottish, notably William Wilberforce (1759–1833), Henry DUNDAS (1742–1811) and David DALE (1739–1806). Thomas TELFORD (1757–1834) was engaged as consultant engineer.

Ultimately a cluster of new communities were created in the north including Ullapool on Loch Broom, Tobermory on Mull, Lochbay on Skye and Pulteneytown in Caithness. Although initially successful, the British Fisheries Society went into relative decline after the 1830s, the settlements were progressively sold off to local landowners, and the society finally wound up in 1893.

• Dunlop, J., The British Fisheries Society 1786–1893, John Donald, 1978.

British Linen Company Established by charter in 1746 at a critical time following the JACOBITE REBELLION of 1745–6, the company — as its name indicates — concerned itself with the financial encouragement of the native linen industry. Although its two competitors, the Bank of Scotland and the Royal Bank of Scotland, resisted an extension of its activities, the British Linen quickly diversified into BANKING. By the 1780s the banking aspect greatly outweighed the linen trade, and a new charter of 1813 recognized this function. However, its title was not changed to the British Linen Bank until as late as 1906. The bank was affiliated with Barclays Bank from 1919 and ultimately united with the Bank of Scotland in 1969.

Broadcasting, see BAIRD, JOHN LOGIE; JOHNSTON, THOMAS REITH, LORD

Brougham and Vaux, Lord, Henry Peter (1778—1868) Born in Edinburgh in 1778, Henry Brougham was a son of the Scottish ENLIGHTENMENT who became a prominent intellectual, politician and reformer on the wider British stage. Educated at the University of Edinburgh, he first studied science, then turned to law, being admitted to the Faculty of Advocates in 1800. After practising law for some time he joined Francis JEFFREY (1773–1850) and others in the establishment of the EDINBURGH REVIEW (1802), initially non-political, it increasingly supported the WHIGS after 1808. The journal became a significant platform for Brougham's campaigns in support of the anti-slavery movement, EDUCATION and legal reform. In 1803 Brougham published what was to become an influential work, *An Inquiry into the Colonial Policy of the European Powers*, and that same year moved to London, quickly becoming an intimate of the great abolitionist, William Wilberforce (1759–1833), and other reformers. He was called to the English bar in 1808 and began a long and distinguished legal career, which reached its zenith with his defence of Queen Caroline, wife of George IV, in 1820.

Brougham first entered Parliament in 1809 and soon established a reputation among the Whigs for his radical independence of mind — supporting numerous reform agitations of the day including electoral reform. After the General Election of 1830 he was raised to the peerage as Lord Chancellor in the Whig ministry of Lord Grey (1764–1845) and he played an important role in the successful passage of the first REFORM ACT in 1832. He subsequently lost office on the dismissal of the Melbourne (1779–1848) Government in 1834 — partly, it was believed, because of his reforming zeal. He failed to regain office but nevertheless maintained throughout years of political isolation a life-long interest in education, judicial reform and the abolition of slavery — as well as a prodigious literary output — until his death in 1868. Considering his non-aristocratic background and strong radical views, which were hardly fashionable in parliamentary circles, Brougham's achievements were significant. His life and work might well be compared with that of another practical reformer and near contemporary, Robert OWEN (1771–1858).

• *Stewart, R., Henry Brougham: The Public Career of Henry Brougham, 1778–1868, Bodley Head, 1985.*

Bruce, Edward (c.1276—1318) He was the younger brother of ROBERT I (1274–1324). Described by one historian as 'more chivalrous than sagacious' (he could be pretty ferocious, too) he played a significant role in the decade from 1308 to 1318.

In June 1313 he negotiated, not necessarily with his brother's approval, the pact with the English commander of Stirling Castle wherby the latter would surrender that fortress if he had not been relieved by Edward II by Midsummer's Day, 1314. Subsequently, at the battle of BANNOCKBURN, where he was in command of one of the main units of the Scottish army, Edward distinguished himself by countering an English cavalry charge in which its leader, the Earl of Gloucester was killed.

In April 1315 a parliament meeting at Ayr recognized Edward as heir presumptive should his brother die childless. The same assembly also approved a royal decision to invade Ireland and Edward's appointment as commander of the Scottish forces. The motives behind Robert I's Irish policy have provoked considerable controversy; perhaps he wanted Edward out of the way; possibly he desired to assist his Irish kinsmen (the king's second marriage was to a daughter of the Earl of Ulster) and also strengthen cultural and historical links with Ireland: more likely, the king hoped his brother's presence would embarrass Edward II and that English hegemony could be replaced by Scottish.

At first it looked as though the latter aim might be realized since in 1315 and 1316 Edward experienced considerable success against his Anglo-Irish opponents. Indeed, at a ceremony near Dundalk on 2 May 1316, Edward was actually declared High King of Ireland. But the tide turned against the Scots and any hope of a successful outcome vanished with Edward's death at Fochart near Dundalk in October 1318.

• *Barrow, G.W.S., Robert Bruce and the Community of the Realm of Scotland, Edinburgh University Press, 1988.*
• *Nicholson, R., Scotland: The Later Middle Ages, Oliver and Boyd, 1974.*

Bruce, Robert, 'the Competitor' (1210—95) As Lord of Annandale, he was the son of Isabella, the second daughter of David Earl of Huntingdon (c.1144—1219) and the grandfather of ROBERT I (1274—1329).

Following the death of ALEXANDER III (1241—86), he claimed the throne on the basis of his descent from David I (c.1084—1153) while at the same time denied MARGARET the Maid of Norway's (c.1283—90) claim through her being descended from a female line. He and his supporters formalized his claims by signing the Turnberry Bond in September 1286.

In 1289 he was closely involved with the preliminaries of the Treaty of BIRGHAM while on the Maid of Norway's death he became one of the leading COMPETITORS for the throne of Scotland. Edward I's verdict in favour of his great rival JOHN BALLIOL (c.1250—1313) left him and his family bitterly disappointed.

• *Barrow, G.W.S., Kingship and Unity: Scotland 1000—1306, Edinburgh University Press, 1981.*

Buchan, John (1875—1940) Buchan was one of the most prominent Scots of his generation, combining the literary activities for which he is best known with a diverse political and diplomatic career. Born in Perth, the son of a FREE CHURCH minister, he attended Glasgow then Oxford universities, being called to the Bar in 1901. Meantime, while still studying, he had already published extensively, including two historical novels, *John Burnet of Barnes* (1898), set in the BORDERS where he spent much his youth, and *The Lost Lady* (1899), a tale of the 1745 JACOBITE REBELLION. By 1898 he already had an entry in *Who's Who* and was clearly a man of promise and ambition. He then worked in London as a lawyer, at the same time building up his literary career and a network of connections with the social and political elite. The years 1901–03 were spent in South Africa working as an administrator in the office of Lord Milner, where his responsibilities (enormous for someone of his age) included land settlement and the (highly controversial) Boer refugee camps. Buchan's political and personal experiences in the reconstruction era following the Boer War further shaped his ideas and writing.

After returning from South Africa, Buchan for a time again combined the law with literary activities, eventually joining the Edinburgh publishing firm of Nelson's as chief literary editor in 1907. With his extensive contacts he secured books from many prominent authors and became a key figure in Nelson's business. He also maintained a huge output of books, articles and reviews and made his first serious attempt to enter politics as Unionist candidate for Peebleshire and Selkirk, a LIBERAL stronghold.

During WORLD WAR I, Buchan was initially a Major in the Intelligence Corps (1916), then subordinate director, Ministry of Information, which gave him further direct experience of international intrigue and propaganda

that proved useful in later novels. Possibly influenced by Erskine Childers's *Riddle of the Sands* (1903), Buchan produced *The Thirty-Nine Steps* (1915), an early example of his 'shockers' or spy-thrillers. Subsequent novels featuring Buchan's famous hero, Richard Hannay, were *Greenmantle* (1916), *Mr Standfast* (1919), and *The Three Hostages* (1924). It seems unlikely that Buchan himself believed the racist, imperialist and jingoistic views which he represented Hannay to possess, but he was certainly conservative in outlook. Like some of his contemporaries, including BALFOUR (1848–1930), he had strong pro-Zionist sympathies. He also produced a multi-volume history of the war, later abridged and updated after the event.

Buchan became Conservative MP for the Scottish Universities, 1927–35, but although he was held in high regard by senior figures like Stanley Baldwin and Ramsay MACDONALD, never attained political office. His ultimate reward for what he saw as a lifetime of public service (having sought an honour for years), was to be created Lord Tweedsmuir and made Governor General of Canada, a post he filled with distinction from 1935 until his death. In the interim he wrote some creditable historical biographies, notably of Montrose (1928), Sir Walter Scott (1932) and Cromwell (1934). While much of his work reflects the prevailing imperialist ideology of his time, Buchan is nevertheless remembered as a great storyteller, whose thrillers transferred well to the screen. Given his enormous talent and connections with the elite his political career was less successful; it might well be contrasted with that of his more controversial associate, Philip KERR, Marquis of Lothian.

• *Lownie, A., John Buchan, Constable, 1995.*

• *Smith, Janet A., John Buchan, Hart-Davis, 1965 (Oxford University Press, 1985).*

• *Smith, Janet A., John Buchan and his World, Thames & Hudson, 1979.*

burghs By the sixteenth century burghs could be clearly classified as either royal burghs or burghs of barony. Another group, burghs of regality, were not a separate category but simply places where a secular lord or a religious corporation had been given extensive judicial powers. Later developments were police burghs, established by various police acts in the nineteenth century, and parliamentary burghs, created as a result of the REFORM ACT (1832). Royal burghs, of which there were sixty-six by the time of the Treaty of UNION (1707), had initially been given the sole right by the Crown to trade overseas and to retail foreign goods as well as considerable privileges in the retailing of native commodities. Moreover their royal charters also allowed them to have burgh courts which could handle a wide range of minor offences, from lapses in Kirk discipline to breaches of the POOR LAW. Such burghs were also in possession of certain political powers: they elected their own town councils and they sent burgesses to Parliament as well as to the CONVENTION OF ROYAL BURGHS.

By 1707, although there were over 200 burghs of barony, most of them were very small and sparsely populated settlements. Thus, while Edinburgh had a population of about 30,000 in the later seventeenth century and Glasgow, Aberdeen and Dundee each had around 10,000 to 12,000 inhabitants, the total population of burghs of barony such as Kilmaurs in Ayrshire or Langholm in Dumfriesshire was only a tiny fraction of these figures.

There were also other distinctions between the two types of burghs. Burghs of barony, for instance, were excluded from trading overseas or retailing foreign goods, at least until the second half of the seventeenth century when legislation considerably relaxed these restrictions. Moreover, although the arrangements for local government were similar, representation in Parliament and at the Convention of Royal Burghs was confined to royal burghs.

Within either type of burgh the essential social division was between burgesses and non-burgesses. The former, a small minority of the burghal population, possessed all the existing political powers and privileges whereas the others, that is the majority residing in any burgh, lacked any rights whatsoever. To become a burgess it was necessary to be a member of one of the merchant or craft GUILDS. Here, the merchants were the dominant social group, strenuously resisting attempts by the crafts to improve their position. However, by the end of the sixteenth century, the latter group had apparently begun to obtain a greater say in burgh affairs as many burghs adopted a formula laid down in Edinburgh in

1584. There, following disturbances in 1582, legislation was passed giving the crafts, among other concessions, representation on the town council. None the less, in practice this does not appear to have made much difference; a wealthy clique of merchants in Edinburgh and elsewhere usually retained complete control. Thus the burghs with their councils either re-electing themselves annually or ensuring in some way or other that merchant interests prevailed, remained notorious during the seventeenth and eighteenth centuries for chicanery and corruption.

In the wake of the great Reform Act, the Burgh Reform Act (1833) introduced elections for the appointment of town councils — which had previously been dominated by self-perpetuating elites of prominent citizens and local landowners. The Local Government Act of 1929 created three different categories of burgh based on size: the four cities of Aberdeen, Dundee, Edinburgh and Glasgow; 19 large burghs; and 178 small burghs. The reorganization of local government in 1975 brought about the demise of the burghs as separate entities when they were amalgamated with the new district councils. Individually and collectively the burghs have played an important role in Scottish history since the sixteenth century. This is reflected in the history of burghs like Stirling, Edinburgh, Linlithgow, St Andrews, Glasgow, and others associated with great events. Together the burghs were a vital element in POPULATION expansion and URBANIZATION and hence contributed substantially to social and economic development.

• Fox, R., 'Urban Development, 1100–1700' in Whittington, G. and Whyte, I.D. (eds.), An Historical Geography of Scotland, Academic Press, 1983.
• Mackenzie, W.M., The Scottish Burghs, Oliver & Boyd, 1949.
• Macqueen, H.L. and McNeill, P.G.B. (eds.), Atlas of Scottish History to 1707, University of Edinburgh/Scottish Medievalists, 1996.
• Pryde, G.S., The Burghs of Scotland, Oxford University Press, 1965.

Burns, Robert (1759—96)   As a major literary figure, Burns was also historically important — though less for what he said and did during a lifetime of dramatic political and economic change than for his longer-term influence after his death. His own life reflected in microcosm the changes that accompanied the AGRICULTURAL REVOLUTION and INDUSTRIAL REVOLUTION. Born in Alloway, Ayrshire, in 1759, Burns, when not being exposed to formal education, worked on the land from an early age. The family tried a succession of apparently unprofitable farms before Burns turned briefly to work as a dresser of flax, used in the LINEN industry.

Following the success of his poems — first published in the 'Kilmarnock Edition' of 1786 — Burns decided against EMIGRATION to the plantations of the West Indies and headed instead for Edinburgh to receive tributes from learned and fashionable figures of the Scottish ENLIGHTENMENT. He spent a year or so in Edinburgh or travelling elsewhere in Scotland before returning to the soil. After farming at Ellisland near Dumfries, Burns received an excise appointment in the town in 1791. Robert Burns was at first a supporter of the FRENCH REVOLUTION though his reforming sympathies got him into deep trouble with the excise authorities and he was lucky to escape dismissal in 1792. After the outbreak of war in 1793, Burns played an active role in the Royal Dumfries Volunteers and, when he died in 1796, was given a military funeral. After his death Burns came to be regarded as a patriotic nationalist and political reformer. Certainly his defence of the common man through poetry and song had a profound influence both on Scottish popular culture and on attitudes to democracy and equality since the early nineteenth century.

• *Carswell, C., The Life of Robert Burns, Canongate Books, 1990.*

• *Daiches, D., Robert Burns and his World, Thames & Hudson, 1971.*

• *Fowler, R.H., Robert Burns, Routledge, 1988.*

• *McIntyre, I., Dirt and Deity: A Life of Robert Burns, HarperCollins, 1995.*

• *Mackay, J., Burns, Mainstream, 1992.*

C

Caledonian Canal, see CANALS; TELFORD

Cameronians The followers of Richard Cameron (1648—80) formed the remnant of the COVENANTERS who still challenged the religious policy of CHARLES II (1630—85) in the 1680s. By the Sanquhar Declaration, issued shortly before their leader's death at Airds Moss near Kilmarnock in July 1680, they renounced their allegiance to the king. Then, in 1684, with their Apologetical Declaration they openly declared war on the government. Those who survived the 'KILLING TIME' to take advantage of the TOLERATION ACT of JAMES VII (1633—1701) were few in number but just as imbued with religious fanaticism as their martyred leaders, Cargill (1619—81) and Renwick (1662—88). Although their three remaining ministers defected and accepted the terms of the REVOLUTION SETTLEMENT, most Cameronians rejected it to become a small SECT outwith the CHURCH OF SCOTLAND. During the eighteenth century some Cameronians joined the breakaway Presbyterian Church, formed after the first Secession in 1733, while most of the others became members of the Reformed Presbyterian Church established in 1743. Most of this latter body eventually merged with the FREE CHURCH in 1876.

• Cowan, I., The Scottish Covenanters, Weidenfeld & Nicolson, 1976.
• Drummond, A.L. and Bulloch, J., The Scottish Church, 1688—1873, St Andrew Press, 1973.

Campbell, Archibald, eighth Earl and first Marquis of Argyll (1607—61) When, as Lord Lorne, he had his hereditary SHERIFFSHIP taken from him, Archibald Campbell joined the ranks of other disaffected noblemen who reckoned they had been treated unfairly by CHARLES I (1600—49). He also disapproved strongly of the king's religious policy, deliberately absenting himself from the first reading of the PRAYER BOOK at St Giles, in July 1637. He was a signatory of the NATIONAL COVENANT, quickly becoming a leading figure in the Covenanting movement. However by the early 1640s there were doubts among some of his colleagues regarding his real motives. JAMES GRAHAM, Marquis of Montrose (1612—50), his strongest critic, alleged, for instance, that his actions were mainly influenced by a desire to further the already extensive interests of the Campbells. The enmity between Montrose and Argyll reached a climax during the former's brilliant campaign on behalf of the Crown in 1644 and 1645 when the Campbells sustained heavy losses. He opposed the ENGAGEMENT and following the defeat of the Engagers at Preston in August 1648 he played a major part in forming the fanatical government that passed the sweeping ACT OF CLASSES. After the setback to the extremists at Dunbar, he came to terms with Charles II (1630–85) and crowned him at Scone in January 1651. However, during the CROMWELLIAN UNION, Argyll pursued an ambivalent course and it was his compliance with the English administration, including the assistance he gave in suppressing the Glencairn Rising, that led to his execution on Charles II's return.

• *Willcock, J., The Great Marquess, Oliphant, 1903.*

Campbell, Archibald, ninth Earl of Argyll (1629–85) The son of Archibald CAMPBELL, eighth Earl of Argyll (1607–61) he opposed the CROMWELLIAN UNION, being present at the battle of Dunbar and also participating in the GLENCAIRN RISING. Despite his father's execution in 1661 he soon found favour with Charles II (1630–85) and all his family possessions were restored to him in 1669. Thereafter his acquisitive behaviour in the southwestern HIGHLANDS provoked considerable resentment among various clans, which was eventually utilized by the DUKE OF YORK (1633–1701) in his capacity as King's Commissioner. Thus in December 1681 Argyll's equivocal reply to the oath attached to the TEST ACT provided an opportunity for the Duke to have him arrested,

accused of treason and sentenced to death. The Earl escaped to Holland, but the motive behind the royal attack on him would appear to have been a desire to win over the various clan chieftains hostile to the Campbells. In 1685, on the Duke of York's accession to the throne, Argyll undertook the 'Argyll Rising', a futile, badly prepared rebellion that lacked any popular support within the country. The inevitable outcome was his capture and execution in June 1685.

Campbell, John, first Earl of Breadalbane, see GLENCOE MASSACRE

Campbell, John, second Duke of Argyll (1678–1743) Appointed Queen's Commissioner to Parliament in 1705, he supported the Treaty of UNION in return for extensive royal favours to himself and his family. Thus, his services were only acquired after he had been promised considerable financial rewards, promoted to major-general in the royal army and elevated to the dukedom of Greenwich. At the same time he also insisted that his brother Archibald (1682–1761) should become Earl of Islay.

Following the Union, despite his opposition to the MALT TAX and his support for dismantling the arrangements of 1707, he decided to back the Hanoverian cause and, in return, was appointed commander-in-chief in Scotland. In 1715 'Red John of the Battles' dealt effectively with the JACOBITE REBELLION, skilfully using Stirling as a base from which to block the advance of the JACOBITES and ultimately thwarting the rebel army at SHERIFFMUIR.

Although he continued to pursue his military career, becoming a field marshal in the British Army in 1736, his later life was largely devoted to politics. Here, as a result of extensive patronage as well as electoral corruption, and ably abetted in all this by his brother Islay and Duncan FORBES (1685–1747), he controlled, at his death, about half the constituencies in the country. Unquestionably Scotland in these years experienced the dubious benefits of political 'management' by the Argylls.

Campbell-Bannerman, Sir Henry (1836—1908) Henry Campbell (who in 1871 added his mother's maiden name to that of his father) was born in Glasgow, the son of a prosperous draper. Educated at Glasgow University and Trinity College, Cambridge, he worked in his father's business until 1868, when he was elected the LIBERAL MP for Stirling Burghs. He held a succession of posts in Liberal administrations of the day — as financial secretary at the War Office (1871–74, 1880–82), parliamentary and financial secretary for the Admiralty (1882–84), Chief Secretary for Ireland (1884–85), and Secretary of State for War (1886, 1892–95). In the last post he instituted various reforms, but the allegation that the War Office was inadequately supplied with cordite caused the defeat of ROSEBERY'S (1847–1929) administration.

Campbell-Bannerman became leader of the Liberals in the Commons in 1899, when the party was badly disunited. The Boer War created tensions between the imperialists and those who supported the Boers — but this situation resolved itself with the end of the war in 1902. Campbell-Bannerman was more careful in his handling of Irish Home Rule.

When Arthur BALFOUR (1848–1930) and his Conservative administration resigned in 1905, the Liberals were returned with a large majority in the ensuing General Election and Campbell-Bannerman became prime minister. Much of the radical legislation proposed by his administration ran into trouble in the Lords, though it did secure the passage of the Trade Disputes Act (1906), which gave TRADE UNIONS the right to strike. The following year Campbell-Bannerman's health deteriorated and only seventeen days before his death he resigned in favour of H.H. ASQUITH (1852–1928).

• *Wilson, J., CB: A Life of Sir Henry Campbell-Bannerman, Constable, 1973.*

Canada, see CLEARANCES; EMIGRATION; GALT; SELKIRK; WORLD WAR II

canals The four canals built in the Lowlands made a substantial contribution to the development of AGRICULTURE, INDUSTRY and trade in the Forth and Clyde valleys and were particularly useful to the COAL and IRON industries.

The earliest was the Forth and Clyde, an Act of Parliament for its construction being obtained in 1768, and prominent engineers such as John Smeaton (1724–92), James Brindley (1716–72) and James WATT (1736–1819) were consulted about the route. Partly because there were so many interested parties, including the CARRON COMPANY, the project was dogged with financial difficulties; but by 1775 the canal was open from Grangemouth, near the mouth of the River Carron, to Stockingfield, north of the River Kelvin near Glasgow. Twenty-two years after the cutting of the first sod, the thirty-five mile canal was open from sea to sea in July 1790, with an important branch carrying navigation to Port Dundas in Glasgow and beyond to a junction with the Monkland Canal. Until the onslaught of RAILWAYS competition, the Forth and Clyde had an important carrying trade — both in goods and passengers.

The Monkland Canal, twelve miles in length, was a short but nevertheless vital link as a coal carrier, opening up the mines of North Lanarkshire in the parishes of Old and New Monkland. Begun in 1770, with Watt acting as consultant, it was opened along its full length in 1793. It carried not only coal, but also general merchandise, manure and lime from nearby Glasgow.

Several other canals were projected while the Forth and Clyde and the Monkland were under construction, but only two of any consequence (discounting the Crinan Canal in Argyll, opened 1801) were actually built. The Glasgow, Paisley and Johnstone Canal (opened 1811) was the eastern section of a much more ambitious plan to link Glasgow with Ardrossan harbour on the lower Firth of Clyde; while the Edinburgh and Glasgow Union Canal, often known simply as the Union Canal (opened 1822), linked up with the Forth and Clyde

at Port Downie near Falkirk. Both RENNIE (1761–1866) and TELFORD (1757–1834) were consulted, though much of the canal was the work of Hugh Baird, the Company's engineer. The Union Canal has a number of notable engineering features including a 650-metre long tunnel at Falkirk and three outstanding aqueducts over the River Avon, the River Almond and the Water of Leith.

Many schemes for a waterway linking the Moray Firth with the west coast via the lochs of the Great Glen had been proposed before the essentially strategic demands of shipping revived interest in a canal during the FRENCH REVOLUTION and NAPOLEONIC WARS (1793–1815). An Act of Parliament (1803) granted £20,000 towards the cost of the project, with management entrusted to a Board of Commissioners. Telford was appointed principal engineer, and after surveying the route and consulting Watt and Rennie (who had advised on similar schemes), work began in 1804. Like the Forth and Clyde, the project was dogged by financial and engineering difficulties. When finally opened from sea to sea in 1822 the sixty-mile long waterway had cost over £800,000 — a huge sum by the standards of the day. It never became an important waterway, yet, in the long term, the Caledonian Canal proved useful to FISHING boats and coasters.

In the face of railway competition the Lowland canals slowly declined, though the Forth and Clyde still carried nearly 700,000 tons of goods in 1913. It closed to navigation fifty years later in 1963, leaving only two commercial waterways, the Crinan and the Caledonian. While the other canals were officially 'remaindered' there was considerable interest in their recreational potential and many conservation schemes resulted during the 1970s and 80s.

• *Cameron, A.D., The Caledonian Canal, Canongate Academic, 1994.*
• *Donnachie, I., Roads and Canals 1700—1900, Holmes McDougall, 1976.*
• *Lindsay, J., The Canals of Scotland, David & Charles, 1968.*

Canterbury, Quitclaim of (1189)
This notable charter represented a major achievement by WILLIAM I, effectively cancelling the Treaty of Falaise. By the agreement Richard I, anxious to join the CRUSADES, released the Scottish king from all agreements enacted by Henry II. In return for a substantial payment of 10,000 marks which would help to finance his campaign, Richard, in a carefully worded document, restored many Scottish rights. According to Duncan a number of questions remained unanswered about homage and allegiance for the Scottish kingdom but the quitclaim made William I 'master of his own subjects in his own kingdom!' Contemporaries thought it certainly removed 'the yoke of Henry's dominion and servitude' and was thus of considerable significance in consolidating the late twelfth and early-thirteenth century kingdom.

Carham, Battle of (1018) Carham, southwest of Coldstream, was the site of one of numerous battles of the early medieval period fought between the Scots and the English. On this occasion MALCOLM II, by beating a Northumbrian force,

reversed the earlier defeat at Durham in 1006. The victory consolidated Scottish territory in Lothian and the Tweed came to delimit the eastern Scottish BORDER.

Carlyle, Thomas (1795—1881)
Next to Walter SCOTT (1771–1832) Carlyle was probably the major literary figure of the nineteenth century and, like Scott, Carlyle owed much of his success to his love of history and the educational traditions of his native land. He was the son of a mason at Ecclefechan, Dumfriesshire, where he attended the parish school before going on to Annan Academy and then entering the University of Edinburgh in 1809. He studied mathematics, then taught for a while at both Annan and Kirkcaldy before returning to Edinburgh in 1819 to read law. Thereafter he combined tutoring and travelling with a literary career, contributing to the *London Magazine* and *The Edinburgh Review*, as well as translating and reviewing German literature — including Goethe and Schiller.

Moving to London permanently in 1834 he committed himself to a full-time literary career. The publication of his *French Revolution* (1837) made his reputation. It would have appeared sooner had not his acquaintance, John Stuart Mill (1806–73), accidentally burned the manuscript of the first volume. This was followed by other renowned works on *Chartism* (1839), *Past and Present* (1843), *Oliver Cromwell* (1845), and *Frederick the Great* (1858–61). Carlyle was a powerful, if conservative, social critic. His views on the impact of industrialization and secularization of society were especially influential in an age of apparently high moral values.

• *Campbell, I., Thomas Carlyle, Longman, 1978.*

• *Rosenburg, J.D., Carlyle and the Burden of History, Oxford University Press, 1985.*

Carnegie, Andrew (1835—1919) Carnegie was the archetypal self-made man who rose from bobbin-boy in a COTTON factory to become a giant of the American iron and steel industry famed for his philanthropy and the establishment of foundations for EDUCATION and research. Born in Dunfermline, the son of a LINEN weaver, Carnegie emigrated to the United States with his family in 1848, settling in Allegheny, Pennsylvania. He worked in a cotton factory, later becoming an engine tender, then a telegraph messenger and operator. In 1853 he joined the Pennsylvania Railroad Company and quickly rose to management. He was also associated with the Pullman Company and was partly responsible for introducing sleeping cars to American railroads.

The Civil War helped extend and consolidate his business interests and by 1864 he had a stake in oil — as well as iron, railway and engineering works made prosperous by wartime demand. Visiting England in 1867 he quickly realized the potential of the Bessemer process and by 1873 his own enterprise concentrated on steel manufacture. Less than a decade later he was the leading American ironmaster, his company being worth five million dollars, and his personal stake 2.7 million. The company prospered despite the depression of 1892 and the bloody strikes that accompanied it — largely due to vigorous management and the protection afforded by US tariffs. By 1899 the Carnegie Steel Company was making 40 million dollars profit and was sold to the US Steel Corporation in 1901 for £89 million — £60 million being Carnegie's personal share.

Carnegie had earlier articulated his views on philanthropy through *The Gospel of Wealth* (1900), 'the man who dies rich dies disgraced', and he proceeded to dispose of his own riches on a variety of leisure and educational projects. These ranged from public baths, parks and libraries in his native and adopted lands — to major endowments for research, such as the Carnegie Trusts. The Carnegie Dunfermline Trust was established 'to bring into the lives of the toiling masses of Dunfermline more sweetness and light'. He ultimately bought the Skibo estate in Sutherland and played the Highland laird during periodic visits until his death in 1919.

• *Wall, J.F., Andrew Carnegie, Oxford University Press, 1970.*

Carron Company Carron, near Falkirk, saw the birth of the modern Scottish IRON industry with the foundation during the Seven Years' War of the Carron Ironworks, dating from 1759. The company's principle partners were William Cadell Sr (1708—77), a Cockenzie merchant with interests in the Swedish iron and timber trades, his son, William Cadell Jr (1737—1819), Dr John Roebuck (1718—94), and Samuel Garbett (1717—1803), the last two already being joint-partners in several enterprises, including sulphuric acid works in Birmingham and at Prestonpans (1749). Cadell Sr had the local knowledge, Roebuck could deploy the necessary technical skills, while Garbett provided the business expertise. Carron Company had an initial capital of £12,000, with provision for its increase to £24,000. A decade later more than £150,000 had been invested in the works, making it a large enterprise by contemporary standards.

Carron differed from earlier iron-making enterprises both in its scale and its techniques. It used local iron ores and adopted coke-smelting, the latter developed half a century earlier by Abraham Darby (1678–1717) at Coalbrookdale, Shropshire. Much of the expertise and skilled labour was initially imported from England with production being concentrated on cannon manufacture. Technical problems associated with casting and boring dogged Carron's fortunes for some years, but in the longer term the 'Carronade' became the company's most famous product – used, for example, by Admiral Lord Nelson (1758–1805) on the *Victory* and other commands. Carron also supplied an iron cylinder for an experimental steam-engine developed in 1765 by James WATT (1736–1819).

Carron Company – which was closely associated for some time with Cadell's plant at Cramond on the River Almond, near Edinburgh – continued as a general iron manufacturer until its closure in 1982. Although historically important, little of the early plant survives, though parts of the complex water-supply system can still be seen.

Carron Company provides an interesting case-study of business enterprise during the early stages of the INDUSTRIAL REVOLUTION, and from this viewpoint might be compared with a similar example from the cotton industry, NEW LANARK.
•*Campbell, R.H., Carron Company, Oliver & Boyd, 1961.*

Carstaires, William, see MEDICINE

Carstares, William (1649–1715) Son of a presbyterian minister who had fled to Holland after Green, Carstares returned to Scotland in the mid-1670s after completing his education at Leyden. His activities against CHARLES II (1630–85) led to his arrest and imprisonment from 1675 to 1679, while his subsequent involvement in the Rye House plot, an English conspiracy against the king, resulted in him being re-arrested and tortured. By not revealing the complicity of WILLIAM III (1650–1702) in this affair he assured himself of the permanent gratitude of the Dutch monarch, accompanying him to England in 1688 as his personal chaplain. Consequently Carstares played a major role in advising William's government over the religious aspects of the REVOLUTION SETTLEMENT, persuading the king to accept a moderate presbyterian church system. However, despite his influence, which earned him the title of 'Cardinal Carstares', he was unable to prevent the abolition of lay PATRONAGE, a measure that he believed would give too much power to the extremists in the Kirk. Four times moderator of the GENERAL ASSEMBLY, he remained a significant figure in the succeeding reign and the acceptance by the Church of the controversial

TOLERATION ACT (1712) owed much to his efforts. In 1703 he also became principal of Edinburgh University, where his replacement of the outdated regent system by professors in charge of their own subjects was a significant and overdue reform.

•*Dunlop, A.I., William Carstares, Oliver & Boyd, 1967.*

Casket Letters In December 1568 during the enquiry being held at Westminster into the complicity of MARY (1542–87) in the murder of Henry Stewart, Lord DARNLEY (1546–67) a silver box was produced by MORAY (1531–70), the leading Scottish commissioner, which allegedly had been discovered in June 1567 in the possession of a servant of James HEPBURN, fourth Earl of Bothwell (c.1535–78). The contents, it was claimed, comprised eight letters from Mary to Bothwell, a number of 'sonnets' and two marriage contracts. All these were supposed to have been perused by MORTON (c.1516–81), Atholl (d.1579), MAR (c.1510–72), Glencairn (d.1574), MAITLAND OF LETHINGTON (c.1525–73) and other notables present at the opening of the casket. Clearly the regent hoped that this evidence would provide overwhelming proof that Mary knew the details of the conspiracy against her husband, was Bothwell's mistress before events at Kirk o' Field, had contracted to marry him before his acquittal for murder or his divorce, and that her claims that she had been abducted by him were bogus.

On the other hand, ever since their presentation there has been controversy about the validity of Moray's evidence, not least because of the delay of eighteen months in presenting it. An additional drawback for any modern assessment has been the fact that the originals disappeared before the end of the sixteenth century and that only copies made by the clerks at Westminster survive. However, the general consensus is that some of the letters were correspondence between Mary and Bothwell, others were written by Mary to someone else, some were addressed to Bothwell by another person and that in certain of them forgery had been committed by an unknown hand.

•*Davison, M.H.A., The Casket Letters, Vision Press, 1965.*
•*Donaldson, G., The First Trial of Mary Queen of Scots, Batsford, 1969.*

Catholic Church Proscribed by the REFORMATION Parliament in 1560, the Catholic Church found itself struggling under the handicap of weak leadership and poor organization. Thus, some of its clergy, for instance Alexander Gordon, Bishop of Galloway (c.1516–75), joined the reformers, others like James Beaton, Archbishop of Glasgow (c.1523–1603) went into exile, while its head, John HAMILTON, Archbishop of St Andrews (1512–71), was executed. In the next century it was only in remote parts of the HIGHLANDS and the northeast where certain itinerant priests had established congregations that the Catholic faith survived. This situation persisted for much of the eighteenth century although there was now a seminary in Glenlivet having so-called 'heather priests'. Moreover, the aftermath of the 1745 JACOBITE REBELLION and the beginning of the CLEARANCES led to considerable emigration among the Catholic population in the Highlands. None the less, a century later this demographic decline had been more than offset by the arrival of large numbers of Irish immigrants into the Lowlands, especially after the Irish famine of the 1840s. The very size of the Catholic population, around 300,000 by 1820, posed severe problems to a church admittedly now benefiting from the relaxation of restrictions against it but faced with serious divisions between its hierarchy and the ordinary priests. To some extent these difficulties were gradually overcome after 1878 when the bishops assumed territorial titles and the clergy, generally, began to devote more of their energies to building new churches and schools.

The EDUCATION Act (1918), which among its several important provisions allowed Catholic schools the privilege of coming under the management of the education authorities while retaining control of the appointment of teachers and religious education, was undoubtedly a major triumph for the Church. It has tended to ensure the continuation of a sectarian educational system within a Catholic population that by the 1990s numbered 800,000. See also CHURCH.

•*McRoberts, D., Modern Scottish Catholicism, J. S. Burns, 1979.*
•*Johnson, C., Developments in the Roman Catholic Church in Scotland 1789—1829, John Donald, 1985.*

cattle Historically, cattle were important indicators of wealth — especially among the Highland CLANS and in the BORDERS. Cattle

'lifting' or rustling were age-old activities, generating much lawlessness. Later both cattle and cattle trade were vital elements in the development of both AGRICULTURE and the export economy during the seventeenth and eighteenth centuries. Pastoral agriculture was always important in the west of Scotland and in the HIGHLANDS and islands, but became a major economic activity after the UNION in 1707. Early ENCLOSURE in the Lowlands was directed at cattle feeding.

A significant trade developed during the eighteenth century from the Highlands to the Lowlands — and further south across the Border to markets in England — invariably over drove roads linking the major 'trysts', or market places, such as that at Falkirk. The later development of steam shipping and ultimately of the RAILWAYS put paid to the droving trade — but nevertheless pastoral agriculture (both cattle and sheep) remained the mainstay of farming in many parts of Scotland.

•*Haldane, A.R.B., The Drove Roads of Scotland, House of Lochar, 1995.*

Caulfield, Major William (d.1767)
In 1732 Caulfield came to Scotland to serve under his Irish compatriot, General WADE (1673—1748) and shortly afterwards was appointed Inspector of Roads. In this capacity he personally supervised the building of around 700 miles of roads as well as numerous bridges in the central and western HIGHLANDS. Two of his main achievements were the routes from Dumbarton to Fort William and that from Blairgowrie to Fort George, near Inverness. Like Wade,

who is sometimes credited with roads that were actually constructed by Caulfield and his men, his efforts brought few economic benefits to the areas affected. Primarily part of a system of military roadways, many of them had fallen into disuse by the end of the eighteenth century.

• Haldane, A.R.B., New Ways Through the Glens, House of Lochar, 1995.

census The first official census was undertaken in 1801, parish ministers throughout Scotland playing the same prominent role they had exercised in the compilation of the first STATISTICAL ACCOUNT in the 1790s. An earlier enumeration had been made in 1755 by the Rev. Dr Alexander WEBSTER (1707–84) and his associate, Rev. Dr Robert Wallace (1697–1771). Sir John SINCLAIR (1754–1835) compiled an estimate for 1795, based on the returns to the Statistical Account; while Patrick COLQUHOUN (1745–1820) produced other data (based apparently on his own calculations) – but neither of these efforts was systematic nor comprehensive. Official estimates of POPULATION had been made elsewhere in Europe, for example, in Sweden (1749) and Austria (1754), and it was the same fiscal and strategic requirements that lay behind the first national census of 1801 – during the NAPOLEONIC WARS. From 1801 there was a census every ten years until 1931 and, owing to the intervention of WORLD WAR II, again from 1951.

Historically the information sought varied: the number of persons of each sex was consistently obtained, but ages were neglected until 1821 and included in every census since 1841. Marital status was included for the first time in 1851. The 1841 census is of particular interest because it included data about native place as well as place of residence – hence giving the researcher some indication of MIGRATION patterns that can be married up with surviving parish registers. The census is clearly an important historical source in the range of information and statistical data it provides – and is thus much consulted by the researcher.

Chalmers, Dr Thomas (1780–1847) Thomas Chalmers was one of the most distinguished ecclesiastic politicians and social reformers of his generation and a leader of the movement that brought about the DISRUPTION and the establishment of the FREE CHURCH in 1843. Born in Anstruther, Fife, in 1780, the sixth of fourteen children, he was educated at the parish school and then the University of St Andrews. Typical of the broad EDUCATION followed at the time, he studied first mathematics and science, then divinity. On graduating he began his career as minister of Kilmany, Fife, in 1803 – though he continued to teach mathematics and chemistry at St Andrews. He was later an unsuccessful candidate for chairs at both St Andrews and Edinburgh.

Kilmany was to Chalmers what New Lanark was to Robert Owen – a test-bed for his ideas about practical theology. Social conditions and the problems of the poor were as important to him as his success as an evangelical preacher, and it was at Kilmany that he realized the importance of the parish as a unit of administration for poor relief — as much as for preaching the ministry. During his time at Kilmany he also found time to publish widely — including a book entitled *An Inquiry into the Extent & Stability of National Resources* (1808), an essay on 'Christianity' for the *Edinburgh Encyclopaedia* (1813), and a pamphlet on *The Influence of Bible Societies on the Temporal Necessities of the Poor.*

Meanwhile, his fame as a preacher spread far and wide and in 1815 he moved to the prestigious charge of the Tron Kirk in Glasgow. Two years later he took London by storm, greatly impressing Wilberforce (1759–1833), Canning (1770–1827) and other distinguished persons. Back in Glasgow, preaching against heathenism was combined with efforts to rescue the less fortunate from degradation and poverty. After moving to the new parish of St Johns in 1820, Chalmers implemented his 'parish system' of relief. He divided the parish into twenty-five proportions, each under an elder who supervised poor relief paid from church collections. He also established — for modest fees — a system of comprehensive education in two day schools and fifty Sunday schools. If cost was the sole consideration his scheme was certainly a success for the annual poor relief budget was reduced from £1,400 to less than £300 — figures that would undoubtedly impress those in authority both in Glasgow and elsewhere. A major work on *The Civic and Christian Economy of Large Towns* and a series of articles on pauperism for *The Edinburgh Review* sprang from this period.

Chalmers then returned to academic life, accepting the offer of a chair in moral philosophy at his alma mater in St Andrews in 1823, later moving to Edinburgh as professor of divinity in 1828. Thereafter he became increasingly involved in church politics, particularly the issue of PATRONAGE, which was hotly debated and contested throughout the 1830s. The so-called 'Ten Years' Conflict' led ultimately to the severing of the Free Church from the established Church in the Disruption of 1843, when Chalmers became first Moderator of the new Church's General Assembly as well as principal of the Divinity College. Although so clearly a radical evangelist, Chalmers was also innately conservative, being decidedly opposed to the first REFORM ACT.

•*Brown, S. J., Thomas Chalmers and the Godly Commonwealth in Scotland, Oxford University Press, 1982.*

Charles I (1600–49)   Born in November 1600, the second son of JAMES VI (1566–1625), Charles became the heir apparent on the death of Henry, his eldest brother, in 1612. Although born in Dunfermline he only visited Scotland on two occasions when he was king; in 1633 he came to Edinburgh for his long-delayed coronation, returning in 1641 to participate in the event known as the Incident, an unsuccessful attempt at undermining the position of his Scottish adversaries.

In his absence the policies he promoted provoked growing antagonism towards the Crown from an increasingly wide spectrum of the population. Landowners and the nobility in particular were greatly perturbed by the ACT OF REVOCATION introduced in 1625, which seemed to endanger their rights to the numerous church properties in their possession since the 1540s. Charles did not seriously intend a wholesale denudation of these acquisitions but merely wished to devise a system whereby some of this wealth could be utilized to improve the financial status of the post-REFORMATION Church. Royal income would also benefit in a small way as well. But the whole business was tackled in an unfortunate manner causing widespread suspicion and resentment among an influential portion of the community. The revocation of certain hereditary sheriffdoms, for instance those in the hands of the Gordon and Hamilton families, and an apparent preference for ecclesiastical councillors — Archbishop SPOTTISWOODE (1565–1639), appointed chancellor in 1635, was the first post-Reformation churchman to hold such a position — were political grievances to augment those concerning property among the nobility.

Another cause of complaint was financial, with the practice of regular TAXATION begun by James VI and continued by Charles being an especially contentious policy. The king only requested contributions in 1625, 1630 and 1633 but since these grants were spread over four years it virtually amounted to annual taxation. Besides, a larger number of the population was now affected since his father's expedient of taxing annual rents was continued by his son.

Linked to the general disgruntlement over fiscal policy were the grievances peculiar to the city of Edinburgh whose citizens, although welcoming metropolitan status in 1633 were much less enthusiastic about footing the bill for the king's coronation. Nor did they approve of increasing the ministers' stipends in the city, particularly since they had just recently done so. But their major objection was to having to bear all the expense of the new parliament house that Charles wished built in the capital and which ultimately cost £127,000.

However, it was the king's religious innovations that effectively united most of the nation against the Crown. The CODE OF CANONS (1636) and the PRAYER BOOK (1637) provoked a serious reaction throughout most of the country culminating in the signing of the NATIONAL COVENANT in February 1638. A royal attempt at conciliation shortly afterwards proved fruitless as the GENERAL ASSEMBLY, meeting for the first time for twenty years in November 1638, not only proscribed the Prayer Book and the Code of Canons but also denounced the FIVE ARTICLES OF PERTH and the whole episcopal apparatus.

Attempts by Charles to restore his position forcibly (the first and second BISHOPS' WARS (1639–40) failed disastrously. As the situation deteriorated in England the king had little alternative but to sign the Treaty of RIPON (August 1640) ending the second Bishops' War and eventually submit, in 1641, to its final humiliating terms.

For the duration of the first Civil

War (1642–6) Scotland was administered by the king's Covenanting opponents headed by the egregious Archibald CAMPBELL, eighth Earl of Argyll (1607–61). An attempt by Argyll's enemy MONTROSE (1612–50) to rally the royalists in Scotland ultimately came to grief at the battle of PHILIPHAUGH in 1645. None the less, by the time of the outbreak of the second Civil War in 1648 there had emerged a significant faction more sympathetic to the royalist cause; this was partly a result of growing doubts about the constitutional aspects of the 1641 settlement, dissatisfaction and disillusionment with the SOLEMN LEAGUE AND COVENANT (1643), and increasing suspicion about Argyll's real motives. Thus, when Charles, in the negotiations held at Carisbrook in December 1647, known as the ENGAGEMENT, indicated his willingness to experiment with Presbyterianism in England for three years and also grant Scottish merchants certain commercial benefits he won over the Scottish delegation to his side. The outcome was a divided state with the 'Engagers' supporting the king and the 'Anti-Engagers', the majority of the General Assembly, opposing him.

By the date of his execution in January 1649, the Engagers, carrying out their part of the bargain, had been defeated by Cromwell's (1599–1658) forces at Preston (August 1648) permitting Argyll and the 'Anti-Engagers' to seize power. The latter quickly introduced swingeing legislation, the ACT OF CLASSES, against their opponents and Scotland, bedevilled by factional divisions, was about to

experience the CROMWELLIAN UNION.

• *Donaldson, G., Scotland: James V to James VII, Oliver & Boyd, 1965.*
• *Lee, M., The Road to Revolution: Scotland under Charles I, 1625–37, University of Illinois Press, 1985.*
• *Mitchison, R., Lordship to Patronage, Edward Arnold, 1984.*

Charles II (1630—85) Born 1630, the eldest son of CHARLES I (1600–49) and Henrietta Maria (1609–69). He was crowned King of Scots in January 1651 but did not become ruler of both countries until the breakdown of the republican government gave him his opportunity in May 1660.

The RESTORATION SETTLEMENT that followed his accession to the throne of both kingdoms almost immediately created problems for his administration, especially over religion. Here, while the objectives of the PROTESTORS were only those of a smallish minority, the bulk of the country shared the hopes of the RESOLUTIONERS for the maintenance of a presbyterian polity within Scotland. Unfortunately the Act Rescissory (1661) and the subsequent religious statutes restoring bishops and reviving lay PATRONAGE all indicated Charles II's preference for a moderate Episcopalian church settlement. A return to the days of JAMES VI (1566–1625) was intended where the kirk sessions, presbyteries and synods co-existed with the bishops and only the GENERAL ASSEMBLY no longer functioned. None the less such proposals were instantly unpopular with a substantial number of the clergy and laity especially those of Protestor persuasion. Consequently, around 270 ministers were deprived for their opposition to lay patronage or episcopal discipline and their adherence to the covenants. Initially the government took a tough line towards these COVENANTERS as measures like the so-called 'Bishop's Dragnet' and the Mile Act underline.

When this policy was accompanied by the stationing and billeting of troops in disaffected areas like southwest Scotland where illegal conventicles proliferated, it provoked resentment that culminated in the ill-starred PENTLAND RISING (1666). However, in 1667 an amnesty was granted to most of those involved in the events of the preceding year and for a time thereafter. Lauderdale (1616–82), who by 1669 had become royal commissioner, pursued a more conciliatory line. Those clergy who had been deprived were given an opportunity to return to the Church, although with some strings attached, and by 1672 around 140 ministers had accepted this offer. Meanwhile, more draconian measures against those who refused to accept the royal indulgences were being placed on the statute book including fines for landowners who permitted conventicles to be held on their estates and the death penalty for field preachers who participated at such meetings. These repressive tactics began to be put into effect around 1674 but there was clearly still considerable support for the Covenanting cause in Fife, the Lothians and the southwest. Matters began to come to a head in 1678 when the government decided to resort to the highly unpopular military expedient of quartering troops, some of them

from the HIGHLANDS, in Renfrewshire and Ayrshire.

The presence of this 'HIGHLAND HOST' only served to worsen an already deteriorating situation and, following the murder of Archbishop SHARP (1618–79) and a skirmish between troops under CLAVERHOUSE (1648–89) and Covenanters at Drumclog, Ayrshire, in June 1679, a full-scale rising was underway. Three weeks later the Covenanters were decisively beaten at BOTHWELL BRIDGE (1679) but the Duke of Monmouth (1649–85), briefly in charge of Scottish affairs, returned to a policy of conciliation and won over a further number of recalcitrant ministers by his religious concessions. Henceforth, only a small fanatical group of ministers and their flocks were openly in contention with Charles II's administration. Known as CAMERONIANS they were subsequently suppressed in the 1680s by Claverhouse and his dragoons, a period often referred to in Covenanting hagiographies as the 'KILLING TIME'. What caused further justifiable resentment among the majority of the population was the controversial Test Act (1681), largely the work of the Catholic JAMES, Duke of York (1633–1701) who was now Royal Commissioner in Scotland. The terms of this Act were frequently enforced in a brutal fashion by Claverhouse who paid scant attention to whether his victims were anarchic Cameronians or merely opponents of the detested statute.

The Act Rescissory also had great political significance since it repealed the constitutional limitations imposed on the king by the legislation of 1640 and restored the Crown to its former position. But Charles constantly remained remote from Scottish affairs in London and it was his Privy Council and Lauderdale in particular who really benefited from the Restoration Settlement. However, if for the king's ministers it meant frequent opportunities to indulge in corruption and peculation, the reign of Charles II also witnessed the appearance of some signs of vitality in the Scottish PARLIAMENT. Thus, as a reaction to Lauderdale's venal regime, there emerged an opposition faction prepared to challenge the powers of the Committee of the Articles and exercise this influence against the royal government on a hitherto unprecedented scale. Hence Lauderdale's failure in 1669 to win sufficient support for any of his proposed legislation, including terms for an Anglo-Scottish union.

In economic affairs there was evidence of some recovery from the nadir of the CROMWELLIAN UNION but little sign of any spectacular improvement. This was especially the case with overseas trade where the English Navigation Act (1661), restricting English imports to native ships or those of the country of origin, proved a major obstacle. Therefore, the main commercial development was the increased activity in non-royal burghs, recognized by Charles II's government, which in 1672 granted certain limited trading privileges to burghs of regality and barony. The latter, like the rest of the kingdom, paid the 'cess', the monthly tax on land introduced during the Cromwellian Union, which now became a permanent feature of the finan-

cial system. Special officials known as Commissioners of Supply were appointed to administer it.

• *Donaldson, G., Scotland: James V to James VII, Oliver & Boyd, 1965.*
• *Ferguson, W., Scotland's Relations with England, John Donald, 1977.*
• *Mitchison, R., Lordship to Patronage, Edward Arnold, 1983.*

Chartism   The Chartist movement emerged from the continuing agitation for parliamentary reform following the passage of the first REFORM ACT in 1832. During the decade 1838–48, it brought together in one national organization with a clearly articulated set of objectives diverse groups and individuals in what became one of the earliest and most significant popular movements of the nineteenth century. The immediate aspirations of the Chartists were published in the 'People's Charter' (1838) and articulated more specifically in the 'Six Points', which sought an extension of the franchise, an end to property qualifications, election of an annual parliament, the secret ballot, a more equal distribution of seats, and the payment of MPs.

The Chartist movement in Scotland inherited a long radical tradition that stretched back to Thomas MUIR (1765–99), the Scottish FRIENDS OF THE PEOPLE, the CORRESPONDING SOCIETIES, and the UNITED SCOTSMEN of the 1790s. It drew support both from the disillusioned middle class, who felt let down by the failure of the Reform Act to extend the franchise far enough to serve their own interests, and from the working class — especially the artisans — who had gained nothing politically and seemed to be under increasing economic pressure as the INDUSTRIAL REVOLUTION progressed and mechanization eroded their status. Among the groups attracted to Chartism were former RADICALS, OWENITES, CO-OPERATORS, trade unionists, temperance advocates, and members of the contemporaneous ANTI-CORN LAW LEAGUE.

From the outset there were close links between Scottish Chartism and the English movement, particularly between branches in Glasgow and Edinburgh and the Birmingham Political Union, which played an important initiating role nationally. Chartism was embraced with enthusiasm north of the Border and by the beginning of 1839 there were upwards of eighty local associations in towns as far apart as Elgin and Dumfries — as well as numerous branches in the four major cities. Scottish delegates played a prominent part in the Convention of the Industrious Classes called in London by Thomas Attwood, MP (1783–1856), Feargus O'Connor (1794–1855) and other English Chartist leaders in February 1839, though the failure of the first National Petition in July of that year highlighted major divisions of opinion concerning tactics among the leadership and the rank and file. Some — notably the middle-class support — considered the best way of achieving their objectives was by 'moral force' or peaceful persuasion, while the more militant and radical regarded 'physical force' as essential. Among the Scottish Chartist leadership the Rev. Patrick BREWSTER (1788–1859) of the Abbey Church, Paisley and John Fraser, editor of the leading Chartist paper, the *True Scotsman,*

represented 'moral force', whereas Dr John TAYLOR (1805–42) was one of the leading advocates of 'physical force'. In general 'moral force' prevailed, even after the shift of leadership from Edinburgh to the more militant Glasgow and Paisley.

There were quite distinctive features in the Scottish agitation: a powerful Chartist press including the *True Scotsman,* the *Scottish Patriot,* and the *Chartist Circular;* good attention to local organization; the maintenance of close relations with the trade unions, and a strong emphasis on educational and moral aspects — seen in Christian-style Chartist churches, Chartist temperance associations, and Chartist co-operatives.

Like many other popular movements of the period the fortunes of Chartism were partly dictated by the economic cycle and partly by the enthusiasm generated by charismatic leaders like O'Connor, who had many Scottish admirers. With the rejection of the Second Petition in May 1842 the movement declined and revived only briefly in a final flurry of activity in 1848, the year of the great revolutions throughout much of Europe. The monster demonstration at Kennington in London had its Scottish counterpart on Calton Hill, Edinburgh, attended by an estimated gathering of 10,000.

Chartism in Scotland — as in England — was long regarded as a failure at least in terms of fulfilling the 'Six Points', its apparently poor national organization, and the inevitable factions that dogged the movement throughout its history. Although Chartism may have failed in the short term, in the longer term its political and cultural ideas had considerable influence. At least some of its objectives were achieved with the second Reform Act (1868) and ultimately most in 1884. Many Chartists became prominent radicals, co-operators, trade unionists and pioneers of the Scottish labour movement later in the nineteenth century.

• *Jones, D., Chartism and the Chartists, Allen Line, 1975.*
• *Thompson, D., The Chartists, Temple Smith, 1984.*
• *Wilson, A., The Chartist Movement in Scotland, Manchester University Press, 1970.*

Chaseabout Raid This was the name given to describe the short-lived rebellion in August– September 1565 that occurred following the marriage of MARY (1542–87) to DARNLEY (1546–67). MORAY (1531–70), who was the key figure in the insurrection, had previously been in touch with disaffected noblemen, such as Argyll (1538–73) and CHATELHERAULT (c.1516–75), as well as Queen Elizabeth (1533–1603). He appealed for support on the ground that he was defending the Protestant faith and the English alliance. Undoubtedly he and MAITLAND of Lethington (c.1525–73) were distressed at the breach in Anglo-Scottish relations caused by the Queen's marriage, but there were obviously personal motives as well behind Moray's stance and that of some of his fellow magnates. Darnley's promotion, for instance, could only lessen their influence over Mary, while in the case of the Hamiltons it was a serious blow to that family's claims to the succession.

Mary handled the crisis in commendable fashion: by giving guarantees regarding the Kirk, she detached MORTON (c.1516–81), Cassillis (1541–76), Lindsay (d.1589) and Ruthven (c.1520– 66); by releasing Huntly (d.1576) from custody and restoring BOTHWELL (1536–78) to her council she won over two former opponents; by personally leading her forces against the rebels and taking a firm line against them the Queen ensured they would receive little support. Thus, early in October 1565, Moray retreated into England, his attempt at destabilizing Mary's regime a total failure. The only significant aspect of the episode was that it encouraged the Queen to rely to a greater extent on non-aristocratic officials such as RICCIO (c.1533–66) in her administration.

• *Donaldson, G., Scotland: James V to James VII, Oliver & Boyd, 1965.*
• *Fraser, A., Mary, Queen of Scots, Weidenfeld & Nicolson, 1969.*

Chatelherault, Duke of, see HAMILTON

Churchill, Winston, see JOHNSTON; REITH; TEMPERANCE; WORLD WAR II

church William the Conqueror's invasion of Scotland in 1072 during which he compelled MALCOLM III (c.1031–93) to pay homage to him might easily have resulted in the Scottish medieval church coming under the control of England. That it did not become absorbed into the English ecclesiastical system was partly because of the attitude of certain Scottish kings, notably Malcolm III and ALEXANDER I (1107–24) who resisted attempts at enforcing formal submission to the archbishop of York, but primarily through the efforts of the Scottish church itself.

By the twelfth century, bishoprics had been established at Aberdeen, Brechin, Caithness, Dunblane, Glasgow, Moray, Ross, Whithorn and St Andrews. However, the independence of the Scottish episcopate was seriously challenged by the Treaty of Falaise (1174) whereby WILLIAM (1143–1214) recognized Henry II as his feudal overlord. None the less by this date the papacy had come round to supporting the independence of the Scottish church from York and the bull *Cum Universi* (1192) confirmed that this was official papal policy.

Scotland had no archbishopric until St Andrews was created in 1472 but by the 13th century the church had persuaded Rome to recognize its independence from England. Churchmen played leading roles both in the administration of the kingdom and, particulary during the WARS OF INDEPENDENCE, defending and protecting what has been described as Scotland's 'identity'.

• *Webster, B., Medieval Scotland: The Making of an Identity, 1997.*

Church of Scotland, see ACT OF REVOCATION; BOOK OF DISCIPLINE; CHALMERS; CODE OF CANONS; COVENANTERS; DISRUPTION; GENERAL ASSEMBLY; KNOX; MELVILLE; NATIONAL COVENANT; PRAYER BOOK; REFORMATION; RESTORATION SETTLEMENT; REVOLUTION SETTLEMENT; SECTS; THIRDS OF BENEFICES; TOLERATION ACT; TREATY OF UNION

Civil War (1570—73)   The assassination of MORAY (1531–70) sparked off a period of conflict that was to persist intermittently until Edinburgh Castle fell to a joint Anglo-Scottish force in May 1573. On the one side were the 'king's men', all those who supported the deposition of MARY (1542–87) and the accession of JAMES VI (1566–1625); opposing them were the 'Queen's men', the Marians who wanted Mary's restoration. In some ways the latter were the more powerful faction in 1570, being able to count among their numbers important families such as the Hamiltons, Gordons and, initially at least, the Campbells. The king, on the other hand, could rely on the various branches of the Stewarts, although the Earl of Atholl (d.1579) was a notable exception, as well as the house of Douglas where MORTON (c.1516–81) was the outstanding figure. The actual course of the hostilities was uneven with bitter fighting particularly around Edinburgh, the besieged capital, punctuated by truces from September 1570 to March 1571 and again from July 1572 to March 1573. Undoubtedly the most significant aspect of the Civil War was the gradual decline in support for Mary. This commenced around mid–1571 when Argyll (c.1538–73), as well as some Ayrshire noblemen defected, and culminated with the Pacification of PERTH in February 1573 when Huntly and the Hamiltons gave up the struggle. The last stage was the siege of Edinburgh where Morton found it necessary to recruit English assistance in order to defeat KIRKCALDY OF GRANGE (c.1520–73), MAITLAND (c.1525–73) and their small garrison.

• *Tytler, P.F., History of Scotland III, W. Nimmo, 1866.*

clans In the HIGHLANDS the traditional clan structure survived — albeit in much-modified form — as late as the JACOBITE Risings of the 'Fifteen and 'Forty-Five, when some chiefs could still mobilize clansmen in warfare. There were several different concepts and variants of the clan but at its heart was kinship and loyalty to the chief. Although there might be many who shared the same descent and even surname, not all clansmen need necessarily have been kin. In a large clan — like the Campbells or Mackenzies — there might be many septs or cadet branches. Yet the myth of common ancestry was nevertheless a powerful one and the reigning chief commanded both great respect and unquestioning loyalty.

Apart from kinship the clan was invariably bound to its chief by the system of land-holding — for the chief's power derived mainly from land ownership and its allocation to clansmen and other supporters. The clan lands might be large or small, unified or widely scattered, depending on the status of the chief. In the larger clans, chiefs employed TACKSMEN to administer the lands and collect rents — by the sixteenth century increasingly in cash rather than kind.

The Highland clans — like some of their BORDER counterparts — had traditionally been unruly, so the Scottish Crown embarked on a series of long-term efforts to bring Lowland-style law and order to what one sixteenth-century commentator described as the 'Wild Scots'. JAMES IV (1473–1513) had made frequent expeditions to the Highlands, forfeiting the Lordship of the Isles and breaking up its power over a widespread area in 1493. By the early 1500s the Campbells, Gordons and Mackenzies had emerged as the most powerful kinships, but their dominance seems to have had little overall effect on petty clan warfare, which continued apace throughout the sixteenth century. Assuming the attitude of feudal lords, the most powerful clan chiefs used their positions and manpower to extend their political and territorial influence — much like the Lowland magnates and lairds.

The next monarch to tackle the clans seriously was JAMES VI (1566–1625), who attempted — with some success — to impose law and order on the Highlands and suppress the more unruly chiefs. His efforts included colonization schemes in Kintyre and Lewis similar to those undertaken during the ULSTER PLANTATIONS. Perhaps more effective were the Statutes of IONA (1609), which sought to prohibit firearms and large retinues, maintain the Church and education, and suppress bards and strong drink. Later the chiefs were ordered to have their sons educated in the Lowlands — a move assumed likely to produce more civilized behaviour.

During the seventeenth century the clan economy was exposed to Lowland capitalism for the first time on any scale, mainly through the development of the cattle trade. This increasing market-orientation continued to modify traditional agriculture and the way of life well into the nineteenth century. Just as important in the erosion of tradition were the increasingly divided loyalties among the clans — many had remained CATHOLIC, while others eschewed the old religion in favour of Presbyterianism. So the clansmen — with their reputation for violence, skill in arms and guerrilla warfare — featured prominently in many of the battles and lesser skirmishes that characterized the Presbyterian revolution, the CROMWELLIAN UNION, and the restored monarchy, notably the Royalist ventures of MONTROSE (1644–5 and 1650) and DUNDEE (1689).

In the aftermath of the REVOLUTION SETTLEMENT pro-Catholic clans became increasingly committed JACOBITES, though the powerful influence exercised by WILLIAM III's Lowland politicians over some of the clans was seen at its most treacherous in the infamous events at GLENCOE in 1692. The Jacobite clans, notably the Macgregors, Macdonalds, Macphersons, Stewarts and Robertsons, continued to support the Catholic cause after the Hanovarian succession and played a prominent role in the JACOBITE REBELLIONS. After the ultimate disaster at CULLODEN (1746) more rigorous laws were passed against the clansmen. Even the kilt was banned and the pipes condemned under the renewed DISARMING ACT (1716), which had its origins in the aftermath of the Fifteen. Many Jacobite chiefs lost their lands to government, a transfer that created the FORFEITED ESTATES. Most were sold off, but some restored in 1784.

It was economic development, mainly agriculture, fishing and kelp, that modified and ultimately destroyed what remained of the traditional mode of social organization and associated land use with the CLEARANCES of the late eighteenth and nineteenth centuries. Extensive EMIGRATION followed and many clan chiefs lost their remaining lands. Those who stayed — including the powerful Campbells, Sutherlands, Mackenzies and Gordons — developed their estates on Lowland lines, carrying out improvement and building planned villages, ostensibly to house displaced clansmen. Something of the traditional way of life survived in the crofting communities, although there was much hardship and suffering due to population pressure and the potato famine. The crofter's position was greatly improved by the Crofters' Act (1886).

There was something of a clan revival in Victorian times, especially through the establishment of clan societies and the wearing of the tartan. Ties of kinship were reasserted and many clans now have a world-wide network of membership. The significant part played by the clans in Scottish history is therefore increasingly better documented and appreciated.

• Devine, T.M., Clanship to Crofters' War, Manchester University Press, 1994.
• Grant, I.F., The Lordship of the Isles, 1935, reprinted Mercat Press, 1982.
• Grimble, I., Clans and Chiefs, Blond and Briggs, 1980.
• Macinnes, A.I., Clanship, Commerce and the House of Stuart, Tuckwell Press, 1996.
• Moncreiffe, I., The Highland Clans, Barrie and Jenkins, 1982.

• *The History of the Highland Clans, Dunedin Multimedia, 1996.*

Claverhouse, John, see GRAHAM OF CLAVERHOUSE

Clearances The clearances are popularly identified with the eviction of the Highlanders from their traditional lands during the eighteenth and nineteenth centuries to make way for agricultural IMPROVEMENT — mainly the grazing of sheep and deer. The term has also come to symbolize the destruction of what remained of the clans, clan life and Gaeldom generally in the aftermath of Hanoverian suppression following the JACOBITE REBELLIONS of the 'Fifteen and the 'Forty-Five.

Although the term 'clearance' was never actually applied at the time, similar events associated with ENCLOSURE occurred in the Lowlands and elsewhere, so the Highland clearances need to be seen in the wider context of capitalist modernization accompanying the AGRICULTURAL REVOLUTION. Indeed there were many parallel experiences in Ireland and on the Continent (Norway, for example) during the nineteenth century — and even into the present century in southern Europe (for example, in Spain, Italy and Greece). Like the Highlands most of these regions had experienced rapid POPULATION growth, pressure on available cultivable land, and acute poverty — resulting in enforced MIGRATION. Migration is a significant theme throughout, for over-population (or congestion, as it was called) was a major concern of the CROFTERS' COMMISSION in the 1880s — long after the major clearances. The clearances have been the subject of greater controversy and more myths than perhaps any other theme in Scottish history (discounting perhaps the Reformation and the Union). The historical debate has generated considerable heat — with a notable divide opened between the 'optimists' and the 'pessimists'. On the one hand is the view that the clansmen or crofters were being offered new opportunities in new lands, while on the other they are seen as victims of wicked and grasping lairds working in collusion with self-seeking TACKSMEN and submissive clergy. Recently, a new generation of historians have added fuel to a fire already well-stoked by those presenting the clearances in a more literary or dramatic genre.

A historically balanced view needs to take account of three major aspects: (i) the context and causes; (ii) the actual events; (iii) the aftermath.

(i) Try as we might, it is hard to escape the fact that subsistence AGRICULTURE in the Highlands could hardly support its pre-eighteenth century population, far less the growing numbers of later in the century. Indeed some have argued that the impact of crop failure and famine, especially in the 1840s, would have been even more disastrous if the population had remained at its pre-clearance level. Considerable misunderstanding surrounds this basic point, for much of the early migration was essentially seasonal, as folk came to Lowland towns seeking work, or to farms for harvest labour. Add to this the desire of landowners to improve their estates on Lowland lines and we have powerful incentives to encourage more permanent migration. The wickedness of the lairds and tacksmen is much discussed, but some did exhibit varying degrees of paternalism and humanity. Moreover, not all lairds were anxious to evict their people for sheep. Some actually opposed migration — partly because they faced falling rents or losing labour from potentially profitable enterprises like FISHING, KELP manufacture, or work in PLANNED VILLAGES on the coast.

Yet the encouragement to migrate further afield was a logical extension of existing custom, especially when the motive was the preservation of a way of life, language, religion and traditions — even on the other side of the Atlantic. Some CATHOLIC clergy in the Western Isles, for example, favoured migration to Canada as a way of preserving religion and language within a cohesive community. Several of the early 'clearances', or more properly migrations, were organized by the clergy, Catholic and Protestant — not as tools of the lairds, but as firm believers in the God-given virtue of their enterprise. We also tend to overlook the fact that the view of settlers in the United States and Canada (an increasingly important focus of Scottish migration after the American War of Independence) was often positive — for the search for land and a new way of life are perfectly understandable. This must certainly have motivated many in the later, and admittedly brutal, clearances, such as those of the Sutherland estates at the beginning of the nineteenth century.

Something else that needs to be borne in mind is that the cultural

and economic pressures to migrate were offset to some extent by economic opportunities for those who remained behind. The increased exposure of the Highlands to economic growth in the Lowlands, the continued expansion of the CATTLE trade, the development of WOOL and LINEN industries, fishing and kelp, demonstrated the potential for activities other than subsistence agriculture. Although these and other developments brought some employment they did little to solve the fundamental problem of over-population. Hence the immediate causes of the clearances were essentially economic in origin.

(ii) There were several clearly identifiable stages in the clearance movement:

(a) From 1740, on a small scale, mainly on the initiative of the tacksmen, who probably recognized more clearly than most the increasing pressure on cultivable land.

(b) After the 1760s when the introduction of Lowland-style sheep farming accelerated clearance, spreading rapidly from the Southern Highlands into the Central and Western Highlands. The earliest large-scale clearances took place in the 1770s and 1780s.

(c) Much larger-scale clearance during and after the NAPOLEONIC WARS, notably in the 1820s. It was then that the harshness of wholesale clearance from the glens and straths was most acute — witness the circumstances in Sutherland and Ross-shire at that time.

(d) Later in the nineteenth century sporadic and occasional numerically large instances, especially in the distress of the famine years during the 1840s.

In all of this there was much suffering and hardship — though at the same time life on poor, unproductive land must have been hard enough. Given a population explosion — partly, as in Ireland, the result of potato cultivation — the limit to numbers the land could support must have been reached. The motives of the landlords are well documented. As far as the people are concerned, Meek's work tells us a great deal more than was previously known about the alternative voice of Gaelic social protest. Certainly the desire for land and the preservation of a way of life were uppermost — even if the ultimate solution lay in emigration.

Another angle on the clearances that has been consistently overlooked until recently was the treatment meted out to native peoples by the settlers. Several historians have indicated that the barbarities committed against Highland peasants during the clearances need to be seen in the wider context of prevailing morality, especially the treatment of the North American Indian, the Australian Aborigine, and the Maori of New Zealand. Though it should be pointed out that land-hungry Highlanders were by no means the only white settlers who committed atrocities against native races.

(iii) The clearances left much bitterness, still part and parcel of Highland mythology after two hundred years. Considering the scale of the upheaval it is surprising that there was so little popular reaction or conflict — some see this as reflecting the stranglehold of the tacksmen and clergy over much of the local population. Indeed, the aftermath saw considerable unrest, especially in food riots and demonstrations during the famine of the 1840s, and in the stand against evictions that continued until the late nineteenth century.

The emergence of direct political action — especially the formation of the Highland Land League — was influenced both by the extension of the franchise and similar events in Ireland. Although the problem of poverty and depopulation remained, the passing of the Crofters' Act in 1886 highlights the success of political RADICALISM in its fight to preserve what remained of traditional lifestyles in the Highlands.

•*Bumsted, J.M., The People's Clearance: Highland Emigration to North America, Edinburgh University Press, 1982.*
•*Hunter, J., The Making of the Crofting Community, John Donald, 1976.*
•*Meek, D.E., Tuath Is Tighearna. Tenants and Landlords, Scottish Academic Press, 1995.*
•*Richards, E., A History of the Highland Clearances Vol 1: Agrarian Transformation and the Evictions 1746—1886, Croom Helm, 1982.*
•*Richards, E. A History of the Highland Clearances Vol 2: Emigration, Protest, Reasons, Croom Helm, 1985.*

Clerk-Maxwell, James (1831—79)

Clerk-Maxwell was one of the most prominent Scottish scientists of his generation. He became the first professor of experimental physics at Cambridge University in 1871. Born in Edinburgh, he was educated at the Edinburgh Academy and the university there. Before he was twenty he had already communicated three papers on physics to the Royal Society of Edinburgh, and in 1850 left for Cambridge.

He was briefly a fellow of Trinity College in 1855, but by the time he was 25 he was professor of natural philosophy at Aberdeen. He moved to King's College, London, in 1860. Clerk-Maxwell began his researches into electricity and electromagnetism in 1856 and continued them until his death at the early age of 48. Like William Thomson, Lord KELVIN (1824–1907), he realized the enormous potential of electricity — but unlike Kelvin confined his activities to pure research rather than practical applications.

Clydebank Blitz, see WORLD WAR II

coal Coal-mining pre-dates the INDUSTRIAL REVOLUTION by many centuries and was already well-established, though still relatively small-scale, in the Lothians, Fife and Ayrshire by the time of the REFORMATION. Pit-depths were limited by available technology, drainage being the most persistent problem, which could be solved only by horse-gins and buckets or by adits sunk at appropriate points to carry off water by gravity. Hence most coal was won from shallow measures by bell-shaped pits or by pit and adit.

During the seventeenth century the shores of the Forth became studded with coal-mines — expansion being directly related to increasing domestic and industrial demand generated by POPULATION growth. Coal was needed for SALT production and a variety of manufacturing processes including BREWING, pottery, glass and soap. One of the largest enterprises of this period was that of Sir George Bruce (d.1625), who developed coal-mining and salt manufacture at Culross. Coal was also being mined in the west of Scotland around Glasgow and in north Ayrshire — and in the latter district was again closely related to the salt industry at Saltcoats, which also became an early centre of export to Ireland.

Although production continued to expand slowly during the early eighteenth century and attracted capital from, among others, the YORK BUILDINGS COMPANY and from major landowners, it was not until the foundation of the CARRON COMPANY in 1759 that Scottish coal-mining experienced sustained development. Indeed, the rise of the IRON industry, coupled with improved mining techniques, greatly influenced development during the early Industrial Revolution.

Throughout the nineteenth century the coal industry increased still further in scale, partly due, as elsewhere, to the application of steam power, and partly to the demands of the wrought iron industry and, from 1830, the railways. The industry became more localized and concentrated in Lanarkshire, Ayrshire and Fife, with the last becoming increasingly dependent on the export trade to Europe. Mining settlements, such as those of north Lanarkshire and north Ayrshire, grew rapidly — often attracting Irish as well as more local MIGRATION. Piecemeal growth generated widespread social problems, given the harshness of working conditions and the inadequate provision generally made by the coal-masters. TRADE UNIONISM developed early to seek improvements.

In the longer term, and especially after 1870, the Scottish coal industry's main problem actually centred on its close relationship with the iron and steel industry, which experienced fluctuating fortunes and was increasingly exposed to foreign competition from Germany, France and the United States. The Scottish coalfield became less and less competitive compared with others elsewhere in Britain, and, indeed, no matter how efficient it proved, its fundamental problems were neglected by both management and labour. WORLD WAR I emphasized the reliance on traditional industries and technology, and although there was some rationalization and diversification in the 1920s and 30s, it was at considerable social cost in the form of redundancies. More mechanization, in newer, deeper pits went ahead.

After nationalization under the National Coal Board in 1947 the industry became even more concentrated as older fields were abandoned as uneconomic and as competition from cheaper fuels increased during the 1950s and 60s. After the energy crisis of the 1970s the success of the Scottish coal industry became increasingly tied to the electric power industry and a revival of exports, particularly to Northern Ireland.

• Duckham, B.F., A History of the Scottish Coal Industry: Volume I 1700—1815, David & Charles, 1970.

Cockburn, John, of Ormiston (1679—1758) John Cockburn was the eldest son of Adam Cockburn, Lord Justice Clerk and a Lord of Session. John Cockburn was himself a member of the last

Scottish Parliament and was a Commissioner for the Treaty of UNION in 1707 — later becoming an MP in the United Kingdom Parliament until 1741.

As proprietor of the Ormiston estate in East Lothian he was an early and prominent advocate of agricultural IMPROVEMENT. On assuming management of the estate in 1714 he began granting extended leases to his tenants, a move designed as an incentive to new methods. He pioneered enclosure, systematic crop rotations, and introduced new varieties of grasses and root crops like the turnip and potato on his estate. He followed agrarian improvements with the development of a planned village at Ormiston — where flax growing and the LINEN industry were actively encouraged.

Although relatively unsuccessful financially — for in a time of inflation long leases worked to the benefit of the tenants rather than himself — Cockburn was a man of some vision and enterprise for his time. He is sometimes regarded as the 'Father of Scottish Agriculture'. Whether or not this can still be sustained in the light of more detailed research on earlier developments during the seventeenth century and on the other eighteenth century 'improvers' is doubtful. Yet Cockburn's contribution to agricultural change need not be underrated.

• Symon, J.A., Scottish Farming: Past and Present, Oliver & Boyd, 1959.

Code of Canons (1636) CHARLES I's (1600—49) coronation ceremony in Edinburgh in 1633 with its unfamiliar and unpopular Anglican ritual was a clear warning of the king's preference for a less austere form of worship. Not long afterwards he suggested to the Scottish bishops the urgent need for a PRAYER BOOK modelled on English lines. Its preparation took longer than expected and the Code of Canons, meant in fact to accompany the liturgy, was issued a year earlier. Apart from the emphasis placed on the royal supremacy, the instructions principally caused dismay because of the omissions that there seemed to be. Thus, kirk sessions, presbyteries and the GENERAL ASSEMBLY were ignored and, moreover, acceptance was demanded of a liturgy as yet unpublished. Therefore, to most presbyteries the Canons were unacceptable and they became one of the causes of religious unrest in the later 1630s.

• Dickinson, W.C. and Donaldson, G. (eds.), A Source Book of Scottish History III, Nelson, 1961.
• Foster, W.R., The Church before the Covenants, Scottish Academic Press, 1975.

coinage, see CURRENCY

College of Justice, see COURT OF SESSION

Colquhoun, Patrick (1745—1820) Colquhoun was a prominent Glasgow and London merchant, one of the 'new men' of the INDUSTRIAL REVOLUTION, and a propagandist for reform of the police, EDUCATION and POOR RELIEF. After a spell in Virginia (1761—6) he returned to settle in Glasgow as a COTTON merchant, associating with the TOBACCO Lords and other prominent members of the com-

mercial community, including David DALE (1739—1806). In 1776 he helped raise a regiment to fight the insurgents during the AMERICAN WAR OF INDEPENDENCE. Colquhoun was afterwards provost of Glasgow (1782), first chairman of the Chamber of Commerce and Manufactures (1783) and chairman of the management committee of the FORTH AND CLYDE CANAL.

Glasgow proved too small a stage and in 1789 he moved to London, where he quickly became an establishment figure — partly through the influence of his friend Henry DUNDAS (1742—1811). He subsequently concerned himself with law and order and social reform publishing *A Treatise on the Police of the Metropolis* (1796), *A New System of Education for the Labouring Poor* (1806), and *A Treatise on the Population, Wealth, Power and Resources of the British Empire* (1814). He was no radical, however, being a strong advocate of stability and control. His views might be usefully contrasted with those of Robert OWEN (1771—1858), the social reformer, whom he almost certainly knew through business and social connections.

Commissioners of Supply This office originated after the RESTORATION, in 1667, when the first permanent commissioners were appointed to allocate the 'cess', or land tax, among their fellow landowners. Qualification was ownership of land at the level of £100 per annum. Failure to execute this function effectively, particularly in the eighteenth century, did not preclude these officials being given numerous administrative duties. These included assisting in educational provision, helping in the supervision of roads and bridges, collecting 'rogue money' for the upkeep of prisons and also bringing criminals to justice. A less commendable activity of some commissioners was in the county elections where a favourite device was corrupt valuations to create fictitious votes for certain candidates.

The Valuation of Land Act (1854), which introduced the rating system, in existence in Scotland until 1989, greatly reduced the importance of officials whose role in local government had become increasingly difficult to distinguish from that of JUSTICES OF THE PEACE and SHERIFFS. With the establishment of county councils in 1889 the commissioners virtually became redundant, although they still worked in co-operation with county councillors on joint police committees until 1929.

• *Whetstone, A.E., Scottish County Government in the Eighteenth and Nineteenth Centuries, John Donald, 1981.*

Company of Scotland Scotland's economy had recovered to some extent from its dire condition in the CROMWELLIAN UNION during the next twenty years. But in the 1690s under WILLIAM III (1650–1702) the combined effects of European mercantilist policies and the French wars were beginning to create serious economic problems. The English Navigation Act (1661), for example, which restricted goods brought into England to English vessels or ships of the country of origin was a serious drawback to Scottish trade, especially with the American colonies and West Indies.

Despite a certain amount of illicit trading with these regions there was growing pressure on the government by Scots merchants for the development of Scottish colonies. Indeed, unsuccessful steps in this direction were taken in the 1680s, at East New Jersey and South Carolina. However, an Act of PARLIAMENT of 1693 finally cleared the way for the setting up of overseas trading companies, hence the formation of the Company of Scotland in 1695.

With its monopoly rights to all trade between Scotland, America, Africa and Asia, not to mention its exemptions from customs, the new venture was an attractive proposition. In fact, much of the initial interest was shown by English speculators. Moreover, William III, eager to distract attention from the massacre of GLENCOE, was also sympathetic to it. But his attitude quickly changed when the powerful East India Company and other commercial interests, alarmed at a possible threat to their privileges, put pressure on the king to insist on the withdrawal of the English investment.

Accordingly, it was only in 1696, once all foreign backing had disappeared, that the Darien Scheme, the plan devised by William PATERSON (1658–1719) for a Scottish colony on the isthmus of Darien in Central America got off the ground. Paterson's ambitious stratagem involved the establishment of a settlement at Darien that would become an entrepot for the trade of both Europe and the East. Its main weaknesses were inadequate preparation and organization. Thus the 3,000 settlers who set sail in 1698 and 1699 lacked any knowledge of the prevailing tropical conditions and inevitably suffered huge losses from sickness and disease. A further problem was the claim to sovereignty over the territory made by Spain, which resulted in the second expedition being attacked by Spanish forces. Moreover, since Spanish amity was a prerequisite of William III's continental diplomacy, the English government refused to give any assistance whatsoever to the colonists.

The Darien disaster created a serious breach in Anglo-Scottish relations. The numerous Scottish investors made the king their scapegoat while in Parliament his opponents made life difficult for faithful servants like QUEENSBERRY (1662–1711) and SEAFIELD (1664–1730). However, William survived the crisis, largely because of the various divisions existing within the opposition, particularly between Presbyterians and JACOBITES. Thus a bill dismissing Spanish claims to Darien and reasserting the rights of the Company of Scotland was defeated, much to the king's relief.

In this manner did William III's foreign policy survive but he was well aware how precarious the situation had been in 1701–2 and what future problems could arise so long as two separate parliaments existed.

At the same time the vicissitudes of the Company of Scotland intensified Scottish dislike of their Dutch monarch and gave a major boost to the Jacobite cause.
• *Ferguson, W., Scotland: 1689 to the Present, Oliver & Boyd, 1968.*
• *Hart, F.R., The Disaster of Darien, Constable, 1929.*

Competitors   The death of MARGARET, Maid of Norway (c.1283–90) saw thirteen different claimants emerge for the Scottish crown. However, the two most eligible candidates were John BALLIOL (1250–1313) and Robert BRUCE (1210–95). Dominating the debate about the succession was Edward I who persuaded all the contestants or 'Competitors' to agree to his adjudication on the issue. The legal examination of the 'Great Cause' began at BERWICK in August 1291 under Edward's supervision with a final verdict in favour of John Balliol being announced on 12 November 1292. The subsequent coronation of Balliol on St Andrew's Day 1292 was soon overshadowed by Edward I's claims to overlordship of Scotland.
• *Stones, E.L.G. and Simpson, G. (eds.), Edward I and the Throne of Scotland, 1978.*

Comyn, John (d.1306)   John Comyn was the son of John, Lord of Badenoch (d.1303) and was usually known as the 'Red' Comyn. He was a member of the most powerful baronial dynasty in thirteenth century Scotland, his father having been both a COMPETITOR and GUARDIAN while the 'Red' Comyn was also a Guardian in the unsettled period after his brother-in-law, John Balliol's (c.1250–1313) abdication. Eventually he played his part in the unsuccessful attempts at resistance against Edward I being a reluctant signatory of the agreement reached at Perth in Febuary 1304 with the English king.

Two years later on 10 February 1306 at Greyfriars Church, Dumfries, Comyn and Robert

BRUCE (1274–1329) met for discussions purportedly about combining their forces against the English. Previous meetings had been acrimonious affairs but this one outdid the others when Bruce stabbed and killed his rival.

• *Barrow, G.W.S., Robert Bruce and the Community of the Realm of Scotland, Edinburgh University Press, 1988.*
• *Young, A., Robert Bruce's Rivals: The Comyns 1212–1314, Tuckwell Press, 1997.*

Conservative Party The Conservative Party (see TORIES) dates from 1834 when Robert Peel (1788–1850) first linked a programme of moderate reform with traditional notions of respect for long-established institutions. In Scotland the Conservatives were trying to recover from the impact of the REFORM ACT, which had greatly favoured the LIBERALS, but their only real success came in the counties where landowners still exercised considerable power and influence over voters. An all-time low was reached in the 1850s when the party all but collapsed.

Nevertheless there was a belated recognition of the need for fresh policies and reorganization in advance of the second Reform Act, with a National Constitutional Association established in 1867. From 1868 a committee to coordinate electoral activities set to work and a year later the potential vote of industrial workers in the West was being canvassed through the Glasgow Working Men's Conservative Association. Disraeli (1804–81) himself had to promote a programme of social reform relevant to Scotland — with some effect in the short term. In the 1874 General Election the Conservatives did well, taking their total of MPs to nineteen — the only major gains in thirty years. The votes were won in the BURGHS rather than the counties and significantly Glasgow returned one Conservative — to break a Liberal monopoly established since 1832. Despite this improvement the party ended up in 1880 with fewer Scottish MPs than it had returned in 1868. Even in 1886, when Gladstone (1809–98) was routed elsewhere, the Liberal vote held up remarkably well and the Conservatives could return only twelve Scottish MPs. 'Scotland,' as Fry observed, 'still mistrusted Conservatism.' But the split in Liberal ranks over Irish Home Rule would prove a major element in favour of the Conservative Party — which came increasingly to be associated with Unionism — whether Irish or Scottish.

Although the Conservatives or Unionists held power at Westminster for over a decade between 1895 and 1905 under Salisbury (1830–1903) and BALFOUR (1848–1930) the party had a generally lean time of it north of the Border. After the 1906 General Election they returned only eight Scottish members, though with their number enhanced by four Liberal-Unionists they could command 38 per cent of the Scottish vote. A separate Scottish Unionist Party, founded in 1911, set about a major reorganization nationally and in the constituencies, and, as Harvie observes, 'Unionist cohesiveness ultimately triumphed over Liberal disorder.'

Despite the problems of the DEPRESSION, Unionist administrators of the inter-war period proved quite reformist in their Scottish dealings. This was most obvious in the work of Walter ELLIOT (1885–1958) at the SCOTTISH OFFICE, particularly in the reform of central and local government. The Local Government Act of 1929 had far reaching consequences for local democracy.

In the 1945 General Election the Unionists returned twenty-five Scottish members taking 37 per cent of the vote, and this share was maintained or exceeded until 1974. Even in 1966, the highpoint of post-war Labourism, twenty Unionist MPs sat for Scottish constituencies. They and their Party found the rise of the SCOTTISH NATIONAL PARTY just as much of a challenge as LABOUR but, despite a positive report on devolution by a committee under the chairmanship of Sir Alec Douglas Home in 1970, inaction was the order of the day. Most Conservatives ultimately supported the 'No' Campaign, which was boosted before the 1979 referendum by Home's personal repudiation of devolution.

The party experienced mixed fortunes during the 1980s, for although the Thatcher governments commanded strong support in England, Conservative policies were mostly rejected by Scottish voters.

The unpopularity of the Conservatives was based on the belief that they were an anti-Scottish party. There was hostility to many Tory policies. The governments under both Thatcher and her successor, John Major, were widely perceived to be using Scotland as a test-bed for such controversial policies as the ill-fated Poll Tax, introduced to Scotland in 1989, one year ahead of the rest of the UK.

However, this unpopularity was not immediately apparent in electoral terms for having gained 24 per cent of the votes (and 10 seats) in the 1987 General Election, the Tories actually increased their vote in 1992 to over 25 per cent, returning 11 MPs to Westminster. Under John Major the Scottish party's virtual rejection of devolution proved ultimately disastrous. Despite obtaining over 17 per cent of the vote in the 1997 General Election, not a single MP was returned from Scotland. The party re-grouped and with pro-devolutionists in the ascendency saw Conservative MSPs returned to the Scottish PARLIAMENT in 1999. In the 2001 General Election Tory fortunes in Scotland improved little, with one MP returned.

• Fry, M., *Patronage and Principle: A Political History of Modern Scotland*, Aberdeen University Press, 1987.
• Harvie, C., *No Gods and Precious Few Heroes: Scotland 1914–1980*, Edward Arnold, 1981.
• Hutchison, I.G.C., *A Political History of Scotland: 1832–1924*, John Donald, 1986.

Convention of Royal Burghs
Although regular meetings of the royal BURGHS were not held until the middle of the sixteenth century the forerunner for such gatherings is believed to have been the medieval Court of the Four Burghs. This was a body originally comprising in the thirteenth century the towns of Berwick, Edinburgh, Roxburgh and Stirling,

which handled disputes between the burghs and appeals from their courts. However, from the year 1578, there is a record of annual meetings of the convention in Edinburgh where the burgh representatives attempted to regulate trade and commerce. One of their concerns, for example, was the organization of the STAPLE at Veere. By the time of the Treaty of UNION the convention, with the decline of many of the royal burghs, had lost much of its influence, although in the 1720s and again in the 1740s it put pressure on the government to provide assistance or protection for the linen industry.
• *Pagan T., The Conventions of the Royal Burghs of Scotland, Glasgow University Press, 1926.*

Co-operatives Early co-operative societies initially derived much from the ideas of self-help generated by craft guilds, benefit and friendly societies, mainly dating from the eighteenth century. As early as 1769, for example, the weavers of Fenwick, Ayrshire, co-operated in the purchase of oatmeal. Other early instances of consumer co-operation in 'victualling societies' included those at Govan (c.1777) and Bridgeton (c.1800), both in Glasgow. The later Lennoxtown Victualling Society (1812) was one of the first to pay dividends in proportion to purchases.

The development of co-operatives during the early nineteenth century was given considerable impetus by the existence of the 'truck system', whereby workers were paid by tokens or notes exchangeable for goods at the company store. The OWENITES took

up the idea in the 1820s and there were several subsequent experiments on co-operative principles — including the short-lived Orbiston Community. Alexander Campbell (1796–1870), a prominent Owenite, became a leading propagandist of co-operation, and it was further popularized by the Chartists during the 1830s and 1840s. One of the earliest examples was the Hawick Chartist Provision Store, established in 1839.

The modern consumer co-operative movement traces its origins to the Rochdale Owenite pioneers who established their store in 1844. Although many of the social ideals slowly vanished, co-operatives were soon widespread, especially in urban, industrial districts of the Scottish Lowlands. A Scottish Co-operative Wholesale Society — designed to provide retail societies with goods at wholesale prices and hence eliminate the middleman — was started in 1868. Control was vested in representatives of local societies. By 1900 the SCWS had become a major commercial force in its own right — with factories, farms and other enterprises under its control. The 'Co-op' (or 'Store') and the 'Divi' had become established institutions of working — and lower-middle-class life.

Although many of these enterprises were great commercial successes, the co-operative spirit of an earlier era continued to be kept alive in youth movements, women's movements, libraries, evening classes and concerts. The social function of co-operatives therefore remained strong, particularly in smaller communities. Another related area of self-help was the co-operative HOUSING movement — active in several Scottish towns and cities during the later-Victorian era. Co-operative building societies erected artisan's dwellings in Edinburgh during the 1860s and in Rutherglen in 1874.

Other forms of co-operation that became increasingly important during the nineteenth century were the friendly societies and the benefit activities of trade unions. These provided basic insurance for workers prior to the introduction of the Welfare State — and some of the original organizations still perform similar functions to the present day.

• *Kinloch, J. and Butt, J., History of the Scottish Co-operative Wholesale Society Ltd, SCWS, 1981.*

Corn Laws, see AGRICULTURE; ANTI-CORN LAW LEAGUE

Corresponding Societies Numerous reform clubs, some calling themselves 'corresponding societies' because of their avowed intention to correspond with similar clubs throughout Britain, were established in the 1790s. The most prominent nationally was the London Corresponding Society, founded by a prominent Scottish Radical, Thomas Hardy (1752—1832). In common with other English reform organizations the LCS had close links with the FRIENDS OF THE PEOPLE and sent delegates to its conventions in Scotland, notably the last attended by Joseph GERRALD (1760—96) and Maurice MARGAROT (1745—1815).

cotton Cotton textiles was one of the leading sectors of the INDUSTRIAL REVOLUTION in Scotland

and contributed substantially to the rise of Glasgow and the west of Scotland as the nexus of economic growth during the period 1780—1830. At the same time the cotton spinning industry and the associated handloom weaving trade were widely dispersed throughout the Lowlands. In the pre-factory or domestic phase before 1775 cotton was grafted on to the existing LINEN industry, producing hybrid yarns. Raw materials from the plantations of the North American colonies and the West Indies were imported to Glasgow and other Clyde ports by merchants like David DALE (1739—1806). Cotton imports rose steadily from 106,000 lbs in 1755 to 628,000 lbs in 1785.

The growth of mass production cotton spinning in the Scottish Lowlands was owed to imported technology and expertise allied to local entrepreneurship, capital, labour and water power. The key innovations came from England: the spinning jenny, developed by James Hargreaves (d.1778); the water-frame of Richard Arkwright (1732—92); and the spinning mule of Samuel Crompton (1753—1827). The earliest mills based on Arkwright's water-frame were established at Penicuik (1778) and Rothesay (1779). By the early 1780s there were another half dozen mills, but still on a fairly small scale.

The major country spinning mills using water power were built in the 1780s. Arkwright had some difficulty enforcing his patent in Scotland, but he sought partnerships with Scottish businessmen willing to invest in his invention. He briefly joined forces with Dale in the establishment of one of the largest mills at NEW LANARK (1785), built on the River Clyde. Other large units were set up on prime water-power sites in Ayrshire, Lanarkshire, Perthshire and elsewhere. By 1787 — two years after Arkwright's patent was cancelled — there were nineteen mills. Growth thereafter was so rapid that c.1795 there were no fewer than 91 mills with half that number located in Lanarkshire and Renfrewshire.

Gradually, as steam power began to dominate after the early 1800s, the industry concentrated increasingly in Glasgow, and by 1839 the city and neighbourhood had 98 out of a total of 192 mills. The power loom gradually eliminated the handloom weaver — an early casualty of technical change — and after 1830 many plants integrated both spinning and weaving. An important finishing industry — bleaching, dyeing and printing — developed to service the cotton and other textile trades, concentrating itself in Renfrewshire and the Vale of Leven.

The Scottish cotton industry slowly declined after 1860, mainly due to an amalgam of increasing competition, over-specialization, higher costs, falling profits and a consequent failure to re-equip with new machinery — problems later all too familiar in other sectors of Scottish industry. The overwhelming dominance of Lancashire as the greatest cotton goods producer always worked against the Scottish cotton industry, to the extent that a leading sector of early industrialization was virtually eliminated by 1914.

• *Chapman, S.D., The Cotton Industry in the Industrial Revolution, Macmillan, 1972.*

• *Knox, W., Hanging by a Thread: The Scottish Cotton Industry, c.1850—1914, Carnegie Publishing, 1995.*

• *Lythe, S.G.E. and Butt, J., An Economic History of Scotland 1100—1939, Blackie, 1975.*

Court of Justiciary   In the late sixteenth century JAMES VI (1566—1625) had unsuccessfully attempted to introduce a system of itinerant justices hearing criminal cases in various parts of the country and CHARLES I (1600—49) actually got as far as appointing eight senators of the College of Justice to undertake such visitations. However, the modern court dates from the legal reorganization that took place in the reign of CHARLES II (1630—85) in 1672 when the Lord Justice-General and Lord Justice-Clerk were joined by five senators who became commissioners of justiciary. The latter, accompanied by the Lord Justice-Clerk, were to make annual circuits, holding their courts in specified towns throughout Scotland. In the nineteenth century all the lords of session became commissioners of justiciary so that today's High Court is staffed by the same twenty-one judges who serve the COURT OF SESSION.

• *An Introduction to Scottish Legal History, Stair Society, 1958.*

Court of Session   During the reign of JAMES IV (1473—1513) the first steps towards establishing a central civil court were taken and latterly certain numbers of his council, known as Lords of Session, were meeting in Edinburgh on a regular basis. However, it was not until the reign of JAMES V (1512—42) that this embryonic Court of Session was placed on a permanent footing. James V, taking full advantage of the various vicissitudes afflicting the papacy in that era, eventually, in 1535, succeeded in obtaining papal confirmation for the establishment of a College of Justice. Under the arrangements made, the king, in return for a guarantee of his loyalty to the Church, would receive £72,000 from clerical taxation, with another £1,400 a year to provide salaries for the judges of his new college. The latter was to consist of a president with fourteen Lords of Session or 'senators', half of whom were to be ecclesiastics, although this stipulation was rescinded in 1640. Until 1604 the court was peripatetic, the whole kingdom being divided into quarters visited in turn between June and October each year. Additional or 'extraordinary' Lords of Session were appointed until 1723, while in 1831 the number of judges was reduced to thirteen. At the same time, the court, which had been organized into two divisions in 1808, was now rearranged into an Outer House of five judges hearing individual civil cases and an Inner House of two divisions, presided over by the Lord President and Lord Justice-Clerk respectively, which would hear appeals. In recent years the total number of judges has been increased to twenty-one.

• *Dickinson, W.C., Donaldson, G. and Milne, I. (eds.), A Source Book of Scottish History II, Nelson, 1958.*
• *Hannay R.K., The College of Justice, H.M. Register House, 1932.*

Covenanters The signatories and supporters of the NATIONAL COVENANT and the SOLEMN LEAGUE AND COVENANT were the earliest Covenanters but the description is particularly used to refer to those who found the RESTORATION SETTLEMENT unacceptable. The bulk of this opposition came from clergy and laity of PROTESTOR persuasion with the main basis of their objections being the revival of episcopacy, State control of the Church and the rejection of the former covenants. The key issue was lay PATRONAGE and with its return the necessity for ministers to obtain both presentation from a patron as well as episcopal collation. February 1663 was the final deadline for coming to terms with these arrangements and thereafter any clergy who had failed to do so were deprived.

The 262 'outed' ministers, approximately a quarter of the total ministry, were replaced by recently qualified graduates of questionable calibre, the so-called 'curates'. Meanwhile, despite government restrictions, many deprived clergy continued to hold services at illegal conventicles, which were often attended by large congregations, especially in the southwest. In order to disperse such gatherings and collect the fines imposed by the 'Bishops' Dragnet', the authorities dispatched troops into the disaffected areas, provoking the ill-fated PENTLAND RISING (1666). Henceforth, at least for a time, more conciliatory tactics were adopted, with bishops like Robert Leighton (1611—84) of Dunblane advocating further alterations in the religious settlement to make it more acceptable to the Covenanters. However, Lauderdale (1616—82), who had the final word, preferred offering indulgences that allowed dissident clergy to return to the Church, albeit subject to certain qualifications. Under this arrangement about 130 ministers rejoined. Those who held out were now increasingly subject to the harsh legislation placed in the statute book in the early 1670s whereby landowners could be fined for allowing conventicles to be held on their territory and ultimately had to give guarantees for the behaviour of their tenants. In addition, unlicensed ministers and their congregations would be fined, any clergyman who presided at a conventicle could face the death penalty, all baptisms must be performed by licensed ministers and ordination by a Covenanting churchman was declared illegal.

Despite these measures, support for the Covenanters grew, at least in the southwest where the introduction of the unpopular 'HIGHLAND HOST' in 1678 caused further resentment. Latent antagonism became open revolt the following year when the murder of Archbishop SHARP (1618—79) in May 1679 and the defeat of a small government force under CLAVER-HOUSE (1648—89) at Drumclog, Ayrshire, in June was the signal for a full-scale Covenanter rebellion. Easily defeated at BOTHWELL BRIDGE by a royal army commanded by the Duke of Monmouth (1649—85), the Covenanters were treated leniently.

Thus, only those who refused to promise that they would eschew further rebellious action were sentenced to transportation in the Barbados (most of them to be drowned en route off Orkney). For the remainder, Monmouth's concil-

iatory policy gave them the opportunity of accepting a third indulgence, which permitted, among other things, indoor conventicles.

These concessions effectively broke the back of the Covenanting movement since those who remained in rebellion were the intransigents who were soon to become known as CAMERONIANS. Unfortunately the introduction of the Test Act (1681) heralded further repressive measures, especially in the southwest, where Claverhouse's units frequently failed to distinguish between those who were Cameronians and those Presbyterians who merely opposed the contentious TEST ACT or had connections with the 1679 uprising.

• *Buckroyd, J., Church and State in Scotland, 1660—81, John Donald, 1980.*
• *Cowan, I.B., The Scottish Covenanters, Weidenfeld & Nicolson, 1967.*
• *Dickinson, W.C. and Donaldson, G. (eds.), A Source Book of Scottish History III, Nelson, 1961.*
• *Donaldson, G., Scotland: James V to James VII, Oliver & Boyd, 1965.*

Craig, James, see NEW TOWN OF EDINBURGH

Craik, William, of Arbigland (1703—98) William Craik was a notable landowner and practitioner of agricultural IMPROVEMENT in his native Galloway. Apparently influenced by Jethro Tull's (1674—1741) work on husbandry, he devised his own drilling machinery for crop sowing and himself became an advocate of more intensive land use. Later, about 1745, he introduced root crops, notably the turnip, to southwest Scotland. His example was emulated by other progressive landowners throughout the Scottish BORDERS and in Cumbria.

Crinan Canal, see CANALS

Crofters' Commission (The Napier Commission) The increasing discontent following the Highland CLEARANCES and later evictions drew public attention to the crofters' plight. Lack of tenure and congestion in some districts led to riots and land raids — the so-called 'Crofters' War' of the 1880s. On the political front the Highland Land Law Reform Association or Highland Land League (1882) commanded widespread support, as did the Crofters' Party, a group of breakaway LIBERALS.

Faced with the prospect of coercion on Irish lines, Gladstone (1809—98) appointed the Royal Commission on the Crofters and Cottars of Scotland under Lord Napier (1819—98), an ex-Indian Civil Servant. This duly heard evidence throughout the HIGHLANDS during 1883—4 and the resulting report catalogued the general distress of land and people.

The recommendations were radical for their time but did not go far enough for the Highland Land League, which sought similar provisions to those of the Irish Land Act (1881), conceding tenure, fair rents and rights of inheritance.

Ultimately — and with political considerations uppermost — Gladstone's Crofters' Holdings Act (1886) gave security of tenure, fixed rents, the right to inherit, bequeath or assign crofts, as well as the right to compensation for improvements. A Crofters' Commission was established to safeguard these rights and deal with disputes. It was not immediately successful, for land redistribution and the development of crofts on cleared land remained significant grievances. On Lewis, the Park deer raid (1887) was perhaps the most famous effort to repossess former crofts which had been turned into a sporting estate.

Subsequent legislation greatly strengthened the commission's powers and ultimately led to the creation of new crofts in many parts of the Highlands. The commission was superseded by the Scottish Land Court in 1911.

The Crofters' Commission can be seen as a belated attempt to restore something of the social and economic fabric of the Highlands so denuded by the earlier clearances and MIGRATION. Although created for essentially political ends, historically it was a long-term success and did much to revive — in modified form — a long traditional way of life in the Highlands and other parts of the north and west.

• *Cameron, E.A., Land for the People? The British Government and the Scottish Highlands, 1880—1925, Tuckwell Press, 1996.*
• *Devine, T.M., Clanship to Crofters' War, Manchester University Press, 1994.*
• *Hunter, J., The Making of the Crofting Community, John Donald, 1976.*

Cromwell, Oliver, see CROMWELLIAN UNION; DUNBAR; ENGAGEMENT

Cromwellian Union (1652—60) The execution of CHARLES I (1600—49) in 1649 in conjunction with the continued refusal of Cromwell (1599—1658) and the Independents to honour the terms of the

SOLEMN LEAGUE AND COVENANT guaranteed Anglo-Scottish conflict. Indeed, by summer 1650, the COVENANTERS had persuaded a reluctant but desperate Charles II (1630–85) to agree to their demands only for their army to be defeated by Cromwell at the battle of DUNBAR in September. This defeat was followed by a gradual English conquest of the country, Edinburgh was taken in December, and by the time another Scottish force, which had evaded the main English army and advanced into England, had been overwhelmed at Worcester in September 1651, Scottish resistance was over. Consequently, the union effectively began in 1652. In that year the Commonwealth government ordered the Scottish BURGHS and counties to elect representatives to recognize the union and thereafter to send a committee to London to discuss its terms. However there was no real consultation and the subsequent arrangements were concluded without the consent of the Scottish PARLIAMENT or the people.

At the outset a system of military government existed but this was superseded in 1655 by a small council, which although dominated by military personnel like General MONCK (1608–70) did at least contain two Scotsmen. The COURT OF SESSION was abolished to be replaced for a period by martial law but eventually a supreme court with about a dozen judges was established to handle criminal and exchequer offences. At a local level, in a move to restrict the influence of the predominantly royalist landowners, the ancient baron courts were greatly reduced

in power while JUSTICES OF THE PEACE, tentatively brought in by JAMES VI (1566–1625), were reintroduced. They were given wide powers, some of them over ecclesiastical misdemeanours in an obvious effort to reduce the powers of the Covenanting clergy.

There was also an English army of occupation permanently based in the country. This varied in size from a large contingent of around 18,000 men in 1654, owing to the threat from the GLENCAIRN RISING, to normally about half that number. They were stationed in five main garrisons, Ayr, Leith, Perth, Inverlochy and Inverness, with numerous subsidiary units scattered over the countryside. Unquestionably they made a substantial contribution to the improvement of law and order, which all contemporary commentators agree was a notable feature of this era and which even applied to such notorious spots as the HIGHLANDS and Islands.

Unfortunately a more orderly society was only achieved by a greatly increased financial burden being placed on many of the population. Initially, as a contribution towards the upkeep of its army, Cromwell's government demanded £10,000 a month reduced to £6,000 in 1657 following the intervention of a sympathetic General Monck. In normal circumstances this would undoubtedly have been regarded as an excessive financial imposition, but with many leading noble families in dire straits either as a result of their involvement in the events of the 1640s or more recently the Glencairn insurrection, such fiscal demands were even more crippling and unpopular.

Nor, since the economic consequences of the union were generally adverse, were the commercial classes any better prepared to face increased taxation. Scotland might have gained the right to trade freely with English colonies overseas but as Scottish merchants did not own any transatlantic vessels this advantage was outweighed by an unfavourable English foreign policy. This resulted in trade restrictions in some of Scotland's traditional markets, such as France and Holland, and when accompanied by embargoes on such important Scottish exports as wool and hides meant economic disaster for England's partner. Certainly, even if some commercial interests did petition for the retention of the union in 1659–60, there were very few economic advantages discernible from it in the preceding decade.

In religion, the anti-royalist PROTESTORS were initially preferred by Cromwell's administration to their opponents, the RESOLUTIONERS. However, the intransigence of most of the former towards the policy of religious toleration followed by the Commonwealth government resulted in the Resolutioners becoming more favourably regarded. In fact, after the death of Cromwell in 1658 and the unstable political situation that ensued, it was to be James Sharp (1618–79), a leading Resolutioner, who was to play a key role in the discussions surrounding the RESTORATION SETTLEMENT.

- *Donaldson, G., Scotland: James V to James VII, Oliver & Boyd, 1965.*
- *Dow, F., Cromwellian Scotland, 1651–60, John Donald, 1980.*
- *Grainger, J., Cromwell Against the Scots, Tuckwell Press, 1997.*

Crusades The Crusades were part of a long-term conflict between Christian and Muslim states for control of the Mediterranean, which had begun with the emergence of Islam in the seventh century. Its focus was the Holy Land in Jerusalem sacred to Christians and a centre of pilgrimage from the time of Constantine the Great. By the eleventh century, Western pilgrims were being challenged to such an extent by the Muslims that in 1095 Pope Urban II preached in favour of a holy war. This effectively launched the First Crusade 1096–1099, and was followed by a series throughout the twelfth and thirteenth centuries, the Second 1145–49, the Third 1187–92, the Fourth 1198–1204, with many important later campaigns including Louis IX's crusade of 1248–54, and 1267–70. According to Duncan the Scots who participated in the first crusade were noted for their faith and 'lack of knightly equipment', which may have reflected the huge distances crusaders had to travel. The Scots subsequently seemed reluctant to finance or participate in a crusade to recover Jerusalem, which had been captured by Saladin in 1187 and generally the number of participants in crusading is unknown. The CHURCH raised awareness, however, and Scots nobles are known to have taken the cross and played a role in many of the complex campaigns. These included Patrick, Earl of Dunbar, who set out to join Louis IX's crusade, but died of disease at Marseilles in 1248, the Earl of Atholl who died at

Carthage in 1269, Sir Alexander Seton whose squire was made prisoner by the Saracens in 1270, and Adam, Earl of Carrick, who died at Acre in 1270. It is not known whether papal and Church attempts to raise revenue for the crusades had much success in Scotland, but it has been suggested by earlier historians that geographical isolation might have been a factor, as well as the continuing Anglo-Scottish conflicts. However modern scholarship indicates that the crusades were as influential on people's thinking in Scotland as elsewhere and that interest in them was maintained until the sixteenth century.

Most other noble families were probably touched in some way by the crusades as participation was not only an expression of faith but a test of valour. The power of the former is seen in ROBERT I's desire to have his embalmed heart carried to the Holy Sepulchre by Sir James Douglas. Douglas, accompanied by many Scottish knights, eventually reached Spain in 1330 where they joined the campaign against the Moors of Granada. At the battle of Tebas de Ardales Douglas and others were killed in action, his bones and the heart of Bruce being duly returned as revered artefacts in their native land.

The royal families of Scotland were all involved in crusading in some form. WILLIAM I's grandfather on his mother Ada's side, was captured by the Turks during the disastrous second crusade, and his brother DAVID may have personally fought the Saracens in the Holy Land, later becoming the fictional hero of Sir Walter SCOTT's novel, *The Talisman*.

Cullen, William (1710–90) Cullen was a prominent figure of the Scottish ENLIGHTENMENT who greatly influenced the development of MEDICINE and medical teaching. He was born in Hamilton, where his father was factor to the Duke of Hamilton. After a spell at the University of Glasgow studying medicine he went to London in 1729 and joined a merchant ship as surgeon. Returning to Hamilton in 1736 — partly thanks to the patronage of the Duke and Duchess — he practised surgery and soon became a man of some standing as a magistrate. He graduated MD at Glasgow in 1740 and moved there in 1744 to lecture on medicine and related subjects. Joseph BLACK (1728–99) became a student and life-long associate.

Cullen was appointed professor of medicine at Glasgow in 1751, moving to Edinburgh as professor of chemistry four years later. He built up a reputation as a formidable and inspiring teacher — not only of chemistry but also of clinical medicine. A series of lectures, published in 1771 without his authority, was subsequently reissued, and there were many later editions. Although he made few radical discoveries Cullen was much honoured during his lifetime and his teaching and publications influenced several generations, helping to put Scottish scholars at the forefront of medical science in the late-eighteenth and early-nineteenth centuries.

Culloden, Battle of (16 April 1746) The JACOBITE and Hanoverian forces encountered each other five miles southeast of

Inverness at Drummossie Moor, part of the estate of Duncan FORBES (1685–1747), Lord President of the Court of Session, on Wednesday, 16 April 1746. Both in military strength and physical fitness the government army was considerably superior to its adversaries. Thus, while the Jacobites possibly had about 5,000 infantrymen, about 100 cavalry and a dozen assorted pieces of ordnance, their antagonists had in the region of 8,000 infantrymen, 800 cavalry and 120 guns. Moreover many of the Highlanders were hungry and exhausted, having spent most of the previous evening participating in a fruitless attempt at a surprise attack on their opponents. The terrain of the battlefield also suited the powerful artillery and cavalry of Cumberland (1721–65), a fact appreciated by MURRAY (c.1700–60), one of the leading Jacobite officers, but ignored by the YOUNG PRETENDER (1720–88). Not surprisingly the actual conflict, which began about one o'clock in the afternoon, was a short-lived affair. The opening salvoes of the Duke's artillery inflicted many casualties while the Highlanders' great tactical weapon, the charge, proved ineffective against the well-drilled troops of the British Army. By two o'clock it was virtually all over; Cumberland had lost about 300 men whereas the Jacobite losses were to be at least four times that figure, a considerable number of them the victims of the indiscriminate shooting of prisoners and wounded that took place after the battle itself.

The subsequent pillaging and devastation of the HIGHLANDS in the weeks thereafter did little to enhance the reputation of either the government, or its principal agent, the aptly nicknamed 'Butcher' Cumberland.

• *Prebble J., Culloden, Secker & Warburg, 1961.*
• *Tomasson, K. and Buist, F., Battles of the 45, Batsford, 1962.*

Cunninghame-Grahame, Robert Bontine (1852—1936)

Cunninghame-Grahame was a flamboyant figure whose colourful reputation was largely the result of his exploits and his accounts of them in various parts of the world, especially South America. Hence his soubriquet 'Don Roberto'. At certain stages in his career he also played some part in Scottish political affairs.

In 1884 on his father's death he returned from cattle rearing in Argentina to take over and ultimately dispose of the family estate at Gartmore in Dunbartonshire. In 1886 he successfully stood as a LIBERAL candidate for North West Lanark. As an MP Cunninghame-Grahame has been described as a 'socialistic radical' with his sympathies lying with those sections of his party who supported working-class interests. Thus in November 1887, despite his political status not to mention also being a JP and Deputy-Lieutenant of Dunbartonshire, he was arrested for his involvement in the celebrated riots in Trafalgar Square and subsequently jailed for six weeks. In May 1888 he became the president of the Scottish LABOUR party, providing them with welcome financial support.

In 1892 Cunninghame-Grahame lost his parliamentary seat and spent his time travelling in South

America, the USA, Spain and Morocco. His accounts of his experiences were widely read and he enjoyed the friendship of such eminent literary celebrities as Joseph Conrad, William Morris and George Bernard Shaw. An opponent of the Boer War, he none the less volunteered but was, not surprisingly, rejected for service in WORLD WAR I.

In 1928 Cunninghame-Grahame made his final appearance in Scottish politics when in May he was appointed president of the National Party of Scotland an amalgamation of certain existing nationalist groups. Shortly afterwards when he contested the Glasgow University rectorial election he put up a very creditable performance against the favourite, Stanley Baldwin, the Prime Minister.

Cunnninghame-Grahame died in Buenos Aires in 1936 and after a spectacular funeral there he was brought back to be buried at Inchmahome Priory on the Lake of Menteith, a fitting resting place for someone who claimed descent from ROBERT II (1316—1390).
• *Schiffley, A.F.T., Don Roberto, London 1937.*
• *Watts, C., & Davies, L., Cunninghame-Grahame, London, 1979.*

Cumberland, Duke of, see CULLODEN; FORBES; JACOBITE REBELLIONS

currency By the sixteenth century the Scottish currency, which in the medieval period had been approximately equivalent in value to England's, had depreciated considerably. This trend, partly a result of constant debasement in the later fifteenth century and throughout the sixteenth, as well as various other economic factors, meant that by the date of the Treaty of UNION there was a vast disparity between the Scottish and English coinage.
• *Stewart, I.H., The Scottish Coinage, Spink, 1967.*

D

Dale, David (1739—1806)   Dale was one of the most prominent entrepreneurs of the INDUSTRIAL REVOLUTION era in Scotland, being particularly associated with the development of the COTTON industry. In many ways he followed the classic route to success, beginning in a humble way as a weaver's apprentice and ending up a successful mill-master with widespread business interests. Born in Stewarton, Ayrshire, in 1739, he was first apprenticed to a Paisley weaver and then became an itinerant weaver's agent on the putting-out system — distributing LINEN yarn and collecting the finished cloth from domestic workers. Around 1743 he moved to Glasgow as clerk to a silk merchant and later became a partner in a fine linen yarn business. Eventually he bought out his partner and built up his own prosperous business, quickly becoming a major figure in the commercial development of Glasgow. Given his knowledge of the trade, Dale was quick to invest in the new cotton spinning machinery after its introduction to Scotland in the late 1770s and joined Richard Arkwright (1732—92) in a short-lived partnership to build NEW LANARK (1783—5), which became one of the largest water-powered country spinning mills in Scotland.

His position as cashier at the Glasgow branch of the Royal Bank of Scotland from 1783 gave him a unique opportunity to check the credit-rating of customers, in particular those fellow merchants — mostly foreign traders — with whom he later participated in joint cotton spinning ventures at Catrine (Ayrshire), Newton Stewart (Galloway) and Spinningdale (Sutherland) among other places. He also had the advantage of further capital by marriage to the family of Campbell of Jura. By the standards of the time he and his resident management made good social provision at New Lanark — notably in diet, housing and schooling — much of which was later claimed by his son-in-law, Robert OWEN (1771—1858), who became manager of the mills and community when Dale sold out to an English partnership in 1799. Much influenced by his religion and his association with the SECESSION kirk, popularly styled the 'Old Scotch Independents' (c.1768), Dale was apparently a man of genuinely philanthropic spirit. He might readily be compared with another successful entrepreneur of a later generation, Andrew CARNEGIE (1835—1919).

•*McLaren, D.J., David Dale of New Lanark: A Bright Luminary to Scotland, Heatherbank Press, 1983.*

Dalrymple, Sir John, first Earl of Stair (1648—1707) Son of Sir James Dalrymple, first Viscount Stair (1619–95), a lord president of the Court of Session and author of the magisterial legal treatise *Institutions of the Law of Scotland*. He became an advocate in 1672, distinguished himself by his defence of the NINTH EARL OF ARGYLL (1629–85) in 1681 and despite his father's sympathies for the COVENANTERS, which resulted in the latter's exile in Holland, was appointed Lord Advocate in 1687 by JAMES VII (1633–1701). None the less he supported the accession of WILLIAM III (1650–1702) and was one of the three commissioners sent by Parliament to London in 1689 to offer William and his wife the Scottish Crown. Both father and son were rewarded for their loyalty by a grateful monarch, the one being re-appointed Lord President and the other, Lord Advocate. In 1690 he became Master of Stair and the following year was given along with the Earl of Melville (1636–1707) the joint secretaryship of Scotland. In this capacity, with the breakdown of the attempts at a settlement by Breadalbane (1635–1717) in the summer of 1691, his decision to make an example of the Macdonalds of GLENCOE and the subsequent Massacre not only tarnished his reputation but ultimately led to his downfall in 1695. Latterly he supported the TREATY OF UNION and in 1703 his services to the Crown were further recognized when he received his earldom from QUEEN ANNE (1665–1714).

Darien Scheme, see COMPANY OF SCOTLAND

Darnley, Lord, see STEWART, HENRY, LORD DARNLEY

David I (c.1085—1153), King of Scots 1124—53 David I was one of the most prominent of the early monarchs. The youngest son of MALCOLM III and MARGARET he succeeded to the throne on the death of his brother, ALEXANDER I. Reflecting the strong links with the English royal family, David was raised and educated at Henry I's court. The bond was further strengthened by his marriage in 1113 to Matilda, a great-niece of William the Conqueror, and through whom he became Earl of Huntingdon. On becoming king David initiated what some historians have described as a major revolution, encouraging Anglo-NORMAN settlement and culture, redefining the law and government on Anglo-Norman principles, refining and extending the role of the church, developing BURGHS as centres of trade and fiscal and monetary reform. These were classic instruments of Normanization, but again as modern scholars point out, in Scotland they were not imposed by force as the English did in Wales and Ireland. Not only this, David was evidently astute enough to combine the new order with existing Celtic power structures and elite. The most notable manifestations of David's reign were the innumerable and potentially powerful lordships headed by Anglo-Norman nobles and their kin he created, an administrative system headed by a variety of officials operating at national and local levels, sheriffs, for example, the establishment of ten important MONASTIC HOUSES including the

Cistercian Melrose and Newbattle, the Augustinian Jedburgh and Holyrood, and a string of BURGHS including Aberdeen, Berwick and Edinburgh.

Many of the burghs were established settlements or defensive sites and the castle and Church together came to typify the Scoto-Norman burgh, as at Lanark, possibly one of David's creations. He also introduced the first Scottish currency. Beyond the confines of Scotland itself, David capitalized on the disruptions that occurred in England during the reign of Stephen and succeeded in gaining control of much of the north as far south as the river Tees, notably Northumbria and Durham. Unfortunately David's heir, the only surviving son, Earl Henry, died in 1152, predeceasing him by only a year. The future of the kingdom David had developed was therefore more uncertain than it might have been, as his young grandson MALCOLM IV succeeded. Most scholarly assessments of David see him as playing a vital role in beginning the transformation of Scotland into a feudal European monarchy, though still integrating (and increasingly absorbing) Celtic traditions.

• Barrow, G.W.S., The Anglo-Norman Era in Scotland, Oxford University Press, 1980.
• Barrow, G.W.S., The Kingdom of the Scots, Edward Arnold, 1973.
• Barrow, G.W.S., Kingship and Unity. Scotland 1000—1306, Edward Arnold, 1981.
• Barrow, G.W.S., Scotland and its Neighbours in the Middle Ages, 1992.
• Pryde, G.S., The Burghs of Scotland, Oxford University Press, 1965.
• Ritchie, R.L.G., The Normans in Scotland, Edinburgh University Press, 1954.

David II (1324—71) Son of ROBERT I (1274—1329) he succeeded to the throne in 1329 as a minor and was soon faced with another serious challenge to Scottish independence from the new English king, Edward III. The principal agent of what has been described as Edward III's policy of 'destabilization' was Edward Balliol (c.1283—1364) son of JOHN (1250—1313) briefly King of Scots in the 1290s. Although Balliol, backed by various disaffected sections of the Scottish nobility usually known as the 'Disinherited', had some initial success at Dupplin, Perthshire in 1332, it was Edward III's decisive victory over a Scottish army at Halidon Hill near Berwick the following year which really mattered. As a result of this success, Balliol was placed as an English vassal on the Scottish throne and much of southern Scotland including Edinburgh was garrisoned by English forces. David II himself was sent for his own safety to France.

That Scottish independence survived was largely due to two factors. Firstly, Edward III was constantly preoccupied with France; secondly, Sir Andrew Murray (d.1338) son of Sir William WALLACE'S (1270—1305) ally, waged an effective guerilla war against the occupying forces. Victory at Culblean, Aberdeenshire in 1335 was followed by further successes so that when David II returned to Scotland in 1341 much of the English threat had been removed. This situation prevailed until 1346 when David II's defeat and capture at NEVILLE'S CROSS, near Durham plunged his country into a second major crisis.

David II's release in 1357, on agreement to pay a ransom, allowed him a period, before his sudden death in 1371, to restore royal government. This he seems to have done in a reasonably effective manner, suppressing a serious rebellion over his proposed marriage plans in 1363 and achieving some sort of recovery of the royal finances. Neither of his two marriages produced any heirs, one of the few problems at least which his successor Robert II (1316–90) did not have.

• *Nicholson, R., Scotland: The Later Middle Ages, Oliver & Boyd, 1974.*
• *Lynch, M., Scotland: A New History, Century, 1991.*

depression   While Scotland — in common with the rest of Europe — has suffered many economic downturns since the sixteenth century the most significant by far was the slump shared with other industrialized countries during the 1920s and 30s. It is to this period that the expression usually refers. Indeed, Scotland's economic problems during the inter-war years — a microcosm of the British experience — help to explain many of the social and political developments of the period itself and of the years immediately following WORLD WAR II.

The problems of industrial structure were certainly deep-seated, with Scotland's reliance on the traditional industries, like COAL, IRON and STEEL, SHIPBUILDING, heavy ENGINEERING and textiles dating back to the INDUSTRIAL REVOLUTION. Old-fashioned technology and perhaps even more traditional management and patterns of industrial relations held out little hope for modernization. At the same time demand during WORLD WAR I simply compounded the problems of an economy over-dependent on out-dated heavy industry. As elsewhere in Britain — on Tyneside, Merseyside, or in South Wales, for example, the loss of export markets during and after the war could be regarded as a central short-term factor contributing to Scotland's economic problems — yet longer-term forces seem altogether more significant. Scotland — and Clydeside in particular — had probably lost her status as 'Workshop of the Empire' long before 1914. This was partly a result of competition from foreign rivals, notably the United States and Germany, and partly the result of industrial development in the colonies. Moreover, Scotland also shared in the failure of enterprise that seemed characteristic of the late Victorian and Edwardian eras. If things seemed gloomy after the collapse of a short post-war boom between 1919 and 1921 they got much worse as Scotland slid into a depression, characterized by alarming levels of unemployment and a widening gap with the British experience. The actual number in employment only reached its 1929 level as late as 1935, with any real recovery delayed until 1936, rather than 1934 for Britain in general. Differences in industrial structure were also reflected in lower productivity and persistently lower earnings, so the social consequences of the depression were more deeply felt in Scotland than elsewhere, with the possible exceptions of South Wales and

Tyneside, which shared similar problems. More positively, the Thirties saw a modest growth of 'new' industries, which by 1935 represented about 11 per cent of net output. Even this development left over 30 per cent of the labour force in Scotland's traditional trades of coal-mining, iron and steel, shipbuilding, heavy engineering and textiles. The upturn when it came was based largely on improved exports and rearmament, though even in 1939 unemployment — at 13fi per cent — exceeded the 1929 level.

Against this background Scotland in the inter-war years presented pockets of deep poverty, severe over-crowding, disease and poor diet. Infant mortality rates were among the worst of any industrial country, and Scotland was one of the worst housed areas in Britain. These two features alone could hardly merit self-congratulation on the part of any government, whether or not it understood the causes. But governments of the period — Tory or Labour — could hardly be blamed for their failure to understand the causes of industrial collapse and unemployment, when the underlying economic mechanisms were just beginning to be identified by theoreticians like J. M. Keynes. No one could deny the severity of social distress caused by the depression, yet thinking about the period is coloured by misery and despair, while more optimistic developments are often overlooked. Some good emerged from the inter-war years in Scotland, especially the political will for improvement through schemes designed to aid the Distressed Areas and assist AGRICULTURE.

Although the problem of unemployment inevitably dominated the thinking of politicians local and national, modest efforts were also made in such fields as slum clearance, HOUSING, health and EDUCATION. Given the scale of the problems in places like Glasgow and Dundee — and conditions were actually worse in some of the distressed colliery districts — the attempt at improvement was too little too late (a catch-phrase for the period), but at least the framework was laid for more positive developments in the future.

•*Harvie, C.T., No Gods and Precious Few Heroes: Scotland 1914—1980, Edward Arnold, 1981.*
•*MacDougall, I., Voices from the Hunger Marches, Polygon, 1991.*
•*Smout, T. C., A Century of the Scottish People 1830—1950, HarperCollins, 1986.*

Devolution, see HOME RULE; SCOTTISH NATIONAL PARTY

Devorgilla (c.1209—1289) Devorgilla was the daughter of Alan, lord of Galloway (d.1234) and Margaret, eldest daughter of David, earl of Huntingdon (c.1144—1219). She married John Balliol (d.1269) and was the mother of King JOHN (1250—1313) who, as a COMPETITOR, was indebted to her for the strength of his claim to the Scottish throne.

A notably virtuous and pious lady, she, with her husband, was responsible for the building of Baillol College at Oxford while she herself founded Sweetheart or New Abbey in Kirkcudbright, the last Cistercian MONASTERY to be built in Scotland.

•*Nicholson, R., Scotland: The Later Middle Ages, Oliver & Boyd, 1974.*

Dewar, Donald (1937—2000)
Reaching the peak of his political
career as First Minister in the
Scottish PARLIAMENT only a year
before his death, Dewar was in
some ways an unlikely leader as
was his road to that position. Along
with JOHN SMITH, his contemporary
at Glasgow University, Dewar graduated in law and developed a life-
long interest in LABOUR politics.

After practising as a lawyer
Dewar entered parliament as MP
for Aberdeen South (1966—70)
and in 1967 was appointed Parliamentary Private Secretary to Tony
Crosland. After 1970 Dewar was
out of parliament till in a famous
by-election victory he was returned
for Garscadden in 1978. He was
successively chairman of the select
committee on Scottish Affairs
(1980—81), a member of the
Scottish front bench team (1981—
83), Opposition Spokesman on
Scottish Affairs (1983—92), and
then at Social Security (1992
onwards). Smith had become
leader of the opposition in 1992
and after his death in 1994 Dewar
followed in his footsteps as a proponent of devolution.

Something of a shambolic figure
and holding traditional views,
Dewar seemed personally and ide-
ologically ill-suited to the New
Labour government, but nevertheless in 1997 he joined Tony Blair's
cabinet as Secretary of State for
Scotland. Blair immediately set
him the task of drawing up a fresh
devolution bill and seeing through
a referendum on the proposals.
Introducing the Scotland Act
Dewar uttered the memorable
phrase, 'There shall be a Scottish
parliament', adding, 'I like that.'

Events moved rapidly following a
referendum in 1998 and elections
(on a mix of first past the post and
proportional representation) and
in 1999 the Scottish Parliament
was convened for the first time
since 1707. A coalition of Labour
and LIBERAL parties was headed by
Dewar as First Minister. Dewar's
resourcefulness and tact saw the
parliament through its early days,
but unfortunately, like his friend
Smith, he did not live long enough
to exercise the influence he might
have done in the longer term.

Disarming Act   The Disarming Act
was one of a series of measures
passed by the Hanoverian government in the aftermath of the first
JACOBITE REBELLION in 1715. Both it
and its successors were designed
to suppress the Highland CLANS
and maintain law and order. The
first Act (1716) imposed fines for
possessing arms and invited their
surrender, while a later act (1725)
premitted search and seizure of
weapons.   Following the 'Forty-
Five, the Act was renewed more
rigorously, even banning the kilt
and condeming the pipes.   The Act
against the kilt and the bagpipes
was ultimately repealed in 1782.

Disraeli, Benjamin, see CONSERV-
ATIVE PARTY

Disruption (1843)   Around 1833
the Kirk entered an era of intense
controversy, the so-called 'Ten Year
Conflict', which culminated in the
Disruption, one of the major
events in Scotland during the nineteenth century. Essentially this
breakaway was a consequence of
the growing strength of the conservative-minded Evangelicals, who
were primarily responsible for the
passing at Westminster in 1834 of

the contentious Chapel and Veto Acts. The former legislation permitted ministers attached to chapels of ease or extension churches to participate in the church courts while the latter obliged presbyteries to accept any objections made to a presentee by a majority of the male heads of families within a congregation. Several parishes were now involved in bitter wrangles at the COURT OF SESSION culminating in 1843 with the Stewarton case, which resulted in yet another setback for the Evangelicals. This decision, which saw a repudiation of the Chapel Act, was the last straw and shortly afterwards at the GENERAL ASSEMBLY of that year, Thomas CHALMERS (1780–1847) and 470 ministers, over one third of the clergy, seceded from the established Church.

Apart from the serious damage to the membership of the Kirk, which lost about 40 per cent of its communicants, the Disruption had important repercussions for the administration of poor relief, being largely responsible for the introduction of the POOR LAW (1845), while in education the new FREE CHURCH constructed numerous schools to provide instruction for its congregations.

•Brown, S.J. and Fry, M. (eds.), Scotland in the Age of Disruption, Edinburgh University Press, 1993.
•Drummond, A.L. and Bulloch, J., The Scottish Church, 1688–1843, St Andrew Press, 1973.
•Ferguson, W., Scotland: 1689 to the Present, Oliver & Boyd, 1968.

distilling Like the other significant Scottish drink industry of brewing, whisky distilling is an ancient activity and its early history is shrouded both in mystery and myth. By the sixteenth century 'aqua vitae' or 'usque baugh' in Gaelic, claimed by some to be Irish in origin, was being distilled on a considerable scale in small pot stills, mainly in the HIGHLANDS. Such was the extent of manufacture that several Acts of PARLIAMENT were passed to restrict malt-making for distilling in times of poor harvest or famine. The first excise duty on spirits was imposed by Parliament in 1644 and it was revived at various times during the late seventeenth century. This indicates — even at this early date — not only the powerful influence of legislation on the industry's fortunes, but also its close relationship to agriculture both in the Highlands and the Lowlands.

After the UNION of 1707 the revenue from excise on spirits was incorporated with income from other duties under the Board of Excise — the total being used to defray the costs of civil administration in Scotland. As equivalent English duties were gradually extended north of the Border, the malt tax was introduced in 1713, ultimately provoking popular protest in the MALT TAX Riots of 1725. Paradoxically the imposition of the malt tax encouraged the consumption of wines and spirits, contraband as well as home-produced. Official statistics suggest that production rose from 100,000 to 250,000 gallons during the years 1708–37, mostly, it seems, for domestic consumption. Another impetus to distilling arose from the Gin Act (1736), which greatly increased the duty on English or imported Dutch gin — Scots whisky was exempt. A boom in the 1740s and early 1750s raised official annual production to over half a million gallons.

A period of crisis marked by a ban on legal distilling due to harvest failure during 1757–60 led to the relative decline of commercial distilleries and the corresponding rise of private stills and smuggling. With the tightening up of legislation against illicit manufacture licensed distilling recovered during the 1770s and 80s. Many large-scale distilleries were established during this period to fulfill the demand of a growing population in both the Highlands and the Lowlands. Whisky exports — mainly to England — became increasingly important. Despite troubled times during the French Revolutionary and Napoleonic Wars (1793–1815) the commercial industry expanded dramatically, official production rising from 1.25 to over 3 million gallons between 1800 and 1815.

Legislation of 1822–3, notably the Excise Act (1823) greatly changed the character of the industry, and, together with the development of the patent still, confirmed an already established trend away from the illicit or perhaps very small licensed distillery, serving the local market, towards the much larger legally-recognized business whose owner was often involved in other enterprises.

The scene was thus set for an era of enormous expansion. By the mid-nineteenth century this was beginning to bring problems of overcapacity and over-production that were to bedevil the industry for many years to come, particularly in times of economic DEPRESSION. This situation was hardly helped by the rise of the TEMPERANCE Movement, which in the longer term led to a net decline in domestic consumption. Later in Victorian times — when blending stands out as the most significant innovation — the search for overseas markets was critical to sustained growth. Despite these problems, production rose from 9 million gallons in 1850 to a peak of 25 million gallons at the turn of the century.

Nearly half a century of adversity after 1900 brought progressive rationalization, accompanied by many closures or failures during the depression of the 1920s and 30s. After WORLD WAR II the industry revived thanks to increased affluence at home and the continuing appeal of Scotch — especially the single malts — as a prestigious drink internationally. Much of the historic tradition survives and in long-established centres of production like Speyside and Islay many of the old distilleries are still at work manufacturing the golden liquid.

• Craig, H.C., The Scotch Whisky Industry Record, Index Publishing Ltd., 1994.
• Moss, M.S. and Hume, J.R., The Making of Scotch Whisky, James & James, 1981.
• Weir, R., The History of the Distillers Company, 1877–1939, Oxford University Press, 1995.

Douglas, Archibald, fifth Earl of Angus (c.1449—1513?) Although Chancellor between 1492 and 1497 in the reign of JAMES IV (1473–1513), he is best known for his involvement in the mysterious events at LAUDER BRIDGE in July 1482. This was the occasion when a number of the household of JAMES III (1452—88) were hanged by the king's opponents and the latter was taken as a prisoner to Edinburgh Castle. However, the definitive biography of the king plays down the role of Angus, placing much of the responsibility on the earls of ATHOLL and Buchan. Moreover, his nickname "Bell the cat" after the medieval fable of the mice placing a bell on their feline enemy would appear to have been a later embellishment invented by David Hume of Godscroft (c.1560-1630), a seventeenth century historian of the house of Douglas.

He was the father of Gavin Douglas (1474—1522) ecclesiastic and noted RENAISSANCE scholar; his other sons all predeceased him, two of them being killed at FLODDEN in September 1513.
• *MacDougall N., James III: A Political Study, 1982.*

Douglas, Archibald, sixth Earl of Angus, see JAMES V; MORTON; PINKIE, BATTLE OF

Douglas, James, fourth Earl of Morton (c.1516—81) The second son of George Douglas of Pittendreich (1490—1552) and a brother of Archibald, sixth Earl of Angus (c.1489—1557), he obtained his title through his marriage to a daughter of James Douglas, third Earl of Morton (d.1552). Although one of the original LORDS OF THE CONGREGATION, he acted cautiously during the REFORMATION crisis and only officially joined the reformers in May 1560. During the personal reign of MARY (1542—87) he became Chancellor in 1563, but his complicity in the murder of RICCIO (c.1533—66) led to his dismissal by the Queen. He was closely involved in the plot against DARNLEY (1546—67) and following Mary's abdication played a major role in the regencies of MORAY (1531—70) and his successors. Thus in November 1572 following the death of MAR (c.1510—72) he was the obvious choice as regent, a title he retained until his overthrow in March 1578. In fact, he soon recovered his position and from June 1578 until December 1580 when he was suddenly arrested and charged with his involvement in the Darnley conspiracy, he remained in charge of the kingdom. As regent, he kept a firm grip on the nobility, administered the borders effectively and resolutely adhered to an English alliance which, at the outset of his administration, had been instrumental in overcoming KIRKCALDY OF GRANGE (c.1520—73) and the remaining Marians in Edinburgh Castle. As for the Kirk, while he was certainly guilty of various malpractices, he did reform the system for collecting THIRDS OF BENEFICES.

At the same time he strongly resisted the challenge to royal authority presented by MELVILLE (1545—1622) and the SECOND BOOK OF DISCIPLINE. However, latterly, his position was gradually undermined by his opponents among the magnates especially the royal favourite Esmé STEWART, Duke of Lennox (c.1542—83) and his colleague James STEWART, Earl of Arran (c.1545—96). This pair, with his other numerous enemies, were responsible for his arrest in December 1580 and ultimately for his execution in June 1581.

Hewitt, G.R., Scotland under Morton, John Donald, 1981.

Douglas, James, second Duke of Queensberry (1662—1711)

Although he had served as Royal Commissioner under WILLIAM III (1650–1702) and had been entrusted with damping down anti-English feelings over the COMPANY OF SCOTLAND, he really came to prominence during the reign of Queen ANNE (1665–1714). Thus, between 1702 and 1707 he played a key role in steering the Treaty of UNION through PARLIAMENT, hence his nickname, the 'Union Duke'. Initially, in 1703, he sustained two serious setbacks when his opponents pushed through, against his wishes, the ACT OF SECURITY and the ACT ANENT PEACE AND WAR. In desperation he resorted to the so-called 'Queensberry Plot', a futile attempt to incriminate rivals such as the fourth Duke of HAMILTON (1658–1712), SEAFIELD (1664–1730) and TWEEDDALE (1645–1713) in a JACOBITE conspiracy. This resulted in his temporary eclipse, but in 1706 the Queen and her ministers had little alternative but to ask the Duke and his henchman MAR (1675–1732) to pilot the arrangements for the Union through their final stages. Queensberry, well aware that success in this mission could only strengthen his influence and position in the Scottish political scene didn't fail his English masters. Aided by a liberal distribution of English money and the divided nature of the opposition he achieved his objective. A grateful Queen Anne rewarded him with the dukedom of Dover.

Douglas-Home, Sir Alex (1903—1995)

The Earl of Home (later Sir Alex Douglas-Home then as a Life Peer, Lord Home), despite a long and distinguished career in politics, was a rather unlikely candidate to become Prime Minister. But in 1963 to the surprise of many of his colleagues in the CONSERVATIVE Party (especially Rab Butler, the cabinet favourite), he succeeded Harold MACMILLAN, who resigned due to illness.

Educated at Eton and Oxford, Douglas-Home came from virtually the last generation of Anglo-Scottish grandees to gain high office through hereditary privilege, though he began his political career as MP for South Lanark in 1931, later claiming, in one of several memorable gaffes, 'I lived among the miners for twenty years.'

After appointments as parliamentary private secretary at the Scottish Office (1933) then to the Chancellor of the Exchequer (1936), Douglas-Home first came to prominence as an aide to Neville Chamberlain during the appeasement era of the later 1930s. He was present during the Munich talks with Adolf Hitler and when Chamberlain arrived back in England by aeroplane and clutching the famous note, Douglas-Home could be seen hovering in the background. He succeeded to the earldom in 1951 and for the next twelve years continued his political career from the House of Lords.

With the Conservatives returned to power in 1951 Douglas-Home became Minister of State at the SCOTTISH OFFICE (1951–55), then Secretary of State at the Commonwealth Office (1955–60). Between 1960 and 1963 he was at the Foreign Office, where given the prevailing Cold War between West and East he was a convinced anti-Communist. While suspicious of the Soviets and supporting nuclear weapons, he also played an important role in the Test Ban treaty of 1963. It was at this point that events forced him even further into the limelight.

To succeed the ailing Macmillan he had to resign his peerage and enter parliament, a safe seat being found for him at Kinross by the retiral of the sitting MP. While certain of election, at the same time he was criticized as a carpet-bagger and became the subject of bitter satire generated by some of the other candidates, including Willy Rushton (assisted by the publisher, John Calder). The then recently established satirical magazine, *Private Eye*, produced an infamous poster showing a skull-like portrait of Home, who even before entering office had fallen victim to a wave of anti-establishment criticism and satire.

There followed what amounted to a year-long election campaign during which Douglas-Home was confronted by the formidable intellect of the LABOUR leader, Harold Wilson. Confessing to 'counting with matchsticks' when it came to economics, he was on safer ground on foreign and defence affairs and was generally regarded as sincere if rather out of touch. The Conservatives narrowly lost the 1964 election, which was much to his credit given the economic problems and legacy of scandals he inherited from the Macmillan era.

But Douglas-Home showed remarkable powers of survival and during the Heath administration was back at the Foreign Office, 1970–74, where he played an important role in Britain's negotiations to enter the Common Market in 1973. He published several reflective books including an autobiography, *The Way the Wind Blows*, in 1976.

drove roads, see CATTLE; ROADS; TRANSPORT

Drummond, George (1687–1766) George Drummond was a prominent Edinburgh citizen during the Age of ENLIGHTENMENT, was six times Lord Provost of the city, and played an important role in the planning of the NEW TOWN. Apparently he was something of a genius with figures because, when only eighteen years of age, he provided data for a committee of the Scottish PARLIAMENT set up to negotiate the financial details of the UNION. This expertise clearly paid off, for in 1707 Drummond was appointed Accountant-General of Excise, when it was introduced to Scotland, becoming a Commissioner of Customs in 1723, at a salary of £1,000 per annum.

Drummond's career advanced rapidly thanks to his Hanoverian sympathies – which led him to raise a company of volunteers against the JACOBITES in 1715. His activity on the town council must also have helped: he became Lord Provost for the first time in 1725. Drummond later organized civic resistance against the Jacobites during the 'FORTY-FIVE and after Sir John Cope's defeat at PRESTONPANS alerted the government directly to the danger of the situation.

George Drummond was influential in the appointment of many eminent figures to the University of Edinburgh, in the establishment of the Royal Infirmary (1736), and in major public works, such as the draining of the North Loch and the construction of what became the North Bridge (1763) connecting Old and New Towns. The building of the New Town itself was begun just before his death.

Dunbar, Battle of (3 September 1650) The decision of the clerical faction, in command of affairs in Scotland since the end of 1648, to recognize Charles II (1630—85), provided he adhered to the SOLEMN LEAGUE AND COVENANT, resulted in Cromwell (1599—1658) coming northwards to deal with the situation. However he found LESLIE (d.1682) a difficult adversary who carried out a scorched earth policy in East Lothian before retreating behind strong defensive positions between Leith and Edinburgh. Cromwell's army, frustrated by these tactics and suffering from outbreaks of sickness among its ranks, withdrew to the seaport of Dunbar. The Covenanting forces followed them, taking up a strong position on Doon Hill overlooking the town itself. On 2 September 1650 Leslie moved his army down the hillside to the plain below only to be caught out by a surprise attack at dawn the next day when the Scots suffered 3,000 casualties and had 10,000 men taken prisoner. The Scottish general's strategy has often been questioned, although it has frequently been alleged that he was unduly influenced by clerical pressure to launch an assault on the English. Undoubtedly his army was greatly understrength as a result of several religious purges made during August, although some PROTESTORS later claimed they had been too lenient. On the other hand he was also concerned about the effects of the prolonged wet weather on his troops as well as the approach of the harvest season, which would inevitably reduce his military strength further. Besides, having an army of over 20,000 men, about twice the size of Cromwell's forces, he must have been fairly confident of victory. His defeat was a significant one, greatly undermining the authority of the Kirk leaders and ultimately ensuring the imposition of the CROMWELLIAN UNION. •*Douglas, W.S., Cromwell's Scottish Campaigns, E. Stock, 1899.*

Duncan, Rev. Dr Henry (1774— 1846) Henry Duncan, best known as the founder of the savings BANK movement, but also a prominent POOR LAW reformer, anti-slavery advocate, CATHOLIC emancipist, and Free churchman, was born a son of the manse at Lochrutton in the Stewartry of Kirkcudbright, where several generations of his family had ministered. Duncan attended Dumfries Academy and was then sent to St Andrews University in 1788. Clearly undecided about his future he left after two years and through a relative, Dr James Currie (1756— 1805), later the biographer of Robert BURNS (1759—1796), obtained a post as a banker's clerk in Liverpool. After three years he returned to Scotland and in 1793 became a student of theology, partly at the University of Edinburgh and partly in Glasgow.

He became a licenciate in the presbytery of Dumfries in 1798 and minister of nearby Ruthwell a year later in 1799.

From the outset he was preoccupied by the problem of rural poverty in his parish and in 1804 revived a local friendly society, which would give its members some independence from poor relief in hard times. Given his background, it was a logical step from this to the establishment of the Savings bank at Ruthwell in 1810. Such was its success that even in a relatively poor neighbourhood deposits rose from £150 to over £900 in the first four years.

Just before his savings bank initiative Duncan, a man of considerable literary skill, founded the weekly *Dumfries & Galloway Courier* (1809), his brothers providing the initial capital. For seven years he edited what became one of the most influential and successful journals of the Scottish provincial PRESS and he used it as a means of propaganda for the savings bank movement, poor law reform and other worthy causes. In fact, his initiative was followed up widely, particularly after the publication of a pamphlet *On the Nature and Advantages of Parish Banks* (1815) and the subsequent SAVINGS BANK ACT (1819). Duncan was made a DD by St Andrews in 1823.

Unusual for a minister of the Established Kirk, Henry Duncan was a notable Catholic emancipist and anti-slaver. His RADICALISM was also voiced in his views about PATRONAGE, whereby a minister might be imposed on a congregation at the whim of the local landowner or heritor. He played a significant role in the events leading up to the Disruption and the establishment of the FREE CHURCH in 1843. Duncan was also something of a novelist publishing two widely-read works, *The Young Country Weaver* (1819) and *William Douglas, or the Scottish Exiles* (1826). He had an interest in antiquities and restored the famous Ruthwell Cross, which can still he seen at his former church. Duncan's career and interests might be compared with those of the great churchman Dr Thomas CHALMERS (1780—1847), a near contemporary. Surprisingly, there is no modern biography.

Dundas, Henry, Viscount Melville (1742—1811) Dundas was born into a distinguished legal family and at the height of his career became one of the most powerful political figures in late eighteenth and early nineteenth-century Scotland. Such was his prestige and power of patronage that he was nicknamed 'Harry the Ninth' or the 'Uncrowned King of Scotland' — and, indeed, the Dundas dynasty remained highly influential long after his demise.

Dundas was educated at the High School of Edinburgh and the University of Edinburgh, being admitted as an advocate in 1763. Family connections ensured rapid career development, for he became in turn Solicitor General for Scotland (1766), MP for Midlothian (1774—90), and Lord Advocate (1775—83). From the outset he proved politically astute. Despite disagreements over policy (for example on concessions to the American colonies, which he opposed, and Catholic emancipation, which he favoured) and changes in ministry under North, Rockingham and Shelburne, he managed not only to maintain his position, but also greatly extend his influence.

In 1782 he successfully carried a resolution that Warren Hastings (1732–1818) be recalled from India and removed from office. The same year he was made a Privy Counsellor and Treasurer of the Navy (1782–83 and 1784–1800). He also became Keeper of the Signet of Scotland, which gave him further powers of patronage, securing jobs and favours for relatives, friends and political supporters.

His own friendship and support of William Pitt (1759–1806) won him further high office as Home Secretary (1791–94), president of the Board of Control, managing Indian affairs (1793–1801), and Secretary of State for War (1794–1801). In this last office he played a prominent role during the dangerous era of the FRENCH REVOLUTION and NAPOLEONIC WARS – masterminding the Egyptian campaign of 1801 against the advice of both Pitt and George III. At the same time he took a hard line against those propagating revolutionary ideas in Scotland and was instrumental in the prosecution of Thomas MUIR (1765–99) and other RADICALS.

Following Pitt's resignation in 1801 Dundas also demitted office, though such was the extent of his support for the new prime minister, Henry Addington (1757–1844), that his management of the 1802 election returned no fewer than forty-three TORIES to two WHIGS for the Scottish seats.

Allegedly to Pitt's surprise he afterwards accepted a peerage as Viscount Melville. Dundas was subsequently First Lord of the Admiralty under Pitt (1804–5). His career ended under a cloud for he was impeached after a commission revealed that large sums of public money had been applied to uses other than the navy during his extended period as treasurer. Although acquitted, he never again held high office and died in 1811.

Dundas was undoubtedly one of the major political figures of his generation, both in Scotland and beyond. This was achieved through a judicious manipulation of the electoral system that continued until the first REFORM ACT and by the extensive patronage that came with high office. For nearly thirty years he was the most influential man in Scotland, acting as election agent for the government, controlling the election of the Scottish Representative Peers as well as members of the House of Commons.

•Fry, M., The Dundas Despotism, Edinburgh University Press, 1992.
•Furber, H., Henry Dundas, First Viscount Melville 1742–1811, Oxford University Press, 1931.
•Matheson, C., The Life of Henry Dundas, First Viscount Melville 1742–1811, Constable, 1933.
•Sunter, R.M., Patronage and Politics in Scotland, 1707–1832, John Donald, 1986.

Dundee, see HOUSING; INDUSTRIAL REVOLUTION; INDUSTRY; JUTE; MIGRATION; PRESS; URBANIZATION

Dundee, Viscount, see GRAHAM OF CLAVERHOUSE

E

Edgar (1097–1107) Edgar was the son of MALCOLM III (Canmore) and MARGARET, who with his brothers, Duncan, ALEXANDER I and DAVID I, were to rule in succession until the mid-twelfth century. In the chaos that followed the death of Malcolm III, the confused reigns of Duncan II (1094) and Donald Ban (1093, 1094–7), Edgar, with support from William Rufus and Anglo-NORMAN forces, seized the throne. Donald was captured and disposed of, with Edgar initiating a ten-year rule, apparently as a subservient to the English king, hence relying on foreign support. After what proved a peaceful reign Edgar died unmarried and childless, being succeeded by his brother as ALEXANDER I.
•Barrow,G.W.S., Kingship and Unity. Scotland 1000–1306, Edward Arnold, 1981.

Edinburgh see INDUSTRIAL REVOLUTION; INDUSTRY; HOUSING; MIGRATION; SHIPBUILDING; URBANIZATION

Edinburgh Review *The Edinburgh Review* was an influential middle-class periodical founded in 1802 by the WHIGS Henry Erskine (1746–1817), the prominent lawyer and reformer, and Francis JEFFREY (1773–1850), the judge and critic. Jeffrey edited it from 1803–29 and was himself a major contributor. Henry BROUGHAM (1778–1868) and Francis Horner (1778–1817) also wrote for it. The periodical concentrated on contemporary issues and exerted some influence on popular movements of the day such as the pressure for political REFORM.

Edinburgh, Treaty of (1560) This was signed on 6 July by English and French envoys marking the end of hostilities in the Scottish REFORMATION. However, its principal terms were political rather than religious. Thus the English and French governments recognized Elizabeth (1533–1603) as rightful Queen of England while MARY, QUEEN OF SCOTS (1542–87), by ceasing to use the English coat of arms, implicitly recognized Elizabeth as well. There were also a number of additional clauses or 'concessions' attached to the agreement, mostly concerned with such details as the dismantling of French fortifications, a prohibition on any foreigners holding office in the government and a guarantee that there would be no reprisals against any of the reformers. The only reference to ecclesiastical matters came in the section authorizing a meeting of the Estates to discuss current religious controversies. This, of course, was a highly significant article in the Treaty since it was the subsequent Reformation

PARLIAMENT meeting in August 1560 that established Protestantism in Scotland.

• *Dickinson, W.C., Scotland from Earliest Times to 1603, Oxford University Press, 1977.*
• *Donaldson, G., Scotland: James V to James VII, Oliver & Boyd, 1965.*

education Considerable controversy surrounds the history of Scottish education since the sixteenth century, notably the debates centring on its supposed democratic traditions dating back to the REFORMATION, relative levels of literacy compared with England and the Continent, the impact of the ENLIGHTENMENT, the quantity and quality of educational provision during the eighteenth and early nineteenth centuries, and the role of universities and scientific and technical education since the INDUSTRIAL REVOLUTION. Consistent themes in the longer term also include secularization, anglicization, expediency and control. The pre-Reformation legacy presented a mixed bag of choral song-schools associated with cathedrals, abbeys or other ecclesiastic institutions and grammar schools in the BURGHS, together with the three universities of St Andrews (1411), Glasgow (1451) and Aberdeen (1495). All three were small and their curricula old-fashioned by contemporary European standards. This traditional approach was reflected in an Act of PARLIAMENT (1496) — one of the earliest education acts in Europe — which made it compulsory for men of substance to send their eldest sons to schools and colleges to learn Latin, the arts and law. This might be regarded as 'vocational' in that it taught a potential elite more about government and keeping the upper hand. The reformers realized the potential of education and in the First BOOK OF DISCIPLINE (1560–61) John KNOX (1512–72) and his associates included a programme that envisaged a properly endowed school in every parish. However, little real progress was made in basic education — mainly because of lack of adequate funding. Money was to come from the reformation of the church and monasteries but it was frittered away. At the same time the universities were reformed with some success and new institutions established in Edinburgh (1583) and at Marischal College, Aberdeen (1593). During the seventeenth century there were further modest developments, starting with an Act of the PRIVY COUNCIL (1616) that backed the Kirk's plea for a school in each parish 'where convenient means may be had'. A later act in 1633 reaffirmed this objective and decreed that heritors or landowners should be taxed to fund the schools. Evasion was tightened up in 1646 — with the result that basic educational provision was further extended throughout much of the Lowlands before the RESTORATION. The 1696 Act for the Settling of Schools was substantially a reiteration of the 1646 Act, but also empowered presbyteries to call on the COMMISSIONERS OF SUPPLY in the counties should heritors fail to provide a parish school. Education — in a variety of forms — was a growth industry during the eighteenth century, reflecting modernization in general and the ideas of the Scottish Enlightenment in particular. For all this the Kirk maintained authority over the schools and the poorly paid dominie often doubled as the session clerk or precentor. Nevertheless, the parochial school provided good, cheap elementary education for most classes and both sexes.

Burgh grammar schools or the increasingly fashionable academies — usually controlled by the town councils — functioned as secondary schools. From both parochial and grammar schools the ubiquitous lad o' pairts might proceed to university to further his education. Private institutions licensed by the Kirk included dame schools, adventure schools, writing schools and charity schools — all providing some form of elementary education. Edinburgh, with its Royal High School, established during the reign of JAMES VI, became a significant centre of schooling, while at a humbler level most towns of any size like Perth (1761), Dundee (1786), Inverness (1788), and Elgin (1791) boasted a decent school serving the neighbourhood. The HIGHLANDS remained relatively neglected until the Society in Scotland for Propagating Christian Knowledge (SSPCK) was founded in 1709 and later with the help of the BOARD OF TRUSTEES and the Commissioners for the FORFEITED ESTATES extended its work of establishing schools throughout the north of Scotland.

Scottish universities also entered a phase of rapid expansion, with the relatively low fees and the teaching of useful subjects like medicine, science, philosophy and law proving attractive to large numbers of students — including many English and Irish Nonconformists barred from

Oxford, Cambridge and Trinity College, Dublin. All but St Andrews, which remained small, shared this growth. Glasgow saw its numbers rise from 400 in 1702 to 1,240 by 1824, while Edinburgh grew from 400 about 1700 to 1,300 in 1800 and 2,300 in 1824. Among the professoriate were some of the most powerful intellects of the Scottish Enlightenment, including Joseph BLACK (1728–99), William CULLEN (1710–90), Adam FERGUSSON (1723–1816), and Adam SMITH (1723–90). Scottish university education, while soundly based on theory, had a very practical bent, though the curriculum later came to be regarded as lacking the depth of that offered by Oxford, Cambridge and continental institutions.

During the nineteenth century there were many important developments that came partly in response to demand from an education-hungry population and partly to meet the more general needs of industrialization. In the first category were schools for the poor opened in the city slums, such as the ragged schools established by Sheriff Watson in Aberdeen in 1841, by Dr Thomas GUTHRIE (1803–73) in Edinburgh in 1847, and the Sunday schools provided by David Stow (1793–1864), a Glasgow merchant-philanthropist, encouraged by the great Thomas CHALMERS (1780–1847). Schools generally remained closely allied to the Kirk, which spearheaded a drive to open more institutions nationally during the 1830s and 40s.

Technical education developed from the work of John ANDERSON (1726–96) and others, leading to the establishment of facilities like Anderson's Institution in Glasgow and a School of Arts (later the Heriot-Watt College) in Edinburgh (1821) teaching mathematics, science and drawing. Mechanics' institutes and libraries for the improvement of working men sprang up in considerable numbers during the 1820s and 30s. Despite these developments enormous gaps remained, especially in the industrial towns and cities where working-class children often left school at the age of eight or nine. In Glasgow as late as 1867 about half the children aged five to ten did not attend school at all. Even in the countryside attendance was a problem, for as many as two-fifths of the children of agricultural labourers were uneducated or withdrawn from school at twelve or thirteen.

Inevitably education became enmeshed in Church politics and sectarianism during and after the DISRUPTION. The Free Church set up its own schools, joining those of the Church of Scotland and lesser sects including the United Presbyterians, Episcopalians and Catholics. There was much unnecessary overlap, many institutions were under-funded and apparently unable to provide a basic education for the majority of the population. This situation could only be remedied in the longer term by a national, publicly-funded system.

The Education Act of 1872 made education compulsory from five to thirteen years of age, placed burgh and parochial schools under the supervision of school boards elected by rate-payers every three years and provided public funding by parliamentary grants and school rates. Those too poor to pay fees or buy books were given assistance from the parish rates. Many of the voluntary schools were integrated in the public system, leaving only Catholic, Episcopalian and English-style fee-paying schools or 'public' schools in the private sector. A Scotch Education Department (so-styled 1872–1918) with a corps of officials – HM Inspectors of Schools – was set up to oversee the development of a supposedly egalitarian and uniform system. Compulsory education was enforced and extended by later acts: in 1883 the leaving age was raised to fourteen and in 1891 fees in elementary schools were abolished. A national curriculum for secondary education – the Leaving Certificate – was introduced in 1888.

In the twentieth century three major Education Acts of 1908, 1918 and 1946 sought to improve the basic system established in 1872, but it was a slow business dogged by expediency and reorganization. Elected local education authorities and school management boards replaced the old school boards in 1918 – only to be swept away under the Local Government (Scotland) Act (1929), which introduced the Education Committees of County Councils. Under the provisions of the 1918 Act a leaving age of fifteen was proposed and Catholic schools – while retaining their religious distinction – were integrated in the State system.

For Scotland the 1918 Act was perhaps as important as the later equivalent to the English Education Act (the Butler Act, 1944), enacted two years later in 1946.

This sought greater uniformity of provision, enforced fifteen as the school-leaving age and gave Education Committees enhanced powers over schools, libraries and further education – the last scandalously neglected until the 1960s. In the post-war years after 1945 an acute teacher shortage was alleviated by Special Recruitment schemes. A new school curriculum was delayed until the 1960s – and reorganization on comprehensive lines only began in the 1970s.

Finally, higher education expanded dramatically following the Robbins Report of 1963. The technical colleges of Glasgow and Edinburgh were chartered as the University of Strathclyde (1964) and Heriot-Watt University (1966), while Queen's College, Dundee separated from St Andrews to become the University of Dundee (1967). The new University of Stirling opened in 1967. The Open University (1969), a UK-wide distance education institution with a high proportion of Scottish students, began teaching in 1970. There was an accompanying expansion of teacher education, of scientific and technical education in the Central Institutions directly funded by the Scottish Education Department, and a belated investment in vocational education, ultimately backed up by a modular curriculum, formulated in the 1980s.

Like many of the major themes in Scottish history that of education – and particularly educational opportunity – is shrouded in myth. There can be no denying its pioneering achievements in terms of elementary education, the eminence of its universities during the

Age of Enlightenment, or the skill of great men of medicine, science, law, the church and industry during the Victorian era. But for all the claims voiced about its democratic traditions the system was hardly ever egalitarian. As T.C. Smout observes, education was generally regarded as 'a matter of low social priority once the perceived needs of the middle classes had been attended to and once a channel had been opened for a limited number of working-class children to use (secondary) school and university as a means of upward social mobility'.

•*Anderson, R.D., Education and Opportunity in Victorian Scotland: Schools and Universities, Oxford University Press, 1983.*
•*Anderson, R.D., Education and the Scottish People, 1750–1918, Oxford University Press, 1995.*
•*Houston, R.A., Scottish Literacy and the Scottish Identity, Cambridge University Press, 1986.*
•*Smout, T.C., A Century of the Scottish People 1830–1950, HarperCollins, 1986.*

Elliot, Walter (1885—1958) If, as Christopher Harvie suggests, there were precious few heroes in Scottish political life during the first half of the twentieth century Elliot could certainly be counted as one of them. After attending the University of Glasgow, where he studied science and medicine, and made friends with John BOYD ORR, later Lord Boyd Orr (1880–1971), James MAXTON (1885–1946), and James Bridie (1888–1951). His interest in scientific research was apparently only matched by his enthusiasm for union debates about issues of the day. During WORLD WAR I he served in France as a medical officer in the Royal

Scots Greys, being decorated MC for valour.

In the Coupon Election of 1918 Elliot was elected as CONSERVATIVE MP for Lanark, becoming private secretary to the Under Secretary of Health for Scotland in 1919 — a post he himself occupied briefly in 1923 and again from 1924 to 1926. From 1924 to 1945 and 1950 to 1958 he was MP for Glasgow Kelvingrove, a bastion of Tory Unionism in a sea of socialism. In 1926 he became Under Secretary of State for Scotland and also played a prominent part in the Empire Marketing Board (1926). He was able for a time to combine politics with his research, working on nutritional problems with his associate Boyd at the Rowett Research Institute in Aberdeen.

After the collapse of the second LABOUR Government, Elliot became Financial Secretary to the Treasury (1931), then Minister for Agriculture and Fisheries (1932–36), where he helped pioneer marketing boards. He was Secretary of State for Scotland from 1936 to 1938, a period that saw notable moves towards devolution of the SCOTTISH OFFICE to Edinburgh. Elliot's meteoric rise in the political firmament ended with his appointment as Minister of Health (1936–40). Although he was violently opposed to appeasement with Hitler, he stayed on in the Chamberlain government, thinking he could do more good from within the Cabinet. Unfortunately for him, when Churchill came to power he was dropped from office.

Elliot spent part of WORLD WAR II as Director of Public Relations at the War Office (1941–2) and later became Chairman of the Public Accounts Committee (1942–3). Thereafter he became increasingly interested in international affairs, particularly in West Africa, where he led a commission on higher education, 1942–3. He was a great supporter of the state of Israel and a prominent advocate of the NATO alliance.

Latterly Elliot came to be regarded as something of an elder statesman and was much honoured — first by a C.H. in 1952 and then by numerous honourary degrees. He was also a successful journalist and broadcaster. His career might well be compared with that of his near contemporary, the Labour politician Tom JOHNSTON (1881–1965), who also became Secretary of State for Scotland. A biographical memoir by Sir Colin Coote, *A Companion of Honour*, was published in 1965.
•*Harvie, C., No Gods and Precious Few Heroes: Scotland 1914—1980, Edward Arnold, 1981.*

emigration   Scottish emigration must be seen as part of the great European exodus since the eighteenth century to areas of recent white settlement — mainly (but not exclusively) in North America, Australasia and South Africa. It was at first a response to rural POPULATION pressure, a decline in mortality, changes in land use (such as ENCLOSURES), and eviction — typified by the Highland CLEARANCES, but also occurring in the Lowlands. Emigration from Scotland began early by European standards, and the country shares second place numerically with Norway — Ireland being the clear leader.

The roots of emigration and colonization lie in the early seventeenth century PLANTATION in Ulster and long-traditional connections with England and Continental Europe. The Nova Scotia colony (established 1629) was the earliest Scottish settlement of any size in the New World, but it was soon followed by others elsewhere in the American colonies. Emigration to North America gathered pace after 1750, with substantial Highland migration to British North America, and especially to Canada following the AMERICAN WAR OF INDEPENDENCE. The Earl of SELKIRK (1771– 1820) was one of many landowners who encouraged Scottish migration to Canada – a favoured destination at the time.

The momentum was maintained throughout the nineteenth and into the early twentieth century – peaking in the 1850s, 1880s, early 1900s and during the DEPRESSION of the 1920s. North America was the most significant destination throughout, though Australia and New Zealand were also important and Scots contributed substantially to the development of both countries. After WORLD WAR II emigration continued at a high level in the later 1940s and the 1950s – the majority settling in the United States, Canada, Australia and New Zealand under government-sponsored migration schemes.

• Bumstead, J., The People's Clearance, Edinburgh University Press, 1982.
• Cage, R. (ed.), The Scots Abroad: Labour, Capital, Enterprise, 1750– 1914, Croom Helm, 1985.
• Devine, T.M. (ed.), Scottish Emigration and Scottish Society, John Donald, 1992.
• Dobson, D., Scottish Emigration to Colonial America, 1607–1785, University of Georgia Press, 1994.
• Donaldson, G., The Scots Overseas, Robert Hale, 1966.
• Karras, A.L., Sojourners in the Sun: Scottish Migrants in Jamaica and the Chesapeake, 1740–1800, Cornell University Press, 1992.
• McLean, M., The People of Glengarry: Highlanders in Transition, 1745– 1820, McGill-Queen's University Press, 1991.
• Meyer, D., The Highland Scots of North Carolina, 1732–1776, University of North Carolina Press, 1961.
• Prentis, M., The Scots in Australia, Sydney University Press, 1983.
• Prentis, M., Squatters and Saints: Scotland and the making of Australia, Dunedin Multimedia, 1996.

enclosure The enclosure of land into unified holdings by stone dykes, hedges or fences was age-old but is particularly associated with the IMPROVEMENT that occurred during the AGRICULTURAL REVOLUTION of the eighteenth and early part of the nineteenth centuries. Some enclosure – mainly for stock grazing – was undertaken during the seventeenth century, Sir David Dunbar of Baldoon in Wigtownshire being one of several Lowland landowners who pioneered enclosure of their home farms or estates. The Scottish PARLIAMENT encouraged enclosure through various enactments before its demise in 1707.

Consolidation of holdings and the extension of farming beyond the INFIELDS and OUTFIELDS of the traditional ferme-toun on to common land and wasteland generally went hand in hand with enclosure – and sometimes brought about the decline of old-established settlements. There was a spell of resistance by the Levellers in Galloway during the 1720s, but elsewhere protest seems to have been relatively limited. Most of the evidence would indicate that enclosure actually created job opportunities in the countryside since improved agriculture was still very labour-intensive. Nevertheless, rural-urban MIGRATION became a prominent feature of Scottish demography during the latter half of the eighteenth century. As in England the rate of enclosure varied from time to time and from district to district-starting in the south and east and moving west and north. The first peak occurred in the 1760s, the second about 1810, and the momentum thereafter maintained until the 1850s. Parliamentary regulation was much less important than in England, with landowners themselves playing a significant role in the proceedings of their own volition. Thus Scottish enclosure differed somewhat in its timing and impact from the English experience.

Engagement (26—27 December 1647) By the latter part of 1647 it was becoming obvious that Cromwell (1599—1658) and the Independents had no intention of carrying out the terms of the SOLEMN LEAGUE AND COVENANT. Accordingly certain noblemen, notably Lauderdale (1616—82) and HAMILTON (1606—49), concerned in any case about the growing ascendancy of the Kirk, contacted CHARLES I (1600—49) who although a prisoner of the Parliamentarians was still able to sign the Engagement. Thus the king, in return for promising to introduce Presbyterianism for a trial period of three years in England and granting various economic concessions, would receive Scottish military aid. As it happened both LEVEN (c.1580—1661) and David LESLIE, Lord Newark (d.1682) the two principal Covenanting generals refused to join the Engagers and an inferior force led by Hamilton was easily overcome by Cromwell at Preston in August 1648. The significance of the episode was twofold: it decisively marked the serious division that had occurred in the ranks of the Covenanting opposition, and the defeat of the more moderate Engagers allowed the fanatics to seize power. Shortly afterwards in January 1649 the ACT OF CLASSES was passed.
• *Stevenson, D., Revolution and Counter Revolution in Scotland, 1644— 51, Royal Historical Society, 1977.*

engineering Before the era of the INDUSTRIAL REVOLUTION engineering in the modern sense was limited to the work of clock-makers, millwrights and masons. Indeed much of the construction work that accompanied industrialization — such as large water-powered COTTON spinning mills, iron works, or steam-engines — was undertaken by such craftsmen. Specialization between mechanical and civil engineering appeared early, though some of the pioneering Scottish engineers like James WATT (1736—1819), John RENNIE (1761—1821) and Thomas TELFORD (1757—1834), were remarkably versatile — building anything from small water-wheels and steam-engines to CANALS, roads and bridges. The mechanical engineering industry as such developed rapidly after 1780 to build and service the machines of industry, notably in TEXTILES, IRON, and COAL, and mainly concentrated around Glasgow and neighbouring industrial districts. Engineering affinity with the Scottish iron industry became still closer with the development of James Neilson's (1792–1865) hot blast process, the rise of the local wrought iron industry and the construction of the RAILWAYS. SHIPBUILDING and marine engineering benefited from innovations by William SYMINGTON (1763–1831), Henry BELL (1767–1830), and Robert NAPIER (1791–1876), among others.

The great hey-day of Scottish heavy engineering – allied to the progress of the iron, steel and coal industries – came during the Victorian era, when Clydeside was described as the 'Workshop of the Empire'. The area specialized in industrial engines and machines, castings, iron and steel plate, merchant and naval ships, and locomotives for British, imperial and other overseas railways. Many large-scale projects, such as railway and bridge building, were overseen by Scottish engineers world-wide. William BEARDMORE (1856–1936) was one of the leading figures of this period.

While heavy mechanical and civil engineering were at the forefront of technology for a time the Scottish industry was soon overtaken by developments elsewhere. Insufficient expansion occurred in electrical, chemical or light engineering much before 1914, although there were some modest developments in the consumer goods sector, such as the Singer sewing machine (manufactured in a huge complex at Clydebank from the 1880s), optical instruments, cycle and motor car production.

During the twentieth century the engineering industry experienced mixed fortunes during two World Wars, the economic DEPRESSION and a traumatic period of reconstruction, which modified it out of all recognition from its Victorian aspect. While heavy engineering, and particularly shipbuilding, declined, there was a corresponding increase in light engineering, not always with much long-term success given the failure of vehicle building at Linwood, Renfrewshire, and Bathgate, West Lothian. Electronic, oil-related, and high technology engineering figured prominently during the 1970s and 80s.

- *Hume, J.R. and Moss, M., Workshop of the British Empire: Engineering and Shipbuilding in the West of Scotland, Heinemann, 1977.*
- *Slaven, A., The Development of the West of Scotland 1750–1860, Routledge & Kegan Paul, 1975.*
- *Swinfen, D., The Fall of the Tay Bridge, Mercat Press, 1994.*

Enlightenment   During the latter half of the eighteenth century and for part of the early nineteenth there was a remarkable surge in culture. Though confined to the urban middle class and the aristocracy, it embraced EDUCATION, philosophy, art, architecture and literature. There were also significant developments in science and technology, and notable contributions to the new social sciences, especially economics. The Scottish experience was much in line with the European, though the Scots certainly made a forceful contribution to the advance of Reason. This brief account is in three sections which (i) examine something of the origins of the Scottish Enlightenment; (ii) chart the main developments in each sphere; and, (iii) make some assessment of the impact of Enlightenment ideas on eighteenth-century Scotland.

(i) According to one historian of the Enlightenment, Chitnis, Scotland provided a particularly sympathetic environment in which the new ideas of 'Reason' became established. His view is that the roots of the movement lay deep in the nation's history — especially in the law, the educational system in schools and universities, and in the Church — all institutions that had developed along Continental rather than English lines. Scottish law was grounded in social law and social philosophy; and the legal profession was dominant in politics and economic affairs. In education — an extremely important influence on Enlightenment ideas — the arts were again distinctly philosophical. MEDICINE was concerned as much with research and teaching, as with caring and curing; while in science the concentration was on the physical and natural, with an emphasis on the application of ideas. The new 'social sciences' — economics, history, politics and sociology — sprang from the same philosophical tradition that prevailed in the arts. The Church dominated the social affairs of the nation, yet at the same time (as Chitnis shows) theology was probably the original 'social science', paving the way for the secular sciences of the eigh-

teenth century. Many churchmen were distinguished men of letters, and this remained so well into the nineteenth century.

(ii) Scotland in the eighteenth century saw significant developments in the sciences, social sciences and culture generally. We only have space here to note the main features, but these can be followed up in greater detail in the cross-references and bibliography. Firstly, science made great strides and Scottish practitioners were essentially applied scientists, marrying research and teaching with practical application. Science had obvious links to technology and industry in the work of chemists and engineers. Outstanding were James Hutton (1726–97) in geology, David Gregory (1661–1708) in mathematics, Joseph BLACK (1728–99) in chemistry and physics, and James WATT (1736–1819) in engineering. Secondly, in philosophy the major figure was, of course, David HUME (1711–1776), author of *A Treatise of Human Nature* (1739–1740) and *Essays, Moral and Political* (1741–42). Hume was greatly influenced by the European philosophy of the age, as were his near contemporaries Francis Hutcheson (1694–1746), Thomas Reid (1710–96), George Campbell (1719–96), and Dugald Stewart (1753–1828), who together represented an important school of Scottish philosophy. Thirdly, the leading social scientists had a sound grounding in the arts, philosophy or theology, notably Adam SMITH (1723–90), Adam FERGUSSON (1723–1816), John Millar (1735–1801), and William ROBERTSON (1721–93). Smith's outstanding contribution, *The Wealth of Nations* (1776), established political economy as one of the leading social sciences. Lastly, there were many important developments in culture. In literature notable contributions were made by the poets Allan Ramsay (1686–1758), James Thomson (1700–48), Robert Fergusson (1750–74), and Robert BURNS (1759–96), while Tobias Smollett (1721–71), and others worked in the novel genre. Literary styles changed greatly in the period, from the Classical, through transitional, to Romantic — the last seen at its best in the vernacular poems of Burns.

Art and architecture also reflected the styles of the age. Art was dominated by Classicism — reflected in both portraiture and landscapes — produced, for example, by Allan Ramsay Jr (1713–84), Henry Raeburn (1796–1823), David Allan (1744–96), Alexander (1758–1840) and Patrick (1787–1831) Nasmyth, and Gavin Hamilton (1730–97). The Scottish contribution to architecture was perhaps more significant — seen at best in the works of Sir William Bruce (d.1710), Colin Campbell (d.1729), James Gibbs (1682–1754), Robert Mylne (1734–1811), and, above all, William (d.1748) and Robert ADAM (1728–92). In urban planning remarkable strides were made — from the grandeur of Edinburgh's planned NEW TOWN to the modest estate villages built all over the Lowlands.

(iii) Several historians — including those cited here — have their own assessment of the Scottish Enlightenment, but they mostly agree that the advances in science and culture can hardly be seen in isolation from general social and economic change. Some have argued that Enlightenment culture was essentially elitist, but while this might be true of art and architecture, it was hardly the case in the sciences, which contributed much to technology and industry. Scottish education — while hardly respected at every level of society imbued with a so-called democratic tradition — nevertheless reinforced its position as a leading national institution, with schools and universities more committed to applied (or 'useful') arts and sciences than their English counterparts. Enlightenment ideas of Reason and Order fitted in well with the new efficiency in agriculture and industry, and hence contributed in some measure to economic growth during the eighteenth century, notably to the AGRICULTURAL REVOLUTION and the INDUSTRIAL REVOLUTION. Pressure for political reform also owed much to Enlightenment ideas combined with ripples from the AMERICAN WAR OF INDEPENDENCE and the FRENCH REVOLUTION.

Finally, many major figures of Scottish life and letters during the first half of the nineteenth century were educated in the philosophy and outlook of the Scottish Enlightenment, which thus had a long-term impact on cultural, social, economic and political developments.

•*Allan, D., Virtue, Learning and the Scottish Enlightenment, Edinburgh University Press, 1993.*

•*Chitnis, A.C., The Scottish Enlightenment: A Social History, Croom Helm, 1976.*

•*Daiches, D., Jones, P. and Jones, J. (eds.), A Hotbed of Genius: The*

Scottish Enlightenment, Edinburgh University Press, 1986.
• *Davie, G.E., The Democratic Intellect: Scotland and her Universities in the Nineteenth Century, Edinburgh University Press, 1961.*
• *Davie, G.E., The Scottish Enlightenment, Historical Association, 1981.*
• *Devine, T.M. (ed.), Improvement and Enlightenment, John Donald, 1989.*
• *Devine, T.M. and Young, J.R. (eds.), Eighteenth-Century Scotland, Tuckwell Press, 1999.*
• *Hook, A. and Sher, R. (eds.), The Glasgow Enlightenment, Tuckwell Press, 1995.*
• *Lenman, B., Integration, Enlightenment and Industrialisation 1746– 1832, Edward Arnold, 1981.*

Episcopal Church, see CHARLES I; CHARLES II; FIVE ARTICLES OF PERTH; JAMES VI; RESTORATION SETTLEMENT; REVOLUTION SETTLEMENT; SECTS; SHARP; SPOTTISWOODE; TOLERATION ACT; WILLIAM

Erskine, Henry, see EDINBURGH REVIEW

Erskine, John, sixth Lord, first Earl of Mar (c.1510—72) John Erskine succeeded his father in 1552 and like him was given custody of Edinburgh Castle. Although sympathetic to the objectives of the LORDS OF THE CONGREGATION, he allowed MARY OF GUISE (1516–60) to seek refuge in the fortress in April 1560. In 1565 he was given the vacant earldom of Mar, previously held by James STEWART (1531–70) who had surrendered it in favour of the earldom of Moray in 1562. He assisted in the suppression of the CHASEABOUT RAID and two years later played a prominent part in the overthrow of BOTHWELL (c.1535–78) and MARY

(1542–87). At the coronation of JAMES VI (1566–1625) at Stirling in July 1567 Mar's role was to carry the infant king during the ceremony. In September 1571 he survived the attack on Stirling by Mary's supporters that resulted in the death of Regent LENNOX (1516–71) by taking shelter in his recently constructed townhouse (Mar's Wark). He was now appointed regent by popular consent although his short-lived administration was an unspectacular one overshadowed by the dominant figure of MORTON (c.1516–81). Much of his time was spent trying to recover Edinburgh from the Marians and his main achievement before his death in October 1572 was to reach an agreement with KNOX (c.1512–72) and the other religious leaders over the functions of bishops in the reformed Kirk.

Erskine, John, sixth Earl of Mar (1675—1732) A staunch advocate of the Treaty of UNION, Erskine played a major role in the events leading up to it. Thus, in 1705, when he became Secretary of State, he was active in drafting the preliminary stages of the Treaty and was probably mainly responsible for the decision that Queen ANNE (1665–1714) should nominate the Scottish commissioners for the subsequent negotiations affecting the Union. As a commissioner himself he was heavily involved in bribing anti-Union noblemen to end their opposition and once it was all over remained one of the Queen's principal Scottish confidants until the demise of the PRIVY COUNCIL in 1708. In 1714, although he supported the Hanoverian succession, he failed to make any impression on the new king and was deprived of his secretaryship. In pique, he now took up the cause of the JACOBITES, organizing a rally of prominent members of the nobility in support of James Francis STEWART, the Old Pretender (1688–1766) at Braemar in August 1715. However, once the rebellion got under way Mar proved to be an unimpressive leader who allowed himself to be outmanoeuvred by John CAMPBELL, second Duke of Argyll (1678–1743). After SHERIFF-MUIR his revolt ground to a halt. February 1716 witnessed the departure for France of 'Bobbing John', so-called on account of his penchant for changing sides; with his estates forfeited he was to remain an exile for the rest of his life.

Estates, Convention of The term seems to have regular usage from the reign of JAMES V (1512–42) by which date it had superseded the earlier General Council. This was the name given to meetings of lords and prelates, summoned to discuss the affairs of the kingdom, and possessing financial and legislative powers comparable to PARLIAMENT. The practice introduced in the early sixteenth century of including representatives of the BURGHS in the composition of conventions apparently led to the change in nomenclature. Nevertheless for the rest of that century there were still significant differences between a convention and a parliament; the former remained a more selective institution while it continued to lack the judicial functions belonging to the latter. However, in the seventeenth century the distinctions became less obvious, especially as burgh representation increased and meetings became more formal with twenty days notice being given beforehand. Thus, while conventions were still called for specific purposes, mainly related to taxation, and could not proceed to discuss other issues, there was latterly little to distinguish between them and meetings of Parliament. The convention, for instance, brought together in 1689 to undertake the REVOLUTION SETTLEMENT was simply converted into a parliament by means of a letter from WILLIAM III (1650–1702).

• Dickinson, W.C. and Donaldson, G. (eds.), *A Source Book of Scottish History III*, Nelson, 1963.
• Donaldson, G., *Scotland: James V to James VII*, Oliver & Boyd, 1965.
• Rait, R.S., *The Parliaments of Scotland*, Maclehose, Jackson, 1924.

F

Falkirk, Battle of (22 July 1298)
Following his victory at STIRLING
BRIDGE in September 1297,
WALLACE (c.1270–1305) had pursued the traditional Scottish tactics
of harrying the Anglo-Scottish borders. In retaliation, and in a determined effort to retreive his
position, Edward I gathered
together a powerful army in the
summer of 1298 for the reconquest
of Scotland.

The opposing forces met on 22
July 1298 near Falkirk where
English superiority in archery triumphed over Wallace's infantry.
The latter, drawn up with their
long spears in a hedgehog like formation were no match for the
accurate delivery of Edward's
archers.

Wallace's defeat signalled the
end of his brief period as a
GUARDIAN, while for Scotland it
marked a further stage in Edward
I's efforts to subjugate the country
during the WARS OF INDEPENDENCE.
• *Barron, E., The Scottish War of
Independence, 1937.*
• *Barrow, G.W.S., Robert Bruce and the
Community of the Realm of Scotland,
Edinburgh University Press, 1988.*
• *Watson, F., Under the Hammer:
Edward I and Scotland, 1286–1307,
Tuckwell Press, 1998.*

famine Famine and disease — as
elsewhere throughout much of
Europe — went hand in hand in
early modern Scotland, acting as
checks on POPULATION expansion.
On many occasions during the sixteenth to eighteenth centuries
famine generally resulted from harvest failure. This was often accentuated by reliance on one food crop,
either oats or potatoes, the latter
widely cultivated after 1750 in both
the Lowlands and the HIGHLANDS.

The incidence of famine varied
widely, the worst periods being the
1570s, 1590s, 1630s, 1640s and
1690s. The last great seventeenth-century dearth, popularly known
as 'King WILLIAM's ill years' brought
widespread mortality and MIGRATION to better favoured districts —
and may even have influenced
negotiations for the Treaty of
UNION with England.

Crop failures were also common
in the latter half of the eighteenth
and early nineteenth century,
though the economy and the
authorities were by that time better
organized to cope with such emergencies. By far the worst was that
which occurred at the same time as
the Great Hunger in Ireland during
the 1840s when famine affected
much of the northern Highlands
and Islands. In the longer term,
this led to the investigations of economic and social conditions by the
CROFTERS' COMMISSION and the
introduction of the crofters' right
to tenure.

• *Devine, T.M., The Great Highland Famine: Hunger, Emigration and the Scottish Highlands in the Nineteenth Century, John Donald, 1988.*

Fergusson, Adam (1723—1816) Adam Fergusson, the philosopher and one of the key figures of the Scottish ENLIGHTENMENT, was born in 1723. Like many other successful men of his generation he was a son of the manse, his father being parish minister at Logierait, Perthshire. At first he was educated at home then sent to the grammar school in Perth. Although quite common at the time he went at the early age of sixteen to the nearby St Andrews University, transferring to Edinburgh to study theology in 1743. There he met several other young men, who like himself were later to become distinguished thinkers and writers, including William Robertson (1721—93), the historian, and John Home (1722—1808), the playwright.

Apparently he was able to combine the study of divinity with a part-time post as private secretary to Lord Milton — right-hand man to the powerful Lord Islay (1682—1761), Walpole's manager in Scotland. Connections in high places — and most probably some knowledge of Gaelic — subsequently helped Fergusson obtain the post of deputy chaplain to the Black Watch Regiment, then the 43rd and later the famous 42nd Regiment. Soon after he became full chaplain to his regiment and engaged in combat at the battle of Fontenoy in Flanders, 11 May 1745. In 1746 one of his sermons — translated from Gaelic into English — was published in London. Much of it was devoted to

a violent denunciation of the JACOBITES, Charles Edward STEWART, the Young Pretender, and the Catholic Church.

Fergusson remained in military service at home and overseas until 1754, but, failing to secure a parish, resigned the ministry and returned to Edinburgh. He succeeded another friend and associate, David HUME (1711—76), as Advocates' Librarian. He became professor of natural philosophy at Edinburgh University in 1759 and was soon a renowned teacher and member of the lively society that typified Edinburgh in the Age of Enlightenment. In 1764 he moved to the chair of mental and moral philosophy and two years later, in 1766, married Katherine Burnett, a niece of Joseph BLACK (1728—99), the chemist.

Most of Fergusson's major works were published during the time he taught at Edinburgh, including an *Essay on the History of Civil Society* (1767), *Institutes of Moral Philosophy* (1769), and *Remarks... on 'Observations on the Nature of Civil Liberty'* (1776). In the last Fergusson proposed peace terms for the North American colonists engaged in the AMERICAN WAR OF INDEPENDENCE. Indeed two years later in 1778 Fergusson travelled to Philadelphia with the British commission sent to negotiate with the American revolutionaries — but to no apparent effect.

He resigned his chair in 1785 and devoted much of his time thereafter to writing, revising his earlier works, and playing host to intellectuals and writers. The young Walter SCOTT (1771—1832) met Robert BURNS (1759—96) at Fergusson's house during the winter of 1786–7. His retirement was spent variously in Edinburgh, Peebles and then St Andrews, where he died in 1816. Fergusson was a significant member of the Scottish 'common sense' school of philosophy and is regarded as a forerunner of modern sociology.

'Fifteen, the, see JACOBITE REBELLIONS

fishing Historically fishing was a long-established activity round the Scottish coast, in the lochs and off the Hebrides and Northern Isles, where it generally complimented subsistence farming or crofting. As the historian of the industry has indicated, Scotland was certainly well-favoured for the development of a large-scale fishing trade, being located in one of the most prolific sectors of the European continental shelf with seas of moderate depth readily fished for herring, haddock and cod by small vessels. The country was fortunate in that the annual movement of herring round the coast worked greatly to the advantage of the Scottish fisherfolk, giving opportunities for catches everywhere at some time of the year.

By the seventeenth century, fish had become an important Scottish export, but the wealth of the offshore grounds also benefited the Dutch, who were especially active in the North Sea. Indeed the success of the Dutch caused much alarm and encouraged government policy to promote native fisheries, notably by the Board of Trustees for Fisheries and Manufactures (1727). Although bounties (or grants) were offered on vessels fitted out for the herring fishing, other legislation on fishing prac-

tices and the high duty on salt needed for curing continued to handicap the industry. The establishment of the BRITISH FISHERIES SOCIETY in 1786 coincided with a new attitude. Bounties were promised on herring catches and on fish exports and soon after the Salt Laws were relaxed in favour of the fishermen.

During the nineteenth century the fishing industry experienced dramatic expansion and by the 1850s the herring fishery of the east coast was the largest in Europe. The fishing POPULATION and communities grew accordingly, with Aberdeen, Peterhead, Fraserburgh, Wick and Stornoway becoming the main fishing ports. As with agricultural produce the growth of the market for fresh fish coincided with the development of the RAILWAYS and of refrigeration and this encouraged the introduction of steam trawling after 1880. Deep-sea fishing had earlier been pioneered by whalers working from Dundee and Peterhead.

By 1914 the industry was large-scale, capital-intensive and much dependent on foreign exports. It experienced the same painful adjustment to changing circumstances as other industries during the DEPRESSION. Falling prices and deteriorating equipment were the main problems, so that by 1939 the Scottish fishing industry had shrunk back substantially from its peak at the turn of the century. Herring fishing never regained its previous significance even when revitalization ultimately came after 1945, and white fishing became the mainstay of the industry.
• *Gray, M., The Fishing Industries of Scotland, 1790–1914: A Study in*

Regional Adaptation, Oxford University Press, 1978.

Five Articles of Perth (1618)
JAMES VI (1566–1625), once he had succeeded in restoring bishops to the Kirk, turned his attention to liturgical reform. Two aspects particularly concerned the king: firstly, the need to alter and to revise the Book of Common Order, the official service book of the reformed church; secondly, a desire to restore certain practices that had been universal before the REFORMATION and which were to be found in some other Protestant churches. Thus James wished to see such festivals as Christmas, Good Friday and Easter being observed, to have private baptism and communion recognized, to have episcopal examination and blessing of children and, most controversially of all, to introduce kneeling during communion. While his provisions regarding private sacraments were contrary to the Presbyterian emphasis on the role of the congregation and those dealing with the Christian calendar offended some of the more uncompromisingly radical clergy, it was kneeling at communion that provoked the most serious opposition. To many, both ministers and laymen, this seemed unacceptably reminiscent of the mass and it was mainly hostility to this measure that saw the Articles initially rejected by a GENERAL ASSEMBLY at St Andrews in November 1617. Infuriated, the king summoned another Assembly at Perth in August 1618 where, after considerable royal intimidation, a majority of the clergy accepted the Articles. They were ratified by PARLIAMENT in 1621 on the understanding that James would desist from any further innovations. Accordingly, the other liturgical changes being considered never materialized during the remainder of the king's lifetime.

• *Cowan, I.B., 'Five Articles of Perth' in Shaw, D. (ed.), Reformation and Revolution, St Andrew Press, 1967.*

Fleming, Sir Alexander (1881–1955) Alexander Fleming, the noted bacteriologist, who pioneered important developments in MEDICINE and the use of antibiotics, was born near Darvel, Ayrshire, in 1881, the son of a farmer. His early schooling was in Darvel and at Kilmarnock Academy, but at the age of fourteen he and his two younger brothers were sent to live in London with an older brother of the family, who had himself become a doctor. During the following two years he attended the Polytechnic Institute in Regents Street, then worked for four years as a clerk in a shipping office in the City. With his brother's encouragement he became a student at St Mary's Hospital Medical School, University of London, where he ultimately qualified with distinction in 1908.

Fleming then began research on anti-bacterial substances that would be non-toxic to human tissue. His understanding of the problems involved was greatly enhanced by his spell as a lieutenant and later a captain in the Royal Army Medical Corps during WORLD WAR I — especially the difficulties posed by care of the wounded in field hospitals and the dangers of cross-infection. After the war he returned to research and teaching, becoming a lecturer at St Mary's in 1920 and later professor of bacteriology at the University of London.

In 1921 Fleming made an important breakthrough in his work when he observed and isolated lysozyme, an enzyme found in animal tissues and secretions, like tears and saliva, which has antibiotic qualities. Some years later, in September 1928, Fleming made his most famous discovery when he noticed a bacteria-free circle around a mould that was contaminating a culture. On further investigation he found that a substance in the mould prevented the growth of bacteria even if diluted a thousand times. He described this 'chance observation' in a paper in the British Journal of Experimental Pathology (1929), calling the substance 'penicillin'. Fleming's basic discovery paved the way for the antibiotic treatment of infectious and other diseases, though it was left to others to follow through the research to the isolation, purification and production stages.

Many honours were subsequently conferred on Fleming, most notably his election to a Fellowship of the Royal Society (1943), a knighthood (1944) and his share of the Nobel Prize for Physiology or Medicine with the Australian Sir Howard Florey (1898–1968) and the German Ernst B. Chain (1906–79) in 1945. Innumerable honorary degrees and honorary citizenships were bestowed upon him. Fleming was certainly a brilliant observer and scientist, but more recently both his personality and his work have become subjects of controversy.

• *Macfarlane, G., Alexander Fleming: The Man and the Myth, Oxford University Press, 1985.*

Fletcher, Andrew, of Saltoun (1653—1716) Elected a Member of PARLIAMENT for Haddingtonshire (East Lothian) in 1678, his early opposition to the policies of Lauderdale (1618–82) and the Duke of YORK (1633–1701) signalled the start of a career distinguished for its outspoken attitude to those in power, especially the English government. Fletcher's main concern was the radical reform of Scotland, which he believed could only come about if that country had greater independence from its neighbour. Not surprisingly he supported the formation of the COMPANY OF SCOTLAND but it was to be the discussions surrounding the Treaty of UNION that placed him in the forefront of Scottish politics. Here, as a leading figure in the Country party he did his utmost by speeches and producing pamphlets to resist any plans for an 'incorporating' union with England, proposing instead a federal solution that would have given Scotland more freedom from centralized control. At the same time he used the debates on union as an opportunity to put forward a series of sweeping reforms. His proposals or 'Limitations' included an extensive reduction in royal authority, an executive, chosen by Parliament, which would be responsible to the legislature, and a widespread diminution in the powers and privileges of the nobility. Thwarted in his objectives, he retired from politics after 1707 to devote himself to farming and agrarian reform.

• *Mackenzie, W.C., Andrew Fletcher of Saltoun, Porpoise Press, 1935.*
• *Scott, P.H., Andrew Fletcher and the Treaty of Union, John Donald, 1992.*

Flodden, Battle of (9 September 1513) The French, faced in 1511 with the formidable threat of a Holy League that included England, were keen to renew the AULD ALLIANCE. Thus, in July 1512, promises of assistance for his proposed crusade against the Ottoman empire and of support for any rightful claim to the English Crown swayed JAMES IV (1473–1513), seriously aggrieved in any case at the death of one of his admirals, Andrew Barton (d.1511) at English hands, to align with Louis XII (1462–1515).

Although the king of France hoped in 1513 for a Scottish attack as soon as the English invasion took place it was not until July that James released his fleet to sail to his ally's assistance, attacking en route the English garrison at Carrickfergus. As for James IV's military campaign, it did not get under way properly until 19 August when, possibly stung into action by the reverse known as the 'Ill-Raid', a badly executed foray into England by Lord Home (d.1516), the royal army left Edinburgh. By 4 September the border had been crossed and Norham Castle as well as the strongholds of Etal, Wark and Ford, had been taken.

On the morning of 9 September the Scottish army was situated in a strong position on Flodden hill with the English forces led by Howard (1443–1524) and his son Surrey (1473–1554) disadvantageously placed below them close to the banks of the River Till. During the course of the morning the English commanders moved their men across the river to a point behind their opponents forcing James, who had failed to counter this manoeuvre, to withdraw his forces to the edge of Branxton hill.

Here, on the afternoon of 9 September, the two armies, numbering perhaps 20,000 men apiece, now faced each other. The strategic advantage still lay with James since his army overlooked the English but he was hampered by an artillery depleted of its best gunners for the sake of the Auld Alliance. This proved to be a major weakness since it was a devastatingly accurate English bombardment that forced the king to abandon his position and lead the fatal assault downhill. Here in the ensuing hand-to-hand fighting the long Scottish spears were found to be inferior to the halberds of their adversaries. Scottish casualties were very heavy; not only was James IV killed, but so too was his natural son, Alexander (1493–1513), Archbishop of St Andrews, along with two abbots, 11 earls, 15 lords and many others.

In the short term, the main political importance of the disaster was that the country was bedevilled with all the problems inherent in the long minority of JAMES V (1512–42). At the same time there were deeper implications since thereafter many of the nobility had serious reservations about the benefits of the Franco-Scottish alliance.

• *Mackie, R.L., King James IV of Scotland, Oliver & Boyd, 1958.*
• *Nicholson, R., Scotland: The Later Middle Ages, Oliver & Boyd, 1974.*

Forbes, Duncan (1685—1747) Appointed SHERIFF of Midlothian in 1709, he first came to prominence in the aftermath of the 1715 JACOBITE REBELLION. Forbes, although a staunch anti-Jacobite throughout his career, objected to Scottish Jacobites being tried by English courts, a situation that had arisen following the refusal of the Lord Advocate and his colleagues to prosecute the rebels. In 1725 he became Lord Advocate and almost immediately was closely involved in the SHAWFIELD RIOTS where his arrest of the provost and bailies of Glasgow was criticized in some quarters on the grounds that he had exceeded his powers. In the PORTEOUS AFFAIR (1736) he did his best to ameliorate the punitive measures taken by the Crown against Edinburgh and its magistrates. A year later he was appointed Lord President, stamping his presence on the COURT OF SESSION by ensuring it operated more efficiently; in these years he was also closely connected with John CAMPBELL, second Duke of Argyll (1678—1743), both in his political 'management' of Scotland and in encouraging improvements in AGRICULTURE on the Duke's estates. In 1745, during the Jacobite uprising, he was instrumental in dissuading many of the northern CLANS from joining Charles Edward STEWART, The Young Pretender (1720—88).

However, despite these valiant efforts on behalf of the Hanoverian government he was treated with great hostility by the odious Cumberland (1721—65).

• *Menary, G., Duncan Forbes, Maclehose, 1936.*

forfeited estates Following the JACOBITE REBELLIONS of 1715 and 1745 the lands of Stewart followers throughout the HIGHLANDS and Islands were forfeited to the government. Many of the estates were sold to the YORK BUILDINGS COMPANY and others, while a Board of Annexed Estates administered the remaining thirteen (ranging in size from tiny Monaltie in Aberdeenshire to the huge Perth estate), all 'inalienably' annexed to the British government in 1752. The unpaid commissioners — drawn primarily from loyal Scottish gentry — were to manage the estates and apply the income from rents 'for civilizing the inhabitants on the said estates, and other parts of the Highlands and Islands of Scotland, and promoting amongst them the Protestant religion, good government, industry and manufactures, and the principles of duty and loyalty to His Majesty, his heirs and successors'. They tried, but to little effect.

The main concerns of the board were agricultural IMPROVEMENT, the development of the LINEN industry, FISHING and communications. Only in the last area were they particularly successful during the later years of their administration. Much of the income from the estates helped in the construction of roads, bridges and harbours. Indeed, the historian of the Jacobite estates has proved that a substantial injection of capital was made in Scotland by the payment of debts on the estates by the Treasury and by public spending of the capital repaid by owners resuming possession. Much of the capital was spent on public works, notably the FORTH AND CLYDE CANAL and harbour improvements along the east coast.

The estates were returned to the original owners or their heirs in 1784, although one estate — that of Lovat — was returned as early as 1774. Thereafter the HIGHLAND AND AGRICULTURAL SOCIETY and the BRITISH FISHERIES SOCIETY became important forces for improvement in the north of Scotland.
• Smith, A.M., Jacobite Estates of the 'Forty-Five, John Donald, 1982.

Forth and Clyde Canal, see CANALS; FORFEITED ESTATES; INDUSTRIAL REVOLUTION; SYMINGTON

'Forty-Five, the, see JACOBITE REBELLIONS

Fraser, Simon, eleventh Lord Lovat (c.1667—1747) A cousin of Hugh, ninth Lord Lovat (d.1696), he successfully contrived to have his own father, Thomas Fraser of Beaufort (d.1699), succeed to the title. However, after further devious and unscrupulous actions which included forcibly marrying the widow of the ninth lord and ostentatiously supporting the Hanoverian cause in 1715, he officially succeeded as the eleventh Lord Lovat. Earlier, he had actually appeared to be an adherent of James Francis STEWART, the Old Pretender (1688–1766), but on being sent by the French as their agent in 1703 he had promptly betrayed the JACOBITE plans to QUEENSBERRY (1662–1711) in the hope of currying favour with the royal minister. As a result, on his return to France, he was incarcerated until the eve of the 'Fifteen revolt. Thereafter, with his title secure, he remained in Scotland acting for a time as adviser to

General WADE (1673–1748). The suppression of the Jacobite clans was Lovat's main recommendation, advice mainly influenced by his desire for the government to restore the independent Companies of Highlanders, one of which he had commanded. Although he initially adopted a cautious approach to the appeals of Charles Edward STEWART (1720–88) for his support, he eventually became sufficiently implicated to feel it necessary to go into hiding after CULLODEN. Captured on Loch Morar he was taken to London, found guilty of treason and executed in April 1747.
• Mackay, D.N., Trial of Simon, Lord Lovat of the '45, Edinburgh, 1911.
• Mackenzie, W.C., Simon Fraser, Chapman, 1908.

Free Church, see CHALMERS; DISRUPTION; HIGHLANDS; SECTS

French Revolution The French Revolution of 1789 was welcomed enthusiastically by groups of Scottish RADICALS — both middle and working-class — who adhered to its ideals of liberty, equality and fraternity. It was regarded by some as an example for the advance of political reform in Britain, though there was much equivocation on the part of the moderates following the abolition of the French monarchy (1792) and the execution of Louis XVI the following year.

The most significant Scottish support came from the FRIENDS OF THE PEOPLE, though there were several CORRESPONDING SOCIETIES and other shadier organizations, including the UNITED SCOTSMEN.

Most went underground or disappeared completely following

government suppression but the ideology of the French Revolution nevertheless influenced many later reform movements in Scotland after 1815.

• *Crawford, T., Boswell, Burns and the French Revolution, Saltire Society, 1990.*

• *Meikle, H., Scotland and the French Revolution, James Maclehose and Sons, 1912.*

Friends of the People   In the aftermath of the FRENCH REVOLUTION (1789), particularly during 1792–4, there occurred the first of two peaks of activity by RADICALS in Scotland — favouring political reform in advance of the first REFORM ACT in 1832. Support for the French Revolution came initially from the middle class, but after the publication of *The Rights of Man* by Thomas Paine (1737–1809) in 1791 and its banning by government in 1792, the movement assumed a much more radical character. Many societies and clubs supporting the revolution and its principles were set up in Scotland at this time. One reform society, calling itself the Friends of the People and modelled to some extent on the London CORRESPONDING SOCIETY was established in Edinburgh in 1792. It was soon followed by others throughout Scotland.

During 1792–3 the Friends of the People held three conventions, organized on broadly similar lines to the French National Assembly. The first convention, held in Edinburgh, drew delegates from over eighty branches. Thomas MUIR (1765–99), the radical advocate, later convicted and transported for sedition, played a prominent part. At the second convention the Rev. Thomas Fyshe PALMER (1747–1802), a Unitarian clergyman from Dundee, was among the leaders, while the third convention — held in autumn 1793 — was led by two English delegates, Joseph GERRALD (1760–96) and Maurice MARGAROT (1745–1815), with William SKIRVING (d.1796) as secretary.

In subsequent sedition trials before the infamous Robert MACQUEEN, Lord Braxfield all were convicted and transported to the convict colony in New South Wales — being described afterwards by sympathizers as the 'SCOTTISH MARTYRS'. By 1793 Britain was at war with France so the suppression of the Friends of the People was inevitable. Its direct contact with French republicanism and the National Assembly had been limited to exchanges of correspondence on matters of mutual concern and to one short visit by Muir. Certainly its programme of universal male suffrage and annual parliaments was revolutionary for its time. The movement had drawn its support from middle-class and artisan Radicals — much as CHARTISM did in the 1830s and 40s. Despite failing to achieve its objectives the movement and its leaders continued to inspire many Radicals during the early nineteenth century.

G

Gallacher, William, see RED CLYDESIDE

Galt, John (1779—1839) John Galt, best known for his novels of Scottish life and manners, though also closely associated with the development of Upper Canada (modern Ontario), was born in Irvine, Ayrshire, in 1779, son of a sea captain in the colonial trade. The family moved to Greenock c.1790 where Galt completed his education at the grammar school before becoming a clerk in the customs house. He later obtained a similar post with a local merchant and started to publish occasional journalism and epic poetry. In 1803 he moved to London where his brother was already established — briefly combining a business partnership with writing before entering Lincoln's Inn to study for the bar. He later abandoned the law, and, partly for health reasons, set out in 1809 on a tour of the Mediterranean. Apparently avoiding the disruptions caused by the Napoleonic War he visited Gibraltar, Sicily, Sardinia, Malta, Greece and Turkey. During his travels he met Lord Byron (1788—1824). Returning to England in 1811 he devoted some time to writing about his trip in two works, *Voyages and Travels* and *Letters from the Levant*.

From then on Galt combined a variety of business interests with writing. In 1815 he was appointed secretary of the Royal Caledonian Asylum, a charitable institution run by the Highland Society of London. He also used his parliamentary connections by acting as consultant to the Edinburgh and Glasgow Union Canal Company. He had little real literary success until the publication — initially in *Blackwood's Magazine* — of his novel *The Ayrshire Legatees* (1821), which took the form of a letter-series containing some highly amusing anecdotes. His masterpiece, written some years before but temporarily shelved, *The Annals of the Parish* (1821) was the record of a fictitious country minister describing the changes experienced in his parish some decades earlier during the AGRICULTURAL REVOLUTION and the INDUSTRIAL REVOLUTION. These were followed by *The Provost* (1822) and *The Entail* (1823) which, like the earlier novels, showed Galt's vigorous style and abundant imagination, combined with humour and sympathetic observation.

Meantime Galt's work in London led to his appointment as agent for the organization of EMIGRATION to Upper Canada, associated with the Canada Company, of which he became commissioner-secretary.

He spent much of the period 1826 to 1829 in Ontario, where he founded the town of Guelph, at the centre of a rich farming area. He also opened up much of the surrounding country by pioneering road construction. However, like the Earl of SELKIRK (1771–1820) he quarrelled with the colonial government and some of the settlers and was recalled to London to face charges of negligence.

Galt spent the remainder of his life — save one effort to found an American land company — in literary activities, including a spell as the editor of a Tory newspaper. One of his last novels, *The Member* (1832), was among the first to deal with corruption in parliamentary elections preceding the Reform Act. He retired to Greenock, where he died in 1839. Galt's literary career might be compared with that of his more famous near-contemporary, Sir Walter Scott (1771–1832).

• *Whatley, C.(ed.), John Galt, 1779–1839, Ramsay Head Press, 1979.*

General Assembly In the First BOOK OF DISCIPLINE there was only the vaguest of references to any assembly of the reformed Kirk. Besides, what evolved at the first meeting, usually taken to have been held in Edinburgh on the 20 December 1560, was a body consisting of commissioners from the nobility, barons, lairds and burghs joined by the members of the Kirk. These then were the 'godly magistrates' whose guidance was believed to be necessary during the reign of the Catholic Queen MARY (1542–87). However, the accession of JAMES VI (1566–1625) and the subsequent return to the king-dom of Andrew MELVILLE (1545–1622) brought demands for a more radical polity, including an assembly whose composition would be restricted to ministers and elders. James fought a prolonged contest with the Melvillians insisting on his right to decide not only when assemblies should meet but also their location. Latterly, after 1618, and the forcing through of the FIVE ARTICLES OF PERTH, the king ceased summoning assemblies, a policy continued by CHARLES I (1600–49) until the crisis provoked by the signing of the National Covenant in 1638. The CROMWELLIAN UNION witnessed the start of another lengthy period of inactivity from 1653 to 1690 when, with the REVOLUTION SETTLEMENT, general assemblies were finally restored along the lines sought by Melville.

• *Shaw, D., The General Assemblies of the Church of Scotland, 1560–1600, St Andrew Press, 1964.*

General Strike (1926) The General Strike of 4–12 May 1926 was the culmination of several years bitter industrial strife in the early twenties and of the efforts of the militant miners' union, led nationally by A.J. Cook (1883–1931), to gain support from other workers in key industries, such as TRANSPORT, the docks and ENGINEERING. The strike arose from the basic economic problems of the coal industry during a painful period of readjustment following WORLD WAR I — most notably the attempts of the coal masters to enforce wage-cuts and longer hours on the miners, accompanied by local and national lock-outs. The Scottish miners had particularly good reasons for their militancy throughout this period as working conditions were generally worse and wage rates often lower than those elsewhere in the British coalfields. Over the years these facts had been acknowledged by several government commissions, including a Royal Commission headed by Sir Herbert Samuel (1870–1963), which reported in March 1926.

Meantime, the Trades Union Congress (TUC) had empowered its General Council to intervene in any dispute involving large numbers of workers and pledged support to the miners. In reality the vacillations among the TUC and STUC leadership as well as uncertainties among other 'front line' union leaders in transport, printing and the docks caused confusion about overall aims and objectives. In general, the leadership was badly prepared — except in the coalfields where 'Councils of Action' were organized to enforce picketing, control food supplies, and set up food kitchens. Most unions made virtually no preparations until a few days before the strike began. The government, on the other hand, was well organized: the SCOTTISH OFFICE and the Lord Advocate set up an Emergency Organization with Scotland divided into five regions whose officials could call on the police and troops to crush disorder and volunteers of the right-wing Organization for the Maintenance of Supplies to keep things moving.

The Samuel Commission saw no immediate solution to the industry's difficulties except cuts in wages, hedged about with concessions, which included a national wage scale and no increase in

hours. On this basis negotiations were conducted between the miners' leaders, the owners and the government — which was already providing a substantial subsidy to the industry. After a series of round-the-clock confrontations the government suddenly broke off negotiations on the pretext that typesetters at the *Daily Mail* had refused to print an editorial calling for resistance to the threatened General Strike. The strike began on 4 May, when railways, transport, docks, metal trades, building, printing and power industries were closed down.

The Scottish response to the call for a General Strike seems to have been good. Transport was most immediately affected with trains stopped throughout Scotland and urban transport severely curtailed. On the whole LNER system north of the Border, only two trains ran on the first day of the strike; and only seven on the LMS network. Motor buses, recently introduced on the roads and invariably driven by their owners (as there were still many one-man operators), offered an alternative form of transport. Students and other volunteers kept some city tram services running. The trams were easy to drive, but this black-leg labour provoked conflicts between strikers and police. In some places, like Glasgow, trams, buses and other vehicles were either overturned or stoned. Numerous arrests were made. The response by dockers was solid, all the ports being deserted. Troops were much in evidence in waterfront neighbourhoods of Glasgow and Clydeside, Leith, Dundee, Aberdeen and elsewhere. While the printers struck in large numbers, closing most of the press, there was some confusion among the construction workers. Two important groups, the engineers and shipbuilders, did not join until the last day of the strike. This Patrick Dollan (1885–1963) later described as 'an error of tactics', since the engineers and ship-builders represented such influential groups in the labour movement.

Overall there was a high level of participation and militancy in Scotland — reflected not only in widespread disturbance, but also in the buildup of armed forces should intervention prove necessary. In the event the strike lasted only nine days and there was 'complete bewilderment' among Scottish strikers when they heard of the TUC's decision to call it off. In the aftermath many Scottish workers were victimized and the miners had to fight on alone for many months before being driven back to work in utter desperation and on the owners' terms. Opinion among Scottish trade unionists on the General Strike was divided. What was an unwise and costly blunder to some was regarded by others as 'a memory of unselfish devotion, of unflinching courage, of unlimited faith in the power of the workers'.

• *Macdougall, I. (ed.), Essays in Scottish Labour History: A Tribute to W.H. Marwick, John Donald, 1978.*

Gerrald, Joseph (1760—96) The son of an Irish planter, Joseph Gerrald was born in St Christopher, West Indies, and educated in London. He subsequently returned to the West Indies, but falling on hard times, moved to the United States, where he apparently practised law in Pennsylvania for four years. During this time he associated with Thomas Paine (1737–1809), author of *The Rights of Man*. He settled back in England in 1788 and was soon involved with the radical reform movements of the day. Gerrald became a prominent member of the London Corresponding Society and it was as one of two delegates of this body that he attended the National Convention of the FRIENDS OF THE PEOPLE in 1793 — Maurice MARGAROT (1745–1815) being his associate. Having played such a prominent part in the proceedings Gerrald was a likely target for the authorities and at his trial before Robert MACQUEEN, Lord Braxfield in March 1794 he was found guilty of sedition and sentenced to 14 years transportation in Australia.

After his sentence he spent over a year in Newgate prison and did not reach New South Wales until November 1795. By that time he was seriously ill and died in the house of a fellow exile, Thomas Fyshe PALMER (1747–1802), in March 1796.

Gladstone, William, see ASQUITH; CONSERVATIVE PARTY; CROFTER'S COMMISSION; LIBERAL PARTY

Glasgow, see INDUSTRIAL REVOLUTION; INDUSTRY; HOUSING; MIGRATION; SHIPBUILDING; URBANIZATION

Glasgow Assembly (1638) The signing of the National Covenant in February 1638 and in the weeks thereafter by much of the nation convinced CHARLES I (1600–49) that he must make concessions to his Covenanting opponents. Thus in September the king consented to the withdrawal of the PRAYER BOOK, the CODE OF CANONS, and the Court of High Commission and the FIVE ARTICLES OF PERTH. He also agreed to a meeting of the General Assembly, the first for twenty years, being held in Glasgow. The problem of the composition of this assembly was resolved by the dominant Covenanting faction insisting on adherence to an Act of 1597 that stipulated the presence of clerical and lay representatives with the addition of commissioners from the royal BURGHS. Eventually 142 ministers and 98 members of the laity attended the assembly when it met in Glasgow Cathedral in November 1638. In no sense was it a democratic gathering since none of the bishops risked attending and many ministers were forbidden to appear for having accepted the religious policies of the Crown. Not surprisingly, a serious disagreement soon arose between HAMILTON (1606—49), the royal commissioner, and the Moderator, Alexander HENDERSON (1583—1646) over the future of the bishops in the Church. The cause of the majority of members, who were strongly anti-episcopal, was greatly strengthened when Johnston of Wariston (1611—63) produced old registers condemning episcopacy. Hamilton vainly tried to have the assembly dissolved but the members pressed ahead, not only annulling the Prayer Book and other royal innovations but also abolishing bishops.

The stage was now set for a confrontation between Kirk and State with both sides mobilizing for the first BISHOPS' WAR.

• Dickinson, W.C. and Donaldson, G. (eds.), *A Source Book of Scottish History III*, Nelson, 1961.
• Donaldson, G., *Scotland: James V to James VII*, Oliver & Boyd, 1965.
• Stevenson, D., *The Scottish Revolution, 1637—44*, David & Charles, 1973.

Glasgow Herald, see PRESS

Glencairn Rising (1653—4) This royalist inspired attempt at insurrection was the only serious threat to the CROMWELLIAN UNION. Glencairn (c.1610—64), who arrived in Scotland in August 1653 with the official backing of CHARLES II (1630—85) for this rebellion, won support both from certain Lowland families and from a number of clan chiefs. Inevitably, of course, the motives of the latter were varied, including dislike of any governmental initiatives at controlling their actions not to mention suspicion of ARGYLL (1607—61) and his policy. However, despite the addition of Middleton (c.1608—74) as military commander there was a lack of co-ordination and determination about the whole enterprise that ensured the rising was comparatively easily suppressed by the English authorities. The final setback came at Dalnaspidal in July 1654 when a force under Middleton was defeated by MONCK (1608—70). The main consequence of the rebellion was the worsening financial circumstances of various noble families as the occupying government confiscated their property and levied fines from them.
• Dow, F., *Cromwellian Scotland*, John Donald, 1980.

Glencoe Massacre (13 February 1692) In the aftermath of the

Jacobite rebellion of 1689, the government of WILLIAM III (1650–1702) alternated its policy towards the HIGHLANDS between one of military subjugation, hence the construction of Fort William, and one of trying to win over the leading CLAN chieftains by financial inducements. Thus, during the summer of 1691, John Campbell, Earl of Breadalbane (1635–1717), acting on the instructions of the Scottish Secretary of State, the Master of Stair (1648–1707) strove to negotiate some kind of settlement with various chiefs. But a combination of intransigence and lingering hopes of French support for the Jacobites, not to mention obstructive tactics from the army commanders, prevented any agreement being reached. Stair became impatient and insisted that all the rebels must take an oath of allegience to the Crown by 7 January 1692 or otherwise risk military action against themselves. MacIan of Glencoe's (d.1692) failure to comply with this order by the prescribed date, even though he had a justifiable excuse and was not the only offender, was sufficient pretext for the Secretary to decide to vent his wrath on the troublesome MacDonalds. Accordingly, in a warrant issued by Stair and signed by the king, the army at Fort William was given instructions to carry out a massacre. The precise methods to be employed were not outlined in the communique – and consequently it was left to the officers on the spot to devise a suitable stratagem. Their response was to send Campbell of Glenlyon (1632–96) into Glencoe with 120 men of Argyll's Regiment and after being billeted with the MacDonalds for a fortnight order him to slaughter them. As it happened the whole sordid affair was bungled since the units supposedly linking up with Glenlyon failed to arrive on time and only MacIan and thirty-seven other members of his clan were killed.

The massacre had serious repercussions for the government since, although it was initially regarded as yet another internecine feud, it soon became apparent the administration was deeply implicated. Eventually Stair was dismissed but more significantly the Jacobite cause in the Highlands was given a tremendous fillip while the prestige of William III plummeted.

•*Hopkins, P., Glencoe and the End of the Highland War, John Donald, 1986.*
•*MacDonald, D., Slaughter under Trust, Hale, 1965.*

Gordon, George, fourth Earl of Huntly (c.1510—62) During the reigns of JAMES IV (1473–1513) and JAMES V (1512–42), the Gordons became one of the most powerful families not only in the northeast but also in the country generally. To a large extent this was a result of deliberate royal policy, which devolved considerable powers on magnates such as the Campbells and Gordons while expecting them in return to maintain order over their unruly territories. The questionable wisdom of such tactics was illustrated in the latter stages of the career of the fourth earl.

George Gordon succeeded to his earldom on his grandfather's death in 1524 and, although mostly on good terms with James V, accompanying him, for instance, on his northern expedition in

1540, he fell from favour for alleged incompetence after his defeat of the English at Haddon Rig in August 1542. In 1543 he became one of the Council of Regency and despite being opposed to the anglophile policies of ARRAN (c.1516–75) he was appointed Chancellor in 1546 in a conciliatory move by the Regent. He was captured at PINKIE in September 1547 but freed soon afterwards on payment of a ransom. Although displeased at losing his chancellorship to a member of the French entourage of MARY OF GUISE (1516–60) he only joined the LORDS OF THE CONGREGATION in 1560. While, unlike his brother Alexander, Bishop of Galloway (1516–75), he showed little enthusiasm for Protestantism, it was annoyance at Lord James Stewart (1531–70) acquiring the earldom of Moray, which the Gordons had been administering, that provoked his rebellious behaviour in 1562. (see James STEWART, Earl of Moray) Thus, following violent action against the Ogilvy family, MARY (1542–87) herself accompanied a royal expedition to the northeast that ultimately saw the Gordons defeated at Corrichie, near Aberdeen, on 28 October.

The Earl died shortly after the battle while his third son, John, (d.1562) was executed. The earldom was inherited by his eldest son, George (d.1576), the father of the sixth Earl (1562–1636) who, as one of the NORTHERN EARLS, was to cause serious problems for JAMES VI (1566–1625) in the 1590s.

Gowrie Conspiracy (5 August 1600) According to JAMES VI (1566–1625) he was invited on 5 August 1600 to Gowrie Castle at Perth by Alexander, Master of Ruthven (c.1581–1600), to meet someone who possessed a remarkable quantity of gold. But on arriving at the castle, again, so the king claimed, he discovered the real purpose of the invitation was to assassinate him. However, his shouts for assistance were heard by his retainers and in the ensuing melee both the Master and his brother, John, Earl of Gowrie (c.1577–1600) were conveniently killed.

What really happened will always remain a mystery but it was not the first time that the powerful Ruthven family had seized the king. In fact, William, Earl of Gowrie (c.1541–84), had done precisely this in 1582. On the other hand it could simply have been some sudden dispute between the parties that sparked off the violence, perhaps regarding the money the Crown owed the Ruthvens. What is undeniable is that James used the incident as a means of testing the loyalty of the Edinburgh clergy who were required to summon their congregations and offer prayers for the royal deliverance. Robert Bruce (c.1554–1631), the solitary minister who persisted in refusing to do this, was banished to Inverness for his recalcitrance.

• *Willson, D.H ., King James VI and I, Jonathan Cape, 1956.*

Gowrie, Earl of, see RUTHVEN RAID

Graham, James, Marquis of Montrose (1612—50) A signatory of the NATIONAL COVENANT Montrose was prominent in the

Covenanting movement both during 1638 and in the First and Second BISHOPS' WARS (1639—40). However, by 1640, reservations about the advisability of such constitutional measures as the abolition of the Committee of the Articles and the introduction of the Triennial Act were beginning to affect his attitude. Moreover he disliked and distrusted Archibald CAMPBELL, eighth Earl and first Marquis of Argyll (1607—61), one of the leading Covenanters, and drew up the Cumbernauld Bond wherein he and several other noblemen denounced the Chief of the Campbells. This action earned him temporary imprisonment. In 1643 Montrose strongly opposed the SOLEMN LEAGUE AND COVENANT and shortly after it was signed made overtures to CHARLES I (1600—49). Thus, in February 1644, he was appointed Lieutenant-General of royalist forces in Scotland and for nearly a year from September 1644 to August 1645 conducted an audacious campaign mainly in the HIGHLANDS on behalf of the Crown. His first victory over the various Covenanting forces sent against him was at Tippermuir to be followed by further successes at Fyvie, Inverlochy, where he defeated his old adversary Argyll, Auldearn, Alford and finally at Kilsyth.

However, in September 1645, a government army commanded by David LESLIE, Lord Newark (d.1682) and reinforced by Scottish veterans from the English Civil War easily routed a force under Montrose, from which there had been many desertions, at PHILIPHAUGH near Selkirk. In fact,

brilliant as his generalship undoubtedly was, it made little real impact in Lowland Scotland, largely because of Montrose's reliance on Highland and Irish troops. The latter, commanded by Alastair MacDonald (d.1647) were too closely associated by most Lowlanders with the recent massacre of Protestants in Ulster.

Montrose returned from exile in 1650 to lead another royalist rising but he was easily defeated at Carbisdale in Sutherland, captured soon afterwards and executed at Edinburgh on 21 August 1650.
• *Cowan, E.J., Montrose: For Covenant and King, Weidenfeld & Nicolson, 1977.*

Graham, John, of Claverhouse

(1648—89) His early career was as a professional soldier in the French and Dutch armies but by 1677 he was in command of units being used by the government to suppress the COVENANTERS in the southwest of Scotland. Despite his defeat at Drumclog, Ayrshire, in June 1679, he remained in favour and from 1682 he was in charge of enforcing religious policy in the same part of the country. Here, as SHERIFF of Wigtown, by the prosecution of those who refused to take the TEST ACT (1681) or who were CAMERONIANS, he earned himself the title 'Bloody Clavers'. However, while he certainly was very active during the so-called 'KILLING TIME', he apparently was not personally responsible for the death of very many people. In 1688 the Crown's high opinion of his services was underlined by his elevation to Viscount Dundee. The following year he repaid this promotion by loyally supporting JAMES

VII (1633–1701) and leading the Highland clans who formed the JACOBITE army challenging WILLIAM (1650–1702). Although, under Claverhouse's able leadership, this army defeated the government forces of General Mackay (c.1640–92) at KILLIECRANKIE, his death in the battle destroyed any hopes the Jacobites had of seizing the initiative in Scotland.

• *Linklater, M. and Hesketh, C., For King and Conscience: John Graham of Claverhouse, Viscount Dundee, Weidenfeld & Nicholson, 1989.*
• *Terry, C.S., John Graham of Claverhouse, Constable, 1905.*

Grant, Archibald, of Monymusk (1696—1778) Grant was the son of a distinguished Lord in Session, Lord Cullen, who was entrusted with his father's estate in Aberdeenshire about 1716 and soon became an energetic and persuasive advocate of agricultural IMPROVEMENT. Apart from duties as MP for Aberdeenshire, Grant devoted much of his time to the Monymusk estate, introducing ENCLOSURES, drainage, crop rotations, new grasses and root crops. At first many of his tenants resisted the changes. Some of the new fences and dykes on the estate were pulled down in night raids resembling the activities of the LEVELLERS in southwest Scotland, but Grant's apparently well-meaning paternalism prevailed — especially through the granting of long leases that gave the tenants an opportunity to benefit from the changes. Unlike many landowners, he seems to have been motivated more by humanity than profit, to the extent that when John Wesley (1703–91) visited the district in 1761 he had nothing but praise for the social conditions of the people on Grant's estate.

Grierson, John (1898—1972) Grierson was a Scottish schoolmaster's son who, following service in minesweepers in WORLD WAR I, became a prominent student at Glasgow University, winning a Rockefeller Research Fellowship for post graduate study in the USA. It was while attending Chicago, Wisconsin and Columbia Universities that he became interested in propaganda techniques and the impact of the modern media on society.

Returning to Britain in 1927, Grierson joined the Empire Marketing Board, initially as director of its film unit. Greatly influenced by contemporary filmmakers such as Eisenstein and Flaherty, he used the EMB as a platform for what he described as 'the creative interpretation of reality' — in other words, the documentary. Moreover the foundations of the documentary film in Britain were undoubtedly laid in 1929 with Grierson's epic of the North Sea herring fleet, *The Drifters*.

In 1934 the GPO took over the EMB film unit and in 1936 it released *Night Mail* one of the most memorable of a long line of documentaries which Grierson either produced or supervised. In 1938 he became the first Commissioner of the Canadian National Film Board and spent WORLD WAR II expanding and developing film-making in Canada.

After the war Grierson was Director of Mass Communications for UNESCO (1946–1948), and Controller of films at the Central

Office of Information; in 1957, he was attracted to television and for a number of years presented the documentary series *This Wonderful World* on Scottish Television. Here he continued to treat social issues in the realistic style which was to be the keynote of his brilliant career.

•*H. Forsyth Hardy, John Grierson London 1978.*

Grimond, Joseph, Lord (1913—93)   'Jo' Grimond, son of a wealthy Dundee jute manufacturer, was educated at Eton and Oxford. In 1950 at a time when the Liberal party was in headlong decline he won the Orkney and Shetland seat for them and was to remain MP for there for the next 33 years.

In 1956 Grimond became leader of the Liberals and for a short period thereafter there appeared to be some signs of a revival in the party's fortunes. Thus, in 1964 they won two seats in Scotland from the Conservatives while the following year David Steel captured Roxburgh, Selkirk and Peebles in a by-election. But the Liberal's leader was more interested in United Kingdom and European issues than Scottish ones. Discussions with the SCOTTISH NATIONAL PARTY about the possibility of an electoral pact broke down and in 1967 he decided to resign the leadership of the Liberals.

Grimond remained a highly popular MP with his constituents until his retiral in 1983 when he was elevated to the peerage.

Guardians   This was a term principally in circulation in the late thirteenth and early fourteenth centuries being comparable in meaning to 'Lieutenant' or 'Regent'. Its first use was after the death of ALEXANDER III (1241—86) whereupon after a meeting of the nobility at Scone, six Guardians were appointed.

John Balliol's (1250—1313) accession in 1292 made these appointments redundant but the collapse of his reign in 1295 and the creation of a council of twelve bishops, earls and barons would seem to have signalled the appearance of another quasi-body of Guardians. However, WALLACE (c.1270—1305) was apparently sole Guardian in 1297—98.

Edward I's dominance of Scottish affairs saw the position virtually disappear, although it was briefly revived in the early years of the reign of ROBERT II (1316—90).

•*Nicolson, R., Scotland: the Later Middle Ages, Oliver & Boyd, 1974.*

guilds   By the sixteenth century, merchant and craft guilds had become permanent features of most Scottish BURGHS. Both types of guild had similar monopolistic objectives; the merchants wanted to preserve their rights to trade overseas and sell foreign commodities whereas the craftsmen sought to protect themselves from other competitors. Entry to a merchant guild was only possible following a period of apprenticeship and thereafter by paying a hefty entrance fee. Here, being a merchant's son was of great assistance, as otherwise there could be some delay. Another possibility was marriage to the daughter of a merchant. An individual on becoming a member of a merchant guild joined, at least in theory, the ranks of the privileged group of burgesses who controlled the burghs. In practice the merchants in most towns were usually a very diverse body and it was normally a small coterie of the most affluent members who controlled everything. In short, town councils and burgess representation in PARLIAMENT was largely the prerogative of a small minority within any merchant guild. This situation, with its obvious opportunities for graft and corruption, frequently exploited to the utmost, was to remain unaltered until the Burgh REFORM ACT (1833). Craft guilds, once they had become 'incorporated trades' by receiving their seal of cause from the town council, could go ahead with drafting rules and regulations, raising funds from their members and appointing deacons to preside over their disciplinary courts. Disputes between the different crafts were settled at meetings of all the incorporated trades under the chairmanship of a deacon convener. The number of craft guilds in the larger burghs was usually seven but some smaller burghs had none at all. Glasgow and Edinburgh, on the other hand, had fourteen. Guild membership, never very substantial, varied between the different crafts; in Glasgow in the early seventeenth century, for example, the tailors, maltsters and shoemakers had the biggest numbers. Entry to the craft guilds followed a lengthy training and probationary period lasting about thirteen years. Nor, apart from having some sort of insurance against poverty, did becoming a fully-fledged member open up such a vast range of opportunities. The wealthier craftsmen tended to overshadow their poorer brethren and these organizations were largely in the hands of a craft aristocracy who reaped most of the benefits. The craft guilds continued to flourish until the advent of the INDUSTRIAL REVOLUTION in the eighteenth century made their restrictive practices and exclusive privileges completely obsolete.

• Lynch, M., Edinburgh and the Reformation, John Donald, 1981.
• Mackenzie, W.M., The Scottish Burghs, Oliver & Boyd, 1949.
• Smout, T.C., History of the Scottish People, 1560—1830, HarperCollins, 1969.

Guthrie, Dr Thomas (1803—73) Like Thomas CHALMERS (1780—1847) Guthrie was a prominent Free Churchman, a propagandist of POOR LAW reform, and a notable pioneer of working-class education. Guthrie was born in Brechin, the son of a successful merchant, and received his early education in the town. In 1815, although only twelve years of age, he was sent off to the University of Edinburgh where he first studied the natural sciences before turning to divinity. He was licensed to preach by the presbytery of Brechin in 1825 but turned down what he described as 'one of the largest charges and best livings in Scotland' in favour of a spell of foreign travel. He spent the winter of 1826—27 in Paris using introductions from his father's friend, Joseph Hume, MP (1777—1855), to move in intellectual circles and attend lectures at the Sorbonne. Among other notables, he associated with Say, the political economist, and Buchon, editor of the *Constitutionnel*.

Returning home to Brechin he worked for a time in the local

provincial bank until in 1830 he secured from William Maule (1771–1852), the Whig MP for Forfarshire and a local landowner, the living of Arbirlot. Following the precepts of Dr Henry DUNCAN (1774–1846), he established a savings bank and also turned his knowledge of MEDICINE to good account in caring for his parishioners. He quickly became a popular preacher and public speaker throughout the Arbroath district and before long his fame reached Edinburgh. Thanks to his connections he moved in 1837 to Old Greyfriars, a parish in the crowded and squalid Old Town. 'I can never forget the hideous scene of starvation and sin that lay before me,' he wrote, 'and after visiting till my heart was sick, came up the College Wynd with the idea that I might well have gone to be a missionary among the Hindoos (sic) on the banks of the Ganges.' He implemented a series of social reforms in the new parish of St John's, carved out from the old parish of Greyfriars — a church (1840), schools, and a rota of district visitors, like that introduced by Chalmers in Glasgow.

Always of a RADICAL persuasion, Guthrie was soon drawn into the debates about PATRONAGE and evangelicalism that were to lead to the DISRUPTION (1843) and the establishment of the FREE CHURCH. His eloquence was used to good effect not only in the propaganda war waged by the non-intrusionists, but also, in the aftermath of the Disruption, in the fund-raising campaign undertaken by the Free Church to build kirks, manses and schools.

Guthrie then turned his attention to education and became what Samuel Smiles (1812–1904) called the 'apostle of the ragged school movement'. His *Plea for Ragged Schools*, or *Prevention is Better Than Cure* (1847) drew attention to the plight of poor children and the problem of juvenile delinquency. His campaign was taken up by the PRESS and such periodicals as *The Edinburgh Review*, resulting in a fund that led to the establishment of a ragged school where poor children were fed, clothed and given training. This was a forerunner of the industrial schools set up with government funding after 1866.

Guthrie supported a wide range of other social reforms, notably the TEMPERANCE Movement, the half-holiday movement, and better working-class housing. He was also a prominent ecumenical. Thanks to a powerful personality, brilliant preaching and oratory, combined with connections in high places, Guthrie profoundly influenced major social reforms of his era. He retired from the ministry in 1864 and for the rest of his life became a social missionary and propagandist — mainly through the pages of the *Sunday Magazine*, which he edited for a time.

H

Haddington, Treaty of (1548)

The Duke of Somerset (c.1506–52) in charge of England in the years 1547–49 continued the policy towards Scotland known as the 'ROUGH WOOING'. Accordingly, in September 1547, the English decisively defeated a Scottish force at the battle of PINKIE. The Earl of ARRAN (c.1516–75) faced with an English occupation of the Lowlands and unable to rely on many of his own countrymen turned again to France for further assistance. Thus on 7 July 1548 at a meeting of French and Scottish representatives near Haddington, the main English headquarters, it was agreed that in return for French military aid, the Scottish government would send their queen, MARY (1542–87), to France where she would ultimately be married to the Dauphin. At the same time, Arran also took good care to look after his Hamilton family interests; his own financial peccadiloes were to be overlooked, his governorship of the kingdom during Mary's minority was guaranteed and he was to receive the dukedom of Chatelherault. His half-brother JOHN (1512–71) was to have his appointment as archbishop of St Andrews confirmed, with the French withdrawing any obstacles at Rome to this.

Militarily the treaty was not particularly significant since the English withdrawal in September 1549 was more for other considerations than the efforts of the Franco-Scottish forces. On the other hand it did underline the sterility of English policy towards Scotland in those years and how it only helped towards the latter increasingly becoming a French satellite.

• *Dickinson, W.C., Donaldson G. and Milne, I. (eds.), A Source Book of Scottish History II, Nelson, 1963.*
• *Donaldson, G., Scotland: James V to James VII, Oliver & Boyd, 1965.*

Haig, Douglas, Earl Haig (1861—1928)

Haig, the most prominent, but by the judgement of some, most infamous of the British military leaders of his generation, was Field-Marshal and Commander-in-Chief of the British Land Forces during much of WORLD WAR I. He was born in Edinburgh, son of John Haig, head of a successful whisky DISTILLING family with its roots in Berwickshire. Haig was at first educated in Edinburgh then went via a preparatory school in Warwickshire to Clifton College. From 1880 he studied at Brasenose College, Oxford, before deciding on a military career and going to the Royal Military College, Sandhurst, in 1884. There he distinguished himself by winning the

Anson Memorial Sword and was afterwards commissioned into the 7th Hussars.

Haig went to India with his regiment in 1886 and there he worked his way through the ranks, gaining considerable field and staff experience. During various periods of home leave he obtained permission to attend cavalry manoeuvres both in France and Germany, and on one occasion he and fellow officers dined with Kaiser William II. After a period at the Staff College, Haig had his first experience of active service in the Sudan (1898), followed rapidly by the South African War (1899—1902), where he served under Major-General French (1852—1925). For his services in the war he was promoted to colonel, became a Commander of the Bath and ADC to King Edward VII (1841—1910). In 1903 he embarked again for India, serving in various administrative posts under Earl Kitchener (1850—1916), notably as inspector-general of cavalry. He was himself given the rank of major-general, thus becoming the youngest officer of that rank in the British or Indian armies.

In 1905 Haig married the Hon. Dorothy Vivian, one of the maids of honour to Queen Alexandria. He returned briefly to India before taking up an important post at the War Office as Director of Military Training (1906—9). There he helped R.B. HALDANE (1856—1928), the Secretary of State for War, establish a general staff, form a Territorial Force as a reserve counter-part of the regular army, and organize an Expeditionary Force to be deployed in event of war. 'By organizing, war may be prevented,' wrote Haig in his diary. After a further period in India as Chief of Staff (1909—11) he returned as commander at Aldershot.

On the outbreak of World War I in August 1914 Haig commanded the 1st Army Corps of the British Expeditionary Force to France and fought in the early battles at Mons, on the Meuse, and at Ypres, where appalling losses were sustained. Towards the end of 1915 he succeeded Sir John French as British Commander-in-Chief on the Western Front. Haig proved to be a stubborn and unimaginative commander, well-regarded by his fellow-officers, but despised by the Prime Minister, Lloyd George (1863—1945), who thought that he wasted lives in the stalemate of trench warfare.

Not until 1918 did either side make much progress. In March Hindenburg and Ludendorff launched a series of offensives aimed at victory in the west before the Americans could arrive in strength. They failed, despite initial success. The French under Marshall Foch (1851—1929), the new Allied Generalissimo, launched the first counteroffensive — followed by Haig's own breakthrough on the Somme. From then on the Allies hammered the enemy until the German capitulation on 11 November. Haig's determination and tenacity had paid off — but at enormous human cost.

Created Earl Haig in 1919 and given a grant of £100,000 by a grateful nation, he spent much of his retirement in work for disabled servicemen, introducing the Poppy Day Appeal, which became associated both with Remembrance Day and his own name. He served for a time as president of the British Legion. The ancestral home of the Haigs at Bemersyde was purchased on his behalf by public subscription and when he died he was buried nearby in Dryburgh Abbey.

• *De Groot, G.J., Douglas Haig, 1861–1928, Unwin Hyman, 1988.*

• *Sixsmith, E.K.G., Douglas Haig, Weidenfeld & Nicolson, 1976.*

Haldane, Richard Burdon, Viscount Haldane (1856—1928)

Haldane, one of the most prominent Scottish politicians of his generation, who became Secretary of State for War 1905–12, was born in Edinburgh and educated at Edinburgh Academy and Edinburgh and Gottingen Universities, graduating in philosophy. Thereafter he went to London to study law, being called to the bar in 1879, and gradually established his reputation as a lawyer specializing in parliamentary work. He became a QC in 1890 and in the course of his legal career advised on many important cases relating to subjects as diverse as the government of Quebec, Scottish petroleum, and the United FREE CHURCH of Scotland (1904).

Meantime his political career had begun in 1885 when he was elected as LIBERAL MP for East Lothian, a seat he held until 1911, when he went to the House of Lords. He was associated with the liberal-imperialists who worked for the Liberal League led by Lord ROSEBERY (1847–1929) and also including H.H. ASQUITH (1852–1928) and Sir Edward Grey (1862–1933). On the formation of the Liberal government in December 1905 Haldane served as Secretary of State for War under Sir Henry CAMPBELL-BANNERMAN (1836–1908) and latterly under Asquith.

On taking office he recognized that 'formidable problems' confronted him, particularly given the criticisms of both the War Office and the army following the South African War (1899–1902) and the concern of his Cabinet colleagues over the level of military spending. Nevertheless he made an extensive study of military reform and saw through the legislation (1907) by which, in the words of Spiers, 'existing forces, regular and auxiliary, could function more effectively in war without becoming an intolerable peacetime burden'. Reforms included the formation of an Imperial General Staff, an Officers' Training Corps, and the Territorial Army. In 1912 Haldane led a mission to Germany seeking to ease the tensions that accompanied the arms race — but to little effect. This event and his intimate knowledge both of the language and the country led him to be nicknamed 'Minister for Germany' in the popular press. During WORLD WAR I his apparent enthusiasm for Anglo-German understanding was to contribute to his downfall.

In 1912 Haldane became Lord Chancellor and during his period in office again addressed himself to reform — this time of legal and constitutional issues and of the House of Lords, though the latter was never pursued. In 1915, on the formation of the Coalition Government under Asquith, Haldane was dropped from office — the 'scapegoat for Liberalism', as one of his biographers has described him.

Asquith's decision to exclude Haldane from the reconstituted ministry — a matter of considerable controversy — was based partly on his identification with German culture and the press campaign against him, and partly it seems by the fact that Haldane continued to be closely identified with reform. In short, his face no longer fitted.

Not surprisingly, Haldane became increasingly estranged from the official Liberal Party, devoting himself primarily to educational reform and the modernization of public administration. He identified himself with Labour and in the 1923 General Election openly campaigned on behalf of Labour candidates. When Ramsay MACDONALD (1866–1937) formed the first Labour government Haldane became Lord Chancellor for the second time. Haldane's public life was linked to the declining fortunes of the Liberal Party, but nevertheless he remained committed to the reforming zeal that characterized Liberal ideology in the early 1900s.

• Ross, S.E., Lord Haldane, Scapegoat for Liberalism, Columbia University Press, 1969.
• Spiers, F.M., Haldane: An Army Reformer, Edinburgh University Press, 1980.

Hamilton, Sir Ian (1853—1947)
General Sir Ian Hamilton, though born in Corfu where his father was serving as an officer with the Gordon Highlanders, spent his boyhood in Argyll. Entering the army in 1875 he subsequently saw action in India, Afghanistan, Sudan, Burma and South Africa. During this period Hamilton was mentioned in dispatches on three occasions and also recommended for a Victoria Cross. At the same he

displayed for a soldier an unfashionable interest music, painting and literature and, later, his own version of events in the Dardanelles, Gallipoli Diary, would be published after WORLD WAR I. In 1914 he was recalled by general Kitchener from Malta where he had been commander of the Mediterranean forces, to take over Britain's wartime defences. In March 1915, aged 62, Hamilton was appointed commander of the Mediterranean Expeditionary Force; he was ordered to capture Constantinople with the questionable assurance that if he did he would 'not only win a campaign, but the war.'

However the Gallipoli offensive ended in disaster with the evacuation of Hamilton's armies and his own dismissal beforehand. Undoubtedly Hamilton was bedevilled by the poor quality of many of his subordinates such as generals Hunter-Weston and Stopford. Yet, by his inability to exercise sufficient control over them, he too must take some of the blame for the Gallipoli fiasco. Unfortunately, as A.J.P. Taylor succinctly observed, 'he was too polite to be a good general in the field.'

• James R. Rhodes, Gallipoli, London, 1965.

Hamilton, James, second Earl of Arran, Duke of Chatelherault (c.1516—75) He succeeded his father, James, first Earl of Arran (?1477–1529), in January 1543 and, following the death of JAMES V (1512–42), become Governor during the minority of MARY, QUEEN OF SCOTS (1542–87). The hallmarks of his regency were inconstancy and a keen eye for the interests of his family. Thus in 1543 he initially favoured an English alliance but by the end of the year he had repudiated the Treaty of Greenwich signed between the two countries. This change of heart was the consequence of a variety of factors, the strength of his political rivals MARY OF GUISE (1516–60) and BEATON (1494–1546), the advice of his influential natural brother, John Hamilton (1512–71), and not least, the arrival in Scotland of Matthew, Earl of Lennox (1516–71). The latter was next in line to the succession after Arran and since there was always some doubt about the validity of the divorce of the Regent's father, Lennox could be utilized by his opponents as a serious rival. His volte-face was largely responsible for Henry VIII (1491–1547) adopting the policy known as the 'ROUGH WOOING'. By the end of 1547 and shortly after the battle of PINKIE, Arran was openly supporting France. Again, his motives were predominantly personal, namely the promise of a French dukedom if he would agree to Mary ultimately marrying the Dauphin and being sent to France. These terms and certain others were incorporated in the Treaty of HADDINGTON July 1548 and in February 1549 Arran became Duke of Chatelherault. By 1553, Mary of Guise was in a strong enough position to persuade the Duke to surrender his regency to her. Her inducements included various financial rewards, ecclesiastical preferments for his family and a guarantee of support for his dynastic claims.

Chatelherault joined the LORDS OF THE CONGREGATION in September 1559 once his son JAMES, Earl of Arran (1538–1609), had been released from French custody. Not surprisingly he opposed Mary's marriage to DARNLEY (1546–67) joining MORAY (1531–70) and the others in the CHASEABOUT RAID in August–September 1565. After its defeat he retired to his duchy in France, remaining abroad until 1569 when he returned to become a supporter of the exiled Mary. He was imprisoned by Moray's government in August 1569 and his last significant action was to be a signatory of the Treaty of PERTH in February 1573, which finally brought the civil war in Scotland to an end.

Hamilton, James, third Earl of Arran (1538—1609)   The eldest son of James HAMILTON, second Earl of Arran, Duke of Chatelherault (c.1516–75) his elevation to his earldom is usually dated from the time of his father's acquisition of his French duchy in 1549. Earlier, he had been put forward as a possible husband of both Elizabeth (1533–1603) and MARY (1542–87). Henry VIII (1491–1547) had offered this as an inducement for his father's support in the negotiations for an Anglo-Scottish alliance and once these arrangements had been repudiated the alternative proposition was equally attractive to the ambitious Hamiltons. He was held hostage at the siege of ST ANDREWS CASTLE, which partly accounts for the Regent's inept handling of this episode in 1546–7, and thereafter he spent much of his time in France in pursuit of elusive French heiresses. Being converted to Protestantism he returned, not without some difficulty, to Scotland in 1559, joined the LORDS OF THE CONGREGATION and was a signatory to the Treaty of BERWICK. In 1560–61 he was again suggested as a husband of Elizabeth, whom he had actually met on his homeward journey in 1559, but a Scottish mission to London to pursue his case met with no success. His name was once more linked with Mary but by 1562 there were already signs of the madness from which he suffered for the rest of his life. In 1581 he was temporarily deprived of his title by James STEWART, Earl of Arran (c.1545–96) but it was restored in 1585 on the latter's downfall.

Hamilton, James, third Marquis and first Duke of (1606—49) Born in England where his father, James, the second Marquis (1589–1625) had been rewarded for his services to JAMES VI (1566–1625) by the earldom of Cambridge, he became an English privy councillor in 1628. Following service in the armies of Sweden in the early 1630s, he was appointed commissioner to the GENERAL ASSEMBLY in 1638 when his efforts on behalf of CHARLES I (1600—49) were conspicuously unsuccessful. Thus the members ignored his condemnation of their actions and proceeded to abolish episcopacy in the Church. In 1639 he was in charge of the royal fleet operating off the east coast of Scotland in the first BISHOPS' WAR but the plan to land troops in support of the royalist Huntly (c.1592–1649) encountered little success.

He returned to Scotland in 1642 on a mission to exploit any divisions among the Covenanting leadership and so prevent Scottish intervention on behalf of the English Parliamentarians. His endeavours were appreciated by the king who bestowed a dukedom on the Marquis in April 1643 but the signing of the SOLEMN LEAGUE AND COVENANT later that year caused Charles to revise his opinions of Hamilton. Accordingly, in 1644, he was arrested and imprisoned for the remainder of the first Civil War. Despite this treatment he remained loyal to the Crown, being an enthusiastic supporter of the ENGAGEMENT and commanding the forces defeated at Preston in August 1648. Indeed his loyalty proved to be his downfall since he was executed in London by the Parliamentarians on 9 March 1649.

Hamilton, James Douglas, fourth Duke of (1658—1712) Although a son of the formidable Duchess Anne (1632–1716) he displayed few of his mother's qualities and his whole career was characterized by irresolute and capricious behaviour. This was notably the case during his period as leader of the Country Party between 1702 and 1707 when on two critical occasions in 1706 and 1707 he completely failed to provide the leadership that the opposition was seeking. Thus, in September 1706, having given his support to the proposal that the Scottish PARLIAMENT should select its own commissioners for the discussions on the Treaty of UNION he suddenly changed his mind and moved that Queen ANNE (1665–1714) should undertake this function. Again, in January 1707, at a vital stage in the negotiations, when his support was required for a proposed withdrawal from the assembly by all the members of the opposition, he wavered at the last minute and refused to give the necessary lead. This may have been the result of government pressure on him behind the scenes because of his secret dealings with the Jacobites — he claimed he had severe toothache at one point — but it undoubtedly had the effect of ensuring the collapse of any successful protest against the Union within Scotland. Latterly, before his sudden death in a fatal duel with Lord Mohun (1675–1712), he was at the centre of the dispute over his new peerage. Created Duke of Brandon in 1711 in return for supporting the TORIES, the opposition in the Lords proceeded to deny Hamilton the right to an hereditary seat in the House. This caused immense resentment among all sections of the Scottish nobility and had considerable bearing on the subsequent campaign in 1713 to annul the Treaty of Union.

Hamilton, John (1512—71) A natural son of James Hamilton, first Earl of Arran (c.1477–1529), he first came to prominence during the regency of his half-brother James HAMILTON, second Earl of Arran (c.1516–75) when, on his return from the Continent, he was persuaded to give his support to the rival Francophile faction headed by MARY OF GUISE (1516–60) and Cardinal BEATON (c.1494–1546). Consequently, he contributed towards Arran's decision to repudiate the Treaty of Greenwich signed with HENRY VIII (1491–1547). In 1547, having previously been Commendator of Paisley and, briefly, Bishop of Dunkeld, he became the last archbishop of St

Andrews before the REFORMATION. His summoning of provincial Councils of the Church in 1549, 1552 and 1559 was a notable, if unsuccessful, attempt at remedying some of its more glaring abuses. The Catechism, issued under his authority in 1552, was an essentially moderate and conciliatory publication as far as many aspects of doctrine were concerned. None the less, Hamilton refused to join the LORDS OF THE CONGREGATION and remained aloof from events in 1560 when the Reformation took place. Thus, the rest of his career was an undistinguished one; he was imprisoned by MARY (1542–87) between 1563 and 1565 for celebrating mass but, with the rest of his family, became a committed Marian after her deposition; he played an active role in the CIVIL WAR and was closely implicated in the assassination of MORAY (1531–70). These activities were largely responsible for the decision to have him hanged at Stirling in April 1571, following his capture at Dumbarton Castle.
•*Herkless, J. and Hannay, R.K., The Archbishops of St Andrews, Blackwood, 1915.*

Hardie, Andrew, see RADICAL WAR

Hardie, James Keir (1856—1915) Hardie was one of the leading members of the early labour movement, to which he made a significant contribution both in Scotland and beyond. Like J. Ramsay MACDONALD (1866–1937), Hardie, born in 1856, was illegitimate, the son of Mary Keir, a farm servant in a small village near the COAL mining town of Holytown in Lanarkshire. Three years later his mother married David Hardie, a ship's carpenter, and the boy took his stepfather's surname. Two of Hardie's brothers subsequently played their own modest roles in the labour movement.

When Hardie was five the family moved to Glasgow where his step-father found irregular work in the shipyards. The family was so poor that Hardie never had any regular education and by the time he was seven was working as a message boy. Several years later — in the aftermath of a lock-out in the ship-yards — David Hardie could get no work and went back to sea. The family went to Newarthill, Lanarkshire, where young Hardie's grandmother lived. Hardie got a job in the mine as a 'trapper' — opening and closing doors under-ground. He attended night school and began to read avidly, mainly Scottish history and the works of Thomas CARLYLE (1795—1881) and Robert BURNS (1759—96). He said that his socialism derived much from the latter: 'I owe more to Burns than to any man living or dead.'

By the time Hardie was in his late teens the family moved to the pit village of Quarter, near Hamilton, where he became a hewer in the local colliery. Like many other Labour politicians he embraced temperance work and this gave him his first public platform. It was a logical step from this to trade unionism and Hardie became the miners' spokesman. Inevitably, this led to his dismissal and in 1878 he opened a tobacconist's shop in Hamilton and began writing for the PRESS in a RADICAL paper, the *Glasgow Weekly Mail*. Following his marriage in 1879 he became corresponding secretary and later

agent of the Lanarkshire miners. Although he could soon claim to be National Secretary of the Scottish Miners, the reality was that he and others like Alexander Macdonald (1823—81) were to have a long struggle to unionize the pits.

After a strike in the Lanarkshire coalfield in 1880, Hardie moved to Ayrshire, where he lived in Cumnock, continued his union work among the miners, and wrote for the *Ardrossan & Saltcoats Herald* and an offshoot, the *Cumnock News,* which he later edited. He also threw himself into LIBERAL politics, although he gradu-ally became disillusioned and turned slowly to socialism. In 1887 he was nominated as the miners' candidate for North Ayrshire. His relationship with official Liberalism continued to be ambivalent during the Mid-Lanark by-election of 1888 when he stood as an Independent Labour candidate. Soon after he helped found the Scottish LABOUR Party and became increasingly involved in the political work of the Trades Union Congress.

This made his name known out-side Scotland and he was then adopted as a candidate in West Ham — winning the seat as an Independent Labour MP in the General Election of 1892. In an unlikely gesture Andrew CARNEGIE (1835—1919) contributed £100 to his election fund. Hardie's first term in Parliament (1892—95) was characterized by speeches in sup-port of the unemployed and labour — as well the famous 'Royal Baby' speech (1894) when he protested against the time-wasting over a motion of congratulation to the Duke and Duchess of York on the birth of a son. This made Hardie a national, if notorious and enigmatic, figure.

Hardie founded the Independent Labour Party (ILP) in 1893 and much influenced the socialist objectives of its programme. He edited the weekly *Labour Leader* from 1894–1904 and the rest of his time was devoted mainly to propaganda and speech-making the length and breadth of the country. He was defeated at the General Election of 1895, partly because he had been preoccupied with national affairs and spent so little time in West Ham. He returned to Parliament as MP for Merthyr Tydfil in 1900, which was also the year he played a leading role in the establishment of the Labour Representation Committee. He became leader of the Parliamentary Labour Party in 1906, when the great reforming Liberal government came to power. Thirty Labour MPs were elected and several important figures entered Westminster, including Ramsay MacDonald and Philip Snowden (1864–1937).

Thereafter Hardie was gradually worn down by years of incessant travelling, hundreds of meetings, irregular meals and illness. Despite these difficulties he made an important contribution to the development of international co-operation and pacifism among socialist parties in Britain and on the Continent. He was temperamentally unsuited to the leadership of the parliamentary party and resigned in 1911 when MacDonald took over. The outbreak of WORLD WAR I shattered many of Hardie's lifetime beliefs and he died, supposedly of a broken heart and

betrayed by many of his comrades, in 1915. In retrospect Keir Hardie's work was by no means destroyed in 1914, for World War I was vital to the rise of the Labour Party, putting it in a much stronger position to make the breakthrough in terms of votes and form a minority government with Liberal support in 1924.

•*Benn C., Keir Hardie, Hutchinson, 1992.*
•*McLean, I., Keir Hardie, Allen Lane, 1975.*
•*Morgan, K.O., Keir Hardie, Radical and Socialist, Weidenfeld & Nicolson, 1975.*
•*Reid, F., Keir Hardie: The Making of a Socialist, Croom Helm, 1978.*

Hay, John, second Marquis of Tweeddale (1645—1713) A member of the Privy Council in the reign of WILLIAM III (1650–1702) Hay came to prominence in the events leading to the Treaty of UNION. Initially a notable member of the opposition or Country Party, he was chosen as Royal Commissioner in July 1704 on the understanding that he and his followers, who were soon to be known as the New Party, would help to resolve the political impasse created by the proposed ACT OF SECURITY. However, Tweeddale found it impossible to persuade either his faction or the opposition to concede any dilution of the bill and in August 1704 had to agree to accept an Act of Security virtually unaltered from the original. Although he failed to guarantee the Hanoverian succession he was still regarded favourably by the English government, possibly because he was more honest than most of his

Scottish colleagues, and it was only his weak handling of the WORCESTER AFFAIR early in 1705 that brought about his dismissal. By that date his own party, now also entitled the Squadrone Volante, was seriously divided, especially over its reaction to the ALIEN ACT, and he had forfeited most of their support as well.

hearth tax rolls   Dating from 1683–4, the hearth tax rolls give lists of hearths, with the names of householders, and thus provide a useful source of population and genealogical data. Those who paid tax, those who failed to do so, and the poor are listed. The extant rolls are almost complete for Scotland — excluding the northern counties (except Sutherland, for which returns survive). They can be compared with the POLL TAX RETURNS and the CENSUS records.

Henderson, Alexander (1583— 1646)   Appointed minister of Leuchars, Fife in 1612, Henderson became prominent in the events leading to the signing of the NATIONAL COVENANT. Thus, in 1637, following the introduction of the PRAYER BOOK, he was a signatory along with Balmerino (d.1649), Loudon (1598–1663) and another minister, David Dickson (1583– 1663), of a petition requesting that CHARLES I (1600–49) should suspend bishops from his Privy Council for the duration of the Prayer Book controversy. In February 1638 he was one of the authors of the National Covenant while, later that year, he was moderator at the momentous GLASGOW ASSEMBLY. During the first BISHOPS' WAR (1639) he was one of the commissioners who negotiated the Pacification of Berwick with the king. In 1641 Charles, in a vain effort to detach Henderson and certain others from the Covenanting cause promoted him to Dean of the Chapel Royal, at Holyrood. In 1643, before the signing of the SOLEMN LEAGUE AND COVENANT, he and Loudon visited Charles to warn him that the only way he could prevent Scottish support for the English Parliamentarians was by making drastic changes in the Anglican Church. Later that year he was one of the leading Scottish delegates at the WESTMINSTER ASSEMBLY.

Henderson, although dedicated to the principles of the National Covenant, was not a religious fanatic and his influence on events, in contrast with some of his colleagues, was essentially a moderating one.

• *Orr, R. L., Alexander Henderson, Hodder & Stoughton, 1919.*

Hepburn, James, fourth Earl of Bothwell (c.1535—78) Hepburn succeeded in 1556, on the death of his father, to the earldom and also the hereditary offices of admiral, Sheriff of Berwickshire, Haddingtonshire and Edinburgh, as well as the custody of Crichton and Hailes castles. Although a Protestant he supported MARY OF GUISE (1516– 60) against the LORDS OF THE CONGREGATION causing considerable damage to their fortunes in October 1559 by his seizure of English bullion intended for them. He played little significant part in events between 1561 and 1565 but was recalled in that year to MARY'S (1542–87) government to render assistance against the CHASEABOUT RAID. He now assumed a more important role in the nation's affairs being present with Huntly (d.1576), Argyll (1538–73), MAITLAND (c.1525–73) and other notables at Craigmillar Castle in November 1566 when the fate of DARNLEY (1546–67) was discussed at some length. His actual contribution to events at Kirk o' Field in February 1567 must remain conjectural but he was certainly very closely involved in the murder and regarded by many as a key suspect. However an attempt in April by Lennox (1516–71) to make him stand trial was thwarted by the presence of so many Hepburns in Edinburgh. The next month, having ended his marriage to a daughter of Huntly by obtaining a divorce from the Commissary Court, not to mention a decree of nullity from the court of the Archbishop of St Andrews as well, Bothwell was in a position to fulfil his major objective, namely marriage to the Queen. Thus on 15 May he married Mary at Holyrood and almost immediately precipitated the inevitable jealous reaction from other leading magnates that plunged the country into a brief civil war.

When the opposing forces met at Carberry, near Musselburgh, Bothwell suggested deciding the issue by personal combat but the Queen preferred to surrender in return for a safe conduct for her consort. The latter was soon forced to seek refuge in Orkney and Shetland – a dukedom to which he had been appointed in May – and thereafter in Norway. He died in prison at Dragsholm Castle, Zeeland, in 1578, the victim of the vengeance of the kinsmen of a Danish woman whom he had wronged in his dissolute earlier career.

• *Gore-Brown, R.F., Lord Bothwell, Collins, 1937.*

heritable jurisdictions   Early Scottish kings encouraged the delegation of their judicial authority by granting heritable jurisdictions to various noblemen. Thus some magnates were granted regalities with courts that could handle all offences except treason, while others were given baronies.

In addition, the office of SHERIFF frequently remained in the hands of the same family. By the eighteenth century, while some regalities had been forfeited and others, along with the baronies, had lost most of their power and influence, there still existed a bewildering complexity of legal bodies. However, it was because heritable courts operated to a greater extent in the HIGHLANDS not to mention the support given by certain sections of the nobility for the JACOBITES, that finally convinced the London government of the necessity for a long overdue overhaul of the judicial system. Accordingly, in 1747, heritable jurisdictions were to all intents and purposes abolished and their functions in future were to be performed by Justices of the Peace, COMMISSIONERS OF SUPPLY and government officials.

• *Whetstone, A., Scottish County Government in the Eighteenth and Nineteenth Centuries, John Donald, 1981.*

Highlands   In geographical terms the large mountainous area in the centre and west of Scotland whose height separates it from the fertile lowlands of the north east, the Forth and Clyde plain and the southern uplands. In the sixteenth and seventeenth centuries it largely marked the linguistic division between Gaelic and English while also presenting, containing as it did about one-third of the country's population, serious administrative problems to such kings as JAMES IV (1473–1513), JAMES V (1512–42) and JAMES VI (1566–1625). Their solution, to a large extent, was to rely on powerful families like the Campbells and Mackenzies to govern on the Crown's behalf. After the REFORMATION the Highlands became one of the few parts of the kingdom where the Catholic Church survived, although this only partly explains the support given by many of the clans to the JACOBITE REBELLIONS. Thereafter, the population was seriously reduced by the effects of the CLEARANCES not to mention the extensive recruiting of Highland REGIMENTS in these years. Towards the end of the nineteenth century, at least until the passing of the Crofters' Act (1886), the grievances of the crofting community were a major issue creating bitter hostility towards certain landowners. Today it is a region dominated in some parts by the doctrines of the FREE CHURCH and mainly dependent on tourism for a livelihood.

• *Clyde, R., From Rebel to Hero: The Image of the Highlander, Tuckwell Press, 1995.*

• *Devine, T.M., From Clanship to Crofters' War: the Social Transformation of the Scottish Highlands, Manchester University Press, 1994.*

• *Fenyo, K., Contempt, Sympathy and Romance, Tuckwell Press, 1999.*

Highland and Agricultural Society Many local or regional agricultural societies were established in Scotland during the Age of IMPROVEMENT, but the Highland Society of Edinburgh (as it was originally called), founded in 1784, proved one of the longest-lasting and most influential. Its membership was national, noblemen and gentlemen of rank, property and professional eminence', including the ubiquitous Sir John SINCLAIR (1754–1835). While its initial objects were improving the HIGHLANDS and Islands and preserving their language and culture, it concentrated mainly on AGRICULTURE, publishing influential transactions and offering prizes for essays describing good practice in husbandry and land use. During the nineteenth century it gradually expanded its activities and its annual show became a highlight of the farming calendar.

• *Davidson, J.D.G., The Royal Highland and Agricultural Society of Scotland. A Short History: 1784–1984, RHASS, 1984.*

Highland Host (1678) Although some of the dissident Presbyterian clergy accepted the Indulgences proffered by Lauderdale (1616–82), there was a determined minority of ministers who rejected all such offers. Since suppression of their illegal conventicles posed certain difficulties to the government's existing military strength, Lauderdale devised the expedient early in 1678 of billeting detachments of Highland troops, as well as some Lowland militia, in the strongly covenanting areas of Renfrewshire and Ayrshire. This was the highly unpopular

'Highland Host', designed to put pressure on both landowners and tenants in the districts affected. In fact it did nothing to abate the activity of the COVENANTERS and, although this policy only lasted for five weeks, it contributed to the growing unrest in the southwest of Scotland that erupted into rebellion in 1679.
• *Elder, J.R., The Highland Host of 1678, Aberdeen University Press, 1914.*

Highland Land League, see CLEARANCES; CROFTERS' COMMISSION

home rule   The earliest efforts to bring a measure of home rule by devolving Scottish decision-making from Westminster coincided with parallel moves in Ireland, with the rise of popular Scottish nationalism, Highland radicalism and Lowland socialism during the 1880s. The Prime Minister, Gladstone (1809–1898), responded positively to the agitation – as he had to the CROFTERS' COMMISSION findings – by re-establishing the post of Secretary for Scotland and setting up the SCOTTISH OFFICE in 1885. Although the party lacked a logical policy, the Scottish LIBERALS broadly supported home rule and some of their number played a prominent part in the Scottish Home Rule Association, founded in 1886. The Scottish LABOUR movement had home rule for Scotland as one of the key points in its early programmes and it remained on the agenda of INDEPENDENT LABOUR PARTY conferences for many years.

Another notable politician, Lord ROSEBERY (1847–1929), was at first an advocate of devolution, though he had abandoned the cause long before he became Prime Minister in 1894. However, the same year

the House of Commons passed by a small majority a motion in favour of 'a legislature in Scotland for dealing with purely Scottish affairs, while retaining intact the power and supremacy of the Imperial Parliament'. In the event, a Scottish Grand Committee was established to deal with essentially non-controversial Scottish bills, and though all Scottish MPs sat on it their number could be supplemented by others at any time to preserve the prevailing party balance.

Although the great reforming Liberal governments under CAMPBELL-BANNERMAN (1836–1908) and Asquith (1852–1928) were sympathetic to Scottish Home Rule, other measures took priority. Yet no fewer than six bills for home rule were introduced in Parliament between 1908 and 1914. Although the majority of Scottish MPs voted in favour none got beyond a second reading. The same was true of the inter-war period: on nine occasions bills or motions proposing home rule in some form were presented to Parliament but were ultimately thrown out.

Meantime, the Scottish Home Rule Association was revived in 1917 by Roland Muirhead (1868–1964) and growing nationalist sentiment throughout the twenties led to the formation of the National Party of Scotland in 1928. It amalgamated with the later Scottish Self-Government Party (1932) to form the SCOTTISH NATIONAL PARTY in 1934.

Although home rule was hardly an issue of any party political consequence the government was forced into acknowledging the increasing burden of Scottish business raising the status of the

Secretary for Scotland to that of Secretary of State and giving him additional junior ministerial support in 1926.

In 1939 the Scottish Office was transferred from Whitehall to St Andrew's House in Edinburgh.

Tom JOHNSTON (1881–1965), when Secretary of State 1941–45, greatly enhanced its powers over economic and social affairs.

None of these developments assuaged the home rulers, particularly those closely associated with the Scottish Convention during the late 1940s and early 50s. Several headline provoking incidents involving nationalists included the removal of the Stone of Destiny from Westminster Abbey and its brief repatriation to Scotland in 1950. Politically such gestures had little impact for neither Labour (having long abandoned it in any case) nor the Tories had much truck with home rule during the 1950s and 60s.

With economic troubles and the nationalist revival home rule became a major issue again during the 1970s — causing renewed confusion and vacillation among the British political parties. Although independence remained a top priority for the SNP, with the Welsh nationalist party, Plaid Cymru, it helped force the Labour government's hand on devolution for Scotland and Wales. The Act to establish a Scottish Assembly was given the Royal Assent in 1978 — though subject to a referendum with a 40 per cent threshold in favour. The referendum in 1979 showed 33 per cent in favour and 31 per cent against, so the devolution initiative failed. With the early demise of the Labour government

and the return of a Conservative administration devolution slipped from the political agenda. Support for home rule revived during the 1980s and 90s, notably through the work of the Campaign for a Scottish Assembly.

Following the return of a Labour government in 1997 another referendum resulted in a majority favouring the establishment of a Scottish Parliament. The first election was held and the parliament duly convened in 1999. For further details see entries under PARLIAMENT, LABOUR PARTY, SCOTTISH NATIONAL PARTY and CONSERVATIVE PARTY.

•*Fry, M., Patronage and Principle: A Political History of Modern Scotland, Aberdeen University Press, 1987.*
•*Harvie, C., No Gods and Precious Few Heroes: Scotland 1914–1980, Edward Arnold, 1981.*
•*Jones, C. (ed.), The Scots and Parliament, Edinburgh University Press, 1996.*

housing   Although by the mid-eighteenth century Scotland was still essentially a rural society URBANIZATION had been a feature since the early modern era. The urban population was concentrated in the BURGHS and growing numbers of planned villages. Edinburgh, the largest centre, was perhaps an exception in the pre-industrial era, as it was growing quite rapidly from the beginning of the eighteenth century and soon showed some of the problems that were encountered later by others towns. There the press of population and increasingly unsanitary conditions in the tenements of the Old Town led to the building of the NEW TOWN, with its classical

Georgian squares and housing, peopled by the middle and upper classes. Given the impact of the INDUSTRIAL REVOLUTION rapid urbanization followed especially in the central lowlands, notably in Glasgow and Dundee, though many other industrial towns, such as Paisley and Kirkcaldy, also expanded rapidly. MIGRATION from surrounding rural districts, from the HIGHLANDS and from Ireland largely accounted for the increase in urban population. Given the close juxtaposition of industry with dwellings, the housing stock in town centres rapidly became overcrowded, creating slum conditions. Stone tenement housing, often of three or four stories, became common, partly because of the high cost of the land feu and partly because of Scottish property law. Hence, as elsewhere in continental Europe (but unlike the English cottage style back-to-back housing, which had its own problems) best use could be made of expensive land near towns centres and workplaces. But the tenement resulted in very high densities, often in single rooms or 'single-ends', as they were commonly known. For middle-class critics tenement life brought with it the horrors of ill-health, immorality and crime. It certainly led to gross overcrowding where infectious diseases, notably TB, could readily be transmitted from one individual to another. Victorian civic pride (perhaps also shame and fear) led to important local slum clearance programmes under improvement acts for Glasgow (1866) and then Edinburgh (1875), which rid some parts of the city centres of overcrowding, but effectively transferred the problems to neighbouring districts. At this time there were also some early efforts to provide worker's housing in places like Edinburgh (1860s) and Rutherglen (1870s) where CO-OPERATIVE building projects resulted in artisan colonies. But the resort was generally to rented accommodation in streets of tenement dwellings, typical of the later Victorian building boom in Scotland. A Royal Commission on the Housing of the Working Classes (1885) concluded that Scottish conditions were different from those in England and that housing and related improvements depended strongly on local civic initiatives but that this varied enormously from town to town. Meantime the bulk of new housing, including that for the middle class, continued to be built by private landlords and speculators and often in suburbs served either by RAILWAY or tramway. Working class housing was typically overcrowded, some of the worst occurring in the mining and iron districts of places like Coatbridge and Motherwell where there were large immigrant populations. The work of a Royal Commission on the state of Scottish housing was interrupted by WORLD WAR I, during which the Rent Strike of 1915 drew attention not only to high rents but also the generally appalling housing conditions in some parts of the country. Following the Royal Commission's report in 1917 the government announced a crash programme of reconstruction and slum clearance, to build state-subsidized local authority housing. Over 200,000 new houses were needed to replace the slums and for more general needs, the Scottish quota of the 'homes fit for heroes' promised by the government. A start was made but the onset of economic DEPRESSION meant that by the early 1920s only about 25,000 houses had been completed. The WHEATLEY Act sought to encourage further building and this policy was continued by the succeeding CONSERVATIVE government. By 1928 Scottish local authorities were building 20,000 houses annually and it was predicted that the earlier Royal Commission's target would be met by the mid-1930s. These programmes resulted in the first major housing estates, often with 'garden city' planning typical of the period. After WORLD WAR II post-war reconstruction under the third LABOUR administration resulted in greater government intervention in town and country planning and housing policy. Major slum clearance programmes in the cities and towns were accompanied by overspill schemes, resettling population in towns beyond the major conurbations, and the development from the late 1940s of the NEW TOWNS. These initiatives were continued by subsequent governments, but while they created new communities and new jobs, they also contributed to the decline of the older communities, where tenements were pulled down to be replaced by high-rise, often even higher density housing. Population was also invariably decanted to suburban housing schemes lacking the facilities previously available in the re-developed inner city districts. While such policies were either reversed or modified after the 1970s, the legacy of these schemes

was sometimes deprivation, the very thing planners and local authorities had set out to alleviate.

•Begg, T., Fifty Special Years: A Study in Scottish Housing, Melland, 1987.
•Begg, T. and Carruthers, A.(eds.), The Scottish Home, National Museums of Scotland, 1996.
•Gauldie, E., Cruel Habitations. A History of Working Class Housing, 1780—1914, Allen & Unwin, 1974.
•Rodger, R. (ed.), Scottish Housing in the Twentieth Century, 1989.

hospitals, see MEDICINE

Hudson's Bay Company, see SELKIRK

Hume, David (1711—76) David Hume, perhaps the most notable and controversial figure of the Scottish ENLIGHTENMENT, was born in Edinburgh in 1811, the son of Joseph Hume of Ninewells, a Berwickshire laird who had married the daughter of Lord Newton, a judge of the Court of Session. Attending the University of Edinburgh, supposedly to study law, he seems to have spent most of the time in literary and philosophical pursuits. After a brief period working in the office of a Bristol merchant, in 1734 he reached a turning point in his career and went to France. There he devoted himself to study and writing his first major philosophical work, *A Treatise of Human Nature* (1739—40). He returned to London to supervise its publication. The *Treatise* is considered the most outstanding book written by any British philosopher, but in Hume's own time it was a flop. It fell, as he put it, 'stillborn from the press'. Hume's *Treatise* was divided into three books: 'Of

Understanding'; 'Of the Passions'; and 'Of Morals'. Overall, this was an attempt to formulate a complete philosophical system: Book I aimed at explaining man's process of knowing and dealt with the origin of ideas, space and time, causality and scepticism; Book II tried to explain the emotional in man, giving reason a subordinate role in the process; while Book III looked at moral goodness and considered human behaviour in the light of its consequences to oneself and others. Hume later repudiated much of the *Treatise* as juvenile, though it remained a work of vital importance to the development of empiricism.

He moved back to Edinburgh in 1740, working there and at Ninewells on his next venture, *Essays, Moral and Political* (1741–42), which had a better reception. He was encouraged to apply for the chair of moral philosophy at Edinburgh in 1744 but objections were raised on the grounds of both heresy and atheism — with the *Treatise* cited as evidence. Disappointed, he resumed a wandering life, returning periodically to London and Scotland. First he was tutor to the Marquess of Annandale (1745–46), then served as secretary to General James Sinclair (d.1762) in Brittany (1746) and on ambassadorial missions to Vienna and Turin (1748–49).

Several important philosophical works derived from this period. A further *Three Essays, Moral and Political* (1748) and *Philosophical Essays Concerning Human Understanding* (also 1748). The latter was a re-working of Book I of the *Treatise*, to which he later added the controversial essay, 'On

Miracles', which denied that a miracle could be proved by any weight of evidence. This work is now better known as *An Enquiry Concerning Human Understanding*, the title given it in Hume's revision of 1758. Book III of the Treatise was also rewritten and popularized in *An Enquiry Concerning the Principles of Morals* (1751).

Following the publication of these books — which are generally regarded as his most mature works — he settled again in Edinburgh where he lived from 1751–63. Adam SMITH (1723–90), the political economist, tried to get Hume appointed as his successor to the chair of logic at the University of Glasgow, but as before he was regarded as suspiciously anti-establishment and atheistic. Yet in 1752, thanks to influence in high places, he was appointed keeper of the Advocates' Library and this gave him the opportunity for further literary ventures — philosophical and historical. His *Political Discourses* (1752) included some important statements on economics, anticipating the work of Smith in *The Wealth of Nations*, while the six-volume *History of England* (1754–62) brought him much wider publicity. Another book, *Four Dissertations* (1757) incorporated a re-working of Book II of the *Treatise*. In 1761 the Vatican banned all his books, though James Boswell (1740–95) regarded him as the greatest writer in Britain.

In 1763 Hume became secretary to the British ambassador to France, the Earl of Hertford. While in Paris he was universally honoured in the salons and at court.

For a period in 1765 he was chargé d'affaires at the embassy and when he returned to London in 1766 he brought with him the eminent French philosopher Jean-Jacques Rousseau (1712–78). They later quarrelled and Rousseau returned to France. During 1767–68 Hume was under-secretary to Henry Conway (1721–95).

Hume returned again to Edinburgh in 1769, where he joined his old circle of acquaintances and fellow-literati, entertained visiting dignitaries in his EDINBURGH NEW TOWN residence, revised his earlier writings, and wrote his autobiography. He died in 1776 and was buried on Calton Hill. Hume was regarded by his contemporaries as an outstanding thinker and this reputation has been revived thanks to his continuing influence on modern philosophy.

• *Mossner, F.C., The Life of David Hume, Oxford University Press, 1980.*

Hunter, William, see MEDICINE

Huntly, Earl of, see GORDON, GEORGE, FOURTH EARL OF HUNTLY

I

immigration A number of immigrant groups from outwith the British isles have settled in Scotland during the modern period.

The first known Jewish resident in Scotland was Abraham of Edinburgh, who is recorded as having lent £80 to Robert de Quincy in 1171. A document dated 11 November of that year attests to the agreement between Robert de Quincy and the monks of Newbattle Abbey under which he grants them his lands for twenty years in return for helping him to pay debts to 'Abraham the Jew'. There is little evidence of Jews resident in Scotland in the medieval period, though English-based traders and merchants may have been visitors (or 'sojourners'). Scotland lacked the anti-Jewish laws that existed in England and other countries.

Jews began to resettle in England from 1656, and by the mid-eighteenth century they numbered several thousand, growing with the arrival of Sephardic and Ashkenazi Jews. Small settlements existed in England provincial towns, but none in Scotland. From the seventeenth century, Scottish universities began to attract Jewish medical students from England and further abroad, as students here were not required to take a religious oath.

Many came to study but did not graduate; the first Jewish graduate of Glasgow University was Levi Myers of South Carolina, who received a medical degree in 1787. Some years later another South Carolinian, Mordechai Marx, became the first Jewish undergraduate at Glasgow; he studied Arts.

Jewish settlement in Scotland was nevertheless slow to develop. From the late eighteenth century, English Jews (typically merchants) made regular though brief visits to Glasgow and by 1800 an increasing number began to settle permanently. Jewish agents of Hamburg TEXTILE and shipping companies set up offices in Dundee and Glasgow in the early nineteenth century, but the German Jews did not form a distinct community as in Bradford. There is some dispute regarding the first Jew to settle permanently in Glasgow. Herman Lion, an Edinburgh-based chiropodist and dentist, settled in Glasgow in April 1790. His business involved the relief of suffering: ingrown toenails, corns, and rotting teeth. Another accorded this distinction is Isaac Cohen, who was admitted as burgess in September 1812; he is credited with the introduction of the silk hat into Scotland.

The formal establishment of Jewish communities in Glasgow and Edinburgh came only in early nineteenth century. Jewish artisan and merchant families from England and the Continent began to settle and achieve diverse employment; a synagogue was established in Edinburgh in 1816. The Glasgow Hebrew Congregation was founded in September 1823 and the first Jewish burial ground in the city was established at Necropolis in 1831 with the blessing of the Merchants' House of Glasgow — evidence of good relations with the newcomers.

In the 1830s, Presbyterian evangelical bodies began to send missionaries amongst the Jews; a Scottish branch of the Society for the Promotion of Christianity to the Jews was formed in 1838, and recorded that '...only in recent years has the Jewish cause been brought into the view of the Church of Scotland.' According to 1831 census, the Jewish community of Glasgow stood at forty-seven; eleven had come from Prussian Poland, twelve from Germany, three from Holland, fifteen from England, and five were Glasgow natives (presumably children).

By 1850, there were around 200 Jews in Glasgow, and according to Collins, 'one of Glasgow's strengths proved to be this acceptance of people of ability without regard to their origins.' A synagogue was founded in Dundee in the 1870s and a Jewish burial ground established there in 1888. By mid-century, most incoming Jews were from Lithuania and formed the main body of Scottish Jewry. The growth of Scottish Jewry coincided with growth of the economy, POPULATION, and cities of the country, and was accordingly cen-

tred on Glasgow. From the 1880s, pogroms and forced expulsions forced thousands of Jews to flee the Baltic, Poland, Russia, Ukraine, Germany and elsewhere in eastern and central Europe. Again, most of those arriving in Scotland were Lithuanian, but nearly all were Yiddish speakers and quickly outnumbered the settled Jewish community in Garnethill, Glasgow (which had been three-quarters Polish descent). These later arrivals established a prominent Yiddish speaking community in Gorbals. Scottish Jews formed relief and welfare bodies to aid the refugees, and received support from the Establishment: most of the guests at the Ball of the Glasgow Hebrew Philanthropic Society were non-Jews. In Glasgow, the Jewish community expanded from a base of 40 families in 1870 to 4,000 in 1897 and to 6,500–8,000 by 1902. There were said to be as many as 10,000 Jewish refugees in Scotland at the turn of the century.

A pattern is discernable amongst the experiences of these refugees. Typically, distressed persons would receive assistance from Scottish Jewish bodies upon arrival, and once able, most would continue on to America and following World War I, a number left for Palestine and the United States. From the 1920s, over 1,000 Jewish refugees arrived in Scotland, and added to an already strong presence in certain areas: in 1933, Gorbals Public School had 327 Jewish students out of total of 997.

Scottish Jews organized boycotts of German goods, and Glasgow became known as a stronghold of British Zionism. In the late 1930s, a number of refugees were interned as suspected Nazi sympathizers but were soon released. Those from Germany did not receive a warm welcome from the established (and largely Lithuanian) Jewish communities, but the groups were united by the war's end. In the years that followed, more affluent Jews felt secure enough to leave enclaves such as the Gorbals for non-Jewish neighbourhoods, and particularly in the southern suburbs of Glasgow.

Jews were not the only Lithuanians to reach Scotland. At the end of the nineteenth century, imperial designs on the Baltic states led to an intense period of 'Russification'. A large number of Roman Catholic peasants were forced to leave Lithuania, most of them for the United States, but for reasons imperfectly understood, perhaps as many as several thousand disembarked at the ports of Leith and Dundee. Arriving from the 1880s until around 1905, most went to Lanarkshire where the men sought work in MINING or other industrial work. A number went to Bellshill to face local resentment at their attempts to find work; according to Smout, the Lithuanians 'found their strange names anglicized (sic) like "Joe Gorilla" by their fellow workers, and were for a time ostracized as blacklegs and job-stealers — Keir HARDIE himself gave evidence to a Select Committee on Immigration as to the menace of these "hordes from the East" flooding into the IRONWORKS and coalmines.

Typically, the first immigrants were single men, who found work and sent for friends and family: this familiar process is known as chain migration. They were accused of lowering wages, and were used as poorly-paid strikebreakers; however, by 1910 most had gained membership in TRADE UNIONS. The Lithuanian community became well established, with its own shops, newspapers, and religious observances. This period of integration was not to last. In the end, there was no great barrier between the Lithuanians and other Scots, and the process of assimilation quickened after 1945. Fourth-generation Lithuanians are now adults, and the old language has nearly disappeared.

There were few Italians residing in Scotland until the 'explosion' of emigration from rural Italy in the 1880s and 1890s as a result of growing demographic pressure on that country's outmoded agrarian structure. Most Italian immigrants came from the province of Frosinone in the Lazzio region and Lucca in Tuscany; chains of migration were established in the late nineteenth century between certain villages (such as Barga in Lucca) and places in Scotland that survived though to the 1970s, interrupted only by WORLD WAR II. A key factor in the successful integration of Italian immigration into Scottish society was their decision to pursue distinctive occupations. In any country, immigrants seen to take employment away from the native-born will be a focus for resentment. With an important exception, Italian migrants made themselves welcome largely through their pursuit of the catering business.

Earlier immigrants had established themselves as the sponsors for later arrivals. These *padroni* (or fathers, patrons) encouraged the importation and sale of consignments of chestnuts through street sales. Italian vendors in London began to sell ice cream from the 1850s, a move quickly followed by their Scottish counterparts. Here, itinerant street sellers had acquired shops by the turn of century, by which time nearly all Italians had gone into catering, with small ice cream shops becoming the norm. A notable ice cream padrone was Leopoldo Giuliani of Barga, who arrived in Glasgow in the 1880s; by 1900 he was the richest Italian in Scotland and owned sixty cafes and shops. A large number of boys were brought over from Italy to staff the premises — around ten per shop. Italian immigration to Scotland peaked just prior to the WORLD WAR I, and by the 1930s, nearly every Italian family owned at least one ice cream, sweet or chip shop. A social institution was born which ruthlessly exploited the Scots' love for sweet and fried foods and was temperance-friendly as well; the Italian community had acquired a 'clean-cut' reputation. By the 1930s, Italian migrants and their offspring were gradually moving into the professions.

While the Italian community in Scotland was formed as a result of economic forces, political events nearly caused its extinction. The roots of Italian fascism lay in World War I, and once in power, Mussolini used his embassies to reach the Italian diaspora in Europe and the Americas; fascism exploited the nostalgia and patriotism of the expatriates. The Glasgow fascist club or fascio (the Casa d'Italia), founded in 1922 by Italian war veterans, was the most important in Britain after London, and took impressive premises in Park Circus in 1935; it was the cultural centre of the Italian community. On Mussolini's orders, a census was taken in 1933 by Italian consular officials of the Italians resident in Scotland, revealing that 50% were full members of Fascist Party. Italians in Britain began to feel a growing anti-Fascist sentiment, with some wishing to become naturalized as a mark of loyalty.

Mussolini declared war on the Allies on 10 June 1940, sparking off anti-Italian riots throughout Britain. Italian-owned shops were looted and burned in Edinburgh, Govan, Tradeshill and Maryhill in Glasgow and in Port Glasgow, Gourock, and Greenock. The disorder was to continue for two days. As a result of Churchill's directive to 'collar the lot', Italian-born men aged 17–60 (along with some German and Austrian Jews) were rounded up for internment; most were in custody by 11 June and were sent to camps in England. Several hundred were taken to Liverpool and put aboard the *Arandora Star*, a ship carrying British wounded, German prisoners, and internees to Canada. Tragically, the ship was torpedoed and sank on 2 July 1940 with many Scottish dead. The internees, among them survivors of the *Arandora Star*, were released in 1944.

The war was nearly the end of the Italian community in Scotland, but a re-integration with the public at large came soon after. According to Italian Consulate figures for 1991 of Italian-born persons and those of Italian origin, 3,492 (or

40% of Scottish total) reside in Glasgow and environs; in the Edinburgh area, 2,200; Aberdeen, 300; Dundee, 400; Perth and Stirling, 150; Fife, 345; an additional 17% in smaller centres; or approximately 23,000.

Poles were the last large group of immigrants to come to Scotland before the arrival of Asians. Probably fewer than one hundred Poles were resident here through to the 1930s. After the Nazi invasion of France, approximately 20,000 Polish servicemen and 3,000 civilians were evacuated to Britain along with the Polish government-in-exile. The Polish First Army Corps was formed in Scotland and the 10th Armoured Cavalry Brigade, a tank unit without a single tank, was charged with defending the Scottish coast from Montrose to Dundee, with its headquarters at Forfar. The 1st Armoured Division was sent to towns in the Borders and Midlothian soon after formation.

Employment and accommodation were found in Scotland for Polish women, and the Scottish Polish Society was formed in 1940. The Polish presence in Britain had its critics, and newspapers 'with the exception of the Catholic and some Liberal and Scottish papers' began to lose sympathy with them and their cause, and in Scotland, some believed the Poles to be 'Papist spies'. Later, Poles who had deserted or were captured during the fighting in western Europe were formed into reserve corps in Scotland in 1944–45, and while 'too late to go into action', they nevertheless 'greatly helped to swell Polish unpopularity in that country.'

By May 1945, half of the Polish land forces in Britain (out of a total of 50,000) were stationed in Scotland. Under the terms agreed at the Yalta Conference in February 1945, Poland came under Soviet control, and some months later, the American and British governments switched their recognition of the Polish government-in-exile in London to the Provisional Government for National Unity in Warsaw. General Stanislaw Maczek, commander of the First Polish Armoured Division (formed in Scotland in 1942) denounced the new Communist government in Poland and declared his refusal to return; a large proportion of the Scottish-based Polish soldiers followed his example. The Labour government in Britain had believed that most Polish servicemen wanted to return home and began to plan the process of demobilization, repatriation and resettlement, and centres were set up at Polkemmet in West Lothian and at 'Duke's Camp' near Inveraray.

In all, some 240,000 Polish soldiers under British control were demobilized, but only 105,000 chose repatriation. Of those that remained, most joined the Polish Resettlement Corps, under which they received basic English-language instruction, industrial training, and job placement. Early in 1947, seventy-four hostels were set up in Scotland to provide housing for PRC members, most of whom engaged in agricultural work (although few were to remain on the land). There were some 2,000 Poles in the Lothians and the Borders, and another 1,400 in Lanarkshire.

These reluctant migrants found themselves in an unenviable position. They detested the Soviet domination of Poland, and once the Iron Curtain had fallen, the Communist government in Warsaw regarded them as something of a foreign legion to be used at some point against the forces of the 'popular democracy'. Any thought of return was out of the question. In Scotland, socialism and a general pro-Soviet feeling experienced a high-water mark in the post-war years, and the often-expressed wish of Polish ex-soldiers to fight the Soviets was not deemed politically correct. According to a Scottish Polish writer, 'some Scottish trade unionists and others sympathetic to the Soviet Union regarded the men of the Polish Second Corps as "Fascists and Jew-baiters", who would be paid either to live in idleness or to compete for Scottish jobs.' The Polish immigrants were assertively Roman CATHOLIC, and the Polish Catholic Mission in Scotland was founded in 1947 by the Archbishop of Edinburgh. Efforts by Polish men to gain work in the coal mines were fiercely resisted by the NUM, but by the 1950s, anti-Polish sentiment was on the wane.

The Poles were not the only war migrants to come to Scotland. During World War II, thousands of western Ukrainians joined the Ukrainian Division of the German army to fight Stalin. Many were captured by British forces, and around 1,000 were put in a POW camp in Haddington (East Lothian) where they were employed in agricultural work. Upon their release in 1948, a number went to England or overseas, but those that remained found work in collieries, the Edinburgh trams, or stayed on the land. A Ukrainian (Roman Catholic) church was founded in the early 1960s, and in the spirit of reconciliation, the Ukrainian ex-servicemen's club in Edinburgh has both former Ukrainian Division and Red Army members.

In 1993, there were around sixty Ukrainian ex-POWs in Edinburgh area, out of several hundred Ukrainians in the city.

Chinese people first came to Britain in the early nineteenth century as seamen aboard merchant ships. The 1851 Census for England and Wales recorded seventy-eight 'China-born aliens' and some may have resided in Scottish ports. In addition, anecdotal evidence suggests that in the nineteenth century, Scottish households returning home from the Far East after long sojourns brought their Chinese servants with them. Nevertheless, while English cities had small but well-defined Chinese communities from the nineteenth century, there is no evidence of sustained Chinese settlement in Scotland before the 1950s. At that time, large numbers of Chinese immigrants (mostly single men) arrived in Britain from Hong Kong with the collapse of traditional farming in the rural villages of the colony, a movement which coincided with a growing demand for Chinese food in this country. In the late 1950s and early 1960s, single Chinese men came to Scotland from London, Manchester, Liverpool and other English centres and opened restaurants. Their original intention may have been to earn enough money to return to Hong Kong in comfortable circumstances, but the success of the family-based catering ventures combined with tighter immigration laws led many of the migrants to bring their wives, children, and in time other relatives from Asia to settle in Scotland.

By the 1990s the Chinese were thought to be the largest ethnic minority group in Glasgow after Indians and Pakistanis, and the largest such community in Edinburgh. The Chinese population in Scotland were notably more dispersed than other ethnic groups. One factor in the 'separateness' of the Chinese in Scotland their concentration in the catering industry and the lack of English amongst older immigrants.

In 1979 Britain accepted some 22,000 refugees from Vietnam, most of whom left in the years following the war in that country — 'the boat people'. According to estimates, approximately 1,500 came to Scotland, but relatively few were to stay. Familiar causes for out-migration from Scotland (climate and unemployment) are suggested, together with a misguided housing policy of dispersing the refugees in council estates (perhaps only one or two families in each), throughout the country; whatever the reason, most of the Vietnamese resettled in areas of Manchester, Birmingham, Leeds, and London which had considerable Vietnamese communities. Of those that remained in Scotland, an estimated 100–300, most were from Vietnam's minority ethnic Chinese population and integrated with the existing Chinese community; perhaps only three or four ethnic Vietnamese families remained by the early 1990s.

The first people from the Indian subcontinent to settle in Scotland were the Gypsies; thought to originate from a tribe in northern India, they were noted officially in 1505. As in the case of the Chinese, the first Indians in modern times to arrive in Scotland were seamen with the East India Company or as the servants of Scottish families. Typically, foreign seamen, or 'lascars', were made redundant upon a ships' arrival in a Scottish port, to be rehired only when another ship was ready to sail; those left temporarily stranded had to find housing and employment. Some were to remain, and by the twentieth century, small communities had formed in the cities. In the 1920s, there were about 40–50 Indians, most of them male, lascars and ex-servants, living in Glasgow. The city was to become the primary centre of Asian settlement in Scotland; there were only eight or ten Indians (other than students) resident in Edinburgh in c.1935 and all were pedlars. Immigrants commonly discover that their choice of occupation will largely determine their reception, and by taking 'distinctive' employment can avoid the accusation of depriving their hosts of jobs. Many Indian men became pedlars and worked throughout the country.

Perhaps due to the predominance of Scots in Indian higher education, the Scottish universities attracted numbers of Indian students; the Edinburgh Indian Association, whose papers are preserved at Edinburgh University Library, dates from 1883. Jainti Dass Saggar from Punjab arrived in Dundee in 1919 to study MEDICINE, and took up practice in 1923; he was perhaps the only Indian resident in the city until joined by his brother, who had likewise come to study medicine in 1926. Jainti Dass Saggar became active in the Labour Party and married a daughter of a local bailie and town councillor; he was elected to the town council in 1936. At a time when eight to ten Indians (excluding students) lived in Edinburgh c.1935, their number in the Gorbals in 1940 is estimated at around 400. According to the 1961 Census, 4,000 Asians resided in Glasgow and 300 in Edinburgh (of these, 100 were Pakistani and 200 were Indian).

The pattern of immigration to Britain from the Indian subcontinent changed from a small but steady inflow in the late 1940s and early 1950s with independence and the partition of the subcontinent to a 'sudden rush to beat the ban' placed on immigration by the British Government in the early 1960s. Recently-arrived Asian men found work as bus conductors and construction workers, while the pedlars became shopkeepers and restauranteurs. During the 1960s, many Indians and Pakistanis from England resettled in Scotland. Unlike their Chinese counterparts, few of the South Asian migrants contemplated returning home on a permanent basis. From the 1970s, Asians in Scotland began to move into trade and commerce and spread into towns and villages across the country. Young Asians began a gradual move into the professions (ideally, medicine) and other non-commercial employment, a trend accelerated in the 1980s. Broadly speaking, the ethos of the Scottish Asian community has consisted of religious adherence and the maintenance of tradition, hard work and family-owned businesses, and keeping up ties with home whilst integrating with other Scots. Despite the demonstrable fallacy of 'there is no racism here', Scotland is viewed favourably by Asians throughout Britain.

• Caplan, J., Memories of the Gorbals, Pentland Press, 1991.
• Carswell, A., For Your Freedom and Ours: Poland, Scotland, and the Second World War, National Museums of Scotland, 1993.
• Collins, K., Second City Jewry: The Jews of Glasgow in the age of expansion, 1790—1919, Aberdeen University Press, 1990.
• Colpi, T., The Italian Factor: The Italian Community in Britain, Mainstream, 1991.
• Daiches, D., Two Worlds, Canongate Press, 1987.
• Edward, M., Who Belongs to Glasgow: 200 Years of Migration, Glasgow City Libraries, 1993.
• Maan, B., The New Scots: The Story of Asians in Scotland, John Donald, 1992.
• Miles, R., et al, It's a Long Story, Asian Action Group Tayside, 1992.
• Murray, J. and Stockdale D. (eds.), The Miles tae Dundee: Stories of a city and its people, Dundee Art Galleries and Museums, 1990.
• Strachura, P. (ed.), Themes of Modern Polish History, Polish Social and Educational Society [Glasgow], 1992.
• Zubrzycki, J., Polish Immigrants in Great Britain: a study of adjustment, The Hague, 1956.

improvement 'Improvement' was the commonplace label for the modernization of AGRICULTURE and farming practice, especially in the century 1750—1850. It involved not only the enclosure of traditional INFIELDS, OUTFIELDS and moorland into consolidated holdings, but also the application of capital to large-scale improvements in land use and management. The legal basis for improvement was founded in a series of Acts of PARLIAMENT passed before the UNION — notably those of 1685 and 1695. Although predominantly a feature of the eighteenth-century AGRICULTURAL REVOLUTION, 'improvement' had been underway in the most progressive districts of the Lowlands, for example in parts of the Lothians and Fife, since the seventeenth century — and it continued in more backward areas well into the nineteenth century.

Apart from enclosure the major features of improvement were in husbandry and crop rotation, the diffusion of new crops, and a more scientific approach to livestock breeding. In common with the English experience there were big changes in land use brought about by drainage, dyke building, hedging, afforestation, ROAD building and planned villages — all significant features of estate improvement. Enlightened landowners took an active hand in improvement and among the leading practitioners were Andrew FLETCHER of Saltoun (1655—1716), John COCKBURN of Ormiston (1679—1758), William CRAIK of Arbigland (1703—98), John, Earl of STAIR (1673—1747), Lord KAMES (1696—1782), and Sir Archibald GRANT of Monymusk (1696—1778) — though there were many lesser figures. They had later emulators in the HIGHLANDS at the time of the CLEARANCES.

The BOARD OF TRUSTEES FOR FISHERIES AND MANUFACTURES exercised some influence (through a system of bounties) on the growth of crops like flax for use in the LINEN industry, but most of the evidence would indicate that local agricultural societies were the main means of transmitting knowledge of the new techniques. The greatest Scottish propagandist was the ubiquitous Sir John SINCLAIR (1754—1835), who was prominent in both the BOARD OF AGRICULTURE and the HIGHLAND AND AGRICULTURAL SOCIETY. Scottish innovators also contributed to such limited mechanization as occurred, including James Small, inventor of the swing plough (c.1760), Andrew MEIKLE (1719—1811), pioneer of the threshing mill, and the Rev. Patrick Bell (1799—1869), who developed the reaping machine.

While influenced to a very considerable degree by a spirit of enquiry typical of the Scottish ENLIGHTENMENT, improvement was strongly commercial and preached the capitalization of agriculture. It can thus be seen as playing a similar role in agriculture as technological and scientific innovation in industry.

• *Hamilton, H., An Economic History of Scotland in the Eighteenth Century, Oxford University Press, 1963.*
• *Phillipson, N.T. and Mitchison, R. (eds.), Scotland in the Age of Improvement, Edinburgh University Press, 1970.*

Independent Labour Party The ILP, founded by James Keir HARDIE (1856—1915) in 1893, was the logical successor to earlier organizations like the Labour Electoral Association, designed to return working-class representatives to Parliament free of any connection with the LIBERALS. Ramsay MACDONALD (1866–1937) was another early pioneer and organizer. Initially the ILP had no direct association with the trade union movement, but in 1900 it became an affiliate of the Labour Representation Committee, the forerunner of the LABOUR PARTY, established in 1906.

From the beginning — and partly thanks to Hardie and his successors — the ILP had strong grassroots support in Scotland. This was maintained by good local organization and propaganda work in which John WHEATLEY (1869–1930), James MAXTON (1885–1946) and Tom JOHNSTON (1882–1965) were prominent. Johnston's paper, *Forward*, was the main Scottish organ of the party. They and many of their colleagues were returned as ILP or Labour MPs in the General Election of 1922.

Throughout the next decade the ILP's relationship with the Labour Party was uneasy as the party and its leadership swung further to the left and became more vociferous in its denunciation of MacDonald's gradualism and the inability of government to deal with the effects of the DEPRESSION. Indeed, the ILP's parliamentary representatives were never bound to obey the Labour Party whip in the House of Commons and this proved particularly irksome during the periods of Labour minority government in 1924 and 1929–31. Maxton was chairman of the party between 1926–31 and again 1934–39.

Until its ultimate disaffiliation from the Labour Party in 1932 the ILP was an important source of intellectual and ideological leadership for the left but thereafter its influence slowly waned. Only Maxton and a few close associates refused to throw in their hand with the Labour Party and negotiations to rejoin broke down over the rearmament issue in 1938. When Maxton died in 1946 its two remaining members, Campbell Stephen (1884–1948) and John McGovern (1887–1968) took the Labour whip.

While the later history of the ILP was fraught with dissention and contributed little to the unity of the left either in Scotland or on the wider British stage, there can be little doubt that the party and its activists made an important contribution to the Scottish labour movement during the first forty years of its existence.

•*McKinlay, A. and Morris, R.J. (eds.), The ILP on Clydeside, 1893–1932, Manchester University Press, 1991.*

Industrial Revolution   Scotland was much affected by the Age of Revolutions, by the ideas of the Scottish ENLIGHTENMENT, by the AMERICAN WAR OF INDEPENDENCE and the FRENCH REVOLUTION, but above all by the revolution in industry that occurred in the late eighteenth and early nineteenth centuries. Four main aspects deserve consideration:

(i) the concept of the Industrial Revolution and how the changes affected Scotland between 1780 and 1820;

(ii) the main developments in the period of 'proto-industrialization' preceding large-scale industrialization before 1780;

(iii) the key sectors of Scottish industrialization, including TEX-

TILES, COAL and IRON;

(iv) the immediate social impact of industrialization.

(i) This is a complex subject, mainly because industrialization was part and parcel of the whole process of economic growth, involving not only an Industrial Revolution, but also new developments in AGRICULTURE, commerce and TRANSPORT. The period, for long described as the 'Industrial Revolution', saw the introduction for the first time on a large scale of mass-manufacture, applying new technology largely imported from south of the border, and in particular leading to the growth of the 'Factory System' in textiles. Scotland already had a well-established textile trade, particularly wool and LINEN cloth production, but the new element was mechanization using water power and steam power as prime movers. In both coal and iron there was parallel growth, partly stimulated by general home demand, and partly by the strategic needs of the French Revolution and the NAPOLEONIC WARS, 1793–1815.

The Industrial Revolution — somewhat later in Scotland than in England — saw the 'take-off' of these key sectors into what some economic historians have described as 'self-sustained growth', and helped lay the basis for further expansion after an initial spurt of activity before 1820. Not only this, demand was stimulated for the products of other sectors, notably agriculture, and processing industries like flour milling, drink, leather goods, etc. None of this growth — essentially concentrated in the Lowlands and especially around Glasgow — would have been possible without significant inputs of capital, entrepreneurship and labour. Capital came mainly from agriculture and existing commercial and industrial enterprises, with BANKS playing a significant role in its mobilization and application to new developments. Entrepreneurship was a quality Scots apparently had in abundance and some businessmen, landowners and lawyers (among others) were quick to see the potential profits to be made from dynamic enterprise.

Labour was more of a problem in the industrialization process than one might think, though there was no shortage of skills in textiles and coal-mining. More problematic was the attraction of labour to the new textile mills and ironworks — many in remote locations. Problems of retaining labour, and of discipline, were often solved by resort to paternalistic PLANNED VILLAGES, like NEW LANARK. Finally, resources were geographically concentrated in the Lowlands, which made capitalist exploitation easier, given the development of transport facilities like the new turnpike ROADS, canals, improved harbours and, ultimately, RAILWAYS — a Transport Revolution coinciding with industrialization.

(ii) Historians have long realized that the concept of an 'Industrial Revolution' is something of a misnomer, because there is increasing evidence of longer-term development — in other words various stages of 'proto-industrialization', which in Scotland would find their origin earlier in the eighteenth century if not before. Agriculture certainly had a critical part to play, as had consumer industries like

DISTILLING, BREWING, milling, SALT, pottery, leather and textiles — all of which were becoming increasingly geared towards expanding urban and export markets long before the 1780s. Heat-using industries — including lime burning and the nascent iron trade — stimulated further demand for coal, while urban building programmes led to expansion of stone quarrying and the timber trade. Finally, the problem of access to English and export markets overseas had been solved by the Treaty of UNION, so an environment for potential growth existed as early as the 1700s.

(iii) In the textile industry there were few 'dark satanic mills' before the 1820s, quite the contrary. Most of the early spinning mills using Arkwright's water frame were established in the countryside on rivers like the Clyde and Tay. New Lanark was the example par excellence of the planned industrial community, developed by the financier-entrepreneur David DALE (1739–1806) from 1783, and managed by Robert OWEN (1771–1858), the social reformer, after 1800. Yet much of the evidence would indicate that the larger mills were still atypical and that a fair proportion of the output was still concentrated in smaller units even by the 1800s. Only after 1815 did cotton production really become concentrated in urban mills around Glasgow and Paisley, though both linen and wool were still essentially rural or small-town enterprises. Alongside factory production there was a parallel development of the domestic sector — notably hand-loom weaving. This soon became the first real casualty of mechanization brought about by the introduction of the power loom.

Both coal and iron industries were closely related geographically and in terms of technology, for the application of coke smelting (as opposed to the use of charcoal) stimulated coal-mining. Steam-engines — themselves coal-using — were applied to haulage and drainage in mines, and adapted for blasting air into furnaces. The first large coke-smelting plant was established at CARRON Ironworks (1759) near Falkirk, followed by later works at Wilsontown, Muirkirk, Shotts, and on the Clyde, near Glasgow. Coal-mining was widespread and still small-scale throughout the Lowlands, though the opening of the Monkland and then the Forth and Clyde canals greatly stimulated production in north Lanarkshire and Stirlingshire.

(iv) All of this was achieved at considerable social cost, though it has to be admitted (perhaps surprisingly) that the social climate was one of stability rather than conflict. The idea that people flocked to work in the new mills, mines and furnaces is certainly open to question; folk had to be persuaded and even cajoled into working as cotton spinners, colliers or furnace hands. Labour certainly came from the HIGHLANDS and from Ireland on a seasonal basis at first, later by MIGRATION settling permanently in the Lowlands. But with the new skills and opportunities came the threat of cyclical unemployment, something that few had experienced in the subsistence life of the crofts or COTTON farms. As regards the standard of living of the working class it is difficult to make meaningful generalizations beyond the obvious fact that for some things got better, while for other groups the opposite was the case. The standard of living controversy in the Scottish context remains to be resolved.

URBANIZATION brought new challenges — the problem of the poor, bad HOUSING, health and sanitation — most of which were already identifiable. But solutions, if only partial, were beginning to be found later in the nineteenth century, when things had got much worse. Glasgow's social problems during the late eighteenth and early nineteenth centuries were perhaps atypical — but only in terms of scale, for other towns shared the same difficulties.

While it would be easy to exaggerate the immediate consequences of new and imported technology and modes of production, there can be little doubt that both combined to make a considerable impact on the economy of the Scottish Lowlands, notably on the textile, coal and iron industries. Some sectors and large parts of the countryside — including the Highlands — were at first unaffected, though gradually the spirit of modernization spread everywhere. Given the relatively late start, industrialization in Scotland proceeded rapidly. The process was thus more concentrated than in England — a phenomenon seen in other peripheral industrial regions of Continental Europe such as Silesia or Sweden.

•*Campbell, R.H., Scotland Since 1707: the Rise of an Industrial Society, 2nd ed., John Donald, 1985.*
•*Lenman, B., Integration, Enlightenment and Industrialisation: Scotland 1746— 1832, Edward Arnold, 1981.*
•*Lythe, S.G.E. and Butt, J., An Economic History of Scotland 1100—1939, Blackie & Son, 1975.*
•*Whatley, C., The Industrial Revolution in Scotland, Cambridge University Press, 1997.*

industry, early   Industry in the sense of manufactures ushered in by the eighteenth-century INDUSTRIAL REVOLUTION were absent in medieval and early modern Scotland. The universal fuels were timber and peat, though COAL was known and evidently mined from the early medieval era. Monastic charters of the twelfth and thirteenth centry mention grants of coal workings. These record coal working rights by Holyrood (c.1200), Newbattle (1210), Dunfermline (1291), and Paisely (1294), the last given rights of digging sea coal. Later Aenaes Silvius (Pope Pius II) made an inadvertant reference to coal by noting that the poor in Scotland went away with joy on their faces after receiving stones, which were actually loads of coal, as alms. Early coal working was closely related to SALT manufacture by evaporation of sea water, for example, along the shores of the Forth estuary. Other significant heat using activities were IRON working, mainly for weapons and tools, pottery manufacture, and BREWING. Milling was another widespread activity, often reserved in the classic feudal system to BURGHS or local nobles. WOOL and leather were both important primary products for local manufacture and export.

industry   Prior to the INDUSTRIAL REVOLUTION of the late eighteenth and early nineteenth centuries

Scotland had an essentially rural, subsistence economy based on AGRICULTURE. Such industrial activities as there were depended for their raw materials on primary products, like wool or animal skins. The ancient BURGHS — either ports or inland market centres — had long-established crafts (organized in GUILDS) which were involved in primitive manufacturing. In those areas where it could be readily worked given the prevailing level of technology, COAL was used as a fuel. Other minerals, such as gold and silver, iron and lead were intermittently worked in the Southern Uplands and the Highlands.

One of the first industries to expand was coal-mining, for as timber reserves (and even turf) became increasingly exhausted in parts of the Lowlands coal was the most obvious substitute for domestic use and in heat-using industries like BREWING, glass-making, lead smelting or SALT manufacture. As the separate entries for coal and salt make clear, there was a close relationship between the two sectors. This was maintained well into the eighteenth century, especially along the shores of the Forth where the majority of the salt works were located. Sir George Bruce (d.1625) was an early pioneer at Culross — though later works were on a larger scale.

During the latter half of the seventeenth century — and partly as a result of parliamentary encouragement — various industrial experiments were undertaken, both by native Scots and by English capitalists who had migrated north. The most prominent was the woollen cloth industry promoted by a small group of apparently short-lived companies, of which the best-known were at Newmills, near Haddington (1681–1713) and Glasgow (1699–1704). Other TEXTILE-related enterprises included LINEN manufacture, paper and rope-making.

More permanent economic growth and industrial expansion occurred during the eighteenth century as a prelude to the Industrial Revolution, beginning about 1780. One of the first activities to benefit was linen — encouraged and supported by the Board of Trustees, while the basis of the modern iron industry was laid by the CARRON COMPANY near Falkirk in 1759. This led in turn to the expansion of coal-mining, which was greatly assisted by the development of improved TRANSPORT and then steam power.

During the classic Industrial Revolution era mass-manufacture of COTTON yarn was the most obvious manifestation of the Factory System, but important inventions also occurred in iron-making, ENGINEERING, chemicals, SHIPBUILDING and consumer industries, among others. Indeed, the foundations of the Scottish industrial economy in the Victorian period — with its emphasis on coal, iron, engineering and textiles (including wool) — had been laid by 1830.

While these great staples continued to expand and innovate the industrial economy remained relatively buoyant. Despite foreign competition Scotland could still claim to be the workshop of the Empire even as late as 1900. Retrospectively, however, there seems to have been an over-concentration of capital and skill on a narrow range of sectors, and, after the 1870s, a failure to adopt new techniques of production and management. Most of the problems that were manifest before the turn of the century were compounded by the demands of WORLD WAR I and the subsequent depression.

Scottish industry experienced mixed fortunes after WORLD WAR II as older sectors like mining and shipbuilding contracted. During the 1950s and 60s attempts at diversification into vehicle manufacture, for example, proved both costly and inappropriate. While North Sea oil-related activities temporarily bolstered steel, heavy engineering and shipbuilding in the 70s, there was greater long-term success in the high-technology spheres of electronics and light engineering located in either the NEW TOWNS or greenfield sites elsewhere. For related subjects see the previous entry and entries under specific industries.

•*Lythe, S.G.E. and Butt, J., An Economic History of Scotland 1100—1939, Blackie, 1975.*
•*Payne, P.L., Growth and Contraction: Scottish Industry, c.1860—1990, Economic and Social History Society of Scotland, 1992.*

infield   In the traditional mode of AGRICULTURE the infield was the land nearest the town or settlement and sometimes under continual cultivation. The infield was seldom enclosed and was divided into RUNRIGS or crude strips, which were allocated among the tenants annually or at longer intervals. The infield received most of the manure and the main cereal crops grown before the eighteenth cen-

tury were bere (a species of barley) and oats. Peas, beans or kail were grown in gardens adjoining the houses. Beyond the infield lay the OUTFIELD, usually pasture, but as time passed increasingly improved for cultivation intakes to an existing town or new settlement.

Inglis, Elsie Maud (1864—1917)

Elsie Inglis, suffragette and humanitarian, was born in India. She lived there until 1875 when the family moved to Hobart, Tasmania. In 1878 they returned to Scotland, settling in Edinburgh, where Elsie Inglis continued her education. Following a year in Paris, and with her father's encouragement, she embarked on her medical studies. The Edinburgh School of Medicine for Women opened in 1886 and Inglis studied there until 1889 when its founder, Sophia Jex-Blake (1840—1912) dismissed two students for a trivial offence. Outraged, Inglis, her father and some well-connected friends established the Edinburgh Medical College for Women and she herself completed her clinical training at Glasgow Royal Infirmary.

Moving to London in 1892 Inglis was appointed to the New Hospital for Women (now the Elizabeth Garrett Anderson) before returning to the Bruntsfield Hospital in Edinburgh. She ultimately lectured in gynaecology at the Medical College for Women and in 1901 opened a small teaching hospital for women, offering obstetric anaesthesia in childbirth to the poor.

Meantime, Elsie Inglis had become active in the women's suffrage movement, devoting much of her spare time to speaking and lecturing on the enfranchisement of women. She helped found the Federation of Scottish Suffrage Societies and on the outbreak of WORLD WAR I in 1914 harnessed the movement to war work. She appealed for funds and established the Scottish Women's Hospitals to provide hospital units staffed by women.

The first unit left for France in November 1914 with a second going to Serbia in January 1915. Eventually fourteen hospital units served in France, Serbia, Corsica, Salonika, Romania, Russia and Malta. During 1915—16 Elsie Inglis herself worked with a unit in Serbia and when that war zone was overrun by Austrians she was detained in conditions of considerable privation until American diplomacy secured her release. Later she returned to Russia and Serbia, but by the end of 1917 she was dying of cancer.

Much honoured by the grateful Russians and Serbs for her dedication and valour she was not utterly neglected by her native land. Arthur BALFOUR (1848—1930), then Secretary of State for Foreign Affairs, said in tribute that she displayed, 'a wonderful compound of enthusiasm, strength of purpose and kindliness. In the history of this World War, alike by what she did and by the heroism, driving power and the simplicity by which she did it, Elsie Inglis has earned an everlasting place of honour.'
• Crawford, A. (ed.), The European Biographical Dictionary of British Women, Europa Publications, 1983.
• Crofton, E., The Women of Royaumont: A Scottish Women's Hospital on the Western Front, Tuckwell Press, 1997.

• Lawrence, M., Shadow of Swords: A Biography of Elsie Inglis, Michael Joseph, 1971.

Iona, Statutes of (1609) In controlling the HIGHLANDS and Islands JAMES VI (1566—1625) relied to a great extent on the assistance and co-operation of powerful clans like the Campbells and McKenzies. However, in some areas an alternative strategy was adopted, notably in the Western Isles, where Andrew Knox (1559—1633), Bishop of the Isles, strongly disapproved of the Campbell hegemony. Thus, in 1608, he led an expedition to Mull, tricked the local chieftain and various others into boarding his ship and then had them incarcerated in various prisons in Central Scotland. He made their release the following year dependent on their signing a series of statutes whose terms included supporting the reformed Kirk, suppressing beggars and vagabonds, not to mention bards who encouraged clan feuds, reducing their retinues and sending their sons to the Lowlands to be educated. The agreement was consolidated by the chiefs putting their names to a General Band in which the signatories acknowledged the authority of the king and gave guarantees of their loyalty to him. Renewed in 1616, it would seem that, at least in this part of the Highlands, James VI had some success in asserting royal control.
• Dickinson, W.C. and Donaldson, G. (eds.), A Source Book of Scottish History III, Nelson, 1961.

iron Historically, iron was important for the manufacture of weapons and more everyday implements. Iron-smelting in bloomeries, or primitive furnaces, was well-established in various Highland locations by the seventeenth century. Then, as later, the prime attraction, apart from readily exploited iron ore, was charcoal provided by the still extensive woodlands of the region. Indeed, the scarcity of wood led to the relative decline of the English iron industry, ultimately forcing ironmasters to look elsewhere for fuel supplies.

The charcoal phase of the Scottish iron industry was dominated by English entrepreneurs — many from Lancashire and Cumbria — who established blast furnaces at several sites throughout the Highlands. Most were short lived, though one continued in production for over a century. At the earliest, Invergarry (1727), the partnership had the use of the local woodlands for thirty-one years and supplied the furnace with ore imported by sea and packhorse from Lancashire. Another, Abernethy (1730), was established on the banks of the River Nethy and used ore mined near Tomintoul in Banff — the only venture completely independent of outside materials. Two later and more successful ventures followed at Bonawe (1753) near Taynuilt and Furnace (1775), both in Argyll. The former has been preserved as a historic monument.

The modern Scottish iron industry dates from 1759 when the CARRON COMPANY established a plant near Falkirk to exploit local iron ores using the coke-smelting techniques developed earlier at Coalbrookdale by Abraham Darby

(1678–1717). With the Seven Years' War (1756–63) raging, the manufacture of munitions was a priority. The first guns were cast in 1761. Carron was followed by a series of plant located in various parts of the Central Lowlands, notably Lanarkshire and Ayrshire. An important iron manufacturing industry — producing everything from a spade to a steam-engine — sprang up as the INDUSTRIAL REVOLUTION created a growing demand for iron products. Scottish inventors contributed to the subsequent expansion of the industry, including David Mushet (1772–1847), who discovered the value of local blackband ironstone, and James Neilson (1792–1865), who introduced the hot blast for smelting iron ore in 1828.

The application of Neilson's hot blast and the use of blackband iron ores greatly reduced the costs of the Scottish iron industry at a time when both home and overseas demand for pig iron was increasing. After 1830 entrepreneurs like the Bairds of Gartsherrie, the Dixons of Govan and Houldsworths of Coltness, established large enterprises controlling not only the ironworks, but also iron and coal-mines. By 1845 Scotland supplied 25 per cent of Britain's output of pig iron. Thereafter production was sustained using both local and imported ores with pig iron output rising from 797,000 tons in 1857 to a peak of 1,206,000 in 1869. After a slump in the 1880s it stood at the same level in 1914. Although a very high proportion of Scottish pig iron output left Scotland without being processed further, about a third was absorbed by RAILWAYS and the ENGINEERING and SHIPBUILDING industries.

The Scottish steel industry dates from the 1870s and owed its growth to the Siemens open-hearth process using imported ores and allied to the rise of steel shipbuilding on the Clyde. In 1885 output was 241,000 tons, with ten firms producing 20 per cent of all British steel. By 1900 production had risen to 964,000 tons — more than a third of all British steel produced by the Siemens process.

While the two World Wars, interrupted by the DEPRESSION, helped maintain the Scottish iron and steel industry, it became increasingly moribund. The period since 1945 saw the industry adapt to changing economic circumstances including new technology and the challenge of foreign competition. As was the experience in coal-mining, shipbuilding and engineering, this brought about large-scale rationalization and plant closures — often at considerable cost to those communities that formerly relied on the industry for their livelihoods.

• Campbell, R.H., The Rise and Fall of Scottish Industry 1707—1939, John Donald, 1980.
• Payne, P.L., Colvilles and the Scottish Steel Industry, Oxford University Press, 1979.
• Slaven, A., The Development of the West of Scotland 1750—1860, Routledge & Kegan Paul, 1975.

Ireland There were many complex demographic, linguistic, kin, religious, political and trading links between Ireland and Scotland in the medieval and modern eras. See specifically MIGRATION.

Isles The Northern Isles of Orkney and Shetland were both settled in prehistoric times, from which a valuable heritage survives. Norse or Viking settlement occurred and even after their withdrawal from the south and west of the mainland and from the Western Isles following the battle of LARGS, the islands were part of the kingdom of Denmark-Norway.

Under the marriage settlement of JAMES III to Margaret, daughter of Christian I of Norway and Denmark, the islands were annexed to Scotland by 1472. By this time Scottish nobility had already established themselves there and were to set the agendas for the differing deveopment of both island groups in subsequent centuries.

The Western Isles played a more significant role in the history of medieval Scotland. The kingdom of the Isles, centred on the Isle of Man, was essentially Norse, but by the twelfth century, the elites were a mixed race of former Vikings and Celtic nobilities. The most prominent and successful was Somerled, who conquered the Isles between 1156–58, and was duly recognized by Norway as 'King of the Isles'. The Isles effectively passed to Scotland in 1266, but in the subsequent disorder associated with the WARS OF INDEPENDENCE, there was continuing lawlessness and confrontation between the Crown and various kin groups of the MacDonalds, who also confronted each other in a succesion of power struggles, as well as taking differing sides in the wars. The MacDonalds of Islay were designating themselves 'LORDS OF THE ISLES' by the fourteenth century, though not officially recognized until the following century.

The Isles and their leaders, in common with the HIGHLANDS more generally, were a constant source of trouble for a series of Scottish monarchs. John, first Lord of the Isles, took the side of Edward Balliol, in his attempts to gain the throne in the 1320s and 30s. Donald, second Lord, united Islanders and Highlanders in a battle against Lowlanders at Harlaw in 1411. Alexander, third Lord, proved a major challenge to JAMES I in his efforts to subdue the Highlands. His son, John, the fourth and last Lord, led a rebellion against James II in 1452, and later in 1462 joined forces with the Earl of Douglas in attempting to undermine James III by signing the Treaty of WESTMINSTER-ARDTORNISH. John also caused trouble for JAMES IV, surrendering in 1494.

• Grant, I.F., The Lordship of the Isles, Mercat Press, 1982.

• McDonald, R.A., The Kingdom of the Isles: Scotland's Western Seaboard in the Central Middle Ages c.1110–c.1336, Tuckwell Press, 1997.

J

Jacobites Originally the supporters of JAMES VII (1633–1701) after he was deposed by WILLIAM III (1650–1702) and his wife, Mary (1662–94), in 1688, the derivation of the word is from 'Jacobus', the Latin for James. Undoubtedly the term was used pejoratively by their enemies. Thus, just as in the Bible, Jacob had deceived his father, Isaac, so James VII and his wife, Mary of Modena (1658–1718), had tricked their British subjects by smuggling a child into the royal palace at the time of the birth of their son, James Francis STEWART, the Old Pretender (1688–1766). At least this was the WHIG version of the event. Support for the Stewart cause continued to exist in the north and northeast of Scotland, as the various JACOBITE REBELLIONS testify, until the decisive defeat at CULLODEN in 1746. Thereafter, as the economic advantages of the Treaty of UNION became more apparent and the anti-Jacobite measures taken by the government began to take effect, Jacobitism gradually withered away.

• *Gibson, J.S., Playing the Scottish Card: The Franco-Jacobite Invasion of 1708, Edinburgh University Press, 1988.*
• *McLynn, F., The Jacobites, Routledge and Kegan Paul, 1985.*
• *Petrie, C., The Jacobite Movement, Eyre & Spottiswoode, 1959.*
• *Szechi, D., The Jacobites in Britain and Europe, 1688–1788, Manchester University Press, 1994.*

Jacobite Rebellions The first rebellion was that led by John GRAHAM of Claverhouse (1648–89) in 1689 but its leader's death at KILLIECRANKIE effectively ensured its collapse. It was ultimately crushed by troops under General Mackay (c.1640–92) in Cromdale (Morayshire). Subsequently there were two serious risings in 1715 and 1745 as well as an abortive attempt in 1719.

1715 Rebellion Although Queen ANNE (1665–1714) died on 1 August 1714, the leading Scottish JACOBITES, particularly MAR (1675–1732) were more interested at this juncture in seeking favours from the new monarch, George I (1660–1727) than organizing any rebellion. Thus it was not until a year later, by which date 'Bobbing John', as Mar was aptly nicknamed, had quarrelled with the king, that the Jacobite rising got underway. At the end of August 1715 Mar proclaimed his loyalty to James Francis STEWART, the 'Old Pretender' (1688–1766) winning the support of powerful noblemen in the northeast such as Huntly (1643–1716) and the Earl Marischal (1692–1778), certain western CLANS, including the Mackintoshes, MacDonalds and Camerons as well as a small group of Jacobites in the southwest led by Viscount Kenmure (d.1716). The motives for participating in the revolt varied widely; for some, recent controversial legislation such as the TOLERATION ACT and the Patronage Act, the introduction of the MALT TAX in Scotland not to mention the Act for Ensuring Loyalty by which known Jacobites had to take an oath of allegiance to the Crown, had made them discontented; for others, like the tenants and servants of Mar and his allies there was often little alternative; for certain other families there was the belief that the insurrection might provide an opportunity to recover their position.

In short, devotion to the Jacobite cause was by no means the only reason for coming out in the 'Fifteen. Unfortunately for the Stewarts, Mar was a weak, indecisive general who failed to take advantage of the poor conditions of the main government strongholds north of the Border. Consequently his army was decisively checked at SHERIFFMUIR on 13 November by John CAMPBELL, second Duke of Argyll (1678–1743), the Hanoverian commander and his loyal troops. Thereafter the rising rapidly disintegrated despite the arrival at Peterhead in December of the 'Old Pretender'. In the north, at Inverness, Simon FRASER (c.1667–1747) captured Inverness, which allowed the Hanoverian forces in that area to suppress the rebels in the HIGHLANDS and the northeast Lowlands. Meanwhile in the southwest, an attempt to link up with English Jacobites in Cumberland ended disastrously in surrender at Preston in November. Finally, in February 1716, the 'Old Pretender' who had not proved to be an inspiring figurehead, departed for France to be followed by other leading Jacobites.

1719 Rebellion In 1719 the Spanish government, as part of a proposed, large-scale invasion of England, arranged a diversionary attack on northwest Scotland in support of the Jacobites. Thus, about 300 Spanish troops accompanied by some of the Scottish survivors of the 1715 rebellion, notably James Keith (1696–1758) and his brother, the Earl Marischal, were landed on the mainland near Glenshiel (Inverness-shire). The main support for the clans came from the Mackenzies under their chieftain the Earl of Seaforth (d.1740) but the rising was easily suppressed by government forces.

1745 Rebellion For some considerable time after the 1715 and 1719 revolts there was little Jacobite activity in the Highlands where such countermeasures as the military road building undertaken by General WADE (1673–1748) and the formation of independent companies of loyal Highlanders proved relatively effective. However, the outbreak of war involving Britain and France in 1739 raised Stewart hopes of French assistance for their cause. Thus, in 1743, Murray of Broughton (1715–77), secretary of the Jacobite Association, persuaded many of the clan chieftains to agree to support Charles Edward STEWART, the Young Pretender (1720–88), the son of the 'Old Pretender', provided he could guarantee French military aid. In fact, the following year, it was only adverse weather conditions that thwarted just such an expedition.

By 1745 the French had altered their strategy and when the 'Young Pretender' landed in July at Eriskay in the Outer Hebrides he lacked that most essential prerequisite, adequate French assistance. However, the Prince had considerable powers of persuasion and in August when he raised his standard at Glenfinnan in Inverness-shire he could rely on extensive support from the central and west Highlands as well as much of northeast Scotland. In the latter area where some of his following was the result of forcible recruitment by local lairds, Episcopalian sympathies were a prominent factor. Elsewhere, such clans as the MacDonalds, Camerons and Mackintoshes were influenced by genuine loyalty to the Stewarts, as well as, in some instances, affection for the Catholic religion; for other clans, such as the Macgregors, there was the feeling that they had nothing to lose by participating in the insurrection.

By the end of September, with the government army led by General Sir John Cope (d.1760) routed at PRESTONPANS, most of the Lowlands, although its inhabitants were primarily anti-Jacobite, was in the hands of the rebels. There followed the invasion of England where, despite reaching Derby by December, the Prince failed to rally anything remotely like the Jacobite support that was anticipated.

The subsequent retreat and the brilliant rearguard action at Falkirk in January 1746 were simply a prelude to the disaster that befell the Jacobite army at CULLODEN in April.

The aftermath of this defeat was considerable; a few of the leading Jacobites, namely Simon Fraser, and lords Balmerino (1688–1746) and Kilmarnock (1704–1746) were executed but most of the others including LORD GEORGE MURRAY (c.1700–60) their most able general and the Young Pretender himself escaped after various vicissitudes to the Continent; the lands of many of those involved in the rising were seized by the government to be administered by the Commissioners of the FORFEITED ESTATES; there was, as after 1715, a Disarming Act that imposed heavy fines on anyone caught in possession of arms, while by another statute wearing Highland dress, because of its warlike association, was proscribed; finally, by the Act abolishing HERITABLE JURISDICTION, the legal powers possessed by some of the clan chieftains were removed. The principal victim, however, was the old clan system. Although crumbling before the 1745 rebellion, the measures taken by the authorities caused its rapid disintegration as the great clan leaders lost their patriarchal powers and became mere landowners.

•*Ferguson, W., Scotland, 1689 to the Present, Oliver & Boyd, 1968.*
•*Lenman, B., The Jacobite Risings in Britain, 1689–1746, Eyre Methuen, 1980.*

James I (1394—1437) James, the third son of King ROBERT III, was born at Dunfermline in July 1394. He was born into the battle for power that surrounded his ailing father, the main participants being his brother, David, Duke of Rothesay and his uncle, Robert STEWART, Duke of Albany. Rothesay ran the country for his father between 1399 and 1402 but was deposed by Albany, imprisoned at Falkland, soon dying in suspicious circumstances. Meantime James's elder brother Robert had also died and he had become heir to the throne. By 1405–6 civil war had broken out between Albany and Douglas on the one hand and the king on the other. The young prince fled to the Bass Rock and was on his way to France when he was captured at sea and handed over to Henry IV of England. A fortnight later on 4 April, Robert III died and James, aged 12, became king, though in the circumstances uncrowned for eighteen years.

As a hostage James continued his education, observing English royal government at first hand, and later serving in the French campaigns of Henry V (1420–21). Albany ruled as governor, evidently ignoring James's early pleas for release. Plans for this had been well advanced before the death of Henry IV in 1413, but James (partly because of the complexities of international politics, especially between England and France) had to wait another eleven years before his return to Scotland. Meantime Albany had died and his son Murdoch, a co-hostage of the king's, had been released in 1416 and returned to Scotland eventually succeeding his father as governor.

James himself was released under the terms of the Treaty of LONDON (1423). When he returned to Scotland in April 1424, accompanied by his English wife, Joan Beaufort, his main objective was imposing centralised authority on English lines. A secondary aim was imposing further TAXATION to pay for his ransom and sending off Scottish nobles as hostages to England. He also wanted revenge on those who had usurped royal authority and done so little to secure his release. Inevitably his agenda did little to enhance his relationship with the Scottish elite. Murdoch, two of his sons, and another noble, Lennox were eliminated in a state execution at Stirling, and the king later moved against other magnates, including, with mixed fortunes, the HIGHLAND chiefs. At Inverness in 1428 many were arrested and imprisoned. Alexander, Lord of the Isles escaped and later defeated the king's forces led by the Earl of Mar at Inverlochy in 1431. Other potential threats were dealt with as they arose, notably the Earl of Douglas in 1431 and the Earl of March in 1434.

Although James was engaged in a constant power struggle he did succeed in imposing law and order, and raising royal revenues. Apparently the money raised to redeem the hostages in England, whom James largely ignored, was disposed of either in conspicuous consumption, such as the fortified Linlithgow Palace, the Charterhouse in Perth, artillery and other weaponry, as well as luxuries for himself and his court. However, James was also a man of culture, a representative of the Scottish Renaissance in literature and music. The romantic poem 'The Kingis Quair' (King's Book) is supposed to have been written by him.

Given his attempts to maintain good relations with England, his siege of Roxburgh in 1436 seemed illogical. When it failed, and James continued his assault on noble privileges, his many enemies seized their opportunity. On 21 February 1437 James was assassinated at the Dominican Friary at Perth, having failed to escape via a sewer running beneath his apartment. The visiting Bishop of Urbino afterwards declared the king a martyr and the (mainly Albany Stewart) assassins were caught and cruelly executed. Thus while James was hardly popular because of his attempts to impose strong government, the attempted coup and assassination failed to overthrow the Stewart monarchy. *Brown, M., James I, Tuckwell Press, 1994.*

James II (1430—60) Born in 1430 at Holyrood, James was the son of JAMES I. Succeeding to the throne at the age of six, James was the fourth Stewart monarch. Crowned in March 1437 he reigned till 1460. He inherited a shaky legacy as his three predecessors had either succumbed to overthrow or assassination. The first seven years of the minority were dominated by periodic civil unrest, much of it a backlash against the efforts of his father to assert royal authority over the most powerful nobles and impose TAXATION. He gained real authority in 1449, the year of his marriage to Mary of Gueldres, a niece of Philip of Burgundy. Four of his sisters were already married to powerful European families in France, the Low Countries and Austria, a situation which clearly gave external credence to his own regime and helped him assert his authority at home.

James is the first Scottish monarch for whom a credible image survives, a portrait painted in 1458 for his sister, Eleanor of Austria. It shows a confident and ruthless looking individual, qualities which were reflected in the policies he pursued in Scotland and beyond. He certainly raised the authority and prestige of the crown, turning the warring nobility against the English rather than himself and, judging by the many charters he signed, travelling extensively throughout the kingdom in peace and war.

The most significant development for the crown was his success in eliminating one of the most powerful families, the Black Douglases, personally assassinating William, the eighth earl, who had been given promises of safety to attend a meeting at Stirling in 1452. This was part of the second phase of the civil war between James and the Douglases which flared up on three occasions between 1451 and 1455, and ended in the downfall of the Douglases. The great castle at Threave was the last Douglas stronghold to surrender in 1455. Thereafter Galloway was administered for the crown by the Abbot of Dundrennan Abbey.

James spent the next five years engaged in other initiatives designed to consolidate his authority. He organised an unsuccessful attack on the Isle of Man, undertook a series of BORDER raids, interfered in the dispute between the Yorkists and the Lancastrians which had resulted in the Wars of the Roses, and tried to have Orkney and Shetland, the northern ISLES, ceded to Scotland in a marriage alliance for his son. A gift he received from Philip of Burgundy in 1457, the huge cannon known as 'Mons Meg', seemed apposite.

In August 1460 James was killed besieging Roxburgh (held by the English from the 1330s), apparently by an exploding cannon. As a modern study puts it, 'an appropriate end for a man who made war for most of his short life, either on his own subjects or against the English'. His personal rule had lasted only eleven years.

• Brown, M., The Black Douglases, Tuckwell Press, 1998.
• McGladdery, C., James II, John Donald, 1990.

James III (1452—88) The eldest son of JAMES II and Mary of Gueldres, James was born in 1452 at St Andrews. His birth ensured the succession at a critical time in his father's reign. Soon after his father's death and the Scots success in besieging Roxburgh castle, James was crowned at nearby Kelso Abbey. The minority (1460—69) was headed at first by Mary as guardian and, in terms of diplomacy with England, proved successful, for the Scots gained Berwick in 1461 from a Lancastrian force and later backed the victors of the Wars of the Roses, the Yorkists. Later James II's territorial and marital aims were fulfilled by the treaty of Copenhagen (1468) which arranged James's marriage to Margaret, daughter of Christian I of Denmark and Norway. The dowry was the earldom of Orkney and the lordship of Shetland, both of which were annexed by 1472. Prior to the permanent loss of Berwick in 1482, this was the greatest geographical extent of medieval Scotland.

Otherwise, in 1466 James survived a coup orchestrated by the powerful Boyd family, who had used the opportunity of the king's minority to advance their position by marriage both into the royal family and to other powerful nobles. The Boyds were toppled in 1469, the year of James's marriage, and the beginning of his majority. Most of the confiscated lands came to the crown. James's relationship with both magnates and PARLIAMENT was uneasy due partly to his reluctance to travel round the country (perhaps thinking he might be safer in Edinburgh) and partly to efforts to raise revenue through TAXATION. Other challenges to royal authority came later from James's blood relations, his two brothers, John, Earl of Mar, and Alexander, Duke of Albany. They certainly stirred up trouble for the king, until Albany eventually fled to France in 1479 and Mar was accused of treason, imprisoned and died in dubious circumstances sometime during the winter of 1479–80.

Albany wasted little time in challenging the king. In 1482, supported by an English army sent by Edward IV, Albany moved north to invade Scotland. This caused a major crisis and led to another coup when James, heading south to meet the English, was seized at Lauder and incarcerated in Edinburgh castle. Loyal nobles in the north helped him regain power, but the mistrust continued, especially after the king passed a Treasons Act (1484), introducing punitive measures against those opposing him. When the southern nobles, with his teenage son, James, as figurehead, staged yet another rebellion, the north again came to his support. He linked up with them after crossing the Forth on Sir Andrew WOOD's ships. He died at the 'field of Stirling' or the battle of SAUCHIEBURN, 11 June 1488, his own inferior force defeated and the king apparently assassinated after he fled by an adversary disguised as a priest.

As with many of the early Scottish monarchs, perceptions of James have changed, mainly because modern research has overturned impressions conveyed by sixteenth-century writers anxious to sustain the continuity and legitimacy of the Stewart succession. Much was made of his pacific image (or at least his opposition to war, which does not really stand scrutiny), but given his record this seems unlikely. His interest in culture, helping to sustain the Scottish Renaissance, is also difficult to prove. James failed, not because of his policies, many of which were later adopted by his son, JAMES IV, but because of his personality. However, says his modern biographer, 'he did fulfill one of the classic duties of a medieval king, that of leader in war'. The historical perception that 'he combined the ruthlessness and acquisitiveness of his grandfather with the unpleasantness of his grandson' made him no better or worse than other early monarchs. • *MacDougall, N., James III. A Political Study, John Donald, 1982.*

James IV (1473—1513) Born 17 March 1473, the son of JAMES III (1452—88) and Margaret (c.1457—86) of Denmark, he became king on his father's death at Sauchieburn, near Stirling on 11 June 1488. Although the Homes and Hepburns, two of the leading families to rebel against James III, were briefly in a dominant position, his son, nearly sixteen at his accession, soon displayed an independent spirit. By the early years of the 1490s he was clearly in control of his kingdom.

Two turbulent areas traditionally requiring the attention of any Scottish monarch, especially at the outset of his reign, were the HIGHLANDS and ISLES and the BORDERS. In the north the lack of royal authority was underlined by the depredations and destruction of the MacDonalds and Mackenzies as they pursued their family vendetta across the countryside. James IV's initial response in 1493 was to deprive the MacDonalds of Islay of their Lordship of the Isles and launch a number of royal expeditions into the region. These were obviously of limited value since as late as 1504—5 Donald Dubh (c.1480—1545), an illegitimate grandson of John (d.1498), the forfeited Lord of the Isles, was engaged in trying to recover his family's title. In fact, James became convinced a better policy was delegating authority in the Highlands to some of the principal families, such as the Campbells and Gordons. This was an expedient with short-term advantages but which in the long run had the disadvantage of creating both overmighty subjects and further unrest among the other Highland clans.

In the borders the king did his utmost to restore some sort of law and order to a region normally notorious for its disorder. He personally accompanied several 'raids' into the area, and while on occasions not averse to dispensing summary justice he generally pre-

ferred less drastic and more conciliatory methods. Thus bonds, that is
guarantees of good behaviour from
certain families on pain of forfeiting lands or possessions, and
pledges, whereby hostages were
taken from some Borderers, were
often employed. Moreover, in
order to boost the treasury and
also as a placatory gesture, the
death penalty was frequently remitted on payment of a heavy fine or
'composition'.

Elsewhere, in his handling of the
CHURCH and the royal finances,
James IV showed his determination
to enforce as far as possible the
authority of the Crown. Thus, in
his relations with the Church, the
king not only insisted on a second
archbishopbric of Glasgow being
founded but also that the concession over ecclesiastical appointments won from the papacy by his
father should be renewed. This
allowed him to promote a number
of questionable candidates, his illegitimate son Alexander (d.1513),
for instance, became Archbishop of
St Andrews in 1504, and to indulge
in the deleterious practice of granting commendatorships of abbeys.

As regards his financial policy,
James, apart from a very substantial
marriage dowry, relied mainly on
his income from the profits of justice, his taxation of the clergy and
an increasingly extensive feuing of
the crown lands. The latter, of
course, was again only a short-term
expedient.

James IV like his father before
him, and as was also to be the case
with his son JAMES V (1512–42),
gave considerable encouragement
to cultural developments within
his kingdom. Accordingly, poets
like William Dunbar (c.1460–

1514) and Gavin Douglas (1474–
1522), notable scholars such as
John MAJOR (1467–1550) and
Hector Boece (c.1465–1536) benefited from royal patronage of one
kind or another. Boece, in fact,
became principal of the newly
founded King's College, Aberdeen,
the first Scottish UNIVERSITY to have
a separate MEDICAL faculty and also
to admit members of the laity. The
addition in 1512 of St Leonard's
College at the University of St
Andrews, largely through the
efforts of his talented natural son
Alexander, illustrates his interest in
education, a facet of his personality
observable previously in Alexander's earlier tuition at Padua
under the great Erasmus (c.1466–
1536). However, his EDUCATION Act
(1496) was drafted more with
improvements in the judicial
system in mind as was his promotion of the first Scottish printing
press at Edinburgh in 1507, which
he hoped would publish a compilation of the nation's laws. Various
architectural improvements were
also undertaken at the main royal
palaces, including the completion
of the Great Hall begun by his
father at Stirling, although it is his
interest in naval building for which
James is best remembered. The
construction, for example, of the
Great Michael, reputedly the
largest warship afloat in Europe,
was certainly no mean achievement.

In his relations with the other
major European powers the state-
craft of James IV is more open to
question. He revived the AULD
ALLIANCE in March 1492, an
insignificant action since England
and France had settled their current differences by the end of that

year. In 1495–96, he welcomed the arrival of the Yorkist pretender Perkin Warbeck (d.1499) but expeditions with him into England proved to be futile forays that failed to realize their presumed objective, the recovery of Berwick. None the less he was at least persuaded thereafter by the more sagacious Henry VII (1457–1509) to enter into the negotiations for an improvement in Anglo-Scottish relations, which ultimately produced the Treaty of Perpetual Peace (1502). This settlement, whose main feature was to be the marriage the following year of James to Henry's daughter Margaret (1489–1541) definitely resulted in an improved atmosphere in the relations between the two kingdoms that was to last until the English king's death in 1509. Besides, this wedding was eventually to result in the UNION OF THE CROWNS a century later.

However, the accession of Henry VIII (1491–1547), and particularly his adherence in 1511 to the Holy League against France, witnessed a revival of the Auld Alliance. James, obsessed with grandiose schemes for joint Christian action against the sinister encroachment of the Ottoman empire naively accepted a guarantee of support for his campaign from the king of France, once Scotland had assisted her old ally against the English. The disaster at FLODDEN on 9 September 1513 and James IV's own death in battle were the unfortunate outcome of the final misjudgement made by the king in his essentially flawed approach to foreign policy.
• *MacDougall, N., James IV, John Donald, 1989.*
• *Mackie, R.L., King James IV of*

Scotland, Oliver & Boyd, 1958.
• *Nicholson, R., Scotland: The Later Middle Ages, Oliver & Boyd, 1974.*

James V (1512—42) James was born April 1512 and succeeded to the throne in September 1513 following the death of his father, JAMES IV (1473–1513), at FLODDEN. During his minority (1513–28) the country was governed by a series of different administrations; his mother, Margaret Tudor (1489–1541), was in charge until her unpopular marriage to Archibald DOUGLAS, Earl of Angus (1489–1557), in August 1514 when the other nobility urgently invited John, Duke of Albany (c.1484–1536), to return as governor. Albany's stewardship ended in September 1524 to be followed by four years of internal conflict between the nobility in which the seizure of James by Angus in 1526 marked the ascendancy of the Douglases. This situation continued until James contrived to escape from them in May 1528.

A feature of his domestic administration was his increasing reliance on ecclesiastics and non-aristocratic councillors like Gavin Dunbar (c.1495–1547), Archbishop of Glasgow, David BEATON (c.1494–1546), Archbishop of St Andrews, and Oliver Sinclair of Pitcairns (d.1560). This was less deliberate policy than a reflection of the growing divisions between himself and many of the nobility. Understandably he detested the Douglases, whose principal members were exiled, although his execution in 1537 of distant relatives like Lady Glamis and the Master of Forbes seems unduly harsh. But his administration of the BORDERS, where he attempted to restore law and order by punitive methods including the imprisoning or fining of leading members of the Hepburns, Homes, Maxwells and Scotts caused particular antagonism. Doubtless for many of them the treatment they received was warranted but that it was impolitic to create such a mood of general resentment was underlined by the poor performance of these families and others on behalf of the Crown in the crisis of 1542. Outwith the Borders, various other families suffered at the hands of a king who had become notoriously avaricious and in the eyes of many lairds and noblemen richly deserved the description bestowed on him of 'ill-beloved'. In the HIGHLANDS, apart from some royal visits including one spectacular expedition in 1540, James V depended on the well-tried expedient of utilizing local magnates to stifle unrest. The only notable departure was the temporary eclipse of the Campbells in the 1530s in favour of the MacDonalds of Islay.

James V's relations with the clergy were complex; on the one hand they objected to footing the bill for his grandiose plans for a COLLEGE OF JUSTICE but on the other they welcomed the presence of prelates on his council, not to mention his tough stance against heresy. They were powerless to prevent his granting commendatorships to his illegitimate children for Kelso and Melrose abbeys as well as the priories of Coldingham, Holyrood and St Andrews.

As far as the bulk of the population were concerned, James V may well have been a reasonably popular figure. His issuing of letters pro- tecting some tenants from eviction by landowners, his proposals for a reduction of mortuary payments and teinds and his penchant for disguising himself in order to go among ordinary folk as the 'Gudeman of Ballengeich' were all actions likely to enhance his reputation. So too, despite its shortcomings, was his determination to reduce border turbulence. Another facet of his character is revealed by his patronage of architecture best observed in the Renaissance-style additions to Falkland, Linlithgow and Stirling not to mention his encouragement of the anti-clerical author of 'The Thrie Estates', Sir David LINDSAY (c.1486–1553).

In his foreign policy James V favoured the AULD ALLIANCE party because of his Francophile chancellor, Dunbar, as well as the continuing influence of Albany, and partly as a counter to the pro-English Douglases. Primarily his reasons were financial since a decent dowry would go some way to solving the financial problems created by his long minority. With Henry VIII (1491–1547) and the French allied against the Pope and the Holy Roman Emperor in the early 1530s, it was not until 1537 that James could marry Madeleine (1520–37) the daughter of Francis I (1494–1547). On her premature demise he quickly arranged another marriage to MARY OF GUISE (1515–60) in 1538. Until 1541 James resisted attempts by Henry VIII to weaken the Franco-Scottish entente, doubtless satisfied he had established financial control over the clergy without the need for any dissolution of the monasteries. His failure to appear at a meeting arranged between Henry and him-

self for September 1541 led to a complete breakdown in Anglo-Scottish relations culminating in defeat at SOLWAY MOSS on 24 November 1542. The nobility, especially those from the Borders, had either reacted adversely to the king's frontier policy or still suffered from a 'Flodden complex'. James died suddenly three weeks after this setback leaving as his heir the infant MARY (1542–87) and bequeathing Scotland the uncertainties of another long minority.
• *Donaldson, G., Scotland: James V to James VII, Oliver & Boyd, 1965*
• *Donaldson, G., Scottish Kings, Batsford, 1967.*

James VI (1566—1625) Born June 1566, son of MARY, QUEEN OF SCOTS (1542–87) and Henry STEWART, Lord Darnley (1546–67) he succeeded to the throne on the deposition of Mary in July 1567. The four regencies of MORAY (1531–70), Matthew STEWART, Earl of Lennox (1516–71), MAR (c.1510–72) and MORTON (c.1516–81) were followed by a period of factional conflict until 1585 when his personal rule commenced.

In government, James relied on a combination of his own not inconsiderable talents as a ruler and a PRIVY COUNCIL in which he placed increasing dependence on non-aristocratic individuals whose loyalty and good service were rewarded by promotion into the ranks of the nobility. MAITLAND OF THIRLESTANE (1543–95) is an early example of a policy, arguably adopted to counteract the power of some of the great magnates, and he was followed by numerous others, for example James Elphinstone (1553–1612), Alex-

ander Seton (1555–1622), Walter Stewart (d.1617) and, most notably of all, Thomas Hamilton (1563–1637). They were conveniently elevated to the peerage in the aftermath of the Act of Annexation (1587). By 1603 and the UNION OF THE CROWNS this system of administration was working quite effectively, although whether James ruled Scotland thereafter as easily as he claimed ('with his pen') is questionable. Certainly he continued to exercise considerable authority by maintaining a loyal Privy Council and keeping a firm grip on both the COLLEGE OF JUSTICE and PARLIAMENT.

In religion, once he had overcome the threats to his position presented by Francis STEWART, Earl of Bothwell (1563–1612) and the Catholic NORTHERN EARLS, James was in a better position to take on the task of restoring episcopal polity within the Church. Under the leadership of Andrew MELVILLE (1545–1622) the post-Reformation Kirk had become Presbyterian but from the mid-1590s the king moved over to the offensive against the Melvillians and by 1603 had effectively restored bishops to Parliament. The arrest and banishment of several leading Presbyterian clergy in 1605 followed by the arrest in London of Melville the next year paved the way for the readmission of bishops to the Kirk by a docile General Assembly in 1610. To control the Church by insisting on episcopacy made good political sense but imposing various changes in liturgy and observance by the FIVE ARTICLES OF PERTH (1618) showed less wisdom. At least James was sufficiently astute not to insist on their enforcement.

In the HIGHLANDS and Islands James pursued the traditional, if oft-criticized policy of relying extensively on the great families like the Campbells and Mac-Kenzies. An alternative expedient, the issue of commissions of fire and sword, was used against the notoriously violent clan Macgregor. One noteworthy departure was the deployment of certain able royal officials in particular areas; thus, Andrew Knox (1559–1633), in his capacity as Bishop of the Isles, assisted in their pacification by persuading several clan chieftains to sign the IONA BOND (1609); James Law (c.1560–l632) while Bishop of Orkney ended the corrupt regime of Lord Robert STEWART (1533–93) and his family; Bishop Alexander Forbes (1564–1617) also performed services for the Crown in the unruly diocese of Caithness. On the other hand, attempts at improving law and order by settling Lowland families on the Isle of Lewis were a complete failure.

Undoubtedly one of James VI's major accomplishments was to settle the BORDERS. This was essentially a consequence of his position after 1603 as king of both Scotland and England, which permitted closer co-operation between the two governments. Thus, by 1605, an Anglo-Scottish force was operating effectively against lawbreakers on the frontier and its eventual disbandment in 1621 only underlines the success of the king's border policy.

In the country generally the description 'King James's Peace' is often given to the last three decades or so of his reign. Certainly there was still an undercurrent of violence as legislation against feuding and keeping large retinues indicates. There was also the mysterious GOWRIE CONSPIRACY (1600). There is plenty of evidence of inflation, plague, food shortages and widespread vagabondage. The 1590s were years when WITCHCRAFT persecutions flourished. None the less clear signs of a more settled and orderly society are provided by such varied developments as the more elaborate and luxurious domestic architecture of the period, the introduction in 1617 of a register of sasines listing all transactions in heritable property, the much greater number of parish churches keeping records of births, marriages and deaths, not to mention the relatively unsuccessful innovation of setting up JUSTICES OF THE PEACE. The increase in commercial prosperity is reflected in the building or restoration of several east coast harbours to cater for expansion in the COAL, SALT and TEXTILE industries.

New enterprises, such as leather-making, glass manufacture and soap-making were encouraged by either the granting of royal monopolies or patents and the introduction of skilled foreign craftsmen. Success was limited while royal attempts at creating economic unity with England came to nought as did the one experiment at colonial expansion in Nova Scotia in 1622–3.

James married Anne of Denmark (1574–1619) in 1589 and they had seven children. Consequently, at his death in 1625 Scotland for once avoided a lengthy minority since the succession went to his eldest surviving son, CHARLES I (1600–49).

• *Brown, K., Bloodfeud in Scotland,*

1573—1625, John Donald, 1986.

• *Donaldson, G., James V to James VII, Oliver & Boyd, 1965.*

• *Goodare, J. and Lynch, M. (eds.), The Reign of James VI, Tuckwell Press, 1999.*

• *Lee, M., Jr., Government by Pen, University of Illinois Press, 1980.*

• *Smith, A.G.R.(ed.), The Reign of James VI and I, Macmillan, 1973.*

• *Willson, D.H., King James VI & I, Jonathan Cape, 1956.*

James VII (1633—1701) Born October 1633, the second son of CHARLES I (1600—49). As Duke of York he was sent to Scotland by his brother CHARLES II (1630—85) in 1679 and again in 1681 when he was responsible for the renewal of repressive measures against the COVENANTERS as well as the drafting of the controversial TEST ACT (1681).

His reign began auspiciously enough in February 1685 with PARLIAMENT readily consenting to further punitive action against the Covenanters and with little support throughout the country for the rising of Archibald CAMPBELL, ninth earl of Argyll, shortly afterwards. But by 1686, when there were distinct reservations in Parliament about his proposal to give toleration to Catholics in return for free trade with England, the situation was clearly changing. Moreover proclamations in August 1686 and January 1687 relaxing the penal laws against his co-religionists only produced further criticism. It was also noted that Protestant officials like QUEENS-BERRY (1637—95) and MACKENZIE OF ROSEHAUGH (1648—1716) were dismissed whereas Romanist converts like Perth (1648—1716) and Melfort (1649—1714) were pro-

moted. In June 1687 James had to extend his indulgences to embrace Presbyterians as well. The effect this had was to bring about a sudden revival in Presbyterianism while at the same time striking a severe blow against Episcopalianism. None the less, while there was growing opposition to the king's policies within Scotland, it was to be English events that were decisive. Thus the flight abroad of James in December 1688 and his relinquishing of the English throne to WILLIAM III (1650—1702) was the prelude to a Scottish convention in April 1689 declaring that he had forfeited the Scottish crown. James VII died in exile in France in September 1701 leaving his son James STEWART, 'the Old Pretender' (1688—1766), to carry on the Jacobite cause.

• *Belloc, H., James the Second, Faber & Gwyer, 1928.*

• *Donaldson, G., Scotland, James V to James VII, Oliver & Boyd, 1965.*

• *Ferguson, W., Scotland's Relations with England, John Donald, 1977.*

• *Mitchison, R., Lordship to Patronage, Edward Arnold, 1983.*

Jeffrey, Francis, Lord (1773—1850) Like his near contemporary Henry BROUGHAM (1778—1868) Jeffrey was educated during the era and with the ideas of the Scottish ENLIGHTENMENT, attending the universities of Glasgow and Edinburgh before going briefly to Oxford. He entered the legal profession in 1794 but despite his intimacy with many of the Edinburgh elite, including Walter SCOTT (1771—1832), apparently made little headway because of his WHIG sympathies and associations.

Jeffrey helped found the influential *Edinburgh Review* and personally edited and wrote for it during 1803–29. He managed to combine literary activities with both law and politics — becoming first Dean of the Faculty of Advocates then Lord Advocate in the reforming Whig administration of 1830–34. He was successively MP for Malton (1831–32), then after the Reform Act sat for Edinburgh until 1834. He himself played a prominent role in the passage of the Scottish Reform Act and the Burgh REFORM ACT (1833).

In 1834 he eschewed Westminster politics to become, as Lord Jeffrey, a judge of the Court of Session — a position he retained till his death. He gave an important decision in favour of the FREE CHURCH during the DISRUPTION. Jeffrey maintained a life-long interest in literature and criticism and selected contributions to the *Edinburgh Review* were published in 1844 and 1853.

Johnston, Archibald, of Wariston (1611—63) A lawyer who came to prominence as a key figure in the framing of the NATIONAL COVENANT whose signing in February 1638 he was to describe in his diary as 'that glorious marriage day of the kingdom with God'. Such religious fanaticism was to be one of his main characteristics, especially in the ensuing conflict with CHARLES I (1600—49). Thus, as Clerk to the GENERAL ASSEMBLY at Glasgow in November 1638, his ability to produce ancient registers condemning episcopacy had a considerable bearing on the assembly's decision to depose bishops. Again, as a member of the Covenanting delegation that negotiated the Pacification of Berwick

(1639) he was extremely critical of the king, although his attitude on that occasion did not deter Charles from promoting him Lord of Session in 1641. He was also given a knighthood in a further royal attempt to create a king's party in Scotland. Later in the 1640s he was one of the commissioners present at the WESTMINSTER ASSEMBLY. He became Lord Advocate in 1646 and Lord Clerk-Register in 1649. Initially during the CROMWELLIAN UNION he was, as a PROTESTOR, opposed to the regime but latterly he came to terms with it and sat in the last two parliaments of the Protectorate. However, this allegiance to the republicans was to have fatal consequences since following the RESTORATION SETTLEMENT he was condemned to death in his absence and being arrested in France, was eventually brought back to this country to be executed at Edinburgh in July 1663.

Johnston, Thomas (1881—1965) Like Walter ELLIOT (1888–1958), a near-contemporary, Johnston was one of the few Scottish politicians of his generation to achieve high office — becoming Lord Privy Seal in the second LABOUR administration and Secretary of State for Scotland (1941–5) under Churchill (1875–1965) in the wartime coalition government. Johnston was born in Kirkintilloch and educated at the local school before going to Lenzie Academy.

Although he had a natural talent for writing and considered going to university, he at first settled for clerical jobs until becoming a printer and editor of two local weekly newspapers. Much influenced by socialism, he and some associates founded *Forward*, the influential left-wing weekly, which he afterwards edited for twenty-five years. In 1913 Johnston became a town councillor in Kirkintilloch — where he was instrumental in establishing a successful municipal bank.

Meantime, in 1907, Johnston had gone to the University of Glasgow as a non-graduating student. While there he was chairman of the Socialist Society and ran the campaign of James Keir HARDIE (1856– 1915) for the rectorship — as well as associating with James MAXTON (1885–1946), who was also a student at the time.

Under Johnston's editorship *Forward* was vigorous in its denunciation of WORLD WAR I, and in a famous incident in 1916 the newspaper was suspended for publishing what was certainly a very accurate report of a noisy meeting between Lloyd George (1865–1945) and TRADE UNIONISTS from the Clydeside engineering shops and shipyards during one of his visits to Glasgow. Publication was resumed some weeks later.

The Forward Publishing Company, as Johnston called it, also produced books and pamphlets on socialist topics written by himself and his associates. One of the earliest was *The Case for Women's Suffrage and Objections Answered* (1907), and his most successful by far, *Our Scots Noble Families* (1909), a venomous attack on the Scottish landed aristocracy. Sales of *Noble Families* were estimated at between 100,000 and 120,000 copies and helped significantly to increase Labour support in Scotland. Later in life Johnston repudiated much that he had written — and it is even said that he tried to buy up existing copies before they fell into the hands of the unsuspecting aristocrats with whom he by then associated. Another important book and a pioneering labour history, *The History of the Scottish Working Class*, appeared in 1923.

After failing to get elected for Clackmannanshire and West Stirlingshire in the Coupon Election of 1918, Johnston became its MP in the great landslide that took RED CLYDESIDE to Westminster in 1922. He held the seat until the defeat of the first Labour government in 1924. Soon after he was returned at a by-election in Dundee, where his TEMPERANCE sympathies worked to his advantage. In 1929 he abandoned his faction-ridden constituency in Dundee and returned to the relative calm of West Stirlingshire, which he continued to represent (with one break 1931–35) for the rest of his parliamentary career.

Johnston had a well-developed interest in colonial affairs and in 1926 visited India to investigate both the conditions among jute workers and the rise of Indian nationalism. He was highly critical of the Indian capitalist elite — but otherwise seems to have had very orthodox views about self-determination. He was apparently opposed to the Congress Party and much of the work of Gandhi (1869–1948).

In the second minority Labour government Johnston became Under-Secretary of State for Scotland, when his main concern was unemployment, and later Lord Privy Seal with a seat in the Cabinet. Following the establishment of the National Government and his defeat in the General Election of 1931 he was out of Parliament until 1935. He spent much of his time, when not engaged in politics, writing *The Financiers and the Nation* (1934), which advocated nationalization of the banking system.

With war looming Johnston, in 1939, was made Regional Commissioner for Civil Defence in Scotland. Early in 1941 Churchill appointed him Secretary of State for Scotland with wide-ranging powers hardly typical of the office but necessary in the wartime emergency. Johnston, supported by a Council of State and assisted by the Scottish Council on Industry, set about the economic and social regeneration of Scotland. Even in wartime much was achieved — notably the development of the North of Scotland Hydro-Electric Board in 1943 and the creation of 700 new enterprises employing 90,000 people between 1942 and 1945. Johnston, a passionate Home Ruler, believed he 'got Scotland's wishes and opinions respected and listened to, as they had not been since the Union'.

After 1945, and having turned down both the post of Viceroy of India and a peerage, Johnston led a busy public life, being at different times chairman of the North of Scotland Hydro-Electric Board, the Scottish Tourist Board, and the Broadcasting Council for Scotland. Beatrice Webb (1858–1943) once described Johnston as 'the best of the Clyde lot', and discounting John WHEATLEY (1869–1930) this seems a fair description. He certainly was one of the few to make a dynamic contribution to Scottish economic and social life in his generation.

*•Johnston, T., Memories, Collins, 1952.
•Knox, W., (ed.), Scottish Labour Leaders 1918–39, Mainstream, 1984.
• Walker, G., Tom Johnston, Manchester University Press, 1988.*

Justices of the Peace   Although they were first proposed by JAMES VI (1566–1625) in 1587 there was no serious attempt at introducing JPs until 1609. But, except during the period of the CROMWELLIAN UNION, they made little impact largely because of competition from existing bodies such as the SHERIFF courts, BARON COURTS and burgh courts. After the Treaty of Union with the abolition of the PRIVY COUNCIL and, in 1747, with the ending of HERITABLE JURISDICTIONS, the justices played a greater part in local government and their duties became more extensive. Settling wage disputes, overseeing WEIGHTS AND MEASURES, suppressing riots, assisting with the administration of prisons and almshouses, supervising the maintenance of roads and bridges and helping with the provisions of the POOR LAW were just some of the tasks that these officials, often in conjunction with the COMMISSIONERS OF SUPPLY, were expected to undertake. James VI had initially recruited them from the ranks of the larger landowners but by the nineteenth century, merchants and businessmen were being appointed as well.

In 1830, for instance, as the struggle for parliamentary reform intensified and the authorities feared outbreaks of disorder the number of justices rose dramatically to 5,600. Increasingly, however, in the later nineteenth

century, their functions were taken over by other bodies and latterly, until local government was completely overhauled in 1974–75, one of their main duties was administering the licensing laws.
• *Whetstone, A.E., Scottish County Government in the Eighteenth and Nineteenth Centuries, John Donald, 1981.*

justiciar   As the name suggests this royal official was the officer delegated by the monarch to dispense justice and also supervise the work of SHERIFFS.

The office was established under royal authority in the twelfth century, numbers varying between two or three at any one time covering three areas of Lothian, Scotia and Galloway. The justiciars went on 'ayre' travelling around their respective districts to supervise justice and hear law suits themselves. The justiciars' functions were ultimately assumed by the Justice General.

jute   Like COTTON manufacture, jute was grafted onto the long-established LINEN industry, notably in Dundee and surroundings where coarse linen — canvas, sailcloth — were the dominant textiles. Jute was first imported to Dundee in 1822 but technical problems prevented its manufacture for at least a decade. Initially the fibre was mixed with flax, then pure jute cloth was produced around 1848 by James Ayton, a linen master.

Jute manufacture expanded rapidly during the 1850s and 60s — thanks partly to industrial demand and partly to the growth of the related linoleum industry in Kirkcaldy. Imports of raw material rose from 9,000 tons in 1848 to 60,000 by 1868 and 170,000 in 1900. The number of mills tripled between 1862 and 1875, with employment reaching an estimated 40,000 — three-quarters being female — in 1890. Long before this, Dundee itself had become a jute-dominated town with 90 per cent of its production being exported from the large integrated mills that dominated the skyline. Not without justification Dundee was christened 'Juteopolis'.

Dundee's monopoly of world jute manufacture was brief. Foreign competition from India and the Continent presented an increasing challenge after the 1880s and by WORLD WAR I had reached serious proportions. Typical of many entrepreneurs of their day the jute producers exploited the workforce by paying low wages and failing to invest in new technology so the impact of the DEPRESSION was profound. Previously high profits slumped and the recession brought high unemployment among the jute workers. Substantial reconstruction followed WORLD WAR II, but the industry slowly declined in the face of competition from new materials. Nevertheless, by the 1970s an impressive degree of diversification had been achieved in what remained of the industry, including the manufacture of polypropylene — incongruously the strongest modern rival to jute.
• *Lenman, B., Lythe, C. and Gauldie, E., Dundee and its Textile Industry 1850–1914, Abertay Historical Society, 1969.*
• *Walker, W., Juteopolis: Dundee and its Textile Workers, 1885–1923, Scottish Academic Press, 1979.*

K

Kames, Henry Home, Lord (1696—1782) Henry Home was a leading figure of the Scottish Enlightenment and like his near-contemporary, John Cockburn (1679–1758), an early practitioner of agricultural improvement. Home, the son of a Berwickshire laird, trained as a lawyer, becoming a Lord of Session in 1752. In common with many other Enlightenment figures his interests were catholic and he produced numerous works on antiquarian, legal and philosophical subjects, most notably his Essays on the *Principles of Morality and Natural Religion* (1751).

He first practised agricultural improvement on his Berwickshire estate, but when his wife inherited Blair Drummond, Perthshire, in 1766 he undertook much more extensive developments there. These included large-scale drainage, enclosure, fallowing, introduction of grasses and clovers, woodland plantations, road and bridge building. Kames subsequently published *The Gentleman Farmer* (1776) and advocated the teaching of agricultural science at the University of Edinburgh.

● *Ross, I.S., Lord Kames and the Scotland of His Day, Oxford University Press, 1972.*

Keith, Sir Robert (died 1346) Little is known of his early life but Keith played an important role in the Wars of Independence and the subsequent history of Anglo-Scottish relations. Although receiving the lands of Keith from King John in 1294 he had switched loyalty by 1308 when he linked up with Robert Bruce. Later he became a Justiciar and Marischal. Commanding cavalry at Bannockburn, he played a significant part in the Scottish victory over the English in 1314. Subsequently luck was not on his side for at Neville's Cross, another major confrontation between the Scots, led by David II, and the English, Keith was killed and the king captured.

kelp The kelp industry — gathering and burning seaweed to produce potash for use in the chemical industry — became important in parts of the Highlands and Islands during the eighteenth century. Kelping was seasonal, labour-intensive, and at its height geographically widespread — though the major centres were the Western Isles, Skye, Mull and the west coast north of Kyle of Lochalsh.

Kelping was established in North Uist about 1735 and slowly spread elsewhere. The first important phase of expansion began about

1770, later peaking between 1790 and 1820, thanks to high prices commanded during the FRENCH REVOLUTIONARY and NAPOLEONIC WARS when imports were either costly or difficult. The industry, therefore, not only provided short-term employment for a large labour force, but also generated substantial profits for some of the clan chiefs and landowners.

In the aftermath of decline there was much hardship and it is generally acknowledged that in the longer term the kelp industry contributed to the problem of over-population — leading ultimately to the large-scale emigration that accompanied the CLEARANCES.

•*Gray, M., The Highland Economy 1750—1850, Oliver & Boyd, 1957.*
•*Youngson, A.J., After the Forty-Five: The Economic Impact on the Scottish Highlands, Edinburgh University Press, 1973.*

Kelvin, Lord, William Thomson (1824—1907)

William Thomson, Lord Kelvin, was one of the most distinguished scientists and inventors of the Victorian era. He was born in Belfast, son of James Thomson, professor of mathematics at the Royal Institution. In 1832 his father moved to the chair of mathematics at the University of Glasgow and a few years later he himself began his studies there. In 1841, while still only seventeen, he entered Peterhouse, Cambridge, and embarked on a brilliant academic career that was to make him professor of natural philosophy at Glasgow by 1846 and a Fellow of the ROYAL SOCIETY by 1851.

His work on mathematical physics led him to investigate the theory that work and heat were convertible and between 1851 and 1854 he formulated the two great laws of thermodynamics — equivalence and transformation — later working on the doctrine of available energy. He and his colleagues then turned to electrical energy and experimentation, including early work on X-rays.

Thomson was always interested in applying science to practical ends, experimenting on electric telegraph cables and inventing the mirror galvanometer. In 1856 he became a director of the Atlantic telegraph company and served as electrician on the Agamemnon, which set out to lay the first cable across the Atlantic. Initially this was unsuccessful, but Thomson supervised the laying of a new cable in 1866, being knighted for his services by a grateful queen and nation. He founded the firm of Kelvin and White to manufacture his inventions and became a wealthy man.

Much of the rest of his life was devoted to research on electricity and magnetism — he published over 600 papers on these and other scientific subjects. He was interested in electrical generation and electric lighting and was particularly struck by the potential of the Niagara Falls for these purposes. Thomson was much honoured, becoming a baron in 1892 and receiving the Order of Merit in 1902. On his death in 1907 he was buried in Westminster Abbey. Strangely, there is no modern biography.

Kennedy, James (c.1408—65)

Kennedy, a nephew of JAMES I, studied at St Andrews and Louvain. He was appointed Bishop of Dunkeld in 1437 and of St Andrews in 1440. In these roles he was evidently conscientious and also travelled in Europe on diplomatic missions, visiting Rome twice. He was an advisor to JAMES II and played a significant role in governance during the minority of JAMES III. He founded St Salvator's College at St Andrews in 1450.

Killiecrankie, Battle of, (27 July 1689)   The first Jacobite rebellion was largely due to the efforts of John GRAHAM of Claverhouse (1648–89), created Viscount of Dundee in November 1688, who had raised the standard of the exiled JAMES VII (1633–1701) on Dundee Law in April 1689. Dundee's only real support came from some of the Highland chiefs and he was only able to conduct guerrilla tactics with any hope of success. However, his capture of Blair Castle in July spurred into action General Mackay (c.1640– 92) the commander of the government forces. Thus, at the head of the Pass of Killiecrankie Mackay's army of about 3,000 men found its route to Blair Atholl blocked by about 2,000 Jacobites. Not for the first time the famous Highland charge proved to be extremely effective, if at some cost in casualties, including Dundee himself. Therefore Killiecrankie turned out to be a pyrrhic victory for the Jacobites since their leader's death ensured the collapse of their revolt.

Lenman, B., The Jacobite Risings in Britain, 1689–1746, Eyre Methuen, 1980.

'Killing Time'   By 1680 the threat posed by the COVENANTERS to the government of Charles II (1630–

85) had been largely countered. Not only had repression taken its toll but other Covenanters had accepted the occasional offer of indulgences made by the authorities. Another such concession had been granted following the decisive defeat of the Covenanters at Bothwell Bridge (1679) leaving only a fanatical remnant led by Richard Cameron (1648–80), the CAMERONIANS, openly defying the government. Since Cameron and his followers renounced their allegiance to the Crown and eventually declared war on the State itself, they were the principal victims of what Wodrow (1679–1734), the historian of the Covenanting era, has entitled the 'Killing Time'. Although this lasted from 1680 to the Toleration Act of James VII (1633–1701) in 1687, it has been estimated that there were only about 100 actual victims, including many leading Cameronians, as well as, possibly, the 'WIGTOWN MARTYRS'. None the less it was an unpleasant episode, especially in the area mainly affected, the southwest of Scotland, where the troops engaged by John GRAHAM of Claverhouse (1648–89) frequently did not enquire too closely into the particulars of those whom they arrested and ill-treated. Thus, numerous ordinary people experienced brutal treatment for such questionable offences as not having taken the bond agreeing to lay down their arms after Bothwell Bridge, for allegedly sheltering Covenanters or for refusing to take the oath attached to the unpopular TEST ACT (1681).

Cowan, I.B., The Scottish Covenanters, Weidenfeld & Nicolson, 1976.

Dickinson, W.C. and Donaldson, G.

(eds.), A Source Book of Scottish History III, Nelson, 1961.

Kirkcaldy, Sir William, of Grange (c.1520—73) The son of Sir James Kirkcaldy of Grange (d.1556), treasurer to James V (1512—42) in the final years of his reign, he inherited his father's antipathy towards Cardinal BEATON (1494—1546) and was one of the Archbishop's assassins in 1546. Taken prisoner after the siege of St Andrews he was sent to France where he eventually distinguished himself as an outstanding military leader. In 1559 he joined the LORDS OF THE CONGREGATION and for the next fourteen years played a major part in most of the main events that took place. Thus, in 1565, he joined the CHASEABOUT RAID, the following year he was involved in the plot against Riccio (c.1533—66), while in 1567 he accepted the surrender of MARY (1542—87) at Carberry and pursued James HEPBURN, Earl of Bothwell (c.1535—78) to the remote Shetlands. However, he ultimately disapproved of Mary's deposition and from 1569 to 1573 became a leading member of the Marians. At the onset of the Civil War, as Provost of Edinburgh and Governor of the Castle — an appointment made by MORAY (1531—70) in recognition of Grange's services at Langside — he was able to ensure the Queen's faction had control of the capital. But his attempt to seize the Regent Lennox (1516—71) in September 1571 ended disastrously and the final collapse of the Marians at the Pacification of PERTH left Maitland (c.1525—73) and himself with a tiny garrison to defend the castle against Morton (c.1516—81) and his English allies. Following the surrender of the fortress in May, Grange was tried for treason, found guilty, and hanged on 3 August 1573.

Knights Templar This military religious order was founded in 1118 during the CRUSADES, to defend Christian pilgrims. It established its headquarters at Temple in Midlothian in 1153, following a grant of land by DAVID I. After the order was suppressed by the Pope in 1312, the property passed to the Knights Hospitallers, who had their base nearby at Torphicen, West Lothian. They also had centres at Kirkliston, West Lothian, and Maryculter, Kincardineshire.

Knox, John (c.1512—72) John Knox was educated at St Andrews University and ordained as a priest. The teachings of George WISHART (c.1513—46), with whom he began to associate, were his earliest introduction to the opinions of the reformers. After the murder of BEATON (c.1494—1546) he eventually joined the cardinal's assassins within St Andrews Castle as their chaplain and following the capture of that fortress by the French was a prisoner on their galleys for two years. Between 1549 and 1553 he was mainly in England establishing a growing reputation for his radical religious outlook but refusing preferment within the Anglican Church. The accession of MARY (1516—58) saw him depart for the Continent where for the next six years he spent much of his time in Geneva absorbing the doctrines of John Calvin (1509—64). However, he did visit Scotland in 1555 when his preaching apparently made a considerable impact on such figures as Argyll (d.1558), Lord Lorne (c.1538–73), Lord James Stewart (1531–70) and William MAITLAND of Lethington (c.1525–73). The upshot was the formation two years later of the LORDS OF THE CONGREGATION and in 1559, after a false start in 1557, Knox returned to play a major role in the REFORMATION. Indeed his fiery sermon delivered in St John's Church, Perth, on 11 May and the violence accompanying it, is usually regarded as marking the commencement of the hostilities that were to last until the signing of the Treaty of Edinburgh. By that date Knox and his colleagues had drafted the First BOOK OF DISCIPLINE, the blueprint for the Reformed Kirk, which was to be largely ignored by the subsequent 'Reformation Parliament' in August 1560.

Thus, the latter part of his career was spent in a constant struggle with the governments of Mary and JAMES VI (1566–1625) endeavouring to obtain their acceptance of the Kirk's proposals for its polity and endowment. His last significant action was to give his approval to the settlement made at Leith in January 1572 when a compromise was reached by the representatives of Church and State over the appointment of bishops.

Knox's literary output was also not insignificant. While his *First Blast of the Trumpet against the Monstrous Regiment of Women* is principally of interest nowadays for its curious title, it did have some contemporary significance since it alienated Elizabeth I of England (1533–1603), who mistakenly believed it was directed against her as well. However, his outstanding achievement undoubtedly was his *History of the Reformation* which, while a personal memoir and certainly exaggerating the reformer's own contribution to various events, is also an invaluable source for the Reformation era.

• *Percy, E., John Knox, Hodder & Stoughton, 1937.*
• *Reid, W.S., Trumpeter of God, Scribners, 1974.*

L

Labour Party   Important antecedents of the Labour
Representation Committee, formed
in 1900, included the Scottish
Parliamentary Labour Party, which
was founded in 1888 by the pioneer socialist J. Keir HARDIE (1856–
1915) and the INDEPENDENT LABOUR
PARTY, which dated from 1893. In
the United Kingdom context the
Labour Representation Committee
included representatives of several
socialist groups like the Social
Democratic Federation and the
Fabian Society, as well as members
of trade unions, united to establish
'a distinct Labour group in
Parliament'.

After its 1906 General Election
victories the Labour Representation Committee was renamed the
Labour Party and J. Ramsay
MACDONALD (1866–1937) became
its first secretary. To add to the confusion a nominally independent
Scottish Labour Party was also
formed in 1906 from the Scottish
Workers' Parliamentary Election
Committee (1900). This ultimately
merged with the British Labour
Party in 1909.

From the outset, Scottish
Labour's relationship with the
British Labour Party, the ILP and
other factions was complex.
Nevertheless it made a significant
contribution to the character of the
Labour Party through leadership,

language and ideology, most
notably in the work of Hardie,
MacDonald, John WHEATLEY
(1869–1930), James MAXTON
(1885–1946), and Patrick Dollan
(1881–1963). The return of a large
number of Scottish Labour MPs in
the General Election of 1922 could
be seen partly as a reward for class
struggles during WORLD WAR I, and
partly as a result of successful propaganda in a deteriorating post-
war economy.

During the 1920s Scottish
Labour made some gains and had
considerable impact locally and
nationally. Men like Wheatley and
Dollan proved to be very successful
politicians – the former at
Westminster, the latter in Glasgow
local government. For many –
especially RED CLYDESIDERS – disillusionment with MacDonald's
gradualism and lack of imaginative
policies to deal with unemployment and social distress soon set
in, leading to the increased alien-
ation of the ILP. Prominent among
the disaffected were Wheatley and
Maxton, and certainly the death of
the former in 1930 robbed the left
of a skilled politician.

The party experienced mixed fortunes in the 1930s as the country
struggled with the DEPRESSION. The
General Election of 1931, following MacDonald's defection from
the Labour Party to form a

'National' government, was an unmitigated disaster, with serious defeats even in traditional strongholds. However, Labour did well in local government — capturing Glasgow in 1933 and also proving successful in other towns during the decade. Many Labour activists worked closely with the Communist Party and other left-wing groups in the battle against unemployment at home and the rise of fascism abroad.

Despite the enthusiasm of Tom JOHNSTON (1881–1965) for administrative devolution during WORLD WAR II, the Labour Party in Scotland became increasingly integrated into the British party after 1945. HOME RULE remained a hardy annual at Scottish conferences for years, but it was finally abandoned in 1958. Though occupying a dominant, but not unchallenged position in the municipal politics of urban-industrial Scotland, the Labour Party's performance was hardly sparkling. The same might be said of its record during the years of Labour government in the 1960s and 70s. Labour's regional policies at first favoured Scotland, especially in terms of new industrial development, but subsequent events nationally and internationally undid most that had been achieved. Continuing economic and social problems served to revive the SCOTTISH NATIONAL PARTY and Labour was forced to do an about-turn on devolution in the late 1970s. In the inevitable shambles of the referendum campaign the Labour Party in Scotland emerged with little credit.

In the 1980s the Labour Party remained the most powerful force in Scottish politics — in contrast to the situation in England, where its vote had been drastically eroded. During the 1980s and 1990s Labour's strength was partly its traditional appeal in its old heartlands and partly a rejection of CONSERVATIVE policies under both Margaret Thatcher and John Major. However, Labour found difficulty with the economy, particularly the decline of heavy industry in areas where its vote was strongest. The SNP, by then more radical, also cost the party votes, especially where home rule tended to divide Labour. Meantime under the leadership of Neil Kinnock, Scots like John SMITH (himself leader 1992–95), helped steer the party through a divisive period by effectively expelling the militant left. As the party swung to the right the left was seen an impediment to attracting middle-class votes Labour needed if it was to be re-elected to government. But Labour, despite gaining forty-nine seats in Scotland at the General Election of 1992, failed to make the breakthrough nationally. Having cast off more of its earlier socialist baggage (including, to some extent, its close relationship with the TRADE UNION movement) and replaced the Red Flag with the red rose, New Labour, under the leadership of Tony Blair, was elected by a large majority in 1997. While success nationally was partly explained by the public's rejection of Tory policies, in Scotland devolution was given high priority in the party's manifesto. In a referendum later that year the establishment of a Scottish Parliament was duly endorsed. Following the election for the Holyrood Parliament in

1999, Labour were the largest party but lacking an overall majority formed a coalition government with the LIBERAL DEMOCRATS. Donald DEWAR, a long-time devolutionist, became the first First Minister.

In summary, there is much to criticize about the activities of the Labour Party in Scotland, though its record in national politics and local government since the 1900s is nevertheless formidable. Much of its initial success was due to the collapse of Radical Liberalism, though it had gained its own momentum in Scotland by 1914. Historically, its socialist ideology has had to give way to pragmatism in the real world – often at the cost of party unity.

• Brown, K.D. (ed.), The First Labour Party 1906–1914, Croom Helm, 1985.
• Donnachie, I., Harvie, C. and Wood, I. (eds.), Forward! Labour Politics in Scotland 1888–1988, Polygon Books, 1989.

land settlement, see AGRICULTURE; DEPRESSION; LEVER

Langside, Battle of, (13 May 1568) The escape of MARY (1542–87) from Lochleven Castle in May 1568 saw the numerous opponents of Regent MORAY (1531–70) and those others responsible for dethroning the Queen rally to her side. Thus at Hamilton on 8 May as many as nine earls, nine bishops, fourteen commendators, seventeen lords and over ninety lairds signed a bond pledging their support. Prominent among them were representatives of the Campbell, Gordon and Hamilton families, the latter committed to pursuing their claims to the succession as advantageously as they could. By all accounts it was the Hamiltons who ill-advisedly precipitated the encounter at Langside, then a village lying to the southwest of Glasgow, as Mary was trying to take her forces to Dumbarton Castle, which was in friendly hands. The conflict itself, on the morning of 13 May, was a short-lived affair in which Moray's numerically inferior army led by MORTON (c.1516–81) and KIRKCALDY OF GRANGE (c.1520–73) took advantage of shortcomings in the ranks of the Marians. Argyll (c.1538–73), their commander, for instance, either became suddenly ill or acted treacherously. Mary, following her defeat, and accompanied by Herries (1512–83) sought refuge in southwest Scotland. Here, since she still patently had a considerable following she made another major miscalculation by deciding to place herself at the mercy of her cousin, Elizabeth (1533–1603).

• Donaldson, G., Mary, Queen of Scots, English Universities Press, 1974.
• Fraser, A., Mary, Queen of Scots, Weidenfeld & Nicolson, 1969.

Largs, Battle of (1263) As one modern historian put it, the Battle of Largs almost has the status of STIRLING BRIDGE or BANNOCKBURN, yet there is considerable controversy about both its causes and scale. The details come from the Norwegian *Hakon's Saga* and Walter Bower's *Scotichronicon*, both of which had reasons to highlight their own versions of events. The battle seems to have been provoked by a series of Scottish attacks on the inner ISLES initiated by ALEXANDER II, who died at Kerrera in 1249 because, it was widely believed, he had attacked the holy ground of Columba. More immediately the year 1262 saw further raids and on Skye, churches were burned and women and children slaughtered. In retaliation Hakon IV, King of Norway, deployed a fleet of 120 vessels (Bower says 160) in the Clyde, raiding coastal settlements and capturing castles in Ayr, and on Arran and Bute. In the battle itself Hakon's raiders were repulsed by the forces of ALEXANDER III, according to Bower, a victory brought about by the intercession of St Margaret herself. While the actual outcome is in doubt, subsequent events were of considerable significance. Hakon died in Orkney during the following winter, Alexander launched further attacks in Caithness, Skye and the Isles in 1264, forcing Hakon's successor, Magnus, to sign the Treaty of PERTH in 1266. The Western Isles and Man passed nominally to the Scots, while Norway kept control of Orkney and Shetland.

Lauder Bridge   The scene of a coup against JAMES III, while heading an army on its way to meet an invading English force sent by Edward IV in support of Albany, James's brother. Several of the king's closest companions and advisors were murdered by a group of nobles led by Archibald DOUGLAS, fifth Earl of Angus, nicknamed 'Bell the Cat'. James himself was held for a time in Edinburgh castle, but ultimately regained control thanks to support from northern magnates.

Lee, Jennie (1904—1988)   Jennie Lee (Janet Bevan, later Baroness Lee) was one of the most memorable women in twentieth-century LABOUR politics. Noted as the wife of the Labour politician, the fiery Welshman, Aneurin Bevan (1897—1960), she herself had a varied political career that began in her youth. Her upbringing in a Fife coal mining community where her grandfather was a TRADE UNION official and her father a miner confirmed her interest in socialist politics.

After studying at Edinburgh University she became a teacher. She continued her political work and in 1929 was elected INDEPENDENT LABOUR MP for North Lanark. During her first brief period in parliament she was closely associated with the Clydesiders, such as James MAXTON and John WHEATLEY, and like them was a thorn in the flesh of the second Labour government headed by Ramsay MACDONALD.

Lee lost her seat in the 1931 election which returned the National Government under MacDonald to Westminster. But she continued to be actively involved in politics and also took up journalism and lecturing. She travelled extensively including visits to the United Sates, the Soviet Union, France and Spain. She was particularly interested in the activities of the Popular Front in France as a model for Labour Party unity in Britain, and in the fortunes of the Spanish republic and the (later) events of the Spanish Civil War, which also divided the left at home. In 1934 she married Bevan, by then MP for Ebbw Vale, in the South Wales coalfield. Her reflections on this period are powerfully conveyed in the book *Tomorrow is a New Day*, published in 1939.

Back in parliament as MP for Cannock following the Labour

landslide of 1945 she was a powerful support to Bevan, who became Minister for Health in the Atlee government and had a key role in the creation of the Welfare State. Bevan resigned over the issue of health charges to pay for increased defence budgets during the Korean War, and later in opposition to the CONSERVATIVE governments of the 1950s he and his wife came to be regarded as the socialist soul of Labour. The 'Bevanites' as they were called formed a party within a party and the Bevans and their supporters were constantly at odds with the leadership, then headed by Hugh Gaitskell. They were reconciled after Bevan in 1957 denounced unilateral nuclear disarmament, although Lee herself had mixed feelings about this. Possibly because she wanted to promote her husband's career she kept out of the limelight, but after he died in 1960 and Labour under Harold Wilson's leadership was elected in 1964 she became more involved in government.

Following his University of the Air speech delivered at Glasgow in 1963 Wilson gave Lee, later Britain's first arts minister (1965), the task of developing the scheme. She subsequently played a major role in setting up The Open University (1969).

In 1980 she published another volume of autobiography entitled MY LIFE WITH NYE, but a franker revelation of their personal and political relationship was subsequently provided by a modern biographer. It is regarded as an outstanding personal and political biography, drawing extensively on testimony and witness of Lee's friends and associates.

•*Hollis, P. and Lee, J., A Life, Oxford University Press, 1997.*

Lennox, Duke of, see STEWART, ESMÉ

Leslie, Alexander, Earl of Leven (c.1580—1661) Reputedly an illegitimate son of a captain of Blair Atholl Castle, Alexander Leslie rose to prominence as a field marshal in the Swedish forces fighting in Germany during the Thirty Years' War (1618—48). The marriage of his son to a daughter of Rothes (c.1600—41), one of the leading adversaries of CHARLES I (1600—49) strengthened his links with the Covenanting cause and he was responsible for organizing the signing of the Covenant by Scottish soldiers serving in Germany. Returning to this country late in 1638 he was actively involved in the military preparations before the First and Second BISHOPS' WARS, playing a major part in both campaigns. In 1641 the king, as part of a vain attempt to split the ranks of his opponents, created him Earl of Leven. None the less, in 1644 he led the Scottish army sent into England in accordance with the military agreement attached to the SOLEMN LEAGUE AND COVENANT. This force, particularly the cavalry commanded by David LESLIE, Lord Newark (d.1682) contributed to the defeat of the Royalists at Marston Moor. His later career was one of mixed fortunes, since although he didn't support the ENGAGEMENT, his allegiance to CHARLES II (1630—85) resulted in his arrest by the English in 1651. He spent three years in the Tower before being released after some pressure by the Swedish government in 1654.

• *Terry, G.S., The Life and Campaigns of Alexander Leslie, Constable, 1899.*

Leslie, David, Lord Newark (d.1682) The grandson of the fifth Earl of Rothes (d.1611), he was yet another Scotsman who served in the Swedish army during the Thirty Years' War (1618—48). He returned to join the Covenanting opposition to CHARLES I (1600—49) and was in charge of the cavalry accompanying the army sent to England in 1644 as part of the outcome of the SOLEMN LEAGUE AND COVENANT. He played a major role in the subsequent battle of Marston Moor while a year later, in September 1645, he commanded the forces that surprised and defeated James GRAHAM, Marquis of Montrose (1612—50) at PHILIP-HAUGH. Regrettably, he must also be held responsible for the slaughter of prisoners and camp followers that took place after that encounter. He refrained from supporting the Engagement but in 1650 was commander of the Covenanting army opposing Cromwell (1599—1658). Although his delaying tactics posed serious problems to the Protector he was ultimately defeated by him at DUNBAR in September 1650. Exactly a year later, commanding the forces supporting CHARLES II (1630—85) he was beaten once again and taken prisoner soon afterwards. He spent the remainder of the 1650s in the Tower, being released at the Restoration and given the Lordship of Newark in 1661 in recognition of his services to the Crown.

Levellers During the 1720s, organized groups of tenant farmers, known by the familiar seventeenth-century term 'Levellers', actively protested against ENCLOSURES by landowners throughout various parts of Galloway in southwest Scotland. This, as their name suggests, was achieved by men and women breaking down stone walls or dykes — as well as confronting the authorities.

The Levellers' action began in the spring of 1724 and was at first concentrated in the Stewartry of Kirkcudbright, spreading later to Wigtownshire — both areas where landlords had enclosed fields for CATTLE grazing on some scale. By all accounts the Levellers and their leaders were well-organized and had the tacit support of several local clergy. Troops from Edinburgh confronted the Levellers near Kirkcudbright on 2 June and in the ensuing confusion the movement was dispersed and its leaders arrested. Sporadic outbreaks of levelling continued throughout Galloway until the autumn, but soon fizzled out. The degree of sympathy among lesser gentry and merchants seems to have done much to reduce the severity of the law when prosecutions were brought in 1725.

The Levellers' Rising in 1724 was the earliest of a series of popular protests, continuing throughout the eighteenth and nineteenth centuries against landlordism and the AGRICULTURAL REVOLUTION — culminating with the reaction in the HIGHLANDS against the CLEARANCES. • *Donnachie, I. and Macleod, I., Old Galloway, David & Charles, 1974.*

Leven, Earl of, see LESLIE, ALEXANDER, EARL OF LEVEN

Lever, William, Viscount Leverhulme (1851—1925) William

Lever, the great soap magnate who established the firm of Lever Brothers and developed the associated PLANNED VILLAGE of Port Sunlight, near Birkenhead, had a short-lived flirtation with the HIGHLANDS and Islands after he acquired the Island of Lewis in 1917 – and later added to his estate by the purchase of Harris in 1919.

Lever seems to have been genuinely concerned about the plight of the crofters – including those returning from WORLD WAR I – and set about a series of regenerative schemes that included investment in farming, tweed manufacture and the fishing industry. The last involved the development of Leverburgh, a fishing village in Harris. Like most of his schemes in the Western Isles, it was short-lived – partly, it was maintained, because the local population resented the intrusion of absentee landlords and demanded their own land to farm as they chose.

Nevertheless, Lever was proud of his association with the islands and when raised to a viscountcy Lord Leverhulme added 'of the Western Isles' to his new designation. In what was to prove a generous gesture he gave the town and surrounding land as a gift to the people of Stornoway in perpetuity. One estimate puts his losses at £1.5 million by the time he finally withdrew in 1923.

• *Nicholson, N., Lord of the Isles: Lord Leverhulme in the Hebrides, Weidenfeld & Nicolson, 1960.*

Liberal Party From the first elections following the Reform Act in 1832 when forty-three out of the fifty-three Scottish constituencies were secured by the WHIGS Scotland was predominantly, though not exclusively, Liberal. Scottish liberalism was generally reformist but from the outset it embraced at least three factions: the paternalist land-owning Whigs; the new middle-class Liberals of the towns and cities; and the working-class Radicals. The Whig landowners favoured a modest extension of the franchise and social improvement in such spheres as the POOR LAW and EDUCATION. Middle-class Liberals, some of whom had supported the ANTI-CORN LAW LEAGUE and CHARTISM, favoured greater sharing of the vote, but little else. The Radicals were interested not only in universal suffrage but also a programme favouring major improvements in working and living conditions including more powerful Factory Acts and greater recognition of TRADE UNIONS and wage bargaining. In the 1840s many Liberals supported the DISRUPTION and joined the FREE CHURCH; while by the 1880s the Radical wing was usually pro HOME RULE for Scotland and upheld TEMPERANCE almost as strongly as the self-help espoused by Samuel SMILES.

Thanks to what Fry calls 'a solid and indispensible bloc of Scots' the Liberal Party held power during 1830–35, most of the period 1846–74, and following Gladstone's (1809–98) famous Midlothian Campaign, more than half of the period 1880–1914. Prominent among their number were Duncan McLaren (1800–86), an MP for Edinburgh (1865–91), who played a key role in securing a better deal for Scotland under the second Reform Act (1868); the aristocrat Lord ROSEBERY (1847–1929), Prime Minister 1894–5, and Sir Henry CAMPBELL-BANNERMAN (1836–1908), Prime Minister 1905–8. Additionally both Gladstone and ASQUITH (1852–1928), Prime Minister 1908–15, sat for Scottish seats. R.B. HALDANE (1856–1928) was a distinguished Secretary of State for War under both Campbell-Bannerman and Asquith, 1905–12.

Given its diversity the Liberal Party was subject to periodic dissention, which gravely weakened its effectiveness in and out of office. Gladstonian Liberalism comprised Free Trade budgets, financial economy, gradual political reform and peaceful foreign and imperial relations. While some of this appealed to the Radicals it was seen by most as essentially gradualist, ignoring major social problems of the day. However, it was the issue of Irish Home Rule that split the party in 1886, with the result that it remained relatively weak for the rest of the century. One positive thing to emerge from this was the CROFTER'S COMMISSION, which responded to similar problems in the HIGHLANDS. While the emergence of organized LABOUR politics was longer term there can be little doubt that the working class enfranchised in the 1884 Reform Act began to turn from Liberalism during this period. Economic problems also tended to shift the balance towards independent Labour action.

Having survived another crisis over the Boer War, the Liberals swept to power in 1906, instituting a series of significant social reforms including National Insurance and old age pensions. These were not enough to save the party from the long-term decline that set in after WORLD WAR I — a major turning point for the Labour Party in Scotland. The Liberal vote in Scotland declined from 28 per cent in 1923 to 18 per cent in 1931, with the low-point being reached in 1955 when the party got 19 per cent of the vote and returned a sole Scottish Liberal MP, the future leader of the party, Jo GRIMOND. Liberal fortunes subsequently revived during the 1960s and 70s, notably in its traditional rural strongholds in the Borders and the Highlands.

Overall the Liberal Party played a significant role in the making of Scottish politics and society during much of the nineteenth and early twentieth centuries and Scottish politicians themselves did much to shape its destiny in Britain as a whole.

• *Fry, M., Patronage and Principle: A Political History of Modern Scotland, Aberdeen University Press, 1987.*

Lindsay, Sir David (1486—1555) A government servant but remembered as a major literary figure, Lindsay was the son of David Lindsay of the Mount, near Cupar, Fife. Little is known of his background but he was a functionary in the court of JAMES IV and during the minority of JAMES V. He was a herald (1530), then Lyon of the court, before being knighted in 1542. His main role seems to have been in ambassadorial missions, which together with his knowledge of the court, church and PARLIAMENT put in him in strong position to assess elite society of the time. The most famous and lengthy was *Ane Satyre of The Three Estates*, which as the name suggests criticised in satire the abuses of church and state, combined with an appeal to the king and other office holders to respect their positions and behave with morality. *Ane Satire* was therefore indirectly an important critique of the excesses of clerical and other office holders in the period preceding the REFORMATION. It also showed that the corruption that had become common-place in court and church had also filtered down to the representatives of the BURGHS. Other works in poem-play style pursued a similar theme.

linen   Linen cloth, manufactured from flax, was the most significant of all the Scottish TEXTILE industries during the eighteenth century and remained important even after the rise of COTTON. As early as the sixteenth century the working of flax and hemp had become a well-established industry, producing everything from table cloth to sail cloth and rope. According to Thomas Morer, writing in 1689, linen had become 'the most noted and beneficial manufacture of the kingdom'. The industry was already concentrated around the Tay and the Clyde and with the coming of the UNION in 1707 the export potential could be readily exploited. Although at first an essentially domestic industry, it was nevertheless highly organized. It benefited from incentives provided by the BOARD OF TRUSTEES for Manufactures, established after the Union, which included subsidies for flax cultivation, bounties or prizes for new techniques or machinery, and the introduction of foreign workers with appropriate skills — like Dutch bleachers and

French cambric weavers. Quality control was a major concern of the Board, which appointed fifty 'stampmasters' to stations throughout the country where all linen offered for sale had to be officially checked and stamped.

The official returns show production rising from 2 million yards in 1728 to 13 million yards in 1770 and 24 million yards in 1800. The industry was widely dispersed but by 1750 the most important areas of production were to be found in Angus, Perth and Fife. The east of Scotland tended to concentrate on coarse yarn and cloth; while the western counties, such as Renfrew, Lanark, Dumbarton and Ayr, had a reputation for the manufacture of fine thread and linen fabric.

As with cotton, mechanization transformed linen into a factory industry. The first process to be mechanized was flax or lint scutching or dressing — a preliminary process carried out in water-powered mills. By 1772 there were over 250 lint mills, one of which at Irvine, Ayrshire, later employed Robert BURNS (1759—96) as a flax dresser. The first mills to spin yarn were established in the 1780s — quickly spreading throughout the industry. However, alongside factory spinning the finishing processes of weaving and bleaching remained relatively primitive and labour-intensive — notably in the handloom weaving sector. This was organized by linen merchants, prominent being the entrepreneur, David DALE (1739—1806), founder of the cotton mills at NEW LANARK. Hand-looms dominated linen weaving even as late as the 1830s. Thanks to the pioneering work of Charles TENNANT (1768—1838) and

201

others, chemical bleaching, dyeing and printing became important industries in their own right.

Linen remained an important industry throughout the nineteenth century, becoming more concentrated in Angus, Fife, Perth, and especially in Dundee, which became a major centre of coarse linen and jute production. Elsewhere, Dunfermline and Ayrshire made a speciality of fine table linen and curtains, while Paisley long dominated the market for linen thread. Several large enterprises emerged in the Victorian era, including Baxters of Dundee and Coates of Paisley. While a degree of paternalism was evident on the part of these and other employers, the condition of labour (mainly women) was generally adverse.

Like the other textile industries linen slowly declined in the face of competition from foreign competition and artificial fibres — but it remained locally significant in Angus, Ayrshire and elsewhere.

• Durie, A.J., The Scottish Linen Industry in the Eighteenth Century, John Donald, 1979.

Lipton, Sir Thomas (1850—1931)

Like many other successful businessmen, Lipton was able to build up a huge enterprise thanks to his boundless energy, organising ability and sharp marketing. Critically, as a youth, he spent four years in the United States, working for part of his stay in a progressive New York grocery store. Returning with $500 savings, and bearing in mind that small businesses could still then be established on modest resources, was able to open his first 'Lipton Market' in Glasgow in

1871. The son of Irish immigrants, he used his Ulster connections to supply high quality diary products and hams, buying in bulk and cutting out middlemen to maximize his returns.

He gradually built the business and by the time he was 40 he had stores all over Britain and had even expanded into tea, coffee and cocoa plantations, which from Sri Lanka supplied his customers. He also had extensive business interests in the US, notably in meat refrigeration and transport. When his main British enterprise went public in 1898 it was worth £2.5 million and his name was by then a household word.

Meantime Lipton had moved to London, climbing the social ladder and associating with royalty, notably with Edward, Prince of Wales. He was rich enough to indulge a passion for yachting and tried five times for the America's Cup without success. While he never won what he described as 'that blooming cup' his two business precepts of 'never take a partner' and 'never accept a loan' certainly paid off, thanks to rising working and lower middle class incomes, changing tastes and improved transport.

Lister, Joseph, see MEDICINE

Lithgow, Sir James (1883—1952)

Son of a successful Port Glasgow shipbuilder, James Lithgow was born in 1883 and educated at the Glasgow Academy and in Paris. When he was sixteen he was apprenticed in the SHIPBUILDING yard and soon earned the nickname 'the Scarlet Runner' — the red-headed lad who did everything twice as fast as any of his workmates. By 1906 he was a partner in his father's firm of Russell & Company, which later became Lithgow's Ltd, with an international reputation for its ships. When their father died in 1908 Lithgow and his younger brother, Henry, were faced with the management of a major enterprise. This they tackled with considerable success during a period that marked the heyday of the Clydeside yards in the years preceding 1914. In 1912 the young Lithgow was elected president of the Clyde Shipbuilder's Association.

While his brother stayed at home to manage the yard Lithgow went off to fight in WORLD WAR I. Joining the Royal Artillery, he was wounded, promoted to lieutenant-colonel and awarded the MC for bravery. He became director of merchant shipping at the Admiralty in 1917. When not managing the business, much of Lithgow's time in the ensuing post-war years and during the depression was spent trying to help industry adjust to the recession. In 1930 he became chairman of the National Ship-builder's Security Ltd and was also involved in the rescue of William BEARDMORE & Company and the Fairfield Shipbuilding and Engineering Company. A determined and tough negotiator, Lithgow involved himself extensively in industrial relations nationally and internationally. He was the British delegate to the International Labour Organization in Geneva, 1922—25 and again 1933—35.

During WORLD WAR II Lithgow was controller of merchant shipbuilding and repairs, and for a time was also in charge of tank production. Later he became president of the Iron and Steel Federation (1943—45) and devoted his time to planning post-war reconstruction. Lithgow was created a baronet in 1925 and made a freeman of Port Glasgow in 1951. James Lithgow can be regarded as one of the most successful twentieth-century Scottish industrialists, whose acute instinct for survival was reflected in many spheres beyond the shipyards of the Clyde.
• *Reid, J.M., James Lithgow, Master of Work, Hutchinson, 1964.*

Livingston, Sir Alexander (d.1450) A member of the influential Livingston family, Sir Alexander Livingston, emerged as a power broker during the minority of JAMES II. Initially he cooperated with another powerful figure, Sir William Crichton, whom he ultimately replaced as a key adviser to the crown. Like Crichton he played a role in the campaign against the Douglases. Both he and his kin gained a variety of offices of state during the later stages of the king's minority, but probably having alienated others in the process, Livingston was overthrown when the king himself took control c.1449.

Livingstone, David (1813—73) Like Mungo PARK (1771—1806), David Livingstone achieved fame as an African explorer, opening up the 'Dark Continent' to European contact and imperialism. Born in Blantyre, Lanarkshire, he worked in the COTTON mills there from the age of ten, receiving his education at night school and by wide reading, mainly in the classics and science. Imbued with enormous determination and all the virtues of self-help Livingstone decided in 1834 to become a medical missionary and supported himself studying at Anderson's College and the University of Glasgow. There he met William Thompson, later Lord KELVIN (1824–1907) and James 'Paraffin' YOUNG (1811–83), the latter a life-long supporter. He continued his studies in London, where, in 1838, he was accepted by the London Missionary Society. The outbreak of the Opium War (1839–42) prevented him going to China, but Robert Moffat (1795–1883), a famous Scottish missionary in Southern Africa, influenced his decision to serve there. He arrived in Cape Town early in 1841.

Livingstone's early missionary journey 1841–49 had the objectives of eradicating slavery and spreading the gospel through what he called 'native agents', mainly in the Cape frontier and in the Transvaal and Kalahari. His contribution to the expedition that discovered Lake Ngami in 1849 was recognized both by a gold medal from the Royal Geographical Society and by its continued support of later explorations. Livingstone had married Moffat's daughter, Mary, in 1845 and she accompanied him on many of his travels before returning to Britain with their family in 1852. In three subsequent journeys Livingstone set out to 'open up a path into the interior' or perish in the attempt. The first, the Luanda-Quelimane expedition (1856) involved a hazardous journey westwards from what is now modern Angola to Mozambique, in the course of which he discovered and named the mighty Victoria Falls on the Zambesi river. He came home to a rapturous welcome and his story of *Missionary Travels and Researches in South Africa* (1857) became an instant bestseller.

Severing his connection with the London Missionary Society he returned to Quelimane as British Consul. He then set out on the Zambesi expedition (1858–64), a well-equipped enterprise including six Europeans, among whom was his brother, Charles. Although Livingstone's leadership was criticized and it failed to fulfil all of its objectives, the expedition nevertheless gathered useful information about the Zambesi and Lake Nyasa regions, which was later to prove of considerable significance in the colonization of British Central Africa. Livingstone and his brother published their *Narrative of an Expedition to the Zambesi and its Tributaries* in 1865.

Finally, against medical advice, Livingstone returned to Africa in 1866 and set out on his quest for the Nile. This involved exploration of much of the lakes region and the headwaters of the Lualaba, a tributary of the Congo. The sick and failing Livingstone was found on 23 October 1871 by Henry M. Stanley (1841–1904), a correspondent of the *New York Herald*, sent to look for him. For a while they continued the expedition together, then Livingstone went on alone. He died in May 1873 and his body was brought by his servants to the coast where it was shipped to Britain. Livingstone was buried in Westminster Abbey in 1874. His discoveries were of major significance for the development of much of southern Africa and he can legitimately be considered as much a pioneer of African nationalism as a tool of European imperialism.

• *Ransford, O., David Livingstone: The Dark Interior, John Murray, 1978.*

Lloyd George, David, see ASQUITH; HAIG; JOHNSTON, THOMAS; RED CLYDESIDE; WORLD WAR I

London, Treaty of (1423) Signed 4 December 1423, this important treaty released JAMES I from imprisonment as a hostage in England. Shortly before succeeding his father, ROBERT III, as king, 4 April 1406, he had been captured by the English on his way to France. The treaty laid down the terms of his ultimate release in April 1424, when he was allowed to return to Scotland. The ransom was set at £40,000 'of good legal money of England', payable in installments. 10,000 merks (a merk was rarely a coin but used in currency calculations and equal to 13s 4d) had to be paid 'in the Church of St Paul, London' within six months of his return, but the same amount was actually remitted as the dowry of Joan Beaufort, whom James married in February 1424. TAXATION in Scotland raised a large sum for the ransom but it seems only 9,500 merks were handed over. The rest remained unpaid. More significant perhaps was the fact that some of the Scottish nobles likely to make trouble for James continued to be held hostage, thus making easier the imposition of royal authority.

Lordship of the Isles, see JAMES IV, ISLES

Lords of the Articles, see PARLIAMENT

Lords of the Congregation In December 1557 a number of Scottish nobles, namely Argyll (d.1558), his son, Lord Lorne (1538–73), Glencairn (d.1574), MORTON (c.1516–81) and Erskine of Dun (c.1538–91) signed the 'First Bond' in which they proclaimed their intentions of supporting the cause of the REFORMATION. Thus the aforementioned were the original Lords of the Congregation but the term is also applied to denote all those who in 1559–60 joined the party challenging the religious policy of the regent, MARY OF GUISE (1516–60).

• *Dickinson, W.C., Donaldson, G. and Milne, I.A. (eds.), A Source Book of Scottish History II, Nelson, 1958.*

Lothian, Philip Kerr, Lord (1882—1940) Philip Kerr in his early career was a leading figure in the Round Table, a group founded in 1910 by former members of Lord Milner's staff or 'kindergarden' who shared the latter's imperial ideals. Between 1916 and 1921 Kerr was Lloyd George's private secretary and ultimately an influential member of the prime minister's enlarged secretariat known as the 'garden suburb' on account of its temporary premises in Downing Street. He was also one of the premier's main advisers at the Paris Peace Conference in 1919. Here, although initially a staunch advocate of the League of Nations' principles, his attitude changed when it became apparent that the US was not going to participate. Latterly he became outspoken opponent of the peace settlement. During the inter-war period Kerr or Lord

Lothian, as he was to become, remained committed to furthering Anglo-American relations and to the whole concept of the Atlantic Alliance. Consequently he was an extremely suitable candidate for British ambassador to the USA, a position which he held from the outbreak of WORLD WAR II. By this date Lord Lothian had apparently abandoned his support for appeasement policies. Here he had taken a stance which had seen him praising Hitler as 'one of the creative figures of this generation' and regarding the Nazi's remilitarization of the Rhineland in 1936 as simply a matter of them 'going into their own backyard'. Lord Lothian died of a heart attack in New York in December 1940, 'a grave loss to the English,' so Goebbels recorded in his Diary.

• *Butler, J.R.M., Lord Lothian, London 1960.*

Loudon Hill, Battle of (1307) This prominent landmark on the moors between Lanarkshire and Ayrshire was the site in May 1307 of a victory by ROBERT Bruce over an English force. As at the conflict in Glentrool earlier in April it is hard to tell how much of a victory this was in the guerrilla campaign fought by Bruce against the English. He and his forces continued to be hunted down.

Lovat, Lord, see FRASER, SIMON

M

McAdam, John Loudon (1756–1836) If Thomas TELFORD (1757–1834) was a giant of civil engineering — canals, aqueducts, bridges and harbours — then McAdam undeniably earned his nickname of 'Colossus of Roads'. A contemporary cartoon carried the following rubric.

Q. 'But who effected this improvement in your paving?', says Mirabel.

A. 'A party of the name of McAdam,' is the reply, 'but coachmen call him the Colossus of Roads.'

Significantly three of McAdam's sons became involved in the family business of ROAD building. McAdam himself came of lesser landed gentry in Ayrshire, where he was born in 1756, the youngest of ten children. Initially educated at Maybole he was sent to America at the age of fourteen to join his uncle, a well-established New York merchant in the colonial trade and a prominent Loyalist. McAdam became a junior partner to his uncle not only in the business but also in a new branch of activity, as agents for the sale of naval prizes. McAdam and his uncle played a leading role in the establishment of the New York Chamber of Commerce and on the outbreak of the AMERICAN WAR OF INDEPENDENCE in 1776 he enlisted as a Loyalist

volunteer. In 1778 he married the daughter of a leading landowner in Long Island. After McAdam returned home in 1783 the contacts he had established in the former colonies were to prove invaluable to his future career both in Scotland and England.

Within a short period of settling in Ayrshire in 1785 McAdam assumed the role of country gentleman, active in local affairs as a turnpike trustee, deputy lieutenant for the county and later raising a group of volunteers when French invasion threatened. As well as road construction he became involved c.1788 with the Earl of Dundonald (1749–1831) in the tar distilling operation of the British Tar Company at Muirkirk.

In 1798 McAdam was appointed naval agent for victualling and supplies in the West of England and moved to Bristol. Although this lucrative opportunity only lasted three years until the Peace of Amiens in 1802, McAdam established important connections with the Bristol mercantile community and continued his consultancy in road building and management.

He gave evidence to the Select Committee on the Turnpike Acts in 1811 and in 1816 was appointed General Surveyor of the Bristol roads. He advised many other turnpike trusts on his road building method, which was based on good drainage and a surface constructed of carefully graded stones, which he published in *Remarks on the Present System of Road-Making* (1816) and a *Practical Essay on the Scientific Repair and Preservation of Roads* (1819).

McAdam's sons became partners in a consultancy that ultimately advised seventy trusts in twenty-eight countries. Much of this work, it seems, was poorly remunerated and although not without means McAdam applied for a government pension. He was granted an ex gratia payment of £4,000 in 1825. In 1827 he was appointed Surveyor General of Roads and given an additional payment for previous outlay. Macadamization of roads contributed substantially to improved TRANSPORT before the age of railways and was widely adopted internationally.

• *Devereux, R., John Loudon McAdam, Oxford University Press, 1936.*
• *Reader, W. J., Macadam: the McAdam Family and the Turnpike Roads, Heinemann, 1980.*

Macbeth (c.1005—57) A famous literary figure, the historical Macbeth, as modern scholars have proved, lived a life of drama during an era when rival kin were challenging each other for power in the north and the Scottish kingdom generally. His struggles for power and his reign coincided with momentous events in England where NORMAN influence was growing, Macbeth himself bringing some of the first Norman knights to Scotland. Avenging his father's death (1020) he killed his cousin, Gille Comgain, clearing the way to become king of Moray in 1032. He then married the widow, Gruoch, who had royal connections, strengthening his own claims through his mother, who was possibly a daughter of MALCOLM II. With no male successor, the dynasty ended with Malcolm's death (or assassination) and the vacuum was filled by Duncan I, son of another daughter of the late king. Following Duncan's disastrous campaign in Northumbria during 1039 Macbeth seized his opportunity, scoring a victory over the king's forces at Pitgaveny near Elgin in 1040. Duncan was mortally wounded or killed by Macbeth, who thus became king. After defeat at the battle of Dunsinnan in 1054 he managed to hold on to the crown but had to allow the return of Duncan's son, MALCOLM 'CANMORE', from exile. Further conflict ensued and in a battle at Lumphanan, Aberdeenshire, Macbeth was killed, almost certainly by Malcolm and Gille Comgain's son, Lulach.

McLaren, Duncan, see LIBERAL PARTY

McCormick, John, see SCOTTISH NATIONAL PARTY, HOME RULE

MacDonald, Alexander, see HARDIE; TRADE UNIONS

MacDonald, Alexander or Alistair, see MONTROSE; PHILIPHAUGH, BATTLE OF

MacDonald, Flora, see STEWART, CHARLES EDWARD, THE YOUNG PRETENDER

MacDonald, James Ramsay (1866—1937) Like another pioneer Socialist, James Keir HARDIE (1856—1915), Ramsay MacDonald, the prominent Labour leader and statesman, was a self-made man, son of an unmarried maid servant in Lossiemouth, Morayshire. He received his elementary education locally until the age of fifteen, but not unusually for the dominie's prize pupil, stayed on from 1881 to 1885 as a pupil-teacher. These four years proved highly formative for he read widely and, despite his youth, became involved in various public activities such as the Lossiemouth Field Club, the Mutual improvement Society, and local politics. In 1885 he responded to an advertisement in *The Scotsman* for a post as assistant to a Bristol clergyman, the Rev. Crofton, who was setting up a Boy's and Young Men's Guild, and was offered the position. MacDonald left home for Bristol wearing a new suit presented by the local draper and, according to Marquand, with 27 shillings in his pocket. During his spare time in Bristol he attended meetings of the Social Democratic Federation, but after only a few months returned to Lossiemouth.

The following year he set out for London and after nearly two years struggling to maintain himself in poorly paid clerical jobs, he was engaged in 1888 as private secretary to Thomas Lough, a RADICAL LIBERAL MP. This gave MacDonald an entre to political circles — as well as invaluable training in party politics and the mechanics of electioneering. He was active for a while in the Scottish HOME RULE Association, and joined the Fabian Society, and a socialist sect called the Fellowship of the New Life. Much of his socialist ideology, it seems, was moulded at this time.

After 1892 MacDonald relied on journalism for a livelihood and became involved In the work of the Labour Electoral Association and then the newly formed INDEPENDENT LABOUR PARTY (1893), where he proved a first-rate organizer. Amid considerable disquiet on the part of local Liberals he stood as an ILP candidate at Southampton in 1895, but was defeated. In 1896 MacDonald made a successful marriage to Margaret Gladstone (d.1911), daughter of Dr John Gladstone FRS, Professor of Chemistry at the Royal Institution, one of the founders of the YMCA and an active Liberal. This opened the door to upper-middle-class radical circles and allowed him to pursue his political career.

MacDonald became secretary of the Labour Representation Committee, forerunner of the LABOUR PARTY, in 1900 and was a close associate of many leading Labour figures including Hardie, Arthur Henderson (1843–1935) and Philip Snowden (1864–1937). One of twenty-nine Labour MPs returned in the General Election of 1906, he became chairman of the ILP, 1906–9, and from 1911 to 1914 led the Parliamentary Labour Party with consummate skill. Since MacDonald and many of his fellow MPs were pacifist and stood out against hostilities in favour of a negotiated peace, WORLD WAR I effectively split Labour. Arthur Henderson took over as leader of the Parliamentary Party while MacDonald and his faction went into limbo.

Although Labour secured over 22 per cent of the vote in the Coupon Election of 1918, MacDonald himself lost his seat, so his return as MP for Aberavon and re-election as leader of the party (thanks to the votes of many RED CLYDESIDERS who later turned against him) were all the more remarkable. Since Labour had twenty-five more seats than the Liberals he found himself Leader of the Opposition and after the indecisive General Election of 1923 agreed to lead a minority Labour government in January 1924 – acting as his own Foreign Secretary. Indeed, foreign affairs pre-occupied MacDonald during the first Labour government's short and ineffective period of office, when John WHEATLEY (1869–1930) was one of the few other ministers to make much impact.

MacDonald's first administration was ended by the election of November 1924 when the affair of the Zinoviev letter severely damaged any hope that Labour might have had of being returned to power. With characteristic deftness he kept control of the party, steering it along the path of gradualism so vocally rejected by James MAXTON (1885–1946) and others on the left. He was again Prime Minister in 1929 but his second administration's incapacity to make even token efforts to deal with the DEPRESSION, unemployment and a worsening financial crisis led to a dramatic split with the party in August 1931.

Ever anxious to prove that both himself and Labour could accept power with responsibility, MacDonald headed a Coalition or 'National' government, which the majority of Labour rejected. MacDonald, increasingly seen as the 'frontman' for a Conservative administration, was villified by all

but a few of his former associates. He staggered on as leader until, worn down by over-work and ill-health, he handed over to Stanley Baldwin (1867–1947) in June 1935.

The ultimate humiliation came in his defeat in the 1935 General Election when Emmanuel Shinwell (1884–1986) beat him at Seaham by a majority of over 20,000. He died while on an Atlantic crossing in 1937 and was buried at Lossiemouth.

Any assessment of MacDonald is inevitably coloured both by his later career and performance as Prime Minister and by the attitude adopted towards him by the party he had apparently betrayed. There can be little doubt, however, that MacDonald made a vital contribution to the early Labour movement, building up Labour as a party of government. Throughout his life his favourite meal was a stolid Scots high tea and, according to Marquand, he stuck as rigidly to the doctrines and assumptions of his youth as he did to that diet. Unfortunately he failed to adapt his views to changing circumstances and like many politicians of the day was unprepared for the problems society faced in the 1920s and 30s. MacDonald's personal achievement, however, was considerable.

• *Marquand, D., Ramsay MacDonald, Jonathan Cape, 1977.*

MacEwan, William, see MEDICINE

MacKay, Hugh, see JACOBITE REBELLIONS; KILLIECRANKIE, BATTLE OF

MacKenzie, Sir George, of Rosehaugh (1636—91) A nephew of Kenneth, third Earl of

Seaforth (d.1678) he became an advocate in 1659 and ultimately was appointed Lord Advocate in 1677. His involvement in cases concerning COVENANTERS in the 1680s earned him the epithet 'Bluidy MacKenzie' but he also had the remarkable distinction of defending Archibald CAMPBELL, eighth Earl of Argyll (1607–61) in 1661 and twenty years later prosecuting his son, Archibald CAMPBELL, ninth Earl of Argyll (1629–85). An author of numerous legal and other works, he is best remembered for founding in 1682 the Advocates Library in Edinburgh, which became the National Library of Scotland in 1925.

•*Lang, A., Sir George MacKenzie, Longmans, 1909.*

MacLean, John (1879—1923) John MacLean, teacher, pioneer socialist and revolutionary nationalist, was born in Pollokshaws, Glasgow, the second youngest of seven children. He attended Pollokshaws Academy and later Queen's Park School — for, despite severe financial difficulties, his widowed mother was determined he would have a good education.

He proved an able pupil and in 1896–7 became a pupil-teacher before entering the FREE CHURCH Training College. Graduating in 1900 he obtained a full-time teaching post. He studied part time at the University of Glasgow, where he met James MAXTON (1885–1946) and took his MA in 1904. He later studied mathematics and science at Glasgow Technical College.

MacLean came to socialism through the Social Democratic Federation, which he joined in 1903, and the Glasgow Teacher's Socialist Society, of which he was a founder member. Like many early socialists he had a strong moral streak, eschewing drink and tobacco, but this was nevertheless mixed with a deep humanitarianism. In the 1900s MacLean became involved with a wide range of socialist organizations and causes throughout the west of Scotland, including the CO-OPERATIVE MOVEMENT, the TRADE UNIONS and the syndicalist Industrial Workers of the World, which inclined him to the concept of 'one big union' to fight capitalism. He was a prominent propagandist for the SDF and lectured tirelessly on Marxist economics, eventually founding the Scottish Labour College in 1916. Although his educational endeavours have probably been exaggerated, he certainly exercised considerable influence on Labour activists before and during WORLD WAR I.

Thanks to his pacifism MacLean became a national figure during the war, which brought him much personal hardship. He spoke out against what he called 'this murder business', supported the Glasgow Rent Strike of 1915, and was ultimately arrested with other militants including William Gallacher (1881–1965) and James Maxton on charges of sedition.

He spent more than a year in prison and on his release returned to his educational work.

According to one biographer, MacLean, on hearing of the Bolshevik Revolution of October–November 1917, was 'too overcome with emotion even to speak'. As the most prominent international socialist, MacLean was duly appointed first Bolshevik Consul in Scotland, but his period of office was cut short by the refusal of the government to recognize his status and by his arrest in April 1918. He was again charged with sedition but this time sentenced to five years at the High Court in Edinburgh. MacLean was sent to Peterhead prison but following a storm of protest was released after serving six months. MacLean was actually at liberty for only nine out of the twenty months following the Armistice — a critical period for the Scottish labour movement. MacLean increasingly disassociated himself from the British Socialist Party and concentrated on revolutionary Scottish nationalism on the Irish model. His 'Tramp Trust Unlimited' (founded 1919) continued his concern for industrial issues, such as the minimum wage, the six-hour day, and full wages for the unemployed. Latterly MacLean's revolutionary position isolated him from many of his former associates and, weakened by imprisonment and ill-health, he died in 1923. Since his death he has become something of a legend — though so far he has had little apparent impact on the ideology of either organized labour or the nationalist movement.

• Howell, D., A Lost Left: Three Studies in Socialism and Nationalism, Manchester University Press, 1986.
• Knox, W., (ed.), Scottish Labour Leaders, Mainstream Publishing, 1984.
• Milton, N., John MacLean, Pluto Press, 1973.
• Young, J.D., John MacLean: Clydeside Socialist, Clydeside Press, 1992.

Macquarie, Lachlan (1762—1824)

Lachlan Macquarie, the most prominent and successful of the early governors of New South Wales, was born on the island of Ulva, near Mull. Macquarie senior was a cousin of the last clan chief and a tenant of the Duke of Argyll, while his mother was the sister of another chief, Murdoch Maclaine. Even these humble family connections were to prove invaluable to Macquarie's career. He volunteered for military service in 1776 and was given an ensigncy the following year in the second battalion of the 84th Regiment, the Royal Highland Emigrants, commanded by a cousin, Colonel (later General) Maclean.

Macquarie served in Nova Scotia, New York and Charleston, ultimately being commissioned lieutenant in the 71st Regiment in 1781. He was then posted to Jamaica, returning to Scotland in 1784 and retired on half-pay. Three years later — and thanks again to the good offices of Maclean — he was made senior lieutenant in the 77th Regiment for service in India. His years in India brought further promotion, extensive administrative experience, and a good marriage, which sadly lasted less than three years, but nevertheless helped his finances. Among the posts he held were paymaster general of troops in the Bombay presidency and military secretary to the governor of Bombay.

During the years 1800–1, at a vital point in the NAPOLEONIC WARS, he was briefly in Egypt where he was deputy-adjutant general of the forces. After a brief period at home 1803–5 he returned to India where he was lieutenant colonel in the 73rd Regiment, 1805–7. When he eventually left India for the last time he came overland via Persia and Russia carrying despatches — to the gratitude of the government on his arrival in England.

By 1808 Macquarie had learned that he would be sent with his regiment to New South Wales, where one of his superiors was to be made governor. Ever anxious for self-promotion he not only asked to be made a colonel but also wrote to Castlereagh (1769–1822), then Secretary of State for the Colonies, asking to be made lieutenant governor — and he was duly appointed. Soon after his superior turned down the governorship and Macquarie was given the job in his place. When he set sail for New South Wales in 1809 Macquarie had explicit instructions stating that 'The Great Objects of attention are to improve the Morals of the Colonists, to encourage Marriage, to provide for Education, to prohibit the use of Spiritous Liquors, to increase the Agriculture and Stock, so as to ensure the certainty of a full supply to the Inhabitants under all Circumstances' — and these he followed as far as possible. Indeed he proved both pragmatic and visionary, promoting public works and buildings, new towns and public morality. He established educational and charitable institutions and attempted a humanitarian policy towards the Aborigines. Macquarie also encouraged the ex-convicts or emancipists by giving them public offices and land grants — to the indignation of immigrant settlers and the military. It was the last innovation that brought Macquarie's administration under government scrutiny in the form of J. G. Bigge (1780–1843), who was

appointed as a commissioner to enquire into the affairs of the colony. By the time Macquarie had quit office and returned home in 1822 his reputation — thanks to the biased Bigge report which took an unfavourable view of the emancipist policy and the "absurd" public works — was already tarnished. He fought back and ultimately obtained a pension. Unfortunately he died before he could collect it in 1824. Macquarie can be regarded as a controversial champion of the emancipists whose term of office ended unhappily — but marked a turning point in Australian history. Macquarie University, Sydney, is named for him.

•*Ritchie, I., Lachlan Macquarie: A Biography, Melbourne University Press, 1986.*

Macqueen, Robert, Lord Braxfield (1722—99)   Robert Macqueen was born in 1722 at Braxfield, near Lanark, in which county his father was sheriff-substitute. He was educated at Lanark Grammar School and the University of Edinburgh, being admitted as an advocate in 1744. He acted as a counsel for the Crown on issues connected with the FORFEITED ESTATES following the 'Forty-Five — and later gained a considerable reputation as an expert on feudal law. Coincident with the ascendancy of Henry DUNDAS (1742—1811), Macqueen became in turn a Lord of Session, with the title of Lord Braxfield (1776), a Lord of Justiciary (1780), and was ultimately promoted to Lord-Justice Clerk in 1788.

Macqueen had a formidable reputation as a judge and presided

over the trials of the 'SCOTTISH MARTYRS', Thomas MUIR (1765–99) and his associates. The harsh sentences he handed down were the subject of parliamentary criticism, though Dundas, for one, supported him. Despite his vigorous defence of law and order, Macqueen himself seems to have been an idiosyncratic character. Whether he was as extreme in his manners and speech as Lord Cockburn (1779–1854) and others later maintained is hard to assess.
• *Osborne, B.D., Braxfield: The Hanging Judge?, Argyll Publishing, 1997.*

Magnus, St (c.1075—c.1117) Magnus was born at a time when more settled, generally Christian, lifestyles prevailed over traditional VIKING ways in the Northern ISLES, but elite kin groups there, as in both Scotland and Norway, were engaged in constant power struggles. His father, Erlend, joint earl of Orkney, was overthrown by Magnus's cousin, Haakon, supported by the Norwegian king, who installed his son as earl. Magnus himself was captured and apparently forced into a life of coastal raiding before escaping, taking refuge in the Scottish court, and then devoting himself to the study of Christianity and prayer. On the death of the Norwegian king, Haakon returned as overlord of Orkney, soon to be joined by Magnus, determined to claim his share of earldom. Magnus was ultimately eliminated by Haakon who, determined to eliminate any rival, murdered him on Egilsay. The cathedral in Kirkwall was dedicated to his memory.

Maitland, Sir John, of Thirlestane (1543—95) A younger brother of William MAITLAND of Lethington (c.1525–73), he supported the Marian cause during the CIVIL WAR and after the surrender of Edinburgh Castle in 1573 was imprisoned by MORTON (c.1516–81) until 1578. In 1579 he joined the anti-Morton faction headed by LENNOX (c.1542–83) and ARRAN (c.1545–96) and in 1581 was appointed a Lord of Session. The RUTHVEN RAID (1582) saw a temporary setback to the progress of his career but once Arran recovered his position in 1583 Maitland's advancement continued and he received the Secretaryship in 1584. In 1587 he became the first person in the sixteenth century who was neither an aristocrat nor a churchman to hold the office of Chancellor. For the rest of his life he remained the principal figure in the governments of JAMES VI (1566–1625). While he didn't achieve the reform of the financial system nor establish control over the HIGHLANDS or the BORDERS in the manner that he had envisaged he had some notable successes. For instance, the alliance with England, negotiated in 1586, was a major achievement, especially significant for James VI as far as the English succession was concerned, while his more conciliatory policy towards the Kirk allowed the administration to concentrate on more serious problems such as the NORTHERN EARLS and BOTHWELL (1563–1612). The king, however, was unappreciative of Maitland's services, regarding him as too powerful and seeing his death as an opportunity to free himself from his influence and rule on his own.

• *Lee, M., John Maitland of Thirlestane, University of Illinois Press, 1959.*

Maitland, William, of Lethington (c.1525—73) Son of Sir Richard Maitland of Lethington (1496–1586), a noted legal and literary figure for much of the sixteenth century, William Maitland was also the older brother of Sir John MAITLAND of Thirlestane (1543–95). He first came into prominence in 1558 when he was appointed Secretary in the administration of MARY OF GUISE (1515–60) and was soon displaying what was to be the most characteristic feature of his political outlook, namely his attachment to an Anglo-Scottish alliance. Thus by the end of 1559 he had transferred his allegiance to the LORDS OF THE CONGREGATION and was closely involved in conversations with Elizabeth (1533–1603) over a proposed match with ARRAN (1538–1609) and, on the return of Mary (1542–87), over the vexed question of the English succession. Mary's decision to marry DARNLEY (1546–67) with the implications it had for his anglophile policies was a serious blow and he eventually became deeply implicated in the Kirk o' Field conspiracy. Indeed, at one point in the proceedings he openly suggested to the Queen that 'other means' rather than strictly judicial ones could be used against her husband. Although he backed MORAY (1531–70) over Mary's abdication and was one of the Regent's commissioners at Elizabeth's subsequent enquiry into Mary's behaviour he was never a deeply committed supporter of the king's party. Accordingly, in 1569, he

joined the Marians and participated on their side in the bitter CIVIL WAR, which was waged intermittently for the next four years. This proved to be a maladroit move since, in one way or another, Mary's followers were gradually eliminated. Consequently, following the PACIFICATION OF PERTH (1573), only KIRKCALDY OF GRANGE (c.1520–73) and Maitland were left to defend the Marian cause from their admittedly formidable position within Edinburgh Castle. But the Regent MORTON (c.1516–81) was able to command English support against the 'castilians' and in May 1573 the garrison was forced to surrender. Maitland died shortly afterwards either as a result of the illness that had incapacitated him for some years or by his own hand. Had he survived his most likely fate would have been a judicial execution.

Major (Mair), John (1467—1550) Born in East Lothian, Major studied at universities in Cambridge and Paris, becoming a professor of theology at Glasgow (1518), St Andrews (1522) and Paris (1525–33). His book entitled *A History of Greater Britain*, published in Paris in 1521, supported Anglo-Scottish relations, though made some attempt at objectivity. Returning to St Andrews, Major wrote theological and philosophical works critical of abuses in the church, so at that level he might be compared with Sir David LINDSAY.

Malcolm I (d. 954) Malcolm was the son of Donald II and was king from c.943 until his death. Clearly ambitious, he secured a grip on Moray, led raids into England as far as Teesdale, and in 945 obtained recognition from Edmond, the king of Wessex, of claims to parts of Strathclyde and Cumbria. His alliance with Britons and Saxons proved abortive, when in 952 they were defeated by Scandinavian forces. He was soon a victim of internal strife, killed by rivals at Fetteresso and later allegedly buried on Iona.

Duncan, A.A.M., Scotland: The Making of the Kingdom, Oliver & Boyd, 1975.

Malcolm II (c.954—1034) Like that of MALCOLM I, Malcolm II's career also had considerable significance both in consolidating the kingdom and defining its boundaries. The son of Kenneth II, Malcolm ultimately resolved the rivalry among the kin group by killing his cousin, Kenneth III, to become king in 1005. He then invaded England as far south as Durham, but was defeated in 1006, possibly following an ineffective siege. A victory at Carham in 1018 gave the Scots control of Lothian and brought Northumbria as far south as the Tweed under Scottish influence. The kingdom of Strathclyde came under his control in 1018 and he may well have appointed his grandson, Duncan I, to rule it. He submitted to Cnut the Great, king of England (1016—35). Further strife resulted in the death of another cousin before he himself either died or was assassinated in 1034.

Duncan, A.A.M., Scotland: The Making of the Kingdom, Oliver & Boyd, 1975.

Malcolm III (c.1031—93) Malcolm 'Canmore' (great head or great leader) was the son of Duncan I, his mother possibly being a member of the Northumbrian elite. While he was still young his father was killed by MACBETH in 1040, and Malcolm was exiled for his own safety in England. He was later assisted by Siward, earl of Northumbria, who led a force into Scotland to defeat Macbeth at Dunsinnan, north of Perth. Canmore thus acquired much territory in southern Scotland but Macbeth was not disposed of until 1057 when he was defeated and killed at Lumphanan, Aberdeenshire. Malcolm next disposed of Lulach, possibly his former ally, who had occupied the throne for a matter of months, becoming king himself in 1058. Twenty years later he further consolidated his position by defeating Lulach's son, who ruled over Moray. Malcolm secured a useful alliance with Thorfinn, earl of Orkney, by marrying his daughter, Ingibjorg, by whom he had three sons, including Duncan II. Evidently long a widower he married secondly Margaret, sister of Edgar Atheling, who together with the Anglo-Saxon royal family, had fled to Scotland after the NORMAN conquest. He raided Northumbria on several occasions possibly in support of his wife's kin and despite having paid homage to William the Conqueror at Abernethy, Perthshire in 1072. His wife, evidently devout, encouraged religious reform and the MONASTIC system, in particular the abbey at Dunfermline. Malcolm and Margaret's family included EDGAR, ALEXANDER I and DAVID I. Shortly after founding Durham cathedral Malcolm was killed in a raid on Alnwick in 1093.

• *Duncan, A.A.M., Scotland: The Making of the Kingdom, Oliver & Boyd, 1975.*

Malcolm IV (1141—65) Malcolm, 'the Maiden', a grandson and successor of DAVID I, became king in 1153 at the age of twelve. The regime continued the NORMAN-IZATION policy, provoking resistance by native Celtic elites, such as Fergus of Galloway and Somerled of Argyll, who probably set out to exploit any weaknesses in the rule of a minor and his supporters. According to modern scholars, the failure of this resistance, which continued for much of the young king's reign, reflected the longer-term success of David I's modernisation programme. Following the civil strife in England over the succession Henry II imposed strong rule, which in 1157 extended to Malcolm surrendering the northern counties of England in return for the earldom of Huntingdon. Malcolm accompanied an English force under Henry to France in 1159. He established the abbey at Coupar Angus in 1162. He died, evidently unmarried in 1165.
• *Duncan, A.A.M., Scotland: The Making of the Kingdom, Oliver & Boyd, 1975.*

Malt Tax In the aftermath of the Treaty of UNION in 1707 the British Parliament sought to equalize taxation between Scotland and England. However, one of several concessions gained by the Scots was freedom from duty on malt (set at 6d per bushel in England) for the duration of the War of the Spanish Succession — if that proved longer than a proposed seven-year exemption. Amid much clamour from Scottish MPs and Representative Peers the malt tax was ultimately extended to Scotland in 1713 — the duty being set at a lower rate of 3d per bushel. Apparently collection was so inefficient and the resulting revenue so modest that the government took matters in hand to tighten up the excise system and extend the duty from malt to ale and beer at 6d per barrel. Despite a deluge of petitions from all over Scotland this took effect in June 1725. Popular protest was immediate and widespread, notably in Glasgow and Edinburgh. In the former city the house of Donald Campbell of Shawfield (c.1671–1753), the local MP, was wrecked and troops fired on the mob; while in the capital there was a brewers strike.

Similar protests against the rising cost of living recurred later in the eighteenth century, mainly as Meal Mobs and food riots, and typically involving raids on mills, granaries and ships loading or carrying grain. A number occurred in the period of high prices and inflation during the NAPOLEONIC WARS and during the FAMINE years of the 1840s.

manrent, bonds of These were agreements generally made between a laird and a nobleman in the fifteenth and sixteenth centuries whereby the lesser man promised to assist the more powerful. The latter reciprocated by guaranteeing to provide his protection and support, a fact that was underlined in the formal contract or bond signed between the two parties.
• *Wormald, J., Lords and Men in Scotland: Bonds of Manrent 1442– 1603, John Donald, 1986.*

Mar, Donald, Earl of (d.1332) Mar was a nephew of ROBERT I, who was captured during the WARS OF INDEPENDENCE in 1306 and held hostage in England.

He was exchanged for Scottish hostages after BANNOCKBURN, but refused to return. It is thought that he provided a useful line of contact with Edward II prior to his return in 1327. Mar, along with Moray and Douglas, was subsequently involved in the Weardale campaign of 1327, during which the young Edward III was almost captured by the Scots. During the minority of DAVID II he was appointed GUARDIAN in 1332 by did not survive long in this role since he was defeated and killed by an English force headed by Edward Balliol at the battle of Dupplin, Perthshire on 12 August that year.

Mar, Earl of, see ERSKINE, ELEVENTH EARL OF MAR

marches Historically the border with England, was less clearly defined than that of Wales with England, to which the term also applies. This led to long-term conflict (seen, for example, in the BATTLE OF THE STANDARD) until the signing of the Treaty of YORK (1237), under the terms of which Alexander II gave up Scottish claims to the northern counties of England. The Scottish marches were divided into three areas of administration and control, East, Middle and West, each with wardens appointed by the Crown. But the marches continued to be noted on both sides of the border for strife between rival kin groups, banditry and cattle lifting, a situation that continued as late as the seventeenth century. While the BORDER itself became more clearly defined following the UNION OF THE CROWNS in 1603, the Anglo-Scottish marches was one of the last areas of the British Isles outside the HIGHLANDS and IRELAND where the rule of law was imposed with difficulty.

Margaret, 'Maid of Norway' (c.1283—90) Margaret was the daughter of Margaret, ALEXANDER III's (1241—86) daughter and Erik II of Norway. This was a political union, and part of the attempt at improving relations between Norway and Scotland following the Treaty of PERTH (1266).

On Alexander III's death in 1286 Margaret assumed considerable dynastic importance since, with her mother dead and Alexander's two sons having predeceased him, she was the sole heir to the Scottish throne. Admittedly, Alexander III had remarried Yolande, daughter of the Count of Dreux, but there were no children of that union.

By September 1290 when Margaret was en route to Scotland, Edward I had negotiated her future marriage to his own son, Edward, by the Treaty of BIRGHAM. In fact an English delegation to welcome her had travelled as far as Wick when news of Margaret's death in Orkney on 26 September 1290 was received.

•*Nicholson, R., Scotland: The Later Middle Ages, Oliver and Boyd, 1974.*

Margaret, St (c.1046—93) Margaret, queen of MALCOLM III, was born in Hungary following her father, Edward's exile from England during the reign there of

Cnut. Since Hungary had only recently become a Christian country it is thought that Margaret was personally touched by the fervour for the religion which prevailed there and that this affected much of her subsequent life. Margaret returned to England during the reign of her great-uncle, Edward the Confessor, but after her father's death and the NORMAN Conquest in 1066, her own and her kin's positions were uncertain. Her brother, Edgar Atheling, and his supporters staged an unsuccessful revolt against William the Conqueror and the family fled north to Scotland. There Margaret married Malcolm and become mother to three future Scottish kings, EDGAR, ALEXANDER and DAVID. Her religious inclinations led to the establishment of an abbey at Dunfermline, and support for the religious foundations at Iona and St Andrews. Modern scholarship is sceptical about what role if any she may have played as a catalyst for the introduction of English or Continental influences or reforming the existing Celtic church. There can be no doubt that her direct connections with the English royal family, the powerful positions occupied by her family, and her piety, all greatly strengthened the Scottish crown, and in the longer term her canonization in 1250 gave the country a saint of international renown.

Margarot, Maurice (1745—1815)
In common with the other 'SCOTTISH MARTYRS' Margarot had an interesting but complex background. He was born in Devon, where his father was a merchant with an interest in wine, and trad-

ing to France and Portugal. Margarot was educated at the University of Geneva and thereafter worked in the family business. This took him to the West Indies and Portugal — and In the latter he apparently owned property. He was living in France at the outbreak of the FRENCH REVOLUTION.

Returning to England in 1792, he was soon associated with the London CORRESPONDING SOCIETY and later represented it and the United Political Societies of Norwich as a delegate at the National Convention of the FRIENDS OF THE PEOPLE in the autumn of 1793.

After the convention was dispersed by the authorities Margarot was tried for sedition and the following year transported to Australia for fourteen years.

Margarot and his wife — who had accompanied him into exile — returned from New South Wales in 1810, the only one of the 'Scottish Martyrs' to do so. He had earlier complained to the authorities about conditions in the convict colonies and in 1812 gave evidence to a Select Committee of the House of Commons on transportation.

Mary of Guise (1515—60)
Daughter of Claude, Duke of Lorraine (d.1551), Mary was married to Louis, Duke of Longueville (d.1537), in 1534. Three years later, not long after she became a widow, she was the subject of marriage negotiations involving France, Scotland and England in which the diplomacy of BEATON (1494—1546) was responsible for ensuring that she married JAMES V (1512—42) rather than Henry VIII

(1491–1547). This marriage took place in 1538 but it was not until December 1542 that her only surviving child, MARY (1542–87) was born, a week before the death of James V. During the lengthy minority of her daughter the Queen Dowager played a major part in preserving and furthering the interests of the Auld Alliance. With Beaton she helped create a substantial faction that was strongly opposed to the proposed marriage treaty with England. On the cardinal's assassination she was prepared to co-operate with Arran (c. 1516–75) and particularly welcomed the arrangements made at the Treaty of HADDINGTON in 1548 whereby Scotland capitulated to France. In April 1554 she replaced Arran, now Duke of Chatelherault, and was at last free to give full rein to her Francophile policies. Consequently, although she displayed considerable skill in handling the reformers and the nobility, KNOX (c.1512–72) was allowed to return temporarily in 1555 and families like the Campbells and Cunninghams had certain of their members given ecclesiastical preferment there was, none the less, growing resentment within the country at the extent of French infiltration.

Unquestionably the pinnacle of her regency was the French marriage arranged for Mary in 1558 with its clandestine clauses making Scotland likely to become a satellite of France. On the other hand her decision early in 1559 to launch a campaign against heresy, a policy largely based on the recommendation of the French government and the changing international situation, was certainly a maladroit one. She was now faced with a Protestant revolution which, when it eventually received English support in February 1560, was to prove too powerful for her resources. However, becoming seriously ill in April, she sought shelter in Edinburgh Castle held by the neutral Lord Erskine (c.1510–72). Here, on 11 June, she died, as elsewhere at Berwick the English and French envoys were discussing the terms of the Treaty of EDINBURGH. •*Marshall, R.K., Mary of Guise, Collins, 1977.*

Mary, Queen of Scots (1542—87)

Born 8 December 1542, the daughter of JAMES V (1512–42) and MARY OF GUISE (1515–60), Mary became queen on the sudden death of her father six days later. In 1548, in accordance with the terms of the Treaty of HADDINGTON, she was dispatched to France ultimately marrying the Dauphin Francis (1544–60) in 1558.

The latter's accession to the French throne in 1559 meant Mary was briefly to be queen of two kingdoms. Moreover, her claims to the English throne in 1559–60 were the main factor behind the support Elizabeth I (1533–1603) gave to the followers of the REFORMATION in Scotland. Francis II's death in December 1560 resulted in Mary leaving France to commence her personal rule in August 1561. Although Mary refused to ratify the religious legislation passed by PARLIAMENT the previous year and also insisted on private celebration of Mass, she otherwise acted favourably towards the post-Reformation Church. Her most notable contribution to it was the arrangement known as the THIRDS OF BENEFICES, which at least gave the Kirk limited financial provision. Generally, she did little to hinder the progress of the Reformation and only the more implacable reformers such as KNOX (c.1512–72) remained unimpressed with her religious policy. Mary, leaning heavily on the advice and experience of her half-brother, MORAY (1531–70), and her secretary, MAITLAND OF LETHINGTON (c.1525–73), initially handled political affairs competently. In 1562, for instance, she successfully overcame the rebellion by the disaffected and pro-Catholic Earl of Huntly (c.1510–62). Furthermore, during these early years she made numerous royal progresses at least partly designed to strengthen her position and enhance her popularity within the kingdom. As for her remarriage and the question of her claim to the English succession, which were the two main political issues, she found herself in a very complicated situation. Elizabeth on the one hand constantly procrastinated over recognizing Mary as her successor yet at the same time insisted on exercising control over Mary's choice of husband. Thus, in exasperation, Maitland at one point backed the candidature of a Spanish suitor simply to put pressure on Elizabeth by favouring a Spaniard. But this device came to nought when Don Carlos (1544–65) was declared insane. Elizabeth now proposed a match between Mary and her favourite Robert Dudley (1532–88) ostensibly promoting him Earl of Leicester specially for this purpose. Discussions on this unlikely proposition were

still underway when Mary suddenly became infatuated with her cousin Lord DARNLEY (1546–67) who had recently returned to Scotland. In May 1565 his elevation to the Earldom of Ross was regarded as tantamount to a betrothal.

Undoubtedly Mary's decision to marry the worthless Darnley in July 1565 was the first major blunder of her career. Apart from stirring up resentment among some sections of the nobility, including Moray, and provoking the CHASEABOUT RAID it made any agreement with Elizabeth even more unlikely. Worse still it marked the beginning of a period of domestic violence of which the murder of RICCIO (c.1533–66) was but one instance and which also witnessed Darnley's own death at Kirk o' Field in February 1567. While Mary's actual complicity in this mysterious incident is likely to remain a subject of eternal controversy, she unquestionably committed another act of political folly two months afterwards when she married BOTHWELL (1535–78). Not only was her new husband widely regarded as one of Darnley's assassins but his dramatic elevation could only antagonize the other leading magnates and foment further internal discord. In the ensuing conflict at Carberry in June 1567 her opponents proved too strong and following her surrender she was forced to abdicate in favour of her son JAMES VI (1566–1625) at Lochleven Castle on 24 July.

However, Mary's deposition was largely the result of one noble faction headed by MORAY and MORTON (c.1516–81) and her overthrow, unlike Bothwell's downfall, was not greeted with universal acclaim.

Thus, when she escaped from Lochleven in May 1568 numerous followers enthusiastically pledged their allegiance to her. Indeed, instead of fleeing to England after the setback at LANGSIDE she should have carried on the struggle against the 'king's men'. But here, yet again, by deciding to place herself at the mercy of her cousin Elizabeth she made another serious miscalculation. She left behind a formidable body of supporters and leading Marians such as Argyll (c.1538–73), Cassillis (1541–76), Boyd (c.1517–90) and Eglinton (c.1531–85) continued to fight on her behalf until mid-1571. In fact, it was not until 1573 with the PACIFICATION OF PERTH in February and the surrender of Edinburgh Castle by KIRKCALDY OF GRANGE and the last of her followers in May that the Marian party was virtually eliminated.

Meanwhile in England, Mary, following the inconclusive enquiry into the Kirk o' Field affair at which the CASKET LETTERS were produced, remained under house arrest in various residences remote from London. Her eventual involvement in several plots against Elizabeth, but most notably the Babington conspiracy, led to her execution at Fotheringay Castle on 8 February 1587.

• Cowan, I., The Enigma of Mary Stuart, Gollancz, 1971.
• Donaldson, G., Mary, Queen of Scots, English Universities Press, 1974.
• Fraser, A., Mary, Queen of Scots, Weidenfeld & Nicolson, 1969.
• Merriman, M., The Rough Wooings, Tuckwell Press, 1999.

• Wormald, J., Mary, Queen of Scots: A Study in Failure, George Philip, 1988.

Maxton, James (1885—1946) James Maxton, a leading figure in the Independent Labour Party, was born near Glasgow of middle-class parents, both schoolteachers. He was educated at Hutcheson's Grammar School, and though his father died shortly before he went up to Glasgow University, he eventually graduated MA. He became a pupil-teacher and undertook training as a teacher. Coming under the influence of James Keir HARDIE (1856–1915), Philip Snowden (1864–1937) and Ramsay MAC-DONALD (1866–1937), he joined the ILP in Barrhead, Renfrewshire, becoming secretary of the branch and later of the Renfrewshire ILP Federation. He was employed in various schools in Glasgow, though always a thorn in the flesh of the EDUCATION authority because of his radical views. He became involved in early moves to establish teachers' unions in Scotland, notably the Educational Institute of Scotland and the Scottish Socialist Teachers' Society. With the revolutionary socialist John MACLEAN (1879–1923) he gave lectures on socialism, Marxism and economics in the Scottish Labour College.

By the early 1900s he was already an established propagandist for the ILP and other socialist movements of the day. Soon his interests and enthusiasms were national rather than localized in the west of Scotland. Maxton became Chairman of the Scottish ILP Council and a member of the National Council of the party in 1912. Like many socialist and labour leaders of the day he was opposed to WORLD WAR I and was an active propagandist against the war. He was a conscientious objector in 1916, and was actively associated with the Clyde Workers' Committee, organizing strikes in the shipyards, engineering and munitions factories in and around Glasgow, which became known as RED CLYDESIDE. Maxton was arrested, charged with sedition and imprisoned for a year 1916–17.

Maxton was selected as a parliamentary candidate for Montrose Burghs in 1914, but switched to Bridgeton, Glasgow in 1916. He fought the Coupon Election in 1918, but was defeated by a narrow margin (his opponent on that occasion later joined the ILP). Thereafter he was appointed as Divisional Organizer of the ILP and during 1919–22 was a member of the Glasgow Education Authority (which had dismissed him from its service in 1916). He fought throughout for under-privileged children and for improved conditions for teachers. In 1919 he was involved in the famous 'Forty Hours' Strike, but unlike Emmanuel Shinwell (1884–1986) and David Kirkwood (1872–1955), escaped arrest at the George Square demonstration (where the Red Flag was raised, and government tanks and troops stood in nearby streets). In the 1922 Election he became MP for Bridgeton, joining the ranks of a large group of Labour left-wingers, known as the Clydesiders. He opposed MacDonald's election to the leadership of the LABOUR PARTY (and consistently opposed him throughout the period to 1935). Maxton was the natural leader of the left-wing, which lost no oppor-

tunity to press for socialist measures, both in Parliament and in the country at large. Maxton at first had little respect for parliamentary procedure and was more than once suspended from the House of Commons for refusing to withdraw criticism of Conservative colleagues on the government side of the House. On one occasion in 1923 four of the Clydesiders were suspended, Maxton and John WHEATLEY (1869–1930), being among their number. Maxton was critical of the first Labour government (in which Wheatley had a Cabinet post), his criticism being the personality cult and policies lacking socialist vigour.

Maxton was Chairman of the ILP from 1926 to 1931, and again from 1934 to 1939, two periods that in a sense saw the rise and fall of the party as a political force. It had always had an important role in the labour movement as a 'think-tank' for policies and propaganda – in the production of which Maxton himself excelled. He promulgated the 'Socialism in Our Time' campaign after 1925 – a call for truly socialist policies to solve Britain's economic and social ills. The Cook-Maxton Manifesto to the workers of Britain was issued in 1926, following the collapse of the GENERAL STRIKE – in which Maxton was again prominent.

Throughout his parliamentary career he worked against imperialism and was closely associated with the League Against Imperialism and related movements. He was closely in touch with the leaders of Irish nationalism and of Indian nationalism, including Gandhi (1869–1948). His work against imperialism found a platform at many Socialist Internationals, including that at Vienna in 1931, where he was critical of the rise of Fascism in Europe. In the thirties he became a notable anti-Fascist and took part in a memorable debate with Sir Oswald Mosley (1896–1980), chaired by Lloyd George (1865–1945).

Maxton was again highly critical of the second Labour government, especially of its unemployment policy – which was among his key interests. After the formation of the National Government by MacDonald, Maxton led the final break of the ILP with the Labour Party in 1932. This led to the decline of the ILP as a political party – though it remained a powerful source of left-wing socialism. Maxton published two books, *The Life of Lenin* (1932), and *If I Were Dictator* (1935). He also wrote dozens of pamphlets and articles.

His anti-Fascist propaganda took him to Spain in 1937, but although he recognized the dangers posed by Fascism in Germany and elsewhere, he could not change his pacifist views. He supported the appeasement policy of Chamberlain (1869–1940) because he thought it might maintain peace a little longer – and stop British workers fighting German workers in another war for capitalism. He maintained his pacifist propaganda against the wartime Coalition government – but there seems little doubt that this stance was as uncomfortable for the ILP in WORLD WAR II as it had been for the Labour Party itself during 1914–18.

Maxton was certainly a man of unswerving principle, who stood up and fought for what he believed, no matter the personal cost. His fight was for the underprivileged in society, and for the Socialist Revolution. He never lost sight of this vision – nor of his propagandist role for socialism. His left-wing stance and dogmatism undoubtedly cost him office, for his ability was widely recognized. He died in 1946.

•*Brown, G., Maxton: A Biography, Mainstream, 1986.*

•*Knox, W. (ed.), Scottish Labour Leaders 1918–39, Mainstream, 1984.*

Mealmaker, George (1768—1808) Mealmaker was a radical weaver who became secretary of the Dundee FRIENDS OF THE PEOPLE and was later prominent in the UNITED SCOTSMEN. During the sedition trials of Thomas MUIR (1765–99) and his associates in 1793–4 Mealmaker was an active propagandist against the government and the war with the French revolutionaries. By 1796 he was one of the leading organizers of the United Scotsmen – whose aims he outlined in a pamphlet entitled *The Moral and Political Catechism of Man* (1797). Soon Mealmaker was arrested and charged with sedition and administering unlawful oaths. Following trial he was sentenced to fourteen years in Botany Bay. He spent the rest of his life in New South Wales, including four years as a supervisor at the Female Factory in Parramatta. He died in exile in 1808. Mealmaker is often regarded as one of the 'SCOTTISH MARTYRS' – though how much direct contact he had with them is unknown.

medicine Before the eighteenth century medical provision was both primitive and limited, though

Scotland seems to have been no worse off than other parts of Europe. The pre-Reformation Church ran hospitals, such as those in Glasgow, Linlithgow and Stirling, while the authorities in the BURGHS saw their role as one of keeping diseases like bubonic plague, typhus, leprosy or syphilis in check. This is not to say that medical science was nonexistent but it was little taught in the universities before the eighteenth century and most trained medical practitioners were either Scots educated in European institutions or Continental emigres. Other forms of treatment included herbal cures, magic cures, healing wells and healing stones — all relatively useless against anything but minor ailments.

FAMINE and disease went hand-in-hand as two of the great Malthusian checks on population growth. Scotland was regularly visited by epidemics of the 'Black Death', with local attacks quickly becoming a national problem. There were six major outbreaks during the sixteenth century and two during the following century with the last great plague running its course over a five-year period, 1644–49. It apparently came from the south with COVENANTERS returning from the siege of Newcastle in 1644, hitting Edinburgh the following year and working its way northward and westward in subsequent years. Vigorous measures were taken against it but nevertheless many died. In the case of Brechin, for example, an estimated 600 people — about a third of the total population — lost their lives when the plague visited the burgh in 1647.

There were also more positive if modest developments during the late sixteenth and seventeenth centuries, such as a recognition of the needs of the sick under the POOR LAW, the fact that physicians, surgeons and apothecaries generally became more numerous, and the establishment of colleges of physicians and surgeons in both Edinburgh and Glasgow. Medical education was still very limited: the most famous physicians of the time, Archibald Pitcairne (1652–1713) and Sir Robert Sibbald (1641–1722) were both educated in Paris and Leyden. Some of the old ways persisted in the work of quacks, travelling healers and even resort to witchcraft on occasion.

The development of medical science and education was a significant element in the Scottish ENLIGHTENMENT and by the close of the eighteenth century put Scotland at the forefront of medicine internationally. A large number of Scottish doctors trained in Leyden, then Europe's best medical school, returning to lobby for such establishments at home. The universities of Aberdeen, Glasgow, Edinburgh and St Andrews all established medical schools early in the century. The success of the school at Edinburgh (1726) was owed to the drive and enthusiasm of its main founders, William Carstaires (1649–1715), the university principal and an earlier lobbier, Lord Provost George DRUMMOND (1687–1766), and the famous surgeon John Monro (1670–1740). The building of the Royal Infirmary in 1729 was another critical factor, since it became a teaching hospital from the outset. Although Glasgow's school was smaller it nevertheless attracted some eminent teachers, notably the influential William CULLEN (1710–90) and Joseph BLACK (1728–99). The Town's Hospital opened there in 1733.

While many of the improvements that took place during the eighteenth century can be ascribed to medical education, the fall in the death rate is more readily explained by better diet and environmental improvements like decent water-supply. The chances of survival at birth were greatly increased by new techniques of midwifery recommended by William Smellie (1697–1763) and William Hunter (1718–83), both of whom worked in London. A number of diseases remained endemic and flared up from time to time, but one killer, smallpox, could at least be held at bay by vaccination – often carried out by the parish minister, the schoolmaster, or the worldly-wise blacksmith.

The INDUSTRIAL REVOLUTION and URBANIZATION exacerbated still further the problems of health care among a rapidly growing population, particularly the control of disease in overcrowded and often insanitary conditions. For example, there were three major outbreaks of cholera in 1832, 1848 and 1853, and two of typhus in 1837 and 1847. These epidemics prodded a previously complacent middle class and the civic authorities into providing not only improved sanitation and water supply in towns and cities but also building fever and isolation hospitals to nurse the sick. Several diseases were virtually wiped out by 1900, for typhus and smallpox were combatted in turn by new sanitary regulations and

compulsory vaccination. Of the respiratory diseases, tuberculosis remained a major killer until the inter-war years and the discovery of antibiotics.

Although Scottish medical schools lost something of their earlier prestige their graduates continued to make significant contributions to medicine, especially surgery. At the Glasgow Royal Infirmary (established in 1794), Joseph Lister (1827–1912) developed antiseptic surgery during the 1860s; while one of his successors, William MacEwan (1848–1924), carried the procedures a stage further to bring aseptic surgery into being. The use of anaesthesia in childbirth – developed earlier by Sir James YOUNG SIMPSON (1811–70) – combined with reduced infection to produce a great advance in surgery generally. Surgeons were further assisted by the discovery of X-rays, pioneered by William Thomson, Lord KELVIN (1824–1907) and others.

During the early twentieth century there was a gradual extension of medical facilities to the majority of the population, hospital provision and treatment being greatly assisted by government intervention through the National Insurance Acts of 1911 and 1920. Many major problems of health and social welfare were highlighted during both WORLD WAR I and WORLD WAR II and the DEPRESSION so the National Health Service inherited an unenviable burden after 1948. Scottish scientists continued to make a notable contribution to the advance of medicine, the most outstanding figure internationally being Sir Alexander FLEMING (1881–1955), who contributed to the development of the lifesaving antibiotic, penicillin.

• *Dingwall, H., Physicians, Surgeons, and Apothecaries: Medical Practice in Seventeenth-Century Scotland, Tuckwell Press, 1995.*
• *Gray, J.A., The Edinburgh City Hospital, Tuckwell Press, 1999.*
• *Hamilton, D., The Healers: A History of Medicine in Scotland, Canongate, 1981.*
• *Yule, B., Matrons, Medics and Maladies: Edinburgh Royal Informary in the 1840s, Tuckwell Press, 1999.*

Meikle, Andrew (1719—1811) Andrew Meikle was the son of James Meikle, a millwright, who worked mainly in East Lothian, the cradle of IMPROVEMENT and the AGRICULTURAL REVOLUTION in Scotland. After working as a millwright himself he developed some of his father's ideas in the construction of mills and milling machinery. Meikle concentrated mainly on the threshing mill — in which there was considerable interest because of its labour-saving potential. His design of 1786 was widely adopted and improved upon but his failure to secure a patent meant that he profited little from his invention. Sir John SINCLAIR (1754–1835), the great agicultural improver and propagandist, later raised £1,500 for Meikle's benefit in his old age.

Melville, Andrew (1545—1622) Melville attended St Andrews University before finishing his studies at the universities of Paris and Geneva. He taught at Poitiers for three years before proceeding in 1568 to Switzerland where, obtaining the Chair of Humanity at the private College of Geneva, he came under the influence of the cele-

brated theologian Theodore Beza (1519–1605). In 1574 he returned to Scotland to become Principal of Glasgow University and to play a major part in the reorganization of that institution. Thus a charter granted in 1577, the 'Nova Erectio', included in its provisions a system of teaching involving specialist 'regents' for each subject. In 1580 Melville was appointed Principal of St Andrews University where he attempted similar changes in teaching methods and with acolytes at both Glasgow and Aberdeen universities his impact on higher EDUCATION was clearly considerable.

However, Melville is usually better known as a religious reformer responsible for the formation within the Kirk of a powerful faction of younger ministers committed to further major ecclesiastical change. Hence it was the Melvillians who prepared the SECOND BOOK OF DISCIPLINE and who became so bitterly embroiled with the Crown over their adherence to Presbyterianism. Initially as JAMES VI (1566–1625) struggled to assert his authority over his kingdom the Presbyterians seemed to be succeeding in their objectives. Yet by the UNION OF THE CROWNS (1603) the king had seized the initiative, a point even more apparent once he was established in London. Accordingly, in 1605, he summoned Melville and a number of his fellow churchmen before him to discuss their actions in Scotland. James now found the Presbyterian leader, who in the 1590s had once audaciously informed the king that he was merely 'God's silly vassal', unacceptably outspoken and intransi-

gent. Melville was confined in the Tower until 1611 and only released on condition that he spent the rest of his life in exile. He died at Sedan eleven years later.
•*McCrie, T., Life of Andrew Melville, Blackwood, 1899.*

Melville, earls of, see DUNDAS

Menteith, Sir John (Stewart) (d. c.1329)

The younger son of Walter Stewart, who had held the earldom of Menteith in the right of Menteith's mother, c.1260–93. Like many of the Scottish nobility during the WARS OF INDEPENDENCE, Menteith changed sides several times. Modern scholarship regards him as a staunch fighter for the community of Scotland during the GUARDIANSHIP. Although supposedly captured by the English, the exact date of his first change of sides is unclear. He was still regarded as Scottish in September 1303, but by March of 1304 was in the 'peace and confidence' of Edward. The following year he became keeper of Dumbarton castle, one of only two entrusted to Scotsmen. The burgh and sheriff-dom of Dumbarton were also put in his charge. Meantime, the search for Wallace had continued and on 3 August 1305 Menteith's servants captured him in or near Glasgow. Whether or not Menteith can be accused of treachery in handing over Wallace is an open question, since, as one modern historian has pointed out, he was repaying the trust Edward had evidently placed in him.

He was created earl of Lennox by Edward and continued loyal to the English king in his pursuit of ROBERT I. By 1308 or 1309 he had joined Bruce and given up his earl-dom for the lordships of Knapdale and Arran. Menteith was present at the St Andrews PARLIAMENT, 1308–9, which issued declarations in support of Robert I. His name was also cited in the later Declaration of Arbroath in 1320.
•*Barrow, G.W.S., Robert Bruce, Edinburgh University Press, 2nd ed. 1976.*
•*McNamee, C., The Wars of the Bruces. Scotland, England and Ireland 1306–1328, Tuckwell Press, 1997.*

migration Although territorial mobility was very restricted in a pre-industrial society, migration has long been a feature of Scottish POPULATION history.

It was given increased momentum during the AGRICULTURAL REVOLUTION and the INDUSTRIAL REVOLUTION of the eighteenth and early nineteenth centuries. It was characterized — though not exclusively — by movement (sometimes over several generations) from rural, agrarian districts, such as the HIGHLANDS, the northeast and the south, to the urban, industrial Central Lowlands. Temporary migration, mainly from the Highlands and from IRELAND, was very common — often in the short-term to work at the harvest or in bleachworks. Movement was always associated with job opportunities and hence closely related to the economic cycle.

During the nineteenth century there was a substantial flow of migrants from Ireland, mainly to the industrial west of Scotland and to Dundee (where in 1851 the proportion of Irish-born was actually higher than in Glasgow). As with the development of earlier industrial activities around planned villages so the opening of new COAL-mines in Ayrshire and Lanarkshire or the establishment of the shale-oil industry in West Lothian are instances of labour-intensive activities that attracted further substantial migration in the mid-Victorian era.

Migration south of the Border to England has also figured in Scottish demography — though at least until the twentieth century probably at a lower level than emigration overseas. Other significant influences on migration patterns include the impact of WORLD WAR I and WORLD WAR II and the depression of the twenties and thirties — which were accompanied by considerable social upheaval. The post-1945 era saw the development of large communities in the NEW TOWNS and in suburban housing schemes, often destroying the social fabric of older centres in the process. See also IMMIGRATION.

• Devine, T.M. (ed.), Irish Immigration and Scottish Society, John Donald, 1991.
• Gray, M., Scots on the Move: Scots Migrants, 1750—1914, Economic and Social History Society of Scotland, 1990.
• Hunter, J., A Dance Called America: the Scottish Highlands, the United States and Canada, Mainstream Publishing, 1994.
• Stewart, I.A.D. (ed.), From Caledonia to the Pampas, Tuckwell Press, 1999.
• Withers, C.W.J., Urban Highlanders, Tuckwell Press, 1998.

military roads, see CAULFIELD; ROADS; TRANSPORT; WADE

Militia Act   While law and order was threatened by radical ideas after the French Revolution, it was not until the FRENCH REVOLUTION and the NAPOLEONIC WARS that Britain was physically threatened by invasion. During the period 1793—97 the French had achieved a number of successes, while Britain experienced mixed fortunes. There was civil unrest — notably in Ireland — and this was aggravated by naval mutinies among the fleet at Spithead, the Nore, and at Yarmouth. The danger of invasion was ever present and to counter this the government implemented a series of emergency measures, including the Militia Act, the Scottish Militia being formed in 1797.

The act enforced conscription by ballot for men between eighteen and twenty-three and provoked serious disorder. This arose from the fact that militiamen could be drafted overseas and that most of the middle and upper classes were either Volunteers (and thus exempt from conscription) or could afford to buy themselves out. Anti-militia disturbances broke out in many places, as 'Scotland went stark mad', according to one contemporary. Schoolmasters, who had to draw up lists of men for the militia ballot had their homes ransacked and parish registers destroyed.

The most serious riot occurred at Tranent, East Lothian, where colliers and salters resisted the ballot. The disturbance was ruthlessly suppressed by troops, with eleven persons killed and several wounded. Order was restored by the end of the year and further inducements of favourable pay and pensions offered to those who would enlist. The quotas for the Scottish Militia were eventually fixed in March 1798, but it was not until seven months later that all of the 6,000 men were at last mobilized.

• Emsley, C., *British Society and the French Wars 1793—1815*, Macmillan, 1979.

• Logue, K., *Popular Disturbances in Scotland 1780—1815*, John Donald, 1979.

Miller, Hugh (1802—56) Miller, an excellent example of self-help, made a significant contribution to nineteenth-century Scottish geology and also gained something of a reputation as a lay theologian, popular journalist and writer on contemporary issues such as the CHURCH, POOR LAW, EDUCATION, and REFORM. Miller was born in Cromarty, son of a seaman who went down with his small trading vessel when it sunk in the Moray Firth in 1807. Educated at the local school, he was then apprenticed to a stonemason and began to take an interest in geology. After he became a journeyman mason in 1822 he was increasingly attracted to literary activities and published occasional poems and essays, notably *Poems Written in the Leisure Hours of A Journeyman Mason* (1829) and *Letters on the Herring Fishing*, originally written to the *Inverness Courier* the same year.

His literary endeavours made him a local figure and in 1834 helped him enter the middle class as a bank accountant. He was able to continue his interest in both geology and writing — as well as become involved in the debate about ecclesiastical reform, particularly the patronage issue. His *Letter to Lord Brougham from one of the Scotch People* (1839) articulated the popular view prevailing

against patronage and brought him to the attention of the evangelicals in the Church of Scotland.

Miller was offered the editorship of *The Witness*, a twice-weekly newspaper supporting church and other reforms. For some time he wrote this virtually single-handed, covering a vast range of topics. In 1840 *The Witness* carried in serial form Miller's work on *The Old Red Sandstone, or New Walks in an Old Field*, published as a book a year later. This made his reputation as one of the most successful popularizers of science of his generation and this was maintained by further publications, including *Footprints of the Creator* (1847) and *The Testimony of the Rocks*, which appeared posthumously in 1857.

After the DISRUPTION of 1843 *The Witness* was for a time essentially the mouthpiece of the Free Church, but after 1845 Miller became joint-owner and was able to pursue a more independent line. Indeed the paper carried features on a variety of social issues including the condition of the HIGHLANDS, education and the poor, mostly written by Miller himself.

Miller became a controversial figure in the 'creation' debate far in advance of Charles Darwin (1809—1882). His position was very much that of the mainstream Victorian scientists, most of whom, as Rosie says, managed quite happily to reconcile their scientific work with their religious faith. Perhaps defending his position and overwork contributed to the mental strain that led to his demise — though tertiary syphilis may have been responsible. He committed suicide in 1856, a tormented but clearly gifted figure.

• *Miller, H., My Schools and Schoolmasters, J. Robertson, (ed.), B&W Publishing, 1995.*
• *Rosie, G., Hugh Miller: Outrage and Order. A Biography and Selected Writings, Mainstream, 1981.*
• *Shortland, M. (ed.), Hugh Miller and the Contrivers of Victorian Science, Clarendon Press, 1996.*

monastic houses   Abbey and castle were closely linked in the process of NORMANIZATION. Their occupants had much in common, with monks and canons having the same interest in land and agriculture as the Scoto-Norman or Anglo-Norman barons. They seem to have had the same faith in written government, charters, and property rights. Often they were relatives of the new settlers and the connections with Normandy and France generally remained strong. The majority of ecclesiastical foundations were made by French religious communities, though some were off-shoots from England.

While some significant new monasteries, such as Dumfermline, associated with St MARGARET, were earlier, the greatest expansion occurred during the reign of DAVID I, who in a reign of twenty-nine years, founded nineteen. Many of these were established by the Cistercian order, then spreading rapidly over much of the Continent and in England, due to the energy and influence of St Bernard. While seeking solitude, in places like Melrose (1136), the Cistercian and other orders were also practical agriculturalists, developing both arable and sheep farming, the latter for WOOL production. There is also evidence that the abbeys of Holyrood (1128) and Newbattle (1140), exploited COAL and engaged in SALT making. Cistercian abbeys included Culross and Balmerino (both Fife), Coupar-Angus, Glenluce and Sweetheart or New Abbey, founded by DEVORGILLA in 1273 (both Galloway), and Deer (Aberdeenshire). Those founded by the Cluniac order were Paisley and Crossraguel (Ayrshire). The Tironsesian order was responsible for Arbroath, Lindores (Fife), and Kilwinning (Ayrshire).

Despite their apparent unworldliness, some occupants of the religious houses played prominent roles in the king's court and the administration of the kingdom and rose to high office.

Apart from castles, the monasteries were the most substantial architectural relics of the medieval era. Although many fell victim to destruction in subsequent centuries, especially during and after the REFORMATION, much of archaeological and historical interest survives, notably in the BORDERS, Dumfries and Galloway, where the structures are both substantial and in striking natural settings.

• *Dilworth, M., Scottish Monasteries in the Late Middle Ages, Edinburgh University Press, 1995.*
• *Fawcett, R., Scottish Abbeys and Priories, Batsford, 1994.*

Monck, George (1608—70) Monck was an Englishman closely connected with Scottish affairs for over twenty years in the mid-seventeenth century. Thus, after beginning his military career in Holland in the 1630s he served in the army of CHARLES I (1600—49) in the two BISHOPS' WARS (1639—40).

However, having eventually gone over to the Parliamentarian side during the CIVIL WAR, he was a prominent member of the English army that defeated the Scots at DUNBAR (1650). Between 1651 and 1652 he was one of the eight major-generals who controlled the country during the first stage of the CROMWELLIAN UNION, returning in 1654, after a brief absence, to become Commander-in-Chief. He dealt effectively with the GLENCAIRN RISING, not to mention a mutiny among his own forces, and remained a key figure in Scotland until the RESTORATION. It was, for instance, through his intervention that some of the tax burden imposed on the nation was reduced by the Protectorate authorities. In 1660 he withdrew most of his army into England in order to facilitate the smooth return of CHARLES II (1630—85), being rewarded with the dukedom of Albemarle for his endeavours. In the immediate aftermath of the Restoration he continued to exercise some influence in Scottish matters persuading the king to order a complete withdrawal of his forces and also taking a leading role in ensuring the downfall of ARGYLL (1607—61). None the less his advice on the religious settlement was ignored and episcopacy was reinstated.

Montrose, Marquis of, see GRAHAM, JAMES, MARQUIS OF MONTROSE

Moray, earls of, see STEWART, JAMES, EARL OF MORAY

Morton, Earl of, see DOUGLAS, JAMES

Muir, John (1838—1914) John Muir, pioneer of the conservation movement, was born in Dunbar, East Lothian, in 1838. His family emigrated to the United States in 1849 where Muir's subsequent education took him to the University of Wisconsin. He then began a career in industry, but after being blinded in one eye in 1867, began pursuing an interest in natural history. He explored large tracts of the American West, where frontier boundaries were already being defined after the opening of the Trans-continental railroads and the surge of migration after the Civil War. He roamed on foot through many parts of the US, notably the Yosemite region, discovering and writing about natural wonders and then urging federal action to protect them from development. He was able to devote time to this cause thanks to marriage with the daughter of a successful Californian fruit farmer and wine maker and to his own success in farming.

Muir was ultimately responsible for the establishment of Yosemite (1890) and Sequoia National Parks and for the formation of the Sierra Club, the organisation aimed at promoting conservation. Muir's vigorous propaganda campaign was a major influence on President Theodore Roosevelt's decision to increase significantly the amount of protected public land. Muir wrote extensively about his explorations. The John Muir Trust, aimed at acquiring wild land in Britain was set up in 1984 and a country park in East Lothian is named for him.

Muir, Thomas, of Huntershill (1765—99) Son of a farmer-turned-merchant, Muir was born in

Glasgow in 1765, attended the Grammar School there, and in 1782 graduated MA from Glasgow University. He later studied law at Glasgow, but after a dispute with the college authorities over his role in a student protest transferred to Edinburgh University. There he completed his studies and entered the Faculty of Advocates in 1787. Thereafter he rapidly gained the reputation of a man of principle, engaging as counsel in cases of PATRONAGE against local landowners and also appearing gratis for poor clients.

A staunch supporter of the FRENCH REVOLUTION, Muir was soon active in the RADICAL reform movement of the day and played a leading role with William SKIRVING (d. 1796) in the inauguration of the Scottish FRIENDS OF THE PEOPLE in July 1792. Muir thereafter became a prominent propagandist for the Friends of the People, travelling round the country on speaking tours and founding new branches — as well as corresponding with the United Irishmen about a unified campaign for political reform and national independence. By the time of the first National Convention in December 1792 Muir was already a marked man and early in January 1793 he was arrested and charged with sedition.

After interrogation — and perhaps to his own surprise — he was released on bail. Visiting London, Muir found that the moderate WHIGS, panicked by the trial of Louis XVI, were preparing to abandon their support for political reform. Muir then embarked on a mission to persuade the French revolutionaries to abandon plans to execute the king, but his last-minute intervention failed. While in Paris Muir met not only the Girondist leaders, but also Thomas Paine (1737—1809), author of *The Rights of Man*, and Dr William Maxwell, an associate of Robert BURNS. With the declaration of war — and having missed the date set for his trial in Scotland — Muir found himself exiled in France.

In June 1793 he eventually sailed for Ireland where he spent some time in Belfast and Dublin meeting the United Irishmen. Knowing himself outlawed, but apparently determined to stand trial and prove his innocence, Muir returned to Scotland and was immediately arrested. His show trial before the ruthless ROBERT MACQUEEN, Lord Braxfield, was a farce and Muir was found guilty of sedition and sentenced to fourteen years transportation. No time was lost in despatching Muir and three associates, PALMER (1747—1802), Skirving and MARGAROT (1745—1815) to New South Wales.

After two years exile Muir escaped on an American ship in February 1796. He had many adventures and misfortunes in Mexico, Cuba and Spain (where he was badly wounded on the face) and arrived in France in 1797 after the French authorities had negotiated his release. Greeted as a hero by the Directory, and renewing acquaintance with other exiled revolutionaries, Muir lived in Paris until his death — probably from earlier wounds — in 1799.

Although somewhat naive in his attitude to both the British government authorities and the French revolutionaries there is little doubt that Muir remains one of the most important figures in the early

Scottish reform movement and has long been commemorated as the most prominent of the 'SCOTTISH MARTYRS'.

• *Bewley, C., Muir of Huntershill, Oxford University Press, 1981.*

Murdock, William (1754—1839) William Murdock, pioneer of gas lighting, was a typically practical inventor of the INDUSTRIAL REVOLUTION era. Son of a millwright at Cumnock, Ayrshire, he worked with his father until 1777, when he joined the famous firm of engineers Boulton and Watt in Birmingham. After two years at their Soho works he was sent to Cornwall as engineer in charge of the firm's operation of selling and maintaining steam pumping engines.

He began his experiments into the properties of gases in 1792 and continued them after his return to Birmingham in 1799. By 1803 the Soho foundry was regularly lit by gas and Boulton and Watt later manufactured gas-making equipment. Although Murdock read a paper about gas to the Royal Society in 1808 and was later involved in Boulton and Watt's efforts to block a parliamentary bill incorporating the Gas Light and Coke Company in 1809, he seems to have dropped his interest in the process soon after. Murdock also pioneered steam locomotion and was closely involved with James WATT (1736—1819) in improvements to the steam engine.

Murray, Sir Andrew (d.1297) Murray, like WALLACE, became a national hero during and after his death in the WARS OF INDEPENDENCE. He was the son of Sir Andrew Murray, a northern landowner with estates in Invernesshire, Easter Ross and Banffshire. Murray, JUSTICIAR by 1289, and so far as is known loyal to JOHN BALLIOL, was captured by the English probably after the battle of DUNBAR and Balliol's resignation of the kingdom in 1296. He subsequently escaped and like Wallace become a leader of the revolt against the English occupation. He seems to have played a prominent role in linking a series of small scale revolts in Moray, in localities east of the Spey, and in Aberdeen, much as Wallace did in the south.

In the famous victory at STIRLING BRIDGE 11 September 1297, Murray was wounded. Murray's movements after Stirling are unclear, but by October in letters regarding TRADE sent to Hamburg and Lubeck, he and Wallace were being described as 'commanders of the army of the kingdom of Scotland, and the community of that realm'. Unfortunately Murray died in November of that year, probably of his wounds, so his place in history was inevitably more difficult to define than that of his fellow patriot. His son, also Sir Andrew Murray (d.1338), became a GUARDIAN in 1332 during the minority of DAVID II.

• *Barron, E., The Scottish War of Independence, James Nisbet & Co., 1914.*
• *Watson, F., Under the Hammer. Edward I and Scotland 1286—1307, Tuckwell Press, 1998.*

Murray, Lord George (c.1700—60) Son of John, first Duke of Atholl (1659—1724) Murray and his brother the Marquis of Tullibardine (1689—1747) both participated in the earlier JACOBITE REBELLIONS of 1715 and 1719 before joining the rising of 1745. Murray enlisted with Prince Charles Edward STEWART, the Young Pretender (1720—88) on 4 September as lieutenant-general in the Jacobite army sharing overall command with the Duke of Perth (1713—47) and the Prince himself. An able general, if apparently also possessing a prickly personality, he frequently found himself disagreeing with the tactics of Charles and his advisers, especially the Irish officers attached to the army. Thus he opposed the decision to invade England in November and the next month, at Derby, was an outspoken advocate of retreating. He distinguished himself in this orderly withdrawal, playing a major part in the defeat of the advancing Hanoverian forces at Falkirk in January 1746. At CULLODEN he again found himself at odds with his leader and the others since he correctly argued that Drummossie Moor, the scene of the actual conflict, provided too many advantages to the powerful cavalry and artillery units of the Duke of Cumberland (1721—65). Commanding the right wing of the Jacobite forces he survived the battle and ultimately escaped to permanent exile in Holland.

• *Tomasson, K., The Jacobite General, Blackwood, 1958.*

N

Nairne, Caroline, Lady (1766—1845) Lady Nairne was the daughter of a devoted supporter of the JACOBITES, Lawrence Oliphant of Gask whose possessions had become one of the FORFEITED ESTATES after CULLODEN. While her initial enthusiasm for Scottish folk music undoubtedly stemmed from her family upbringing and background, her marriage in 1806 to her cousin major William Nairne was also very significant.

Nairne was Inspector General of Barracks, a sinecure which included an apartment in Holyrood Palace. By 1824 when her husband's forfeited Jacobite title was restored, Lady Nairne, as she now was, had taken full advantage of the opportunities presented to her by living in Edinburgh. Thus by this date she had contacted Robert Purdie the editor of *The Scottish Minstrel,* a six-volume collection of Scottish music. Using the nom de plume 'Mrs Bogan of Bogan' she submitted the lyrics of numerous melodies to Purdie.

Though she wrote or adapted a vast assortment of songs and poems during her lifetime, recognition of her contribution to Scotland's musical heritage only came posthumously. Today, she is best remembered for songs like 'Wi' A Hundred Pipers', 'Caller Herrin' and 'The Laird of Cockpen'.

Napier Commission, see CROFTERS' COMMISSION

Napier, Robert (1791—1876) Robert Napier, who made a significant contribution to Scottish marine ENGINEERING and SHIPBUILDING, was born in Dumbarton in 1791, son of a local blacksmith. Educated at the local grammar school he was later apprenticed to his father. After he himself had become a master smith in 1812 he spent some time working for Robert Stevenson (1772—1850), the noted civil engineer, lighthouse and harbour builder. He then returned to his father's business before setting up on his own in 1815 as an engineer and blacksmith.

Clearly much influenced by his cousin, David Napier (1790—1869), who helped pioneer steam navigation, Napier constructed his first marine engine for the steamship *Leven* for service between Glasgow and Dumbarton in 1823. Three years later he built the engines for the *Eclipse*, which sailed between Glasgow and Belfast. Following his success in a steamboat competition in 1827, his engines were much in demand and he moved to larger premises to build increasingly more powerful marine engines. He supplied engines for the Glasgow Steam Packet Company, which he himself joined in 1830, for the East India Company in 1836, and was the first on the Clyde to construct marine engines for the navy. He was consulted about the feasibility of transatlantic steam shipping and contracted to supply Samuel Cunard (1787–1865) with engines for the three vessels that helped pioneer the Cunard Company. Napier was closely associated with the company for fifteen years.

In 1841 Napier acquired land at Govan and laid the basis for what was later to become the famous shipbuilding firm of Robert Napier and Sons. Over 400 contracts were fulfilled under his management and that of his sons, including iron ships for the Peninsular and Oriental Company and for Cunard Company. He patented many improvements to marine engines and iron ships and his employees included David Elder, John Elder (1826–69), George and James (d.1870) Thomson, William Denny (1847–87) and others who established yards of their own and helped make the Clyde a major international shipbuilding centre.

Latterly Napier's services as a consultant were much sought after, he served as a judge at the Great Exhibition in 1851 and the Paris Exhibition in 1855, received the Legion of Honour from Napoleon III (1808–73) and was also honoured by the king of Denmark. He augmented a large and valuable art collection, which was disposed of on his death. Napier was a typically practical man born of the Industrial Revolution era but also had the considerable entrepre-

neurial skills needed to build and sustain a profitable international shipbuilding enterprise.

Napoleonic Wars The Napoleonic War (1799–1815) — essentially an extension of the FRENCH REVOLUTIONARY WAR (1793–9) coincided with Napoleon's rule as First Consul (1799–1804) and Emperor of France (1804–14). There was a brief period of uneasy peace from 1801 to 1803 following the Treaty of Amiens. The war thus embraces a period of dramatic economic, social and political change in Scotland associated mainly with the AGRICULTURAL REVOLUTION, the INDUSTRIAL REVOLUTION, urbanization, and the growing, though temporarily quiescent, movement for REFORM inspired by the French Revolution itself. Additionally a large proportion of the population was mobilized in the army or navy and played a prominent role in the British government's campaign against France.

Firstly, the war was an important catalyst to economic development across a whole range of sectors, from primary production to manufactures. AGRICULTURE was stimulated by rising prices and rents, which in turn encouraged IMPROVEMENT. In the Lowlands and other areas of arable farming large new areas were brought into production, with cereals in particular pushed to the margin of cultivation. In the HIGHLANDS high prices encouraged both the CATTLE trade and the extension of the CLEARANCES for sheep farming, meat and wool production. The KELP and FISHING industries also prospered — the former product fetching £20 per ton by 1808.

Industries, notably those of strategic importance like agricultural processing (BREWING, DISTILLING, milling, tanning, etc.), COAL and lead-mining, iron manufacture, SHIPBUILDING and TEXTILES were greatly stimulated by increased demand. Of these the iron industry was most obviously affected by demand for munitions such as the cannon produced at the CARRON Ironworks, near Falkirk. Because of the shift to war supply and the rapidly expanding domestic market, the Continental System (1806–9) by which Napoleon tried (with some success) to isolate British merchants from European ports, seems to have had only limited effects on Scotland; though the American War (1812–14) was more damaging, especially to the COTTON trade.

At the close of the war there was a severe economic down-turn, bringing long-term depression and unemployment for the first time on any scale during the Industrial Revolution, greatly heightening social tension and putting severe pressure on the forces of law and order. The much increased rate of industrialization and military participation also had significant social consequences. The war created employment in both town and countryside — and in the latter context hastened the emergence of an urban, industrial workforce.

MIGRATION into the towns in search of work and new opportunities greatly taxed social facilities, particularly such provisions as were made available under the POOR LAW and for housing. In the aftermath demobilization caused major problems of re-adjustment

of the kind seen later following WORLD WAR I.

As elsewhere in Britain, this was an era of high tension — especially during times of threatened invasion. Scotland was heavily fortified, regular troops in the Lowland castles and Highland forts being supported by volunteers and conscripts enlisted under the hated MILITIA ACT. Martello towers similar to those in England and Ireland were built for coastal defence — a good example can be seen in Orkney guarding Scapa Flow. Many French prisoners were held captive in Scotland, notably at Edinburgh Castle, Perth prison (which, like Dartmoor, dates from this period), Penicuik and Lanark. The number of Scots in the ranks was high in proportion to the population and many unfortunates were press-ganged into the navy. Several new regiments were raised — particularly from the Highlands — and played a prominent part in Continental campaigns. Scottish commanders, on land and at sea, finally helped overcome Napoleon in 1815.

Politically, the rise of Napoleon as the autocrat of France, test-bed of the revolution, depressed democrats everywhere. Under Henry DUNDAS (1742–1811) and his successors reformers and agitators were driven underground, though they emerged briefly from time to time in the guise of the United Scotsmen, anti-Militia Act rioters, food rioters or striking cotton spinners. The Napoleonic War, therefore, left a legacy of unfulfilled social and political expectations that were to surface in the difficult post-war era after

1815 and be further nurtured by the RADICALS, OWENITES, ANTI-CORN LAW LEAGUERS and CHARTISTS during the age of reform.

• *Emsley, C., British Society and the French Wars 1793—1815, Macmillan, 1979.*

National Covenant (1638) Drafted by Alexander HENDERSON (1583—1646) and Archibald JOHNSTON of Wariston (1611—63), two leading critics of CHARLES I (1600—49), this document was given its final format in February 1638 by a small group of noblemen headed by Lord Balmerino (d.1649). It was then signed on 28 February and 1 March by various prominent magnates, lairds, ministers and burgesses before being distributed for general subscription throughout the country. It brought to a head the growing campaign against such royal religious innovations as the CODE OF CANONS and the PRAYER BOOK, which had resulted in widespread protests and the formation by the end of 1637 of the curiously named Tables. This was a committee representing different sections of the population based in Edinburgh. Charles refused to acknowledge the mounting criticism of his policies, hence the drawing up of the National Covenant. Much of it was preoccupied with previous legislation, particularly the 'Negative Confession' made by JAMES VI (1566—1625) in 1581 where he had strongly asserted his Protestant principles. Clearly the point was being stressed that Charles should consult PARLIAMENT and the Church rather than behave in an arbitrary manner. Significantly the signatories also pledged themselves to ignore and resist the religious changes introduced by the Crown until such time as they had been discussed by a GENERAL ASSEMBLY and Parliament. Such was the nationwide support for the Covenant that Charles back-pedalled and permitted the Kirk to hold a General Assembly in GLASGOW in November 1638. it was to be this General Assembly whose decisions were to be a major factor in the complete breakdown of relations between Charles and his subjects.

• *Dickinson, W.C. and Donaldson, G. (eds.), A Source Book of Scottish History III, Nelson, 1961.*

• *Donaldson, G., Scotland: James V to James VII, Oliver & Boyd, 1965.*

• *Macinnes, A.I., Charles I and the Making of the Covenanting Movement, John Donald, 1991.*

National Party of Scotland, see HOME RULE; SCOTTISH NATIONAL PARTY

Navigation Acts The Navigation Act, when first passed by the Long Parliament in 1651, was designed to maintain an English monopoly over the colonial trade. Subsequent acts, notably a second Navigation Act (1660), the Frauds Act (1662), the Staple Act (1663) and the Plantation Duties Act (1673), tried to stop the loop-holes in the original Act. These laid down broadly that no goods might be imported from or exported to the colonies except in English-built and English-owned ships, and that certain 'enumerated' products, such as TOBACCO and sugar, might only be shipped direct to England or other English colonies.

Scotland fell under the same exclusion as the Netherlands,

France, Spain and other trading rivals of the English and this was a major irritant to Scottish merchants before 1707. Many Scottish traders — notably those of Glasgow and other Clyde ports — engaged in a growing but still illegal commerce with the North American Colonies and the West Indies, while their exclusion from legal trading also inspired the ill-fated DARIEN SCHEME in Central America (1698–1700). The effects of the Navigation Acts and the exclusion of the Scots from colonial trade figured prominently in subsequent negotiations over the Treaty of UNION.

Neville's Cross, Battle of (1346)
Following successive raids by Scottish forces on England in 1342 and 1345, DAVID II was defeated after a third invasion which ended at Neville's Cross near Durham on 17 October 1346. Wounded by an arrow and captured by his enemies, he was subsequently held prisoner for eleven years. As earlier, following the defeat at Halidon (1333), southern Scotland was invaded by an English army designed to install Edward Balliol as king but he failed to raise enough support from the Scottish elite. Edward III eventually cooled in his support for Balliol who resigned his claim to the throne in 1356. A year later David was released under the terms of the treaty of Berwick.

New Lanark Like the pioneering CARRON Ironworks, the COTTON spinning mills at New Lanark on the River Clyde, 25 miles (40 km) south of Glasgow, are associated with technological innovation and the modernization of production processes during the classic INDUSTRIAL REVOLUTION era. While New Lanark was not the first, it became one of the largest and most important water-powered country spinning mills of its period and was later associated with the work of Robert OWEN (1771–1858), the social reformer.

New Lanark was planned and developed in 1785 by David DALE (1739–1806), a prominent Glasgow merchant-banker, and Richard Arkwright (1732–92), inventor of the water frame — though the latter soon abandoned his interest. Dale and his management made New Lanark a model industrial community with a PLANNED VILLAGE providing housing, school and other social facilities. As was the norm both women and children were employed, some being orphans drawn from institutions. One of Dale's managers, William Kelly, developed special lightweight machinery that could he readily operated by children.

Dale's son-in-law, the entrepreneurial Robert Owen, took over as manager in 1800 and turned New Lanark into a test-bed for his economic and social ideas, notably in man-management, EDUCATION and environmental improvement. Yet many of the innovations Owen claimed for himself had, in fact, been initiated under Dale's regime, though Owen stopped employing children under ten years of age. He also introduced an innovative school curriculum and adult education in the Institute for the Formation of Character, which still stands.

Under Owen, the mills and village at New Lanark became a showplace, much visited by dignitaries and other industrialists with a latent enthusiasm for philanthropy, which clearly could be made to pay profits. Indeed, after several partnership difficulties Owen became sole proprietor of New Lanark and it made him a rich man.

After Owen's withdrawal from the business in the late 1820s New Lanark continued to operate for another 150 years before the closure of the mills in 1968. Subsequently it became the object of a major conservation effort and is now one of the most important industrial monuments in Britain, its status being acknowledged internationally by UNESCO as a World Heritage Site.
• *Donnachie, I. and Hewitt, G., New Lanark: The Dale and Owen Industrial Community since 1785, Edinburgh University Press, 1993.*

New Town of Edinburgh   The late eighteenth-century New Town is perhaps the best physical and architectural manifestation of the Scottish ENLIGHTENMENT, built 1776–1840 to a symmetrical plan characteristic of the period. The original proposals of 1752 owed much to George DRUMMOND (d.1776), while the plan conceived by James Craig (1740–95) dates from 1767. The New Town — in contrast to the Old — was dignified by broad and stately streets and squares, among which George Street and Charlotte Square are perhaps the finest. Some of the most elegant buildings of the great Georgian architect, Robert Adam (1728–92), grace the district, notably Register House, the Old College and many of the houses around Charlotte Square, including Bute House. In George Street

are the Assembly Rooms (1787) and Music Hall (1843), although the most famous street, Princes Street, with its array of shops on the north side, is much altered. Otherwise the original core of the classical New Town is much as it was conceived, though greatly extended southward and northward after the early 1800s. A major conservation scheme has restored much of the New Town's former grandeur.
• *Youngson, A.J., The Making of Classical Edinburgh, Edinburgh University Press, 1966.*

New Towns   The Scottish New Towns grew from the United Kingdom-wide post-war planning movement after 1945, though the idea of such new communities had been canvassed earlier during the DEPRESSION and WORLD WAR II. The New Towns were designed to relieve population pressure, ease slum clearance in the cities, provide greenfield sites for industrial expansion, and generate employment. East Kilbride (1948) was the pioneer, followed by Glenrothes (1949), Cumbernauld (1956), Livingston (1962) and Irvine (1966). A sixth, Stonehouse, was designated but later abandoned. Though experiencing mixed fortunes, the New Towns were generally successful in their aims. This was at considerable cost to the core of older communities — notably Glasgow — from which large numbers were decanted and which took many years to regenerate as a result.

New Zealand, see CLEARANCES; EMIGRATION

Newspapers, see PRESS

Normans   Norman feudalism began to extend its influence in Scotland by imposing itself on existing patterns of social, religious and cultural life long before the twelfth century. But it was during the reign of DAVID I that Norman institutions began to have much greater impact, imposing a new order on the country, particularly throughout the Lowlands. The main manifestations of this were the castle, the SHERIFFDOM, the BURGH, and MONASTIC HOUSES, staffed by landholders, soldiers, administrators, officials, merchants, and members of religious orders. Two other important facets of this were the creation of baronies (with their BARON COURTS) and bishoprics, extending, respectively, the power of landowners and the Church.

Northampton, Treaty of (1328) Following the WARS OF INDEPENDENCE, ROBERT I's struggle for recognition of Scottish independence was brought to a successful conclusion by this agreement. It incorporated the substance of six key points Bruce had communicated to Edward III in October 1327. Commissioners from both sides hammered out the details at Newcastle and York, the treaty being finally agreed to on 17 March 1328 with the English commissioners sent to Holyrood. The treaty was subsequently ratified by the English parliament at Northampton on 4 May. The treaty highlighted some points of vital significance for Anglo-Scottish relations. Central were the English renunciation of sovereignty and a marriage alliance between the future DAVID II and Joan, the young sister of Edward. Though both were minors, this took place at Berwick 12 July 1328. Unfortunately Bruce, after a long illness, died a year later. Subsequent events in Anglo-Scottish relations, as modern research confirms, proved how much of a personal achievement his triumph in the wars and the consolidation of the kingdom had been.

• *Barrow, G.W.S., Robert Bruce, Edinburgh University Press, 2nd edn. 1976.*
• *Lynch, M., Scotland. A New History, Pimlico, 1992.*

North British Railway, see RAILWAYS

Northern Earls   One of the long-standing problems facing JAMES VI (1566–1625) once his minority ended was the threat to royal authority posed by Huntly (1562–1636), Errol (c.1566–1631) and Crawford (c.1567–1607), the so-called 'Northern Earls'. From around 1588 to 1594 these Catholic noblemen and their followers were able to treat the Crown with remarkable impunity. Thus, they sympathized with Philip II (1527–98) over the defeat of his armada, promising support both in 1589 and again in 1593 when a complex conspiracy known as the 'Spanish Blanks' was concocted involving promises of assistance for a Spanish invasion of western Scotland. Even Huntly's murder of the Earl of Moray (c.1560–92) only resulted, as the other incidents had done, in a short spell of imprisonment for the culprit. In fact, it was not until late 1594 that the king took a tougher stance, temporarily driving Huntly and Errol into exile and ultimately, in 1597, forcing them to renounce the Catholic faith.

James VI's vacillation can be accounted for by a reluctance to antagonize English Catholics now that the succession seemed a possibility, a personal attachment to the youthful Huntly and perhaps an ingrained fear of retaliatory assassination. At the same time his preference for patient diplomacy rather than violent solutions to his difficulties should not be underestimated.

• *Willson, D.H., King James VI & I, Jonathan Cape, 1956.*
• *Donaldson, G., Scotland: James V to James VII, Oliver & Boyd, 1965.*

Norway, see LARGS, BATTLE OF; MARGARET, MAID OF NORWAY

Nova Scotia, see EMIGRATION

O

Ogilvie, James, first Earl of Seafield (1664—1730) Originally a JACOBITE at the start of WILLIAM III's (1650—1702) reign, James Ogilvie was soon won over by the Crown and remained a loyal servant until the Treaty of UNION. As Secretary of State he performed sterling service at the height of the crisis involving the COMPANY OF SCOTLAND and again in the reign of Queen ANNE (1665—1714) during the events leading towards the Union. As Chancellor in 1702—4 and 1705—7 he played a major part in furthering the interests of the Queen and her ministers. The ultimate outcome owed a great deal to his efforts and he was suitably rewarded by a grateful English government. Latterly, resentment at the abolition of the PRIVY COUNCIL, annoyance at the decision preventing the admission of Scottish peers with English titles to the House of Lords and the introduction of the MALT TAX in Scotland made Seafield, now fourth Earl of Findlater, increasingly disaffected. Thus, in 1713, he took the lead in moving the bill for the repeal of the Treaty of Union. In 1715 he displayed a certain amount of sympathy for the Jacobites but astutely avoided any open commitment to their cause.

Orkney, see MAGNUS; STEWART, PATRICK, EARL OF ORKNEY

Otterburn, Battle of (1388) This was one of the most important engagements in the ongoing conflicts with England late in the reign of the by then aged and infirm ROBERT II. Fought on 5 August 1388, the Scots under James, second earl of Douglas, and George Dunbar, Earl of March, defeated the English under Henry Percy (nicknamed 'Hotspur'), son of the earl of Northumberland. Percy was captured and Douglas killed. Otterburn was followed by another large-scale raid into England as far as Newcastle, but it ended with the defeat of the Scottish forces at Homildon Hill, near Wooler. This resulted in a truce, with the English consolidating their defence of the northern counties and the Scots abandoning their raids south.

outfield In the traditional mode of AGRICULTURE the outfield, as the name suggests, was the land on the fringes of the 'toun' or settlement that served either as marginal arable land or as pasture. The outfield received little or no manure and in many instances progressively lost its fertility. During the sixteenth and seventeenth centuries some settlement took place on the outfield areas — largely in response to POPULATION growth. Hence some outfield was subject to IMPROVEMENT for more systematic grazing or cultivation.

Owen, Robert (1771—1858)
Robert Owen, entrepreneur, social reformer and visionary, although a Welshman, born at Newtown, Montgomeryshire, spent the most successful and creative stages of his life in Scotland as manager and later owner of the NEW LANARK cotton mills and community. After elementary schooling he spent his early working life in the textile retail trade in Stanford, Lincolnshire, London and then Manchester, to which he moved in 1792. At first he worked in drapery but soon entered a partnership with John Jones in cotton spinning machine manufacture. He then gained useful managerial experience in cotton spinning and became a partner of the Charlton Twist Company. In his spare time he was a member of the Manchester Literary and Philosophical Society and began to learn something of the social and economic ideas of the ENLIGHTENMENT. During a series of business trips to Glasgow and the West of Scotland Owen met David DALE (1739—1806) and visited New Lanark. In 1799 Owen and his partners bought the mills, while he himself married Dale's daughter. By 1800 he was installed as manager of one of the largest cotton spinning plants in Scotland, with a labour force of about 2,000 people.

New Lanark became the test-bed for Owen's social and economic theories. He attempted to improve the general environment by better working conditions in the mills and introducing improved sanitation, HOUSING and EDUCATION. He stopped both the employment of children under ten and the recruitment of pauper apprentices. Most of the innovations were prompted by a desire for improved efficiency, work-flows and output, such as attention to the welfare of women and children, cleanliness and accident prevention in the mills. Owen backed up a system of supervision by overseers with his 'silent monitor', a four-sided wooden block, designed to hang on the machine and coloured white, yellow, blue and black. The colour of the side showing to the front represented 'the conduct of the individual during the preceding day'; white was excellent and black the opposite. Supervisors kept 'books of character', which Owen regularly inspected. What was essentially an exercise in industrial psychology prevented what Owen called 'bad and inferior conduct'. Owen's initial programme of community development among the workers soon extended from environmental improvements to education for child and adult. Again, it is easy to regard expenditure on education as conducive to greater productivity, though Owen's partners never seemed to take his view.

Soon Owen was incorporating the lessons of New Lanark in *A New View of Society; or, Essays on the Principle of the Formation of Human Character* (1813—14), where he set out to demonstrate that humanitarianism need not necessarily prejudice profits if the inner truth that a man's character was formed by his environment was understood. Clearly, in the disturbed atmosphere following the NAPOLEONIC WARS, Owen's claim to be able to produce conforming characters had a certain appeal to the governing class and within a short time he was hob-nobbing with royal dukes and cabinet ministers. After leading movements for Factory and POOR LAW reform Owen initiated an intensive propaganda campaign, proclaiming the idea that *A New View of Society* held the solutions to contemporary social and economic problems. Distress and unemployment would be relieved by the creation of independent, self-supporting communities, which he described as villages of 'unity and mutual cooperation'.

CO-OPERATIVE effort would replace individual competition. These ideas were articulated in *Two Memorials on Behalf of the Working Class* (1818) and refined in the most important statement of his economic philosophy, *Report to the County of Lanark* (1821). A growing and articulate group of Owenites soon put the ideas to the test — including the sole Scottish experiment at Orbiston, Lanarkshire (1825—28).

The remainder of Owen's long life can be divided into three periods. The first, 1825—29, saw Owen's participation at the New Harmony community, Indiana, United States — while other OWENITE communities were established in Devon and in Ireland. Owen left New Lanark and in the second 'Socialist' period (1829—34) became closely associated with working-class movements, principally labour exchanges, consumer co-operatives and trade unions. In the last two years of this phase Owen was associated with the Grand National Consolidated Trades Union, which collapsed in 1834. Lastly, during what might be described as his 'millennialist' period (1835—58), Owen con-

cerned himself with disseminating propaganda about the 'New Society'. Many Owenites associated themselves with the CHARTIST movement until its collapse in 1848. Thereafter Owenism increasingly assumed the character of a religious order led by Owen, the 'Social Father'. Owen was therefore a pragmatic and successful businessman, typical of the INDUSTRIAL REVOLUTION era, but unique in his optimism about a social philosophy that might act as a corrective to its excesses.

• *Butt, J. (ed.), Robert Owen: Prince of Cotton Spinners, David & Charles, 1971.*
• *Donnachie, I., Owen of New Lanark and New Harmony, Tuckwell Press, 2000.*
• *Pollard, S. and Salt, J. (eds.), Robert Owen: Prophet of the Poor, Macmillan, 1971.*

Owenites The Owenites were the followers of Robert OWEN (1771—1858), the social reformer, and were particularly active in Scotland during 1825—35. Owenism embraced a variety of the social ideas of RADICALS — derived mainly from Owen's essays on *A New View of Society* and later writings. In Scotland it manifested itself through communitarianism, suffrage associations, labour exchanges, CO-OPERATIVES, TRADE UNIONS, socialist societies, secular and millenarian churches and institutes as well as a vigorous popular press. As elsewhere in Britain and North America the movement attracted both middle-class and working-class enthusiasts.

The first Owenite community, established at Orbiston, near Motherwell, in 1825 was short-lived but nevertheless influential. Later there were many Owenite societies in the industrial districts — including branches of the National Equitable Labour Exchange (1832) and the Association of All Classes of All Nations (1835).

Although the Owenites never had particularly clear objectives and somewhat lost their way after the demise of the Grand National Consolidated Trade Union, Owen's Scottish followers continued their activities in a variety of social and reform movements including CHARTISM, consumer co-operation, trade unions and other labour associations.

•*Harrison, J.F.C., Robert Owen and the Owenites in Britain and America, Routledge and Kegan Paul, 1969.*

P & Q

Palmer, Thomas Fyshe (1747—1802) Born in Bedfordshire, Palmer was educated at Ely and Eton before enrolling at Queen's College, Cambridge, to prepare for the ministry. He received his BD degree in 1781, but his association with the Church of England was shortlived and he became a Unitarian minister, moving to Scotland in 1783. He was soon a prominent preacher and campaigner for religious toleration.

Palmer joined the Scottish FRIENDS OF THE PEOPLE in Dundee and was closely associated with the publication in 1793 of an address opposing government policies towards the war with France, the raising of taxation, and opposition to political reform. The address also asserted the right of universal suffrage. Palmer was arrested and charged with writing the Dundee address, being described by the Lord Advocate, Robert Dundas (1758—1819), as 'the most determined rebel in Scotland'.

Convicted of sedition he was sentenced to seven years transportation and despite efforts by WHIGS in Parliament to have the judgement reversed was shipped with Thomas MUIR (1765—99) and the other 'SCOTTISH MARTYRS' to New South Wales in 1794. Because of his status as a political prisoner he enjoyed considerable liberty in exile, even undertaking business enterprise in the colony. After his sentence he left for England in 1801, but died as a prisoner-of-war on the Spanish island of Guam in 1802.

Park, Mungo (1771—1806) Mungo Park, physician, explorer and distinguished son of the Scottish ENLIGHTENMENT was born at Foulshiels near Selkirk in 1771. Although his father was a mere tenant farmer, Park was at first educated privately before being sent to Selkirk Grammar School and later apprenticed to a local surgeon. In 1789 he went to the University of Edinburgh where in addition to studying medicine he became fascinated by botany, in which his brother-in-law, James Dickson, was both an expert and associate of Sir Joseph Banks.

After qualifying, Park headed for London and, partly through the good offices of Banks, he obtained a post as assistant surgeon on an East Indiaman, the *Worcester*, bound for Sumatra. Park had the opportunity to pursue research on the botany and natural history of the area and when he returned in 1794 read a paper to the Linnean Society in London describing eight new species of fish he had observed during the voyage.

Banks was also instrumental in

Park's appointment to the first African expedition financed by the Association for the Promotion of Discovery through the Interior of Africa, which had as its main objective the exploration of the Niger. With instructions to trace its course from source to sea, he arrived in the Gambia on 21 June 1795 aboard the brig *Endeavour*. Despite bouts of fever, the hostility of Muslim natives and numerous other privations he was able to make his way from the Gambia to Segu on the Niger during 1796. There he turned back because it was quite clear he would be killed if he tried to go further. Fighting his way back to the Gambia he eventually arrived in England via the West Indies in December 1797 — after an absence of two years and seven months.

Park was honoured by the African Association and feted by London society before returning to Scotland. He spent much of the year 1798 writing an account of his travels, which was published in 1799. The same year he married and later in 1801 he moved to Peebles to practise medicine. He made the acquaintance of both Adam FERGUSSON (1723–1816) and Walter SCOTT (1771–1832).

A second expedition to West Africa was planned for 1805 and Park set out to try again: this time he had with him a company of soldiers. The aim was to buy a boat at Segu, head for midstream and sail seawards without making a landfall: anyone who tried to stop them would have to face the firepower of four dozen muskets. This was a sensible enough plan but no sooner had the expedition set out from the Gambia than the soldiers were struck down by malaria. By the time Park got to Segu only four of the expedition's 46 members were alive. Undaunted, he navigated his way for a thousand miles of the river and it was only when interrupted by the Bussa rapids that the party was attacked and killed — ironically by non-Muslims who apparently thought they were themselves under attack. Park's demise left several questions unanswered about the ultimate destination of the Niger, but he nevertheless pioneered European exploration of the African interior. His career might well be compared with that of David LIVINGSTONE (1813–73), another famous Scottish explorer.

•*Lupton, K., Mungo Park, Oxford University Press, 1978.*

Parliament Summoned by a royal proclamation giving forty days notice, this very formality was originally one of the main distinguishing factors between Parliament and a CONVENTION OF ESTATES. It usually met in Edinburgh or Stirling by the sixteenth century, but with the completion of Parliament House in 1639 always met thereafter in the capital. Except in the 1640s, when the Triennial Act was in force, (repealed 1661), the Crown only called Parliament when it felt it was necessary. TAXATION or major changes in religious policy were two of the most common reasons for a summons. In the early sixteenth century its composition comprised the representatives of the Three Estates, that is from the clergy, nobility and BURGHS, all sitting in a single chamber assembly.

After the REFORMATION there were some alterations to the membership of Parliament. While bishops still attended, as did the commendators who had succeeded the abbots, the practice of erecting such commendators into temporal lordships, adopted by JAMES VI (1566–1625) in 1587, meant that they joined the ranks of the nobility in growing numbers. In the 1630s the controversy over the PRAYER BOOK (1637) and its aftermath resulted in no bishops being present at any of the parliaments held between 1639 and 1660. However, the prelates were restored in 1661 by CHARLES II (1630–85) and it was not until the REVOLUTION SETTLEMENT (1689) that ecclesiastical representation was finally removed.

The nobility, unlike the spiritual estate, strengthened its position, especially during the seventeenth century. In fact by the eve of the Treaty of UNION (1707), as a result of accession by lords of erection and various creations from the ranks of the lairds, the 154 Scottish peers almost equalled their English counterparts in number.

Burgh representation and influence, like that of the magnates, also expanded in the sixteenth and seventeenth centuries. Attendance was primarily restricted to royal burghs but these swelled in number from around forty in 1500 to a total of sixty-six by 1707. Moreover there was a considerable increase in the number of burgesses actually appearing at Parliament and several burghs in the early seventeenth century were sending two members — a practice, from 1621, officially only permissible by Edinburgh. The method of selection remained unaltered with individual town councils nominat-

ing their burgess commissioners.

The main departure in the composition of Parliament took place in the second half of the sixteenth century with the appearance of the county commissioners. Although small barons and freeholders had been encouraged to attend in the reign of JAMES I (1394–1437), this innovation had never caught on and it was not until the lairds became more politically conscious a century later that they showed much interest in constitutional matters. Over one hundred of them flocked to the 'Reformation Parliament' in 1560 but it was not until 1587 that JAMES VI, eager to counter the influence of the Kirk and also grateful for a useful financial subvention, drafted the necessary legislation. This ratified James I's earlier statute and consequently each shire elected two members, with the exception of Clackmannan and Kinross who each had one. Both the franchise and qualifications for sitting as a county member were limited initially to these landowners who were forty-shilling freeholders. Later seventeenth-century legislation widened the franchise to include feuars and certain other categories while in the 1690s some larger counties were allowed to send additional members.

For much of the sixteenth and seventeenth centuries the Crown maintained a very strong grip on Parliament. To some extent this was due to the presence of the numerous individuals who were mere nominees of the Crown such as members of the PRIVY COUNCIL, bishops and noblemen who owed their recent elevation to royal favour. Moreover, in the counties

SHERIFFS could exercise wide influence while in the burghs royal authority was frequently considerable. But undoubtedly it was the body known as the Committee of the Articles that put the king or his royal commissioners into such a decidedly powerful position. Originally the Lords of the Articles had been chosen in various ways, sometimes even by all the Estates, but under James VI it become a system specifically designed to extend royal control. Thus, by 1621, the bishops were choosing eight noblemen who in turn selected eight bishops and between then they chose the burgh and county representatives. Since the bishops were royal appointments and they would only pick magnates sympathetic to the Crown, the extent of royal domination is obvious. Besides, there was the long established tradition of Parliament, once it assembled, allowing the Lords of Articles to be chosen and then adjourning. It reassembled merely to give its assent to bills placed before it and which it had no hand in drafting.

Although there was some dimunition of royal authority during the Covenanting interlude when the Committee of Articles was abolished and Parliament gained control over the executive and judiciary, Charles II's reign saw a return to something like the previous constitutional situation. Thus it was not until the Revolution Settlement and the final abolition of the Committee of Articles that the Scottish parliamentary system really began to show some signs of serious development. In fact, by 1703 all proposed legislation was to be discussed at every stage by the whole assembly. Ironically this included, shortly afterwards, the articles of the Treaty of UNION heralding its demise.

HOME RULE began to appear on the agenda of the LIBERAL and LABOUR parties towards the end of the nineteenth century, but subsequent attempts by politicians in the 1920s and 1930s to introduce greater devolution from Westminster failed. In the post-war era the longer-term success of the SCOTTISH NATIONAL PARTY and the delicate balance of power between Labour and the Liberals in the mid-1970s forced the issue more strongly, resulting in the Scotland and Wales Act of 1978. However the referendum of 1979 did not produce a sufficient majority in favour of devolution and the initiative failed. During the 1980s and 1990s the Campaign for a Scottish Assembly maintained the momentum for devolution, but there was confusion among the parties about their commitment to change. Following the return of a Labour government in 1997, another referendum resulted in a substantial majority favouring the establishment of a Scottish Parliament with limited tax-raising powers. After the first election of MSPs on a mix of first-past-the-post and proportional systems, the Scottish Parliament was reconvened in 1999. A coalition of Labour and Liberal Democrats formed the first administration, with DONALD DEWAR, a long-standing devolutionist who had steered the legislation through Westminster, as First Minister. The SNP under Alex Salmond formed the first opposition. The Scottish Executive took over the powers of the SCOTTISH

OFFICE, leaving the Scotland Office, with much diminished responsibilities, under the Secretary of State for Scotland.

• Dickinson, W.C., Donaldson, G., Milne, I.A. (eds.), A Source Book of Scottish History II and III, Nelson, 1963.

• Donaldson, G., Scotland: James V to James VII, Oliver & Boyd, 1965.

• Rait, R.S., The Parliaments of Scotland, Maclebose, Jackson, 1924.

Paterson, William (1658—1719)

Although born in Dumfriesshire most of Paterson's youth and early career was spent in England. Thus in 1694, having already proposed the formation of the Bank of England, he became one of its original directors. At this juncture the COMPANY OF SCOTLAND attracted his keen interest and when it provoked hostile reaction in England and the withdrawal of English and foreign investment, Paterson strongly advocated the establishment of an independent Scottish colony on the Isthmus of Darien, the so-called 'Darien Scheme'. He accompanied the first expedition in 1698 losing in the process his second wife and son and nearly his own life as well. Despite these experiences he became a staunch supporter of the Treaty of UNION, publishing a pamphlet on the subject and taking a major role in the drafting of the articles relating to trade and finance in the Treaty. After 1707, he was returned as Member of Parliament for Dumfriesshire, but had to surrender his seat following a contested election. Not until 1715 did he receive compensation for the financial losses sustained in the Darien disaster.

patronage Although the FIRST BOOK OF DISCIPLINE proposed the abolition of a system whereby initially the Crown had taken over the right to present ministers of the Kirk, no action had been taken against it. The demand was repeated more forcibly in the SECOND BOOK OF DISCIPLINE, again to little effect, and it was not until 1649 when a radical Presbyterian faction held office that patronage was temporarily abolished. However, the restoration of CHARLES II (1630–85) was to witness legislation restoring patronage. Thus, the Rescissory Act (1661) annulled all parliamentary measures since 1633 and another statute in 1662 officially restored patronage with the requirement that ministers appointed since 1649 must obtain presentation from the patron and episcopal collation. About a quarter of the clergy were subsequently deprived for failing to obey this Act and they became the backbone of the COVENANTERS. The REVOLUTION SETTLEMENT (1690) included among its statutes an Act concerning Patronage by which the individual rights of patrons were to be eliminated and the heritors, or landowners, and the elders were henceforth to present ministers to their charges. This remained the situation until 1712 when the Patronage Act restored to patrons of ecclesiastical benefices the right of presentation. Dissatisfaction in the eighteenth century with the terms of this Act led to the First SECESSION (1733) whereas in the nineteenth century it was a major factor in causing the DISRUPTION. Patronage was finally abolished in 1874 by a Tory government eager to increase its support in Scotland especially from an established Church which was largely CONSERVATIVE in its political allegiance.

• *Donaldson, G., Scotland: James V to James VII, Oliver & Boyd, 1965.*
• *Ferguson, W., Scotland, 1689 to the Present, Oliver & Boyd, 1968.*

Peel, Robert, see CONSERVATIVE PARTY

Pentland Rising (1666) Reaction against the religious arrangements contained within the RESTORATION SETTLEMENT (1661) was an essential ingredient of the hostility to the government displayed by the COVENANTERS in the 1660s. In southwest Scotland the statutes imposing fines for non-attendance at church and prohibiting attendance at conventicles could only be enforced by drafting military units into the area. This policy, involving the quartering of troops on the local population, was highly unpopular. In November 1666 Sir James Turner (c.1615–86), the commander of these forces, was taken prisoner by a group of Covenanters and his seizure was the signal for an armed uprising. The insubstantial rebel army eventually reached Colinton near Edinburgh only to be decisively overwhelmed on 28 November at Rullion Green in the Pentlands by Sir Thomas Dalyell (c.1599–1685) and his government forces. About thirty rebels who refused to take the oath of allegiance were executed and some others were transported to Barbados. The main significance of the rising, which was essentially a badly-armed and poorly-led peasant rebellion, was the arrival in Scotland of

Lauderdale (1616–82) as Scottish commissioner. Under his influence a more conciliatory approach towards the Covenanters was adopted.

• *Cowan, I., The Scottish Covenanters, Weidenfeld & Nicolson, 1976.*
• *Terry, C.S., The Pentland Rising and Rullion Green, Maclehose, 1905.*

Perth, Pacification of (1573) The first major problem facing MORTON (c.1516–81), once he became regent in November 1572, was to bring to an end the CIVIL WAR that had been waged intermittently since 1569. In February 1573, through the good offices of Henry Killigrew (d.1603), the English ambassador, he was able to organize a conference at Perth with the leading supporters of MARY (1542–87). Accordingly, as a result of these discussions an agreement was reached on 23 February with the representatives of the Huntly-Hamilton faction whereby they promised religious conformity, recognized Morton as regent, ended their allegiance to Mary, disbanded their forces and handed over all prisoners and property that they had taken. In return all measures taken against them since June 1567 were to be revoked, they were to have their lands restored and certain individuals, notably Archbishop John HAMILTON (1512–71), were to be rehabilitated. Consequently, Morton could now concentrate his efforts on dealing with KIRKCALDY OF GRANGE (c.1520 –73) and MAITLAND OF LETHINGTON (c.1525–73) who with the garrison of Edinburgh Castle formed the last bastion of Marian support in the country.

• *Hewitt, G.R., Scotland under Morton, John Donald, 1982.*

Perth, Treaty of (1266) Following the battle of LARGS and further confrontations in the north and the ISLES between the Scots under ALEXANDER III and the Norwegian forces of Magnus IV, a negotiated settlement was arranged under a treaty signed at Perth on 2 July 1266. Norway ceded the Western Isles and the Isle of Man to the Scots in return for a lump sum of 4,000 merks and an annual payment of 100 merks. Although the Isles continued to cause the crown problems, the treaty defined the northern and western borders of the kingdom and the peace with Norway led to the subsequent marriage of Alexander's daughter to Magnus's successor, Eric, in 1281. Their daughter was the MARGARET, Maid of Norway.

Philiphaugh, Battle of (13 **September 1645)** The victory of James GRAHAM, Marquis of Montrose (1612–50) at Kilsyth on 15 August 1645 seemingly placed the lieutenant-general of the king's forces in Scotland in an unassailable position while the Committee of Estates, the main organ of the Covenanting opposition, was apparently in complete disarray. None the less Montrose quickly discovered it was impossible to keep his army together; many of the Highlanders began to drift homewards while most of the Irish soldiers under the command of Alexander MacDonald (d.1647) were more interested in pursuing their vendetta against the Campbells in Kintyre. Thus it was a greatly depleted body that was surprised by David LESLIE (d.1682) on 13 September at Philiphaugh near Selkirk and routed by Leslie's civil

war veterans. It was a battle notable for the absence of any quarter by the victors towards the vanquished as well as being the encounter that effectively ensured the collapse of Montrose's revolt.
• *Cowan, E.J., Montrose: For Covenant and King, Weidenfeld & Nicolson, 1977.*

Pinkie, Battle of (9 **September 1547)** Although the English government had failed to intervene in time in July 1547 to assist the beleaguered garrison at ST ANDREWS CASTLE, the ROUGH WOOING was resumed by Protector Somerset (1506–52) shortly afterwards. Thus in September English military and naval forces left Berwick for Scotland. The Protector's army of around 16,000 men was an impressive one, consisting not only of experienced infantrymen, including some foreign mercenaries, but also numerous cavalry and artillery. On the other hand the Scottish forces, despite being larger in numbers, with perhaps around 23,000 men, were poorly armed and very short of cavalry. During the first week of September, Somerset's men captured various small fortresses like Douglas and Innerwick as they advanced along the east coast. By 8 September they were camped near Prestonpans facing a Scottish army, commanded by ARRAN (c.1516–75), which was in a relatively strong situation behind the River Esk and in front of Musselburgh. On the morning of 9 September, the anniversary of Flodden, the Regent ordered Angus (c.1489–1557) who was in charge of the Scottish vanguard, to attack. He did this on the mistaken assumption that Somerset was beginning to retreat, whereas in fact the English commander was endeavouring to move his forces to a strategically superior position on a low hill known as Pinkie Cleuch. In the ensuing conflict English military superiority gradually established itself as Scottish resistance began to crumble in the wake of a devastating artillery bombardment.

The battle became a rout in which Arran possibly lost half his men and had about 1,500, including HUNTLY (c.1510—62) taken prisoner. Somerset followed up his victory by garrisoning some of his troops in certain fortresses on the Forth and Tay. However, this action only served to increase anti-English feelings and strengthen the cause of the AULD ALLIANCE within the country.

• *Donaldson, G., Scotland: James V to James VII, Oliver & Boyd, 1965.*
• *Fergusson, Sir J., 'The Rough Wooing' in The White Hind, Faber, 1963.*
• *Merriman, M., The Rough Wooings, Tuckwell Press, 1999.*

planned villages The planned villages of Scotland — several hundred in total — were essentially products of the AGRICULTURAL REVOLUTION and the INDUSTRIAL REVOLUTION eras, although some were built beforehand. The planned village was a significant instrument of IMPROVEMENT on landed estates and sometimes a means of resettling population dispersed by ENCLOSURE in the Lowlands or by the CLEARANCES in the HIGHLANDS. Others were closely associated with INDUSTRY, sometimes with remotely located enterprises where labour could only be retained by the provision of HOUS-ING, for example in the COTTON, COAL and IRON industries.

Three phases of village building can be identified: 1735—69 (mostly agricultural); 1770—1819 (mainly in the north-east, the Highlands, and in the industrialized Lowlands); and 1820—50 (when a smaller number of new settlements, associated with TRANSPORT and TEXTILE production were developed).

Inveraray (1742), planned and built by the Dukes of Argyll, is a fine example of an early estate village; Gatehouse-of-Fleet, Kirkcudbrightshire (1765), conceived by James Murray of Broughton and Cally, ultimately combined transport, agricultural and industrial functions; while NEW LANARK (1785), developed by David DALE (1739—1806) and later associated with Robert OWEN (1771—1858), the social reformer, is one of the best surviving examples of a purely industrial village. In the Highlands the British Fisheries Society was responsible for creating several planned communities, notably Helmsdale, Tobermory and Ullapool.

The planned villages of the eighteenth and early nineteenth centuries can be regarded both as physical manifestations of good order and efficiency dictated by the ideology of the Scottish ENLIGHTENMENT and as instruments of social control exercised by land owners and industrialists over their workforce.

• *Phillipson, N.T. and Mitchison, R., Scotland in the Age of Improvement, Edinburgh University Press, 1970.*

Plantation of Ulster JAMES VI (1566—1625) in the late 1590s embarked on a scheme for pacifying the HIGHLANDS and Islands by encouraging Lowland lairds to establish townships in areas such as Kintyre, Lochaber and the Isle of Lewis. Although these attempts at 'plantation' in Stornoway and elsewhere came to nought they were to be the forerunners of a more ambitious programme in Ulster.

In that province the flight to the Continent in 1607 of two leading noblemen and the subsequent forfeiture of their estates, provided the incentive for a new royal initiative. Ignoring the advice of Lord Chichester (1563–1625) his Lord Deputy in Ireland, who suggested the statesmanlike solution of dividing the forfeited property among the lesser Irish chieftains, James went ahead with an alternative plan. Convinced that the only way to guarantee religious conformity and national security in this part of Ireland was to have a loyal establishment, and also attracted by a convenient opportunity for rewarding faithful royal servants, the king invited 'undertakers' to submit applications for land in Ulster for the purpose of settling English or Lowland Scots. There was a tremendous response, particularly from many lairds and as a result by the mid-seventeenth century it has been estimated there were between 40,000 and 50,000 Scots living in Ulster.

The immediate consequence of a royal policy that deprived the native population of much of its land and subjected them to foreign domination was the ferocious Irish rebellion of 1641. The long-term effects of James VI's unfortunate action have, of course, persisted until the present day.

• *Maxwell, M.P., The Scottish Migration to Ulster in the reign of James I, Routledge & Kegan Paul, 1973.*
• *Willson, D.H., King James VI & I, Jonathan Cape, 1956.*

police With the increased URBANIZATION that accompanied the INDUSTRIAL REVOLUTION the enforcement of law and order became a more significant objective than it had previously been either in the towns or in the countryside. While suppression of disturbances or riots — for example, against the MALT TAX or the MILITIA ACT — was the main concern of authorities during the eighteenth century, crime prevention and policing became more important in crowded and apparently lawless towns and cities.

Town guards and militia were gradually replaced by regular, preventative police forces along the lines of that introduced in London by Patrick COLQUHOUN (1745–1820). Among the major urban centres, private Acts of Parliament were obtained by Aberdeen in 1795, Glasgow in 1800, Paisley in 1806 and Dundee in 1824. Although to some extent this brought into being what is often called the 'new police' most of the acts also included provision for paving, lighting and cleanliness — associated with old ideas of policing in the eighteenth century.

The first identifiable movement towards a modern police force in rural areas was made by the COMMISSIONERS OF SUPPLY for Ayrshire when, in 1800, they considered a report on 'the general State of the Police of the County'. By 1840 a dozen or so counties had established some sort of rudimentary force.

Given the prevailing level of popular agitation and unrest, the authorities sought to extend institutional policing by the Police Act of 1833; while the later Act of 1857 also had important implications for BURGH policing. It provided for the consolidation of county and burgh forces — hence reducing the proliferation of small, urban police forces. In 1892 a further Act finally repealed all the local police Acts (except for Edinburgh, Glasgow, Aberdeen and Greenock) and restricted the maintenance of a separate force to burghs having a population of 700 and an existing force.

While local police commissioners retained considerable authority, the role of central government through London or Edinburgh considerably increased during the second half of the nineteenth century. Legislation and inspection brought about early centralized regulation — at first through the Home Office in London — and ultimately through the Secretary for Scotland and the SCOTTISH OFFICE.

Poll Tax The historic name of the poll tax, described under POLL TAX RETURNS, was revived by the CONSERVATIVE government in 1989, when it introduced what was essentially a per capita tax to replace local rates. Otherwise known as the Community Charge, the Poll Tax was calculated to spread the local tax burden over a higher proportion of the population than the long-established tax on dwellings and business premises, which itself closely resembled the earlier HEARTH TAX. Introduced in Scotland a year earlier than in England and Wales,

it generated further hostility against Tory policies. Leftists, notably Tommy Sheridan, a Glasgow councillor, later an MSP, played a prominent part in the campaign against the tax. Such was the scale of the revolt that the government was forced into a u-turn (Thatcher having sworn that she never would), then back-tracking and replacing it with a banded rating system closely resembling the previous one. The Poll Tax issue helped galvanize support for opposition parties, notably for LABOUR and the LIBERAL DEMOCRATS nationally, and for the SNP in Scotland itself. Surprisingly, the fact that Labour continued to pursue poll tax debtors in Scotland while an amnesty had been granted elsewhere passed with relatively little comment.

poll tax returns Dating from 1694–5, these list the names and place of residence of every person over sixteen years of age, male and female — but are unfortunately incomplete. The most comprehensive cover the shires of Aberdeen, Banff, Berwick, Orkney, Renfrew, Argyll and Perth; while a variety of returns for parishes elsewhere also survive. They can be compared with the HEARTH TAX ROLLS and the census records. See also the entry on POPULATION.

Poor Law Historically, the Scottish Poor Law differed from that of its southern neighbour in various ways. From the sixteenth century until the mid-Victorian era the Scottish approach to the problems of poverty reflected basic differences of scale and stages of development. The smaller and less-advanced society needed a less formal system of poor relief, although this is not to imply that the Scottish PARLIAMENT, the burghs and the CHURCH neglected the problem or were unwilling to legislate accordingly. It was only when the pressures brought about by the LNDUSTRIAL REVOLUTION and rapid URBANIZATION in the Central Lowlands came after 1800 that the old, informal system began to break down — both as a means of relieving poverty and as a device for social control.

The long-traditional role of the pre-REFORMATION Church in assisting the poor was stressed in the First BOOK OF DISCIPLINE (1560–61) wherein every kirk was instructed to 'provide for the poor within itself'. The authorities, it stressed, were not 'patrons for stubborn and idle beggars, who, running from place to place, make a craft of their begging ... but for the widow and the fatherless, the aged, impotent, or lamed, who neither can nor may travail for their sustenation'. God, the book asserted, would show how this might be 'most easily done', adding that the 'stout and strong beggar be either compelled to work or returned to his native parish.'

Much of this was reiterated in a later and important Act Anent the Poor, passed by the Scottish Parliament in 1574. This began by stressing the relative ineffectiveness of previous legislation and, in a new departure, permitted the levying of a 'stent' or assessment for the poor. Subsequent amendment to the Poor Law included an apparently ineffective Act of 1663 authorizing manufacturers to press vagabonds into service, and another of 1672, authorizing the erection of workhouses.

These various pre-1707 statutes (partly modelled, it seems, on the English Elizabethan Poor Law) and associated legal interpretations gave scope for wide diversity of practice. Although magistrates in the burghs and kirk sessions in country parishes ran the system, they did so by their own lights and consequently there was little uniformity of approach. The respective authorities could choose as they wished to impose legal assessments on the heritors and inhabitants, operate a system of voluntary assessment, use the benefactions left by deceased to the poor fund, issue licenses to beg, or erect a workhouse. They might even choose to assist the able-bodied unemployed — as many apparently did during times of harvest failure and accompanying FAMINE. As one historian of the Scottish Poor Law, Cage, indicates in a modern study, settlements of the poor, setting the poor to work, poor houses and other paraphernalia borrowed from England all existed, but for most authorities in town or countryside the law was remote. Local practice and tradition was what was understood.

The traditional methods of poor relief relied, then, on the able-bodied looking after themselves or being helped by their families in times of trouble. The old, sick, widowed or orphaned might be given modest 'outdoor' relief in their own homes. While this system was hardly ever adequate in a pre-industrial society, it certainly could not cope with the crisis of periodic mass-unemployment that accompanied the INDUSTRIAL REVOLUTION of the late eighteenth and early nineteenth centuries. Migration to the towns and cities soon highlighted the problem, putting increasing pressure on existing social facilities, such as the hospitals and workhouses of Glasgow and Edinburgh and frightening the authorities about how to maintain law and order. Major critics of the old Poor Law included, on the one hand, Patrick COLQUHOUN (1745–1820), the merchant turned social critic, and on the other, Robert OWEN (1771–1858), the entrepreneurial social reformer, who used NEW LANARK as the test-bed for some of his ideas before becoming a propagandist of reform. It counted among its defenders the Rev. Henry DUNCAN (1774–1846), whose energy in his rural parish at Ruthwell, Dumfriesshire, was a model to others, and the famous Dr. Thomas CHALMERS (1780–1847), theologian turned social critic and politician. In 1820 Chalmers actually transferred the traditional rural model (with which Duncan was familiar) to his urban parish of St Johns in Glasgow — apparently to good effect. OWENITE schemes were less successful. Owen's most significant socio-economic statement, *Report to the County of Lanark* (1821), was never adopted, either by those who commissioned it or by anyone else, and the Orbiston Community (1825) was short-lived.

After 1830 the difficulties mounted and poor relief became a major political issue between Whigs and Tories and greatly influenced the Reform Movement and debates generated in turn by the RADICALS, the CHARTISTS, the ANTI-CORN LAW LEAGUE, the TRADE UNIONS and the CO-OPERATORS. The problem of providing for the able-bodied unemployed caught in successive economic depressions forced a revision of the system. After the acute depression of 1843 and the Disruption of the Kirk, a Royal Commission was appointed to investigate the problem of the poor. Although the report was inconclusive, the ensuing Poor Law Amendment Act (1845) brought into being central control through a Board of Supervision and established parochial boards with powers to levy rates for poor relief.

The major legal difference between Scotland and England remained — the relief of the able-bodied. Although boards were gradually made to face reality and care for the 'occasional poor', the system in general was mean and harsh, with minimal provision and subject to a means test. Poor houses were built, with parishes combining to meet the costs: by 1866 there were sixty-six capable of housing around 12,000 persons. However, outdoor relief remained the norm, as it always had because of its economy. This remained the case even after the Board of Supervision was wound up and replaced by the Local Government Board in 1894. In turn this was superseded by the Board of Health, established as a department of State in 1919. Provision remained essentially local throughout the 1920s and 30s, though distinctively Scottish features were disappearing.

Meantime a variety of initiatives by the great reforming LIBERAL government made provision for school meals (1906), medical inspection of school children (1908), old age pension (1909), labour exchanges (1909), and compulsory social insurance under the National Insurance Act (1911). Friendly societies and trade unions increasingly encouraged voluntary self-help, but generally only the better-paid were able to avail themselves of such schemes.

As was the case with MEDICINE, the DEPRESSION highlighted Scotland's acute social problems — poor housing, bad health, high mortality — all aggravated by low incomes, unemployment and poverty, which were as bad as any in Britain. Social surveys of the period show that such conditions were universal in most Scottish industrial towns — and much worse in the colliery districts. The circumstances described forced belated recognition of poverty as an economic phenomenon, rather than a failure of moral purpose — though the stigma of the 'means test' died hard even with the coming of the Welfare State after 1945.

•Cage, R., The Scottish Poor Law 1745—1845, Scottish Academic Press, 1981.

•Checkland, S.G. and Checkland, O., Industry and Ethos: Scotland 1832— 1914, Edward Arnold, 1984.

•Levitt, I., and Smout, T.C., The State of the Scottish Working Class in 1843, Scottish Academic Press, 1979.

population Before the first government CENSUS of 1801 we need to rely on estimates of total population derived from a variety of sources including HEARTH and POLL TAX RETURNS, parish registers, and several unofficial censuses undertaken during the eighteenth century. Civil registration of births,

deaths and marriages was not instituted in Scotland until 1855 so the analysis of fertility and mortality is hazardous — as indeed is the problem of assessing MIGRATION in advance of the 1841 census, the first to include such data.

Since the sixteenth century, Scotland has generally conformed to the wider demographic pattern prevailing in much of Europe. Broadly similar factors operated to transform a largely rural and agrarian population into a predominantly urban and industrial one. The most significant were changes and variations in mortality, fertility and migration.

Historians can only make a calculated guess at population numbers in the seventeenth century. Scotland's population — as Flinn and his associates have proved — was small by European standards and overall population density was low. Roughly 800,000 people lived in Scotland at the beginning of the century, the total probably rising — despite three savage crises in the 1620s, 1640s and 1690s — to about the one million mark by the time of the UNION in 1707.

During the eighteenth century population grew slowly before 1740, perhaps only restoring the level of 1690, preceding the seven 'Ill Years' of harvest failure and FAMINE during that decade. There was marked and sustained growth from the late 1740s, maintained except for a slight dip in the early 1760s until the late 1780s. Thereafter the rate of growth, though still positive, appears to fall slightly in the last decade of the century, reaching 1.6 million at the census of 1801.

Eighteenth-century population

growth can be explained by a combination of economic growth (associated with the AGRICULTURAL REVOLUTION and the INDUSTRIAL REVOLUTION), changes in social organization, and changes in the impact of disease or physical environment. The evidence available indicates the importance of falling mortality brought about by a combination of favourable factors. Firstly, there was no widespread famine, the potato provided an important new food crop in the HIGHLANDS and elsewhere, and better TRANSPORT ensured imports and more efficient distribution of available food. Secondly, the poor relief system was improved. Thirdly, medical and environmental improvement contributed to falling mortality through the provision of infirmaries, dispensaries and vaccination. Finally, higher fertility probably resulted from modest improvements in the standard of living during the latter half of the century. Sources for this period — apart from parish registers — include WEBSTER'S census and the first STATISTICAL ACCOUNT.

Much more accurate data is available to the historian from the first census of 1801. In general during the nineteenth century population growth was faster before 1851, but both the 1870s and 1890s achieved rates comparable with those of the first half of the century. Population rose to 2.9 million in 1851, and reached 4.4 million in 1901.

Migration played an increasingly important role in Scottish demography during the nineteenth century. Migration to other parts of Britain and emigration abroad were both significant — not only those forced by poverty to leave

during and after the CLEARANCES, but also increasing numbers voluntarily seeking new lives and opportunities in North America, Australia, New Zealand and elsewhere. Immigration was less significant numerically, but nevertheless migrants from Ireland, England and Continental Europe helped counterbalance the outward drift.

The Highlands experienced a persistent decline in population from mid-century, following the Famine in the 1840s. Indeed most rural areas, including those in the Lowlands, had reached their peak by 1851, although some country towns (often market and service centres) continued to grow. Improved transport, notably the RAILWAYS, probably encouraged movement to the towns and industrial districts. So changes in population distribution and URBANIZATION were significant features of Victorian Scotland — as they remained into the twentieth century.

Better medical care, improved dietary and living standards produced a slow decline in the death rate from the 1870s, but mortality nevertheless remained higher in Scotland than in England. Throughout the first half of the present century poverty and poor housing were major problems in both urban and rural areas. Loss through emigration continued at a high level and during the years of the DEPRESSION outstripped the natural increase. The census of 1931 showed a net decline on 1921 of 40,000 persons.

Population on the eve of WORLD WAR II in 1939 was estimated at over the 5 million mark and in the post-war years since 1945 has seen a slow increase thanks largely to higher standards of living coupled with better welfare and medical services. Social factors, such as more readily available contraception and legalized abortion, as well as economic factors, have exercised increasing influence on Scotland's demography since the 1950s. Migration, especially south of the Border, remains important, though offset to some extent by a reverse flow in Scotland's direction.

•*Jones, H., 'Population Patterns and Processes from c.1600', in Whittington, G. and Whyte, I.D. (eds.), An Historical Geography of Scotland, Academic Press, 1983.*
•*Flinn, M. (ed.), Scottish Population History from the 17th Century to the 1930s, Cambridge University Press, 1977.*

Porteous Riot (1736)   A new customs and excise system was established in Scotland as a consequence of the Treaty of UNION. Not surprisingly it was highly unpopular and despite its efforts SMUGGLING was still widespread and smugglers held in high regard. In Edinburgh in 1736 at the execution of a prominent smuggler the captain of the city guard, John Porteous (d.1736), faced by a very hostile crowd, ordered his men to open fire. Several citizens were killed and Porteous himself was arrested to stand trial for his actions. When, after being sentenced to death, his execution was delayed there was serious rioting in the city culminating in Porteous being lynched by an infuriated, but apparently well-organized, mob.

Walpole (1676–1745), as Prime Minister, was incensed at this vio-

lent outbreak and it was only through the mediation of John CAMPBELL, second Duke of Argyll (1678–1743) that government action was limited to the city being fined and its provost being permanently disqualified from office. However, the long-term significance of the event was political: the quarrel between Walpole and Argyll and the latter's hostility to the former was ultimately to be a contributory factor in causing the Prime Minister's downfall in 1742.

•*Ferguson, W., Scotland, 1689 to the Present, Oliver & Boyd, 1968.*

Prayer Book (1637)   Intended to be introduced by CHARLES I (1600–49) at the same time as the CODE OF CANONS in 1636 it was not ready until the following year. Its appearance in St Giles on 23 July 1637 provoked a celebrated riot within the cathedral and widespread protests throughout the country. Although it was meant to replace the existing Book of Common Order in existence since the early days of the REFORMATION, much of its contents were perfectly acceptable to even the most ultra-Protestants. But there were controversial sections especially those dealing with the communion service or stipulating additional saints days and festivals not to mention certain ambiguous comments about the use of 'ornaments', which the Crown, exercising its royal supremacy, claimed to have the power to prescribe. Moreover, and this was its most unpopular aspect, it had been imposed on the people without the consent of either the GENERAL ASSEMBLY or PARLIAMENT. Therefore, in conjunction with the

Code of Canons it provided useful ammunition for all those opposed to Charles I's policies and serious religious dissidence commenced with its introduction. None the less, despite a chequered career within the post-Reformation Church the Prayer Book survived within the CHURCH OF SCOTLAND, albeit in a revised format, until this century.

• *Dickinson, W.C. and Donaldson, G. (eds.), A Source Book of Scottish History III, Nelson, 1961.*

• *Stevenson, D., The Scottish Revolution, 1637—44, David & Charles, 1973.*

Press   The Scottish press has a long and distinguished history, and given the apparently high level of literacy and EDUCATION among the population, exercised no small influence on events, at first as agents of the status quo and later, when government control was relaxed, as agents of REFORM.

The earliest Scottish newspaper, the *Edinburgh Gazette,* published 'by authority', appeared from the press of James Watson (d.1722) in 1699. Watson was also responsible for the later *Edinburgh Courant,* a folio broad-sheet of 1705—10. An *Edinburgh Evening Courant* followed in 1718, like other papers of the time ardently loyal to the Hanoverian cause. Newspapers faced two major drawbacks: first, there was the cost of paper and printing; and second, Scottish newspapers, in common with those south of the Border, had to cope with the fiscal controls arising from the Stamp Acts (1712, 1725), which placed a duty on newspapers. Despite these drawbacks the *Caledonian Mercury* (first pub-

lished 1720), started as a twice-weekly journal, soon managed to raise its circulation to such an extent that it could convert to a five times weekly paper from 1726. Another early issue was the *Aberdeen Journal* (1747), the earliest north of the Forth, and the longest continuously published newspaper in Scotland.

From the early 1760s and the time of crisis in the North American Colonies that led ultimately to the AMERICAN WAR OF INDEPENDENCE (1775—83) upwards of fifty newspapers and periodicals circulated in Scotland at different times. Given the importance of the Scottish connection through settlement and commerce (mainly in TOBACCO and COTTON), there was actually greater interest in American than domestic news. The Scottish newspapers were invariably pro-government — including the violently conservative *Glasgow Advertiser* (founded 1783 and later known as the *Herald & Advertiser,* 1801), under its editor, Samuel Hunter (1769—1839), a colonel in the Glasgow Yeomanry.

Later censorship became even tighter and, indeed, at the time of the FRENCH REVOLUTION it is said that bribes were disbursed to writers on the *Caledonian Mercury,* the *Edinburgh Herald*, and other papers to ensure that they toed the government line against any form of Radicalism. Legal and fiscal controls were further tightened during the French Revolutionary and NAPOLEONIC WARS. These included laws designed to prevent the printing and dissemination of seditious literature and greatly increased Stamp Duty.

Despite these constraints a new

reforming press came into being after the 1800s, counting among its titles the *Dundee Advertiser* (1801), the *Aberdeen Chronicle* (1806), and *The Scotsman* (1817). The first was edited from 1811–25 by Robert Rintoul (1787–1858), a founder of the *Spectator*. *The Scotsman* was founded by the brothers John and William Ritchie, who worked in close association with its first editor, Charles MacLaren (1782–1866). These papers addressed significant issues of the day, most critically that of political reform — but with some caution initially, given the enforcement of the Six Acts (1819), restricting the freedom of the press. Provincial papers also grew in numbers and influence, an appropriate and successful example being the *Dumfries & Galloway Courier,* established by the Rev. Henry DUNCAN (1774–1846) of savings bank and poor relief fame.

Although dating back to the publication of the *Scots Magazine* in 1739, another significant feature of this era was the development of the periodical press, including the Whigish *Edinburgh Review* and the TORY-inclined *Blackwood's Magazine* (1817). The former had a subscription list of 12,000 in 1813 and Francis JEFFREY (1773–1850), its dynamic editor, claimed this represented 50,000 readers.

In the aftermath of the first Reform Act there was a great increase in press activity locally and nationally. CHARTIST papers, like the *Scottish Patriot,* the *True Scotsman,* the *Perthshire Chronicle,* and the *John O'Groats Journal,* stimulated reading and debate among artisans about great matters of the day. This reforming tradition was maintained by many pro-LIBERAL newspapers — which broadly reflected the ideology of Scottish middle-class politics throughout the later Victorian era. Both the *Glasgow Herald* (now *The Herald)* and *Scotsman* lent their support to Liberal-Unionism. At the other end of the political spectrum papers like the Independent Labour Party's *Forward,* edited by the indefatigable Tom JOHNSTON (1882–1965), helped advance the cause of socialism.

Scots read newspapers avidly and until the early twentieth century a quite distinctive Scottish press managed to maintain upwards of twenty national titles — all Scottish-owned until the 1920s. English mass-circulation papers, like the *Daily Mail* and *Daily Express* penetrated the market with Scottish editions and set going a trend that continued into the age of electronic publishing in the 1980s and 1990s. After a painful period of closures and rationalization in the 1960s and 1970s the *Glasgow Herald* and *The Scotsman* continued to dominate the quality market, while the *Daily Record* remained relatively unchallenged as the strongest-selling Scottish tabloid. Further north, in Dundee, the long established and successful Thomson & Leng empire, produced a range of popular titles with a distinctively Scottish flavour — notably their flagship newspaper, the mass-circulation *Sunday Post.*

From the historian's viewpoint the press is clearly a valuable source of information — though its authority on many matters needs to be treated with some caution. In one sense newspapers are readily accessible sources for the historian, though invariably so voluminous that accessing specific information can often be both difficult and time-consuming. Several national and a few local papers have been indexed. Strangely, there is no adequate modern study of the Scottish press — apart from one relatively inaccessible monograph.

Prestonpans, Battle of (21 September 1745) The Hanoverian government was badly prepared for the outbreak of the JACOBITE REBELLION of 1745 in that its commander, John Cope (d. 1760), had only about 4,000 troops dispersed in various garrisons throughout Scotland. Consequently, his strategy was to postpone if possible an encounter with Charles Edward STEWART, the Young Pretender (1720—88) until reinforcements arrived from England. However, the rapid advance of the Jacobite army in early September forced Cope to attempt the defence of Edinburgh and a large contingent of his available men was shipped from Aberdeen to Dunbar for this purpose. But his opponents moved too quickly for him, the capital was taken on 17 September and the government commander now had to prepare to face the rebels at Prestonpans a few miles east of Edinburgh. Both armies comprised about 2,300 men and Cope's defeat was largely a result of the skilful tactics adopted by Lord George MURRAY (c.1700—60) and the other Jacobite officers. Thus while Cope anticipated the main Jacobite thrust would come from the east it was a surprise attack from the opposite direction, made possible by the discovery of a route through the marsh in front of the Hanoverian forces that proved decisive. The subsequent Highland charge turned the battle into a rout and within ten minutes the contest was over. The political significance of the event was considerable since with the exception of Edinburgh and Stirling castles the whole of Scotland was now under Jacobite control and their cause, at this juncture, no longer seemed a forlorn hope.

•*Tomasson, K. and Buist, F., Battles of the '45, Batsford, 1962.*

Privy Council The origins of Privy Council lie in the undifferentiated king's council of the middle ages. By the mid-sixteenth century when it was normally meeting twice weekly — in Edinburgh, or wherever the king happened to be — and wielding considerable legislative and judicial powers, it clearly overshadowed PARLIAMENT in importance. Thus significant measures such as the arrangements made for the Kirk in 1562 known as the THIRDS OF BENEFICES, the appointment of wardens in the BORDERS, or the abolition of Norse Law in Orkney and Shetland in 1611 were the work of the Privy Council rather than Parliament. Likewise its judicial functions were wide-ranging and despite the existence of the COLLEGE OF JUSTICE and the COURT OF JUSTICIARY some cases continued to be brought before the council. At the same time it was not really a policy-making body since generally all it did was execute the wishes and decisions of the Crown. This was particularly true after the UNION OF THE CROWNS (1603) when JAMES VI (1566–1625) issued his councils with multifarious instructions, which he expected them to carry out. During the reign of CHARLES II (1630–85) there was also a council for Scottish affairs based in London with Lauderdale (1616–82) acting as its secretary and reducing even further the authority of the Privy Council in Edinburgh.

Nominally its composition was extensive and by the early seventeenth century nearly a hundred councillors were eligible to attend. In practice the actual numbers who did were considerably less and James VI stipulated seven as the minimum for a quorum. Usually there were slightly more than this present, the most active members undoubtedly being State officials such as the chancellor, treasurer, comptroller and secretary and various legal figures. However, CHARLES I (1600–49) decided that judges should no longer be eligible for membership of his councils.

The Privy Council survived the Treaty of UNION (1707) but was abolished soon afterwards in 1708 by the Westminster Parliament.
• *Donaldson, G., Scotland: James V to James VII, Oliver & Boyd, 1965.*

Protestors Their origins are to be found among those clergy who drafted the Western Remonstrance at Dumfries in October 1650 demanding reinforcement of the ACT OF CLASSES. These Remonstrants became known as 'Protestors' when they subsequently objected to the more moderate policies of the rest of the Kirk at the GENERAL ASSEMBLY of 1651 and 1652. During the 1650s they were locked in bitter conflict both with their rivals the RESOLUTIONERS and with the English administration. None the less a few leading Protestors found themselves unable to resist government overtures, notably Johnston of Wariston (1611–63) and Patrick Gillespie (1617–75) who became Principal of Glasgow University. Following the Restoration Settlement, the Protestors formed the backbone of the opposition to it with many of them becoming prominent Covenanters.
• *Donaldson, G., Scotland, James V to James VII, Oliver & Boyd, 1965.*
• *Stevenson, D. (ed.), The Government of Scotland under the Covenanters, 1637–1651, 1982.*

queens, see ANNE; MARGARET; MARY

Queensberry, Duke of, see DOUGLAS, JAMES, SECOND DUKE OF QUEENSBERRY

R

'Radical War'   In the aftermath of the NAPOLEONIC WAR economic recession was accompanied by increased Radical agitation and popular clamour for political REFORM. During the period 1817–19 a wave of riots and demonstrations throughout Britain much alarmed the government, which resorted to the oppressive Six Acts to restore order. This limited ordinary public meetings, the possession of arms and unlawful drilling — and imposed a new tax of 4d a copy on newspapers and pamphlets. While much of the repressive legislation against combinations of workmen or trade unions and the political reform societies never strictly applied under Scottish law, the authorities viewed such organizations with fear and suspicion. As in England, the year 1817 saw a series of sedition and treason trials similar to those of Thomas MUIR (1765–99) and his associates in the 1790s. South of the Border the unrest culminated in the Peterloo Massacre of 1819, while in Scotland the outcome was the so-called 'Radical War' of 1820.

The years 1819–20 were ones of acute economic depression and increasing unemployment, especially among the major casualties of mechanization, like the handloom weavers. This served to inflame working-class agitation over a wide range of non-economic issues. Meantime the authorities had resorted to the use of spies and agents provocateurs to obtain information about the activities of the underground reform movement in Scotland. Mass meetings were held in Glasgow, Paisley and elsewhere during 1819, all closely monitored by the authorities, but it was not until February 1820 that the government acted in the dramatic arrest of twenty-seven members of a Glasgow Radical committee suspected of planning a rising in both Scotland and England.

This only served to increase the tension and on 1 April 1820 placards posted up in Glasgow and surrounding towns called on the people to strike and rise in rebellion to redress their common grievances. Some maintained that this 'Address' to the people was the work of a government agent provocateur, though the historical evidence shows that it was almost certainly the work of a seditious pamphleteer. Strangely it made no direct reference either to Scotland or the conditions there. The strike itself seems to have been remarkably successful, with an estimated 60,000 workers in the West of Scotland standing down for a week. The rising, on the other hand, was a pathetic and misconceived escapade — the result of false information and poor leadership.

On 5 April a party of around fifty Radicals marched east from Glasgow to seize the CARRON Ironworks and secure munitions. En route they joined up with a party from Stirling but at the so-called 'Battle of BONNYMUIR', near Falkirk, the small force was easily scattered by a troop of hussars and local volunteers. Four of the Radicals were wounded and the rest quickly rounded up. Another more modest but equally abortive rising took place in Strathaven, Lanarkshire — the group marching north towards Glasgow to join forces with other Radicals.

In the aftermath of the 'Radical War', fifty prisoners, including the leaders Andrew Hardie, a Glasgow weaver, John Baird, a blacksmith from Condorrat, and James Wilson, another weaver, were tried for treason. Most got off with light sentences, but nineteen were transported to Australia (where they became known collectively as the 'Scottish Insurrectionists'), and the unfortunate Hardie, Baird and Wilson were executed — the last on very slender evidence.

The 'Radical War' represents the second highpoint of the pre-Chartist reform agitation in Scotland. It is sometimes regarded as having direct links with nascent Scottish nationalism and with republicanism, but there is nothing in the historical record to support this view. Nor, apparently, were the circumstances of the 1820 rising particularly related to contemporary events south of the Border. Nevertheless the folk memory gen-erated by the 'Radical War' remains sufficiently powerful for its leaders to be regarded as Scottish martyrs, much like Muir and his associates in the previous generation. See RADICALS.

• *Berresford Ellis, P. and MacA'Ghobhainn, S., The Scottish Insurrection of 1820, Gollancz, 1970.*
• *MacFarlane, M. and MacFarlane, A., The Scottish Radicals: Tried and Transported to Australia for Treason in 1820, Spa Books, 1981.*

Radicals A generic description for those of radical views and commonly used throughout the late eighteenth and much of the nineteenth centuries. Eighteenth-century Radicals were influenced by the new social scientific ideas and secularism of the ENLIGHTENMENT and by the impact of both the FRENCH REVOLUTION and the INDUSTRIAL REVOLUTION. In the 1790s Radicals stood for varying degrees of political change from universal suffrage to outright revolution — embracing such movements as the Scottish FRIENDS OF THE PEOPLE and the UNITED SCOTSMEN.

In the first half of the nineteenth century Radicalism encompassed numerous ideologies and popular movements of the day, notably those advocating parliamentary reform, but including OWENITES, co-operators, TRADE UNIONISTS, and free traders. Radicals were interested in causes as diverse as factory reform, anti-slavery, public health, and Catholic emancipation.

Later in the century, Scottish Radicals were invariably associated with Liberal politics locally and nationally. Many Scottish Liberals were themselves of radical persuasion particularly in their support of social reform, Irish Home Rule, and the problem of the HIGHLANDS. The 'Radical' label continued to be attached to such Liberals even after the formal establishment of Scottish socialist and Labour parties in the 1880s.

Historically the terms 'Radical' and 'Radicalism' meant different things at different times and need to be used with some caution.

railways   The railway in Scotland — as elsewhere — was a major initiator of improved TRANSPORT and contributed substantially to the later stages of the INDUSTRIAL and AGRICULTURAL REVOLUTIONS. It not only directly assisted the development of heavy industries like COAL, IRON and ENGINEERING, but also became an important industry in its own right. Indeed railway, iron and locomotives were major Scottish exports before 1914.

The predecessors of modern railways were the horse wagonways, almost exclusively built to transport coal. The earliest was the Tranent and Cockenzie, built in 1722 by the YORK BUILDINGS COMPANY, which owned the local coal-mines and salt pans. Between then and 1824, thirty other wagonways with a total length of about eighty-five miles were constructed. The largest single project was the Kilmarnock and Troon (1812), a 90-mile-long plate-way on a four-foot gauge. The engineer was William Jessop, who worked with Thomas TELFORD (1757–1834) on the Caledonian Canal. The Kilmarnock and Troon railway not only became the first in Scotland to carry passengers, but also saw the first trial of a steam-locomotive,

supplied by George Stephenson in 1816.

As Robertson, the historian of early railways, shows, the 1820s and 30s marked a transition in the development of Scottish railways, mainly because the new lines extended into traffic other than coal or iron and ultimately became integral parts of the overall railway system. During 1824–35 thirteen companies were authorized, including the important Monkland and Kirkintilloch (1826), Edinburgh and Dalkeith (1831), Dundee and Newtyle (1831–32), Garnkirk and Glasgow (1831), Wishaw and Coltness (1833–34) and Slammanan (1840) lines. Although mostly short and using both horse and steam power, several of these lines directed the first challenge to the canals as industrial carriers.

The 'Railway Mania' hit Scotland later than England, the first major inter-urban line, the Edinburgh and Glasgow, being authorized in 1838 and opened in 1842. A total of eight companies were authorized between 1836 and 1843, but most were of only local importance. It was not until the mid-1840s that the 'mania' really affected Scotland with the incorporation of the Caledonian Railway (1845), the Great North of Scotland Railway (1846), and the North British Railway (1846). The other major lines were the Glasgow and South Western (1850) and the Highland (1865).

The first of the five, the Caledonian Railway, was the northern company of the west coast main line, beginning at Preston and going direct to Glasgow via Carlisle with an offshoot from

Carstairs to Edinburgh. It provided its first through service to London in 1848. The 'Caley' linked with the smaller Scottish Midland Junction and Scottish North Eastern Railways to provide services to Stirling and Perth, and, from 1850, to link Aberdeen and London. It absorbed several early lines in the Clyde Valley, achieving access to Glasgow on both sides of the river. Its major terminus was Buchanan Street Station (1849). The 'Caley' became an important company with lines extending from Carlisle to Aberdeen, Dundee and Edinburgh, as well as Greenock, Callander and Oban. It also controlled a large suburban network around Glasgow.

The Great North of Scotland Railway, despite its name, was the smallest of the five. It originated in a scheme to construct a line from Aberdeen to Inverness, but due to rival schemes only got as far as Elgin. Ultimately its network covered Aberdeen, Moray and Banff with an extension into Inverness on the Speyside branch to Boat of Garten. It was the only railway equipped with electric telegraph throughout its whole length and also pioneered electric lighting. Its most famous branch was the 'Royal' Deeside line to Ballater.

The North British Railway controlled the northern section of the east coast main line, crossing the Border in 1846. It originated in the Berwick-Edinburgh line and by 1865 had acquired the Edinburgh and Glasgow, Monkland, Perth and Dundee, West of Fife, and Edinburgh Railways. The NB was a prime mover in the building of the West Highland line to Fort William and Mallaig (1884 onwards). The

company was responsible for both Tay Bridges, the first being opened on 1 June 1878 and destroyed by a storm on 28 December 1879 with the loss of nearly a hundred lives. A second bridge was built in 1887, within sight of the piers of the original bridge, and nearly 2 1/4 miles long. The rail link north of Edinburgh was completed by 1890 when the Forth Bridge, a major achievement of Victorian engineering, opened after seven years construction.

The Glasgow and South Western Railway was an amalgamation of the Glasgow, Paisley, Kilmarnock and Ayr and the Glasgow, Dumfries and Carlisle Railways, and as its name implies, covered most of Ayr, Dumfries and Galloway. It was a fierce competitor of the 'Caley' — both for traffic to Carlisle and on the Clyde steamer services. It also provided for the Irish short-sea crossing with the Ayr-Stranraer line.

The last of the five, the Highland Railway, originated in the Inverness and Nairn Railway, which opened in 1855, united ten years later with lines from Nairn to Keith (1858), Inverness to Perth (1863), Perth to Dunkeld (1856). Northern and Western extensions created the lines to Wick and Thurso and to Kyle of Lochalsh.

As elsewhere local landowners played a prominent role in railway promotion, notably the Duke of Sutherland, who had his own private train.

The creation of an extensive network in the industrial Lowlands and over-extended branch lines in sparsely populated areas inevitably took its toll. Rationalization occurred with the absorption of the 'big five' into the London Midland Scottish and the London and North Eastern Railways in 1923. In 1948 they themselves were nationalized to become the Scottish Region of British Railways. Many lines, including those in the Borders, Dumfries and Galloway, were closed, often in the face of determined local opposition. Faced with intense competition from the roads and starved of capital by successive governments, railway modernization was delayed until the 1970s.

From the historical viewpoint the railways had a major impact on the economy and urbanization and have left a remarkable legacy in Scotland — a rich heritage of engineering achievement and a major archive housed in the Scottish Record Office. Several preservation schemes have revived abandoned lines, often with working steam locomotives.

• *Gourvish, T.R., Railways and the British Economy 1830—1914, Macmillan, 1980.*
• *Kellet, J.R., The Impact of Railways on Victorian Cities, Routledge and Kegan Paul, 1969.*
• *Robertson, C.J.A., The Origins of the Scottish Railway System 1722—1844, John Donald, 1983.*
• *Thomas, J., A Regional History of the Railways of Great Britain: Vol VI Scotland: the Lowlands and Borders, David & Charles, 1971.*

Ramsay, Allan, see AMERICAN WAR OF INDEPENDENCE

Red Clydeside The name 'Red Clydeside' arose from over eight years of intense labour conflict in the Glasgow area, coinciding with WORLD WAR I and its aftermath, 1914—22. This series of episodes,

as Harvie and McLean have shown, has assumed legendary proportions — almost on the scale of the Covenanters or the Jacobite risings — and its resonance is particularly strong on the Left. Many Labour leaders between the wars, such as James MAXTON (1885—1946), David Kirkwood (1872—1955), Thomas Johnston (1882—1965), Emmanuel Shinwell (1884—1986), John WHEATLEY (1869—1930) and the early Communist activists William Gallagher (1881—1965) and Harry McShane were participants in what the government regarded as subversive activity. Another leading activist was the Scottish socialist revolutionary, John MACLEAN (1879—1923).

Clydeside was historically a major centre of engineering and shipbuilding, dependent on both skilled labour and cheap supplies of iron and steel from nearby Lanarkshire and Ayrshire. Heavy industry in general had weathered several slumps — notably that of 1906—7 — and with the outbreak of war the Clyde became one of the most important suppliers of strategic materials, notably ships' munitions, tanks and aircraft. With recruitment to the Services running at a high level — despite the anti-war movement — industry soon found itself short of labour. Forced to employ the unskilled, women and boys, and increasingly turning to mechanization, trades like engineering soon faced TRADE UNION militancy over 'dilution' and wages.

Thus there arose a series of conflicts during 1915—16 consisting of: (i) the 'tuppence an hour' engineers' strike in February 1915; (ii) the strike at Fairfields shipyard during August 1915; (iii) the Rent Strike (mainly in Glasgow and district) of October-November 1915; and (iv) the imposition of 'dilution' (by semi- or unskilled labour) in the engineering works during January–April 1916, culminating with the deportation (under the Defence of the Realm Act) of those shop stewards who encouraged resistance.

After these brief confrontations with employers, landlords and the government, there followed three years of relative tranquillity until the 'Forty Hours' strike of January-February 1919 — notable for the famous George Square riot of 1 February, when the streets of Glasgow rumbled to the sound of tanks. Finally the General Election of 1922 saw sweeping Labour victories in ten of the Glasgow city seats and others in Dumbarton, Renfrewshire and Lanarkshire. Much of the evidence would indicate that Labour's victory nationally was due to general political realignment away from the Liberals, while the Irish vote was also important in the West of Scotland. The 'Clydeside' MPs may have been radicals but were they neither Marxist Socialists, nor had they been elected by militants.

It might be fairly said that the 'Red Clyde' died with MacLean, though even he became less and less influential. While revolution may have been remote from the industrial troubles of the Clyde, the events of the period — seen by some as the 'glad confident morning' of Scottish socialism — live on in the legend.

•*Harvie, C.T., No Gods and Precious Few Heroes: Scotland 1914—1980, Edward Arnold, 1981.*

•*Kenefick, W. and McIvor, A., Roots of Red Clydeside: Labour Unrest and Industrial Relations in the West of Scotland, John Donald, 1996.*
•*McLean, I., The Legend of Red Clydeside, John Donald, 1983.*

Reform Acts   In the aftermath of the Treaty of UNION, Scotland was represented (or more accurately, under-represented) in the British Parliament by forty-five MPs in the House of Commons, returned under an electoral system almost designed for corruption, and by sixteen Representative Peers in the Lords, generally chosen from the most subservient of the Scots nobility. Scotland had the narrowest franchise of the three kingdoms — roughly 4,000 out of a population of 1.5 million at the close of the eighteenth century. This compared with 17,000 voters in the borough of Westminster and 6,000 in the city of Bristol. The Scottish electorate was then divided between 2,500-odd in the counties and 1,500 in the BURGHS.

In the thirty county seats, the franchise was essentially restricted to the large landowners who either elected themselves or their placemen; while in the burgh seats electoral manipulation was just as bad, with MPs generally chosen by corporations. Burghs were grouped together in a random fashion and by the end of the eighteenth century expanding industrial centres — often ancient burghs like Glasgow, Paisley or Dundee — were grossly underrepresented. The prevailing situation much resembled that in the so-called 'Rotten Boroughs' south of the Border. The whole system was readily controlled in the interest of the government by extensive powers of patronage — managed after 1775 by the shrewd Henry DUNDAS (1742–1811), who commanded huge electoral influence throughout Scotland.

After the FRENCH REVOLUTION, RADICALS and others agitated for political reform, but much of this went underground until the discontent that flared up following the end of the NAPOLEONIC WARS in 1815. Modest reforms by the TORIES in the 1820s were mainly of a fiscal kind and failed to address abuses, either of suffrage or representation. These became major objectives in the WHIG platform, which sought to advance middle-class aspirations for an increased role in government.

The first Scottish Reform Act — partly influenced by the draughtsmanship of Francis JEFFREY (1773–1850) — was passed in 1832. It raised Scottish representation from forty-five to fifty-three, redistributed the seats and extended the franchise to £10 householders in the towns, £10 property owners and £50 tenants in the counties. Although the Scottish electorate jumped dramatically from 5,000 to over 60,000 the working class was still without the vote. In other regards the first Reform Act was defective. Its authors, as the historian Fry has observed, were obsessed by fears of going too far towards democracy, and in some places the reforms made little difference — the small burghs and rural seats being good cases in point. In many counties it merely served to consolidate the power of the landed gentry, the property-owning qualification being set so high and legal trickery the order of the day.

There were numerous challenges to both Whigs and CONSERVATIVES in the 1830s and 1840s, notably CHARTISM, the ANTI-CORN LAW LEAGUE and the TRADE UNIONS, which all sought political reform in their different ways. The Chartists produced the 'People's Charter' (1838) listing their 'Six Points' for reform. Although the Chartists were not immediately successful, in the longer term the second Reform Act, passed under the Conservatives in 1868, fulfilled many of their objectives. It extended the vote to all rate-paying householders and lodgers paying £10 rent for unfurnished rooms in towns and to owners of £5 property and £14 tenants in the counties. Scottish representation was increased to sixty.

Yet the bulk of the rural population and many of the inhabitants of small industrial centres, not large enough to rank as burghs, were still excluded from the franchise. Other abuses were gradually eliminated. The need for secret voting, to prevent both bribery and intimidation by landlords and employers, was vital. During Gladstone's (1809–98) first ministry the Ballot Act (1872) ensured secret voting; while his second ministry saw the Corrupt Practices Act (1883) — preventing unauthorized payments — on to the statute book. A year later the significant third Reform Act of 1884–85 gave male suffrage to all householders in the counties as well as the burghs, adding twelve more members to the Scottish contingent at Westminster and making an extensive re-alignment of parliamentary constituencies based on POPULATION distribution.

Female householders had been given the vote in municipal elections in 1869 but subsequently various Women's Suffrage bills had failed to make much progress in a male-dominated parliament. The concerted campaign of the Suffragette Movement after 1903 and of the Scottish Federation of Women's Suffrage Societies (1906), led by Dr Elsie INGLIS (1864–1917), combined with the vital effort made by women during WORLD WAR I, eventually led to votes for women under the Representation of the People Act (1918). This gave the vote to men over twenty-one and women over thirty, the latter also being allowed to seek election for the first time. Under the Act Scottish MPs were increased to seventy-four (including three university seats) and another notable feature was widespread redistribution of burgh and county constituencies. Later the Equal Franchise Act (1928) brought complete adult suffrage.

The progress of reform and the extension of the franchise clearly had profound political consequences in Scotland and beyond. It directly influenced in turn the fortunes of the great political parties, the Conservatives and the Whig-Liberals, and after the 1880s the relative decline of the Liberals and the rise of the LABOUR PARTY as a major force in Scottish politics. Finally, it should be noted that as a consequence of various other reforms under the Burgh Reform Act (1833) and the Local Government Act (1889) — the latter establishing county councils — local government had been substantially democratized before 1914.

• Fry, M., *Patronage and Principle: A Political History of Modern Scotland*, Aberdeen University Press, 1987.
• Hutchison, I.G.C., *A Political History of Scotland 1832–1924*, John Donald, 1986.

Reformation In August 1560 the Scottish PARLIAMENT passed a series of measures that ended all links with Rome, proscribed the celebration of the Mass and authorized a Protestant confession of faith. The antecedents of these momentous changes, passed by what is significantly usually described as the 'Reformation Parliament', had been in existence for some years beforehand and, in the case of the deterioration of the Church, for a lengthy period.

The CHURCH in Scotland, like its continental counterparts, had been going into a slow decline long before the sixteenth century and inevitably was suffering from the various shortcomings that were common elsewhere. Thus the grinding poverty and ignorance of the majority of the priesthood stood in stark contrast with the affluent worldliness of most of the bishops and monastic heads. The main cause of this impoverishment was an iniquitous procedure whereby the revenues of the individual parishes were absorbed by cathedrals, monasteries, collegiate churches and universities leaving only a meagre pittance for the hapless vicar. This appropriation of benefices had been inaugurated in the twelfth century and had reached its zenith by the sixteenth when an estimated 85 per cent of parishes were affected by it. There had been attempts to curb such developments; an act of Parliament of 1471, for instance, prohibited future appropriations except in the case of collegiate churches.

Unfortunately, this body was the main offender in later years. Accordingly, by the sixteenth century a career in the priesthood had become an unattractive proposition generally by-passed by those with any ability and usually the resort of someone who had failed to get on elsewhere. Not surprisingly, there were numerous reports and allegations that the lower clergy were ill-educated, avaricious and immoral. Impoverishment at parish level also meant that many church buildings and furnishings were dilapidated or neglected.

What of the bishops or conditions within the various regular institutions? Certainly there are some signs among the former of familiar abuses such as pluralism, non-residence, nepotism, simony and immorality and the behaviour of prelates like David BEATON (c.1494–1546), of St Andrews, or Patrick Hepburn Moray, did little to enhance the reputation of the pre-Reformation clergy. Yet it would be unwise to attach too much significance to their peccadilloes. The Scottish hierarchy was no worse than elsewhere and had in its midst some comparatively enlightened figures. One such was Robert Reid (d.1558), Bishop of Orkney and Commendator of Kinloss, who at his death left the funds that ultimately provided the endowment for the University of Edinburgh. Another such was John HAMILTON (1512–71), Beaton's successor at St Andrews, who did his utmost in the decade before 1560 to eliminate some of the worst defects among the clergy.

As for the heads of monasteries and their inmates, there is little evidence to suggest that there was widespread corruption and sinful behaviour within the monastic system or, for that matter, the friaries. Where criticism was certainly justified was in the case of the nunneries, which were universally condemned for their illiteracy and scandalous conduct.

The main stricture that can be made against the bishops and the monastic heads is the worldliness and the inertia that pervaded everywhere. Again, this is hardly surprising when the policy towards the Church adopted by the Crown since the late fifteenth century is taken into account. Both JAMES IV (1473–1513) and JAMES V (1512–42) had made generous use of the arrangement negotiated with the papacy by James III (1452–88) allowing the Scottish monarchy to make major appointments in the Church. Consequently, various royal kinsmen were promoted in this way and James V, following in the footsteps of his father, who had introduced his illegitimate son into the see of St Andrews, filled several abbeys and priories with his natural offspring. By the 1530s James V was extending this policy to include many of the nobility, notably the Hamiltons. Moreover, even if a magnate was unable to gain complete control over a monastery through a commendatorship there were often excellent opportunities for profiting by means of becoming a lay bailie responsible for ecclesiastical property, not to mention the practice of reserving to certain noble families a part of the revenues of a bishopric on the appointment of a new incumbent.

The growing number of noblemen who began to obtain feu charters of church land as the clergy tried to satisfy the financial demands of James V only serves to underline the extent to which the bishoprics and monasteries were becoming secularized. Thus, on the eve of the Reformation, most monasteries were controlled by lay commendators, a situation highly unlikely to promote reform or produce dynamic leadership.

Another significant factor in producing the Reformation was the growth of Protestant opinions within the country, especially from around the mid-1540s. Before that date the impact of Lutheranism was negligible and the execution of Patrick Hamilton (1504—28) for heresy was followed by only a dozen such sentences during the remainder of James V's reign. For much of the 1540s there are instances of sporadic heretical activities in places like Dundee, Perth and their hinterland. The culmination of these was the murder at St Andrews in May 1546, at least partly in revenge for the execution of the Protestant George WISHART (c.1513—16) earlier in the year, of David Beaton, Archbishop of St Andrews. But even the accession of Edward VI (1537—53) followed by the introduction of the Protestant faith into England had little effect on Scotland despite the English strategy of infiltrating translations of the Bible during both the ROUGH WOOING and thereafter. In fact, Protestantism, outwith certain radical enclaves in Angus, Ayrshire, Fife and the Lothians remained a predominantly underground affair still lacking the catalyst that could make it become a serious threat to the established Church. Where it existed in the 1550s, as the visitations of John KNOX (c.1512—72) in these years confirm, it was no longer Lutheran but Calvinist doctrines that it was supporting.

The first real indication of serious opposition to the administration of MARY OF GUISE (1515—60) and her admittedly equivocal support of the Church came in December 1557 when the signing by Argyll (c.1538—73), Lorne (1545—84), Glencairn (d.1574), MORTON (c.1516—81) and Erskine of Dun (c.1509—91) of an agreement known as the 'First Band' wherein the signatories pledged themselves to work for the establishment of a reformed Church. Yet it was not until May 1559 with the return of Knox from France and the attack on the friaries that same month that the Reformation can actually be considered to have got properly under way. By this stage it was apparent that other motives were increasingly playing a significant role, especially political considerations.

Mary of Guise, once she had taken over from CHATELHERAULT (1516—75) in 1554 pursued an astute but incontrovertibly Francophile policy, which had resulted in several Scottish members of the government being replaced by various Frenchmen. Additionally there was the presence of a French military force and the burden of the taxation controversially imposed for its upkeep. For some magnates the marriage of the regent's daughter, MARY, QUEEN OF SCOTS (1542—87), to the Dauphin in 1558 only confirmed their growing fears that Scotland was becoming a French satellite. But the regent handled the marriage issue competently by ensuring that three of the eight commissioners who went to France on this business, Cassillis (1517–58) Lord James STEWART, Earl of Moray (1531–70) and Erskine of Dun, were sympathizers of the reform movement.

In fact, as long as the fanatically Catholic Mary Tudor (1516–58) remained alive, Mary of Guise did little to hinder Protestantism. Thus, in order to embarrass her neighbour and give moral support to France, at war with England and Spain, she did not discourage continental exiles such as Knox and John Willock (d.1585), formerly a Dominican friar at Ayr, from returning. It was only with the accession of the Protestant Elizabeth (1533–1603) and the peace settlement of Cateau-Cambresis in March 1559, ending the Habsburg-Valois conflict, that the Regent seriously altered her policy towards the reformers. Hence the summons to Knox and his fellow preachers to appear before her on 10 May 1559 and their subsequent outlawing for failing to do so. These events effectively marked the beginning of the religious civil war that was to last until July 1560.

During this period while some noblemen such as Argyll and Glencairn were influenced in supporting the rebellion by their religious feelings, with others, like HUNTLY (c.1530–62) or Chatelherault, political considerations predominated. The latter, for instance, diplomatically delayed in joining the rebels until September 1559 by which date his eldest son, the Earl of ARRAN (1537–1609) had escaped

from detention in France. Meanwhile, another prominent figure, the Earl of Morton, spent these months switching from one side to the other. Unquestionably what caused most of the nobility to support Knox and the others was the conviction that it was in their best interests to do so. Not, it should be stressed, with financial objectives uppermost in their thoughts — they had already extensively pillaged the wealth of the Church — but because they realized success would mean the end of the French hegemony in Scotland. This outcome would restore them to their former ascendancy in the government and also strengthen ties with England, an impossible undertaking as long as Mary of Guise was at the helm.

The lairds, while some of them like MAITLAND of Lethington (c.1525–73) welcomed improved Anglo-Scottish relations, were as a class more motivated by social aspirations. Consequently their attendance in large numbers at the Reformation Parliament signified a desire to have a greater voice in national affairs and to play a substantial role in the establishment of the reformed Kirk. The burgesses to some extent shared this outlook, although some of them were doubtless aware of the commercial advantages of stronger ties with England.

Only those furthest down the social ladder had strong economic motives for becoming involved in the Reformation struggle. For this group the financial exactions and devices of the Church had become increasingly intolerable. This, of course, was partly a result of James V's taxation of the clergy, ostensibly for the creation of his new COLLEGE OF JUSTICE, which led to the Church adopting unpopular and harmful expedients. While teinds and mortuary payments were grievances of long standing, the introduction of the feuing system to ecclesiastical lands caused further resentment. This was especially the case with those affected by rent increases imposed by the new feuars, and particularly so by those unfortunate enough to be evicted as part of this process.

At the same time there was always in Scottish society in the sixteenth century a large section of the population in desperate economic circumstances. This body in company with the numerous vagabonds and beggars who roamed the countryside gladly participated in a movement that they conceived as an attack on the wealthiest institution in the kingdom. The various outbreaks of mob violence against churches and friaries that characterized the start of the Reformation bear witness to their involvement.

If the origins of the Reformation consist of an amalgam of religious, political and socio-economic factors, it was English intervention that ensured victory for the Protestant cause. Despite initial success against the Regent's forces, the LORDS OF THE CONGREGATION, as they were called after the 'First Band' of 1557, soon lost their momentum. Before long they were desperately seeking English assistance only to find that Elizabeth, with her own domestic position insecure, was very wary about intervening on behalf of rebels in Scotland. The radical religious opinions of Knox and his outspoken views about female rulers were additional justification for a cautious stance. It was fears of continued French influence in Scotland in conjunction with their support of the claim of Mary, Queen of Scots to the English throne which finally persuaded Elizabeth to take action openly across the Border. The Treaty of BERWICK, February 1560, was the turning point in the religious conflict that ended with the Treaty of EDINBURGH, July 1560. Significantly, the only reference to religion came in the 'concessions' attached to the main body of the political settlement where It was agreed that the Scottish estates should be summoned to discuss ecclesiastical matters and other issues.

The subsequent Reformation Parliament completely neglected some of the major proposals outlined by the reformers in their BOOK OF DISCIPLINE. Thus, questions such as the endowment and organization of the Reformed Kirk remained unresolved and were to bedevil relations between the post-Reformation Church and the State for many years thereafter.

• Cowan, I.B., The Scottish Reformation, Weidenfeld & Nicolson, 1982.
• Donaldson, G., Scotland: James V to James VII, Oliver & Boyd, 1965.
• Donaldson, G., The Scottish Reformation, Cambridge University Press, 1960.
• Kirk, J., Patterns of Reform: Continuity and Change in the Reformation Kirk, 1989.
• Lynch, M., Scotland: A New History, Century, 1991.
• Wormald, J., Court, Kirk and Community, Edward Arnold, 1981.

regiments There was no standing army in Scotland before the

RESTORATION. Therefore, the Crown had to rely on the support of the nobility and a system whereby all able-bodied men between sixteen and sixty years of age were liable for military service for a maximum period of forty days. Many Scotsmen in the sixteenth and seventeenth centuries became mercenaries in the Swedish and Dutch armies, Alexander LESLIE (c.1580–1661) being one notably successful example. The regiments that began to be raised in the later seventeenth century and thereafter were initially known by the name of their founder then by the colonel in charge. Thus the Royal Scots began life as Hepburn's Regiment and later became the Earl of Dumbarton's Regiment of Foot. However, during the reign of WILLIAM III (1650–1702), regiments began to be given numbers based on their rank and seniority; the Royal Scots, accordingly, were now to become the First or Royal Regiment of Foot. The first Highland regiment, the ancestor of the celebrated Black Watch, was raised by GENERAL WADE (1673–1748) in 1739.

In 1881 there was a massive reorganization of the British infantry that involved the linking in pairs of all regiments of the line with a number above 25. The Queen's Own Cameron Highlanders (the 79th) were exempt from these arrangements while another Scottish unit, the 99th, was linked with the 62nd to become part of the Wiltshire Regiment. After World War II there were further changes that were to lead to amalgamations among certain regiments and the disbandment of the Cameronians. The Argyll and Sutherland Highlanders only avoided a similar fate by organizing a tremendous protest campaign.

• Brander, M., *The Scottish Highlanders and their Regiments*, Gleneil Press, 1996.
• Cochrane, P., *Scottish Military Dress*, Blandford, 1987.
• Henderson, D., *Highland Soldier: A Social History of the Highland Regiments, 1820–1920*, John Donald, 1989.
• Henderson, D., *The Scottish Regiments*, HarperCollins, 1993.
• Wood, S., *The Scottish Soldier*, Archive Publications, 1987.

Reith, John, Lord Reith (1889—1971) Like John Logie BAIRD (1886–1946) John Reith was a distinguished pioneer of broadcasting, though in a management rather than an inventive capacity. Reith was a son of the manse, born at Stonehaven, where his father was the FREE CHURCH minister. He was educated at the Glasgow Academy, Gresham's School, Norfolk, and the Royal Technical College, Glasgow, before taking an apprenticeship with the North British Locomotive Company in 1908. In 1914 he worked on the extension of the Royal Dock in London. He joined the 5th Scottish Rifles on the outbreak of WORLD WAR I and spent nearly a year in France before being wounded at the battle of Loos in October 1915, when a sniper's bullet gashed his face. Back home, he worked in the Ministry of Munitions, including an eighteen-month spell in the United States, negotiating contracts for munitions.

After the war Reith was at something of a loose end and toyed with the idea of entering Parliament, either representing the LIBERALS or LABOUR. He worked for a while as general manager of Beardmore's Coatbridge plant, but thereafter moved to London. When the post of general manager of the British Broadcasting Company was advertised he applied and was appointed in December 1922. For the next four years he masterminded the development of commercial broadcasting and then when the British Broadcasting Corporation received its royal charter in 1926 of public service broadcasting. This was no easy task given both the prejudice against it and the lack of precedents — for Reith violently eschewed the American experience of sponsored commercial radio. Reith was determined to create an efficient national service, setting a high moral and educational tone. His dogmatism and determination paid off even in the face of considerable political criticism, for example at the time of the GENERAL STRIKE in 1926. Ten years later in 1936 he inaugurated television.

By 1938 Reith was apparently bored at the BBC and left to become Chairman of Imperial Airways, and later in 1939 held a similar post at the British Overseas Airways Corporation. With the outbreak of WORLD WAR II, Reith held a succession of ministerial posts — information, transport and works. Churchill (1874–1965) added planning and a peerage to this last post in 1942, but Reith found it difficult to work with politicians and his career in government ended with his early dismissal. He spent the rest of the war working at the Admiralty and helped mastermind the D-Day landings.

Although he bitterly regretted his move from the BBC and continued to crave high office, Reith's subsequent public service was considerable, chairing such bodies as the Commonwealth Telecommunications Board, the New Towns Committee, the National Film Finance Corporation and the Colonial Development Corporation. One of his last public appointments was as Lord High Commissioner to the General Assembly of the Church of Scotland in 1967–68 — a post to which he brought both great physical stature and the high moral values he had sought to impose on others throughout his earlier career. Yet Reith was a man of vision and dynamism — undoubtedly one of the most gifted Scots of his generation. The Reith Diaries were published in 1975.

• Milner, R., Reith: The BBC Years, Mainstream, 1983.

Relief Church, see SECTS

Renaissance Scotland was touched by the ideas and culture of the Renaissance (literally 'revival' of art and letters) in a great variety of ways. From its centre in Italy, where the classical tradition was virtually unbroken, and beginning about the start of the fifteenth century, classical styles in art and architecture gradually spread to northern and western Europe. While the two eras of the Renaissance, the Low Renaissance, lasting from c.1400–1500, and the High Renaissance, c.1500–c.1530, apply specifically to Italy, elsewhere the forms continued to flourish for much longer, in Scotland even into the eighteenth century. There was also a significant flowering in literature, notably in poetry and drama. While much of this was essentially elite culture some of it, mainly the drama, reached down to ordinary folk.

Renaissance architectural styles are seen in the palaces or great houses that were built or reconstructed during the fifteenth and sixteenth centuries, notably at Linlithgow, Edinburgh Castle, Stirling Castle (especially 1540–42), Holyroodhouse, and Falkland (especially 1537–41). The Royal Works were particularly productive during the reign of JAMES V. Modern restoration shows the palaces at Stirling and Edinburgh to advantage, especially the great halls. The 'Stirling Heads' are the finest examples of Scottish Renaissance wood carvings to survive. Little art of the period survives, although later tapestries and painted ceilings reflect the styles.

The literature of the period in Scots, to some extent influenced by classical styles, is important, particularly poetry and drama. The poet king, JAMES I, is thought to have been the author of the love poem, 'The Kingis Quair', and possibly of a clutch of rustic poems, including 'Peblis to the Play' and 'Christis Kirk on the Green'. More notable were the great scholars and poets like Gavin Douglas, John Bellenden, Robert Henryson, William Dunbar, Alexander Montgomerie and Alexander Scott. Of greater significance to the study of the social and political history of the period is the work of Sir David LINDSAY, whose verse play, *Ane Satyre of the Thrie Estaitis*, openly criticised corruption among the elites, notably in the church. Culturally, the Reformation was

long thought to have had a detrimental effect on what might be loosly defined as 'renaissance' ideas and styles, but modern scholarship has modified that view. The Renaissance certainly arrived later in Scotland and took off from a lower base-line compared to, say, England, the Netherlands or Germany, mainly because of the limited development of the economy and the smallish elite able to afford or patronise culture. If the economic condition of Scotland is compared to those of Italy and France, it is easy to understand why the poverty of the country meant that Renaissance ideas had less impact, at least in the shorter-term. That is not to say that classical ideas in general did not exercise great influence on later artists and architects, in particular those of the great classical revival in the eighteenth century.

•*Cowan, I.B. and Shaw, D. (eds.), The Renaissance and Reformation in Scotland, Scottish Academic Press, 1983.*

Rennie, John (1761—1821) John Rennie was one of the leading civil engineers of his age and played a large part in designing and building the TRANSPORT system that enabled the INDUSTRIAL REVOLUTION to develop. Rennie, the son of a farmer, was born in East Linton and educated locally before attending the High School in Dunbar. He worked for a while with Andrew MEIKLE (1719–1811), the famous millwright and inventor of the threshing machine, before starting his own business designing and constructing mills. This he managed to maintain on a part-time basis 1780–83 while he studied at the University of Edinburgh. Among his early commissions was an IRON foundry for CARRON COMPANY.

Although Rennie apparently left Edinburgh without graduating he made some useful contacts with Joseph BLACK (1728–99) and John Robison (1739–1805), professors respectively of chemistry and natural philosophy. Both were associates of James WATT (1736–1819) and in 1784 Rennie joined the firm of Boulton and Watt in Birmingham and London as an ENGINEERING consultant. During the next five years, Rennie installed steam-engines and other machinery for Boulton and Watt but after 1789 mainly worked on his own account. He soon established himself as a leading engineer extending his consultancy to include civil and structural engineering, of such schemes as the Kennet and Avon Canal, the Rochdale Canal, the Lancashire Canal, and the Aberdeenshire Canal, the last planned in 1796. Like his contemporary Thomas TELFORD (1757–1834) Rennie was engaged to design and carry out an extensive range of public works apart from canals, including roads, bridges, harbours and water works. Among his early works in Scotland were the Clyde navigation and Glasgow docks, harbours at Saltcoats, Stranraer and Montrose, and several bridges. In 1805 Rennie prepared a report for the Commissioners for Northern Lights on the Bell Rock Lighthouse and he later worked with the resident engineer, Robert Stevenson (1772–1850), during its construction (1807–10).

By this time Rennie had a national and even international reputation advising on public works in Europe and America. Later Scottish schemes included the Edinburgh and Glasgow Union Canal (planned 1814) and Portpatrick harbour (1817). He was joined in the business by two sons, George (1791–1886), and John (1794–1874), the latter becoming a renowned civil engineer in his own right. He inherited his father's qualities of pragmatism and sound business sense and carried on the family tradition of civil engineering into the RAILWAY Age. • *Boucher, C.T.G., John Rennie: The Life and Work of a Great Engineer, Manchester University Press, 1963.*

representative peers By the terms of the Treaty of UNION Scotland was to be represented in the British House of Lords by sixteen peers to be elected at Holyroodhouse by the Scottish peerage. This soon provided an excellent opportunity for political 'management' by the current ministry in London so that those returned were usually those nominated by the government. They were also frequently the recipients of substantial pensions as well. The system of election prevailed until 1963 when the Peerage Act permitted all Scottish peers to attend the House of Lords.

Resolutioners Resolutioners were a seventeenth-century Presbyterian faction that owed its origins to a resolution passed in the GENERAL ASSEMBLY in December 1650 approving the suspension of the ACT OF CLASSES. This contrasted with an earlier decision taken by the more fanatical clergy, known as the PROTESTORS, against such a policy and ensured a period of bitter religious conflict between these rival bodies during the CROMWELLIAN UNION. However, the Resolutioners, although royalist in their sympathies, did at least reach a modus vivendi with the English administration. Thus, in 1655, their ministers gave assurances of loyalty to the regime and agreed to cease offering prayers for the exiled CHARLES II (1630—85). James SHARP (1618—79), one of their leading members, played a major role in the religious discussions and negotiations which were to form a part of the RESTORATION SETTLEMENT.

• *Donaldson, G., Scotland: James V to James VII, Oliver & Boyd, 1965.*
• *Stevenson, D. (ed.), The Government of Scotland under the Covenanters, 1637—1651, 1982.*

Restoration Settlement This was essentially the political and religious legislation that followed the return to the two thrones of CHARLES II (1630—85). The Act Rescissory (1661) annulled all legislation since 1633, which meant that not only was the episcopal system revived (to be confirmed by a series of religious statutes in 1662) but the various limitations on the royal prerogative made in 1640—41 were also rescinded. Thus the Committee of the Articles was restored but the Triennial Act and the legislation whereby royal ministers and officials were answerable to Parliament were repealed. That this did not result in a return to the ineffectual conciliar government of CHARLES I (1600—49) was largely due to the composition of the new administration. Many of its personnel, like

Lauderdale (1616—82) and Middleton (1608—74) were formerly opponents of the Crown and were determined to assert their independence albeit to an accompaniment of blatantly corrupt behaviour.

The popularity or otherwise of the settlement, within Scotland generally, depended on a variety of different factors. For most of the nobility, with the notable exception of Archibald CAMPBELL, eighth Earl and first Marquis of Argyll (1607—61), it provided an opportunity for magnates like Glencairn (1610—64), Rothes (1630—81) and Crawford (1596—1678) to retrieve positions which as Covenanters they had forfeited with the CROMWELLIAN UNION. The bulk of the clergy had serious reservations, the extent of their antagonism depending largely on whether they were RESOLUTIONERS or PROTESTORS. Most of the former although disappointed and dissatisfied with the settlement, were not prepared to challenge it outright whereas the latter found it totally unacceptable. Their dissidence provided the clerical basis for the COVENANTERS. Many of the laity, at least in southwest Scotland, clearly sympathized with these disaffected ministers but elsewhere there was much less hostility towards the religious changes. For a large section of the population, weary of religious controversy and unhappy with the enforced union, the restoration must have brought some hope, not entirely justified, of greater stability and economic improvement.

• *Buckroyd, J., Church and State in Scotland, 1660—81, John Donald, 1980*
• *Donaldson, G., Scotland: James V to James VII, Oliver & Boyd, 1965.*

• *Ferguson, W., Scotland's Relations with England, John Donald, 1977.*

Revolution Settlement (1689—90)

WILLIAM III (1650—1702) and his wife, Mary (1662—94), accepted the English Crown on 13 February 1689 but about a month earlier the new king of England had also agreed to requests to administer Scotland until such time as a convention summoned for the 14 March had discussed the situation. However, although this convention subsequently condemned bishops, the main items in both the Claim of Right and the Articles of Grievances adopted in April were primarily constitutional. Thus, according to the Claim of Right, the ruler must adhere to the Protestant faith, there was to be no TAXATION without the consent of PARLIAMENT, the royal prerogative was to be strictly limited and Parliament itself should meet regularly with the right to freedom of speech guaranteed. As for the Articles of Grievances, their most significant feature was the condemnation of the Lords of the Articles. With the convention also having declared the throne vacant, a delegation from its members was consequently sent to London where, on 11 May, William and Mary accepted their offer of the Scottish Crown.

In June the convention reassembled as a fully-fledged parliament, but although Hamilton (1635—94), the royal commissioner, was prepared to agree to the abolition of episcopacy he was unwilling to concede to demands for the removal of the Lords of the Articles and for the full restoration of the Presbyterian Church. Accordingly Parliament was prorogued until April 1690 and it was not until June and July of that year that the outstanding constitutional and religious issues were finally resolved. William, now pre-occupied with Ireland and concerned about the Scottish Parliament withholding supply, reluctantly allowed Melville (1660—1728), who had replaced Hamilton, to agree to the abolition of the Lords of the Articles and the restoration of Presbyterianism. Thus, lay PATRONAGE was abolished, the ministers ejected in 1662 were restored and the General Assembly was revived. In fact, the main outlines of the religious settlement were based on the so-called 'Golden' Act of 1592, which had permitted the formation of presbyteries within the kingdom.

Therefore, although it initially meant that the Kirk was governed by a small minority of radical ministers, the events of 1689—90 did provide the foundations for the modern CHURCH OF SCOTLAND. The CAMERONIANS were determined to remain outwith the new system but many of the Episcopalian ministers gradually returned, assisted by concessionary legislation in the 1690s and, later, during the eighteenth century.

• *Dickinson, W.C. and Donaldson, G. (eds.), A Source Book of Scottish History III, Nelson, 1961.*
• *Drummond, A.L. and Bulloch, J., The Scottish Church, 1688—1843, St Andrew Press, 1973.*
• *Ferguson, W., Scotland, 1689 to the Present, Oliver & Boyd, 1968.*

Riccio, David (c.1533—66)

Born in Turin, David Riccio accompanied the Savoy ambassador to Scotland in 1561 and first attracted the attention of MARY (1542–87) by his musical accomplishments. By 1565 he had become a secretary attached to the department handling matters relating to Mary's role as dowager-queen of France. Following the defeat of the CHASEABOUT RAID in September 1565 and the Queen's greater reliance on his services due to DARNLEY'S (1546–67) shortcomings, Riccio gradually became the proposed victim in a complex assassination plot. Darnley undoubtedly was the key figure in the whole business since, on the apparently groundless assumptions that Riccio and Mary were lovers, he had become insatiably jealous and wanted the secretary removed. Darnley's vengeful obsession enabled MORAY (1531–70) and some of the Chaseabout Raiders due to stand trial before PARLIAMENT in March 1566 for their misdemeanours to strike a deal with Mary's husband. Thus they would assist him against Riccio and support his claims to a share in royal government if he in return would prevent any action by the Estates against them. Others attracted to the conspiracy included Morton (c.1516–81) and Ruthven (c.1520–66) who objected to foreign influence in the government and, in the former's case, the rumoured possibility that his chancellorship was to be transferred to the Italian. Allegations that the secretary was also a papal agent ensured the support of KNOX (c.1512–72) and others for the enterprise.

The murder of Riccio at Holyrood on the night of 9 March was a particularly squalid episode notable only for Mary's astute handling of the situation in the immediate aftermath. However, the most important and sinister aspect of the Riccio assassination surrounds the actual objectives of the conspirators. Unquestionably the secretary was an insignificant person and it seems highly likely that the real target was either Mary herself or at least the creation of a state of affairs where the queen and her weak husband would be mere puppets manipulated by a powerful noble faction.

• Donaldson, G., Mary, Queen of Scots, English Universities Press, 1974.

• Fraser, A., Mary, Queen of Scots, Weidenfeld & Nicolson, 1969.

Ripon, Treaty of (1641) This is the name usually given to the agreement concluded by CHARLES I (1600–49) and his Covenanting adversaries that officially ended the second BISHOPS' WAR in June 1641. In fact, the discussions about a settlement began at Ripon but the final details were completed in London. Under its terms there were to be no English garrisons at either Berwick or Carlisle, the Scots were to receive an indemnity of £300,000 and the king was to ratify the recent constitutional and ecclesiastical legislation of the Scottish PARLIAMENT. In effect it marked the triumph of the opponents of royal authority in Church and State, as was to be underlined shortly afterwards when Charles had to concede Parliament's right to choose both the PRIVY COUNCIL and the judges.

• Dickinson, W.C. and Donaldson, G. (eds.), A Source Book of Scottish History III, Nelson, 1961.

• Donaldson, G., Scotland: James V to James VII, Oliver & Boyd, 1965.

• Stevenson, D., The Scottish Revolution, 1637—44, David & Charles, 1973.

roads Before the seventeenth century Scotland was a relatively backward and under-developed country and it is hardly surprising that internal transport was primitive. Trade within the country relied heavily on coastal shipping, the most important towns being ports, like Edinburgh, Stirling, Dundee, Perth, Aberdeen, Ayr and Glasgow. Nevertheless a basic network of primitive roads and packhorse routes linked the main burghs and provided such transport as the level of economic activity dictated in the Lowlands. Much of the Highlands remained remote — though the cattle trade had begun to open up drove roads to Lowland markets.

PARLIAMENT, by Acts of 1617, 1661 and 1669, directed local justices of the peace to mend and maintain roads leading to market towns, seaports and parish churches, and later legislation stressed the need for improvement. After the UNION an Act of 1719 emphasized the need for local rather than national action, placing the onus for road building and maintenance as before on JPs and 'overseers' appointed to supervise the ineffectual system of 'statute labour' and local taxation. The system relied on casual labour, often unskilled, of those too poor to pay the fine of 'eighteen pence ... for every day's failure'.

Clearly a fresh approach to the whole problem of internal transport was necessary. This led to the establishment under parliamentary Acts of the turnpike trusts, essentially organized on English lines, to build and maintain roads in their localities and charge appropriate tolls for their use. The first in Edinburgh was established in 1713 — and as agricultural IMPROVEMENT and the INDUSTRIAL REVOLUTION picked up momentum many more trusts came into being.

Meantime, government intervention in the aftermath of the JACOBITE REBELLIONS led to the construction of a network of military roads in the HIGHLANDS. Although the prime motive was strategic — to facilitate the movement of troops through the mountains and glens — the roads contributed to the opening of the region and to economic development, such as the CATTLE trade, KELP and FISHING. The work of the military road builders was co-ordinated by Lieutenant-General George WADE (1673—1748), Commander-in-Chief of the forces in North Britain. Work began in a modest way in 1725, shortly after Wade took command, and by 1760 military engineers built over a thousand miles of road. Another military road was built through Dumfries and Galloway, partly following the line of the existing highway. A Commission for Highland Roads and Bridges, with Thomas TELFORD (1757—1834) as consultant, later continued the work of the military road builders.

During the early stages of industrialization roads provided the main form of transport as canal building was limited by both terrain and cost. Turnpike trusts created or up-graded hundreds of miles of road mainly in the Lowlands — served by stage coaches and carriers, providing services between the main cities and towns. Maintenance costs, particularly on post roads like the Glasgow to Carlisle, were partially offset by central government. Apart from Telford, both John Loudon MCADAM (1756–1836) and John RENNIE (1761–1866) made notable contributions to Scottish road and bridge building during the turnpike era.

Road transport remained important well into the nineteenth century. Even after the 1840s, when the railway first began to present any real challenge, the horse and cart were often of far greater local significance. The railway companies often provided road services to those communities not directly connected to a railhead. Responsibility for road building and maintenance passed to the county councils in 1889 and with the increased demands of the motor car roads became the joint responsibility of local authorities and the SCOTTISH OFFICE.

•*Donnachie, I., Roads and Canals 1770–1900, Holmes McDougall, 1976.*
•*Haldane, A.R.B., New Ways Through the Glens, David & Charles, 1973.*
•*Taylor, W., The Military Roads of Scotland, David & Charles, 1976.*

Robert I (1274—1329) Robert Bruce was the grandson of ROBERT BRUCE 'the Competitor' (1210–95), and son of Robert, earl of Carrick (d.1304) who resigned his earldom to him in 1292.

Like most Scottish noblemen who held territory in England as well as Scotland (in Bruce's case Ireland as well) he pursued an ambivalent policy towards Edward I during the early stages of the WARS OF INDEPENDENCE. Thus, he supported WALLACE (c.1270–1305) in 1297 but submitted to Edward I in 1302. Again, in 1304, he was in England, securing the succession of his English estates following his father's death.

Consequently, it was only after the murder of John COMYN (d 1306) that Bruce emerged as a key figure in the patriotic struggle against England. Crowned at Scone on 25 March 1306 he was soon in serious difficulties, suffering defeat at the hands of English forces at Methven in June and shortly afterwards from the followers of Comyn at Dalry on the Perthshire and Argyll border. Thereafter, he was in exile in Ulster, possibly Orkney as well, returning via Arran to Turnberry in Ayrshire where he landed with a small band of supporters in February 1307. A similar expedition to Loch Ryan headed by his brothers, Thomas and Alexander ended disastrously with their capture and subsequent execution.

In 1307, Bruce, however, was more successful and minor victories at Glen Trool and Loudon in Ayrshire wcre followed in 1308 by more substantial successes. By 1309 Bruce exercised control over two thirds of Scotland although, significantly not over the Lothians nor most of the southern half of the country. Here, it was to be another four or five years before English strongholds at Perth and Dundee were taken and garrisons in the Lothians and Borders such as Linlithgow, Edinburgh, Dunbar and Roxburgh surrendered.

The Scottish victory at BANNOCKBURN in June 1314 was certainly a decisive one since only Berwick now remained in English hands.

None the less, hostilities continued as Edward II refused to recognize Bruce as king of Scotland or abandon his own claims to sovereignty. Bruce retaliated by continuing, on the one hand, the policy of sporadic, but effective, raids on nothern England while on the other, opening a 'second front' in Ireland. This latter move was largely entrusted to his brother Edward (c.1276–1318). His ultimate defeat and death in October 1318 signalled the end of diversionary tactics which at times had been close to success.

It was not until 1323 that a semipermanent truce was arranged with England marking the beginning of a process which was to culminate in the signing of the Treaty of EDINBURGH in 1328 wherein Bruce achieved recognition of Scottish independence and his claim to the throne.

While much of Bruce's career was preoccupied with the struggle against England, there were signs of certain noteworthy social, economic and political developments. For instance, there was a recovery in trade as Exchequer returns bear witness; grants in Feu Ferm to some of the larger burghs such as Aberdeen and Edinburgh suggest a rise in their importance; the influence of ancient families such as the Comyns and Balliols declined to be replaced by faithful royal servants like Thomas Randolph and Sir James Douglas; the church benefited from royal generosity, especially the monasteries, whose decline was temporarily arrested by Bruce's grants to them; the meeting of PARLIAMENT at Cambuskenneth in 1326 with freeholders and burgesses in attendance indicates some widening of the social classes who attended such assemblies.

Bruce died at Cardross, Dunbartonshire on 7 June 1329. He was married twice; firstly to Isabella, daughter of the earl of Mar, their daughter Marjory was subsequently mother of ROBERT II; secondly to Elizabeth daughter of the earl of Ulster. DAVID (1324–71), the son of this marriage, succeeded his father in 1329.

• Barrow, G.W.S., Robert Bruce and the Community of the Realm of Scotland, Edinburgh University Press, 1986.
• McNamee, C., The Wars of the Bruces, 1306–28, 1997.
• Nicholson, R., Scotland: The Later Middle Ages, Oliver & Boyd, 1979.
• Watson, F., Under the Hammer: Edward I and Scotland, 1286–1307, Tuckwell Press, 1998.

Robert II (1316—90)   Robert was the son of Walter, sixth High Steward of Scotland and Marjory, daughter of ROBERT I, and thus the first Stewart monarch. Robert played a role as GUARDIAN of the kingdom during the absence in France and later captivity of DAVID II, notably in the years 1346–57. He was previously regarded as relatively ineffective but at least one chronicler writing in the fifteenth century and modern scholarship take a more positive view. Aged 55, he was old for his time when he eventually succeeded David in 1371.

Although the king was rarely on campaigns, the Scots, led by younger relatives and other nobles, exploited the weakness of the English authorities during the old age of Edward III and the minority of Richard II. The Scots stopped paying the balance of the ransom due for David in 1377 and by the early 1380s had recovered much of the territory previously occupied by the English. At the same time truces were renewed with the English until 1383 and Robert also avoided any involvement in the Hundred Years' War.

Power was increasingly exercised by two of Robert's sons, John, earl of Carrick, and Robert STEWART, earl of Fife, later duke of Albany. In 1381 Carrick was brought into government as heir-presumptive and three years later made lieutenant of the kingdom. At the same time the king was deprived of the control of justice, which under strict supervision of parliament, passed to Carrick. Modern scholarship suggests a coup rather than the inability of Robert to exercise control. The situation which then existed, given that Carrick himself in 1388 was badly injured by a horse, resulting in what Lynch described as a 'lame-duck guardianship', was complex. However, Fife, as guardian seems to have made major efforts to maintain law and order in the north, intervening in disputes in Moray, where another son of the king, Alexander STEWART, earl of Buchan, the notorious 'Wolf of Badenoch', had earlier been censured for lawlessness.

Robert seems to have spent the closing years of his life in Stewart strongholds in the west, notably Rothesay. He died in April 1390, but the evidence which suggested a 'senile kingship', can be revisited to build up a different picture. It could very well be that his death brought to an end a long period of stability and certainly there were subsequent disputes over the succession, involving both Fife and Buchan.

Unfortunately from Robert's two marriages were rival lines of descent which contributed to instability during the closing decade of the fourteenth and the first quarter of the fifteenth centuries.

•*Boardman, S.I., The Early Stewart Kings, Robert II and Robert III, 1371—1406, Tuckwell Press, 1996.*

Robert III (c.1337—1406) The eldest son of ROBERT II, John, earl of Carrick, a GUARDIAN of Scotland, succeeded his father, taking the title Robert, a move no doubt designed to distance himself and the monarchy from any association with his predecessor, King John BALLIOL. His incapacity evidently weakened his rule, and his brother, Robert, earl of Fife, continued as guardian for several years after he acceded. However, even before his enthronement, trouble had broken out in the north, with the king's brother, Alexander STEWART, earl of Buchan, the 'Wolf of Badenoch', leading raids on Forres and burning Elgin cathedral in 1390. Trouble continued in the north and especially in the HIGHLANDS. Faction fighting generally was sporadic during much of Robert's reign.

In 1398 a power struggle began between the kings's brother, Robert STEWART, created duke of Albany, and his elder son, David, who was created duke of Rothesay and in 1399 started to assume a greater role in government as lieutenant of the kingdom for three years. As the modern scholarship suggests the idea that the kingdom was in a state of misgovernment and schism can be countered by the fact that the political community represented a significant third force in governance, able, as Lynch suggests, to monitor carefully the behaviour of a weak king and the rivals for succession. Indeed Rothesay proved energetic but to such an extent that his regime was unpopular. He further alienated Albany, who with the earl of Douglas in January 1402 led a coup, arresting and detaining Rothesay at Falkland. Two months later he was dead, to be followed soon after by another of Albany's rivals, Malcolm Drummond.

The king could do little to check either the restored Albany or the power of the belligerent nobles who led a force to a disastrous battle against the English at Homildon Hill, Northumberland, 14 September 1402. Thereafter Robert, from his base at Rothesay castle, consolidated his power base in the west and in 1406 arranged for his young son, James, to be sent to France for safety. Unfortunately, the future JAMES I was captured and held by the English. Three weeks later, possibly on hearing the news, Robert died, in his own words 'the worst of kings and the most wretched of men in the whole realm'. Historians take a more positive view, pointing to widespread and longer-term economic problems coinciding with factional fighting and succession crises.

• Boardman, S.I., *The Early Stewart Kings, Robert II and Robert III, 1371– 1406, Tuckwell Press, 1996.*

Robertson, William, see AMERICAN WAR OF INDEPENDENCE; ENLIGHTEN-MENT

Rosebery, Archibald, Earl of (1847—1929) Archibald Primrose, Lord Rosebery, was one of the most prominent Liberal politicians of his generation, holding several key Cabinet posts before becoming Prime Minister in 1894. Although born and educated in England, Rosebery maintained family and political connections with Scotland and was one of the few political personalities to take a consistent interest in Scottish affairs. Among his contemporaries at Eton were Arthur BALFOUR (1848–1930) and Lord Randolph Churchill (1849– 94). From 1866 he spent some time at Oxford but never graduated, because, on the death of his grandfather in 1868, he succeeded to the earldom and estates – including Dalmeny, Midlothian.

Declaring himself to be a Liberal in 1869, he began a long parliamentary career in the House of Lords. His early concerns included foreign and imperial affairs, as well as Scotland, whose administration he felt was badly neglected at Westminster. His lobbying paid off and in 1881 he was appointed to an under-secretary's post at the Home Office in charge of Scottish business in the House of Lords. Although he resigned in frustration in 1883, his persistence in pointing out the need for a Scottish minister ultimately brought into being the office of Secretary for Scotland and the creation of the SCOTTISH OFFICE in 1885.

Although he sometimes seemed reluctant, Rosebery's rise up the political ladder was astounding. He was Lord Privy Seal in 1885, Foreign Secretary briefly in 1886 and again during 1892—94, becoming Prime Minister after

Gladstone's (1809–98) resignation, 1894–95. Like other Liberal administrations his was dogged by the question of Irish Home Rule and friction over the reform of the House of Lords. Defeated in the General Election of 1895, Rosebery resigned as leader of the Liberal Party the following year.

After his period in high office he devoted much of his time to political intrigue and manipulation, especially from his Scottish base. His views became increasingly eccentric and after squabbling with CAMPBELL-BANNERMAN (1836–1908) and other former associates he severed himself completely from the Liberal Party in 1905. He denounced Lloyd George's reforming Budget of 1909. He also found time to indulge in horse-racing and won the Derby three times. He produced some passable historical biographies, including works on Sir Robert Peel, Oliver Cromwell, Napoleon and Lord Randolph Churchill.

While Rosebery was hardly a brilliant prime minister, he tried to reunite a Liberal Party shattered by the Irish Question and was a strong advocate of what he described as 'mutual self-respect and mutual independence' within the 'commonwealth of nations' that made up the British Empire.
•*James, R.R., Rosebery: A Biography of Archibald Philip, Fifth Earl of Rosebery, Weidenfeld & Nicolson, 1963.*

Ross, William (1911—1988) Ross was born with LABOUR politics in his blood for his father, a locomotive driver, was a member of the town council in Ayr. His schooldays and teens were touched by the GENERAL STRIKE and the DEPRESSION, when for a time his father was unemployed.

Following in the footsteps of MAXTON, Ross attended Glasgow University graduating in 1932 to become a teacher. In 1936 he was selected as Labour candidate for Ayr.

After the outbreak of WORLD WAR II he enlisted and subsequently had a distinguished military record in India where he served on the North-West Frontier, until seconded to signals GHQ India in Delhi. By 1944 he was cipher officer to Lord Louis Mountbatten, supreme commander, Southeast Asia and accompanied him to Burma and Singapore for the signing of the peace treaty with the Japanese. He was made MBE and left the army with the rank of major.

With his background and connections and rather like Dennis Healey, he was an ideal Labour candidate. Although failing to get elected at Ayr in the 1945 General Election, he succeeded in a by-election at Kilmarnock which he represented between 1946 and 1979. He became parliamentary private secretary to Hector McNeill, Secretary of State for Scotland remaining at the post until the Labour defeat in 1951.

During the long Labour opposition he worked on social issues becoming in 1962 Shadow Secretary of State for Scotland. With the return of Labour in 1964 he occupied this position during the subsequent Wilson administrations. Although essentially a centralist he fought with great determination for the Scottish economy, particularly industrial development, the NEW TOWNS and the regeneration of the HIGHLANDS. The success of the SCOTTISH NATIONAL PARTY, however put home rule or devolution back on the agenda and since Ross strongly resisted this he lost his post when Wilson resigned in 1976.

He subsequently became Lord High Commissioner to the GENERAL ASSEMBLY of the Church of Scotland (1978–80), and a life peer in 1979.

Like MACDONALD and MAXTON of earlier generations Ross stuck to his principles in politics and private life, but despite his modernizing tendencies was essentially a traditionalist — perhaps not surprising in view of his background.

Rough Wooing Whether Henry VIII (1491–1547) ever did have any grandiose imperialist plans for Scotland is questionable and it seems more likely, engaged as he was in a war against France, that he was mainly concerned about the continued existence of the AULD ALLIANCE. Therefore, he was keen to strengthen Anglo-Scottish relations by a marriage alliance between his only son, Edward (1537–53), and the infant MARY, QUEEN OF SCOTS (1542–87). Consequently, when the Treaty of Greenwich (1543), which seemed to have accepted this proposal, was repudiated by the Scottish authorities, Henry decided on forcible implementation of his policy. Thus, in 1544 and 1545, English forces commanded by the Earl of Hertford (c.1506–52) attacked and devastated much of eastern Scotland; hence the 'Rough Wooing', a contemporary expression for these incursions.

While considerable damage, especially to church property, and loss of life were inflicted the invasions were really counter-productive. In fact, far from convincing the Scottish nation of the value of an English alignment, they merely reinforced the bonds with France, as the siege of ST ANDREWS CASTLE (1546–47) was shortly to confirm.
• *Dickinson, W.C., Donaldson, G., Milne, I. (eds.), A Source Book of Scottish History II, Nelson, 1963.*
• *Donaldson, G., Scotland: James V to James VII, Oliver & Boyd, 1965.*

Rullion Green, see PENTLAND RISING

runrig In the traditional mode of AGRICULTURE a typical township was divided into rough strips or parcels of land known as runrigs or rigs. The earliest documentary evidence relating to the term dates from the fifteenth century, although runrig seems to have existed from the twelfth century. In a multiple-tenancy town the rigs in the arable land or INFIELD would traditionally be shared out annually by the landowner or his arbiter. By the late seventeenth century in parts of the Lowlands the re-allocation process was being abandoned in favour of a system identifying a share with its previous occupier.

Despite ENCLOSURE and IMPROVEMENT runrig survived in the Lowlands well into the eighteenth century and even later in less progressive districts. The next logical step came with the consolidation of holdings into the familiar farm units created during the AGRICULTURAL REVOLUTION. The runrig system can be compared with the English open field system — though there were considerable contrasts in tenure and land use.

Ruthven Raid (1582) In August 1582 JAMES VI (1566—1625) became the prisoner of a faction headed by William Ruthven, Earl of Gowrie (c.1514—84), which also included prominent noblemen such as Angus (1555—88), Lindsay (d.1589), Mar (1562—1634) and Thomas Lyon, Master of Glamis (c.1546—1608). While some of the 'raiders' had particular grievances against the Arran-Lennox government, for instance Gowrie, as Treasurer, was owed a huge amount of money, the bond that tended to unite all of them was a serious concern about the real intentions of Lennox, both from a political and religious standpoint. Although the new regime with its pro-English and ultra-Protestant outlook had the backing of the Kirk for its overthrow of the Arran-Lennox administration, it received scant assistance from Elizabeth (1533—1603) or the English government. Thus the following June when the king succeeded in escaping, the 'Raiders' were quickly supplanted by Arran and his supporters. The principal victim of the whole episode was Lennox, who didn't survive his enforced exile in France.

• *Donaldson, G., Scotland: James V to James VII, Oliver & Boyd, 1965.*

S

St Andrews Castle, siege of, (1546—47) The murder of Cardinal BEATON (c.1494–1546) at St Andrews Castle on 29 May 1546 and the seizure of the fortress by KIRKCALDY OF GRANGE (c.1520–73) and his fellow assassins placed the Regent, ARRAN (c.1516–75), in a difficult position. While the incident didn't spark off a Protestant revolt, most of the 'castilians' being too radical or reprobate for any general support, the government would have to take some kind of action, especially as Arran's brother John HAMILTON (1512–71) was bishop-elect of Dunkeld and as those inside also favoured the English marriage arrangements for MARY (1542–87). On the other hand the Regent didn't want the position of MARY OF GUISE (1515–60) strengthened by some form of French intervention while he had also to consider that his eldest son, James HAMILTON, third Earl of Arran (1538–1609), was held as hostage within the castle. Arran's quandary helps to explain the ineffectual measures taken against the rebels in 1546 including the futile attempt at blowing up the stronghold by mining. The members of the garrison were in touch with England and hoped for intervention from that source – it was on this assumption that John KNOX (c.1512–72) entered the castle as chaplain in April 1547. However, it was the kinsmen of the dowager who took the first steps to break the siege by sending a French fleet in July to begin a bombardment of the fortress. On 31 July the castle surrendered and its occupants were either imprisoned or sent to the galleys.

•*Donaldson, G., Scotland: James V to James VII, Oliver & Boyd, 1965.*

salt Historically, salt was an important commodity in Scotland and its manufacture was closely allied to coal-mining. It was partly because of this relationship that its history was long subsumed in that of coal, though, as the historian of the industry shows, salt was not always the junior partner. Given its importance to early industrialization and particularly the history of the Scottish coal and chemical industries, salt manufacture was of considerable economic and social importance – an interesting but apparently misunderstood craft.

The process of salt-making by boiling seawater in lead or iron pans was patently simple, but there was nevertheless considerable diversity in modes of production depending on the scale of the enterprise and on supplies of coal, peat or timber fuels. However, the regional concentration of the industry along the shores of the Firth of Forth emphasized the important relationship of successful salt manufacture to initially cheap and readily-worked coal. Although salt-making was simple it still required some skill, and this had interesting implications for employer-worker relations.

By the 1570s, when the industry was already well-established, the 'Golden Age' of Scottish salt manufacture began. The industry was buoyant for over seventy years, its success built on the export trade (mainly to the Baltic and the Low Countries). Thereafter a patchy prosperity was maintained until 1820, largely by capturing the home market. It was this switch to reliance on the domestic rather than the overseas market that was to give the industry such a significant but hitherto unexplored place in the negotiations preceeding the Treaty of UNION. Finally, the social history of salt making is worth exploring because of the 'slavery' issue, which until recently dominated discussion about labour conditions in the industry.

The work processes and problems, as well as the business of sales and distribution are central to the history of salt-making. Saltworks, enveloped in smoke and steam, were highly concentrated workplaces in an era when most manufacturing was widely dispersed in the domestic system and this too had considerable influence on work-patterns and labour relations. The salt-masters — mainly large landowners in Lothian and Fife — fought a constant battle against the elements and rising fuel costs, as easily got coal was progressively exhausted. Skilled labour was hard to keep — hence

the lifetime bond between master and servant.

Although Scots salt was poor, often wet stuff and would have had few buyers in a perfectly competitive market, thanks to favourable fiscal treatment a substantial industry had been created by the late sixteenth century. Such was the power and influence of the salt-masters that they later secured a domestic monopoly when overseas markets slipped away from them after the middle of the seventeenth century. Hence the political economy of salt played a vital role in the Union as the powerful landowners-cum-salt-masters made very sure that Scottish salt 'might not be ruin'd by the salt made in England', the latter a much superior item and subject to a higher tax.

The modern history vigorously challenges 'the distorted picture of the Scottish salters' circumstances' by examining questions of serfdom, status and the so-called 'Emancipation Acts' of 1775 and 1799, which affected both colliers and salters. What strikes one immediately is the small numbers involved — no more than 350 full-time workers at any time during the 1700s — and that the job was relatively skilled. Legal servitude bound master as much as servant and there is a good case to be made for seeing 'emancipation' as a release for the masters from long-established obligation to the salters — especially rates of pay. Nor could the salters' status be regarded as directly comparable to that of the colliers — but both were to suffer badly in the free market that characterized the later stages of industrialization in the Scottish Lowlands.

• *Whatley, C.A., The Scottish Salt Industry 1570—1850: An Economic and Social History, Aberdeen University Press, 1987.*

Sauchieburn, Battle of (1488) Fought on 11 June 1488, Sauchieburn or 'the field of Stirling' was a battle between factions supporting JAMES III on the one hand, and those supporting his heir. The latter won the day, and in the aftermath of the battle James was either killed or murdered. Historians judge that the rebels had a narrow victory and that the regime installed under the young JAMES IV remained essentially weak with two major revolts against it by before 1490.

Savings Bank, see BANKING; DUNCAN

Scapa Flow   Since the outbreak of WORLD WAR I Scapa Flow had been the main operational base of the British Grand Fleet and in November 1918, as part of the Armistice arrangements, the German High Seas fleet was taken there to await the outcome of the Paris Peace Conference. By the end of the month eleven battleships, five battle cruisers, eight light cruisers and fifty destroyers with their wireless equipment removed, their guns immobilized and most of their fuel confiscated were being guarded by the Battle Cruiser Force augmented by various armed fishing craft. In May 1919 the Battle Squadron took over the role of custodians of a fleet whose redistribution was now causing serious friction among the victorious allies. On board the interned

warships the skeleton crews, unhindered under the terms of the Armistice by the presence of armed guards, had decided to scuttle their ships rather than allow them to fall into Allied hands. Thus, four days before 21 June 1919 when the Armistice officially ended, the commander of the German fleet gave instructions to his men to begin scuttling their ships two hours before noon on the 21st. However the deadline was postponed for forty-eight hours by the Council of Four in Paris and the commander of the British Battle Squadron decided to undertake an extensive tactical exercise with his fleet on the 21st. Accordingly, when the German sailors began opening their sea-cocks and watertight doors the Battle Squadron was steaming into the Pentland Firth. By the evening, despite attempts by the remaining British vessels to force the German crews to stay aboard their ships, which resulted in ten German sailors being killed, ten battleships, all five battle cruisers, four light cruisers and thirty-two destroyers had been scuttled.

No evidence has yet been produced to indicate that the German government had given secret instructions for the destruction of its navy although it unquestionably approved of the action taken. British reaction was initially a mixture exasperation and anger but this quickly changed to relief once it was realized that at least the French and Italians would not be able to acquire most of the ships.

In WORLD WAR II Scapa Flow was again a major naval base, protected by a defensive system known as the Churchill Barrier following the sinking of the *Royal Oak* by U-boat in 1939 .

•*Marder, A.J., From the Dreadnought to Scapa Flow, Oxford University Press, 1970.*

•*Vander, Van D., The Grand Scuttle, Waterfront, 1986.*

Schools, see EDUCATION

Scotsman, The see PRESS

Scott, Sir Walter (1771—1832) Like Robert BURNS (1759–96), Scott was a major literary figure whose impact historically was also of considerable significance. Although born in Edinburgh, Scott came of Border stock and because of an illness that left him lame, spent much of early childhood with relatives in the BORDERS. Thereafter he was educated at the Royal High School and the University of Edinburgh. Studying law, he became an advocate in 1792 and was appointed Sheriff of Selkirk in 1799. (He became Clerk of Session in 1806.)

Meantime, Scott had maintained a life-long interest in literature, especially romantic poetry and ballads. After translating some German poems and a play by Goethe (1750–1832) he published in 1802–3 *The Minstrelsy of the Scottish Border*, which first brought him to public attention. A series of narrative poems followed, beginning with the 'Lay of the Last Minstrel' (1805). His first novel, *Waverley*, which he had begun years before, was published anonymously in 1814. Following its success Scott went from strength to strength, producing a series of novels based on Scottish history and characters ranging from *Guy Mannering* (1815), through *Rob*

Roy (1818), to *A Legend of Montrose* (1819).

This prodigious output was maintained for the rest of his life, partly to maintain the flamboyant lifestyle of a Border laird at Abbotsford, which he acquired in 1812, and partly to repay creditors of the Edinburgh printer and publisher, Constable and Ballantyne, in which Scott was a partner, following its collapse in 1826. He undertook to pay off a debt of over £100,000, ruining his health in the process.

Scott contributed to a revival of interest in Scottish history and culture, reflecting the prevailing Romanticism of his generation. This view of Scotland eschewed the impact of the FRENCH REVOLUTION and closer to home the INDUSTRIAL REVOLUTION in favour of legends from the COVENANTING and JACOBITE eras. Nevertheless, by playing a leading role in the visit of George IV to Scotland, and through his novels, Scott contributed to the maintenance of Scottish culture and nationalism during the rest of the nineteenth century. For other major figures of Scott's era see Thomas CARLYLE (1795—1881), John Galt (1779—1839), and Francis JEFFREY (1773—1850).

•*Anderson, J., Sir Walter Scott and History, Edina Press, 1981.*

•*Ash, M., The Strange Death of Scottish History, Ramsay Head Press, 1980.*

•*Daiches, D., Sir Walter Scott and his World, Thames & Hudson, 1971.*

Scottish Convention, see HOME RULE; SCOTTISH NATIONAL PARTY

Scottish Home Rule Association, see HOME RULE; MacDONALD, RAMSAY

Scottish Labour Party, see HARDIE; LABOUR PARTY

'Scottish Martyrs'   This was the nickname bestowed on Thomas MUIR (1765–99) and his fellow RADICALS, who were sentenced and transported to Botany Bay following a series of sedition trials in 1793–94. In fact, as political prisoners, they received relatively favourable treatment in the colony. A CHARTIST-inspired monument was erected in 1844 at the Calton Cemetery, Edinburgh, as a memorial to Muir and his associates.

Scottish National Party   The Scottish National Party was founded in 1934 – an amalgamation of the National Party of Scotland (established 1928) and the Scottish Self-Government Party (dating from 1932). The former was dominated by ex-INDEPENDENT LABOUR PARTY members including Dr John ('King John') MacCormick (1904–61) and the life-long nationalist, Roland Muirhead (1868–1964), and had secured 5,000 members by 1929. The latter consisted mainly of disillusioned HOME RULE Liberals – the British LIBERAL PARTY having been thrown into further disarray following the establishment of the National Government. Although showing some promise in by-elections the SNP result in the General Election of 1935 was dismal and its membership had fallen to around 2,000 by 1939. During WORLD WAR II the SNP kept up some of its former momentum – eventually winning and briefly holding the Motherwell seat in April 1945, just prior to the great Labour landslide.

While the disillusioned MacCormick's Scottish Convention ini-

tially stole some of the limelight, SNP membership and support grew gradually during the 1950s and 60s and by 1965 the party had around 16,000 members. There was something of a hiatus after the famous Hamilton by-election victory of 1967 – although support grew dramatically in the early 1970s. The two General Elections of 1974 saw the SNP raise its share of the Scottish vote from 22 to 30 per cent and return no fewer than eleven MPs after the October election.

The SNP did much to galvanize the Labour government into introducing devolution for Scotland – but after the debacle of the referendum campaign and an equivocal result in 1979 support for the party temporarily evaporated. In the General Election that year only two SNP MPs were returned, and in the party itself there was much internal recrimination and dissention between left and right wings. Yet the SNP continued to maintain its confirmed place in Scottish politics as the only party favouring independence rather than dependence – considerably influencing the commitment of Labour, Liberal and even some CONSERVATIVE politicians to Scottish devolution. With increased economic difficulties becoming apparent in Scotland the SNP experienced a recovery in its fortunes during the 1980s, culminating in ex-Labour MP Jim Sillar's victory in the 1988 Glasgow Govan by-election.

The debate over home rule or devolution versus independence continued to divide the SNP which had an equivocal relationship with the Campaign for a Scottish Assembly. But anti-Tory feeling and

disillusion with LABOUR'S vacillation on the issue continued to
work in the party's favour and its
vote increased from 14 to 22 per
cent between 1987–97. At the first
election for the Scottish Parliament
in 1999 the SNP emerged as the
largest party after Labour, forming
the official opposition under the
leader, Alex Salmond.

• Brand, J., *The National Movement in Scotland*, Routledge & Kegan Paul, 1978.
• Gallagher, T. (ed.), *Nationalism in the Nineties*, Polygon, 1991.
• Harvie, C., *Scotland and National-ism: Scottish Society and Politics, 1707 to the Present*, 3rd edition, Routledge, 1998.
• Wolfe, J.N. (ed.), *Government and Nationalism in Scotland*, Edinburgh University Press, 1969.

Scottish Office   Following the
Treaty of UNION in 1707 a Secretary
for Scotland was appointed to deal
with Scottish business, while the
Lord Advocate continued to act as
the chief government law officer in
Scotland. In 1746, following the
second JACOBITE REBELLION, the
office of Secretary for Scotland was
abolished and the Lord Advocate
assumed responsibility for most
government business north of the
Border. Thus, as Kellas shows, 'the
key position of Scots law in preserving Scotland's identity in the
government was emphasized.'

During the nineteenth century
and due mainly to pressures of
industrialization, URBANIZATION, and
POPULATION growth, the functions
of local and national government
greatly increased, particularly in
the fields of poor relief, EDUCATION,
public health and the construction
of ROADS. Many BURGHS (and after

the local government reform of
1889, the counties) implemented
major capital schemes to provide
water supply, drainage, gas lighting, hospitals and other civic
improvements. Since it helped to
finance them central government
assumed much greater control
over these activities as the century
progressed. This is seen in the creation of various supervisory boards
like the Board of Supervision for
Poor Relief (1845), the General
Board of Commissioners in Lunacy
(1857), the Scotch Education
Department (1872) and the Prisons
Commission (1877).

Meantime, in 1828, the Home
Secretary had been put in charge
of Scottish administration. Since he
was often ignorant about Scotland
the Lord Advocate remained the
best-informed spokesman about
Scottish affairs and exercised growing powers over the increasingly
complex concerns of government.
This alarmed many Scottish LIBERAL
MPs who regarded the position of
the Lord Advocate, the patronage
he exercised, and the lack of time
for Scottish affairs as wholly unde-
mocratic. These views were partly
stimulated by practical considerations and partly by the rise of
Scottish nationalism and the HOME
RULE movement, supported by key
figures including Lord ROSEBERY
(1847–1929). The Prime Minister,
Gladstone (1809–98), was thus
persuaded to introduce a bill in
1884 setting up the Scottish Office
and reviving the post of Secretary
for Scotland.

Ironically, in 1885 it was a
CONSERVATIVE administration who
appointed the first incumbent, the
Duke of Richmond and Gordon
(1818–1903), and transferred to

his office certain functions of the Home Office, the Privy Council, the Treasury and the Local Government Board. He also became responsible for the boards of supervision already established in Edinburgh. Although both the Lord Advocate's department and the Home Office were constantly on the defensive the Scottish Office gradually extended its influence over a wide range of functions.

Further boards were created to deal with specific areas of administration, notably the Congested Districts (Scotland) Commissioners (1897), responsible for easing social problems in the HIGHLANDS; the Scottish Insurance Commissioners (1911), to implement and supervise the national insurance scheme; the Board of Agriculture (1912); and the Highlands and Islands (Medical Services) Board (1913). Following the Scottish Board of Health, established in 1919, assumed the responsibilities of the Local Government Board for Scotland, the Scottish Insurance Commissioners, and the Highlands and Islands (Medical Services) Board.

From 1892 onwards the Secretary for Scotland had a seat in the Cabinet but it was not until 1926 that he was promoted to one of HM Principal Secretaries of State and dignified with the title Secretary of State for Scotland. A Parliamentary Under-Secretary was also created in 1926 — upgrading a similar post dealing exclusively with health. Others joined him later as the responsibilities widened. Some of the specialized boards were soon promoted to departments. In 1928 the Board of Agriculture, the Board of Health

and the Scottish Prison Commissioners were replaced by the Department of Agriculture for Scotland, the Department of Health for Scotland and the Prisons Department for Scotland — each a statutory body independent of the Secretary of State, but under his control and direction.

Following the recommendations of the Gilmour Committee Report on Scottish Administration (1937) for tighter control of Scottish affairs there was substantial devolution to a new Edinburgh-based Scottish Office, the London office at Dover House being retained to maintain links with Parliament and other Whitehall departments. St Andrew's House, a splendid architectural exercise in art deco, opened in 1939, becoming the Secretary of State's headquarters. At the same time the independent departments were abolished and four new ones directly responsible to him established: the Scottish Home Department; the Department of Health for Scotland; the Scottish Education Department; and the Department of Agriculture and Fisheries for Scotland.

The range of functions exercised by the Scottish Office was greatly extended during WORLD WAR II under the then Secretary of State, Tom JOHNSTON (1881–1965), a noted devolutionist. During the emergency and the years of post-war reconstruction that followed, the Scottish Office played an increasingly important role in encouraging economic developments, for example the building of NEW TOWNS and the North of Scotland Hydro-Electric Board. In 1962, another reorganization brought into being the Scottish

Home and Health Department and the Scottish Development Department to join Education and Agriculture and Fisheries. Ultimately a Scottish Economic Planning Department (renamed the Industry Department for Scotland in 1983) was added to oversee industrial and North Sea oil related developments.

As the Scottish Office expanded and strengthened its corporate existence it exercised an increasingly important role in the governance of Scotland. Not only did it influence the policy of major British government departments in Scotland — like Health, Social Security or Employment — but it had close relations with many other powerful and nominally independent quasi non-governmental organizations unique to Scotland. These included the Scottish Special Housing Association (one of the oldest, dating from 1937), the CROFTERS' COMMISSION (1955), the Highlands and Islands Development Board (1965), later Highland and Island Enterprise and perhaps most influential of all, the Scottish Development Agency (1975), later Scottish Enterprise.

The wide responsibility of the Scottish Office and its ministers (five in total by 1979) was a source of annoyance to advocates of HOME RULE, who, like their Victorian counterparts, viewed its power with suspicion. Indeed, a central issue in the devolution debate of the 1970s and 1980s was the problem of gaining democratic control over a Scottish administrative state that remained essentially unaccountable to the people of Scotland no matter which party held the political reigns in Britain or who occupied the post of Secretary of State for Scotland. Nevertheless, the Scottish Office was more than a device of government and, as Kellas observes, 'the previous statehood of Scotland and the provisions of the Union of 1707 are its heredity, and national consciousness its lifeforce.' These aspects of national identity were subsequently given expression in the establishment of the Scottish Parliament in 1999. Most of the Scottish Office's functions were assumed by the Scottish Executive, while a Scotland Office was established under the Secretary of State for Scotland.

•*Gibson, J.S., The Thistle and the Crown: A History of the Scottish Office, HMSO, 1985.*

•*Keating, M. and Midwinter, A., The Government of Scotland, Mainstream, 1983.*

•*Kellas, J.G., The Scottish Political System, Cambridge University Press, 1984.*

•*Monies, G., Local Government in Scotland, W. Green & Son, 1996.*

•*Walker, D.M., The Scottish Legal System, W. Green & Son, 1981.*

Scottish Trade Union Congress, see GENERAL STRIKE; TRADE UNIONS

Seafield, Earl of, see OGILVIE

secessions, see DISRUPTION; SECTS

sects The REVOLUTION SETTLEMENT established the modern Church of Scotland and of the Protestants only the CAMERONIANS and the Episcopalians remained outside the arrangements. The latter, as the Scottish Episcopal Church, are still in existence while the Cameronians who were to set up their

Reformed Presbyterian Church, merged, or most of them did, with the FREE CHURCH in 1876.

One of the main features of Church history in the eighteenth century was the series of secessions that took place, the first significant breach coming in 1733. The key issue was PATRONAGE. Consequently, a pronouncement by the GENERAL ASSEMBLY in 1731 that the election of ministers should be restricted to heritors and elders, thereby ignoring the wishes of the congregation, provoked vehement protests. Particularly outspoken was Ebenezer Erskine (1680–1754), minister of Stirling, who, with some of his supporters, being suspended by the General Assembly, formed a Secession Church in December 1733. This breakaway movement soon had around twenty ministers and over thirty congregations throughout the Lowland area yet it too was to become bedevilled by factionalism. Thus, in 1744, the Seceders were split over the Burgess oath, which the more conservative-minded among them regarded as showing too much approval of the established Church. Hence they became divided into Burghers and Anti-Burghers, the former led by Erskine and the latter by the fanatical Adam Gib (1713–88). Later in this century there were further disagreements leading to the formation of the Old Light Burghers and Anti-Burghers as well as the New Light Burghers and New Light Anti-Burghers.

The main difference between them was that the 'New Lights' were less insistent on the State having a duty to maintain the Kirk

and in 1820 the two 'New Lights' merged to form the United Secession Church. Meanwhile, in 1761, the second secession occurred when Thomas Gillespie (1708–74) and his colleagues broke away from the Church of Scotland to set up the Relief Church. Gillespie, minister of Carnock near Dunfermline, although at odds with the General Assembly over patronage, was far more liberal in outlook than the earlier Seceders and his new organization rapidly acquired new members.

Undoubtedly patronage remained the outstanding issue in the first half of the nineteenth century and the most dramatic event, the DISRUPTION, in 1843, owed a great deal to that controversy. However, the establishment of the Free Church marked the zenith of the secessionist movement and thereafter there was an increasing tendency towards amalgamation. Thus, in 1847 the Relief Church and the United Secession Church joined together to become the United Presbyterian Church. A few years later in 1852, a majority of the 'Old Lights', who had founded a United Original Secession Church in 1822, aligned themselves with the Free Church.

This century, the union in 1929 of the United Free Church, an alliance of the Free and United Presbyterian Churches made in 1900, with the Church of Scotland has resulted in only a handful of the sects surviving. Accordingly when the remnant of the original Secession Church also rejoined the main body in 1956 there only remained the 'Wee Frees', a branch of the Free Church that had refused to accept the alliance of the Free Church in 1900, and having most of its support in the Highlands and Islands, the United Free Church (the small minority who rejected the union of 1929), the Free Presbyterians, a splinter group of the Free Church, formed in 1892, and the tiny Reformed Presbyterian Church.

Burleigh, J.H.S., A Church History of Scotland, Oxford University Press, 1960.

Brown, C.G., The People in the Pews: Religion and Society in Scotland since 1780, Economic and Social History Society in Scotland, 1993.

Drummond, A.L. and Bulloch, J., The Church in Late Victorian Scotland, St Andrew Press, 1978.

Drummond, A.L. and Bulloch, J., The Church in Victorian Scotland, 1843–73, St Andrew Press, 1975.

Drummond, A.L. and Bulloch, J., The Scottish Church, 1688–1843, St Andrew Press, 1973.

Selkirk, Thomas Douglas, fifth Earl of (1771—1820) Selkirk, a pioneer of Canadian development and a leading advocate of EMIGRATION from the Scottish HIGHLANDS, was born at St Mary's Isle, Kirkcudbright, seventh and youngest son of the fourth Earl of Selkirk. He was educated at Edinburgh University where he was an associate of Walter SCOTT (1771–1832), who became a close friend. Like many landowners he had an interest in estate IMPROVEMENT and following a tour of the Highlands in 1792 developed an enthusiasm for applying the same principles to the social and economic problems of the region. Succeeding his father in 1799 he turned his attention to emigration,

planting his first colony of Highlanders on Prince Edward Island in 1803. Another settlement was established in Upper Canada, at Baldoon, near Lake St Clair — not without resistance from the colonial authorities, who were suspicious of Selkirk's motives.

Back in Scotland, Selkirk published his *Observations on the Present State of the Highlands of Scotland* (1805), took an increasingly active part in local and national politics, and began formulating plans for his most ambitious project — the settlement of the Red River Valley, in what is now Manitoba. He and his brother-in-law, Andrew Wedderburn Colvile, were astute enough to acquire a controlling interest in the Hudson's Bay Company and in 1811 obtained from it a grant of 116,000 square miles of land in the Red River Valley. The first settlers, led by Miles MacDonell, left in 1811 and others followed in 1812–14 and 1815. Fort Douglas, as it was called, became the first major settlement in the North West.

However, the Red River Valley colony represented a major intrusion on the part of the Hudson's Bay Company into territory which had previously been the monopoly of the rival fur trading company, the North West Company. In 1815 the Nor' Westers began a campaign designed to drive the colonists from the Red River, culminating in a battle near Fort Douglas in 1816 in which Robert Semple, the Hudson's Bay Company's agent, and nineteen of the settlers were killed. Meantime, Selkirk had arrived in Canada and with a force of soldiers captured the North

West Company's headquarters at Fort William, and later reinstated his colonists on the Red River. When the battle reached the Canadian courts in 1818 the verdict went against Selkirk — largely it was believed because of vested interests supporting the North West Company — and he was fined £2,000 in damages.

Although he continued the fight in Parliament Selkirk's health deteriorated and he died in France in 1820. Incongruously the two fur companies settled their differences the following year and Selkirk's colony flourished as one of the pioneer communities of modern Manitoba.

• *Bumstead, J.M., The People's Clearance: Highland Emigration to British North America 1770—1815, Edinburgh University Press, 1982.*

Sellar, Patrick (1780—1851) Rightly or wrongly, Patrick Sellar is remembered for his callous treatment of victims of the Highland CLEARANCES. Born in Morayshire, Sellar studied law in Edinburgh. He built up his career as a lawyer and estate factor, notably to the Countess of Sutherland and her husband, Lord Stafford. He became notorious during the clearances which occurred towards the close of the NAPOLEONIC WAR, overseeing the eviction in June 1814 of tenants from Strathnaver. Houses were evidently set alight with elderly residents still inside and leaving them little time to escape, others torched before people could remove possessions and animals. Sellar was prosecuted on charges of arson and culpable homicide and his trial became a cause cèlébre. Progress and moral

improvement were seen as important but the key issues for the defence were the 'trial of strength between abettors of anarchy and misrule and the magistracy as well as the laws of this country'. Sellar was acquitted, and Robert Mackid, the Gaelic-speaking Sheriff-substitute who raised the prosecution at the request of the tenants, was sacked. While this could be regarded as a gross injustice, the whole episode needs to be seen in the context of widespread social unrest and economic disruption following the war and the generally repressive policies of the Liverpool administration throughout Britain and Ireland. The events in Sutherland, along with other incidents during the Clearances, are also documented in Gaelic verse and song, sources largely neglected by writers in English.

• *Grimble, I., The Trial of Patrick Sellar, Routledge & Kegan Paul, 1962 (Saltire Society, 1993).*
• *Richards, E., Patrick Sellar and the Highland Clearances: homicide, eviction and the price of progress, Polygon, 1999.*

shale oil, see YOUNG, JAMES.

Sharp, James (1618—79) Born in Banff in the conservative northeast of Scotland and educated at Aberdeen University, James Sharp's career initially appeared to be heading in the direction of an appointment within the existing episcopal system. But by the mid-1640s he was on the staff of St Andrews University, a decidedly Covenanting establishment, and he became minister of Crail in 1648. In the 1650s he emerged as a leading RESOLUTIONER and was largely responsible for persuading

Cromwell (1599–1658) to transfer his favour towards this faction in preference to the rival PROTESTORS. During the negotiations surrounding the RESTORATION SETTLEMENT he played a distinctly controversial role; to many of his compatriots he appeared to have betrayed them and sacrificed his religious beliefs for the archbishopric of St Andrews, to which he was promoted in 1661. However, it could be argued that he had little choice since the nobility was determined to wreak its revenge on the Presbyterian clergy for all the humiliation that it had endured in previous years. On the other hand he did his personal standing little good by his enthusiastic support for the repressive measures taken by the government against the COVENANTERS and there was an early assassination attempt on him in 1668. His actual murder on 3 May 1679 at Magus Moor near St Andrews was the work of a band of fanatical Covenanters, which included Hackston of Rathillet (d. 1680) among its members. He was dragged from his coach and shot, the incident forming part of the serious unrest that was to culminate in the battle of BOTHWELL BRIDGE in June 1679.

•*Buckroyd, J., James Sharp, Archbishop of St Andrews (1618–79), John Donald, 1987.*

Shawfield Riots (1725)   In 1712, while the War of the Spanish Succession was still in progress there had been an attempt by the government, contrary to the terms of the Treaty of UNION, to impose a MALT TAX on Scotland. This had provoked a strong reaction among much of the population, including the Scottish Members of PARLIAMENT and in 1713 a bill to repeal the Union was only narrowly defeated in the House of Lords. However, in June 1725, Walpole (1676–1745), as an alternative to an English back bench proposal for the imposition of a hefty tax on Scottish ale, substituted a lighter duty of threepence a bushel on malt. This proved to be a highly unpopular measure throughout Scotland with the most spectacular protest occurring at Shawfield, Glasgow, where the property and residence of Daniel Campbell, (c.1671–1753) Member of Parliament for Glasgow Burghs was destroyed because of his supposed sympathy with the detested legislation. There followed an ineffective attempt at restoring law and order by troops from the garrison at Dumbarton, which ended with the Glasgow magistrates arresting the commanding officer for allowing his men to fire on the mob.

In fact, what had greatly exacerbated the whole situation was indecisive action by the Scottish executive. Roxburgh (c.1680–1741) refused to take any action and it was left to the newly appointed Lord Advocate, Duncan FORBES (1685–1747), to take the initiative. The upshot was the fining of the city of Glasgow in order to provide compensation for Campbell of Shawfield and sentences of transportation being passed against some of the leading rioteers. Undoubtedly the significance of the episode, apart from its revelation of certain latent anti-Union sentiment, was the manner in which it underlined the administrative deficiencies created by the abolition of the PRIVY COUNCIL in 1708.

• *Ferguson, W., Scotland: 1689 to the Present, Oliver & Boyd, 1968.*

sheriff   A key figure in the judicial system since the twelfth century. By the sixteenth century it had become an hereditary appointment with the extensive duties that it involved, including outlawing criminals, settling territorial disputes or enforcing TAXATION, being undertaken by various deputies. The Crown rarely tampered with the hereditary aspect of the system and when CHARLES I (1600–49) did deprive the Gordons and certain other families of their hereditary sheriffdoms it was a highly unpopular action. Thus it was not until the aftermath of the JACOBITE REBELLION in 1745–46 that HERITABLE JURISDICTIONS were finally abolished in 1747. Thereafter the country was organized into a series of principal sheriffships with sheriff-substitutes designated for every county town. Today the sheriff-substitute remains the judge before whom both civil and criminal cases are initially heard with more serious charges ultimately being referred to the High Court.

Sheriffmuir, Battle of (13 November 1715)   Although MAR (1675–1732) had announced his support of the JACOBITE cause in August 1715, by the beginning of November he and the bulk of his army were still encamped in Perthshire. This had given John CAMPBELL, second Duke of Argyll (1678–1743), in charge of the government forces, the opportunity to make some hasty defensive preparations although his regiments were still heavily outnumbered by Mar's. On Saturday, 12 November, well aware of his opponent's numerical superiority, Argyll moved most of his men from Stirling Castle to Sheriffmuir above Dunblane where at least the terrain was suitable for his cavalry, the strongest units in his army. Meanwhile, Mar at last stirred himself and the next day the two sides, one consisting largely of about 1,000 clansmen from the northeast of Scotland and the other of around 3,000 professional soldiers and locally recruited levies, encountered each other. While the actual contest was an inconclusive affair, with the left wing on both sides being routed, strategically it was a victory for the Hanoverians. Thus, Mar advanced no further, his followers lost heart and the battle in fact signalled the collapse of the JACOBITE REBELLION of 1715.

• *Lenman, B., The Jacobite Risings in Britain, 1689–1746, Eyre Methuen, 1980.*

Shinwell, Emmanuel, see RED CLYDESIDE

shipbuilding   Shipbuilding on a small-scale was long-established in Scotland but it was not until the early nineteenth century that it grew sufficiently to become of significance to the economy. Its growth was the result of rapid expansion in the Clyde, two favourable factors being the changes in methods of construction (from wood to IRON and steel) and changes in propulsion (from sail to steam and diesel). Frequently developments in the first category are cited as more important, but there seems little doubt that pioneering work in propulsion and marine ENGINEERING gave the Clyde a headstart in steam and iron shipping. The earliest development was the steam-tug *Charlotte Dundas*, designed by William SYMINGTON (1763–1831), and launched on the FORTH AND CLYDE CANAL in 1802. Henry BELL (1767–1830) developed the first practical steamboat for passenger traffic in 1812 and this was soon followed by others as the relatively calm waters of the Firth of Clyde proved ideal for steamboats. One of the earliest iron boats was the *Vulcan* (1818), while the *Fairie Queen* (1831) was a pioneering iron steamer. In 1835 half the tonnage of steamships built in Britain originated on the Clyde — though otherwise the area was still unimportant relative to overall output elsewhere.

By the middle of the nineteenth century the Clyde had overtaken other centres in steam, developed an important marine engineering industry, and begun to finance major shipping companies. Robert NAPIER (1791–1876) was one of several prominent shipbuilding entrepreneurs of the period. Even then, wooden sailing ships were still more important than iron steamships. Port Glasgow and Greenock produced the former, while most of the latter were built in Glasgow and Dumbarton. Clippers, like *Cutty Sark*, remained viable on long routes, where steamers proved costly.

The subsequent development of Scottish shipbuilding — and especially the Clyde yards — was owed to the increased efficiency of boilers, the development of the triple expansion engine, the steam-turbine, and the use of steel in construction. A phase of expansion occurred in the 1880s when steel began to displace iron, just as iron

had wood. Many of the great shipbuilding yards and related marine engineering workshops aided by relatively cheap and highly skilled labour came to prominence in the period before WORLD WAR I. Shipping fleets expanded internationally and naval rearmament brought even more work to the Clyde, with Scottish shipbuilding output reaching a peak of 2.6 million tons, 60 per cent of UK output, in the period 1919–23. Some of the shipyard workers had a reputation for militancy and became associated with the activities of RED CLYDESIDE.

After the war other shipbuilding regions were worse hit than Clydeside and indeed Scotland improved its share of UK output as well as introducing new methods of propulsion in the diesel engine. The Clyde produced 60 per cent of total passenger liner tonnage 1921–38 including the *Queen Mary* (1934) and *Queen Elizabeth* (1939). Again warships provided work during a period of declining international trade, though rationalization took its inevitable toll as well, badly affecting iron and steel.

Shipbuilding experienced mixed fortunes after WORLD WAR II, a period characterized at first by unprecedented prosperity then after 1960 by a collapse that took the industry to the brink of disastrous decline. The latter was owed partly to lack of investment in modernization, indecisive management, and inter-union demarcation disputes, and partly to the overwhelming advantages in prices and delivery dates offered by European and Japanese competitors. The work-in at Upper Clyde Shipbuilders (1971) was one notable instance of worker resistance to the inevitable demise of the yards, some of which were given a stay of execution during the seventies by oil-related or warship construction.

• *Moss, M. S. and Hume, J. R., Workshop of the British Empire: Engineering and Shipbuilding in the West of Scotland, Heinemann, 1977.*
• *Clyde Shipbuilding from Old Photographs, Batsford, 1975.*

Sibbald, Sir Robert, see MEDICINE

sieges Besieging the enemy in castles or other fortifications was a significant military tactic historically and there are numerous examples that can be drawn from Scottish history during the medieval and early modern era. The tactics deployed reflected the prevailing technology, but both the besieged and their enemy had to be well-prepared and well-organised. Apart from the strength of the fortification, the numbers of arms and weaponry, the fundamentals of survival were water and food supplies, the availability of which inavriably determined the length of the siege. Clearly those on the outside could more readily maintain supplies, but this was not always the case, especially in very large and important castles. While the easiest, though longer-term tactic, was simply to starve out the occupants, other means could be resorted to by means battering rams, towers, ladders, ropes, fire, and ultimately artillery to break through the walls. Tunnelling was another option, but as at ST ANDREWS CASTLE, it could be short-circuited by counter-tunnelling to either break out or stop the

besiegers before they broke through. Roxburgh, which was held by the English from the 1330s to 1460, was besieged several times. It was eventually captured after JAMES II had been killed by a cannon explosion during the siege.

Simpson, Sir James Young (1811—70) Simpson, the famous obstetrician who was first to use ether and later chloroform in anaesthesia, was born in Bathgate. His education began at the local school and thereafter he studied MEDICINE at Edinburgh University, graduating MD in 1832. He was a brilliant scholar and by 1839 was appointed to the chair of midwifery in the university.

When news of the use of ether in surgery reached Scotland from the United States and England in 1846, Simpson experimented with it in obstetrics the following January. Later that year he and his assistants tried out chloroform by inhaling it themselves, and used it at Edinburgh Royal Infirmary soon after. While there was much initial resistance it was given royal blessing by Queen Victoria (1819—1901) who was anaesthetized during the birth of her eighth child, Prince Leopold, in 1853.

While Simpson is best remembered for his work in anaesthetics, he also contributed much to obstetrics in general. In 1847 he became a physician to the Queen and was later much honoured at home and abroad. In 1866 he received a baronetcy, the first given to a Scottish medical practitioner.
• *Shepherd, J.A., Simpson and Syme of Edinburgh, E. & S. Livingstone, 1969.*

Sinclair, Sir John, of Ulbster (1754—1835) John Sinclair was a prominent MP (1780–1811), landowner, politician and propagandist of agricultural improvement. He was educated at Edinburgh, Glasgow and Oxford, later entering for the English bar at Lincoln's Inn. He inherited his father's extensive Caithness estates in 1770 and, following a European tour, married and settled at the family seat of Thurso Castle.

Sinclair became involved in estate IMPROVEMENT and local politics, becoming MP for Caithness in 1780 – a position he held for all but a few short periods representing some English constituencies – until 1811. Although he never achieved high political office he nevertheless exercised considerable influence through both personal connections and his publications – notably *A History of the Public Revenue of the British Empire* (1785–89).

He helped establish the BOARD OF AGRICULTURE (1793) and was himself a notable improver, founding PLANNED VILLAGES at Thurso (The New Town, c. 1790) and Hallkirk (c. 1800), as well as writing numerous works on the new agriculture, including a major volume on agriculture in the northern counties of Scotland.

Historically, his major achievement was the compilation of the *Statistical Account of Scotland* (1791–99), a major socio-economic survey of the country at a critical stage in its development during the AGRICULTURAL REVOLUTION and the INDUSTRIAL REVOLUTION. An assiduous pamphleteer, his other interests included monetary reform, the problems of the Highlands, and African exploration. He was also closely associated with the work of the BRITISH FISHERIES SOCIETY.

• *Mitchison, R., Agricultural Sir John: The Life of Sir John Sinclair of Ulbster 1754–1835, Geoffrey Bles, 1962.*

Skirving, William (?—1796)
William Skirving was secretary of the Scottish FRIENDS OF THE PEOPLE and one of the SCOTTISH MARTYRS sentenced for radical activities during the early FRENCH REVOLUTIONARY era. The son of a Lanarkshire farmer, Skirving was educated in Haddington and then at the University of Edinburgh. Eschewing plans to enter the church, he began farming at Damhead and then, after his marriage, at Strathruddie in Fife. He became something of an expert on agricultural IMPROVEMENT, publishing a book on the subject entitled *The Husbandman's Assistant* (1792).

Always something of an enthusiast for political reform he soon joined the Scottish Friends of the People, taking a prominent part as secretary from 1792. After the National Convention of 1793 Skirving was an early victim of the counter – revolution and, convicted of sedition, was transported to Botany Bay for fourteen years. He sailed with MUIR (1765–99) and the others, reaching New South Wales in October 1794. In the colony he farmed for some time but soon his health declined and he died in March 1796 – just a few weeks after the demise of Joseph GERRALD (1760–96), another of the 'Scottish Martyrs'.

Smellie, William, see MEDICINE

Smiles, Samuel (1812—1904)
Born in Haddington, Smiles

studied medicine at Edinburgh University, 1829–32. For a while he worked in his native town, later moving to Leeds to become a surgeon. In 1838 he published his first book, *Physical Education,* and thereafter combined medicine with a variety of other occupations and literary activities. He was editor of the *Leeds Times,* a CHARTIST journal (1838–42), assistant secretary of the Leeds and Thirsk Railway (1845), and, later, Secretary to the South Eastern Railway (1854–66). It is possible his business career was advanced by George Stephenson, whose biography (1857) Smiles wrote. But his most famous book was *Self-Help* (1859), the best known exposition of Victorian values.

Self-Help, as its name suggests, espoused the individualism, effort and enterprise by which all could achieve self-improvement and self-fulfilment, the philosophy which also underpinned the laissez faire thinking of his age. Although aimed at a popular audience it was particularly targeted at aspiring workers, who by dint of effort, EDUCATION, and possibly occupational shifts, could raise themselves further up the social ladder. Based on the middle-class ideals of its era, it was grounded in morality and religion. The book was a huge success, but Smiles came in for much criticism and in the 1866 edition regretted that he had been misunderstood by many in advocating selfishness.

A series of self-improvement titles followed, including *Character* (1871), *Thrift* (1875) and *Duty* (1880). While *Self-Help* was the most famous of his books, by far the most informative was the

substantial *Lives of the Engineers* (1861–62), which clearly built upon his earlier work on Stephenson.

Smiles's career is hard to categorize, but it might usefully be compared with those of LIVINGSTON and CARNEGIE, who were certainly good, if contrasting, examples of nineteenth-century self-help. More generally, self-help had a major impact on attitudes towards the poor and on welfare policies in both Britain and the United States.

• *Garvis, A., Samuel Smiles and the Construction of Victorian Values, Sutton Publishing, 1997.*

• *Gosden, P., Self-Help. Voluntary Associations in Nineteenth-Century Britain, Batsford, 1973.*

Smith, Adam (1723—90) Adam Smith, one of the major figures of the Scottish ENLIGHTENMENT and the leading pioneer of political economy, was born in Kirkcaldy, where his father was a customs officer. After education at the local grammar school Smith began a long association with Glasgow University in 1737 at the age of fourteen. There he studied Latin, Greek, mathematics and moral philosophy. In 1740 he won a Snell Exhibition to Balliol College, Oxford, where he stayed for seven years.

Returning to Scotland he divided his time between Kirkcaldy and Edinburgh, giving lectures on jurisprudence and rhetoric, under the patronage of Lord KAMES (1696–1782). In 1751 he was elected to the chair of logic at Glasgow, and in 1755 became professor of moral philosophy, occupying the latter post for nine years. In 1759 he published his lectures as a book, entitled *The Theory of Moral Sentiments*. He associated with most of the major thinkers of his day and frequently visited Edinburgh where he and David HUME (1711–76) founded the Select Society.

In 1764 he resigned his chair and became tutor to the young Duke of Buccleuch, touring the Continent, 1764–66. On their visit to France, Smith met the leading philosophers, including Quesnay, Turgot and Necker. Although he regarded the young Duke as something of a dullard, the post provided him with a pension and the following six years were spent mostly in Kirkcaldy living with his mother and a cousin. There and in London he devoted himself to writing *The Wealth of Nations*, published in 1776.

The Wealth of Nations is both a pioneering study of economic analysis and of political philosophy, in that it addresses fundamental ideas about self interest and natural liberty. It opens with a discussion of the division of labour, the separation of individual tasks and consequent specialization, as a key factor in economic growth. Smith analyses the nature of economic growth, through exploring the relationship of value and of price in exchanges, and through discussions of wages, profits and rents. He then deals with the accumulation and employment of capital and the merits and drawbacks of different economic systems, especially those fashioned by mercantilists and physiocrats — both of which Smith rejects in favour of the system described as 'natural liberty'. Smith had a minimalist view of the State. It had certain functions, notably the provision of defence and law and order, but apart from a certain minimum of public works, the State should not interfere with market forces. Smith received £500 for the first edition.

In 1778 Smith was appointed one of the Commissioners of Customs in Scotland — a handsome sinecure — and returned to live in Edinburgh. There he maintained his friendship with other Enlightenment figures and devoted his spare time to a wide range of intellectual interests. He became Lord Rector of Glasgow University in 1787. Although he instructed that his manuscripts should be burned a week before his death in 1790, much of his other writing survived and has been published, notably the Glasgow Edition of the Works and Correspondence.
• *Campbell, R.H. and Skinner, A.S., Adam Smith, Croom Helm, 1982.*

Smith, John (1938—94)   Smith was one of several prominent politicians of his generation to emerge from Glasgow University in the 1960s. As a young lawyer (later becoming an advocate) he stood unsuccessfully as LABOUR candidate for East Fife in 1961 and 1964. In 1970 he was duly elected for Lanarkshire North and was its MP (as Monklands East from 1983) till his death. Smith had considerable stature and integrity, which came in useful given the divisive (and often sectarian) local politics of North Lanarkshire. It was these qualities, apart from his considerable ability, which helped him rise rapidly through a series of positions in the Wilson and Callaghan governments at the Scottish Office (1974), the Department of Energy

(1974–76), the Privy Council Office (1976–78), and, finally, as Secretary of State for Trade (1978–79). With Labour in opposition (led in turn by Michael Foot and Neil Kinnock), Smith continued to specialize in economic issues, and despite ill-health was ultimately leader of the Labour Party and the Opposition in 1992. Smith made impressive efforts to raise morale and heal divisions caused by ideological shifts and changing policies within the Labour Party and by the run of election defeats which returned a series of CONSERVATIVE governments (led by Margaret Thatcher and then John Major). Like DEWAR, Smith had a long-term commitment to devolution but his death in 1994 left it with others to advance that cause.

smuggling Described by one historian as 'the national vice of the Scots', smuggling was an ancient trade, rampant long before the UNION of 1707 or the English NAVIGATION ACTS, which limited colonial trade to their own shipping. However, as Smout observes, the Scots were delighted to marry their traditional dislike of customs and excise officials with the patriotic ideal of cheating the English. Smuggling, either by sea or over land, took place with or without the connivance of revenue officers, though concealment was by far the more prevalent. Historically, the favoured goods of the smuggler were spirits, wine and TOBACCO — all subject to high duty and valuable relative to their bulk. Others included Dutch or English TEXTILES (such as fine LINENS), sugar and even SALT, the imported item being far superior to the locally manu-

factured product. Less obviously valuable items smuggled into Scotland from Ireland included CATTLE and corn.

With the increased efficiency and vigilance of the customs and excise during the eighteenth century and the imposition of wide-ranging duties on alcoholic drink (including the MALT TAX) wines and spirits became the most important and profitable products for the smuggler. In addition to drink run ashore in quiet coves a growing trade developed from Ireland and the HIGHLANDS in the products of illicit DISTILLING. Reform of the excise, notably the Small Stills Act (1816), and lowering duty gradually reduced, though did not eradicate, illicit distillation. Given its covert nature it comes as little surprise that there is no serious historical study of smuggling — despite its legendary appeal and oblique associations with such notables as Adam SMITH (1723–90) and Robert Burns (1759–96).

• *Smout, T.C., Scottish Trade on the Eve of Union 1660–1707, Oliver and Boyd, 1963.*

Solemn League and Covenant The outcome of the English Civil War was of crucial importance to the Covenanters since a victory for CHARLES I (1600–49) could only mean that their future position in Scotland would be in serious jeopardy. For the English Parliamentarians, their poor performance in the early stages of the Civil War had made it imperative that by the spring of 1643 they should consider seeking some kind of accommodation with the COVENANTERS. Thus it was Pym (1584–1643) and his Parliamentary colleagues who took the initiative in negotiating an alliance with Archibald CAMPBELL, eighth Earl and first Marquis of Argyll (1607–61) and the other Covenanting leaders, although the latter had also become increasingly attracted to such a proposition. The result was the religious and military pact known as the Solemn League and Covenant.

The ecclesiastical arrangements whereby the Presbyterian system or at least 'the example of the best reformed churches' was to be adopted throughout the British Isles, following a parliamentary victory, were drafted in August. In September they were accepted by Pym's faction despite the ominous reservations of the anti-Presbyterian independents. The military alliance by which the Covenanters committed Scotland to providing 18,000 infantry and 2,000 cavalry was completed in November.

The treaty had differing consequences for the two signatories. For the Parliamentarians its main significance was military since LESLIE (1580–1661) (or, as he now was, the Earl of Leven) and his army played a crucial role in the first major defeat of the Royalists at Marston Moor in 1644. In Scotland it had religious and political repercussions; for many Covenanters there was now an unequivocal commitment to presbyterianize the whole of Britain, a view strengthened by their participation during 1643 in the WESTMINSTER CONFESSION. The failure of the English Parliamentarians to honour the terms of their agreement made conflict inevitable and was to create the conditions that produced the CROMWELLIAN UNION. At the same time not all Covenanters nor all of the nation were behind the 1643 arrangements. Thus, it also served to underline the growing disunity within the country, between those who supported Argyll's party and those, like MONTROSE (1612–50), who suspected or disliked their intentions.

• Donaldson, G., Scotland: James V to James VII, Oliver & Boyd, 1965.
• Ferguson, W., Scotland's Relations with England, John Donald, 1977.
• Stevenson, D., The Scottish Revolution, 1637–44, David & Charles, 1973.

Solway Moss, Battle of (24 November 1542) The failure of JAMES V (1512–42) to attend the conference arranged between Henry VIII (1491–1547) and himself at York in September 1541 led to a breakdown in Anglo-Scottish relations. In August 1542 an initial English assault was effectively repulsed at Haddenrig, between Kelso and Coldstream, by HUNTLY (c.1510–62), only for the king to dismiss his victorious commander, apparently for not pursuing his success further. All that this action did was intensify the discontent and resentment already simmering among many of the nobility. Accordingly, following a second English invasion in October, a planned royal counter-attack came to nought when the leaders of his army refused to advance beyond Fala Muir in the Lammermuir hills. But James persisted and mobilized another force; one contingent commanded by Cardinal BEATON (c.1494–1546) and the king's half-brother, Moray (1500–44), who had replaced Huntly, set off in an easterly direction, while the other led by the king himself left Edinburgh on 21 October for the West March. James, becoming suddenly unwell, remained at Lochmaben. His army with Maxwell (d.1546), the Warden of the West March, and Oliver Sinclair (?d.1560), one of the royal favourites despised by the aristocracy in charge, headed south from Langholm across the Border into England. There on 24 November, just north of Gretna, at Solway Moss they encountered a small group of Borderers under Maxwell's English counterpart. Although there was only a few Scottish casualties the ensuing skirmish was a humiliating one for the Crown with numerous noblemen surrendering without a fight, including Maxwell himself. In fact, the whole sorry episode was a clear indictment of the king's mishandling of his nobility. Most of those captured joined other exiled families such as the Douglases to become the 'Assured Scots', Henry VIII's fifth column of English pensioners who would return shortly to their native land.

• *Donaldson, G., Scotland, James V to James VII, Oliver & Boyd, 1965.*
• *Fraser, G.M., The Steel Bonnets, Pan Books, 1974.*

Spottiswoode, John (1565—1639) John Spottiswoode was the son of the noted reformer of the same name (1510–85) who had been one of the five Superintendents appointed in 1561. Unlike many of the younger ministers in the second half of the sixteenth century he was not an adherent of MELVILLE (1545–1622). His episcopal leanings were noted favourably by JAMES VI (1566–1625)

whom he accompanied to London in 1603 and who shortly afterwards promoted him to the archbishopric of Glasgow. Spottiswoode soon played an active role on the PRIVY COUNCIL, supporting his colleague Bishop Knox (1559–1633) in his actions in the Western HIGHLANDS, which culminated in the Statutes of IONA (1609). In 1615 he was appointed Archbishop of St Andrews but although he approved the FIVE ARTICLES OF PERTH in principle he strongly advised the king to seek the consent of the GENERAL ASSEMBLY before trying to introduce them. His faithful service to the Crown received its highest accolade when he became Chancellor in 1635, the first ecclesiastic to hold this office since the REFORMATION. However, he quickly distanced himself from the religious policy of CHARLES I (1600–49) attacking the Book of Canons and the PRAYER BOOK. After the NATIONAL COVENANT was signed he endeavoured for a time thereafter to act as mediator between the government and the Covenanting opposition, but as the crisis deepened he felt obliged to depart for a self-imposed exile in England. His *History of the Church of Scotland* published posthumously provides an episcopal alternative to the presbyterian writings of David Calderwood (1575–1651).

Stair, John Dalrymple, second Earl (1673—1747) A career soldier and diplomat, Stair was also a pioneer of agricultural IMPROVEMENT. He was educated at the universities of Edinburgh and Leyden and joining the army subsequently fought under Marlborough (1650–1722) in the war against France,

1702–13. After a period engaged on diplomatic missions — including that of ambassador to France — he returned to Scotland in 1720 to settle on his estates.

In 1707 he had inherited the family title and became one of the Scottish REPRESENTATIVE PEERS in the United Kingdom Parliament following the Treaty of UNION. With one interlude (1742–3), when he returned to active service and diplomacy, he afterwards devoted much of his time to agriculture on his estates in West Lothian and Wigtownshire. Probably emulating techniques he had seen at first hand on the Continent, notably the Netherlands, he introduced improved drainage, ENCLOSURES, and root crops — as well as extensive afforestation.

Standard, Battle of (1138) This was a significant clash in the unresolved dispute between the Scots and the English over claims to territory in Northumberland and Cumbria. Fought near Northallerton, North Yorkshire, on 22 August 1138, this defeat of the Scottish forces, by tradition one of the largest ever to invade England up to that time, brought to an end DAVID I's intervention in the English conflict between his niece, Matilda, and that of her rival Stephen.
•*Lynch, M., Scotland: A New History, Pimlico, 1992.*

staple During the fourteenth century Middleburg and Bruges vied as staple ports where basic Scottish exports such as woollen textiles, fish, hides and skins were sent. Then, in the early sixteenth century the market for such goods became Veere or Campveere on the island of Walcheren. Originally the Scottish merchants trading in the staple had been subject to Flemish law but gradually they received extensive privileges having their own courts, kirk and warehouses as well as a conservator specially appointed to look after their interests. During the seventeenth century, Veere gradually became a backwater as northern Dutch ports such as Rotterdam and Amsterdam overtook it in importance. Besides, the pattern of Scottish trade was altering and there was a decline in woollen exports. Coal became more important but it was not a staple. None the less Veere survived the Treaty of UNION and continued as Scotland's staple port until 1799 when it was finally abandoned.
•*Davidson, J. and Gray, A., The Scottish Staple at Veere, Longmans, 1909.*

Statistical Accounts of Scotland Three remarkable series of volumes describing contemporary society and conditions in the 1790s, the 1830s to 1840s and the 1940s to 1960s — each in their way of considerable historical interest and value.

The first (generally known as the Old Statistical Account) was initiated and compiled by Sir John SINCLAIR (1754–1835), who used his influence to persuade ministers throughout Scotland to submit detailed returns on their parishes. His questionaire covered all aspects of social and economic life and those clergy and other contributors who complied with his detailed requests produced invaluable data and descriptions of their localities during an era of dramatic change in AGRICULTURE and INDUS-TRY. Not all were as co-operative as he would have liked, so the parish accounts are inevitably very variable in depth and usefulness.

The production of this massive twenty-one volume work took nearly ten years (1791—99), with Sinclair employing a team of editors and clerks to assist with publication. One major weakness arises from the fact that the parish accounts were published as they became available — rather than in county volumes. A modern reprint has corrected this fault. An index was provided in vol.21 (1799). Sinclair himself later produced the valuable *Analysis of the Statistical Account of Scotland* (1825), which provided an overview of conditions at the time — as well as an update on the original compilation of the 1790s.

The *Second* (or New) *Statistical Account* was a comparable exercise undertaken by a committee of the Society for the Benefit of the Sons and Daughters of the Clergy, compilation and revision being mainly in the late 1830s and early 1840s. A total of fifteen volumes resulted, some containing accounts for several counties. Vol.1 contains an alphabetical list of parishes and vol.15 a general index to the series.

Finally, the *Third Statistical Account of Scotland*, published under the aegis of the Scottish Council for Social Service, the four original Scottish universities and the then local authorities, set out during the late 1940s to follow the same tradition. The early volumes, for example, Ayr, Fife and East Lothian, all provided valuable portraits of post-war society, but editorial problems and delays in

publication meant that later volumes produced in the 1950s and 1960s were dated and, as a result, of variable usefulness.

Stevenson, Robert, see NAPIER; RENNIE

Stevenson, Robert Louis (1850—1894) Stevenson, like BURNS and SCOTT, was a major literary figure whose life and writing are of historical significance because they reflected the prevailing ethos and culture of late nineteenth century Scotland. The Stevensons were distinguished in ENGINEERING, Robert Louis's grandfather, Robert, his father, Thomas, and his uncles, Alan and David, being light house engineers, working mainly for the Commission for Northern Lights.

Born in Edinburgh, ill-health meant that some of his childhood was spent indoors looking out on the streets of the NEW TOWN, whose lamp lighters he immortalised in one of the poems featured in *A Child's Garden of Verses* (1885). As an engineering and law student in Edinburgh he later saw some of the seamier side of urban life, which he deployed to good effect in several of his novels. In 1875 he became an advocate but partly influenced by a tubercular condition, turned his attention to literary activities and travel, mainly in France, where the climate was more congenial than at home. These were combined in the travel essays, *An Inland Voyage* (1878) and *Travels With a Donkey in the Cevennes* (1879). While in France he met Fanny Osborne, an American divorcee, travelled with her to the United States and married in 1880.

His next move was into romance

with *The New Arabian Nights* (1882) and then the enormously successful *Treasure Island* (1883), a stirring pirate yarn. Then with echoes of Mary Shelley's Frankenstein came *The Strange Case of Dr Jekyll and Mr Hyde* which became his best known work. Its psycho-analytic discourse was based on the motif of 'doubling', the fractured self, one good, one evil, a theme popular in Scottish fiction, doubtless influenced by Calvinism. It also drew on stories of Edinburgh body snatchers, and medical and scientific experiments, the consequences were far-reaching and uncontrollable.

A series of historical novels followed: *Kidnapped* (1886), *The Black Arrow* (1888), *The Master of Ballantrae* (1889), *Catriona* (1893), which was a sequel to *Kidnapped*. With the exception of *The Black Arrow*, all dealt with eighteenth-century Scotland, to some extent reflecting the romantic views Victorians then held of the JACOBITE era. The powerful *Weir of Hermiston* and *St Ives* were both unfinished and published posthumously.

Stricken by tuberculosis, Stevenson, his wife and step-son, settled in Samoa (1888–89) where the mild climate delayed what was even by nineteenth century standards a premature death. Stevenson's literary talent lay in moulding Scottish history and the vernacular tradition to contemporary themes, though modern scholarship sees some of his work challenging modernity and the imperial diaspora of which he was part. There is a huge critical and biographical literature.

• *Bell, I., Robert Louis Stevenson: Dreams of Exile, Headline, 1993.*
• *Calder, A., Robert Louis Stevenson: Selected Poems, Penguin, 1998.*
• *McLynn, F.J., Robert Louis Stevenson: A Biography, Hutchinson, 1993.*

Stewart, Alexander, first earl of Buchan (d.1406) The fourth son of ROBERT II (1316–90) Alexander Stewart was appointed Justiciar of nothern Scotland in 1372 and it was his lawless behaviour in that part of the country which earned him the nickname, 'the Wolf of Badenoch'. His title, as first earl of Buchan, came as a result of his marriage to the countess of Ross.

He was a constant thorn in the flesh of both his father, Robert II and his brother ROBERT III (c.1337–1406), his most infamous action occuring in 1390 when, following his excommunication by an exasperated bishop of Moray, he and his highland followers burnt both Forres and Elgin, including the cathedral.
• *Boardman, S., The Early Stewart Kings, Tuckwell Press, 1996.*

Stewart, Charles Edward, the 'Young Pretender' (1720—88) Eldest son of the James Francis STEWART, the Old Pretender (1688–1766) he was born in Rome and by the outbreak of the War of the Austrian Succession in 1739 had become the focus of JACOBITE aspirations and French intrigue. However, when he sailed for Scotland to commence the JACOBITE REBELLION in 1745 he lacked not only the support of France but also most of his troops and stores since the ships carrying them had been forced to return through British naval intervention. None the less the rising went ahead largely due to the persuasive powers of the Prince and with the capture of Edinburgh and the defeat of General Cope (d.1760) at PRESTONPANS the uprising began to taken on a more serious aspect for the WHIG government in London. These fears were intensified by the arrival of the Jacobite army at Derby early in December but the Young Pretender discovered he was unable to persuade Lord George MURRAY (c.1700–60) and his fellow officers to proceed any further. Lack of any French assistance and the presence of a formidable British army under Cumberland (1721–65) in the south not to mention the forces under Field Marshal WADE (1673–1748) behind them in the north of England convinced the Jacobite commanders that retreat was the only feasible strategy. Defeat at CULLODEN in April 1746 forced Charles to seek refuge among his faithful supporters, of whom Flora MacDonald (1722–90) has possibly become the most celebrated, before his departure to France in September. The remainder of his life with its anticlimactic descent into drunken dissipation ensured the complete collapse of the Jacobite cause and must cast serious doubt on whether the Prince remotely deserved the loyalty which so many Highlanders bestowed on him.

• *Kybett, S.M., Bonnie Prince Charlie. Unwin Hyman, 1988.*

Stewart, Esmé, Duke of Lennox (c.1542—83) Esmé Stewart was the son of John Stewart (d.1567), who was a brother of Matthew Stewart, Earl of Lennox (1516—71) the father of Henry STEWART, Lord

Darnley (1546–67). Esmé, therefore, was a cousin of the father of JAMES VI (1566–1625), and by 1579 when he arrived in Scotland from France, where he had inherited his father's title of Lord d'Aubigny, he was the leading representative of the Lennox interest in the Scottish succession.

However, there were other conceivable motives for his appearance in this country not least an invitation from the king as well as the possibility that he was acting secretly on behalf of the French and Spanish governments. Certainly he speedily won the confidence and affection of the impressionable boy king, being rewarded in March 1580 with the Earldom of Lennox, which Robert Stewart (c.1520–86), his elderly uncle, was persuaded to surrender. A year later he became Duke of Lennox and also Keeper of Dumbarton Castle. Yet, although he succeeded in having MORTON (c.1516–81), his principal adversary, overthrown and executed in June 1581, his period of ascendancy was short-lived. Despite placatory gestures such as the Negative Confession, a denunciation of papal doctrines drawn up in January 1581, the Kirk remained hostile. So too did the allies of the ex-Regent, Morton, and it was a combination of some of these opponents who organized the RUTHVEN RAID in August 1582, which took the king out of his control and ensured his downfall. He returned to France, dying there the following year.

Stewart, Francis, fifth Earl of Bothwell (1563—1612) His father was John (d.1563), an illegitimate son of JAMES V (1512–42), while his mother was a sister of James Hepburn, fourth Earl of Bothwell (c.1535–78). As the latter's nephew he appeared to inherit much of his impetuous and dissolute nature yet at the same time displayed a command of several languages and, by his Italianate alterations to Crichton Castle, a keen interest in architecture. He received his earldom in 1581 but it was about a decade later that he came to prominence with his unruly behaviour and disregard of royal authority. By his audacious attacks on royal residences such as Holyrood and Falkland not to mention assaults on the king's person he proved a serious threat to a monarch already hard pressed by the rebellious NORTHERN EARLS. Indeed on two separate occasions he eschewed his Protestant principles to become the ally of Huntly (1562–1636) and Errol (c.1566–1631). JAMES VI (1566–1625) had him forfeited in 1592 for, among other crimes, alleged WITCHCRAFT and unquestionably his departure into continental exile in 1595 removed a nobleman who had become a constant source of embarrassment and concern to the Crown.

Stewart, Henry, Lord Darnley (1546—67) The son of Matthew Stewart, fourth Earl of Lennox (1516–71) and Margaret Douglas (1515–78), the latter being the daughter of Margaret Tudor (1489–51) and ARCHIBALD DOUGLAS, sixth Earl of Angus (c.1489–1557). This placed him next to MARY, QUEEN OF SCOTS (1542–87) in the succession to the English throne.

He was born in England during his father's long exile, arriving in Scotland early in 1565 shortly after the former's rehabilitation. His marriage to Mary which took place on 29 July 1565 following the granting of a papal dispensation necessitated by the couple's propinquity was significant on two counts. Firstly, it endangered to some extent the Anglo-Scottish alliance and the previous diplomacy of MORAY (1531–70) and MAITLAND OF LETHINGTON (c.1525–73) since Elizabeth (1533–1603) looked unkindly on a partnership that seemed a further threat to her position. Secondly, it caused dissension among magnates such as Argyll (c.1538–73), Glencairn (d.1574), Rothes (d.1611) and particularly Moray himself, who observed their influence waning and, miscalculating the support they had among their colleagues, participated in the ill-starred CHASEABOUT RAID of August-September 1565. Darnley's subsequent involvement with Moray and his exiled companions, as well as all the other disaffected noblemen and lairds who participated in the assassination of RICCIO (c.1533–66) only served to underline his total inadequacy to share royal government with Mary. The exact circumstances of his own, predictable, death at Kirk o' Field, Edinburgh, on 10 February 1567 must remain an unsolved mystery.

Undoubtedly, many of the leading families in the country appear to have had a hand in the affair and, without accepting all the controversial evidence of the CASKET LETTERS, it is clear that the Queen herself had some foreknowledge of her husband's death. Equally certainly, Darnley's malignant influence had serious consequences for Mary's personal rule, confirming that her decision to marry him was one of the major mistakes of her career.

• *Bingham, C., Darnley: A History of Henry Stuart, Lord Darnley, Constable, 1995.*
• *Donaldson, G., Mary, Queen of Scots, English Universities Press, 1974.*
• *Fraser, A., Mary, Queen of Scots, Weidenfeld & Nicolson, 1969.*

Stewart, James Francis, the Old Pretender (1688—1766) The only son of JAMES VII (1633–1701) and his second wife, Mary of Modena (1658–1718). He was exiled to France with his family in 1688 and by the beginning of the eighteenth century had become the focus of the JACOBITE claims to the throne. In 1708 he was on board a French fleet cruising off the coast of Scotland but failed to set foot on Scottish soil. He did land at Peterhead in December 1715 but by that date the JACOBITE REBELLION was virtually over. In any case he was an unimpressive figure who did little to inspire enthusiasm among the supporters for his cause. On 4 February 1716 he departed for the Continent to spend most of the rest of his life in exile in Rome.

Stewart, James, Earl of Moray (1531—70) A natural son of JAMES V (1512–42) he attended St Andrews University in the 1540s, accompanied his half-sister, MARY (1542–87), to France in 1548 and was also one of the survivors of the delegation that negotiated her marriage in 1558. He became a Protestant in the mid-1550s joining the LORDS OF THE CONGREGATION

shortly after hostilities with Mary of Guise (1515–60) began in 1559. He was a signatory of the TREATY OF BERWICK in February 1560 and a prominent member of the provisional government before Mary's return to Scotland in 1561. She rewarded his services with the Earldom of Moray in 1562 a decision that helped to precipitate the Huntly rebellion in October of that year. He and Maitland (c.1525–73) were two of the key members of Mary's administration in the early years but her marriage to Henry STEWART, Lord Darnley (1546–67) ended the partnership. The damage done to Anglo-Scottish relations and the challenge to his personal authority persuaded Moray to engage in the ill-advised CHASEABOUT RAID in August 1565. Its failure resulted in his temporary exile in England but he was restored to favour by Mary after the RICCIO (c. 1533–66) murder when she astutely divided the opposition. Although present in November 1566 at Craigmillar Castle where the fate of Darnley was discussed he kept clear of the actual conspiracy. On Mary's abdication in June 1567, the king's party appointed him Regent for the infant JAMES VI (1566–1625) and he ultimately received belated recognition of his title by Elizabeth (1533–1603), following the enquiry into Mary's affairs held towards the end of 1568. The remainder of his regency was bedevilled by opposition from Mary's supporters, particularly the Gordon and Hamilton families, and it was a member of the latter, Hamilton of Bothwell Haugh (d.1580) who assassinated Moray at Linlithgow on 21 January 1570.

•*Lee, M. Jr., James Stewart, Earl of Moray, Columbia University Press, 1953.*

Stewart, Captain James, Earl of Arran (c.1545—96)

A son of Lord Ochiltree (c.1521—92) and a brother-in-law of John KNOX (c.1512—72) — his sister having become the reformer's second wife — he pursued a military career on the Continent until his return to Scotland in 1578. He soon became a member of the faction, led by Esmé STEWART (c.1542—83) opposing MORTON (c.1516—81), dramatically denouncing the ex-Regent before a meeting of the PRIVY COUNCIL on 31 December 1580. In 1581 he was elevated to the Earldom of Arran on the grounds of the insanity of James HAMILTON (1538—1609) and a tenuous claim through descent from a daughter of the first Earl of Arran (c.1477—1529). Although the RUTHVEN RAID led to his being imprisoned, this proved to be only a temporary setback and in 1583 he was restored to the Privy Council. By 1584 he had become chancellor and with MAITLAND OF THIRLESTANE (1543—95) was responsible for royal policy until his downfall a year later. Thus it was Arran's administration that passed the 'Black Acts' against MELVILLE (1545—1622) and the Presbyterians while it also laid the foundations for the league with England, ratified in 1586. His overthrow in November 1585 was a consequence of the political machinations of various enemies, in which Maitland and Patrick, Master of Gray (c.1588—1612), were among the most prominent, not to mention the tendency of JAMES VI (1566—1625) to believe all the gossip and rumours surrounding his former favourite. His death in 1596 was at the hands of a nephew of Morton's.

•*Fergusson, J., Sir, The Man behind Macbeth, Faber and Faber, 1969.*

Stewart, Matthew, fourth Earl of Lennox (1516—71)

In France during the 1530s, Matthew Stewart was persuaded to return to Scotland in 1543 by BEATON (1494—1546) who saw him as a useful counterweight to ARRAN (c.1516—75). His antecedents gave him a strong claim to the throne, especially as there was some doubt regarding the validity of the marriage of Arran's father. However, Lennox preferred to offer his services to England in return for strengthening his dynastic position by obtaining the permission of Henry VIII (1491—1547) to marry Margaret Douglas (1515—78), daughter of Margaret Tudor (1489—1541) and ANGUS (1489—1557). Thus he assisted the English with their ROUGH WOOING, being declared a traitor in 1545 by PARLIAMENT for his actions. He remained in England for twenty years before being rehabilitated by MARY (1542—87) shortly before his son, HENRY STEWART, Lord Darnley (1546—67), also came north. He was prominent on the Queen's side during the CHASEABOUT RAID in August-September 1565 but understandably deserted Mary after his son's murder in February 1567. He was unable to bring JAMES HEPBURN, fourth Earl of Bothwell (c.1535—78) to justice in 1567 but he fought against his former daughter-in-law at LANGSIDE in 1568 and later that year was a member of the prosecution at her 'trial' in England. Following the assassination of MORAY (1531—70) in January 1570 he eventually succeeded as Regent in July largely on the recommendation of Elizabeth (1533—1603). During his brief regency the CIVIL WAR between the government of JAMES VI (1566—1625) and Mary's followers proceeded in sporadic fashion. Lennox's main success was the capture of Dumbarton Castle in April 1571 and the execution of John HAMILTON, Archbishop of St Andrews (1512—71), one of his principal adversaries. His own death occurred on 3 September 1571 when he was mortally wounded at Stirling Castle in a skirmish with Marian opponents led by KIRKCALDY OF GRANGE (c. 1520—73).

Stewart, Patrick, Earl of Orkney (d.1615) He was the eldest surviving son of Robert Stewart (1533—93), one of the illegitimate offspring of JAMES V (1512—42), who had been given the Earldom of Orkney by JAMES VI (1566—1625) in 1581. There had been widespread criticism of Robert's administration of the Northern isles, especially during the Regency of MORTON (c.1516—81), and this was to be renewed even more vociferously under Patrick. The appointment in 1606 of James Law (c.1560—1632) to the vacant see of Orkney signalled a head-on clash between the unruly Earl and royal authority as represented by its upholder, the new bishop. By 1612 Patrick had lost much of his powers; the office of justiciar had been taken from him; Norse law, which he had used unscrupulously in his dealings with the islanders,

was abolished, he was forced to surrender his strongholds, notably his castle in Kirkwall, and he himself was incarcerated in Edinburgh Castle. An attempted rebellion on his behalf by one of his natural sons only served to worsen his plight and he was executed early in 1615.

• *Anderson, P., Black Patie: The Life and Times of Patrick Stewart, 1993.*
• *Donaldson, G., Shetland Life under Earl Patrick, Oliver & Boyd, 1958.*

Stewart, Robert, first Duke of Albany (1339—1420) The third son of ROBERT II (1371—90) by his first marriage to Elizabeth Mure, Robert Stewart was a major figure in Scottish affairs for nearly fifty years.

In the 1370s, in the early years of his father's reign, he helped to spearhead the territorial expansion of the Stewart family, becoming in this period the earl of Fife and Menteith as well as Constable of Stirling castle.

The accession of his brother John as ROBERT III (c.1337—1406) in 1390, a king variously described as 'decrepit' and 'infirm' saw an inevitable increase in his powers. Thus, he became duke of Albany in 1398 and, intermittently was GUARDIAN (1390—93) and Lieutenant (1402—6). The death in suspicious circumstances in 1402 of David, Duke of Rothesay, the heir to the throne only served to strengthen his position further. Meanwhile, in the interval before the accession of JAMES I (1394—1437) in 1406 Albany experienced difficulties both in the north of Scotland and the BORDERS. In the north, his nephew Donald, Lord of the Isles (d.1420) replaced his brother ALEXANDER, the Wolf of Badenoch (d.1406) as principal trouble-maker while in the south an unsuccessful foray against the English at Humbleton in September 1402 saw the capture of numerous Scottish nobleman including his son, Murdoch.

The seizure of James I in 1406, en route to France, meant that Albany assumed control of the country as Governor, a position he retained until his death in 1427. During these years apart from dealing with the heretical activities of John Resby who was burned at the stake in 1407, and reluctantly recognizing Martin V as pope of an united church in 1418, Albany was preoccupied, as before, with affairs in the far north and relations with England. The struggle with Donald, Lord of the Isles ended at Harlaw in 1411 and while the actual outcome of the battle is subject to some debate, Donald did at least submit to royal authority the following year at Lochgilphead. As for the Anglo-Scottish situation, Albany took advantage of Henry IV and Henry V's preoccupation with France to negotiate the return of several leading Scottish nobleman, among them his son, Murdoch. Significantly, however, James I remained an English prisoner.

Unquestionably an extremely powerful and ruthless figure, only the ultimate goal of the Scottish throne eluded Albany and his family.

• *Boardman, S., The Early Stewart Kings — Robert II and Robert III, Tuckwell Press, 1996.*

• *Nicholson, R., Scotland: The Later Middle Ages, Oliver & Boyd, 1974.*

Stewart, Walter, Earl of Atholl (c.1360—1437) Walter Stewart was the younger son of ROBERT II (1316–90) and Euphemia Ross. He actively supported Robert STEWART, duke of Albany (1339–1420) in his Highland campaigns in the 1390s and, following his appointment as earl of Caithness in 1401, he was allegedly closely involved in the death of ROBERT III's (c.1337–1406) son, David, at Falkland Palace in 1402. He became earl of Atholl in 1404 and later, on the return of JAMES I (1394–1437) from exile, earl of Strathearn in 1427. He was in charge of domestic agreements at Blackfriars, Perth on the evening of 21 Febuary 1437 when the increasingly unpopular James I was murdered. However, he lost out in the ensuing power struggle and, along with other leading regicides, including his grandson, the septuagenarian conspirator was executed on 26 March, 1437.

• *Nicholson, R., Scotland: The Later Middle Ages, Oliver & Boyd, 1974.*

Stirling Bridge, Battle of (11 September 1297) This was the first major confrontation in the WARS OF INDEPENDENCE. It took place below Stirling Castle on 11 September 1297 when the forces of Andrew MURRAY (d.1297) and William WALLACE (c.1270–1305) decisively defeated an English army commanded by the earl of Surrey.

This was a significant victory for 'the leaders of the army of the kingdom of Scotland' as Wallace and Moray subsequently described themselves in foreign correspondence, since it ended, if only temporarily, the English occupation of Scotland.

•*Barron, E., The Scottish War of Independence, 1934.*

Succession Acts As the name suggests, this series of acts influenced the line of succession from the Bruces through to the Stewarts. The first in 1315 designated Edward BRUCE, ROBERT I's brother, as heir in preference to his daughter, Marjory. The second, in 1318, following the deaths of both Edward and Marjory, designated Robert Stewart, Marjory's son, should the king himself not have issue. By the third in 1373, the succession to ROBERT II was restricted to his sons and their male heirs, excluding females. Later, when all legitimate male lines gave out MARY did succeed unchallenged following the death of her father, JAMES V in 1542.

Suffragettes, see INGLIS; REFORM ACTS

Symington, William (1763—1831) William Symington, who made a significant contribution to the development of steam navigation, was born at Leadhills, the son on an engineer in the nearby Wanlockhead leadmines. After attending the universities of Glasgow and Edinburgh, he abandoned his aim of entering the ministry and turned to ENGINEERING. In 1786 he experimented with an improved atmospheric engine driving a steam road carriage and soon after became involved in the Dalswinton steamboat project.

This was the brainchild of the energetic banker and inventor, Patrick Miller (1731—1815), who had previously undertaken a series of expensive and privately-funded experiments in ship design at Leith. It seems likely that James Taylor (1757—1825), tutor to the family at Dalswinton, suggested to Miller the advantages of trying out steam-power in place of manually-operated capstans to drive the paddle-wheels of the experimental craft.

As MacLeod points out, this was a co-operative venture, but the respective roles of the three men became a source of acrimonious debate after Miller's death, not least because of the rivalry between Symington, Taylor and another pioneer of steam navigation, Henry BELL (1767—1830) of *Comet* fame. The steamboat trials on Dalswinton Loch, near Dumfries, allegedly in the presence of Robert BURNS (1759—96), who lived nearby, took place in October 1788.

Miller then commissioned Symington to design and supervise the construction at CARRON Ironworks of a much larger engine, which was fitted in a 60-foot double-hulled boat with paddle wheels on the FORTH AND CLYDE CANAL in 1789. It proved a success, moving 'freely and without accident' at a speed of 6.5 mph. This experiment encouraged Symington to develop an engine giving direct drive to the paddle-wheels, which was patented in 1801. The second *Charlotte Dundas* (1803), a 58-foot long vessel with a single paddle-wheel at the stern and fitted out with this engine, was able to tow two sloops for eighteen miles along the Forth and Clyde Canal.

After the withdrawal of his patron, events somewhat overtook him with the launch of Robert Fulton's steamboat on the Hudson in 1807 and Henry Bell's *Comet* on the Clyde in 1812. Symington spent much of his later life as an engineer in Falkirk — before moving to London and dying there in relative obscurity in 1831.

•*Harvey, W.S. and Downs-Rose, E,G., William Symington: Inventor and Engine Builder, Northgate Publishing, 1980.*
•*MacLeod, I. and Neil, J., The Dalswinton Steamboat 1788—1988, T. C. Farries, 1988.*

T

tacksman   In the HIGHLAND context, the tacksman, from the Scots 'tack', meaning a tenure or lease, generally held a lease from the CLAN chief or landowner, subletting to tenants. At first he was essentially the middleman in a military organization, whose prime purpose was to fill the rent-roll with loyal tenants — perhaps relatives or kinsmen of the chief. While this remained important even in the late seventeeth century (and to some extent as late as the JACOBITE REBELLIONS of the 'Fifteen and the 'Forty-Five), it was the tacksman's organizational role within the estate economy that became paramount.

Each tacksman acted as the farmer of rents in his district and under this system large clan chiefs could gather rent from vast and often inaccessible estates. By leasing large segments to intermediaries in this way landowners delegated responsibility for collecting rent from the many small landholders that typified Highland estates. Many tacksmen made a handsome profit as farmers of rent — and much scorn and hatred from the tenants in the process.

The tacksmen played a prominent role in the CLEARANCES of the late eighteenth and early nineteenth centuries. While some exercised humanity in their dealings with the tenants, others were motivated by self-interest and worked in league with estate factors to evict the people.

taxation   Until the reign of JAMES VI (1566–1625) the Crown was normally expected to 'live off its own'. This meant that the income derived from such sources as the crown lands, customs, fines and escheats was supposed to provide enough to meet all the expenses of the royal household as well as all other outlays. The Comptroller was the official responsible for handling the former while the Treasurer took care of the latter. In special circumstances, such as royal marriages or the subjugation of an unruly area like the BORDERS, the Estates in PARLIAMENT would be asked to contribute to an extraordinary tax. In this event half the amount demanded was paid by the clergy, one-third by the nobility and one-sixth by the BURGHS.

Under James VI, who had serious financial problems, taxation came to be a more regular affair affecting a greater proportion of the population. Thus, after the UNION OF THE CROWNS, taxes spread over several years were requested in 1606, 1612, 1617 and again in 1621 with, latterly, an additional levy of 5 per cent placed on all annual rents. This trend continued under

CHARLES I (1600—49) so that by the outbreak of the first BISHOPS' WAR taxation was becoming a regular occurrence. Further important developments took place during the CROMWELLIAN UNION when not only an assessment on land values, eventually fixed at £6,000 a month, was introduced but an excise duty on beer and spirits, originally adopted during the English Civil War, was also collected. The RESTORATION witnessed the continuation of this Cromwellian policy. Thus the assessment or 'cess' as it became known was firmly established as the principle mode of direct taxation, COMMISSIONERS OF SUPPLY being specifically appointed in 1667 for the purpose of assessing the land tax. Likewise, the excise duty continued to be collected and with the customs was to remain the main form of indirect taxation. Apart from occasional additional expedients like poll taxes in the 1690s, the Scottish fiscal system continued to operate in this fashion until it was replaced under the terms of the Treaty of UNION (1707).
• *Dickinson, W.C. and Donaldson, G., A Source Book of Scottish History III, Nelson, 1961.*

Taylor, Dr John (1805—42)   Like the Rev. Patrick BREWSTER (1788—1859), John Taylor was a prominent leader of Scottish CHARTISM. Something of a romantic figure, he seems to have been greatly influenced by the movement's greatest propagandist, Feargus O'Connor (1796—1855). Born in Maybole, Ayrshire, in 1805, Taylor's early career is something of a mystery, though he served as a naval surgeon before becoming involved in

politics after 1830. He unsuccessfully contested a seat in the first parliamentary election following the REFORM ACT, and stood again as a Radical in 1834.

Taylor by this time had embraced both radical journalism and a wide variety of reform movements in the west of Scotland — including radical associations, OWENISM, TRADE UNIONS, the ANTI-CORN LAW LEAGUE, and, ultimately, Chartism itself. Taylor was a 'physical-force' Chartist who became well known for the violence of his oratory, but his career was cut short by poor health in 1840 and he died two years later in 1842.
• *Wilson, A., The Chartist Movement in Scotland, Manchester University Press, 1970.*

Telford, Thomas (1757—1834) Thomas Telford, the major engineer of the INDUSTRIAL REVOLUTION, was a man of prodigious energy and output in the construction of ROADS, bridges, CANALS and harbours throughout Britain and beyond. He had few rivals in his day, excepting perhaps John RENNIE (1761—1821), the other great civil engineering genius. Telford was born in Eskdale and attended the local school until, at the age of fifteen, he was apprenticed as a stonemason. The local landowner, the Duke of Buccleuch was improving the town of Langholm by adding a planned village, New Langholm, and the young Telford was employed building housing there. Like Hugh MILLER (1802—56) he apparently spent his leisure hours reading and writing poetry. During 1780—81 he found work as a journeyman mason constructing the NEW TOWN

OF EDINBURGH, and began to develop an interest in architecture and architectural drawing.

It seems likely that his next move, to London, was assisted by well-connected individuals in the trade for he was introduced to both Robert Adam (1728–92) and Sir William Chambers (1726–96). The latter was architect of Somerset House, which Telford helped to build, 1782–83. He also began to act as a consultant to William Pulteney (1729–1805), a wealthy landowner in Dumfriesshire and Northamptonshire, though he spent the years 1783–86 at Portsmouth Dockyard, superintending the erection of various buildings, including a chapel. He then went to Shrewsbury at Pulteney's behest, first as his architect, then, until 1792, as surveyor of public works locally.

The next decade changed the course of Telford's life and brought him a national reputation – not as an architect but as an engineer. He worked on the Ellesmere and the Shrewsbury Canals, the Severn navigation and London docks. In 1801 – again thanks to Pulteney – he was appointed engineer to the BRITISH FISHERIES SOCIETY and in 1802–3 reported on Highland Communications. When the government established Commissions for Highland Roads and Bridges and for the Caledonian Canal it was to Telford they turned. He designed and built numerous harbours and bridges throughout the HIGHLANDS, notably that at Craigellachie over the River Spey. The Caledonian Canal was begun in 1803, opened to traffic in 1822, but not completed until many years after his death. Telford

worked on many other roads including the Holyhead road and the Glasgow–Carlisle and Carlisle–Portpatrick turnpikes. The building programme in North Wales included the famous Menai Bridge, then the largest suspension bridge of its type, opened in 1826.

Telford was also responsible for the design of the Gotha Canal in Sweden, begun in 1809 and opened after many difficulties in 1832. Indeed his canal work continued to be important even on the eve of the Railway Age. His largest canal project was the Birmingham and Liverpool Junction, constructed between 1826 and 1835 and finished only six months after his death. Telford apparently had an ambivalent attitude to RAILWAYS which, like many contemporaries, he saw as mere extensions of canals. Significantly most of his canals survived the railway age – though his greatest monuments are perhaps his bridges, manifestations in stone and iron of Telford's engineering genius.

• Rolt, L.T.C., Thomas Telford, Penguin, 1985.

temperance High alcohol consumption was common to all classes of Scottish society by the eighteenth century. This was partly a function of social and work-related customs and partly of relatively low levels of taxation combined with lax supervision of retail outlets. Both BREWING and DISTILLING (legal or otherwise) grew dramatically in the late eighteenth and early nineteenth centuries and by 1829 spirit consumption alone was estimated at 5.7 million gallons. Investigators and the authorities not unnaturally related the twin problems of the poor and criminality to drunkenness.

The leading Scottish temperance pioneers were John Dunlop (1789–1869), a Greenock lawyer and philanthropist, and William Collins (1789–1853), a successful printer and publisher and an ardent admirer of Thomas CHALMERS (1780–1847). Dunlop's interest in temperance dated from 1828, when he visited France and was surprised to find morals apparently superior to those of Scotland. He immediately published pamphlets on the subject and launched the first Temperance Society in 1829. Dunlop was soon joined by Collins – a fanatical propagandist of temperance – who travelled widely delivering lectures and used his press to spread the gospel of temperance reformation through tracts and newspapers. The Glasgow City Mission (1826) played a leading role in the attack on intemperance in a city that became the focus of the Scottish temperance movement. Other groups active in the cause included the OWENITES, the CHARTISTS, and CO-OPERATORS – dedicated to moral as well as political and social reform.

While the main platform of the early temperance reformers was against spirits rather than what they described as 'nutritious' liquors, total abstinence or teetotalism was also seen as an important objective. One of the earlier supporters was the Rev. Patrick BREWSTER (1788–1859), the leading Paisley Chartist, who advocated parliamentary legislation to restrict licenses. The Scottish Temperance League was founded in 1844 and

by the 1850s most temperance reformers advocated legislation at a national level and restriction of licenses locally. The first breakthrough came with the Licensing (Scotland) Act – the Forbes Mackenzie Act – of 1853, which introduced Sunday closure and 11 p.m. weekday closing.

Regulation of the drink trade subsequently became a major political issue and temperance was embraced by both LIBERAL and LABOUR parties. Many pioneer Socialists, including Keir HARDIE (1856–1915), John MACLEAN (1879–1923), and Tom JOHNSTON (1881–1965), grew up in the temperance movement or its offshoots, the Band of Hope and the Good Templars. Additionally, there were several CATHOLIC Church organizations dedicated to the cause.

In 1913 the reforming Liberal government passed the Temperance (Scotland) Act, which made possible local veto polls on licensing. Around this time prohibitionist ideas found expression in the Scottish Prohibition Party (1901), whose leading activist, Edwin Scrymgeour (1866–1947), unseated Winston Churchill to become an MP for Dundee in 1922. The first local veto polls under the Temperance (Scotland) Act were held in 1920: several 'dry' areas resulted – but prohibition on American lines was firmly rejected.

Following the report of the Clayson Committee on the Scottish licensing laws (1973), the Licensing (Scotland) Act of 1976 extended opening hours and allowed Sunday and all-day opening. The temperance movement nevertheless remained active in the fight against alcohol abuse – historically a major cause of mortality throughout Scotland.

• *Donnachie, I., A History of the Brewing Industry in Scotland, John Donald, 1979.*
• *King, E., Scotland Sober and Free: The Temperance Movement 1829– 1979, Glasgow Museums & Art Galleries, 1979.*

Tennant, Charles (1768—1838)

Charles Tennant, a leading pioneer of the Scottish chemical industry, was born in Ochiltree, Ayrshire. After a local education he was apprenticed to the silk trade in Kilbarchan, Renfrewshire. He then switched to TEXTILE finishing and bleaching, setting up his own bleachfield near Paisley.

The rapid expansion of the textile industry brought about a search for new methods of bleaching, which received particular encouragement in Scotland from the BOARD OF TRUSTEES. The standard method, advocated by Francis Home's *Experiments in Bleaching*, published in Edinburgh in 1754, was the use of dilute sulphuric acid as a bleaching agent followed by exposure to natural sunlight on the bleachfield. In 1774 chlorine was discovered by the Swedish chemist Carl Wilhelm Scheele (1742–86) and in 1785 the French chemist Claude Louis Berthollet (1748–1822) found that it was a powerful bleaching agent. News of this breakthrough was relayed to James WATT (1736–1819) and others and by the late 1780s, several Scottish bleachworks, including Tennant's, had adopted chlorine bleaching.

In 1798 Tennant himself secured a patent for the production of liquid bleach made from chlorine and slaked lime – though court proceedings during 1802 indicate that the process was widely used. Tennant registered a second patent in 1799 for the production of bleaching powder that could be safely transported. His company set up its chemical works at St Rollox, Glasgow, to manufacture the product. Tennant became a prominent industrialist and in his later years was an active promoter of RAILWAY development in Glasgow and the west of Scotland.

• *Singer, C. (ed.), A History of Technology, Vol IV: The Industrial Revolution c.1750 to c.1850, Oxford University Press, 1958.*

Test Act (1681)

Although the Duke of Monmouth (1649–85), as successor to John Maitland, first duke of Lauderdale (1616–82), had adopted a conciliatory approach towards religious dissidence in the immediate aftermath of the defeat of the Covenanters in 1679, this was a short-lived policy. The illegitimate son of CHARLES II (1630–85) was soon replaced by James, Duke of York (later JAMES VII) (1633–1701), his brother and heir, who quickly reverted to repressive measures. Hence this misguided and ill-conceived statute. Its main articles, apart from insisting that all office holders in Church and State accept the obsolete Confession of Faith enshrined in the REFORMATION (1560), also stipulated acceptance of the royal supremacy over the Church as well as renunciation of all previous covenants and any support for change in civil or ecclesiastical government.

This legislation, while presumably directed against the CAMERONIANS, antagonized many others as well. While two notable opponents were Archibald CAMPBELL, ninth Earl of Argyll (1629–85) and Sir James Dalrymple of Stair (1619–95), many Presbyterians were unhappy about royal supremacy in Church affairs especially when it would subsequently be placed in the hands of the Catholic Duke of York. Over sixty ministers resigned rather than submit to an Act, which in southwest Scotland, at least, was enforced with considerable vigour by GRAHAM of Claverhouse (1648–89) and his forces.

• Cowan, I., The Scottish Covenanters, Weidenfeld & Nicolson, 1976.
• Dickinson, W.C. and Donaldson, G. (eds.), A Source Book of Scottish History III, Nelson, 1961.

textiles Historically textile manufacture was both long-established and of considerable economic importance in Scotland. The oldest activity by far was woollen cloth production, based on local wool resources and commonly pursued by craftsmen in the countryside and BURGHS, where guild organization prevailed among weavers. Attempts were made to expand and improve the industry at various times during the sixteenth and seventeenth centuries, but as was the case with LINEN, little real progress was made before the eighteenth century. Within the limits of what remained an essentially domestic system textiles expanded to the point where mechanization was necessary before a breakthrough could be made to mass-production in a factory system during the Industrial Revolution. For technical reasons this occurred first in COTTON, where spinning was mechanized in water-powered mills like those at NEW LANARK, built by the entrepreneur David DALE (1739–1806) in 1785. Cotton quickly became a mass-manufacture industry concentrated in Glasgow and the west of Scotland and was the lynch-pin of the economy 1780–1820. Linen was soon mechanized, and although more widely dispersed than cotton, was mainly found in the east of Scotland and around Paisley. Prior to the widespread introduction of the power loom after 1830 the textile industry relied to a large extent on a huge corps of handloom weavers – who later became among the first major casualties of industrialization. By 1850 the textile industry embraced wool, cotton, linen and JUTE, the last a peculiar specialism of Dundee and district. Most factories were by then steam-powered, but nevertheless the industry was widespread from Dumfries in the south to Elgin in the north. Subsequently, during the late nineteenth and early twentieth centuries, the Scottish textile industry shared the experience of that south of the Border – exposure to foreign competition and rising raw material costs being the main factors in a long-term decline. Scottish cotton and linen were overwhelmed by Lancashire and Ulster respectively and wool only survived a series of downturns in its fortune during and after the DEPRESSION by increased specialization on luxury products.

• Butt, J. and Ponting, K. (eds.), Scottish Textile History, Aberdeen University Press, 1987.

Thirds of Benefices   The First BOOK OF DISCIPLINE had intended that the post-REFORMATION Church should be endowed with most of the revenues of its unreformed predecessor. However, as this proved to both an unpopular and impracticable proposition, a compromise was adopted in 1562 by MARY (1542–87) and her PRIVY COUNCIL whereby all existing holders of benefices would lose one-third of their income. Thus all former members of the old Church would still retain two-thirds of their wealth while the remainder was to be shared between the State and the Kirk. To some extent this suited both sides; the bishops, realizing they would have to make some kind of contribution had previously suggested surrendering a quarter of their wealth and the financial problems of the reformers were at least now officially recognized by Mary's government. At the same time the arrangement was by no means an ideal one. Apart from the fact that the bulk of Church revenues still remained in the hands of the old ecclesiastical system and that numerous remissions of thirds were also granted, there was the vexed question of the proportion that the Kirk would obtain from the State. Even the granting in 1567 of first claim to the thirds and the right to appoint their own collectors made little difference to KNOX (c.1512–72) and his colleagues since they lacked the organizational ability and strength to make this concession effective. Thus it was not until MORTON (c.1516–81) became Regent in 1572 and the Crown resumed collection of the thirds that there was any financial improvement in the Kirk's position. Under Morton the thirds were more efficiently collected and administered so that the sum available for the stipends of the ministers steadily increased.

As more benefices were acquired by the Kirk during the second half of the sixteenth century the thirds assumed less importance although they were still being collected until the beginning of the next century.
• *Donaldson, G., The Scottish Reformation, Cambridge University Press, 1960.*

Thorfinn, Earl of Orkney (c.1009—c.1065)   Thorfinn is inevitably something of a mythical figure in that much that is known of him derives from the sagas. He was the eldest son of Sigurd, Earl of Orkney, and through his mother, was a grandson of KING MALCOLM II. He fought against his cousin, DUNCAN I, and possibly divided the kingdom with MACBETH. They defeated and killed Duncan. They evidently went to Rome together and on his return Thorfinn built a cathedral for his bishop at Birsay on Orkney. Two sons subsequently fought with Harold Hardrada, king of Norway, at the battle of Stamford Bridge in 1066. His daughter, Ingibjorg, married MALCOLM III.

tobacco   The development of the colonial tobacco trade, from which Scotland was excluded by the NAVIGATION ACTS before the Treaty of UNION, quickly made Glasgow and its satellite ports on the Firth of Clyde an entrepot of international standing. Much of its progress and wealth derived from the North American colonial tobacco trade, orchestrated by an entrepreneurial merchant community based in the city who became known as the 'Tobacco Lords'.

Despite the protestations of JAMES VI (1566–1625), the smoking habit and the taking of snuff both caught on and by the time the Scots were able to trade legally with Virginia and Maryland, tobacco was already big business. Glasgow was well situated from the point of view of collecting cargoes and the tobacco ships could take an increasing range of manufactures – notably linens and iron goods in return. Even acknowledging the existence of SMUGGLING, there was a spectacular increase in the trade. According to official figures imports rose from 15 million lbs in 1755 to 45 million lbs in 1775 – an increase of 300 per cent. Commercial success depended on re-exports, which consistently accounted for two-thirds of total imports, mainly to Europe.

Tobacco – like COTTON – was a plantation crop and many of the planters and their agents were Scots or of Scottish descent. Labour was provided by indentured servants and increasingly with the passage of time by Negro slaves imported from Africa – often via the West Indies where the Scots were also active in the sugar plantations. The 'Tobacco Lords' and planters were sometimes in partnership and several Glasgow merchants themselves owned plantations.

Although the AMERICAN WAR OF INDEPENDENCE brought about the collapse of the tobacco trade and it was never again so important to the Scottish economy, there is little evidence that the Glasgow merchant community sustained heavy losses. A combination of commercial expertise and foresight had prompted many to diversify into general trade or invest in agriculture and industry.

•*Devine, T.M., The Tobacco Lords: A Study of the Tobacco Merchants of Glasgow and their Trading Activities c.1740–90, John Donald, 1975.*

Toleration Act (1712) The leaders of the Kirk had reluctantly been converted to the Treaty of UNION when a guarantee of the security of the Presbyterian system was incorporated into that Treaty. However, the reintroduction of lay PATRONAGE and the passing of the Toleration Act in 1712, both as a result of party manoeuvrings at Westminster, were two serious setbacks. The latter legislation, permitting Episcopal clergy in Scotland to use the liturgy of the Church of England, was largely the work of TORIES in the House of Lords, such as Balmerino (1682–1736) who saw an opportunity for affecting religious change. The significance of the measure was twofold. Firstly, it caused dissension among the Scottish Episcopalians, many of whom did not want their church to be regarded as a mere appendage of the Anglican system, while the non-jurors, that is Episcopalians who would not recognize the REVOLUTION SETTLEMENT, were excluded altogether. Secondly, by authorizing worship not in accordance with the practice of the established Church, it infuriated the Presbyterians who regarded it as a flagrant breach of the Treaty of Union.

•*Drummond, A L. and Bulloch, J., The Scottish Church, 1688–1843, St Andrew Press, 1973.*

• *Ferguson, W., Scotland: 1689 to the Present, Oliver & Boyd, 1968.*

Tories Originally used in Ireland to describe a species of rural brigand, by the date of the REVOLUTION SETTLEMENT this term had become one applied to the most dedicated supporters of the traditional monarchy and the Episcopalian system. Hence its application on occasions to followers of the JACOBITE cause. However, by the early nineteenth century it had completely altered its meaning since it had become a term used by the WHIGS to describe upholders of the Tory ascendancy in Scotland such as the powerful Melville family. From the mid-nineteenth century it has been employed in a pejorative sense against the CONSERVATIVE PARTY or Unionist Party by their political opponents in Scotland and England.
• *Warner, G., The Scottish Tory Party, Weidenfeld and Nicolson, 1988.*

trade It is difficult, if not impossible, to assess the volume of trade in early Scotland, but internally it was probably quite extensive, and externally at least well established with northern Europe and Ireland by the early mediaeval period. The focii of internal trade were the BURGHS — indeed this was one of the main functions of these often modest urban centres. Each of the early burghs exercised some sphere of infleunce over local trade, its extent being a function of its own size and importance.

In the cases of larger centres like Edinburgh, Berwick, Stirling, Perth, Aberdeen, Ayr or Dumfries, which were also ports and invariably engaged in foreign trade or trade with Ireland, the resulting networks might be far wider, regional or even national, so far as this was possible given the primitive inland TRANSPORT system and modest tonnage of vessels that could be deployed either in limited coastal or more distant trade. Rules and regulations for trade were closely monitored by the burghs, which were dominated by merchnats and craftsmen.

The foreign trade of Scotland partly reflected prevailing relations with foreign powers, notably England, France, the Low Countries and the Baltic. This situation is seen in the letter (1297) addressed to the merchants in Lubeck and Hamburg by WALLACE and MURRAY, assuring them that Scotland, then 'recovered by war from the power of the English', was still open to trade. Flemish merchants settled in the east coast burghs, emphasising the importance of trade across the North Sea. The likelihood is that during much of the medieval period Scotland was a net importer of manufactures since INDUSTRY on any scale was very much undeveloped. Nevertheless the Scots established their own STAPLE port in Middleburg and later in Bruges, through which much of the trade in hides, leather, WOOL, SALT, and (later) LINEN and other commodities passed.
• *Reid, N.H. (ed.), Scotland in the Reign of Alexander III 1249—1286, John Donald, 1990.*
• *Simpson, G.G. (ed.), Scotland and the Low Countries 1124—1994, Tuckwell Press, 1994.*

trade unions From the late seventeenth century — although contrary to the common law of Scotland — labour organizations existed in various industries. These combinations of workers were designed partly for mutual protection against masters, and partly as friendly societies providing basic welfare benefits for members during lay-offs or in the event of death. A combination had as its prime functions safeguarding the trade against dilution (as guilds did for craftsmen in the BURGHS) and resisting reductions in wages. One major industrial group, the colliers, provides an excellent illustration of an early workers' combination, for organized strikes in the coal-mines were far from unusual as early as the 1700s. Colliers, like workers in the SALT industry, were supposedly bound to their masters more rigidly than other groups, but in reality did not regard themselves as part of an enslaved community.

Nevertheless, coalmasters and other employers could and did invoke the aid of the law and sometimes the military to enforce contracts with workers. Opposition from employers forced many labour organizations to assume the guise of friendly societies, sometimes called benefit societies or box clubs. Several hundred existed in Scotland throughout the eighteenth century. Most were local and often limited to a single occupation, for example the Journeymen Woolcombers Society of Aberdeen, founded in 1755, and the Fenwick Weavers' Society, which was an early example of the co-operative, dating from 1769. Many of the early friendly societies later developed into trade unions.

With the coming of the INDUSTRIAL REVOLUTION disputes between workmen and employers became more common, especially in the skilled trades. During the 1780s and 90s organized labour was closely identified with growing waves of RADICALISM — partly inspired by the ideas of the Scottish ENLIGHTENMENT, and partly by the events of the FRENCH REVOLUTION — in particular the Scottish FRIENDS OF THE PEOPLE and the UNITED SCOTSMEN. Several strikes occurred during this era — by Glasgow weavers in 1787, by seamen at Aberdeen in 1792, and by miners at Bo'ness in 1796 — all ruthlessly suppressed by the authorities.

This set the tone for the ensuing thirty years, although it is important to emphasize that the Combination Acts (1799–1800), drawn in English terms, did not strictly apply in Scotland. Nevertheless, the legal standing of combinations was weak, even after the repeal of the Acts in England in 1824 brought some easement. Under the common law of Scotland workers still had to contend with the restrictions of the Master & Servant Act (1823). This enforced contracts of employment between master and labour, invariably in favour of the former. In any case the authorities did not look favourably on any disorder within the workplace or otherwise.

Despite the restrictions and the vigilance of the authorities there was considerable trade union activity during this period, notably on the part of printers, cotton spinners, weavers and miners. The Edinburgh printers scored a historic judgement to have their wages fixed by law in the Court of

Session (1804), though the failure of masters to pay 'moderate and reasonable wages' led to a major strike of weavers eight years later in 1812 — centred in Glasgow and the west of Scotland. The strike lasted three months but when funds ran out it was broken and the union leadership charged with organizing an illegal combination. Ultimately, seven of their number were imprisoned and thereafter unions generally adopted a lower profile until the mid-1820s.

An upsurge in unionism accompanied the rise of the REFORM movement, the activities of the OWENITES, and CHARTISM during the 1830s and 1840s. Among the most militant and best organized were the cotton spinners and the miners — both groups being involved in further bitter strikes. Faced with a crisis in the cotton industry during 1836–37 employers forced down wages and introduced non-union labour to effect savings. This resulted in a violent three-month strike. Ultimately it was lost and the five leaders of the Glasgow Cotton Spinners' Union were tried and convicted of violence and sedition. Sentenced to transportation in 1838, they were pardoned after considerable public protest in 1840.

Although local issues dominated the affairs of most unions, the miners had the best organization and generated the most sustained industrial action of the period. An Ayrshire Colliers Union dated back to 1824 and other miners' unions existed elsewhere in Lanarkshire and Fife. A Miners' Association of Great Britain and Ireland was active in Scotland during the 1840s and the impetus was later main-tained against the harsh coalmasters of Lanarkshire and other colliery districts by Alexander MacDonald (1823–81), the prominent miners' leader and one of the first workingmen to enter Parliament in 1874. In the longer term — especially during times of economic prosperity — the miners made substantial gains. The Fife district won an Eight-Hour Day in 1870 and in 1873 MacDonald achieved something resembling a Scottish Federation.

Meantime, 'New Model' unionism on English lines — first seen in the formation of the Amalgamated Society of Engineers (1851) — began to make some impact on Scotland, particularly among skilled operatives like shipwrights, blacksmiths, carpenters and joiners. Trades councils, composed of trade union delegates, became increasingly effective and influential — illustrated best in the coordinating activities of those in Edinburgh (1853), Glasgow (1858), Dundee (1861) and Aberdeen (1868).

In the later Victorian era moves towards new unionism among other less skilled workers reflected developments south of the Border, the farm workers, railwaymen, dockers and carters proving especially active in Scotland. Trade unionism became increasingly associated with LABOUR politics — evidenced in the vigorous defence of the working man by James Keir HARDIE (1836–1915) and his associates during the 1870s and 80s. The 1890s saw several major strikes and lock-outs in Scotland, including those by railwaymen (1890–1), the miners (1894), and the engineers (1897). The Scottish Trades

Union Congress (STUC) was formed in 1897 and subsequently became an important platform for Scottish labour.

Increased militancy was a marked feature of Scottish trade unionism during the early part of the twentieth century — manifesting itself most dramatically in RED CLYDESIDE during and after WORLD WAR I and in the later GENERAL STRIKE of 1926. Politically, Scottish trade unionism swung to the left with the result that Communists came to play an important role in their affairs and leadership. This was especially true during the acute hardship of the depression in the 1930s, when the National Unemployed Workers' Movement was very active in Scotland.

In the post-WORLD WAR II period the climate of economic expansion in the 1950s and 60s brought both increased membership and major gains for the trade unions. Given Labour's hegemony in Scotland the larger unions and the STUC gained greater influence over public affairs and economic policy. During the 1970s, however, the onset of economic recession and the rundown of many of Scotland's older industries brought mixed fortunes for many trade unions. The movement was still able to command mass support of the kind seen over the closure of the Upper Clyde Shipbuilders in 1971 — though sadly it has been unable to prevent the decline of Scottish manufacturing industry.

• *Campbell, A., The Lanarkshire Miners: A Social History of their Trade Unions, 1775—1874, John Donald, 1979.*
• *Fraser, W.H., Conflict and Class:*

Scottish Workers 1700—1838, John Donald, 1988.
• *Gray, R.Q., The Labour Aristocracy in Victorian Edinburgh, Oxford University Press, 1976.*
• *MacDougall, I., Labour in Scotland: A Pictorial History from the Eighteenth Century to the Present, Mainstream, 1985.*

transport   Transport both by land and sea during the medieval period followed even older routes. Although the Roman roads and marching routes have been plotted in detail, knowledge of later landward routes is patchy. Those between the major BURGHS, which were estblished to encourage trade, castles, and religious foundations, were probably quite well defined, as was the route from England into Scotland via Berwick and Dunbar.

The places and dates of charters, signed, for example, by kings and members of the royal entourage, indicate considerable travel by horse and litter, by fairly well defined routes linking the main settlements. There were several important medieval bridges, such as those over the Tweed at Berwick, the Forth at Stirling, the Nith at Dumfries.

Most movement was probably by sea, hence the importance of coastal burghs and fortifications, or those that could be reached by water on the firths of Forth, Tay and Clyde. Queensferry was the most famous river crossing on the route linking Edinburgh and Dunfermline across the Firth of Forth, a journey made by many monarchs of the era, some to their cost.

Transport was historically significant in the early development of TRADE and INDUSTRY as well as the associated growth of burghs and URBANIZATION. In the sixteenth and seventeenth centuries internal transport was primitive, though most of the major centres were linked by some kind of road and bridges and ferries — many dating from the medieval era — facilitated the crossing of rivers and estuaries. On the Forth, for example, the ancient Stirling Bridge was the lowest bridging point, while passage across the wider estuary between Lothian and Fife was possible at Queensferry.

The first element in the Transport Revolution of the eighteenth century was the development after the JACOBITE RISINGS of military roads in the HIGHLANDS and SouthWest, followed by the construction, after 1760, of an extensive turnpike road network throughout the Lowlands. Secondly, during the early stages of the Industrial Revolution a modest but important series of canals were constructed to link industrial centres or develop coal-mining and iron production. In a limited way the CANALS also helped promote agricultural improvement by providing carriage for both fertilizers and produce. Thirdly, after the 1830s the RAILWAYS provided the most important mode of transport, facilitating rapid communication of goods and passengers throughout much of the country by 1850. Lastly, coastal shipping remained significant throughout, with steam shipping being pioneered on the Clyde in the early 1800s. Scottish engineers like John Loudon MCADAM (1756–1836), John RENNIE (1761–1821) and Thomas

TELFORD (1757–1834) made notable contributions to the Transport Revolution.

During the nineteenth century as the railways increased in importance, the canals and shipping declined. Road transport — though remaining locally important — also suffered badly from railway competition and it was not until the development of the internal combustion engine and the motor car that renewed investment occurred. In the longer term this affected the railways, which experienced a period of contraction — both during the depression and in the years following WORLD WAR II. Internal air transport — begun in the inter-war era — became increasingly important after 1945.

Turnberry   Turnberry Castle, on the Firth of Clyde, south of Ayr, was a stronghold of the Earls of Carrick and has important associations with the WARS OF INDEPENDENCE. In September 1286 supporters of Robert Bruce entered a bond upholding his claim to the crown following the death of ALEXANDER III. Bruce, ROBERT I, as he was to become, began his campaign against the English from Turnberry in 1307.

Turnpike Acts   The development of road transport during the eighteenth and early nineteenth centuries was facilitated by Turnpike Acts, which made it possible to raise additional capital for road construction by charging tolls. Under these Acts, turnpike trusts, generally composed of local gentry and merchants, were established to build and maintain roads and bridges, mainly in the Lowlands. The first Turnpike Act in Scotland, for the County of Edinburgh, was passed in 1713, and later between 1750 and 1844 nearly 350 acts relating to other parts of the country were obtained. The civil engineers John Loudon MCADAM (1756–1836), John RENNIE (1761––1821) and Thomas TELFORD (1757–1834) all worked for Scottish trusts. The problems of turnpike trust administration were perhaps less acute than in England, but nevertheless there were many small trusts responsible for short and unprofitable roads. Turnpikes were abolished in 1878 and responsibility for road building and construction was assumed by the county road trustees and thereafter passed to the county councils on the reorganization of local government in 1889.

Tweeddale, Marquis of, see HAY

U & V

Union Canal, see CANALS; GALT; RENNIE

Union of the Crowns (1603) The origins of the claim of JAMES VI (1566–1625) to the English Crown stemmed from his descent from the marriage of JAMES IV (1473–1513) and Margaret Tudor (1489–1541) in 1503. By the 1580s with Queen Elizabeth (1533–1603), the last surviving Tudor, still unmarried and childless, James was becomingly increasingly conscious of the fact that he might succeed her someday. In 1585–86, for instance, during the negotiations for an Anglo-Scottish alliance, the king, acting on the instructions of MAITLAND OF THIRLESTANE (1543–95) pressed unsuccessfully for public recognition of his claim. A decade later, James took a more positive step in his pursuit of the 'great prize' by firmly aligning himself with Robert Cecil, (1563–1612) a key figure on the Queen's council. This policy unquestionably paid off since by the time of Elizabeth's death in March 1603 there was general acceptance of James in English circles as the rightful heir to the throne. The king hurriedly departed for London in April returning only once, in 1617, to his native land. However, although the regal union of 1603 did not become a legislative and administrative one until just over a century later when the Treaty of UNION (1707) incorporated the two nations into a single state, the departure of James VI quickly affected the prestige of the Crown in Scotland. Thus the difficulties experienced by CHARLES I (1600–49) stemmed to a large extent from the determination of the nobles and others to challenge royal absolutism by their own ideas of popular sovereignty.

● *Dickinson, W.C. and Donaldson, G. (eds.), A Source Book of Scottish History III, Nelson, 1961.*
● *Willson, D.H., King James VI and I, Jonathan Cape, 1956.*

Union, Treaty of (1707) JAMES VI (1566–1625) on becoming joint sovereign had made an unsuccessful attempt at establishing closer links between the two countries. The CROMWELLIAN UNION, on the other hand, was an unpopular arrangement forcibly imposed on a reluctant Scottish population. WILLIAM III (1650–1702), as the seventeenth century ended, and his reputation in Scotland plummeted following the massacre of GLENCOE and the DARIEN disaster, had realized the only way to improve Anglo-Scottish relations was a more comprehensive partnership. However, it was to be the reign of ANNE (1665–1714) that, in 1707, was to witness a parliamentary union incorporating the two nations.

Anne inherited a situation where, by the death in 1700 of her only surviving son, succession to the throne had been vested through the Act of Settlement (1701) in the Electress Sophia of Hanover (1630– 1714), the granddaughter of James VI, and her issue. Unfortunately for the Queen there had been no similar legislation by the Scottish Parliament, which understandably felt disgruntled by the English statute and the lack of consultation over the matter. Since, from May 1702, England and France were ranged against each other in the War of the Spanish Succession (1702–13), with the French backing the exiled Stewarts, dynastic differences began to assume major importance. However, efforts by Anne and her government in 1702–3 to negotiate a union came to naught, the stumbling block being the unenthusiastic approach of the English commissioners. Thus discussions between them and the Scottish delegation led by the pro-union Duke of QUEENSBERRY (1662–1711) finally collapsed in January 1703.

Between 1703 and 1705 relations between Anne and the Scottish Parliament steadily deteriorated. This development took place despite a placatory gesture by the government, the Wine Act (1703), permitting Franco-Scottish trade in wartime. Accordingly, the ACT ANENT PEACE AND WAR (1703) stipulated that after Anne's death Parliament could take its own foreign policy decisions while the ACT OF SECURITY (1704) left the question of succession unresolved.

The English Parliament retaliated in February 1705 with the Alien Act. By its main terms the Act of Security must be repealed and if the Hanoverian succession was not accepted or steps had not been taken towards union by Christmas 1705, Anglo-Scottish trade would be suspended. Although the outcome of the WORCESTER AFFAIR (1705) indicates that the initial Scottish response was one of angry defiance, the threat of economic warfare was clearly a powerful factor in changing this stance. Consequently, Parliament, which reassembled in July with John CAMPBELL, second Duke of Argyll (1678–1743) as its new commissioner, had agreed by September to the holding of discussions with England. In other words, the anglophile Court Party led by magnates like MAR (1675–1732) and Seafield (1664–1730) and supported after a fashion by TWEEDDALE (1645–1713) and his vacillating New Party (aptly named the 'squadrone volante') were able to have their proposal for negotiations on an Anglo-Scottish treaty accepted by Parliament.

Furthermore, the possibility of a successful outcome to these discussions was greatly enhanced when HAMILTON (1658–1712), supposedly the leader of the opposition, the Country Party, suggested, for reasons best known to himself that the Queen should nominate the Scottish commissioners. A suspiciously sparsely attended session quickly voted in favour of this recommendation.

By July 1706 the two sides had agreed to the terms of the treaty. The principal features included Scottish acceptance of the Hanoverian succession; the amalgamation of the two parliaments with Scotland's representation reduced from 157 members to 45 plus 16 elected peers in the Lords, although the fate of the PRIVY COUNCIL was postponed until the united parliament reached a decision; complete freedom of trade between both nations and Scottish access to the English colonial empire; standardization of the CURRENCY, WEIGHTS AND MEASURES; £398,000, the so-called 'Equivalent' to be paid by England partly as arrears of salary for office holders and as compensation both for losses incurred in the Darien affair and for Scotland's future funding of the English national debt; the Scottish legal system to remain unaltered.

Between 4 November 1706 and 16 January 1707 all twenty-five articles in the treaty were passed by the Scottish Parliament. The only significant concession was the Act guaranteeing the position of the CHURCH OF SCOTLAND, which had proved necessary if the influential opposition of the Kirk was to be stifled. The Scottish PARLIAMENT was dissolved for the last time on 25 April and the Act of Union came into force in both countries from 1 May 1707.

The question still remains why the Scottish estates surrendered their independence. Clearly economic considerations, the benefits, for instance, which it was hoped would be forthcoming to the cattle trade, the fishing and linen industries as a result of freedom of trade and extended markets played a substantial part in determining the members' actions. Certainly energetic English government pamphleteers like Daniel Defoe

(c.1661–1731) laid great emphasis on such commercial advantages. The Alien Act, moreover, with its threat of economic sanctions was a salutary deterrent to those who might favour an alternative course.

At the same time the English authorities and their principal agents in Scotland, Mar and Seafield, exercised all their considerable talents in 'management' to win the support of a majority of the nobility. Some of these inducements are patently transparent – Argyll obtained an earldom for his brother, Archibald (1682–1761), and had himself promoted to field marshal in Marlborough's (1650–1722) army – but others are less obvious. Unquestionably £20,000 was sent by an anxious government at Westminster, but with the exception of Queensberry, who apparently received £12,000 for arrears owing to him while he was commissioner, exactly how the remainder was distributed is impossible to disentangle. Indubitably anyone who wished to be the recipient of this largesse would have to support the union cause in Parliament. Nor was this the only financial incentive since the Equivalent with its promised guarantee of payment of outstanding salaries and compensation for debts incurred over the Darian fiasco was yet another.

Finally, the divisions and disagreements within the opposition made the task of the Court Party all that much easier. The Country Party, in fact, lacked any cohesion whatsoever and was merely a disparate collection of frustrated place-seeking noblemen, Jacobites, Presbyterians, Episcopalians, discontented Darien investors, and a small sprinkling of radical Parliamentarians like the celebrated FLETCHER of Saltoun (1653–1716). Compensating or conciliating a suitable proportion of these countrymen posed little problem to Mar or his lieutenants. Once this had been done there were no serious obstacles to prevent the union so eagerly sought by the English government and its Scottish sympathizers.

• *Dickinson, W.C. and Donaldson, G., eds., A Source Book of Scottish History III, Nelson, 1961.*

• *Ferguson, W., Scotland: 1689 to the Present, Oliver & Boyd, 1968.*

• *Feguson, W., Scotland's Relations with England, John Donald, 1977.*

• *Riley, P.W.J., The Union of England and Scotland, Manchester University Press, 1978.*

• *Smout, T.C., Scottish Trade on the Eve of Union, Oliver & Boyd, 1963.*

• *Whatley, C.A., 'Bought and Sold for English Gold': Explaining the Union of 1707, Economic and Social History Society of Scotland, 1994.*

United Scotsmen Following the suppression of the FRIENDS OF THE PEOPLE (1793–94) the United Scotsmen, a secret society on the model of the contemporaneous United Irishmen, was formed in 1796–97. They advocated not only universal suffrage and annual parliaments, but also maintaining contact with French and Irish revolutionaries. The United Scotsmen apparently commanded strong working-class support in weaving districts around Glasgow, Paisley, Dunfermline and elsewhere – but after the arrest and conviction in 1798 of their principal leader, George MEALMAKER (1768–1808), a Dundee weaver who had earlier been active in the Friends of the People, the movement was banned in 1799 and crumbled away to nothing by 1802. Mealmaker is often regarded as one of the 'SCOTTISH MARTYRS', for like Thomas MUIR (1765–99) and his companions, he was ultimately transported to the convict colony in New South Wales. By the time he arrived, however, both GERRALD (1760–96) and SKIRVING (1796) had died, and Muir had made his escape to die in France in 1799.

United States of America, see AMERICAN WAR OF INDEPENDENCE; CARNEGIE; CLEARANCES; COTTON; NAVIGATION ACTS; SMUGGLING; TOBACCO; WORLD WAR II

universities The earliest Scottish university was formally established at St Andrews in 1412. It had the support of Bishop Henry Wardlaw, confirmed by papal bull of 1413. It was seen as a means of preventing Scottish students being contaminated by the heresies they might have picked up at English or European universities. Glasgow University was founded in 1451 by Bishop William Turnbull and after a difficult period, was re-established in 1577. King's College, Aberdeen, was founded in 1495 by papal bull granted on a petition of JAMES IV, and subsequently confirmed in its status by William Elphinstone, Bishop of Aberdeen in 1505. Marischal College was founded in 1593, eventually uniting with King's College in 1860. Edinburgh University pre-dated Marischal by decade, having been established in 1582 and begun teaching 1583. For later developments see under EDUCATION.

Upper Clyde Shipbuilders, see SHIPBUILDING; TRADE UNIONS

urbanization From the early creation of BURGHS as market centres in the twelfth century urbanization has figured prominently in Scottish POPULATION history. By the sixteenth century burghs had greatly increased in number and were growing — though the majority were still small by the standards of other European towns and cities. Some of this expansion could be attributed to the REFORMATION, which released large areas of former church land in and around the older burghs.

Various seventeenth century POLL TAX returns and HEARTH TAX returns suggest that there were three tiers in the hierarchy of urban centres: first, the largest burghs headed by Edinburgh, Aberdeen, Glasgow, Dundee, Perth and St Andrews; second, a middle rank of ten or so including Stirling, Ayr, Dumfries, Haddington and Inverness; and last, many small burghs like Culross on the Firth of Forth — an early industrial centre based on COAL and SALT manufacture. Estimates of population are difficult — possibly 30,000 for Edinburgh in 1690, compared with London's 400,000 around the same time.

Towns grew rapidly during the INDUSTRIAL REVOLUTION and thereafter urban growth remained a significant social and economic factor, especially in the Lowlands. There was a notable change in the rank order of the larger towns and cities for the industrial centres like Glasgow, Dundee and Paisley (among others) expanded rapidly during the late eighteenth and early nineteenth centuries. This is not to deny the growth of towns and villages everywhere — a clear function of economic development — in AGRICULTURE as well as INDUSTRY. The numerous PLANNED VILLAGES — though less grand than Edinburgh's classical NEW TOWN — were an interesting exercise in urban development during this era.

Glasgow provides a useful case-study in urban, industrial growth — with many of its associated social problems of overcrowding, poverty and disease. During the Industrial Revolution the city grew rapidly: its population trebled between 1755 and 1801 (from 23,000 to 77,000); and trebled again in the three subsequent decades to 1831 (202,000 at the census of that year). Later expansion was just as dramatic, with a massive influx by MIGRATION from Ireland after the 1840s, so that Glasgow ultimately became the Second City of the Empire and one of the great nineteenth-century international urban centres.

Edinburgh's earlier experience had created the elegant Georgian New Town away from the squalor of the Old Town's ancient tenements. To the existing city and the neighbouring port of Leith more was added, mainly during the late nineteenth-century building boom. There were some interesting exercises in working-class co-operative housing, but the most striking legacy of this era are the ordered tenement suburbs that make the city seem as much a Victorian creation as a Georgian one.

A third city, Dundee, was in some senses a microcosm of the Glasgow experience with its juxtaposition of jute mills, overcrowded tenement housing and elegant middle-class suburbs by the banks of the Tay. In many ways nineteenth-century Dundee was a telling indictment of industrial capitalism at its worst — and a manifestation of the acute social problems urbanization brought in its wake.

The twentieth century saw the relative decline of many small, rural communities (especially beyond the Central Lowlands) — partly this was a function of migration to the larger towns and cities. Suburban growth and the establishment of New Towns became major exercises in planning to tackle the problems of congestion and slum clearance in the older urban centres.

• *Adams, I., The Making of Urban Scotland, Croom Helm, 1978.*
• *Devine, T.M. and Jackson, G. (ed.), Glasgow: Beginnings to 1830, Manchester University Press, 1995.*
• *Gordon, G. and Dicks, B., Scottish Urban History, Aberdeen University Press, 1983.*

Veere or Campvere, see STAPLE

Vikings   Scandanavian influences, social, economic and cultural were of great significance, especially in the Northern and Western ISLES. On the mainland Norse influence was exercised at different times in Caithness, Sutherland, Ross, Skye, Argyll, and along the west coast as far south as Galloway. There was also a substantial and longer-term presence on the Isle of Man. Temporary or permanent MIGRATION across the North Sea was partly the result of rapid POPULATION growth or over-population on the west coast of Norway. Three types of activity in the traditional long boats and often accompanied by violence, charcterize Viking movement: pirate raids on coastal areas; TRADING activities, often extending beyond Scotland and as far as the Mediterranean; overseas settlement, concentrated in the north and west. Many of the leaders of these expeditions, which began in the late eighth century, picking up momentum in the nineth, seem to have been exiles, forced to leave their kin group, possibly banished for offences, or minor branches unlikely to inherit or head a kin group at home. A typical Viking raid, on Iona in 806, was said to have resulted in the massacre of 68 monks and other inhabitants. From the viewpoint of existing society, the influence of Viking activity, raids and then settlement, may well have been of deterioration. In some situations it prevented the further growth of Celtic society. Certainly in Orkney and Shetland it absorbed existing society and culture. In many areas presistent raids hindered trade and prevented the growth of large centres of Celtic culture and religion, especially in the danger areas. Norse society and culture were established firmly in the Northern Isles and there as everywhere in the British Isles was ultimately converted to Christianity. St MAGNUS left the most enduring legacy in Orkney. Much of the Viking story is documented in the numerous contemporary sagas or in the early medieval chronicles. The Battle of LARGS in 1263 saw the final defeat and suppression of all Norse influnce on mainland Scotland, but both Orkney and Shetland remained bastions of Scandanavian influence and rule even after the earldom of Orkney passed to a succession of Scottish earls, beginning in the thirteenth century. However, the Norse earls had begun to inter-marry with Scots nobility and royalty in the late tenth and early eleventh centruries, THORFINN being a famous instance.

•*Ritchie, A., Viking Scotland, Batsford, 1993.*

W & Y

Wade, Field Marshal George (1673—1748) Born in Ireland, Wade served extensively in the Iberian Peninsula during the War of the Spanish Succession (1702—13), eventually reaching the rank of major-general. In 1724, as part of a governmental plan to promote economic growth and also police the Highlands, he was appointed commander-in-chief of military forces in Scotland. Although his first action was to suppress the SHAWFIELD RIOTS (1725) he was soon engaged in the work for which he is best known, an extensive road building operation in the HIGHLANDS. Thus, between 1726 and 1738, assisted by troops who included the REGIMENTS that were to form the Black Watch in 1739, Wade supervised the construction of approximately 250 miles of roads and numerous bridges. While the most celebrated of the latter is the Tay Bridge at Aberfeldy, his principal roads were those along the Great Glen, from Fort Augustus to Inverness and from Dunkeld to Inverness by the route largely followed by the present A9. However, his most spectacular effort, the road from Fort Augustus over the Corrieyairach Pass, has long since been abandoned. Indeed, Wade's roads and those of his successor Caulfield (d.1767) did little to benefit the economy of the Highlands as they were essentially designed as a means of military communication. Ironically, the Jacobites were to use them to good effect in 1745, by which date Wade, now a field marshal, was commander-in-chief in England. His outmanoeuvring by the Highlanders led to his dismissal and the appointment as his replacement of Cumberland (1721—65).

• *Salmond, J.B., Wade in Scotland, Moray Press, 1938.*

wagonways, see RAILWAYS

Wallace, Sir William (c.1270—1305) The second son of Sir Malcolm Wallace of Elderslie (Renfrewshire), William Wallace rose to prominence in 1297 as a leading opponent of the English regime occupying Scotland on behalf of Edward I. Involved earlier that year in an incident at Lanark which saw the English sheriff slain, he was active throughout 1297 in the early stages of the WARS OF INDEPENDENCE. By August he had established links with another resistance movement operating in the north of Scotland commanded by SIR ANDREW MURRAY (d.1297), a powerful figure, heir to extensive territory in Invernesshire and elsewhere. On 11 September 1297 a joint force of Murray's and Wallace's routed an English army led by the Earl of Surrey at the battle of STIRLING BRIDGE and temporarily ended English control of Scotland. Moray died later of his wounds but Wallace was knighted and proclaimed sole GUARDIAN of the kingdom.

His triumph was short-lived since the following year on 22 July 1298, Edward I comprehensively defeated him at the battle of Falkirk. Wallace was briefly active in the next stage of the Wars of Independence in 1304 but had little success before being taking prisoner near Glasgow on 3 August 1305. He was handed over to Edward I by Sir John Menteith (d.1329) and, following a trial at Westminster was hung, drawn and quartered.

Wallace may have acted as a figurehead for the stratagems of others, for example, Robert Wishart, bishop of Glasgow (d.1316) but, nonetheless he deserves credit for inspiring patriotic resistance to English domination and he has remained an icon of the nationalist movement in Scotland.

• *Barrow, G.W.S., Robert Bruce and the Community of the Realm of Scotland, Edinburgh University Press, 1988.*
• *Nicholson, R., Scotland: The Later Middle Ages, Oliver & Boyd,1974.*
• *Watson, F., Under the Hammer: Edward I and Scotland, 1286—1307, Tuckwell Press, 1998.*

Wars of Independence (1296—1328) Arguably the War or Wars of Independence lasted from 1296 to 1424. Nonetheless the signing of the Treaty of EDINBURGH on 17 March 1328 (followed by its subsequent ratification at Northampton) unquestionably was a crucial date in Scotland's struggle to achieve freedom. Therefore, it is worth noting that under the terms of that agreement, Edward III's government conceded that Scotland 'was separate in all things from the kingdom of England and assured forever of its territorial integrity.'

Chronologically, the main stages in the War of Independence were as follows :

1296: Edward I and his army sacked BERWICK, defeated a Scottish force at DUNBAR and conquered the eastern half of the country as far as Elgin.

1297: Risings led by William WALLACE and Andrew MURRAY end in victory over English at the battle of STIRLING BRIDGE.

1298: Wallace defeated at FALKIRK but Edward unable to take advantage because of commitments in France.

1303: Successful English invasion by Edward I.

1304: End of effective Scottish resistance with English capture of Stirling Castle.

1305: Capture and execution of Wallace.

1306: ROBERT Bruce murders John COMYN; Robert crowned king but is defeated at the battles of Methven and Dalry.

1307: Minor victories for Bruce at battles of Glen Trool and Loudon.

1308: Comyns and others defeated at Inverurie and the Pass of Brander.

1309—13: Main English garrisons in Scotland slowly recaptured by Bruce and his supporters.

1314: Battle of BANNOCKBURN; Berwick the only stronghold in English hands.

1315—18: 'Second Front' opened in Ireland by the king's brother BRUCE (c.1276—1318).

1318: Berwick retaken from the English.

1319—21: Anglo-Scottish Truce.

1320: Declaration of ARBROATH.

1323—27: Second Anglo-Scottish Truce.

1328: Treaty of Edinburgh — Northampton.

• *Barron, E.M., The Scottish War of Independence, 1934.*

• *Barrow, C.W.S., Robert Bruce and the Community of the Realm of Scotland, Edinburgh University Press, 1988.*

• *Cameron, S., The Scottish Wars of Independence, Dunedin Multimedia, 1999.*

• *McNamee, C., The Wars of the Bruces, 1306—28, 1997.*

• *Nicholson, R., Scotland: The Later Middle Ages, Oliver & Boyd, 1974.*

• *Watson, F., Under the Hammer: Edward I and Scotland, 1286—1307, Tuckwell Press, 1998.*

Watson-Watt Sir Robert (1892—1973) Robert Watson-Watt was born in Brechin, Angus and educated at Brechin High School and University College, Dundee. During WORLD WAR I he was a meteorologist attached to the Royal Aircraft Factory at Farnborough, his knowledge of radio waves being utilized to provide weather forecasts for the Royal Flying Corps. After the war he was a member of the Department of Science and Industrial Research before the National Physics Laboratory as its Superintendent in 1933.

In 1935 Sir Henry Tizard, recently put in charge of the committee responsible for Britain's air defences, asked Watson-Watt and his colleagues to evaluate the feasibility of devising a 'death ray' that would destroy enemy aircraft.

Watson-Watt's reply was to recommend instead the introduction of a system of radio direction and ranging ('radar'), whereby enemy planes could be detected by the radio wave reflections they emitted. By late 1935 the first radar station was in operation and in 1936 Watson-Watt was appointed head of radar research.

Between 1936 and the outbreak of WORLD WAR II a chain of radar stations, mainly along the east and south coast of England, was built under Watson-Watt's direction. Much of the research was undertaken at Bawdsey Research Station near Felixstowe but some of it was carried out at Dundee, particularly the experiments on radar detection at night. As a result, by the time of the Battle of Britain the Royal Air Force could detect German aircraft as easily in the dark as in the daylight.

For his services in the development of Britain's early warning system Watson-Watt was deservedly knighted in 1942, while his own account of his achievements *Three Steps to Victory* was published in 1957.

• *Brown, R.W., (ed.), Radar Development to 1945, London, 1988.*

Watt, James (1736—1819) James Watt, a famous son of the Scottish ENLIGHTENMENT, who through his development of the steam-engine contributed substantially to the INDUSTRIAL REVOLUTION, was born in Greenock in 1736. His father was a versatile merchant-cum-mathematical instrument maker and after schooling at the local grammar school Watt worked initially in his workshop before being sent to Glasgow then London for further training.

By 1757 he had returned to Glasgow, where the friendship of Andrew Anderson, brother of John Anderson (1726–96), Professor of Natural Philosophy, helped him to secure an appointment as mathematical instrument maker in the university. There he was encouraged in his experiments on the steam-engine by Joseph BLACK (1728–99), beginning with the repair of a model Newcomen engine in 1764. Watt realized that the loss of latent heat was the worst defect of the Newcomen engine and that condensation must be effected in a separate chamber – hence the separate condenser – invented in 1765. In 1768 a small test engine was built in partnership with John Roebuck of CARRON Ironworks and the following year Watt patented his invention. Further development of the steam-engine was delayed because Watt spent much of the period 1766–74 earning his living as a land surveyor, including advising on the routes of several Scottish canals.

In 1768 Watt had been introduced to Matthew Boulton (1728–1809), the Birmingham engineer who became his partner in the further exploitation of the steam-engine after 1775. Watt moved to Birmingham and thereafter rapid progress was made on technical improvements to the steam-engine. Watt himself spent long spells in Cornwall supervising the erection of steam pumping-engines in copper and tin mines. A number of important inventions followed: rotary motion, achieved by the sun-and-planet gear (1781); the double-acting engine (1782); parallel motion (1784); the centrifugal governor (1788), to control the speed of the engine; and the pressure gauge (1790).

Watt's patent had been extended by Parliament in 1775 with the result that Boulton and Watt had virtually sole rights for twenty-five years and became wealthy men. They were elected to Fellowships of the Royal Society in 1785 and Watt was also an eminent member of the Lunar Society in Birmingham. He bought an estate in Radnorshire where he spent most of the time after his retirement in 1800. Watt was honoured by his former employers, Glasgow University, who made him a Doctor of Law in 1806, and by the French Academy of Sciences, when in 1816 he became a foreign associate.

Watt's inventions quickened the pace of industrialization, not only as it affected major industries like COAL, IRON, ENGINEERING and TEXTILES, but also influenced the development of new modes of transport in steam navigation and the railways.

• Robinson, E. and Musson, A.E., *James Watt and the Steam Revolution, Adams & Dart, 1969.*

• Rolt, L.T.C., *James Watt, Batsford, 1962.*

Watt, Robert (?—1794) Watt is a shadowy figure associated with a revolutionary conspiracy hatched in Edinburgh after the demise of the Scottish FRIENDS OF THE PEOPLE and the later sedition trails of 1793–94. Watt had attended meetings of radical societies – including the Friends of the People – and apparently acted as a government informer until his services were dispensed with in 1793. Perhaps for this reason he continued to associate with a small underground group, which drew delegates from various surviving societies. Its Committee of Ways and Means, under Watt's direction, planned an armed insurrection in the spring of 1794. Troops were to be won over, the workers mobilized in support, Edinburgh Castle, the post office, and banks seized, and a provisional government proclaimed. Similar plans had allegedly been drawn up for London and Dublin. The plot was soon discovered. Watt and an associate, David Downie, were tried for treason in August 1794 and ultimately sentenced to death. Others arrested turned king's evidence and were pardoned, Downie was reprieved, but Watt was executed for his part in the plot in October 1794.

Webster, Rev. Dr Alexander (1707—84) Webster, the son of the minister of Edinburgh Tolbooth Kirk, became a minister himself — first at Culross and thereafter at his father's old charge. His strong support of the Hanoverian cause during the JACOBITE REBELLION of 1745—46 made him an establishment figure. Webster was a popular evangelical preacher and also associated with many of the intellectuals of the ENLIGHTENMENT era in Edinburgh.

He shares joint responsibility with a colleague, the Rev. Dr Robert Wallace (1697—1771) — himself something of a statistician — for the compilation in 1755 of the first unofficial census of Scotland. He involved the Society in Scotland for the Propagation of Christian Knowledge in the Highlands and Islands in his scheme, threatening to withdraw charity schools if the clergy did not co-operate. He was also uniquely placed to pressurize ministers elsewhere to comply with his queries: he was acting on behalf of the government; he was then Moderator of the General Assembly of the Church of Scotland; and he was associated with a scheme for the provision of annuities for widows and children of the clergy. According to the census the total population of Scotland in 1755 was 1,265,380 persons.

Webster's later interests included the planning of the NEW TOWN OF EDINBURGH, the problems of the HIGHLANDS and POOR RELIEF. He was a typical Scottish Enlightenment figure in his practical application of both theology and the new 'social sciences'.
•*Kyd, J.G., Scottish Population Statistics, Scottish History Society, 1952.*

weights and measures These were complex with different BURGHS, such as Edinburgh, Stirling, Lanark and Linlithgow originating what became standard weights, capacities (liquid and dry), linear and square measures. Over the centuries these gradually became standardized. Despite various attempts by PARLIAMENT to disentangle the extremely confusing systems throughout Scotland, it was not until the Restoration that a serious attack on the problem was undertaken. Thus, in 1661, a parliamentary commission proposed the introduction of national standards with certain burghs having custody of particular weights or measures. Accordingly, Edinburgh would keep the ell for linear measure, Linlithgow the firlot for dry measure, Lanark the troy stone for weight and Stirling the jug for liquid capacity.

The Treaty of UNION should have brought standardization throughout the United Kingdom but in reality it was not until the nineteenth century, by an Act of 1824, that uniformity was statutorily established and gradually conformed to.
• Robinson, M., A Concise Scottish Dictionary, Aberdeen University Press, 1985.

Westminster Assembly At the same time in 1643 as the negotiations for the SOLEMN LEAGUE AND COVENANT were being conducted, an invitation was sent in June by the English Parliamentarians inviting a Scottish delegation to participate in a conference at Westminster for the reform of the Anglican Church. In August the GENERAL ASSEMBLY accepted the offer and appointed five ministers and three elders as delegates. Accordingly, the clergy were represented by Robert Baillie (1602–62), Robert Douglas (1594–1674), George Gillespie (1613–48), Alexander HENDERSON (1583–1646) and Samuel Rutherford (c.1606–61) and the elders by the Earl of Cassillis (c.1595–1668), Lord Maitland (1616–82) and Archibald JOHNSTON of Wariston (1611–63). While the Scottish commissioners were unhappy not only with their role as observers but also with the religious divisions prevalent among the English members, their attendance had considerable significance. Thus, the subsequent Westminster Confession, approved by the General Assembly in February 1645 became thereafter the religious foundation of the CHURCH OF SCOTLAND. Its Confession of Faith, with its roots firmly embedded in Calvinist doctrine, its catechisms, its Form of Church Government and its Directory of Public Worship have remained essential features of the Scottish Presbyterian Church until the present day.
• Dickinson, W.C. and Donaldson, G., A Source Book of Scottish History III, Nelson, 1961.
• Makey, W., The Church of the Covenant, John Donald, 1979.

Westminster Confession, see WESTMINSTER ASSEMBLY

Westminster-Ardtornish, Treaty of (1462) During the minority of JAMES III, the ISLES remained a source of trouble, weakening the crown and making government difficult. Worse still, the kingdom itself was threatened when John, LORD OF THE ISLES, and his son, Donald, joined forces with the forfeited and exiled James, Earl of Douglas, to sign a treaty with Edward IV. Under its provisions all three became effective pensioners of the king of England on the understanding that if England successfully invaded Scotland the territories north of the Forth would be divided between them. The treaty was signed in London on 13 February and later ratified by Edward at Westminster, 17 March. Ardtornish Castle in Morvern was one of the Lord of the Isles's principal fortresses.

Wheatley, John (1869–1930) John Wheatley, the most formidable physically and intellectually of the RED CLYDESIDERS, was Catholic

Irish, born in County Waterford, where his father was a labourer. When Wheatley was nine, the family — like so many others — migrated to the Lanarkshire coalfield, where his father found work as a miner at Braehead or Bargeddie, near Glasgow. Wheatley was educated at the Roman Catholic school in Ballieston, but poverty forced him down the pit at the age of eleven. However, this did not prevent him continuing his education at night school, reading avidly and teaching himself shorthand. Unlike many pioneer socialists he kept up his church connections and also became interested in Irish Home Rule and the United Irish League.

Like Keir HARDIE (1856–1915), Wheatley was both able and ambitious, and when he was twenty-four he quit the pit, worked for a time as a publican, then joined his brother running a small shop in Shettleston. The business was apparently not very successful and in 1902 Wheatley turned to journalism combined with advertisement sales. He worked for the *Glasgow Observer & Catholic Herald* — and this move was to prove highly influential in his political career.

In 1906 Wheatley went into partnership in a printing and publishing company, Hoxton and Walsh, which by 1911 was a successful and well-capitalized limited company. Later Wheatley broke with his partner and reconstructed the firm under his sole control. He proved to be a remarkably astute manager and in 1921 the business had an annual turnover of £71,000. Wheatley then moved into newspaper publishing, notably the *Glasgow Eastern Standard*, established in 1923, which he used partly for purposes of propaganda.

Meantime, Wheatley had become increasingly involved in local politics, founding the Catholic Socialist Society (1906), joining the INDEPENDENT LABOUR PARTY in 1907, and beginning his association with James MAXTON (1885–1946), who became a close friend, and with Tom JOHNSTON (1881–1965), who got him to write for *Forward*. He became a county councillor in Lanarkshire in 1910 and after 1912 represented Shettleston as a Glasgow city councillor. He devoted himself to social issues, such as health and housing, and during WORLD WAR I played a prominent role in the Rent Strike (1915) and in the activities of the Clyde Workers' Committee. He proved a skilful leader of the Labour group on the Glasgow Corporation.

Although narrowly defeated in the Coupon Election of 1918, Wheatley masterminded the Labour victories that returned both himself and a large number of his associates to Westminster in 1922. His initial support for Ramsay MACDONALD (1866–1937) was rewarded somewhat grudgingly by his appointment as Health Minister in the minority Labour government of 1924. His Housing Act proved to be the only legislative achievement of the short-lived administration.

Thereafter Wheatley, like many of his ILP associates, became increasingly disillusioned with the gradualism of MacDonald, and his actions in support of the left widened still further the gap between himself and the leadership. When MacDonald formed a second administration in 1929 Wheatley was not invited to join. Like Maxton he spent much of his parliamentary time attacking the government from the back benches until his death in 1930. Wheatley was undoubtedly a major figure of the Scottish Labour movement and probably its most intellectual and successful propagandist.

• *Knox, W., Scottish Labour Leaders, Mainstream, 1984.*

• *Wood, I.S., John Wheatley, Manchester University Press, 1990.*

Whigs   The defeat in 1648 of those who supported the ENGAGEMENT provided an opportunity for the extreme Presbyterians to seize power. This episode was derisively entitled the 'Whiggamore's Raid', apparently a reference to the expression 'whiggam' used by the COVENANTERS of southwest Scotland to urge on their steeds. By the later seventeenth century the term 'Whig' was being used to describe the opponents of the religious policies of CHARLES II (1630–85) and JAMES VII (1633–1701) and those who supported the REVOLUTION SETTLEMENT. In the eighteenth century the epithet was used initially to indicate all those who welcomed the establishment of the Hanoverian succession and like John CAMPBELL, second Duke of Argyll (1678–1743) frequently benefited from their support. However, by the end of the century and the start of the nineteenth, with their rivals, the Tories, firmly entrenched in office for many years, the Whigs became the supporters of reform, especially of the Westminster Parliament. The aristocratic connotations surrounding the name caused the party leaders

to change it to LIBERAL in the mid-nineteenth century.

'Wigtown Martyrs'   By 1680 the COVENANTERS who remained in active opposition to the Crown had been reduced by a policy, which had been a mixture of conciliation and repression, to an embittered remnant known as the CAMERONIANS. In 1684 the latter issued their Apologetical Declaration denying royal authority and effectively putting themselves on a war footing with the State. In retaliation, the government introduced the death penalty for anyone who refused to disown the Cameronians' declaration, hence the sentence of death by drowning passed on two recalcitrant Wigtown females, Margaret Lauchleson or Maclachlan (c.1620?–1685) and Margaret Wilson (1667–?1685). Whether or not they actually did expire under the incoming tide of the Solway Firth continues to remain a subject of some controversy.

• *Cowan, I., The Scottish Covenanters, Weidenfeld & Nicolson, 1976.*

William I ('the Lion') (1143–1214)   Independent Scotland's longest reigning monarch, William was the second son of Earl Henry, son of DAVID I. In 1165 at the age of 22 he succeeded his brother, MALCOLM IV. He inherited a mixed legacy, with large areas of the country where royal authority was limited or non-existant or had only been temporarily subdued, like Moray in the north and Galloway in the southwest. Following in his grandfather's footsteps in 1174 he attempted to recover former Scottish territory in Northumbria. He was captured at Alnwick and after being publicly humiliated in Northampton was imprisoned at Falaise in Normandy. By the Treaty of Falaise, William was forced to vow homage to Henry II 'for Scotland and for all his other lands' a much more wider-ranging obligation than previously. The subsequent quit-claim of Canterbury (1189) relieved William of his obligations, but did not solve the longer-term problem of the claims the English monarchs had over their Scottish counterparts, notably during the WARS OF INDEPENDENCE. Meanwhile, William had set about a vigorous policy of supressing revolt and extending royal authority by feudalisation. This involved reorganising and extending SHERIFFDOMS over much of the Lowlands (except the northeast) and building a network of royal castles in Ayrshire, Berwickshire, Dumfriesshire in the south and Perthsire, Moray and Ross in the north. Kin groups like the Bruces, Morvilles and Stewarts were given extensive lordships in the southwest and the north. Subsequent revolts, probably against colonization, were suppressed in the north in 1197, 1202, 1211 and 1214. William's support of the CHURCH was reflected in the foundation of Arbroath abbey (1176), where he was later buried. He was succeeded by his son, Alexander II. The nickname, 'the Lion', seems to have come into common usage after his death, perhaps an attempt to put him on an equal footing historically with King Richard, 'the Lionheart'.

•Lynch, M., Scotland. A New History, Pimlico, 1992.
•Owen, D.D.R., William the Lion, 1143–1214. Kingship and Culture, Tuckwell Press, 1997.

William III (1650—1702) Born 1650, the posthumous son of William II, Prince of Orange. In 1677 he married Mary (1662–94), elder daughter of James VII (1633–1701) by his first wife, Anne Hyde (1637–71). He and Mary accepted the offer of the Scottish Crown on 11 May 1689 (to become, correctly speaking, 'William II' as far as Scotland was concerned). Whether they actually agreed to all the terms of the Claim of Right or the Articles of Grievance drawn up beforehand and presented to them is doubtful. Admittedly, the subsequent REVOLUTION SETTLEMENT (1689–90) certainly restored Presbyterianism and abolished Episcopacy, lay patronage and the Lords of the Articles. On the other hand, these changes only came about following complex manoeuvrings between the various political factions within PARLIAMENT and William's commissioners, Hamilton (1635–94), and later, Melville (1636–1707). The king himself was pre-occupied with the Irish rebellion.

Undoubtedly, the main feature of William III's reign is his increasing unpopularity with his Scottish subjects. The JACOBITES, naturally, were his enemies. Their rising in 1689, although initially successful at KILLIECRANKIE, disintegrated with the death during the battle of John GRAHAM, Viscount Dundee (1648–89) their only competent leader. Thereafter they had generally to rely on royal errors or misjudgements to engender support for their cause. The Episcopalians, if they were not, like most of the bishops, opponents of William from the outset, soon had the Revolution Settlement as a powerful incentive for joining the ranks of the opposition. As for the CAMERONIANS they, not surprisingly, took umbrage with certain aspects of the religious arrangements and remained a hostile body outwith the Church of Scotland. However, the bulk of the population was to lose faith with the king largely on account of two episodes: the GLENCOE MASSACRE (1692) and the DARIEN Scheme.

The Glencoe affair not only ended the career of the unpopular royal secretary, the Master of Stair (1648–1707), but also did grave harm to William's own reputation and standing because of his complicity in this deplorable business. If nothing else it provided a great boost for Jacobitism in the HIGHLANDS. Ironically the king's support of the COMPANY OF SCOTLAND and its ambitious commercial objectives was originally given in order to distract attention from the Glencoe debacle. But William soon abandoned this policy. Pressure from the East India Company and the niceties of an English foreign policy in which Spanish claims to Darien had to be respected proved over-riding considerations. The king, in fact, was not totally to blame for Scotland's colonial disaster in Central America; but the Scottish people, additionally in those years the victims of a series of bad harvests causing widespread economic grievances, unquestionably thought otherwise.

•Ferguson, W., Scotland: 1689 to the Present, Oliver & Boyd, 1968.
•Ferguson, W., Scotland's Relations with England, John Donald, 1977.
•Mitchison, R., Lordship to Patronage, Arnold, 1983.
•Riley, P.W.J., King William and the Scottish Politicians, John Donald, 1979.

Wilson, James, see RADICAL WAR

Wishart, George (c.1513—46)
Wishart's origins and early career are obscure but he is said to have been related to the Wisharts of Pittaro, near Montrose, and to have been educated at King's College, Aberdeen. By the early 1540s his unorthodox religious views had forced him to live abroad where he came into contact with the Swiss reform movement. Consequently, at least according to KNOX (c.1512–72), he rejected all beliefs and practices lacking scriptural warrant, a doctrinal standpoint that was later to be a central feature among Scottish reformers. He spent some time at Cambridge before returning to Scotland in 1543 with the commissioners negotiating the proposed marriage treaty between MARY (1542–87) and the future Edward VI (1537–53). During 1544–45 he was preaching his heretical opinions in areas such as Angus, Fife, Ayrshire and East Lothian where there were some signs of support for his radical views. Early in 1546 he was arrested on the instructions of BEATON (c.1494–1546) at Ormiston in East Lothian and imprisoned in Edinburgh Castle. On 28 February he was tried for heresy before a convocation of bishops at St Andrews and on being found guilty of this offence was burned at the stake on 1 March 1546.

While his execution certainly provided another motive for the subsequent assassination of Beaton shortly afterwards it did not serve as some sort of catalyst for the Reformation. Indeed it acted as a severe curb on heretical activity in Scotland for the time being.

witchcraft Although the first anti-witchcraft legislation appeared shortly after the REFORMATION, serious persecution of witches in Scotland didn't take place until the 1590s with the advent of the celebrated trials in North Berwick. Thereafter the mania displayed itself in several distinct phases with the years 1629–30, 1649–50 and 1661–62 being the most virulent periods. The regions of highest incidence of witchcraft investigations were the Lowlands and the northeast with the Lothians, Fife and Aberdeen areas particularly badly affected. The Highlands and Islands had no known cases.

The procedure in witchcraft allegations was that either the PRIVY COUNCIL issued commissions for a trial or the case was heard by the Court of Justiciary. Between them they examined the hundreds of unfortunate people, mostly women, accused of being the agents of Satan and having committed some Satanic malpractice. Various forms of torture were used to extract confessions including the horrific 'witch-pricking' to discover the 'witchmark', an area of the body supposedly immune to any pain. The victims were usually female, frequently elderly and generally from the lower end of the social scale. The exact number actually found guilty, garrotted and then burned is difficult to ascertain but the most recent estimate of around 1,000 is well below previous, probably exaggerated, figures.

Motives in this country for a witch craze, which was a Continental phenomenon as well, include belief in the whole concept of witchcraft — JAMES VI (1566–1625) produced a short book, *Daemonologie*, on the subject in 1597 — the impact of a Calvinist theology with its strong stance on the subject, not to mention the various socio-economic factors like FAMINE, plague and internal instability that influenced mental attitudes throughout the seventeenth century.

After the spate of witchcraft trials in the early years of the RESTORATION era there was a gradual decline. This was doubtless partly a result of the use of torture to extort confessions becoming illegal in 1662 and leading lawyers such as MACKENZIE of Rosehaugh (1636–91) adopting a more critical attitude towards the methods of inquiry used in such trials. The witchcraft laws were finally repealed in 1736, nine years after the last execution at Dornoch for this offence.

•*Larner, C., Enemies of God, Blackwell, 1981.*
•*Smout, T.C., A History of the Scottish People, Collins, 1969.*

Wood, Sir Andrew (c.1460—1540) Wood was a merchant trading out of Leith, his two known vessels being the *Yellow Carvel* and the *Flower*. He aided JAMES III and was both knighted by him and given lands in Largo, Fife, in 1483. He subsequently served JAMES IV, defeating an English force which had been raiding Scottish ships off the Firth of Forth in 1489. He not only commanded ships on expeditions to enforce royal authority in the western Isles, but also captained the *Great Michael,* the largest Scottish vessel of its time and the flagship of the country's fleet.

wool   Wool was one of the few important exports of medieval Scotland. The monastic orders, especially in the BORDERS, were believed to have developed sheep and wool production from the twelfth century onward. Skilled Flemish immigrants were later partly repsonsible for the development of the cloth trade in the BURGHS.

The modern woollen industry is the longest-established TEXTILE sector, woollen cloth — though inferior to that produced in England — being an item of export by the sixteenth century. Some official attempts were made to encourage the development of the industry when Parliament forbade the export of raw wool in 1581; permitted the 'inbringing' of foreign craftsmen to teach locals the necessary skills (1582); and prohibited the 'hamebringing of Inglis claith' (1597). The burgh records of Edinburgh show that 'Flemings' arrived there in 1588, while the Convention of Estates later urged others to introduce 'craftsmen strangereas' and renewed the ban on the export of wool.

During the seventeenth and much of the eighteenth centuries the woollen industry was almost wholly domestic. There were two main divisions: the country weavers who made coarse plaids and 'hodden grey'; and the burgh guilds, who made better cloth. There were, however, several

attempts to develop some sort of factory system, most notably that of Sir James Stanfield at the short-lived Newmills near Haddington in 1681 and the Woollen Manufactory of Glasgow (1699–1704). This signalled the introduction of mechanized finishing in fulling and dyeing mills driven by water-power — a large number being built with the encouragement of the BOARD OF TRUSTEES. Patrick Lindsay gave a valuable account of the wool trade in the *Interest of Scotland Considered* (1733), describing an industry widely dispersed throughout the Lowlands. Later David Loch's *Essays on Trade* (1778) indicated that regional specialization was already apparent: in the Borders, the towns of Galashiels, Peebles and Selkirk specialized in worsted yarn production; while Kilmarnock concentrated on coarser work, including carpets. Stocking making was important in Dunbar, Tranent, Perth and Inverness. Other important producers included Stirling, Fife, Aberdeen and Moray.

Woollen manufacture was transformed into a factory industry during the INDUSTRIAL REVOLUTION, but mechanization — mainly for technical reasons — was slow relative to COTTON and LINEN. Water and steam-powered spinning mills supported a substantial corps of outworkers, mainly handloom weavers. The introduction of the power loom did not bring about their immediate demise but integrated plant for carding, spinning and weaving became more common after 1830. This development coincided with an upturn in demand for finer quality products, especially hosiery, tweed cloth and checks, made popular by Sir Walter SCOTT (1771–1832) and others. The power loom, in both cloth and hosiery sectors, lowered costs and widened the market to such an extent that by 1876 there were nearly 250 factories employing 22,000 workers. Specialization became more obvious, with tweeds being produced mainly in the Border and Ochil hillfoot towns, hosiery in Hawick and Dumfries, and carpets in Glasgow and Kilmarnock. Tweed manufacture was revived in the Highlands and Islands and typical of the Scottish woollen industry as a whole since the late nineteenth century concentrated on essentially luxury products. With the rationalization that characterized the industry since the depression this tendency has continued.

• Gulvin, C., The Scottish Hosiery and Knitwear Industry 1680–1980, John Donald, 1984.
• Gulvin, C., The Tweedmakers: A History of the Scottish Fancy Woollen Industry, 1603–1914, David & Charles, 1973.

Worcester Affair (1704—5) The Darien disaster had provoked widespread anglophobia and the seizure by the East India Company early in 1704 of the Annandale, the sole remaining vessel belonging to the COMPANY OF SCOTLAND, caused a further serious deterioration in Anglo-Scottish relations. Accordingly, in August 1704, when the English ship Worcester put in to the Firth of Forth before joining a London-bound convoy, it provided an opportunity for retaliation. Thus, the prize was seized and the Worcester's captain and crew accused of complicity in pirat-

ical activities that had caused the loss of the Speedy Return, another merchantman owned by the Company of Scotland. Despite a total lack of any evidence incriminating the captain or his crew they were found guilty by the Court of Admiralty in March 1705 and the captain with two of his crew were hanged at Leith shortly afterwards.

Clearly this whole incident was no less than judicial murder. It had been permitted by a nervous PRIVY COUNCIL faced with a growing anti-English hysteria in which impecunious stockholders of the Company of Scotland were prominent. At the same time the unpopular Alien Act of February 1705, the Westminster Parliament's reply to the ACT OF SECURITY and the ACT ANENT PEACE AND WAR, assuredly did little to prevent the fate of the unfortunate crew of the Worcester.

• Ferguson, W., Scotland's Relations with England, John Donald, 1977.
• Temple, R.C., New Light on the Tragedy of the Worcester, 1704–5, Benn, 1930.

World War I It could be argued that the Great War (1914–18) was as important historically for Scotland as the INDUSTRIAL REVOLUTION or the DISRUPTION. In common with the British experience the war had a major impact on the Scottish economy, on society and on politics — both short and long term. The military participation ratio was high. By one estimate 20 per cent of the 800,000-odd British and Irish dead or missing were Scots. On the home front the war brought considerable industrial, social and political upheaval — particularly to Glasgow and Clydeside. The area was a major centre of the war effort, given the concentration of strategic industries, such as shipbuilding, engineering and munitions. Industrial militancy during the early stages of the war earned the area the revolutionary-sounding nickname of 'RED CLYDESIDE'.

The war effort greatly stimulated Scottish heavy industry and both shipbuilding and engineering were particularly prosperous given the demand for naval and merchant ships, heavy armaments and other machinery of war. New industries, like motor vehicle and aeroplane manufacture were devoted entirely to war work. While heavy munitions were perforce located on Clydeside, light munitions, explosives and aero-engine production were widely dispersed in places safe from Zeppelin raids. A National Munitions Plant at Gretna, Dumfriesshire, was one of the largest in the country.

Other industries had mixed fortunes because of lost markets — with TEXTILES and COAL being prime examples. On the land, AGRICULTURE, though suffering labour shortages due to conscription, helped maintain food supplies — much reduced through loss of vital imports. Everywhere — in factory or on farm — women and boys took the places of men fighting at the front. EDUCATION of children was sometimes much neglected as a result.

While there can be little doubt that many industrialists profited from the war, the labour force, particularly the skilled, also advanced wage rates. Much of the militancy on the Clyde was generated initially by 'dilution' in the engineering workshops as unskilled or semiskilled labour and mechanization threatened an elite corps of workers. This protest manifested itself in the Engineers' Strike of February 1915 and the Fairfields' Strike of November that year — during which the Clyde Workers' Committee played a leading role.

The conflict between the workers and the government came to a climax between December 1915 and April 1916. Lloyd George (1863–1945), as Minister of Munitions, visited Glasgow to meet the shop stewards and try to placate the engineers. His eloquence had little effect and the seizure of *Forward* for reporting an uncensored version of events only served to alienate the workers further. Finally the deepening military crisis brought about enforced dilution and after a short-lived strike at Beardmore's in March there was little further industrial action for the remainder of the war. The Bolshevik Revolution hardly caused a stir: the gaoling of John MACLEAN (1879–1923) caused more concern on humanitarian grounds than enthusiasm for his revolutionary ideals.

Scotland occupied a strategic position in the naval war between Britain and Germany with three major bases at SCAPA FLOW, headquarters of the Grand Fleet, at Invergordon in the Cromarty Firth, and at Rosyth in the Firth of Forth. On the outbreak of war British naval policy was to contain the German High Seas Fleet in the North Sea, and, thinking the German U-boat range was limited, Scapa Flow became the main British base. However, German submarines could, in fact, patrol much of the North Sea and English

Channel, and after a false sighting of a U-boat in Scapa Flow on 1 September 1914 the base was moved to Loch Ewe and then Lough Swilly in Ulster. This proved so remote that the defences at Scapa Flow were strengthened and the Grand Fleet returned to the North Sea. It was from the three Scottish bases that the fleet steamed to its major confrontation with the Germans at Jutland, 31 May–1 June 1916. Scottish waters subsequently saw a great deal of action in the anti-U-boat campaign.

While Ramsay MACDONALD (1866–1937), James MAXTON (1885–1946), and others on the left resisted both the war and the introduction of conscription in 1916, the Scots also contributed substantially to the war on land. Scottish REGIMENTS played a prominent role in the long drawn out trench warfare on the Western Front and in bloody battles like that on the Somme (1916) or the earlier and apparently pointless Gallipoli venture (1915–16). The Scottish National War Memorial at Edinburgh Castle and numerous less flamboyant memorials in towns and villages elsewhere are mute testimony to those who gave their lives in the fighting. Prominent Scots among the military leaders were Sir Ian Hamilton, who commanded the ill-fated Dardanelles expedition and Field Marshal Sir Douglas HAIG (1861–1928), later Earl Haig, who was Commander-in-Chief of the British forces at the end of the war.

The Great War, as Marwick says, was the first total war and in Scotland, as elsewhere, marked an important watershed in modern history. A cataclysmic event in terms of loss of life and destruction of resources, it served as a catalyst to political and social changes on the home front. Politically it contributed to the rise of LABOUR and the demise of the LIBERALS in Scotland; while socially the working class, women and youth became more articulate and influential. Unfortunately the Scottish economy only benefited in the short term, and, it might be argued, the Great War actually delayed modernization of traditional industries, management and labour relations – with the result that the DEPRESSION hit harder than might otherwise have been the case.

•Banks, A., *A Military Atlas of the First World War, Heinemann, 1975.*

•Harvie, C., *No Gods and Precious Few Heroes: Scotland 1914–1980, Edward Arnold, 1981.*

•MacDonald, C.M.M. and McFarland, E., *Scotland and the Great War, Tuckwell Press, 1999.*

•Marwick, A., *The Deluge: British Society and the First World War, Macmillan, 1975.*

World War II   As in the Great War, Scotland shared the wider British experience of World War II (1939–45) and the fight against Adolf Hitler and his allies. Although the casualty rate was about 40 per cent that of WORLD WAR I, a large number of Scottish civilians and merchant mariners also died or were wounded in the conflict. Indeed, as Calder has argued, this was a 'people's war' in which the home front was as critical to ultimate victory as the military breakthrough of 1943–44.

The civilian population felt the immediate impact of the war through such measures as the evacuation of city children and some mothers to the countryside or towns likely to escape the bombing, the black-out, the rationing of food, clothing and other goods, and conscription of young, fit, male workers — except in reserved occupations. Some young men, rather than be called up, chose to work down the COAL mines, where they earned the label 'Bevin Boys' after Ernest Bevin (1881–1951), Minister of Labour in Churchill's Coalition government.

The Home Guard or Local Defence Volunteers mobilized and trained in their spare time those left behind. Others joined the Air Raid Precautions service (ARP) or fire brigade — the latter a more obviously dangerous occupation in wartime than in peace.

Women played an important role on the home front, working in factories, munitions plants, in the Women's Voluntary Services (WVS) or the Women's Land Army — formed to redress labour shortages in AGRICULTURE. Many women joined the forces, serving in the Auxiliary Territorial Service (ATS), the Women's Royal Naval Service (WRNS), the Women's Air Force (WAAF), or nursing units at home or overseas.

The naval bases at Rosyth, Invergordon and SCAPA FLOW continued to be important and, despite the distance from Germany, the first air raid on Britain in October 1939 saw bombs dropped near the Forth Railway Bridge — apparently targetted at naval vessels in Rosyth. On the west coast, Glasgow and the Clyde became vital to Britain's food and military supply from overseas —

especially from the United States and Canada. Convoys under naval protection made the dangerous North Atlantic crossing, while the giant ocean liners, the *Queen Mary* and the *Queen Elizabeth,* served as troopships for the duration of the war. The Soviet Union was later partly supplied from Scottish ports.

Scotland also occupied an important position relative to air strategy in both the North Sea and the North Atlantic. Much of the country became a static aircraft carrier, with numerous airfields and bases constructed along the eastern seaboard facing Germany and Scandinavia. A major sea-plane base was established on the shores of Loch Ryan, Wigtownshire, and at nearby Baldoon there was an important training centre for flyers. Aircraft from west coast bases, like Prestwick, undertook submarine reconaissance and convoy surveillance in the North Atlantic.

For five years, much of Scotland was virtually an armed camp and at one time or another there were many thousands of allied forces — Poles, French, Norwegians and Americans — based in Scotland. Several prisoner-of-war camps — mainly for Italians — were set up in the Lowlands and in Orkney, the most poignant memorial to their existence being the Italian Chapel built in a nissen hut on Burray. Some Italians and Poles, having gained refugee status, subsequently made their homes in Scotland after the war.

Following the conquest of Norway in 1940, the Germans carried out several hit-and-run raids on Shetland (the base for the 'Shetland Bus' to Norway), Orkney and the northeast ports. The heaviest German raid on Clydeside during the blitz of 13–15 March devastated Clydebank and killed over 1,000 people. Only distance saved Glasgow and other Clydeside towns from the punishment inflicted on London, Coventry and many of the south coast ports. On Clydeside, as elsewhere, plans were immediately made for reconstruction when circumstances allowed.

Scots men and women played a distinguished role in the fighting, not only in Europe but also in North Africa and the Far East. Scottish infantry divisions, perhaps less Scottish in character than before, contributed substantially to the campaigns in North Africa, Italy and Normandy that opened up the long road to victory in 1945.

In social and political terms the effects of the war for Scotland were as profound as those springing from World War I — a microcosm of the British experience during years of reconstruction and the creation of the Welfare State in the post-war era. Although there were limits to what could be achieved in wartime, a basis for reconstruction, nationalization and State intervention for the first time on any scale could be seen in the work of Thomas JOHNSTON (1881–1965), Churchill's able Secretary of State for Scotland, 1941–5, and intangible improvements in employment opportunities, health, EDUCATION and HOUSING in deprived localities.

•Addison, P., The Road to 1945. British Politics and the Second World War, Jonathan Cape, 1975.

•Calder, R.A., The People's War, Jonathan Cape, 1969.

•Harvie, C.T., No Gods and Precious

Few Heroes: Scotland 1914–1980, Edward Arnold, 1981.

Wyntoun, Andrew of (c.1355–1422) Andrew Wyntoun, a canon at St Andrews, and later prior of St Serf's, Loch Leven, was one of the earliest historians of Scotland. About 1400 he complied a chronicle of Scotland in verse, which because of the limited sources for the period, has remained an important (if not very reliable) account both of his own time and earlier generations.

York Buildings Company The York Buildings Company was incorporated by an Act of the English Parliament in 1691 to supply water to customers in St James and Piccadilly. The water was drawn from the Thames and stored at waterworks in the grounds of York House. The move from supplying water to fashionable parts of London to the development of the HIGHLANDS was occasioned by the aftermath of the JACOBITE REBELLION of 1715 when the FORFEITED ESTATES were put up for sale. An Act of Parliament in 1719 required purchasers of the forfeited territories to grant annuities on the value of the estates and the York Buildings Company became the vehicle for this arrangement. As Campbell has indicated, there could not have been a more propitious time for such a flotation, given the frenzy of speculation created by the South Sea Bubble.

When this died down the company leased many of the estates and encouraged agricultural IMPROVEMENT, one of their tenants being Sir Archibald GRANT of Monymusk (1696–1778). It also engaged in the timber trade on

Speyside and iron smelting at Abernethy (1728), though the latter was short-lived. Other industrial enterprises in the lowlands included the COAL mines and SALT pans of the exiled Earl of Winton (d.1749).

From the outset the York Buildings Company was a dubious enterprise. It was soon overextended and in even greater debt than the former landowners. After complex bankruptcy proceedings lasting many years the estates were either returned to their former owners or sold. By the end of the eighteenth century many lawyers had profited from litigation involving the company, which was left, as it had begun, with a waterworks. • *Murray, D., The York Buildings Company: A Chapter in Scotch History (1883), new edn. Bratton Publishing, 1973.*

York, Duke of, see JAMES VII

York, Treaty of (1237) In a move that had considerable long-term significance for relations between Scotland and England, Alexander II gave up claims to three counties of northern England, over which there had been dispute for generations. In return he was given estates in Cumberland and Northumberland.

Young, James (1811–83) James 'Paraffin' Young, the notable chemist and mineral oil magnate, was born in Glasgow, where his father was a joiner. At first he was apprenticed to his father but began his formal EDUCATION at the Mechanics' Institute and then at Anderson's University where, in 1830, he studied chemistry under Professor Thomas Graham. By

1832 Young was Graham's laboratory assistant and moved with him to University College, London, where he remained until 1838. Thanks to Graham's recommendation he became manager of Muspratt's Chemical Works, St Helens, moving in 1844 to Tennants, Clow and Company in Manchester. During his time with these two firms he undertook practical chemical research and made what were to prove very useful business contacts.

In 1847 Young investigated oil from a natural spring in a Derbyshire mine, obtaining good quality lamp oil. This led Young and his partners to form Young's Mineral Oil Company and, following further experiments, Young patented his process for the production of mineral oil by the distillation of coal in 1850. From the paraffin produced mineral oil and other by-products could be readily extracted.

The Scottish mineral oil industry was established in 1851 when Young and his partners opened their plant at Boghead near Bathgate to exploit the rich local reserves of cannel coal. Successfully guarding his patent against infringement Young had made a fortune before it expired in 1864. Meantime, attention had turned to oil shales and Young added to his wealth by acquiring extensive leases in the oil-rich districts and creating Young's Paraffin Light and Mineral Oil Company to exploit them in 1865.

Given his dynamism and the euphoria that surrounded the expansion of a new industry it is perhaps surprising that Young withdrew from the business as early as 1870. By modern standards he was a millionaire several times over and having acquired several country estates in Renfrewshire, West Lothian and Kincardineshire, he spent much of his remaining fortune on good works. He endowed a chair of chemistry at his old college and was a staunch patron of his lifelong associate the explorer David LIVINGSTONE (1813–1873). Young's career might be compared with that of Andrew CARNEGIE (1835–1919), the steel baron turned philanthropist.

•*Butt, J., Scottish Men of Science: James 'Paraffin' Young, Scotland's Cultural Heritage, 1983.*
•*Slaven, A. and Checkland, S., Dictionary of Scottish Business Biography 1860–1960: Vol. 1 The Staple Industries, Aberdeen University Press, 1986.*

Young Pretender, see STEWART, PRINCE CHARLES EDWARD

APPENDICES

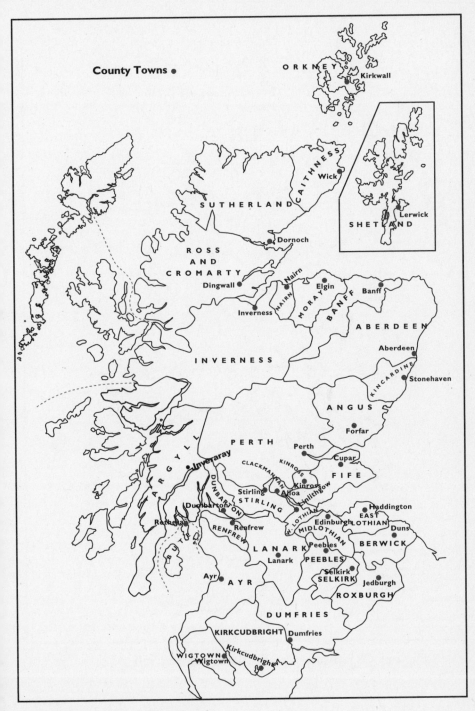

The Old Counties of Scotland

The Religious Organisation of Scotland before 1560

Population Statistics

Census Statistics for Scotland

Year	Population	Pop. per ml^2		Year	Population	Pop. per ml^2/km^{2*}
1801	1,608,420	54		1911	4,760,904	160
1811	1,805,864	60		1921	4,882,497	164
1821	2,091,521	70		1931	4,842,980	163
1831	2,364,386	79		1941	5,095,969**	
1841	2,620,184	88		1951	5,096,415	171
1851	2,888,742	97		1961	5,179,344	174
1861	3,062,294	100		1971	5,228,963	68*
1871	3,360,018	113		1981	5,130,735	66*
1881	3,735,573	125		1991	5,102,400	66*
1891	4,025,647	125				
1901	4,472,103	150				

** No census held; estimated figure.

Population of the Highlands

Statistics given are for the seven Crofting Counties (Argyll, Caithness, Inverness, Ross & Cromarty, Sutherland, Orkney and Zetland)

Year	Population		Year	Population
1811	318,266		1891	360,367
1821	361,184		1901	352,371
1831	388,876		1911	341,535
1841	396,045		1921	325,853
1851	395,540		1931	293,139
1861	380,442		1951	285,786
1871	371,356		1961	277,948
1881	369,453			

Royal Burghs

Royal burghs were those who received their burghal privileges direct from the Crown and who as a consequence, enjoyed various political and economic advantages, not the least of which were considerable and exclusive trading privileges. In many cases, the exact year in which a royal charter was granted is impossible to determine from extant records; often it can be dated only to a particular monarch's reign or a date by which records show that it was operating as a royal burgh, the charter having been granted at some point prior to this.

Burgh	County	Original Grant of Charter
Aberdeen	Aberdeen City	1124–54
Annan	Dumfries	1532
Arbroath	Angus	1178–82
Auchterarder	Perth	1246
Auchtermuchty	Fife	1517
Ayr	Ayr	1203–06
Banff	Banff	1189–98
Brechin	Angus	1165–1171
Burntisland	Fife	1541
Campbeltown	Argyll	1700
Crail	Fife	1178
Cullen	Banff	1589–98
Culross	Fife	1592
Cupar	Fife	1327
Dingwall	Ross & Cromarty	1226–7
Dornoch	Sutherland	1628
Dumbarton	Dunbarton	1222
Dumfries	Dumfries	1186
Dunbar	E. Lothian	1445
Dundee	Dundee City	1191–95
Dunfermline	Fife	1124–27
Edinburgh	Edinburgh City	1124–27
Elgin	Moray	1130–53
*Elie[1] & Earlsferry[2]	Fife	1599[1], 1589[2]
Falkland	Fife	1458
Forfar	Angus	1153–62
Forres	Moray	1130–53
Fortrose	Ross & Cromarty	1590
Glasgow	Glasgow City	1611
Haddington	E. Lothian	1124–53
Inveraray	Argyll	1648
Inverbervie	Kincardine	1341
Inverkeithing	Fife	1153–62

Burgh	County	Original Grant of Charter
Inverness	Inverness	1130–53
Inverurie	Aberdeen	1195
Irvine	Ayr	1372
Jedburgh	Roxburgh	1159–65
*Kilrenny[1], Anstruther Easter[2] & Anstruther Wester[3]	Fife	1578[1], 1583[2], 1587[3]
Kinghorn	Fife	1165–72
Kintore	Aberdeen	1187–1200
Kirkcaldy	Fife	1644
Kirkcudbright	Kirkcudbright	c. 1330
Kirkwall	Orkney	1486
Lanark	Lanark	1153–59
Lauder	Berwick	1502
Linlithgow	W. Lothian	c. 1138
Lochmaben	Dumfries	c. 1447
Montrose	Angus	1124–53
Nairn	Nairn	c. 1190
New Galloway	Kirkcudbright	1630
Newburgh	Fife	1631
North Berwick	E. Lothian	c. 1425
Peebles	Peebles	1153
Perth	Perth	1124–27
Pittenweem	Fife	1541
Queensferry	W. Lothian	1636
Renfrew	Renfrew	1124–47
Rothesay	Bute	1400–01
Rutherglen	Lanark	1124–53
Sanquhar	Dumfries	1598
Selkirk	Selkirk	1328
St Andrews	Fife	1620
Stirling	Stirling	1124–27
Stranraer	Wigtown	1617
Tain	Ross & Cromarty	1439
Whithorn	Wigtown	1511
Wick	Caithness	1589
Wigtown	Wigtown	c. 1292

* These burghs united in 1929.

Secretaries of State for Scotland

1885	The Duke of Richmond	1940	Ernest Brown
1886	G. O. Trevelyan	1941	Tom Johnston
1886	The Earl of Dalhousie	1945	Earl of Roseberry
1886	Arthur J. Balfour	1945	Joseph Westwood
1887	The Marquis of Lothian	1947	Arthur Woodburn
1892	Sir G. O. Trevelyan	1950	Hector MacNeil
1895	Alexander Bruce	1951	James Stuart
1903	Andrew Murray	1957	John S. Maclay
1905	The Marquis of Linlithgow	1962	Michael Noble
1905	John Sinclair	1964	William Ross
1912	T. P. Mackinnon-Wood	1970	Gordon Campbell
1916	Harold John Tennant	1974	William Ross
1916	Robert Munro	1976	Bruce Millan
1922	Viscount Novar	1979	George Younger
1924	William Adamson	1986	Malcolm Rifkind
1924	Sir John Gilmour	1990	Ian Lang
1929	William Adamson	1994	Michael Forsyth
1931	Sir Archibald Sinclair	1997	Donald Dewar
1932	Sir Godfrey Collins	1999	John Reid
1936	Walter Elliot	2001	Helen Liddell
1938	D. J. Colville		

Deputy Secretaries of State for Scotland

This new office was created on 28th July 1998.

1998	Helen Liddell
1999	Office vacant
1999	Brian Wilson

First Ministers of the Scottish Parliament

Unlike at Westminster where the leader of the largest party automatically becomes Prime Minister, the First Minister is voted in by all Members of the Scottish Parliament.

1999	Donald Dewar	2000	Henry McLeish

Scottish Monarchs to 1714

The House of MacAlpin (834–1034)

Kenneth I (Mac Alpin) (r. 843–58)

Donald I (r. 858–62) brother of Kenneth I

Constantine I (r. 862–77) son of Kenneth I

Aed (r. 877–78) son of Kenneth I

Eochaid (r. 878–89) grandson of Kenneth I

Donald II (r. 889–900) son of Constantine I

Constantine II (r. 900–42; d. 952) son of Aed

Malcolm I (r. 942–54) son of Donald II

Indulf (r. 954–62) son of Constantine II

Dubh (r. 962–66) son of Malcolm I

Culen (r. 966–71) son of Indulf

Kenneth II (r. 971–95) son of Malcolm I

Constantine III (r. 995–97) son of Culen

Kenneth III (r. 997–10005) son of Dubh

Malcolm II (r. 1005–34) son of Kenneth II

Note: Not all children are shown on the genealogical charts that follow. Names of monarchs are shown in bold.

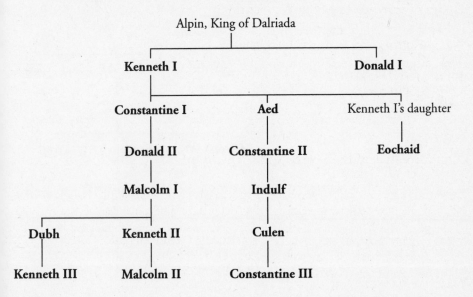

The House of Dunkeld (1034–1290)

Duncan I (r. 1034–40) grandson of Malcolm II
Macbeth (1040–57) grandson of Malcolm II
Lulach (r. 1057–58) great-grandson of Kenneth III
Malcolm III (r. 1058–93) son of Duncan I
Donald II (r. 1093–94; deposed) son of Duncan I
Duncan II (r. 1094) son of Malcolm III
Donald III (restored r. 1094–97) son of Duncan I
Edgar (r. 1097–1107) son of Malcolm III
Alexander I (r. 1107–24) son of Malcolm III
David I (r. 1124–53) son of Malcolm III
Malcolm IV (r. 1153–65) grandson of David I
William I (r. 1165–1214) brother of Malcolm IV
Alexander II (r. 1214–49) son of William I
Alexander III (r. 1249–86) son of Alexander II
Margaret (r. 1286–90) granddaughter of Alexander III

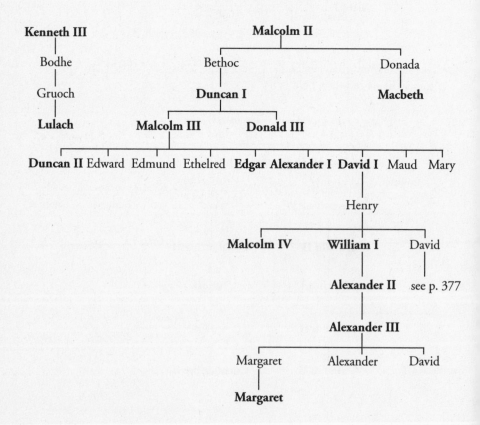

see p. 377

Interregnum (1290–92)

The House of Balliol (1292–96)

John (r. 1292–96) great-great-great grandson of David I

Interregnum (1296–1306)

The House of Bruce (1306–1371)

Robert I (r. 1306–29) great-great-great-great grandson of David I
David II (r. 1329–71) son of Robert I

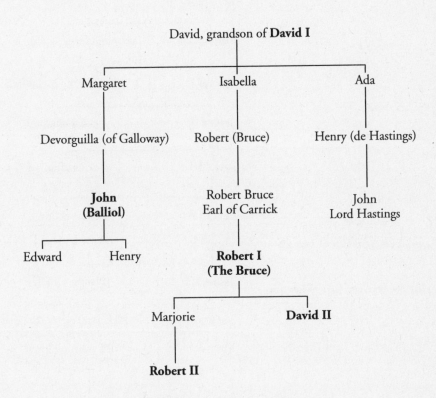

The House of Stewart (1371-1649)

Robert II (r. 1371–90) grandson of Robert I
Robert III (r. 1390–1406) son of Robert II
James I (r. 1406–37) son of Robert III
James II (r. 1437–60) son of James I
James III (r. 1460–88) son of James II
James IV (r. 1488–1515) son of James III
James V (r. 1513–42) son of James IV
Mary I (r. 1542–67) daughter of James V
James VI (r. 1567–1625) son of Mary I
Charles I (r. 1625–49) son of James VI

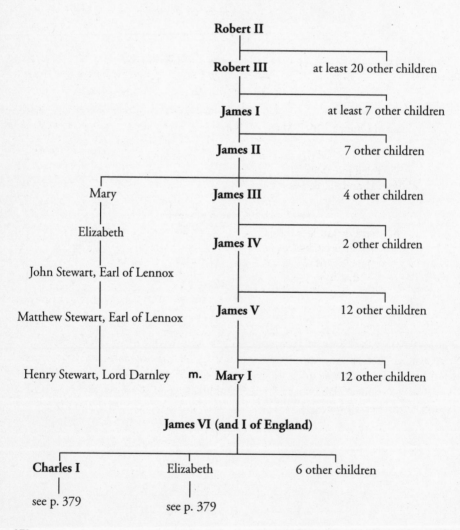

see p. 379

see p. 379

The Commonwealth (1651–53) and Protectorate (1653–60)

Oliver Cromwell (r. 1651–58)
Richard Cromwell (r. 1658–60); son of Oliver

The House of Stewart (1660–1707)

Charles II (r. 1660–85) son of Charles I
James VII (r. 1685–89) brother of Charles II
William II & Mary II (r. 1689–1702; 1689–1694) son-in-law and daughter of James VII
Anne (r. 1702–14) daughter of James VII

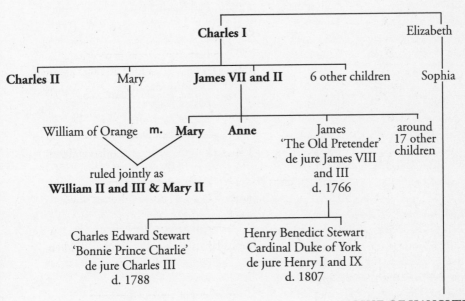

HOUSE OF HANOVER

The accession of the House of Hanover in 1714 ended the line of Scots kings that stretched back almost nine hundred years to the 9th century and began the German line whose descendants still rule today. It has been calculated that in 1714 there were 57 people with a stronger claim to the throne than the Elector of Hanover who succeeded as George I; however, all were Catholic. Their descendants now run into thousands.

Territorial Titles of the Scottish Nobility

Territorial Title	Family Name	Territorial Title	Family Name
Duke of Albany	Stewart	Earl of Lennox	Stewart
Earl of Angus	Douglas	Earl of Leven	Leslie
Duke of Argyll	Campbell	Lord Lorne	Campbell
Earl of Arran	Hamilton	Earl of Lothian	Kerr
Duke of Atholl	Murray	Earl of Loudon	Campbell
Earl of Atholl	Stewart	Lord Lovat	Fraser
Earl of Balcarres	Lindsay	Earl of Mar	Erskine
Lord Balermino	Elphinstone	Earl of Marchmont	Hume
Lord Belhaven	Hamilton	Earl Marischal	Keith
Earl of Bothwell	Hepburn	Earl of Melfort	Drummond
Earl of Breadalbane	Campbell	Earl of Melville	Leslie
Duke of Buccleuch	Scott	Earl of Menteith	Graham
Earl of Bute	Stuart	Lord Methven	Stewart
Earl of Caithness	Sinclair	Duke of Montrose	Graham
Earl of Cassillis	Kennedy	Earl of Moray	Stewart
Duke of Chatelherault	Hamilton	Earl of Morton	Douglas
Earl of Crawford	Lindsay	Lord Ochiltree	Stewart
Earl of Cromarty	Mackenzie	Earl of Perth	Drummond
Viscount Dundee	Graham	Earl of Queensferry	Douglas
Earl of Eglinton	Montgomery	Earl of Rothes	Leslie
Earl of Errol	Hay	Duke of Roxburgh	Kerr
Lord Glamis	Lyon	Earl of Seafield	Ogilvie
Earl of Glencairn	Cunningham	Earl of Seaforth	Mackenzie
Earl of Gowrie	Ruthven	Earl of Stair	Dalrymple
Earl of Huntly	Gordon	Earl of Sutherland	Gordon
Lord Innermeath	Stewart	Viscount Tarbat	Mackenzie
Earl of Islay	Campbell	Earl of Tweeddale	Hay
Duke of Lauderdale	Maitland	Lord Yester	Hay

Religious Houses and Orders in Scotland at the Reformation

Monks

Benedictine: Coldingham, Dunfermline, Iona, Pluscarden
Cluniac: Crossraguel, Paisley
Tiron: Arbroath, Kelso, Kilwinning, Lesmahagow, Lindores
Cistercian: Balmerino, Beauly, Coupar Angus, Culross, Deer, Dundrennan, Glenluce, Kinloss, Melrose, Newbattle, Sweetheart
Valliscaulian: Ardchattan
Carthusian: Perth

Regular Canons

Augustinian: Blantyre, Cambuskenneth, Holyrood, Inchaffray, Inchcolm, Inchmahome, Jedburgh, Monymusk, Portmoak, Pittenweem, St Andrews, Scone
Premonstratensian: Dryburgh, Fearn, Holywood, Soulseat, Tongland, Whithorn
Trinitarian: Aberdeen, Dirleton, Fail, Peebles, Scotlandwell

Mendicant Friars

Dominican: Aberdeen, Ayr, Dundee, Edinburgh, Elgin, Glasgow, Inverness, Montrose, Perth, St Andrews, Stirling, Wigtown
Franciscan: Aberdeen, Ayr, Dumfries, Dundee, Edinburgh, Elgin, Glasgow, Haddington, Inverkeithing, Kirkcudbright, Lanark, Perth, St Andrews, Stirling
Carmelite: Aberdeen, Banff, Edinburgh, Inverbervie, Irvine, Kingussie, Linlithgow, Luffness, Queensferry, Tullilum

Nunneries

Cistercian: Coldstream, Eccles, Elcho, Haddington, Manuel, North Berwick, St Bothans
Augustinian: Iona
Dominican: Sciennes
Franciscan: Aberdour, Dundee

Cathedrals

Secular: Aberdeen, Brechin, Dornoch, Dunblane, Dunkeld, Elgin, Fortrose, Glasgow, Kirkwall, Lismore
Monastic: St Andrews, Whithorn

Source: Cowan, I. B. and Easson, D. E., *Medieval Religious Houses of Scotland*, Longman, 1976.

Secessions from and the Disruption of the Church of Scotland

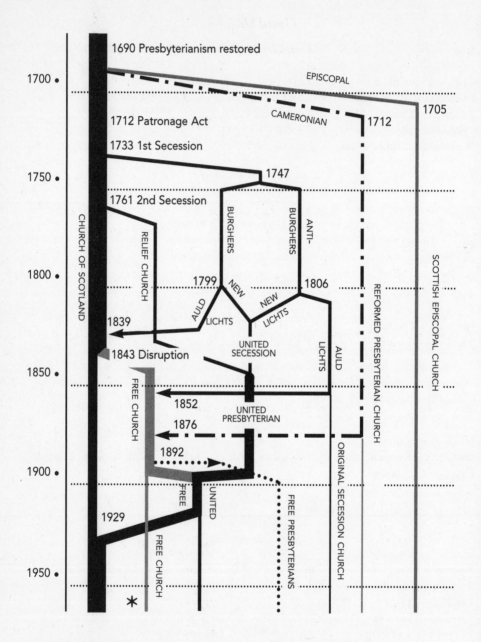

* In 2000, the Free Church was split once again following the breakaway of the Free Church (Continuing) congregations.

Scots Weights, Measures and Money

Liquid Measures

Scots	Equivalent Imperial	Equivalent Metric
1 gill	0.749 gill	0.053 l
4 gills = 1 mutchkin	2.996 gills	0.212 l
2 mutchkins = 1 chopin	1 pint 1.992 gills	0.848 l
2 chopins = 1 pint*	2 pints 3.984 gills	1.696 l
8 pints = 1 gallon	3 gallons 0.25 gills	13.638 l
*1 pint = 104.2034 cub ins	1 pint = 34.659 cub ins	1 litre = 61.027 cub ins

Linear & Square Measures

Scots	Equivalent Imperial	Equivalent Metric
1 inch	1.0016 in	2.54 cm
8.88 in = 1 Scots link	8.8942 in	22.55 cm
12 in = 1 foot	12.0192 in	30.5287 cm
$3^1/_{12}$ feet = 1 ell	37.0598 in ($1^1/_{37}$ yards)	94.1318 cm
6 ells = 1 fall (fa)	6.1766 yards (1.123 poles)	5.6479 m
4 falls = 1 chain	24.7064 yrd (1.123 chains)	22.5916 m
10 chains = 1 furlong	247.064 yrd (1.123 furlongs)	225.916 m
8 furlongs = 1 mile	1976.522 yrd (1.123 miles)	1.8073 km

Scots Weights

Scots	Equivalent Avoirdupois	Equivalent Metric
1 drop	1.093 drains	1.921 g
16 drops = 1 ounce	1 oz 1.5 drains	31 g
16 ounces = 1 pound	1 lb 1 oz 8 drains	496 g
16 pounds = 1 stone	17 lb 8 oz	7.936 kg

Scots Money

Scots	Equivalent Sterling
1 penny	$^1/_{12}$ penny
2 pennies = 1 bodle	$^1/_6$ penny
2 bodles = 1 plack	$^1/_3$ penny
3 bodles = 1 bawbee	$^1/_2$ penny
2 bawbees = 1 shilling	1 penny
13 shillings 4 pence = 1 merk	1 shilling $1^1/_2$ pennies
20 shillings = 1 pound	1 shilling 8 pennies